Teaching in
Further Education

Other Further Education titles available from Cassell:

Teaching in Further Education

An Outline of Principles and Practice

L.B. Curzon

FIFTH EDITION

CASSELL

Cassell
Wellington House
125 Strand
London WC2R 0BB

First published 1976
Fifth edition published 1997
Reprinted 1990, 1991 (twice), 1992, 1993, 1994, 1996

. **British Library Cataloguing in Publication Data**

Curzon, L.B. (Leslie Basil), *1921–*
   Teaching in further education: an outline of principles
   and practice.–5th ed.
   1. Great Britain. Further education institutions. Teaching
   I. Title   II. Series
   374.13

ISBN 0–304–70255–2

Phototypeset by York House Typographic Ltd.

Printed in Great Britain by Redwood Books, Trowbridge, Wilts.

'What would we say of an architect who, in putting up a new building, could not tell you what he was building, whether it was a temple dedicated to the god of truth, love and right, a simple house in which it would be comfortable to live, a handsome though useless ceremonial gateway that those driving through would admire, a gilded hotel for fleecing improvident travellers, a kitchen for cooking victuals, a museum for the custody of rarities, or finally a shed for storing old junk that one no longer needed? You should say the same, too, about an educator who does not know how to define the ends of his educational work for you clearly and precisely.'

K.D. Ushinsky: *Man as the Object of Education* (1868)

'How to live? – that is the essential question for us. Not how to live in the mere material sense only, but in the widest sense. The general problem which comprehends every special problem is – the right ruling of conduct in all directions under all circumstances. In what way to treat the body; in what way to treat the mind; in what way to manage our affairs; in what way to bring up a family; in what way to behave as a citizen; in what way to utilise those sources of happiness which nature supplies – how to use all our faculties to the greatest advantage to ourselves and others – how to live completely? And this being the great thing needful for us to learn is, by consequence, the great thing which education has to teach. To prepare us for complete living is the function which education has to discharge; and the only rational mode of judging of an educational course is to judge in what degree it discharges such function.'

Herbert Spencer: *Education* (1861)

Contents

Introduction to the Fifth Edition

This fifth edition of *Teaching in Further Education* has the same overall aim as previous editions, namely to assist in the important task of making teaching in the colleges of further education more efficient and effective. The specific objective of this edition is to present a structured text outlining some of the principal theories of learning, and examining a number of widely used practices relating to modes of formal instruction in the colleges and similar institutes.

The book has been written with two groups of readers in mind – teachers in training and college staff who are interested in a review and analysis of their professional teaching activities.

The text places a deliberate emphasis on the practical nature of the teaching process. Where theory is discussed, attention is directed to its links with classroom activity. The vital contribution which can be made to the practice of teaching through an examination of established learning theory is given special prominence.

Preparation of a fifth edition has involved a thorough revision of the original material. Many useful suggestions concerning the revision of content, made by lecturers in colleges of further education and teacher-training departments, are embodied in the text. Some aspects of presentation owe much to views expressed at a seminar attended by a group of college lecturers who had studied earlier editions during their professional training.

Features of this new edition include revised chapters dealing with the theories of learning associated with Bruner and Skinner. A new chapter, explaining the concept of intelligence, includes reference to the controversy surrounding the recently published work of Herrnstein and Murray. An extended treatment of the techniques of lesson planning and preparation is given, together with revised material concerning the sequencing of instruction. Computer-aided learning is reconsidered and the important metaphorical concept of 'the teacher as manager' is explored in detail. Notes and reference material have been updated and the appendix on 'Topics for Discussion' has a new content.

This is essentially a *general* text, involving an exposition of the elements of instruction common to the courses offered currently in colleges of further education in the United Kingdom. It does not include, therefore, any prescriptive advice concerning specific examinations or national syllabuses and schemes of work: it deals with fundamental matters which will be of interest to all members of college teaching staffs, no matter what may be the precise titles or content of the courses with which they are involved.

L.B. Curzon
Oxford, 1997

Part One

An Overview of the Teaching-Learning Process

Chapter 1

Education, Teaching and Learning

Of all the men we meet with, nine parts of ten are what they are, good or evil, useful or not, by their education (Locke, 1695).

The objective of this text is the articulation and examination of the main general principles and practices associated with the work of our colleges of further education. It reflects the author's values and beliefs, tempered by experience, in relation to the purposes and forms of education. Dewey's words express the rationale of those values and beliefs:

Since life means growth, a living creature lives as truly and positively at one stage as at another, with the same intrinsic fullness and the same absolute claims. Hence education means the enterprise of supplying the conditions which ensure growth, or adequacy of life, irrespective of age (Dewey, 1916).

Argument of the text

The argument of the text flows from a *rejection* of those concepts of education which effectively downgrade the formal aspects of instruction, an uncompromising *assertion* of the value of the work of the colleges, and an *affirmation* of the importance of techniques of instruction in enabling students to enter upon and enrich their heritage, thus contributing to human progress which is viewed in these pages as the essential aim of education.

The principles which are reflected intentionally in the text may be set out in the form of a sorites; they are, in unelaborated form, as follows:

- without vision a people will undoubtedly perish;
- formal education can contribute in significant fashion to the breadth and acuity of that vision;
- colleges of further education and similar types of institution can assist in the broadening of the nature and quality of formal education;
- the effectiveness of the colleges can be heightened by the training of staff in the

theory and practice of instruction in general, and teaching techniques in particular.

Acceptance of these principles would seem to require acknowledgment of the force of Oakeshott's dictum: 'The price of the intelligent activity which constitutes being human is learning ... A man is what he learns to become: this is the human condition.'

Arrangement of the text

The argument of the text is presented in six parts. In Part One definitions of the subject area are considered and teaching is discussed in terms of an amalgam of science and art. In Part Two aspects of educational psychology are examined and an attempt is made to indicate the direct relationship of some psychological theories to instructional activity in college classrooms. Part Three concentrates on communication and control in the classroom: these aspects of the teaching-learning process are seen as central to its efficiency. In Part Four the functions of the teacher in his or her role as manager of the instructional process are examined and emphasis is given to specific tasks concerning the student and the learning environment. Part Five outlines and examines key instructional techniques, while Part Six considers the ways in which student performance can be assessed and evaluated.

Introductory remarks on education

The human activity which we call 'education' is based largely in our society on the related processes known as 'teaching' and 'learning'. The formalization of these processes, resulting in their being carried out within schools, colleges and similar institutions, emerges from society's conscious responses to fundamental problems of adaptation and survival.[1] Education in our culture is concerned generally with the handing on of beliefs and moral standards, accumulated knowledge and skills. It has been viewed as 'the nurture of human personality' and as 'investment in human capital'. In its essence it is a recognition of the fact that society's way of life must be *learned* – since an understanding of it is not inherited – by each individual.[2] The process of assimilation of the experiences of earlier generations is at the basis of this task; education assists the younger generation in this process. Learning depends on the individual's experiences within, for example, his or her family, social environment and, more specifically, the educational institutions he or she attends. Teaching involves the provision of those conditions that directly promote effective learning.

When we speak of 'formal education', such as that provided in the colleges of further education, we have in mind, for example, institutions, staff, curricula, programmes, objectives and techniques: these are the *means* associated with the teaching-learning process. The *ends* with which these means are associated are a direct reflection of views of broad social aims. In these pages, the ends of education, involving its rationale, purpose and objectives, concern *human growth*, the signs of which include 'flexibility, openness to new insights, new possibilities, hospitality to novelty, to the imaginative and the creative'. The educational activities appropriate to these ends also involve preparing the student to take his or her place in a changing society, and this means, in Dewey's words, 'to give him command of himself; it means so to train him that he will have the full and ready use of all his capacities; that his eye and ear and hand may be tools ready to command and that his judgment may be capable of grasping the conditions under which it has to work'.[3]

Our study of the theory and practice associated with further education begins with a general consideration of the processes of learning and teaching.

Behaviour

In its general sense, 'behaviour' – a term which figures prominently in this text – has been defined, typically, as 'outward deportment, manners, conduct . . . the manner in which a thing acts' (*Cassell's English Dictionary*). The student's actions in the classroom and the teacher's conduct of the lesson are manifestations of behaviour. Psychologists have defined behaviour in more formal terms.

(a) 'Any response or set of responses made by a living animal' (Evans).[4]
(b) 'The total response, motor and glandular, which an organism makes to any situation with which it is faced' (Drever).[5]
(c) 'The expressed and potential capacity for activity in the physical, mental, and social sphere of life (*Encyclopaedia Britannica*, 1989).
(d) 'Anything an organism does, any of its actions' (Bruno).[6]

Behaviour has been analysed in terms of stimulus and response. A *stimulus* results from some change in an animal's environment. That stimulus is some physical energy change which activates the animal's sense receptors, producing a temporary increase of physiological activity. The animal attempts to adapt to the environmental change: that attempt is a *response*, which may or may not be successful in the circumstances. The response is, therefore, the activities of an animal, usually involving muscles or glands, resulting from a stimulus. The series of observable activities resulting from stimulus-response (S-R) phenomena is known as 'behaviour'. Skinner (see Chapter 6) attempts to define behaviour precisely as 'the movement of an organism or of its parts in a frame of references provided by the organism itself or by various external objects or fields of force'. His definition assumes that all one person can know about another person's awareness and feelings is based on inferences from what that other person *does*. Hence an explanation of 'behaviour' may be provided by a statement of the *functional relationship* between a person's behaviour and those prior events influencing it. By discovering and analysing those prior events that produce relatively enduring changes in people's subsequent behaviour, we are in effect studying the *learning process* that enables them to control themselves and parts of their environment.

The suggestion that the term 'behaviour' be confined to 'the activities of an organism that can be observed by another organism' is not universally accepted (see e.g. Oakeshott's comments on p. 7). Indeed, it epitomizes one of the fundamental differences between the cognitive and behavioural schools of psychology (see pp. 36–8). (Experienced teachers find it difficult to accept that a student's actions tell the *whole* learning story.) Cognitive psychologists argue that unobservable processes, such as those that take place in the brain (thoughts, dreams, etc.) ought to be included in an overall concept of behaviour. On behalf of the behaviourists, Skinner answers in uncompromising fashion:

> Mentalistic explanations allay curiosity and bring enquiry to a stop ... We cannot measure sensations and perceptions as such, but we can measure a person's capacity to discriminate among stimuli, and the *concept* of sensation or perception can then be reduced to the *operation* of discrimination.

For the purposes of this text, we shall consider human behaviour as the *physiological reactions of a person to his or her environmental stimuli.*

Adaptation, survival and learning

The very survival of an animal depends on its ability to adjust and adapt successfully to changes in its environment, that is *to learn.*[7] Whether it be the paramecium which can be observed under a microscope moving into obstacles then displaying its 'blind, fixed avoidance response' by backing away and seemingly approaching again on a different path, or a flock of feeding starlings which scatters in alarm when the wind raises the tattered arm of a scarecrow, or a mouse which, having been defeated in a fight with another, will attempt to run away at the next approach of the victor, the survival of an animal seems to depend on *some tendency to react in ways which are favourable to continued existence.* This tendency is clearly visible in the reactions of a person to physiological needs, such as those arising from thirst or hunger, or to the suspected presence of great danger. An inability to react correctly, to learn how to adapt, is usually incompatible with continued survival. (Dawkins[8] argues that 'we are survival machines – robot vehicles blindly programmed to preserve selfish molecules known as genes'.)

Since an animal's environment is subject to the processes of change, animal behaviour must include the capacities to respond to that change. In more precise terms, if the animal is to survive it must read its environment correctly, must perceive any significant alterations (particularly those spelling a threat) and must make a *correct adjustment or adaptation* to the environmental stimuli. The biologist, Young, considers adaptation as 'the successful incorporation of information about the world'.[9] This vital process necessitates receiving, interpreting and storing information. In effect, the animal must *learn* from its experiences – often a difficult process, and one in which nature may not give a second chance. Learning may be *inferred* from the subsequent reactions of the animal to similar stimuli. The octopus which modifies its reactions after being presented repeatedly with a crab attached to an electrified plate, the child who perceives a link between his cries and the swift appearance of his mother and acts accordingly when he requires attention, have learned how to control important factors in their environment.

The reception, interpretation, storing and retrieval of information are essential operations in the process of control of the environment. In general, the more adequately one is able to carry out these operations, the more precisely one is able to control, and therefore change, the environment according to one's wishes. The formal processes of instruction – teaching and learning – may be viewed therefore as being linked with humanity's continuing attempts to control, change, or adapt to its environment so that its survival is the more assured. (Note the belief, held by some scholars, that what is 'good' for a culture is whatever promotes its survival, so that ethical principles reflect, basically, problems of survival.) It is not hyperbole to suggest that the survival of our species is linked to education.

A note of dissent

Oakeshott (1901–92), in his 1975 essay, *A Place of Learning*, rejects totally the relationship of 'adaptation' to 'learning' presented above. The learning in which we become human differs markedly from the process of organic adaptation to surrounding circumstances. Human learning is not an induced reaction to fortuitous environmental pressures; it is a 'self-imposed task' inspired by a wish to understand and an awareness of our ignorance. It is concerned with ideas, emotions, sensibilities and beliefs; it has nothing to do with organic homeostasis. Human life is much more than a mere process in which an organism grows to maturity; it is 'an adventure in which an individual consciousness confronts the world', and is without a pre-ordained destination. It is 'a predicament and not a journey'. Learning is, for a human being, 'a lifelong engagement' and our world is 'a place of learning' in which educational institutions reflect stages in the engagement to learn.

Teaching and learning in the classroom

Consider four groups of students, typical of those to be found in a college of further education, engaged in the formal activities known as 'the teaching-learning process'.

Group 1

The first group consists of motor vehicle trade apprentices learning the fundamentals of vehicle servicing in preparation for an examination in Vehicle Maintenance, NVQ Level 1.

This class is being held in the college's vehicle workshop, which is equipped with appropriate machinery. Visual aids, in the form of charts and pictorial diagrams are posted on the walls. The ten students are gathered round a demonstration vehicle and the instructor has stated the general lesson objective – the removal and refitting of exhaust manifolds. The instructor has reminded the group of the work done in the previous lesson and is proceeding to an explanation of the sequence of practical steps which will constitute the procedure to be taught. 'First we have to disconnect ... what? Yes, the battery negative lead. Let's do this. John, please disconnect the lead. Next we apply a considerable amount of this penetrating oil to the manifold and exhaust pipe flange nuts and bolts. Watch carefully how this is done ... What has to be done next? Think carefully. Fred, please ... Correct! We unbolt any heat shields or shrouds from the manifold. Here are the necessary tools. Note how I set about this ... Next, from the manifold flange we unbolt ... what? If you are not sure, look at the diagram at the top of the chart behind you ...'

A causal observer of this lesson will see a group of students listening to an instructor and watching his actions. To the trained teacher-observer there is evidence of a carefully structured teaching-learning situation made up of a group of planned activities and based on an analysis of the separate tasks involved in mastering a psychomotor skill. An instructional objective has been defined and the sequence of skill activities to be taught has been arranged. Stimuli have been presented and correct responses elicited and reinforced – the essence of effective instruction. The lesson will continue with a demonstration of further activities and will end with a recapitulation and test.

Group 2

The second group comprises students preparing for the examinations of the Institute of Legal Executives (ILEX), plus others working towards the Intermediate GNVQ in Retail and Distributive Services; they are examining problems relating to theft. The two sets of students have been brought together to share discussion of a topic which is of joint concern.

The students have attended two lectures on the meaning of 'theft' in law: the ILEX students are concerned with the legal implications of the Theft Act 1968; the other students are interested in the handling of suspected shoplifters. The group has heard a reminder of what is meant in law by 'stealing'. The group tutor then states that the purpose of the session is to examine in greater depth what is meant by 'dishonesty'. 'Let's look, first, at this short video. Keep in mind what we mentioned briefly last week about "dishonest conduct".' A video is shown, illustrating the behaviour of a customer in a supermarket: he puts two small items in his pocket and does not pay for them. On leaving the supermarket, he is stopped by a store supervisor. He is then heard telling the supervisor that the goods are of very small value and that he will pay for them there and then. The video is stopped at that point.

The tutor then speaks: 'ILEX students, please choose a reporter, form yourselves into a discussion group, and be ready to tell me in fifteen minutes' time whether you think that the offence of stealing under the 1968 statute can be made out. Distributive trades students, please choose a reporter and be prepared to tell me how, as store managers, you would deal with the situation which has arisen.'

Here may be discerned a prepared scheme of instruction, based on a variety of stimuli and aimed at involving students in the processes of cognitive and affective learning (the former concerned with the analysis and comprehension of facts, the latter with responding and evaluating). The students' activities are directed in overall manner towards attainment of the general instructional objective.

Group 3

The third group is made up of A level students engaged in studying that section of a syllabus in economics which is based on the trade cycle. The teacher's objective is to make the students aware of a quasi-rhythmical pattern and periodicity of movements in production. An overhead projector is being used to display a graph illustrating employment statistics during the first half of the nineteenth century. Time has been allowed for observation of the graph, questions have been raised and answered and the teacher is developing the lesson from that point. The precise instructional objective for this part of the lesson is: 'the students shall recall, after the lesson has ended, the types of period which make up the trade cycle'. '... Look carefully at the movement of the curve between 1900 and 1940 ... Note the red arrows which I am marking in so as to show the peaks in 1909, 1921 and 1933. Note, next, the green arrows which I am using to mark troughs ... Which years ought to be marked? ... Good! Mark them on your graphs. Listen now to a short extract from this recording of a recent broadcast on "Unemployment and the trade cycle". Listen, in particular, to the speaker's definition of the trade cycle in his second sentence, and keep it in mind.'

In this lesson a variety of techniques is employed. Eyes, ears and the associated senses are involved in the process of receiving and interpreting information. Powers of comprehension and deduction are being exercised and the students are moving – as the result of a deliberate plan formulated by the teacher – to a level of understanding higher than that which existed when the lesson commenced. A test, which will be administered towards the end of the lesson, will measure and evaluate that level, so that teacher and students will be aware of progress and attainment.

Group 4

The fourth group comprises six nurses and four other health worker students who are working through a module on 'Physiology for Health Care' as a part of their course designed for the GVNQ BTEC Advanced Certificate in Health and Social Care; they are examining the structure of the human skeleton. They are seated at computer screens, working through a short revision course. The computer program deals with the names of the bones and principal parts of the pelvic girdle. Each student is working at his or her own pace and is guided by the program along a prepared route designed to lead to a specific level of knowledge. The program includes sequences of illustrations, diagrams and multiple choice questions. A correct answer is followed by a short reinforcing statement and an instruction that the correct answer is to be copied into the student's workbook. The class tutor moves among the students, asking questions and checking and evaluating written answers; the tutor also adds explanations of various matters appearing in the program.

In this lesson, individually presented units of instruction are eliciting responses which will aid the processes of retention and recall – the essence of revision. Correct responses prepare the way for further stimuli; incorrect responses are analysed prior to a further set of questions. A planned sequence of activities related to the

communication of information – reception, comprehension, retention and retrieval
– is the basis of this type of instruction.[10]

Elements of the teaching-learning process

An analysis of the teaching-learning situations described above will show the
existence of the component elements of the system referred to as the 'formal
classroom situation' (with which succeeding chapters will be largely concerned).
Those elements include the following:

1. A *learner*, whose nervous systems, senses and muscles are operating in sequen-
    ces of patterned activity, which we speak of as *behaviour*.
2. A *teacher*, selecting and organizing instructional methods, consciously planning
    and controlling a situation directed to the achievement of optimum student
    learning.
3. A *series of learning objectives*, related to students' anticipated and desired
    behavioural changes. We may consider objectives as 'intended learning out-
    comes', the level of attainment of which can be observed and measured (see
    Chapters 13 and 30).
4. A *sequence of S-R situations* affecting teacher and learner, resulting in persistent
    and observable changes in the learner's behaviour from which we may infer
    'learning'. That learning is directed by the teacher towards an enhancement of
    students' cognitive, affective and psychomotor abilities.
5. *Reinforcement* of that behaviour. By 'reinforcement' (see Chapter 6) we refer to
    an activity which increases the likelihood that some event will occur again.
6. The *monitoring, assessment and evaluation* of the learner's changes in behaviour
    in relation to the objectives of the learning process. (These specialized activities
    are fundamental to the process of '*control*' (see Chapter 12) without which the
    teaching-learning process must be less than adequate.)

Definitions of learning

How should 'learning' be defined? Dictionaries provide a general, if superficial,
guide. 'Knowledge acquired by study' (*Cassell's English Dictionary*) is a typical
dictionary definition. More specific definitions have come from educational psychologists. The following are examples.

(a) 'Any activities that develop new knowledge and abilities in the individual who
    carries them out, or else cause old knowledge and abilities to acquire new
    qualities' (Galperin, 1965).[11]
(b) 'A process of reorganisation of sensory-feedback patterning which shifts the
    learner's level of control over his own behaviour in relation to the objects and
    events of the environment' (Smith, 1966).[12]
(c) 'The process by which an activity originates or is changed through reacting to an

encountered situation, provided that the characteristics of the change in activity cannot be explained on the basis of native response tendencies, maturation or temporary states of the organism (e.g. fatigue, drugs, etc.)' (Hilgard and Bower, 1981).[13]

(d) 'What occurs when a person makes sense out of what he encounters or experiences in interacting with self, others and the environment' (Brubaker, 1982).[14]

(e) 'A change in human disposition or capability, which persists over a period of time, and which is not simply ascribable to the process of growth' (Gagné, 1983).[15]

(f) 'Learning is becoming capable of doing some correct or suitable thing in *any* situations of certain general sorts. It is becoming prepared for *variable* calls within certain ranges' (Ryle, 1983).[16]

(g) 'Learning is a relatively permanent change in behaviour or in behavioural potentiality that results from experience and cannot be attributed to temporary body states such as those induced by illness, fatigue or drugs' (Hergenhahn, 1997).[17]

(h) 'The alteration of behaviour as a result of individual experience. When an organism can perceive and change its behaviour, it is said to learn' (*Encyclopaedia Britannica*, 1989).

(i) 'The acquisition and retention of knowledge and habits of thought in a way that permits them to be employed in a useful way after the initial exposure has been terminated' (Saunders and Walstad, 1990).[18]

(j) 'The active creation of knowledge structures from personal experience' (Biehler, 1993).[19]

Running through definitions of this type are the following assertions: the nature of learning is inferred from *changes in behaviour*; learning occurs as the result of given *experiences* which precede changes in behaviour; learning involves '*behaviour potentiality*' (that is, the capacity to perform some act at a future time, as contrasted with 'performance' which concerns the translation of potentiality into behaviour); the modification of behaviour involved in learning is of a *relatively permanent nature*.

For the purposes of this text, we shall consider learning as '*the apparent modification of a person's behaviour through his activities and experiences, so that his knowledge, skills and attitudes, including modes of adjustment, towards his environment are changed, more or less permanently*'.

It will be obvious that not *all* behaviour is learned. The so-called 'emotional responses' that have value to the human being are basically unlearned: the neonate's crying is not learned in the sense noted above. Some psychologists speak of 'prepared learning' and 'unprepared learning'. The former category is based on the view that we seem to be prepared in a biological sense for certain types of learning which have a high survival value, e.g. learning to walk and talk. Unprepared learning involves learning about one's world, e.g. learning to read, to perform complex skills – the type of learning which seems not immediately related to survival. Behaviour resulting from unprepared learning generally requires motivational support in the form of services provided by specialized educational institutions, organized so as to produce effective learning.[20]

Oakeshott on learning

Oakeshott views learning as an activity which is possible only to an individual who is 'capable of choice and self-direction' in relation to his or her impulses and environment. It allows one to come to know oneself and one's surroundings; it is interminable and relates to conduct, not behaviour. The world which surrounds an individual consists not of mere abstractions but of beliefs. One can enter and 'possess' one's world only through the activities which constitute learning, and this involves being taught. It is only through the transactions which emerge from the process of learning ('doing and submitting at the same time') that one's world becomes comprehensible.

The significance of an analysis of the teaching-learning process for the teacher

The implications of what has been stated above are obviously important for the practising teacher involved in the day-to-day activities of the classroom, laboratory and workshop. Learning – often thought of as a mysterious, incomprehensible event – emerges from the definitions presented above as a very complex process, but one which, nevertheless, lends itself to analysis and which is generally amenable to the techniques of scientific investigation. The activities which may be inferred as having occurred when changes in a learner's behaviour are observed have been made the subject of close and continuous enquiry. It is useful for the practising teacher to be aware of the research and conclusions of the experimental psychologists in the area of the study of human learning.

Since the learning process can be understood to a large extent, it can be guided in considerable measure (but never completely: Dewey reminds us that perhaps the greatest of all pedagogical fallacies is 'the notion that a person learns only the particular thing he is studying at the time'). The task of the teacher is no longer limited to the imparting of information with the hope that it will be comprehended and remembered. That task has to be seen in terms of *planning* those conditions and activities which will result, as far as possible, in effective learning. The guidance of the learning process, which comes from an analysis of its constituent elements, necessitates activities known collectively as '*control*'. Control is based on *monitoring* (or *measuring*), *assessing* and *adjusting* – specific tasks which are fundamental to successful classroom teaching (see Chapter 12).

The passing on of information can no longer constitute the teacher's entire responsibility. His role is seen in this text as involving responsibility for the vital, interpersonal processes of communication which are at the very centre of the teaching-learning situation. The teacher as *communicator* figures prominently in some of the chapters which follow. The teacher as *manager*, with a direct responsibility for the planning and deployment of resources, also features significantly in these pages.

The call for the abolition of formal education

Teachers are aware of the barrage of criticism which descends around their heads from time to time. 'Black papers', political pronouncements and newspaper editorials suggest that educational institutions are directly responsible for declining standards. Much more significant, however, than ephemeral criticism of this nature, is the fundamental attack on the very nature of formal education which has appeared in recent years. The movement for 'deschooling', which characterizes formal education as 'anti-human', and views the teaching profession as involved in 'the subversion of true education', has as its most prominent advocate Ivan Illich (b. 1926), a former Catholic priest and vice-president of the Catholic University of Puerto Rico. In his celebrated *Deschooling Society*,[21] Illich recommends the total abolition of formal education and the teaching profession as at present constituted.

Society, says Illich, has degraded its members by imposing on them a concept (and practice) of education which is alien, and sets of institutions (schools, etc.) which are 'vicious'. These institutions are producing 'non-people'; their task seems to be to process people for employment in a fundamentally flawed market-place economy. 'Hidden curricula' produce a people who are alienated from true learning. The situation demands a revolutionary change – 'deschooling'.

In a 'deschooled society', learning would be totally *non-formal*. 'Learning webs', based on society's resources, would take into account the 'four sources of real learning' – things, models, peers and elders. 'Skills exchanges' would be set up, based on 'free skills centres' open to the public. 'Educational administrators' (who would *not* include 'the many persons now attracted to teaching who are profoundly authoritative') would give advice on learning to those who asked for it; they would help learners to find the paths which would lead fastest to their goals. The basic question for society, in relation to education, would be: 'What kinds of things and people might learners want to be in contact with in order to learn?'

Freire (b. 1929), teacher, theologian and philosopher, has collaborated with Illich and has set out his views on the necessity for the abolition of formal education in *Pedagogy of the Oppressed* (1973).[22] Although his main concern is with the necessity to remove the poverty and degradation of the 'third world' in Latin America, his general analysis of formal education is applicable, he claims, to educational systems in all countries. Because formal education involves a superordinate-subordinate relationship between teacher and student, it has become irrelevant in an era in which people must exercise for themselves their creative and critical powers. Instructional programmes based upon the fettering of potentialities, in the interests of an exploiting class, are intolerable. The formal classroom, the ritualized processes of instruction in further and higher education, deprive the masses of the possibility of achieving 'conscientization' – the attitude that enables individuals to build an appreciation of autonomy and self-responsibility.

The process of 'conscientization' can grow only when traditional schooling and the passivity and conformity which it is designed to intensify are abolished. A 'problem-posing education', which involves a continuous process of 'unveiling of reality', must be created and, in this type of education, the dispossessed will study by involvement at an informal level with those who are willing to teach. The 'problem-posing education' which will replace formal institutions and their curricula will be carried on 'neither *for* nor *about* the oppressed but *with* them'.

Criticism of Illich and Freire has been harsh. Bowen suggests that 'in dispensing with the school, there is the real danger of dispensing with culture and civilisation'.[23] Some critics have drawn attention to the total failure of Illich to work out the practical implications of the 'teaching webs'. Freire has been denounced as a Tolstoyan in the age of electronically controlled mass communication, unable to understand the dependence of the technologies which are essential for the material development of the 'third world' upon the advanced knowledge which he affects to despise. It has been said of both men that their programmes would deprive the poor of Latin America of the very processes which are needed if their poverty is to disappear.

The impetus of the deschooling movement seems to have diminished, but teachers ought to be aware of the existence of educational philosophies which question their role in, and value to, society.

The chapters which follow rest upon a rejection of the philosophy of deschooling; they accept the need for a recognition of formal instructional techniques as powerful means of 'initiating students into exactitudes of thought' and creating the basis for informed choice, thereby assisting in the realization of human potential.

Notes and references

1. See generally for this chapter: *Education, Culture, Economy and Society* ed. A.H. Halsey (OUP, 1997); *Means and Ends in Education* by B. Cohen (Allen & Unwin, 1983); *The Philosophy of Education* ed. R.S. Peters (OUP, 1973); *Education, Society and Human Nature* by A. O'Hear (Routledge, 1981); *Democracy and Education* by J. Dewey (Macmillan, 1961); *The Voice of Liberal Learning – M. Oakeshott on Education* ed. T. Fuller (Yale UP, 1989). (Note that the dates of publication given in these pages refer to the editions used in preparation of this text.)

2. See *Cultural Transmission and Evolution* by L. Cavalli-Sforza (Princeton UP, 1981). Note Oakeshott's description of teaching as 'the deliberate and intentional initiation of a pupil into the world of human achievement': cited in *The Voice of Liberal Learning* by T. Fuller (Yale UP, 1989).

3. 'My pedagogic creed' by J. Dewey in *Dewey on Education* ed. M.S. Dworkin (Columbia UP, 1967).

4. *Psychology: Dictionary of the Mind, Brain and Behaviour* (Arrow Books, 1978).

5. *Dictionary of Psychology* (Penguin, 1979).

6. *Dictionary of Key Words in Psychology* by F.J. Bruno (Routledge & Kegan Paul, 1986).

7. See e.g. *Animal Behaviour* by N. Tinbergen (Time-Life, 1965); *Unravelling Animal Behaviour* by M.S. Dawkins (Longman, 1986); *The Ant and the Peacock* by H. Cronin (CUP, 1991); *The Life of Mammals* by J. Young (OUP, 1967); *Place and Purpose in Nature* by G. Williams (Weidenfeld, 1996); *The Shape of Life* by R.A. Raff (University

of Chicago Press, 1996); *The Web of Life* by F. Capra (Harper Collins, 1997); *Physiology of Behaviour* by N. Carlson (Allyn & Bacon, 1994).

8. *The Selfish Gene* (OUP, 1976).
9. *The Life of Mammals* (OUP, 1967).
10. See 'Teaching cycles and strategies' by C. Power in *The International Encyclopaedia of Teaching and Teacher Education* (Pergamon, 1987), referred to in later chapter notes of this text as *IETE*.
11. *Psychology of Teaching* (USSR Publishing House, 1965).
12. *Cybernetic Principles of Learning and Educational Design* (Holt, Rinehart & Winston, 1966).
13. *Theories of Learning* (Prentice-Hall, 1981).
14. *Curriculum Planning* (Scott, Foresman, 1982).
15. *The Conditions of Learning* (Holt-Saunders, 1983).
16. *The Concept of Mind* (Penguin, 1983).
17. *An Introduction to Theories of Learning* (Prentice-Hall, 1988, 1997).
18. *The Principles of Economics Course* (McGraw Hill, 1990).
19. *Psychology Applied to Teaching* (Houghton Mifflin, 1993). See also 'Conceptions of Learning' by E. Beatty. *International Journal of Educational Research*, 1992, *19*.
20. See *The Process of Learning* by J. Biggs and R. Telfer (Prentice-Hall, 1987).
21. Pub. Calder and Boyars (1971).
22. See *The Texts of Paolo Freire* by P.V. Taylor (Routledge, 1993); *Teachers as Cultural Workers* by P. Freire (Plymbridge, 1997).
23. *Theories of Education* by J. Bowen and P. Hobson (Wiley, 1987).

Chapter 2

The Science and Art of Teaching

> To distinguish between science and art is not to put them into competition but to recognise the distinctive ways in which they operate . . . The distinction is important, if for no other reason than to show the extent to which each has been and can be used in educational enquiry (Eisner, 1979).

In this chapter we ask the fundamental question: is teaching a science, an art, or an amalgam of both? This is a vital matter for educational theory and practice: upon the answer ought to depend an appropriate approach to the training of teachers, and the relevant criteria for the evaluation of a teacher's performance.[1] We consider also the relevance and utility of theory, keeping in mind the suggestion of Williams[2] that it is time, perhaps, to view theory and practice in education as two sides of the same coin, 'or maybe, more like a Möbius strip'.

'Teaching' is defined in this chapter in formal terms and attention is drawn to four matters of particular importance for readers of this text: the use of definitions, the use of analogies and models, the significance of 'perception' in relation to the interpretation of teaching theory, and the evaluation of theories.

The common elements of 'teaching', 'training' and 'instruction' – a matter of some importance in the colleges of further education – are mentioned, and the significance of the concepts is noted.

The relevance and utility of theory

The relevance of theory to teaching practice is not always obvious to many teachers. The young teacher, fresh from his or her training course, overwhelmed by novel experiences, is often unable immediately to link the reality of the classroom with the theories he or she has learned. The experienced teacher, hard-pressed to maintain standards in the face of unimaginative administrative decisions, may feel that there is 'no time for theory conceived at a far, comfortable distance from the chalk face'. Both teachers epitomize those for whom difficulties in accepting theory make the reception and translation of theory into practice impossible. Yet, if teaching is accepted as even a 'partial science', theory cannot be neglected, for no valid science can be constructed without a theoretical basis. Set out below are some frequently posed questions on this topic.

'Principles', 'axioms', 'theorems', 'hypotheses', 'theories' ... What exactly do these terms mean?

These words are often used conterminously in books dealing with teaching theory. They can be differentiated, however. A *principle* is a generalization that provides a guide to conduct or procedure, e.g. the principle that effective teaching demands control of the classroom situation. An *axiom* is a self-evident principle that is, apparently, not open to dispute (but see p. 26), e.g. the axiom that lack of motivation makes for learning difficulties. A *theorem* is a proposition admitting of rational proof which is usually necessary to succeeding steps in some structure of reasoning, e.g. the theorem that it is possible to test and assess the level of a student's intelligence. *Hypotheses* are unconfirmed assumptions, e.g. the suggestions that spatial arrangements in a classroom directly affect student learning. A *theory* is a system of ideas attempting to explain a group of phenomena, such as the processes of learning. Kerlinger[3] suggests that a theory is a 'set of interrelated constructs (concepts), definitions and propositions that present a systematic view of phenomena by specifying relations among variables, with the purpose of explaining and predicting the phenomena'. Hull (see p. 60) writes of a theory as a 'systematic, deductive derivation of secondary principles of observable phenomena from a relatively small number of primary principles or postulates, much as secondary principles or theories of geometry are ultimately derived from a few original definitions and primary principles called axioms'.

Why do teaching theoreticians employ so much jargon? Why can't they use everyday language?

A specialized body of knowledge tends to generate and use its own technical terminology. Consider, for example, the use of words such as 'energy' in physics, 'market' in economics, 'duty' in jurisprudence. The knowledge on which teaching theory rests is of a highly specialized nature. Psychology, neurology, biology have all contributed to teaching-learning theory. It is not easy to substitute 'everyday language' for technical terms and yet maintain acceptable standards of precision. As an example, attempt to replace with everyday language terms such as 'conditioning', 'encoding' and 'reinforcement'.

Why is there so much fundamental disagreement among teaching-learning theoreticians? They don't agree even on the meaning of basic terms, such as 'education'.

Teaching is a complex activity, varying outwardly from one situation to another, so that it is not easy to explain or define its nature with precision – hence much of the disagreement. (Try, as an exercise in definition, to bring under one conceptual heading the modes of instruction involved in showing a child how to tie her shoelaces, teaching a student the use of a typewriter, and explaining to an adult the concept of 'idiom'. Attempt, further, to recall how you 'learned' to tell the time, to use a calculator, to drive a car.) Not all theoreticians and practising teachers perceive events in the same way; hence, interpretations of events differ. Disagreement is not necessarily a sign of an ineffective, sterile body of knowledge: differences in the interpretation of quantum theory have not prevented great advances in physics. Terms such as 'education' overlap several disciplines, such as the 'inexact sciences' of sociology and political theory, hence the frequent arguments as to its precise meaning. Jurists continue to dispute the very meaning of the term 'law'; economists often disagree as to the meaning of the term 'economics'. Lack of agreement on definitions does not imply total uncertainty within a discipline; it may indicate, rather, the existence of a number of approaches to the areas of knowledge embraced by that discipline. Miller argues:[4] 'A situation in which different explanatory frameworks are in the field, attributing contrary explanations to phenomena, is no crisis. For accepting a theory, approach or explanation only requires belief in its adequacy to cope with the phenomena.'

Some teaching-learning theory seems to be based on the work of writers who lived many centuries ago. Plato, Aristotle, Locke ... what relevance have they in an age which they could not have envisaged?

> He who would confine his thought to present time will not understand present reality (Michelet, 1833).

Contemporary educational theory did not spring into existence, fully armed with principles and axioms, in the 1970s or 1980s. Today, we as teachers and theoreticians see as sharply as we do, not because of any superior acuity of vision, not because we are wiser than our ancestors, but because, in many areas of theory and practice, we 'stand on their shoulders'. What and how *they* perceived is often interwoven with *our* thought patterns, even though we may be unaware of the debt.[5] Today's practice and burgeoning theory in educational writing cannot be understood fully without reference to ideas rooted in the ancestry of that theory. (Note the statement of Weimer[6] that almost every learning theory propounded in this century is based on the associative principles first expounded by Aristotle.) As the historian, Maitland, reminds us: 'Today we study the day before yesterday, in order that yesterday may not paralyze today, and today may not paralyze tomorrow'.

Do practical people, such as teachers, really need theory?

Substitute for the word 'teachers', the words 'surgeons' or 'airline pilots' – who are 'practical people' – and the restricted basis of the question is exposed. If practice is the 'how', theory is the 'why'. Successful practitioners in the field will be the better equipped for their tasks if they understand both the 'how' and the 'why'. Theory and practice often go hand in hand; indeed, theory may be based upon 'distilled practice'. Fontenelle reminds us that 'to despise theory is to have the excessively vain pretension to do without knowing what one does, and to speak without knowing what one says'. The economist, Keynes, an outstanding example of a theoretician and a 'practical person', warned in emphatic terms against the self-styled 'men of practice' who, while affecting to abhor theory, are unconsciously guided by the ideas of 'defunct scribblers'. How many generations of unacknowledged and unknown theoreticians, one wonders, have fashioned the views of the 'practical teachers' who declare sincerely that 'carrot and stick' is the only real answer to problems of student motivation? Indeed, teachers, like all other professional workers, cannot escape the pervasive nature of theory. Popper observes: 'All observations (and, even more, all experiments) are theory-impregnated: they are interpretations in the light of theories'.

Theory, argues Anderson, serves many functions: it seeks to describe and explain phenomena 'in a parsimonious way' (that is, by using as few assumptions as possible in the explanation) and stimulates novel ways of thinking about those phenomena. Its significance is summed up well by the biologist and teacher, Jacob:[7]

> For an object to be accessible to investigation, it is not sufficient just to perceive it. A theory prepared to accommodate it must also exist. In the dialogue between theory and experience, theory always has the first word.

An important note of caution comes from over one and a half centuries ago and was formulated by a theoretician in a very different field of activity:

> In the same way as many plants only bear fruit when they do not shoot too high, so in the practical arts the theoretical leaves and flowers must not be made to sprout too far, but kept near to experience, which is their proper soil.

If a teacher's actions succeed in practice, why bother to theorize? Isn't there some truth in the jibe that educational theoreticians are people who say: 'I agree that it works in practice, but I wonder if it works in theory'?

Without knowing *why* a course of action is successful, without understanding the significance of its content and context, one may make mistakes in the future when the actions are again performed, in a fundamentally different environment, for example. Polanyi, commenting on the history of science, has made trenchant observations on the 'practice-is-all-you-need' school:

> Almost every major systematic error which has deluded men for thousands of years relied on practical experience ... Horoscopes ... the cures of witch doctors and of medical practitioners before the advent of modern medicine, were all firmly established through the centuries in the eyes of the public by their supposed practical success. The scientific method was devised precisely for the purpose of elucidating the nature of things under more carefully controlled conditions and by more rigorous criteria than are present in the situations created by practical problems.[8]

'Teachers are born, not made, and theory can never help those who lack the innate talent to teach.' What of this?

This argument, often presented in apodictic, sibylline style, has been used in its time to downgrade and devalue the work of teacher-training institutions, industrial training boards, seminars aimed at the improvement of teaching practice – and books on teaching! There is, however, much evidence to suggest that improved understanding and practice can and do stem directly from instruction in theoretical principles of teaching. The argument rests on an unwarranted belief in the existence of innate, unimprovable qualities of the teacher. The very concept of teaching fundamentals in any subject area as an aid to the comprehension and improvement of practical activity – the successful foundation of many generations of teaching practice – is not compatible with the idea underlying the 'born, not made' aphorism. To carry the idea to its conclusion would be to negate the very concepts of teaching and learning as activities designed to build on, and improve, our genetic inheritance.

Are the principles of teaching and learning as set out in these pages, for example, universally applicable?

Probably yes. There is little in the literature or in the practical experience of teachers to suggest, for example, that cognitive theory has no application in countries south of the equator or that the transfer of learning does not operate outside Europe! Problems related to difficulties in retrieving and reinstating learned information are fundamentally the same for students in Bolton, Berlin or Beijing. What *is* of considerable significance, however, in relation to this question, is the relevant 'cultural and social overlay'.[9] Thus, the excessive reliance of many students in southeast Asia on rote learning, the emphasis on memorization of texts in the traditional schools of theocratic states, the extensive use of electronic aids in the American classroom, tend to create different learning *styles and patterns* and produce associated types of teaching skill. But these differences do not arise from any variations in learning *processes*, as set out in these pages; rather do they reflect a diversity of cultural backgrounds. None of the learning theories and modes of tuition referred to in this text has an exclusively 'local' or 'national' significance.[10]

Definitions of teaching

A typical dictionary definition of 'teaching' is given in *Cassell's English Dictionary*: 'causing a person to learn or acquire knowledge or skill'. The activity is defined in terms of causation, with some end in view. A selection of more formal definitions is set out below.

(a) 'Intended behaviour for which the aim is to induce learning' (Scheffler, 1960).[11]

(b) 'Teaching is aimed at changing the ways in which other persons can or will behave' (Gage, 1963).[12]

(c) 'That array of activities the teacher employs to transform intentions and curriculum materials into ... conditions that promote learning' (Eisner, 1979).[13]

(d) 'Teaching involves implementing strategies that are designed to lead learners to the attainment of certain goals. In general these strategies involve communication, leadership, motivation and control (discipline or management)' (Lefrancois, 1985).[14]

(e) 'Teaching denotes action undertaken with the intention of bringing about learning in another' (Robertson, 1987).[15]

(f) 'Teaching is an interpersonal, interactive activity, typically involving verbal communication, which is undertaken for the purpose of helping one or more students learn or change the ways in which they can or will behave' (Anderson and Burns, 1989).[16]

For the purposes of this text we define teaching in terms related directly to the concept of learning, as stated on p. 12 above: *'a system of activities intended to induce learning, comprising the deliberate and methodical creation and control of those conditions in which learning does occur'.*

It should be noted that teaching is seen as a *system* of activities, not a single action. Power states that teaching assumes its distinctive character and meaning not in isolated behaviour 'but in sequences of interrelated acts'.[17] 'Teaching cycles' characterize most sequential patterns of classroom activity: the cycles are based on 'episodes' intended by the teacher to induce certain types of activity and to produce learning states. Teaching is considered by Power to be the systematic series of activities through which the teacher seeks to interpret his specific tasks in relation to modification of the learner's state of knowledge.[18]

Teaching: art or science?

Discussion with almost any group of practising teachers in further education will reveal fundamental differences of opinion on the classification of 'teaching' as an art or science. Some will insist that teaching is a scientific application of tested theory; some will argue that it is essentially a performance on the 'classroom stage' that can be characterized as aesthetic, so that it has to be considered as a form of art;[19] some will maintain that it is a hybrid, an art with a scientific basis, or a science with overtones of artistic impression;[20] some will reject 'art' and 'science' as having any place in the purely practical, day-to-day teaching activity in the colleges. Others will be amazed to learn that their teaching activities can be classified as partaking of the nature of either science or art – rather like Molière's Monsieur Jourdain who was surprised to find that he had been 'speaking prose' all his life!

Observation of a series of teaching activities in a typical college of further education will generally reveal a variety of approaches (see pp. 7, 8). One successful lesson may have been prepared carefully on the basis of an analysis of student needs, culminating in a listing of learning objectives (see Chapter 14); teaching strategy and tactics will have played their part in a planned utilization of class time. Another successful lesson may have been characterized by a seemingly casual approach in which the teacher has employed his or her skills in a deliberate attempt to discover 'ends through action'; his or her activities would bring to mind the description of the artist as 'one who plays hide-and-seek but does not know what he seeks until he finds it'.

The distinction between teaching as art and science is typified in the approaches of Highet (1977),[21] Eisner (1979) and Skinner (1968).[22] Highet is vehement in his denunciation of the application of the aims and methods of science to learners as individuals. This is seen as a 'dangerous' tendency: a scientific relationship between human beings must be inadequate. So-called 'scientific teaching' will be inadequate 'as long as both teachers and pupils are human beings'.

Eisner enumerates four senses in which teaching should be considered an art. First, it is an art in the sense that the teacher 'can perform with such skill and grace' that for teacher and student alike the performance provides an intrinsic form of expression – the lesson has the overtones of an aesthetic experience. (Note that Biehler argues that teaching is an art because it involves emotions and values, and these 'cannot be objectively and systematically manipulated'.) Secondly, teaching is an art in the sense that teachers in their professional work must exercise qualitative judgments in the interest of achieving qualitative ends. 'Classroom qualities such as tempo, tone, climate, pace of discussion and forward movement' require the exercise by the teacher of qualitative forms of intelligence. Thirdly, teaching, like any other art, involves a tension between automaticity and inventiveness. The teacher has to use his or her repertoires and routines in an innovative way so as to deal inventively with what happens in class. Finally, teaching is an art in the sense that many of its ends are emergent – they are not preconceived; they emerge in the course of interaction with students. Opportunities for the creation of 'ends in process' require models of teaching akin to other arts.

Skinner (see Chapter 6) argues that successful teaching can be the result only of the conscious and judicious application of scientifically validated theory to classroom situations. Successful teaching does not happen fortuitously; it emerges when the teacher has made, and understood, a correct analysis of student behaviour in terms of the complex interplay of elementary concepts and principles. When behaviour is understood, an appropriate instructional methodology must be sought in order that it might be modified where necessary on the basis of desired ends. On the practising teacher and the scientist investigating classroom behaviour will fall the joint tasks of observing fact, formulating theory, applying it and then reinterpreting both fact and theory.

Fundamental to this text is the belief that the practice of teaching ought to move to a position in which it can be seen as based openly on an application of theory reflecting the reality of the classroom and its environment, and that such theory and practice ought to be subjected to continuous, severe criticism. The critical, methodical appraisal of teaching principles and practice would seem to be a prerequisite for the construction of a comprehensive theory of teaching, whether it be considered as science or art. One thing, however, is almost certain – teaching, because of its very nature, can never be an *exact* practice. (In any event, it is as well to remember Solow's comment: 'All theory depends on assumptions which are not quite true. That is what makes it theory.')

To provide a scientific basis for teaching may be essential – but this is not enough. The correct application of scientific principles so as to achieve desired ends partakes of an art – the exercise of a human skill involving mastery of technique *and* aesthetic appreciation. The violinist who is skilled in techniques of finger positions, who has a good knowledge of acoustics and harmonics, cannot guarantee a tolerable, let alone an artistically valid, performance. The teacher who understands perfectly the theories of learning, cannot promise an effective lesson. Musician and teacher require something over and above appropriate, scientific technique and under-standing – they need the capacities of judgment, perception and interpretation, which can emerge only after much experience and which are akin to the developed powers of the artist.

In this text, teaching is seen as involving a blend of science *and* art; both enter into the provision of the conditions for effective learning.[23] Costa sums up this view: 'Teaching is a synthesis, not a separation – a synthesis of the human mind's rational *and* intuitive capabilities. Neither is comprehended in the other, nor can either be reduced to the other. Both are necessary, supplementing one another for a fuller understanding of the realities of teaching and of learning.'[24]

Some problems arising from the text

We mention briefly below some problems related to the method of presentation in the text of the concept of 'teaching': they concern the use of definitions, the utilization of analogies and models, the process of 'perception', and the evaluation of theory.

The use of definitions

A swift perusal of the text will indicate that definitions have been used very widely for two purposes: first, to supply the meaning of a term that might otherwise not be understood (e.g. 'behaviourism'); secondly, to restrict the meaning of a term that has several meanings, in order to prevent ambiguity (e.g. 'reinforcement'). (Note Hobbes' comment in *Leviathan* (1651): 'In the right definition of name lies the first use of speech, which is the acquisition of science; and in wrong or no definitions lies the first abuse, from which proceed all false and senseless tenets'.) But to 'know a definition' is no indication that the concept with which it deals has been assimilated. Such knowledge 'may be purely formal without any understanding of the system of essential attributes that underline it and without any ability to apply it' (Talyzina). The definitions appearing in this or any other text on teaching require continuous and critical examination in the light of theory and practice in the classroom if they are to be of any value to the practising teacher.

The philosopher Popper has questioned the widespread dogma that definition is essential to plain, clear thinking.[25] He claims that a definition cannot really establish the meaning of a term; it can only shift the problem of meaning back to the defining terms, so that arguments about whether a definition is correct or not 'can only lead to an empty controversy about words'. (Consider, in this context, the definition: 'Teaching is the process of assisting students to learn'.)

The definitions used in this text prove, in themselves, nothing. Their use is intended to concentrate the attention of the reader on what is believed to be the essential nature of that which is being defined. In relation to the study of teaching principles, the definition acts as a focus of meaning, and nothing more.

The utilization of analogies and models

An *analogy* is a process of reasoning, of explaining from what seems to be a parallel case; resemblances are found between new experiences and established, familiar facts.[26] In physics, for example, Huygens (1629–95) explained the wave theory of light in terms of a well-known concept of sound as a 'wave phenomenon'; in the study of teaching we speak of the teacher's role as akin to that of 'guide and manager'. A *model* (see the comments on p. 135 by Deutsch) is an interpretation (usually detailed) of a relatively complicated system (S_1) in terms of a simpler known system (S_2), so that the workings of S_1 are recognized by reference to the interplay of elements in S_2. Texts on teaching are replete with models: see, for example, the models of communication, control and memory in Chapters 11, 12 and 17.

The physicist, Oppenheimer (1904–67), writes of the use of analogy in the following terms: 'Whether or not we talk of discovery or of invention, analogy is inevitable in human thought, because we come to new things in science with what equipment we have, which is how we have learned to think, and above all how we have learned to think about the relatedness of things. We cannot, coming into something new, deal with it except on the basis of the familiar and the old-fashioned.'

Argument by analogy has its dangers. To consider the teacher as a 'guide' does not imply that all the functions of a guide should be read into the tasks of the teacher; indeed, assumed resemblances may not, in fact, be actual resemblances. Perception of the role of the teacher in terms of a 'controller of a system' may seem inadequate when one takes into account the nature of that which is being controlled. Similarly, the model does not represent reality in its entirety: the processes of storage of information in the student's memory, for example, bear no resemblance whatsoever to the process of storing physical items in containers. The utilization of models and analogies in relation to explanations of the teaching process must be examined very carefully when they appear in a textbook.[27]

The process of perception

The term 'perception' appears in many places in this text. Student A 'perceives' his teacher as an excellent tutor, devoted to his class and his subject; student B 'perceives' him as a dour, humourless martinet. Student X, after reading Chapter 6 of this book 'perceives' Skinner's doctrine of behaviourism as a valuable contribution to the study of human beings; student Y 'perceives' the doctrine as a pernicious attack on human dignity.

The verb 'perceive' is used above to refer to interpretation in terms of one's background, values, prior learning, etc. But perception and interpretation are not the same; in Kuhn's words: 'What perception leaves for interpretation to complete depends drastically on the nature and amount of prior experience and training'.[28] In the formal sense, perception refers to the translation of sensory stimuli into organized, meaningful experience.[29] In these pages the term is generally used in its non-formal sense: 'perception' of a theory, a lesson, a teacher's abilities, will reflect not only objective reality, but also the values and past associated experiences of the perceiver.

Evaluating theories of instruction

Many theories of instruction are presented in these pages and the question of evaluation must arise. How ought we to decide whether or not to accept a complex theory relating to instructional practice? In his Nobel lecture of 1988, the econometrician, Allais,[30] suggested the following approach to the examination of theories, based upon the principles of 'scientific method': the importance of this approach extends far beyond the subject matter of this text. The steps in Allais' approach are as follows:

1. Reduce the theory to its component hypotheses, which should be well-defined.
2. Examine each hypothesis so that its consequences may be deduced.
3. Confront the consequences with observed data. This is the 'golden rule' for the evaluation of theory. 'Any theory whatever, if not verified by empirical evidence, has no scientific value and should be rejected.'

Allais suggests an extensive use of theoretical models (see p. 135) in the presentation and evaluation of hypotheses. No general theory can be understood, he states, if it is not illustrated by models which make possible the *implications* of its constituent hypotheses. Indeed, 'the more general a theory, the more its illustration by models ensures a full understanding of its significance and scope.'

Popper, in his analysis of the investigation of theory, insists that 'enquiry begins with *problems*, not observations'. We begin with a problem (P_1), to which we seek to offer a tentative solution, a tentative theory (TT). The theory is subjected to intensive criticism so as to eliminate error (EE). The theory and its critical revision produce new problems (P_2):

$$P_1 \rightarrow TT \rightarrow EE \rightarrow P_2 \ldots$$

So 'real enquiry begins and ends with problems'. (Readers may care to evaluate, in the light of this analysis, the theories of instruction associated with Skinner and Bruner, for example.)[31]

Kuhn[32] suggests a five-standards set of criteria for evaluating the adequacy of a theory:

- it should be accurate within its domain, that is, its consequences should be in agreement with experiments and observations;
- it should be consistent internally and with other related, currently accepted theories;
- it should be broad in scope;
- it should be relatively simple, 'bringing order to otherwise isolated phenomena';
- it should stimulate new research.

A note on 'the givens' in expositions of teaching theory

Teachers will find in their reading of some educational theory that, all too often, an exposition will involve the acceptance of unproven data ('We all know that . . .'; 'One must admit that . . .'; 'It goes without saying that . . .'). Is it necessary that so-called 'unchallengeable assumptions' be examined if a theory appears to depend on them?

In his inaugural address at the University of St Andrews, delivered in 1867, John Stuart Mill advised his audience of tutors and students to beware of the 'conceptual necessaries' and the '*a priori* givens' in expositions of theory:

> To question all things; never to turn away from any difficulty; to accept no doctrine either from ourselves or from other people without a rigid scrutiny by negative criticism, letting no fallacy, or incoherence, or confusion of thought, slip by unperceived; above all, to insist upon having the meaning of a word clearly understood before using it, and the meaning of a proposition before assenting to it; these are the lessons we learn from the ancient dialecticians.

This is valuable advice for those who engage in the evaluation of theory.

The criteria for a theory of instruction

Anderson and Burns[33] have outlined the desiderata of a theory of instruction as follows.

1. It should define the terms included in its postulates and be capable of explaining the past and making predictions as to the future.
2. It should outline precisely its boundaries.
3. It should be verifiable.
4. It should show congruency with existing empirical data relating to the area it seeks to cover.

(See also Bruner's comments on p. 117.)

A note on 'teaching', 'training' and 'instruction'

When we refer in this text to 'teaching' in further education we also have in mind 'training' and 'instruction'. The history of educational development which resulted in the theoretical separation of teaching from training is almost as old as formal education itself and is related to the growth of socio-economic ideas which sought to place manual workers in a different educational and social category from those who worked largely by exercise of intellectual skills. Training became involved with the 'how', teaching with the 'why'; the former activity was concerned with the acquisition of appropriate patterns of habits in limited situations, the latter was said to be related to 'development of the whole person'. According to Peters, 'training' was seen largely as a matter of 'knowing how' rather than of 'knowing that', of knack rather than of understanding. ' "Education" implies that a man's outlook is transformed by what he knows [whereas] "training" suggests the acquisition of appropriate appraisals and habits of response in limited conventional situations [and] lacks the wider cognitive implications of "education" ': *Ethics and Education* (1966).

In practice, however, it is often difficult to separate the 'how' and the 'why': they go together and should be taught together.[34] Consider three activities taking place simultaneously in classrooms in a college of further education: in one room nursing students are being shown the techniques of recording details of a patient's condition; in another room personnel managers are listening to a lecture on theories of motivation; in a third room computer engineers are discussing the problems of designing artificial intelligence. Are these persons being trained, taught or instructed? Do the differences depend on the techniques employed in the facilitation of learning? Or does it all depend, in Peters' words, on the criteria to which teacher-learner transactions must conform?

The concept underlying this text is of training and teaching viewed as two sides of the same coin: the principles involved in teaching are applicable almost in their entirety to training. Both activities are devoted to the acquisition of understanding; both can result in human growth; both require a planned approach to the problems of the learner. Stonier[35] suggests that 'training' provides the learner with skills; 'education' provides meta-skills which can be used so as to acquire further skills more easily. The meta-skills allow one to obtain and assimilate information outside one's expertise. The more we educate a student in the use of the meta-skills, the more versatile and accomplished he will become.

The term 'instruction' as used here is not differentiated in any significant fashion from the terms 'teaching' and 'training'. 'Theories of instruction' are construed as 'theories of teaching and training'; see, for example, Gagné's statement that instruction is 'a set of events that affect learners in such a way that learning is facilitated'. This would be accepted by many teachers as a description of the essence of the teaching and training processes. Note, too, Smith's comment, in *Definitions of Teaching* (1987): 'All can agree that training and instruction comprise what is called teaching ... Training may and often does involve instruction – giving information in the form of directions, reasons and evidence – and is thereby a form of teaching.'

In summary, teaching, training and instruction are similar and their rationale is the intensification of the rate of human development – the essence of educational activity.

Notes and references

1. See generally for this chapter: *The Educational Imagination* by E.W. Eisner (Collier-Macmillan, 1979); *Experience and Education* by J. Dewey (Macmillan, 1938); *Human Learning* by T. Leahey and R.J. Harris (Prentice-Hall, 1989); *The Art of Teaching* by G. Highet (Methuen, 1977); *Psychology Applied to Teaching* by R.F. Biehler (Houghton Mifflin, 1993); *Education and Training* by T. Heaton (Macmillan, 1996).
2. 'Teaching' in *Theory into Practice* (Ohio State University, 1982, 2).
3. *Foundations of Behavioural Research* (Holt, Rinehart & Winston, 1973).
4. *Fact and Method* (Princeton UP, 1984).
5. No less a figure than Francis Bacon declared in his *Wisdom of the Ancients* (1690) that 'It matters not what has been done; our business is to see what can be done'. Little was to be gained from 'the darkness of antiquity'.
6. *American Psychologist* (1973, 28).
7. *The Logic of Living Systems* (Allen Lane, 1974).
8. *Personal Knowledge* (Routledge & Kegan Paul, 1958).
9. See e.g. Herbert Spencer's *The Study of Sociology* (1873): 'The average opinion in any age and country is a function of the social structure of that age and country'; and Margaret Mead's *Growing-up in New Guinea* (1930), in which she refers to the 'cultural walls within which an individual can operate'.
10. See, on this topic, 'Chinese teachers' views of western language teaching: context informs paradigms' by B. Burnaby and Y. Sun in *TESOL Quarterly* (1989, 2). See also 'The impact of foreign experts, methodology and materials on English language study in China' by T. Scovel in *Language Learning and Communication* (1983, 2).
11. *The Language of Education* (Thomas, 1960).
12. *Handbook of Research on Teaching* (Rand McNally, 1963).
13. *Op. cit.* (1979).
14. *Psychology for Teaching* (Wadsworth, 1985).
15. See *IETE*.
16. *Research in Classrooms* (Pergamon, 1989).
17. 'Teaching cycles and strategies' in *IETE*.
18. See 'Definitions of teaching' in *IETE*.
19. See 'College classrooms as dramatic arenas' in *Mastering the Techniques of Teaching* by J. Lowman (Jossey-Bass, 1984).
20. Lord Beveridge, in *The Art of Scientific Investigation* (Heinemann, 1951) was emphatic in his view of the practice of science as demanding a large element of art.
21. *The Art of Teaching* (Methuen, 1977).
22. *The Technology of Teaching* (Prentice-Hall, 1968).
23. See 'Teaching: art or science?' by M. J. Dunkin in *IETE*.
24. *Using What We Know About Teaching* (Harper & Row, 1984).
25. See e.g. *The Open Society and Its Enemies* (Routledge & Kegan Paul, 1966). Short accounts of Popper's interesting views on learning appear in *Theory and Reality* ed. H. Albert (Mohr, 1972) and *Theories of Learning* by B. Hergenhahn (Prentice-Hall, 1997).
26. R. Dawkins, in *The Blind Watchmaker* (Penguin, 1988) – a restatement of evolutionary theory – comments that the human mind 'is an inveterate analogiser', and that people

seem compulsively drawn to imagine meanings in slight similarities among processes of very different natures. For a detailed treatment, see *The Role of Analogy, Model and Metaphor in Science* by W.H. Leatherdale (Elsevier, 1974). The use of analogies in teaching is well established and popular. In a private communication to the author, Dr Peter Suber of Earlham College, Richmond, Indiana, USA, has set out a number of interesting 'analogy exercises' for teaching the fundamentals of legal reasoning. For the use of analogies in advanced intelligence tests, see *Intelligence, the Psychometric View* by P. Kline (Routledge, 1996).

27. See e.g. *Practical Logic* by M. Beardsley (Prentice-Hall, 1950).

28. *The Structures of Scientific Revolution* (Chicago UP, 1970). See also *Perception* by R. Sekuler and R. Blake (McGraw-Hill, 1990).

29. See *Mind in Science* by R.L. Gregory (Penguin, 1981), in which perception is analysed in terms of data from sensory signals, read so as to provide further data which in turn will generate perceptual hypotheses. J. Searle, in *Minds, Brains and Science* (Penguin, 1989) – the Reith Lectures for 1984 – suggests, in terms of particular interest to the class teacher, that perception is a function of expectation, so that a student who expects to see something may see it more readily. The student's moods and emotions affect how and what he perceives. See *Perception* ed. K. Atkins (OUP, 1996); *The Artful Eye* by R. Gregory and J. Harris (OUP, 1996). Note also the interesting comment by Titchener in *Experimental Psychology* (Macmillan, 1927): 'We never have a perception. Consciousness is a shifting tangle of processes, themselves inconstant, and the "perception" is a little bit of pattern ravelled out from the tangle and artificially fixed for scientific scrutiny'.

30. See *Methodus*, June 1990.

31. See *Learning from Error: Popper's Psychology of Learning* by W. Berkson (Open Court, 1984).

32. *Op. cit.* (1970).

33. *Op. cit.* (1989).

34. The author's experiences as a member of an industrial training board (now defunct) included countless inconclusive discussions on the question of the differences between 'education' and 'training'. Among the more popular ideas canvassed was a 'situation theory' – whether an instructional event was 'education' or 'training' depended on *where it took place*, so that a lecture on management given in a firm's training department was 'training', whereas the same lecture given by the same lecturer to the same group in a college lecture theatre was 'education'!

35. *The Wealth of Information* (Methuen, 1981).

Part Two

Aspects of Educational Psychology

Chapter 3

The Nature of Psychology and Theories of Learning

> Of all the fast-moving current trends, surely the most general is the continued movement of psychology in the direction of becoming a science – in the sense in which chemistry became a science in the nineteenth century and physiology and embryology became sciences in the late ninetenth and early twentieth centuries (Murphy, 1979).

Responsibility for the provision and control of the conditions for effective learning is presented in this text as a principal duty of the practising teacher in further education. It is important, therefore, that the teacher shall consider some of the important answers given by educational psychologists to the fundamental problem: *How does the human being learn?*[1]

Psychology, which studies questions of this nature, and its more recent offshoot, educational psychology, may assist in the clarification of problems – which is the first step along the road to their solution. For the teacher approaching psychology for the first time, four caveats are necessary. First, the literature is vast and seems to be increasing at an exponential rate, so that selective reading is essential. Secondly, contemporary learning theory is highly eclectic and characterized by a wide range of hypotheses, often of a conflicting, if not contradictory, nature. The teacher who is searching for a single uncomplicated answer to questions arising from the teaching-learning process is likely to be disappointed. Thirdly, the vocabulary of psychology is extremely complex and technical terms abound. Some words used by psychologists (e.g. 'personality', 'thought', 'insight') are at variance with their everyday use and many phrases have become estranged from their origins (e.g. 'retention and retrieval', 'creativity and intelligence', 'conditioning of behaviour'). Fourthly, a knowledge of psychological principles is, on its own, no guarantee of success in the classroom; it must be allied with appropriate techniques if instruction is to be successful. A note of caution was sounded by William James in his 1923 *Talks to Teachers*:

> I say ... that you make a great, a very great mistake, if you think that psychology, being the science of the mind's laws ... is something from which you can deduce definite programs and schemes and methods of instruction for immediate schoolroom use. Psychology is a science, and teaching is an art; and sciences never generate arts directly

out of themselves. *An intermediate inventive mind must make the application by using its originality.*

Defining psychology

The boundaries of the study known as 'psychology' are very wide; at its periphery it impinges on, for example, philosophy, neurology and linguistics. The problem of definition is intensified by the need to find an umbrella expression which will cover the views of psychologists who believe that mind is the central area of their study, and of those psychologists who deny the very existence of mind. It may be useful to note the contents headings of a short standard text on elementary psychology as an example; content can assist in fixing the boundaries from which definition might emerge. The following are typical examples of contents headings: sensation-perception; motivation; emotion; innate patterns; learning; thinking; intelligence; personality; behaviour pathology.

The term 'psychology' seems to have been coined in 1595 by Otho Casmannus to indicate 'study of the mind or soul'.[2] Today's general dictionaries include the following definitions: 'the study of human experience'; 'the science of human nature'; 'the study of how the human animal senses, perceives, feels, thinks, acts'; 'humanity's attempt to understand itself'. Specialist texts define psychology in ways which reflect the impact of a variety of modern doctrines on 'the science of mind'. Consider the following examples.

(a) 'The science of mental life, both of its phenomena and of their conditions . . . The phenomena are such things as we call feelings, desires, cognitions, reasoning and the like' (William James, 1890).[3]

(b) 'That division of natural science which takes human behaviour – the doings and sayings, both learned and unlearned – as its subject matter' (Watson, 1919).[4]

(c) 'The scientific study of the behaviour of living creatures in their contact with the outer world' (Koffka, 1925).[5]

(d) 'The scientific study of behaviour. Its subject matter includes behavioural processes that are observable, such as gestures, speech, and physiological changes, and processes that can only be inferred as thoughts and dreams' (Clark, 1970).[6]

(e) 'The study of the more complex forms of integration or organization in behaviour ... this includes also the study of processes such as learning, emotion, or perception that are involved in organizing the behaviour. "Integration" or "organization" refers to the pattern or combination of different segments of behaviour in relation to each other and to external events impinging on the organism' (Hebb, 1972).[7]

(f) 'The scientific analysis of human mental processes and memory structures in order to understand human behaviour' (Mayer, 1981).[8]

For the purposes of this text, psychology is defined as *'the science which attempts to discover the general laws which can explain the behaviour of living organisms'.*

Branches of psychology

A variety of specialized branches has grown from the general body of psychology. Thus, *social psychology* investigates the influence of groups and institutions upon individual behaviour; *industrial psychology* applies psychological principles to the analysis and solution of work-related problems; *physiological psychology* studies the bodily foundations of human behaviour. *Educational psychology* seeks to apply appropriate psychological principles to problems arising from the theory and practice of education. It is concerned with problems such as: What is the nature of learning? How do we learn? How does motivation affect learning? How do we remember and why do we forget?[9]

Educational psychologists adopt a variety of modes of investigation. The *experimental method* involves the selection and manipulation of variables, the study of responses, the control of extraneous influences and the interpretation of resultant data.[10] *Naturalistic observation* – the examination of events in an unmanipulated environment – constitutes another technique of investigation. The study of *case histories* from schools and colleges, the use of *tests* and *surveys*, are other forms of studying problems of educational psychology.

The pervasive nature of psychology will be clear to college staff who specialize in subject areas such as sociology, management and marketing, and design. In each of these areas psychological theories play a role. Areas of study formerly far removed from psychology now feel its impact. For example, developments in economics, such as the theory of rational expectations and indifference analysis, owe much to psychological principles; jurisprudence now has its own 'psychological school' based on the work of Petrazycki (1864–1931).

Contemporary educational psychology is concerned essentially with an investigation of the psychological foundations and characteristics of those activities which appear to constitute the teaching-learning process. In recent times educational psychologists have extended their use of statistical methods of enquiry into areas such as the precise measurement of intelligence, and have widened their techniques of experimental investigation. The significance of experimental psychology in relation to educational enquiry, which grew from the investigative techniques of Wundt (1832–1920) as applied to physiological psychology, was noted by one of his students, Titchener (see p. 86) in his observation, made in 1929:

> It is worth remembering that, despite all the psychological systems from Aristotle down, it is only since the appearance of experimental psychology and its attainment of impersonal results that the special technologies of mind have sprung into vigorous being.

The emergence of schools of learning theory

Psychology has not yet attained the level of a unified science; to some observers it is merely a collection of disparate studies with widely differing theoretical foundations, techniques of investigation and methods of interpreting empirical data. Divisions seem much deeper and controversy much more intense among psychologists than among research workers in many other disciplines.

One of the most important causes of basic controversy in psychology has resulted from the growth of 'dualism', that is the concept of mind and matter as two entirely distinct entities. Descartes (1596–1650) taught that mind and body were different, although they interacted, that is they affected each other.[11] Watson (see Chapter 4) denounced the mind-body problem as essentially false. 'Mind' was no more than the activity of the brain (i.e. a consequence of its anatomy and physiology) and the nervous system. Psychology continues to reflect this fundamental division of opinion. At one extreme of interpretation is the concept of mind as a myth (note, for example, Ryle's 'ghost in the machine'); at the other extreme is the view of mind as a reality, as an 'irreducible principle of innate consciousness'.[12]

Controversies of this nature have affected educational psychology profoundly. Behaviourism arose as a reaction to learning being interpreted as mere mental functioning. Cognitive psychology holds fast to the significance of the internal processing of thoughts and images at the level of consciousness. Schools of psychology, each internally united by agreement on a specific approach to problems of learning, have emerged; some of the most important are mentioned below. (It should be noted, however, that there is overlap of views in some of the schools and that it is not always easy to allocate a psychologist to a specific school, e.g. behaviourism or cognitivism.)

Behaviourist psychology: 'Why don't we make what we can observe the real field of psychology?' (Watson)

Behaviorism involves a mechanistic, materialist view of psychology as the study of observable, objectively measurable behaviour. (Note the comments of Lashley, 1923:[13] 'To me the essence of behaviourism is the belief that the study of man will reveal nothing except what is adequately describable in the concepts of mechanics and chemistry, and this far outweighs the question of the method by which the study is conducted'.) Behaviourism teaches that the explanation, prediction and control of behaviour are possible without reference to concepts involving consciousness. It has a distinguished ancestry: Heraclitus, Democritus, Hobbes and Locke have been claimed as earlier philosophers from whose reasoning modern behaviourism has emerged. Fundamental to behaviourism is the view that man may be perceived as a biological machine; he reacts to appropriate stimuli in ways which may be observed and analysed; his behaviour stems from his adaptation to external events in the physical world.

Skinner differentiates 'methodological' and 'radical' behaviourists.[14] The former may have accepted the existence of process generally referred to as 'mind', but do not deal with them because these processes are not 'publicly observable' and statements concerning them cannot be confirmed. The latter state unambiguously that so-called mental activities are no more than 'explanatory fictions'.

Behaviourist learning theory focuses attention on stimulus-response (S-R) events and on the significance of contiguity, repetition and reinforcement leading to conditioning. Behaviourist psychology applied to the classroom calls for detailed systematic methods and sequences of instruction aimed at the shaping of behaviour.

Behaviourists selected for comment in Chapters 4, 5 and 6 include Pavlov, Watson, Thorndike, Guthrie, Hull, Tolman, Skinner and Gagné.

Purposive and neo-behaviourism: 'The more we know about the behaviour of others, the better we understand ourselves' (Skinner)

Some educational psychologists have suggested that behaviour is generally directed to some goal: people behave as if they have some *purpose*. Such behaviour, often directed by anticipations of consequences based on past experience, can be related to the nature of goals to be sought and the means to attain those goals. Behaviour might be described, therefore, as 'purposive'. ('Human behaviour can be genuinely purposive because only human beings guide their behaviour by a knowledge of what happened before they were born and a preconception of what may happen after they are dead; thus only human beings find their way by a light that illumines more than the patch of ground they stand on': Medawar, *The Life Science* (1997).)

The neo-behaviourists have investigated the significance of reinforced, or conditioned, responses in relation to the S-R bond. In relation to teaching they stress the importance of the teacher's role in effecting successive and systematic modification of changes in the students' environment so as to increase the probability of the appearance of desired responses in their behavioural patterns.

Gestalt psychology: 'Nature is neither kernel nor shell – she is everything at once' (Goethe)

Gestalt psychology is concerned with the significance of organized forms and patterns in human perception, thinking and learning. Understanding and the perception of relationships within organized entities are the very essence of learning. For the psychologist, the study of *molar* behaviour (behaviour of the whole organism) is likely to be more productive than concentration on *molecular* behaviour (behaviour analysed in terms of single events). Shifting the emphasis away from what the Gestaltists considered to be the crudities of behaviourism, they would ask not, '*What* has the student learned to do?', but '*How* has the student learned to perceive this new situation?' It is the teacher's task to assist in the promotion of 'insightful learning' and to act so that students might develop and extend the quality of their insights.

To apply the principles of this type of psychology to the classroom demands awareness of the unified nature of the teaching-learning situation, the shifting, but vital, nature of the teacher-student relationship, the importance of studying the perceptual responses of students to their environment and the construction of a system of instruction which will allow students to understand subjects as coherent wholes, rather than as collections of apparently unrelated procedures. The teacher's function is seen as helping students to perceive environment, to make an intelligent response to it, and to enrich their personalities. Koffka, Köhler and Wertheimer are discussed in Chapter 7.

Cognitive psychology: 'I think, therefore I am' (Descartes)

The term 'cognition' derives from *cogito* – to think; it involves, essentially, 'know-ing', and has been defined by Neisser as 'all the processes by which the sensory input is transformed, reduced, elaborated, stored, recovered and used'. Cognitive psychol-ogy aims at uncovering and understanding the internal activities underlying cognition, motivation, organization of memory, etc. These internal activities are said to result from internal structures and *can* be known. S-R theory is rejected as a simplistic and inadequate attempt to explain away the rich varieties of human perception and consciousness.

Cognitive psychologists assume that, in the interactions of an organism and its environment, not only is there a change in the overt behaviour of the organism but there is also a change in its knowledge of the environment; this latter change affects present responses and future attitudes to the environment. The student should be viewed as a purposive individual in continuing interaction with his social and psychological environment. Learning is essentially a process of interaction as a result of which the learner attains fresh insights ('cognitive structures') and sheds or modifies old ones. It is the task of the teacher to assist the student in restructuring and enriching his insights.

Cognitive learning theory suggests to the teacher a responsibility for designing instruction so that exploration and the discovery of relationships shall be encour-aged and understanding shall result. The integration of knowledge will assist in leading the student toward his 'total development' – a primary goal of education. (In the 1980s, the cognitive school began to give particular attention to the use of computer simulation in attempts to model the central processes of human cognitive organization. Thus, Anderson, in *The Architecture of Cognition* (1983), used a simulation to provide evidence of the existence in human beings of 'a unitary system of higher-level cognition' which operates over the entire range of individual mental life and comprises 'declarative knowledge' (how we 'know about' something) and 'procedural knowledge' (how we 'know how' to do something).) Dewey, Bruner, Ausubel and Vygotsky are discussed in Chapters 8 and 9.

Humanistic psychology: 'Freedom makes a difference' (Rogers)

The total rejection by some psychologists of behaviourism on the one hand and psychoanalysis on the other, brought about in America a 'third force' designed to present psychology in the context of a 'complete vision of human life'. Social failures and a perceived betrayal of humanity's hopes in the twentieth century required a fresh interpretation; psychology was to be viewed as concerned with spontaneity, creativity, mental health, growth and the fulfilment of potential.

In educational terms humanistic psychology calls for a quality of teaching which will allow students to make conscious choices in an environment characterized by freedom. The teacher will act as a 'facilitator', relating to his students in a 'person-centred manner', based on empathic understanding – a sensitive awareness of how the student perceives his environment. The modes of enquiry of humanistic psychology are directed to a study of human values and 'authentic relationships' among teachers and students. The founders of this school of educational psychology, Maslow and Rogers, are discussed in Chapter 10.

The defunct school of Soviet educational psychology

Prior to *glasnost* and the subsequent collapse of the USSR in the early 1990s, there existed a renowned school of Soviet educational psychology which claimed to be in direct line with the earlier, celebrated Russian experimental psychologists, Sechenov, Pavlov and Bekhterev. Educational workers at all levels occupied a special role in the process of developing 'the new Soviet citizen'. A vast bureaucracy linked the Academy of Pedagogical Sciences of the USSR with educational institutions, in which the approved doctrines of educational psychology were translated into practice. Much of the published research work of theoreticians, such as Talyzina, Rubinstein, Landa and Galperin, was also studied in Britain and America.

Educational psychology was viewed, in Marxist terms, as a part of state superstructure, reflecting the characteristics of socialist production. Western doctrines concerning education were rejected decisively: behaviourism was denounced as 'mechanical materialism' which denied the changing nature of mankind; cognitivism was dismissed as ignoring Marx's dictum: 'The phantoms formed in the human brain are but sublimates of their material life process'.

Menchinskaya,[15] a typical representative of Soviet psychology, viewed learning as the 'attainment of concepts'. His research, published in Europe in 1959, reflected experiments carried out in engineering technical colleges. We learn, he argued, through a process of analysis and synthesis. When concepts are formed by the learner, the relation between the levels of analysis and synthesis are changed qualitatively. Where learning elements and procedures are *organized* correctly, independent thinking will be encouraged. Teachers can help in this process by planning instruction which proceeds from the simple to the complex.

Rubinstein's work,[15] published in the 1960s, sought to show that the essence of the teaching-learning process was to be found in *problem-solving*. Building on the work of Menchinskaya, he emphasized the significance of analysis through synthesis. Where students cannot solve problems immediately, they should be encouraged to refer to previously resolved problems (the act of synthesis) and 'confront the existing problem with previous successful practice' (analysis). Effective learning demands the precise classification of the nature of a problem situation, then a selection of the operation which 'is inevitable if a successful solution is to be obtained'. The process demands continual rehearsal of previously acquired knowledge and practice in the application of thinking skills.

In his analysis of learning published in 1966, Landa[15] suggested that learning can be perceived as 'the acquisition of algorithms', that is, a series of operations designed to solve tasks, presented serially and based upon rules and procedures.

Talyzina's work is noted on p. 375. The theories of Galperin are mentioned on p. 111 and linked with those of Vygotsky.

A note on the pattern of development of psychological theories

Vygotsky (see Chapter 8) suggests that a uniform pattern may be discerned in the development of psychological theory. In the first stage, he claims, there emerges an empirical discovery which suggests important revisions of generally held views on thought. A second stage is reached when the discovery is clothed in conceptual form, allowing it to be used in the discussion of some formal theories of psychology. In the third stage, the conceptual form becomes an abstract principle, apparently capable of applicability to psychology as a whole. In its final stage it moves away from psychology and develops pretensions of being a methodology applicable to all types of knowledge. It then merges with some dominant philosophy and generally disintegrates under the weight of its own wide claims.[16]

Readers may wish to refer to a detailed history of some schools of psychology so as to consider their development in the light of Vygotsky's concept of pattern. (They may also care to consider the cynical observations of the physicist Planck (1858–1947): 'An important scientific innovation rarely makes its way by gradually winning over and converting its opponents: it rarely happens that Saul becomes Paul. What does happen is that its opponents gradually die out, and that the growing generation is familiarized with the idea from the beginning.')

Notes and references

1. See generally for this chapter: *Psychology* by G. Leitman (Norton, 1995); *Psychology* by D. Hockenburg (Worth, 1997); *The Oxford Companion to the Mind* ed. R.L. Gregory (OUP, 1990) (referred to in later notes as *OCM*). For reviews of the history of psychology, see: *Historical Introduction to Modern Psychology* by G. Murphy and J. Kovach (Routledge & Kegan Paul, 1979); *The Shaping of Modern Psychology* by L.S. Hearnshaw (Routledge, 1987); *Master Builders of Modern Psychology* by J.D. Keehn (Duckworth, 1996); *A History of Psychology* by L. Benjamin (McGraw-Hill, 1997); *Connections in the History and Systems of Psychology* by B. Thorne and T. Henley (Houghton Mifflin, 1997).
2. Hearnshaw (*op.cit.*) suggests that the word was coined by Goclenius of Marburg (the teacher of Casmannus) in 1590.
3. *The Principles of Psychology* (Rinehart & Winston, 1890).
4. *Behaviourism* (Norton, 1970).
5. *Principles of Gestalt Psychology* (Kegan Paul, 1936).
6. See *Introduction of Psychology* by R.L. Atkinson (Harcourt Brace Jovanovich, 1983).
7. *A Textbook of Psychology* (Saunders, 1972).
8. *The Promise of Cognitive Psychology* (Freeman, 1981).
9. See *Educational Psychology* by R. Slavin (Prentice-Hall, 1988); *Psychology Applied to Teaching* (Houghton Mifflin, 1993); *Educational Psychology* by T. Good and J. Brophy (Longman, 1995).
10. There is a problem in that 'philosophers of science have repeatedly demonstrated that more than one theoretical construction can always be placed upon a given collection of data' (Kuhn).
11. See *Descartes: An Intellectual Biography* by S. Gaukroger (OUP, 1997).
12. An attempted resolution of the problem was presented by Searle in the 1984 Reith

Lectures (see *The Rediscovery of the Mind* (MIT, 1992)). Mental states are features of the brain, he suggests, and may be considered on two levels of description – a higher level (in mental terms), a lower level (in physiological terms). The same causal power of the system may be described 'with perfect consistency' at either level: they are consistent and true. See also *Kinds of Minds* by D.C. Dennett (Weidenfeld, 1996); *Consciousness Explained* by D.C Dennett (Little, Brown, 1991).

13. 'The behaviouristic interpretation of consciousness' in *Psychological Review* (1923).
14. See e.g. his article on 'Behaviourism' in *OCM*.
15. See *Handbook of Contemporary Soviet Psychology* by M. Cole and I. Maltzman (Basic Books, 1969).
16. An interesting view of stages in the development of a science is given by T.S. Kuhn in *The Structure of Scientific Revolutions* (3rd ed.) (Chicago UP, 1997): revolutions in science involve a change from one paradigm to another. A 'paradigm' involves radically changed specific theories and techniques, changes in the kinds of question that theories are expected to answer, and the criteria for judging those answers. See also *The Essential Tension* by T.S. Kuhn (Chicago UP, 1977) and *Revolution in Science* by I.B. Cohen (Harvard UP, 1985).

Chapter 4

The Behaviourist School

If its facts were all at hand, the behaviourist would be able to tell after watching an individual perform an act what the situation is that caused his action (prediction), whereas if organised society decreed that the individual or group should act in a definite, specific way, the behaviourist could arrange the situation or stimulus which would bring about such action (control) (Watson, 1919).

The sources of classical behaviourism[1] (see p. 36) may be found in the philosophical writings of Hobbes,[2] Comte and La Mettrie, and in the laboratory experimental research of Pavlov. Doctrines associated with behaviourism were first systematized in 1913 by Watson (see p. 48) and refined by Thorndike and others; they have provided, in turn, a foundation for today's neo-behaviourism associated principally with Skinner (see p. 75). Classical behaviourism was essentially a reaction against theories based largely on data derived from introspection (i.e. subjects' verbal reports of their reactions and perceptions). Watson insisted on the necessity to discard introspection in favour of a study of *the objectively observable actions* of persons. In this way the science of psychology would become 'a purely objective, experimental branch of natural science'.

Several interlocking concepts were common to the research writings associated with the development of behaviourism in its heyday around 1913–35.

1. Consciousness, mind, mental states were examples of ideas which were to be rejected because they could not be verified. Following La Mettrie (1709–51), who had denied that human beings were essentially different from animals, save in degree, and who saw man as a complicated, wonderful, self-main-taining machine, the early behaviourists rejected mind-body dualism, saying that the problems of human nature could be explained in *purely mechanistic terms*. (Later, biophysics and biochemistry were seen as powerful tools of explanation.)
2. The philosophy of reductionism, which suggested that human activities could be explained in terms of the *behavioural responses of the lower animals* (e.g. rats,

dogs), was seen as offering a valuable approach to the solution of problems involving human behaviour.

3. All behaviour was to be investigated and understood solely in the context of *responses to stimuli* (S-R). Hence the behaviour known as 'learning' might be defined in terms of changes in responses made to stimuli on the basis of the learner's past experiences.

4. The circumstances in which stimuli become linked to overt responses must be a key subject for study.[3] Hence the process of *conditioning*, whereby relationships of responses to stimuli are modified in order to change behaviour, is also an important subject for investigation.

5. Behaviour might be explained as a *function of environmental influences*.

6. The methodology of behaviourism required a *formal, quantitative basis* if scientific method were to characterize psychology.[4] (Note the comment of Whitehead: 'Search for measurable elements among your phenomena, and then search for relations between these measures of physical quantities'.)

7. Behaviourism has as its objective the *prediction and control* of human behaviour.

Pavlov, Watson, Thorndike, Guthrie and Hull made very important contributions to behaviourism which are considered below.

Pavlov: the background

Pavlov (1849–1936), the celebrated Russian physiologist who became director of the Soviet Institute of Physiology, was primarily interested in the circulation of the blood and the processes of the gastro-intestinal system. He showed little interest in psychology as such until his last years. For him, so-called 'mental events' were no more than 'reflex units of behaviour'. As a young man he had been influenced by his fellow countryman, Sechenov (1829–1905), who had written in his *Reflexes of the Brain*: 'All acts of conscious or unconscious life are reflexes ... Only physiology holds the key to the scientific analysis of psychical phenomena'. The study of the nervous systems of animals led him to methods of investigation from which he discovered the techniques of the *conditioning of behaviour*. On the basis of these techniques was erected a new structure of the investigation of aspects of human behaviour and, in particular, the study of aspects of the learning process. For Pavlov, *all* human learning is due to conditioning. His work on the process of conditioning continues to rank very high in the list of contributions made by scientists to an understanding of learning.[5]

According to Pavlov, so-called 'mental phenomena' could be dealt with objectively and scientifically only if it were possible to reduce them to observable, measurable physiological quantities. ('[The behaviour] of higher animals can be successfully studied only if one completely renounces the indefinite formulations of psychology and stands wholly upon a purely objective ground.') The concept of the 'reflex' could be extended so as to embrace not only unlearned responses but also learned reactions. Behaviour in all its varieties was, according to Pavlov, essentially *reflexive*; it was determined by specific events. (His system has been described as 'neurobehavioural'; S-R (i.e. the concept of environmental specifiable stimuli producing responses) is replaced by S-N-R, stimulus-neural process-response.) *Unconditioned reflexes* or responses were inborn types of nervous activity, transmitted by inheritance. (A reflex is described by Miller[6] as 'an involuntary, unlearned predictable response to a given stimulus or class of stimuli, a response that is not influenced by any conscious thought or resolution but that can usually be seen to have some clear purpose in protecting the organism or helping it to adjust to the environment'.) But *conditioned reflexes* or responses (see below) were acquired by an organism during its life; they were not normally inheritable, according to Pavlov. *Human beings learn as the result of conditioning*, and it was this hypothetical process which formed the basis of Pavlov's research.

The process of conditioning studied by Pavlov was derived from the results of his investigation into salivation in dogs.[7] It is said that the incident which gave the initial impetus to this investigation was Pavlov's observation of the reactions of a laboratory dog to the squeaking of a door which was opened daily by a janitor bringing food to the animal – an interesting example of serendipity. Pavlov inverted the parotid salivary gland of a dog so that its secretions could be accumulated in a calibrated glass and measured externally. The animal was placed in a harness and then presented with a stimulus such as the sound of a metronome, bell or tuning fork. Initially, the sound did not seem to elicit any observable response. Later a powdered meat was presented to the dog after a short interval of time following the sound and its salivary fluid was collected and measured. After further trials, in which the sound of the metronome or bell was invariably followed by the presentation of food, the sound alone produced an anticipatory salivary response. Pavlov's discovery has been stated by Razran[8] to be this: 'A stimulus initially inadequate to evoke some reflex may become adequate after it has been administered together with a stimulus adequate to produce the reflex'. This is illustrated in Figure 4.1.

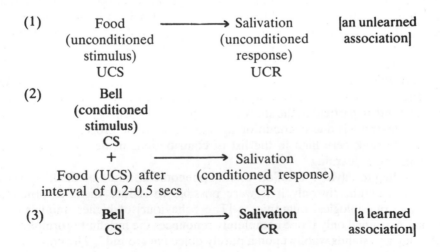

Figure 4.1   The process of conditioning

The components of Pavlovian conditioning that appear in Figure 4.1 may be explained as follows.

(a) UCS. Essentially the UCS elicits a natural response without any prior training (i.e. an innate reflex response).
(b) UCR. This is the response elicited by the UCS; it is often highly reflexive and tends to happen swiftly and automatically when the UCS occurs. Examples: eye blink, knee jerk.
(c) CS. The CS is the (previously neutral) stimulus which eventually comes to elicit a response by 'proper pairing' in time with the UCS; the new response comes to be conditional upon the CS being presented. It must, of course, exist as a stimulus within the subject's sensory range, e.g. it must be visible or audible.
(d) CR. This is the reflex which is elicited when the CS and the UCS are paired. It is also referred to as a 'conditional reflex' because it is conditional upon the presentation of the CS.

Pavlov found that if the paired stimuli (CS + UCS) were presented repeatedly, the CR gradually increased in strength. This conditioning process was seen by Pavlov as a possible explanation of certain aspects of the organization of behaviour. Most environmental stimuli can become conditioned stimuli with direct effects on behaviour. The techniques of conditioning, it was suggested, could be applied to the training of human beings. *Human behaviour might be amenable to the process of moulding on the basis of the controlled establishment of conditioned responses.* Further, in Pavlov's words, 'Any natural phenomena chosen at will may be converted into a conditioned stimulus ... any visual stimulus, any desired sound, any odour ...'. (Popper has suggested an interesting interpretation of Pavlov's experiment, the point of which will not be lost on teachers. He puts forward the idea that the laboratory dogs had 'developed a theory', consciously or unconsciously, that the food would arrive when the bell rang, and that this expectation caused the saliva flow, precisely as did the expectation raised by the smell of the food.)

Pavlov believed that the nervous centres involved in the formation of CRs in man were located on the cortex of the cerebral hemispheres. Temporary connections (including CRs) were formed as the result of 'excitation' or 'irradiation' of stimuli reaching these hemispheres. Stimulation becomes generalized in the hemispheres so that other areas of the cortical region react similarly to the area involved in the original stimulus. A 'cortical mosaic' is produced which will determine the responses of an organism to its environment; as these responses become automatic, a 'dynamic stereotype' has been created. The stereotype makes it easier for the organism to respond to an environment which is largely predictable, but difficulties emerge when the organism is confronted by a new environment. These findings, however, were inferred from behaviour, not from a direct study of the brain; they received little support from other experimental workers.

Pavlov's 'conditioning' is known by many other psychologists as 'associationism' – a term which is central to the work of educational psychologists such as Thorndike. Pavlov wrote, in 1934, in the following terms: 'Are there any grounds for differentiation, for distinguishing between that which the physiologist calls "the temporary connection" and that which the psychologist terms association? They are fully identical; they merge and absorb each other.'

Pavlov's generalizations

Pavlov's studies and research yielded data from which he constructed a series of generalizations ('functional laws'), the most significant of which are as follows.

(a) *Extinction*. The extinction of a CR (that is, its gradual fading and eventual disappearance) is caused by the *inhibition* of the CR, which results from repeated or continued presentation of the CR without the UCS. The initial inhibition, said Pavlov, is temporary only; as the inhibitory state diminishes, the ability of the CS to produce the CR increases.[9] *Disinhibition* emerges as the partial regaining of conditioning (when, for example, a partially or entirely extinguished CS is applied together with some new stimulus). Spontaneous recovery is inferred from a partial reversion of the effects of extinction and the re-appearance of the original conditioning over a period of time.[10]

(b) *Generalization*. This concerns the *partial transfer* of a CR to stimuli similar to the CS (i.e. 'stimulus generalization') and to reflexes similar to the CS (i.e. 'reflex generalization').

(c) *Differentiation*. This involves alternating presentation of the CS, accompanied by the UCS, with presentations of related stimuli unaccompanied by the UCS.

The uniqueness of man

The fact that most of Pavlov's research, which he pursued for over 60 years, was carried out on dogs (although in the final stages of his career he used monkeys and gorillas) should not blind teachers to his deep belief in the unique nature of human beings. He maintained that humans have fewer instincts than animals so that their behaviour is governed by CRs to a very much higher degree. It is possible to condition humans and animals in ways which are similar; but human beings possess, uniquely, the rich treasure-house of language. The animal responds to simple primary signals (i.e. environmental stimuli); humans respond also to the secondary signals conveyed to them in written or spoken form. There is, said Pavlov, no comparison, qualitative or quantitative, between 'the grandiose signality of speech' and animals' stimuli.

Human behaviour cannot be understood totally by referring to the very simple S-R actions of Pavlov's experiments on dogs; nowhere in his writings does Pavlov suggest otherwise.[11] We may learn some important lessons from his study of animals which have application to the human body (described by Pavlov as 'unique in the degree of its self-regulation'), but human beings themselves occupy 'an ontological status superior to that of the animals'. Pavlov, it should not be forgotten, wrote of 'our extra, especially human, higher mentality', and of 'science, the instrument of the higher orientation of man in the surrounding world and in himself'. In 1909 he referred to his disinclination 'to negate anything which relates to the innermost and deepest strivings of the human spirit. Here and now I only defend and affirm the absolute and unquestionable rights of natural scientific thought ... who knows where its possibilities will end!' Thirteen years later he expressed 'a deep, irrevocable and uneradicable conviction that [the study of conditioned reflexes] is the path of the final triumph of the human mind over its last and uppermost problem – full knowledge of the laws and mechanisms of human nature and thus full, true, and permanent happiness ... deliverance from present gloom and the purge of present-day shame in interhuman relations'.

Pavlov's work and the teacher

The major works of Pavlov, such as *Conditioned Reflexes* (1927), have been the basis of continuous study in recent years on the importance of conditioning in the process of learning.[12] Some of Pavlov's deductions from his experimental data have been reassessed, and conditioning is now seen by some psychologists as much more than a mere substitution of one stimulus for another. Conditioned responses differ from unconditioned responses, and the process of conditioning may result in the subject acquiring a new group of stimulus response patterns – a matter of significance for the class teacher whose work includes the presentation of stimuli in a variety of conditions.[13]

It should be noted, further, that Koestler,[14] in rejecting the relevance of Pavlov's work to the study of human learning, suggests that the physiological concept of the conditioned reflex is a fiction which has become an anachronism. He cites Hebb's view that Pavlov's theory ought to be rejected, not because it is too physiological, but because it does not agree with experiments made much later. 'Conditioning' is, according to Koestler, a useful term when applied to 'induced changes in glandular and visceral reactions'; it is merely confusing 'when used in a loose analogical way for other types of learning'.

The mere suggestion that Pavlov's work might have positive lessons for the practice of classroom instruction is rejected firmly by many teachers. Research derived from experiments on mutilated animals should, it is argued, have no application whatsoever to human learners. The atmosphere of the animal laboratory is, and must remain, a world away from that of the classroom and the purposes of the activities therein. Koestler, who sees reductionism as a threat to mankind, criticizes Pavlov who, he says, provided us with new insights into human nature, 'but only into those rather elementary, non-specific aspects ... which we share with dogs, rats or geese, while the specifically and exclusively human aspects which define the unique-ness of our species are left out of the picture'. Further, it is felt by many that the entire concept of conditioning, with its all-too-familiar connection with 'brain washing' (that is, the deliberate influencing of behaviour patterns in persons so as to make them conform to the demands of a political ideology), must have no place in educational activity. The freedoms which must characterize the classroom are incompatible with the philosophy and technology associated with conditioning.

Others, however, see in Pavlov's work a possibility of evolving techniques which, when refined, can be used consciously and conscientiously to shape human intellectual development – an important objective of teaching activity. The excesses of those who have deliberately misused conditioning techniques ought not to be advanced, it is argued, as reasons for forbidding the use in all circumstances of some of those techniques. For Pavlov, learning was inseparable from association; hence, *what* teachers do, *how* they do it, in what *surrounding circumstances* and to what *ends* become significant for the study of instruction.

Environmental stimuli provided *intentionally and unintentionally* by the teacher's performance in the process of instruction may become associated with undesired responses – the authoritarian instructor who arouses a dislike for his subject area and, in so doing, conditions students to a permanent dislike for closely associated subject matter, is an example. (The American psychiatrist, Sullivan (1892–1949) notes in *Conceptions of Modern Psychiatry* (Norton, 1947) that where people say they are 'useless at mathematics', it is almost always a result of having suffered, in the days of their introduction to number, 'so much threat of anxiety, so much anxiety itself, that the whole field of intrinsically mathematical symbol operations has taken on a vague mark of anxiety'.) The moral for the teacher seems clear: ensure as far as possible that stimuli provided by teaching performance become associated with appropriate and desired positive responses by students. This means considering the lesson, its planning and delivery, in all its aspects.

Pavlov's insistence on organisms being studied as wholes, 'in all their interactions', and on biological processes being considered as essentially dependent on the environment, has lessons for teachers wishing to understand the significance of the *setting* of instruction. Human personality is determined, according to Pavlov, by environment, biological inheritance and conditions of upbringing, and a person's general behaviour depends largely on his or her 'acquisitions', that is, the habits he or she has formed. The part that can be played by a teacher in the process of habit formation will be obvious. Planned teaching events, strengthened by other experiences, can exert a decisive influence on that process.

Watson: the background

Watson (1878–1958), professor of experimental and comparative psychology at Johns Hopkins University, Maryland, began his career as a researcher into animal behaviour. It was this background that led him to examine psychology in strict behavioural terms: he had become very interested in the fact that the absence of speech in his laboratory animals compelled him to communicate with them in behavioural terms only. His major works include *Behaviour: An Introduction to Comparative Psychology* (1914); *Psychology from the Standpoint of a Behaviourist* (1919); *Behaviourism* (1925).[15] Psychology, according to Watson, ought to be a purely objective, experimental branch of natural science (the 'science of behaviour') and behaviour could be described adequately in *physiological terms* of S-R, habit formation, etc. Concepts such as 'sensations' and 'feelings' were to be cast aside: 'the behaviourist cannot find consciousness in the test-tube of his science'. 'Instinct', for example, was a term no longer needed in psychology; what was called 'instinct' belonged to learned behaviour, i.e. it was a result largely of training. The introspectionist's question: 'What is the organism *experiencing*?' had to be replaced by the question: 'What is the organism *doing*?' 'Consciousness' was a term of no value, since it merely reflected the mind-body problem, which was of no significance – mind did not exist. Indeed, said Watson, the assumption of consciousness was 'just as unprovable as the ancient concept of man's soul'. 'Thought', he suggested, might be merely 'subvocal speech movements', i.e. small, overt movements of muscles in the vocal apparatus. (The study of language was, said Watson, a vital matter for psychologists.) In making statements of this nature, Watson was adopting the position of the earlier peripheralists, who denied the importance of central cerebral processes in the human being. In Medawar's words,[16] Watson substituted 'the empirical for that which, because it was not presented to the senses, could only be known by inference ... [Behaviourism] supplanted the presumption of privilege in introspective psychology by empirical narrative and reportage.'

The concept of memory was also rejected by Watson; it was 'shot through with all kinds of philosophical and subjective connotations'. Instead of using the term, a behaviourist should speak of 'how much skill has been retained and how much has been lost in a period of no practice'. By 'memory', says Watson, is meant nothing except the fact that when we meet a stimulus again after an absence, 'we do the old habitual thing (say the old words and show the old visceral-emotional behaviour) that we learned to do when we were in the presence of that stimulus in the first place'.

Behaviour takes the whole field of human adjustments as its own, and is to be studied in terms of biologically determined phenomena. (The theoretical goal of psychology should be the prediction and control of behaviour.) Its understanding necessitated a close study of glandular secretions and muscular movements. The principal method of study should be *objective observation and experimentation*. This required a new vocabulary from which subjective terminology would be eliminated; references to 'introspectively observable phenomena', such as sensation, thought and intention, which were said to intervene between stimulus and reaction, would disappear. Belief in the existence of consciousness, Watson reminded his readers, 'goes back to the ancient days of superstition and magic'. The phrase 'being conscious' is merely 'a popular or literary phrase descriptive of the act of naming our universe of objects both inside and outside'.

Watson insists that 'the closest scientific companion of behaviourism is physiology'. But can behaviourism be differentiated from physiology? He argues as follows:

> It is different from physiology only in the grouping of its problems, not in fundamentals or in central viewpoint. Physiology is particularly interested in the functioning of parts of the animal – for example, its digestive, circulatory and nervous systems ... the mechanics of neural and muscular response. Behaviourism, on the other hand, while it is intensely interested in all of the functioning of these parts, is intrinsically interested in what the whole animal will do from morning to night and from night to morning.

Watson and the learning process

According to Watson, human beings are born with some few reflexes and emotional reactions, but no 'instincts' (which are merely S-R links); all other behaviour is the result of building new S-R connections. Habit formation may be analysed in terms of constituent units of conditioned reflexes. Learning, as an aspect of human behaviour, can be studied in terms of the formation of connections in the learner's muscle groups. When S and R occur *at the same time* their interconnections are strengthened and the eventual strength of the connection will depend largely upon the *frequency* of S and R occurring together. S produces activity in a part of the brain, and R emerges as the result of activity in some other part; S-R neural pathways are strengthened when the two parts of the brain are simultaneously activated. But learning produces no new connections in the brain – they exist already, as part of the learner's genetic constitution, and learning may merely make functional a connection that has been latent. Hence our behaviour, personalities and emotional dispositions are all *learned* behaviours. *The human being is no more than the sum of his or her experiences.* (In his later years Watson would move away from an emphasis on the importance of 'frequency', which he was to characterize as 'purely speculative'.)

Given this analysis, conditioning was seen as fundamental to learning. The conditioning of the learner through his environment and experiences, in which the teacher may actively intervene, is the central process in the building of habits, and will determine his or her acquired patterns of behaviour. Heredity and instincts counted for little in Watson's scheme as contributions to human behaviour. Learning becomes an all-important factor in the development and modification of an individual's behaviour.

Watson embodied Pavlov's findings into his theory of learning. Watson believed that young children had no reason to fear animals. In a famous experiment involving conditioning, he showed an 11-month-old child some tame white rats, an experience which the child apparently enjoyed. Later, a rat was presented shortly after a loud noise which frightened the child. After several repetitions of the experience the child showed fear of the rat even in the absence of the distressing noise. Fear was displayed also in the presence of other furry objects. Watson showed later that, by feeding the child with his favourite dishes and introducing the feared animal very gradually into the background and then into the child's direct view, the fears could be extinguished. (However, an account by Harris of the experiment throws doubt on the success of the deconditioning of 'little Albert'.[17]) Kovach suggests that Watson's 'crude experiment' gave credence to the view that 'not only simple motor habits, but important, enduring traits of personality, such as emotional tendencies', might be built into a person through the processes of conditioning.[18]

Habit formation was considered by Watson to be a significant part of learning. He believed that a stimulus in the outside or inside environment will set the individual moving. That individual may do many things before blotting out a stimulus or moving beyond its range. When he gets into the same situation again, 'he can accomplish the one or the other of these results more rapidly and with fewer movements' – we say that he has *learned*, or formed a habit.

Watson's work and the teacher

The behaviourism propagated by Watson and others who share his views has become an object of unceasing criticism by psychologists and teachers. His work is said to have suffered from 'a surfeit of speculation', an absence of data, and over-generalization. It has been condemned as a reductionism which robs man's nature of its dignity, reducing the complexities of human development to mechanistic, deterministic and over-simplified formulae – 'the psychology of muscle twitches'. A recent attack, mounted by Talyzina of Moscow University,[19] reflects the views of many opponents of behaviourism.

> Behaviourists interpret the subject of their studies in a coarse, mechanistic way: having separated behaviour from the psyche, they reduced it to a system of movements. It is true, of course, that movement is part of behaviour, but behaviour may not be reduced to a sum of movements ... Behaviourists did not perceive the qualitatively specific properties in the behaviour of man by comparison with that of animals. They view man not as a social being but as a purely biological one.

Others, however, view the behaviourists' emphasis on the significance of environment and experience as stressing the *positive role of the teacher*. Heredity gives the learner his body only ('... there is no such thing as an inheritance of capacity, talent, temperament, mental constitution and characteristics ... these things depend on training ...'). All else is *acquired*, and the control of the activity of acquisition is important. Control of the learning environment – an essential task of the teacher – becomes a significant factor in the learner's development.

The possibility of the student being conditioned to respond favourably to the circumstances in which he learns – his class environment, his instructor, the content and overtones of the lesson – reminds the teacher of the importance of planning the learning environment and lesson content with care. Each part of the lesson ought to be examined in the teaching-planning stage, and evaluated during class activity, as a contributory factor to the eliciting of those responses which make up desirable criterion behaviour. 'What type of response will be elicited from my students as the result of my teaching activity?' Questions of this nature ought to be posed by the teacher in the preparatory stages of a lesson, and the answers ought to affect subsequent lesson content.

Teachers in further education ought not to forget the possibility of students' attitudes to their lessons being formed as a result of the conditioning process of which Watson wrote. A student's negative attitude to, say, quantitative topics may be the result of his generalization of anxieties resulting from difficulties at an earlier period in his mathematics training. It is, unfortunately, a simple matter for that generalized attitude to take in the wider field of the college curriculum as a whole. Watson's work can also act as a reminder to the teacher to take particular care to avoid creating *intentionally or unintentionally* the anxieties and hostility which may emerge later as a wide, fixed response to formal instruction of any type.

In the flush of enthusiasm, and emphasizing the importance of the environmental determinants of behaviour, Watson claimed that, given a dozen 'healthy infants, well-formed', he would guarantee to train any one of them, chosen at random, to become any type of specialist he might select, 'regardless of his talents, penchants, tendencies, abilities, vocations and race of his ancestors'. Stripped of its zeal and hyperbole, Watson's challenge stands as a reminder of the powerful contribution which can be made by the teacher to the growth and shaping of the learner's personality. Changes in personality, said Watson, can be effected by changing the individual's environment in such a way that new habits have to form. 'The more completely they change, the more personality changes. Few individuals can do all this unaided.' The importance of the teacher's task is implicit in a doctrine of this nature.

Thorndike: the background

Thorndike (1874–1949) was one of the dominant personalities for many years in the study of learning.[20] Almost all his professional life was spent on the staff of a teacher training college. His output was prodigious: a recently compiled list of his works showed more than 500 titles. His major writings include *The Principles of Teaching Based on Psychology* (1906), *Animal Intelligence* (1911) (an expanded version of his doctoral thesis), *The Psychology of Learning* (1913), and *The Fundamentals of Learning* (1932). His main interest was animal psychology and, in particular, intelligence, learning and understanding. 'It is certain that man should try to match his understanding of masses, atoms and cells by understanding of himself.' Thorndike's pattern of experiments with animals ('instrumental conditioning') marked out a route which was followed later by other experimental psychologists, including Skinner (see pp. 75–83); he accepted the general implications of Morgan's statement (*Introduction to Comparative Psychology* (1891)): 'In no case may we interpret an action as the outcome of the exercise of a higher psychical faculty if it can be interpreted as the outcome of the exercise of one which stands lower in the psychological scale'.

The basis of Thorndike's approach to problems of behaviour lay in his beliefs that 'human nature in general is the result of the original nature of man, the laws of learning, and the forces of nature amongst which man lives and learns'; and that *human behaviour could be analysed and studied in terms of S-R units.* All learning involves the formation of *new* S-R connections. The essence of behaviour was to be found in the initiation of events and an individual's reactions to them. 'Mind' was no more than a collective term relating to the activities of the body cells which responded to stimuli, a 'compound of elemental impressions bound together by association'. Behaviour and, therefore, learning were explicable through an understanding of *bonds* between sense impressions and impulses to actions; the task of the psychologist was to discover how such bonds are created. Thorndike's emphasis on S-R bonds led to the categorizing of his theories as 'bond psychology' and 'connectionism'. (As a result of conditioning, specific responses and specific stimuli would be *connected.*) Learning is *direct*: it is not mediated by ideas. Further, quantification should be used in the formulation of psychological theory: 'Whatever exists, exists in some amount and can be measured'.

Thorndike's theories emerged largely from experiments with cats, chicks, dogs and monkeys, but he believed that some universal laws of behaviour could be derived from that work. A human being, in his view, differed from the other animals only in degree and merely in the *abundance of the associations* that he develops between environment and his corresponding motor reactions, as well as in 'the rate with which the associations are formed and the complexities of their inter-relationships'. Human superior intelligence was little more than a reflection of the capacity to form S-R bonds. Degrees of human intelligence were quantitative, not qualitative, and signified varying speeds of bond formation; the more intelligent person has more bonds at his disposal to enable him to deal with problems. Heredity was primarily responsible for human achievement; environment was of secondary importance. Character would triumph over circumstances.[21]

Thorndike's laws of learning

Thorndike's contribution to the theory of learning may be summarized by a statement of his major and subsidiary 'laws'. The *law of effect* was formulated thus: an act which results in an animal experiencing satisfaction in a given situation will generally become associated with that situation, so that when it recurs the act will also be likely to recur. Thorndike defined 'satisfaction' as a state of affairs which the animal does nothing to avoid, often doing things which maintain or renew it. The opposite state of affairs is one which the animal does nothing to preserve, often doing things which put an end to it. An act which results in discomfort tends to be dissociated from the situation, so that when the situation recurs, the act will be less likely to recur. *The greater the satisfaction or discomfort experienced, the greater the degree to which the S-R bond will be strengthened or loosened.* Pleasurable effects, therefore, tend to 'stamp in' associations; unpleasant effects (such as punishment) tend to stamp them out. This law is a break with the doctrines of associationism; it has overtones related to the 'psychological hedonism' of Bentham (1748–1832) and the 'pleasure-pain' principle of Spencer (1820–1903). It is the forerunner of Skinner's principle of reinforcement (see pp. 78–9). The subsequent modification of this law is mentioned below.

According to the *law of exercise*, a response to a situation will generally be more strongly connected with that situation in proportion to the number of times it has been so connected and to the average strength and duration of the connections. In general, therefore, the more frequent the repetition of the time sequence of S and the corresponding R, the more secure will be the connection (the *law of use*). Other things being equal, exercise strengthens the bond between situation and response. (Teachers will see here the hallowed intellectual justification for drill and repetition in, for instance, arithmetical processes.) This law, too, was later modified when Thorndike announced that it was of minor importance. The *law of readiness* suggests that a learner's satisfaction is determined by the extent of his 'preparatory set', that is, his readiness of action; this refers to the dependence of the rate with which a connection is developed or the extent to which it corresponds to the learner's current state.

There were several subsidiary laws. The *law of multiple response* states that a response which fails to produce satisfaction will trigger off another until success results and learning becomes possible. According to the *law of set*, learning is affected by the individual's total attitude or disposition; hence a student's cultural background and present environment are of importance in determining his or her responses. What the learner brings to the learning situation is significant. The *law of selectivity of response* suggests that as the person learns, so he or she becomes capable of ignoring some aspects of a problem and responding to others. ('Such partial or piecemeal activity on the part of a situation is, in human learning, the rule.') The *law of response by analogy* emphasizes that a person's response to a novel situation is determined by innate tendencies to respond, and by elements in similar situations to which he or she has acquired responses in the past. (This principle is known also as the *law of identical elements*; it may help to explain the phenomenon of 'transfer of learning': see pp. 223–6.[22]) The *law of associative shifting* suggested that a learner responds first to a given stimulus, then he may transfer the response by association to a different stimulus which acquires the capacity to elicit the same response. (This seems to be in line with Pavlov's findings.)

The *law of effect* was modified 30 years after its publication when Thorndike abandoned his belief that punishment tended to stamp out S-R bonds. His restatement of the law emphasized that punishment merely caused the learner to modify his behaviour until he discovered some act which resulted in reward. Rewarding a connection strengthened it, whereas punishing it had little direct weakening effect. The *law of exercise* was also modified by Thorndike: practice in itself did not make perfect, but practice in circumstances which allowed the learner to be informed of his results could be valuable in strengthening the S-R links. The *law of spread of effect*, enunciated in 1933, stated that, if an act had pleasurable consequences, the pleasure tended to become associated not only with the act and the eliciting stimulus, but also with other actions which occurred at approximately the same point in time. This principle seemed, to Thorndike, to confirm his belief in the *direct nature of learning*.

Thorndike's work and the teacher

Thorndike's theories have been criticized as crude and over-simplified. In particular, his S-R bond explanation of the basis of learning has been condemned as a mechanical and restricted interpretation of some few aspects of the complexities of human behaviour.[23] His *law of effect* has been criticized by Lindsay and Norman.[24] Their criticism should be studied in the context of Norman's use of the term 'learning' to refer to 'the act of deliberate study of a specific body of material so that the material can be retrieved at will and used with skill'. The 'automatic nature' of learning, in terms of the *law of effect*, explains nothing. It pays no attention to the internal information processing which must be going on during the learning event. The law is too vague about the temporal conditions involved. It seems to ignore the causal relationship which must exist between actions and outcome.

Criticism has been directed against those aspects of Thorndike's work which were derived specifically from his experimental work with monkeys. The fallacy of attributing higher cognitive functions to animals has been noted repeatedly by those who warn against anthropomorphic interpretations of animal behaviour. Harlow, for example, notes: 'The monkey's learning capabilities can give us little or no information concerning human language, and only incomplete information relating to thinking'.[25] Klein interprets Harlow's observation as meaning that 'the scope of animal psychology can never be extended far enough to include the totality of human psychology'.[26] Thorndike, it has been argued, was much given to far-ranging extrapolations of his animal studies which, in the event, vitiated the force of his theories concerning human responses to stimuli.

Many psychologists and teachers, however, see Thorndike's work as that of an important pioneer, mapping a route for others who followed. Thorndike's general view of the relationship of psychology to teaching is significant. He viewed psychology as part of the necessary basis of a scientific approach to the practice of teaching and wrote: 'Just as the science and art of agriculture depend upon chemistry and botany, so the art of education depends upon physiology and psychology'.

There is much in Thorndike's work which is of relevance to the day-to-day tasks of the class teacher. Its emphasis on the significance of the S-R bond reminds the teacher of the importance of viewing *all* his activities (intended and otherwise) as contributions to the learning process. An orderly classroom, learning objectives based on progress from simple to complex concepts, producing a 'satisfying state of affairs' for the learner, with regular examinations, a 'dominant' teacher using positive control, would characterize a Thorndike-type teaching-learning situation. It would resemble the real world outside the classroom as far as possible. Lesson planning, instructing and evaluation of attainment emerge in the light of Thorndike's analysis as related directly to those responses which make up learning. ('Consider the situation the student faces and the response you wish to connect with it ... Put together and exercise what should go together, and reward desirable connections.')

Thorndike's modification of the *law of effect*, which stressed external reward as a more effective factor than punishment in the modification of a learner's behaviour, has an obvious lesson for the teacher. Further, the *law of exercise* suggests the importance of 'doing' and of repetition in the learning process, and its modification emphasizes the futility of thoughtless rote learning; repetition without reinforcement will not enhance learning. The *law of readiness* stresses the importance of preparation for learning and serves to remind the class teacher of the vital part played in the learning process by *motivation* and of his responsibility for the strengthening of a student's readiness to learn. A student's interest in his work, and in improvement, can be conducive to learning; significance of subject matter to the student can affect that interest. The necessity of flexibility of approach by the learner and the value of trial and error learning (i.e. the formation of S-R bonds by random selecting and connecting) emerge from Thorndike's *law of multiple response*. The *law of selectivity of response* underlines the importance of arranging instruction so that students can discriminate among lesson components on the basis of selective attention. His demonstration of the significance of 'response by analogy' reminds the teacher of the responsibility for arranging the conditions of learning so that the identification of common elements in a variety of situations may result in strengthening the ability to generalize.

Thorndike's views on understanding and insight are also of great interest to the teacher. Understanding grows out of habits acquired at an early stage in the learner's development. It may be fostered by teaching the learner 'appropriate connections'. Insight, the understanding of a new situation immediately is no 'unpredictable spasm'; it arises on the basis of appropriate habits and the understanding of analogies. ('Nowhere are the bonds acquired with old situations more surely revealed in action than when a new situation appears.') Learning is incremental, says Thorndike. It occurs in small steps rather than in large jumps; it is direct and not mediated by reasoning. The technique of attempting to instruct by mere lecturing can be unproductive and the commonest error of the inexperienced teacher is 'to expect pupils to know immediately what they have been told'. Telling is not teaching!

> Both theory and practice need emphatic and frequent reminders that man's learning is fundamentally the action of the laws of readiness, exercise and effect ... If we begin by fabricating imaginary powers and faculties, or if we avoid thought by loose and empty terms, or if we stay lost in wonder at the extraordinary versatility and inventiveness of the higher forms of learning, we shall never understand man's progress or control his education ... Strange as it may sound, man is free only in a world whose every event he can understand and foresee. Only so can he guide it. We are captains of our own souls only in so far as they act in perfect law so that we can understand and foresee every response which we will make to every situation.[27]

Guthrie: the background

Guthrie (1886–1959) became professor of psychology at the University of Washington after a period of study of philosophy. He had been influenced by some philosophical writings which suggested that a number of the more important problems concerning 'mind' could be translated into concepts of behaviour and comprehended accordingly. His definitive work was *The Psychology of Learning* (1935).[28]

For Guthrie, explanations had to 'summarise sequences of observable events'; an acceptable explanation would state the general class of which some particular sequence is an instance–and nothing else. Human behaviour was to be explained precisely in terms of *control by eliciting stimuli*; a change in S-R connections could be understood and explained on the basis of simple, mechanistic laws. Some behaviour seemed to Guthrie to be goal-directed, but this was not to be explained in non-physical terms. A person's intention to reach some goal could be explained in terms of maintaining stimuli that keep the organism active and allow muscular readiness to respond and muscular readiness to accept the consequences of that response. Similarly, attention can be explained in physical terms as a variety of responses orienting sense receptors towards stimuli. 'What is being noticed becomes a signal for what is being done.'

Learning, said Guthrie, could be defined as '*the alteration in behaviour that results from experience'.* Observable and nameable events have to be studied in order to understand learning. In particular, a knowledge of the fundamentals of learning required an awareness of the nature and interplay of stimuli and responses.

Guthrie and the learning process

Guthrie's theory of learning is based on the concept of there being one kind of learning only, and on one general principle, that of *simultaneous contiguous conditioning*: '*A combination of stimuli which has accompanied a movement will on its recurrence tend to be followed by that movement.*' The principle has been paraphrased by Hill thus: 'If you do something in a given situation, the next time you are in that situation you will tend to do the same thing again'. Whether the response emerges as the result of an unconditioned stimulus or in any other way is of no matter, according to Guthrie. Provided that the conditioned stimulus and reaction occur together (i.e. in contiguity), learning will take place.[29]

If it is argued that stimuli precede responses (so that they are not in contiguity), Guthrie then appeals to the concept of movement-produced stimuli (MPS). The presentation of S elicits a 'miniature R' which acts as a S for another R, and so on until finally an observable R is elicited and emitted. Each MPS is in continuous contiguity with the preceding and following movements, that is, the initial S and R are in contiguity. Guthrie had in mind the 'molecular' small movements which go to make a skilled performance. Later in his career Guthrie revised his law of contiguity to read: what is being noticed becomes a signal for what is being done. This suggested his recognition of an organism's responding *selectively* to a small portion of the large number of stimuli confronting it.

A further law states that '*a stimulus pattern gains its full associative strength on the occasion of its first pairing with a response*'. The implications are clear: reinforcement plays no part in the learning process, and practice adds nothing to the strength of the S-R bond, which is of the all-or-nothing type. 'One experience is sufficient to establish an association.' A S-R bond is there or not there, and no intermediate variation in its strength can be inferred. '*Learning occurs normally in one associative episode.*' But teachers have observed repeatedly the force of the adage: 'practice makes perfect'. Guthrie retorts: all that practice can do is to ensure that R will occur under a variety of differing circumstances. Mere repetition (the essence of much practice) is futile if the stimuli are the same from one practice test to another.

> The reason that long practice and many repetitions are required to establish certain skills is that these really require many specific movements to be attached to many different stimulus situations. A skill is not simple habit, but a large collection of habits that achieve a certain result in many and varied circumstances.

Forgetting is interpreted by Guthrie as 'a case of the failure of response to a cue'. The teacher can presumably induce forgetting by creating a situation in which the student makes a new response to the same set of stimuli. Once he or she has made the new response, the student replaces the old R with the new R. Forgetting is not a passive fading of S-R associations contingent on the lapse of time, but requires 'active unlearning', which consists of learning to do something else in the circumstances; hence 'all forgetting must involve new learning'.

Guthrie's views on 'punishment'

The term 'punishment' is used in behaviourist psychological theories to indicate 'the use of some aversive event contingent on the occurrence of an inappropriate behaviour'. Effective 'punishment' (in the college classroom, a reprimand, for example) will result in a decline in the frequency or intensity of the undesired behaviour. Guthrie takes an interesting position in this matter: its implications for the teacher will be apparent. Punishment, he says, is effective in a conflict situation only where incompatible responses occur to the punishing S. 'Punishment that produces only emotional excitement will tend to fixate the punished R.'

Guthrie advises that, if the teacher wishes to discourage a type of behaviour, an attempt to *discover the cues* leading to that behaviour should be made. The teacher should then arrange a situation so that the undesired behaviour will *not* occur in the presence of those cues. 'This is all that is involved in the skilful use of ... punishment.'

The eradication of habits

Guthrie's system of learning does not allow for the breaking of habits, but merely for their *replacement*. Three such techniques are mentioned in his writings, constituting a topic of considerable interest to teachers. Essentially, the modification and eradication of undesirable habits involve discovering the type of S which evokes the undesirable R, and then discovering some method of producing a dissimilar R in the presence of each S. It should be noted that the use of 'punishments' is *not* a constituent feature of these methods.

1. *The 'threshold' (or 'toleration') method.* Present the S you wish to have disregarded, but only in a weak fashion so that the undesirable S is not elicited. Then increase S to full strength in gradual fashion so that R never occurs (i.e. the stimulus is always below the 'threshold of the response'). At this point the undesired habit is assumed to have been replaced by an incompatible habit.
2. *The 'fatigue' (or 'flooding') method.* Present the S repeatedly so as to elicit the undesired R, until the R is fatigued. Then continue the presentation until a new R (perhaps a mere non-response) emerges. The undesirable habit should then have been replaced.
3. *The 'incompatible response' (or 'counter-conditioning') method.* Present the S that has brought about the undesirable R at the same time as another S that will produce an incompatible response. The original S will then become linked with the new desirable R.

Guthrie's work and the teacher

Guthrie has not escaped the general criticisms levelled at behaviourists. Critics point to the real-life complexities of behaviour, particularly in the classroom, and argue that such behaviour is not explained by contiguity theory. (Guthrie stressed the importance of practising acquired skills in the *exact conditions* under which tests will take place). Not all teachers are convinced that if a learner does something in a given situation, he or she will tend to do the same thing again when next in a similar situation.

But the significance of Guthrie's concept of learning should not be overlooked in its entirety. His insistence on particular responses to particular stimuli serves to remind the class teacher of the importance of the *combination of stimuli* resulting from a carefully arranged classroom environment and teaching activity. It emphasizes, too, the overall significance of presenting stimuli in a *planned* way. Essentially, the teacher should act so as to ensure that students behave in a particular way and, while they are doing so, the appropriate stimuli to be associated with that behaviour should be presented.

Guthrie stresses the importance of attempting to elicit desired patterns of behaviour in specific situations. Preparation for formal examinations, for example, involves practising (and relearning) in a situation which should have a close resemblance to that of the actual examination. Situation simulations, which require a precise analysis of S and R, can play a very important role in those class activities related to preparation for particular situations. Indeed, an implication of Guthrie's theory might be that, if we accept the necessity to plan instruction so that it should approximate as closely as possible to likely, future real-life circumstances, then perhaps teachers are too dominant a part of the instructional process. Where a teacher dominates, the students' responses will be cued to the sight of the teacher and the sound of his or her voice. In the teacher's absence the desired R, in content and strength, might not be elicited. It seems, therefore, that the teacher ought to be as small a part of the S situation as is consistent with class control requirements.

Teachers will note Guthrie's views that rewards and punishments are of little significance (since there is no important place in his theory for the concept of reinforcement) and in themselves are neither good nor bad. Whether they are effective or ineffective will be determined by what they cause the learner to *do*.

On the subject of class control, Guthrie has interesting advice for the teacher. He notes the military maxim that one should never give an order that one does not expect to be obeyed. The teacher should remember that each time he gives an order and something other than obedience follows, 'associative inhibition' tends to attach to that order. 'If a teacher makes a request for silence in the room and it is disregarded, the request actually becomes a signal for disturbance.' 'Nearly all arguments, by giving the opponent practice in defending the "wrong" side, make the teacher the signal for opposition.'

Guthrie's observations on the process of learning continue to have much relevance for the teaching-learning situation in our colleges. 'We learn only what we ourselves do. Students, in solving problems, must engage in activities other than watching.' Mere drill as a component of instruction negates true learning: repeating responses time after time is to no advantage unless the surrounding circumstances are changed. What is really vital in the learning situation is the control of stimuli so that desired responses might emerge. 'Students do not learn what was in a lecture or a book. They learn only what the lecture or book caused them to do.' *What a person does is what a person will learn.*

Hull: the background

Hull (1885–1952) was an American psychologist (although an engineer by training) who worked firmly within the behaviourist tradition as it applied to adaptive behaviour. He taught at Yale and later headed a team at the Institute of Human Relations where he directed research on the place of learning in the conduct of social affairs. His theoretical roots were in the Pavlovian S-R system and its explanation of learning. Hull's major writings were *Principles of Behaviour* (1943), *Essentials of Behaviour* (1951) and *A Behaviour System* (1952).[30]

An important aspect of Hull's work is its quantitative, deductive character. He was concerned with the utilization of scientific method in his enquiries; postulates were set out, deductions of an empirically verifiable nature would be inferred from the postulates, and the deductions would then be tested, confirmed, modified or rejected. The theoretician had the task of formulating postulates in a manner which would produce exact, precisely stated deductions. Hull believed that a significant offshoot of all theoretical research was the research it generated. The work of his followers, such as Spence and Mowrer[31] testifies to the quality of his research. His work dominated the psychology of learning in America between 1930–50.

Hull's contribution to learning theory

The fundamental function of behaviour in an animal, said Hull, is to enable it to deal with its biological problems. Needs (e.g. for food) produce a reaction in the form of activity; the resultant particular behaviour, which reduces those needs, is gradually learned so that adaptation by the animal to its environment is assured. Basic physiological needs produce *drives* (i.e. the psychological correlates of the needs) which Hull classified as primary or secondary. Primary drives are those which are immediately necessary if the animal is to survive. Secondary drives emerge as offshoots from the process of satisfaction of primary needs. In an emergency situation, therefore, inborn response tendencies act as an automatic adaptive behavioural mechanism; a 'second mechanism' is constituted by the *capacity to learn* – in Hull's words, 'a slightly slower means of adapting to acute situations'. Habits are formed when drive-reduction (which reduces organic needs and follows the attainment of a goal) is perceived as rewarding; habit strength is determined by the strength of associations between stimuli and responses.

Hull found the simple S-R model unsatisfactory. He postulated in symbolic terms a S-O-R connection (where O represents the *significance of variables*). These variables, which will affect the nature, shape and intensity of a response to a stimulus, were inferred as; 'independent', e.g. history of any prior training of the organism in previous similar situations, the amount of reward available; 'intervening', e.g. inhibition, habit strength, stimulus strength; 'dependent', e.g. response latency (how long did the response take?), probability of response. ('Intervening variables' of this type are 'unobservable entities', logically interrelated and, according to Hull, experimentally verifiable.)

Learning should be viewed basically in terms of *habit* which may be considered as a function of reinforcement. Drive reduction, with its accompanying satisfaction, is an important reinforcer; the process of repeated drive reductions will 'stamp in' the learning. Learning does not take place following a single trial; indeed, a number of trials may be found necessary before the results of that learning move beyond the threshold and are recognized in the learner's performance.

Hull's work and the teacher

Hull's drive theory, based on the concept of the existence within individuals of relatively intensive internal forces which motivate most types of behaviour, and his view of the strength of S-R associations as dependent on innate habit strength and acquired habit strength, have ramifications which can extend to the classroom. Thus, the motivation of behaviour is seen as resulting from intense arousal; the ability to produce the arousal necessary for learning can be developed by appropriate environmental stimuli. Here is a rationale for the activities of those teachers who aim deliberately at the arousal and maintenance of interest in a lesson by a planned, structured environment. The perceived value of rewards, Hull suggests, clearly influences the intensity of behaviour. The teacher who is considering the utilization of a system of 'rewards' as a reinforcement of desired behaviour will be interested in Hull's controversial view of reinforcement and drive reduction as almost synonymous.

Hull's work will remind the teacher of the need for 'distributed practice' so that inhibition will not appear during the process of learning. Topics to be taught should be placed in the timetable so that the subjects that are most dissimilar will succeed one another, e.g. English, physics, history, maths. In this way learner fatigue should be reduced.

Behaviour in the learning situation is thought of by many practising teachers as an outcome of drive and cognitive processes. Hull emphasizes the drive component and notes the importance of the intervening variables in the process of learning. In terms of the behaviourist tradition which Hull enriched, he extended the analytical value of the S-R behavioural model and paved the way for a deeper understanding of the drive stimuli which he held to be at the basis of the phenomenon of learning.

Notes and references

1. See generally for this chapter: *An Introduction to Theories of Learning* by B.R. Hergenhahn (Prentice-Hall, 1997); *Learning Theories for Teachers* by M.L Bigge (Harper & Row, 1976); *Theories of Learning* by G. Bower and E.H. Hilgard (Prentice-Hall, 1981); *Learning Theory* by R.C. Bolles (Holt, Rinehart & Winston, 1979); *Psychology: Theory and Applications* by P. Banyard (Chapman & Hall, 1994); *Psychology of Learning and Behaviour* by B. Schwartz and S. Robbins (Norton 1995); *A Materialist Theory of the Mind* by D. Armstrong (Routledge, 1993); *Contemporary Learning Theory and Research* by R. Tarpy (McGraw-Hill, 1997); *The Psychology of Learning* by J.T. Walker (Prentice-Hall, 1996).

2. 'Life is but a motion of the limbs ... for what is the heart but a spring, and the nerves but so many strings, and the joints so many wheels, giving motion to the whole body': *Leviathan* (1651).

3. 'When we describe people as exercising qualities of mind, we are not referring to occult episodes of which their overt acts and utterances are effects; we are referring to these overt acts and utterances themselves': *The Concept of Mind* by G. Ryle (Penguin, 1983).

4. See, in particular, the work of Hull, as in *A Behaviour System* (Yale UP, 1952).

5. See *Pavlov, a Biography* by B. Babkin (Chicago UP, 1949); *Pavlov* by J. Gray (Fontana, 1979).

6. *Psychology* (Penguin, 1972).

7. See *Lectures on Conditioned Reflexes* (Liveright Press, 1928).

8. Article on Pavlov in *Encyclopaedia of Social Sciences*.

9. See 'Pavlovian conditioning' by R. Rescorla in *Psychological Review* (1988, *43*).

10. See the recent work of Bouton, set out in 'Context, ambiguity and classical conditioning' (*Current Directions in Psychological Science*, 1994, *3*). The difficulties involved in clinical practices based upon Pavlov's concept of extinction are discussed in *Psychology of Learning and Behaviour* by B. Schwartz and S. Robbins (Norton, 1995).

11. See the reported work of Roessler in *American Journal of Psychology* (1943, *56*).

12. See, 'Pavlov's conceptualisation of learning' by G. Windholz in *American Journal of Psychology* (1992, *102*).

13. Some research workers, e.g. Bolles (*op. cit.*) doubt the mechanist-associationist explanation of Pavlovian conditioning and suggest that a cognitive explanation might be more satisfactory. It can no longer be taken for granted, says Bolles, that conditioning produces an automatic connection of some response to the CS; it may be that what is learned in the Pavlovian situation is not a response at all, but merely an expectancy that a certain response will be followed by some reinforcement. Note also the work of Garcia ('Relation of cue to consequence' in *Psychonomic Science*, 1966, *4*), suggesting that *genetic endowment* affects the type of associations made by an organism.

14. *The Act of Creation* (Arkana, 1989).

15. See *J.B. Watson* by D. Cohen (Routledge, 1979).

16. *The Art of the Soluble* (Constable, 1967).

17. See 'Whatever happened to little Albert?' by B. Harris in *American Psychologist* (1979, *34*). A replication of the experiment was reported by E.O. Bregman in *Journal of Genetic Psychology* (1934, *45*). See also 'Phobias and preparedness' by M. Seligman in *Biological Boundaries of Learning* ed. M. Seligman and J. Hager (Appleton, 1972).

18. *Historical Introduction to Modern Psychology* by J. Kovach (Routledge, 1979).

19. *The Psychology of Learning* (Progress Publishers, 1981).

20. See *The Sane Positivist – a Biography of Thorndike* by G. Joncich (Wesleyan UP, 1968).

21. See *Human Nature and the Social Order* (Macmillan, 1940).

22. Thorndike seemed to suggest that education produces highly specific rather than general skills. 'A man may be a tip-top musician, but in other respects an imbecile; he may be a gifted poet, but an ignoramus in music; he may have a wonderful memory for figures and only a mediocre memory for localities, poetry or human faces': *The Principles of Teaching* (Seiler, 1906).

23. There is now a growing belief among psychologists that behaviour is not controlled by stimuli, but by internally organized 'programmes'; the programming may reflect social culture. See e.g. *The Selfish Gene* by R. Dawkins (Granada, 1978).

24. *Human Information Processing: An Introduction to Psychology* (Academic Press, 1977).

25. 'The development of learning in the Rhesus Monkey' in *American Scientist* (1959, *47*).

26. *A History of Scientific Psychology* (Routledge, 1970).

27. *Psychology of Learning* by Thorndike (Teachers College Press, 1913).

28. See also *Educational Psychology* by Guthrie and Powers (Ronald Press, 1950).

29. See Guthrie's 'Association by Contiguity' in *Psychology* ed. S. Koch (McGraw-Hill, 1959); *Learning Theory* by R. Bolles (Holt, 1979); 'Formalization and clarification of a theory of learning' by V. Voeks in *Journal of Psychology* (1950, *30*).

30. See 'Clark L. Hull' by S. Koch in *Modern Learning Theory*, ed. W. Estes (Appleton, 1954); *Systems and Theories of Psychology* by J. Chaplin and T Krawiec (Holt, 1970); *Learning: A Survey of Psychological Interpretations* by W.F. Hill (Harper & Row, 1990).

31. See 'The Hull-Spence approach' in *Psychology* ed. S. Koch (McGraw-Hill, 1959); Spence's *Behaviour Theory and Learning* (Prentice-Hall, 1960). See also Mowrer's *Learning Theory and Behaviour* (Wiley, 1960) in which – unusually for a behaviourist – he finds a place in learning theory for the emotions, which he describes as 'a high order of intelligence . . . [and of] quite extraordinary importance in the total economy of living organisms'.

Chapter 5

The Neo-behaviourist School (1)

It is often said that a scientific view of man leads to wounded vanity, a sense of hopelessness, and nostalgia. But no theory changes what it is a theory about; man remains what he has always been. And a new theory may change what can be done with its subject matter. A scientific view of man offers exciting possibilities. We have not yet seen what man can make of man (Skinner, 1979).

Early behaviourist doctrines have been extended and modified by psychologists and research workers such as Tolman, Skinner and Gagné, who are discussed in this chapter and the next.[1] Tolman's views, rooted firmly in the principles of behaviourism, but acknowledging some cognitivist doctrine, flowered in unique fashion and were categorized as 'purposive behaviourism'. Skinner brought novel types of experiment and scientific technology to the detailed study of the learning process viewed in strict behavioural terms[2] and created a theory based on 'operant reinforcement'. Gagné examined the instructional technology needed for competency-based education and developed a psychology, based upon behaviourism, related to the observable circumstances that obtain when acts of learning occur. Each of these psychologists has affected the principles and practice of teaching in our schools and colleges.

Purposive behaviourism, associated with Tolman, represented a break with the Watson S-R tradition. In Tolman's words: 'Although I was sold on objectivism and behaviourism as *the* method in psychology ... I rejected the extreme peripheralism and muscle-twitchism of Watson.' All animal and human learning seemed to Tolman to involve a basic goal-seeking trend; but no teleological implications should be read into this view. In simple terms, an organism responded selectively and purposefully to its environment.

The neo-behaviourists, exemplified by Skinner (the *theoretician* concerned with the principles of learning) and Gagné (the *practitioner* concerned with the design of instruction), moved away from the simplistic approach of Watson. Skinner's 'radical behaviourism' was, in effect, a break with traditional psychology. Neo-behaviourism insisted that truth was to be found in observations, rather than in the interpretation of observations. Behaviour is controlled very largely by the environment. Indeed, Leahey suggests a paraphrase of Shakespeare in Skinner's terminology: 'The fault, dear Brutus, lies in our contingencies of reinforcement, not ourselves'.[3] Gagné stresses the importance of contiguity and reinforcement, and the effect on individual human development of systematically designed instruction.

Blackman[4] gives a classification of the components of a behavioural approach to teaching as follows: the concern of teaching is with the observable, that is, what the student actually does; behaviour is, for the most part, learned; learning means a change in behaviour (we can know that learning has taken place only by observing student behaviour); learning is governed by the law of effect (based on the repetition of behaviour followed by consequences which are found desirable); the context in which behaviour appears is of much significance.

Tolman: the background

Tolman (1886–1959) taught psychology at the University of California. Because of his highly individual, eclectic approach to the study of behaviour and his findings, he is claimed by both behaviourist and cognitive schools as an advocate of their teachings. It has been said of him: 'He was methodologically a behaviourist, but metaphysically a cognitive theorist'.[5] He opposed the views of the S-R 'fundamentalist' associationists: for him, the S-R association was not an objective fact, it was no more than an *inference*. The act of behaviour had to be studied in a *molar* (i.e. large-scale), rather than a *molecular*, way. As a behaviourist he rejected introspection as a mode of inquiry, but the mechanistic views of the early behaviourists seemed too simple for an adequate explanation of behaviour, which he saw as *holistic* (i.e. capable of explanation in terms of the whole system). Not all the problems considered by the introspective (cognitive) psychologists were to be rejected, since motivational and perceptual variables, for example, affected the process of learning in that they intervened between environmental stimuli and observable responses.

His major work, *Purposive Behaviour in Animals and Men* (1932), emphasized his view of behaviourism and 'purpose' in behaviour. 'The motives which lead to the assertion of a behaviourism are simple. All that can ever actually be observed in fellow human beings and in the lower animals is behaviour.' We do not merely respond to stimuli, we move towards goals related to our beliefs and our attitudes. 'Organisms pursue goal objects by selecting certain means-object routes.' We can understand behaviour only by examining an entire *sequence* of varied behaviour with some predictable end; we have to examine the whole so as to understand how the sequence is put together and the end achieved. 'Behaviour reeks of purpose.' Early behaviourists had viewed anything intervening between stimulus and response as itself in the nature of a response. Tolman rejected this as too simple an explanation, and viewed the determination of behaviour as a result of environmental stimuli and physiological states *plus* the intervention of variables (which he termed 'cognitions'). (Intervening variables include demands and appetites.) Cognitions, demands, appetites, etc., combined so as to produce responses. Behaviour was 'docile', that is, flexible and not invariant, and adaptable to changing circumstances. But Tolman stressed that purposive behaviour, although molar and not molecular, *was* none the less a behaviourism. 'Stimuli and responses and the behaviour-determinants of response are all that it finds time to study.'

In thinking about anything a person uses a 'cognitive map', that is, a general appreciation of relationships among different stimuli and a *set of expectancies* about the meaning of those relationships. Such a map was a symbolic representation of the person's environment – physiological, psychological and social – and his possible relations to it. The map would be constructed on the basis of the person's specific goals (or 'purposes'). Goal objects have motivating qualities; the presence of a preferred goal object may result in a performance superior to that elicited by the presence of a less desirable goal object. The *expectations* concerning a goal object are of great importance.

Tolman and the learning process

Learning, according to Tolman, was the *acquisition of expectancies*. By an 'expectancy' he meant that, in the presence of a certain 'sign', a particular behaviour will produce a particular consequence. We 'learn' when we establish a series of expectations concerning the contiguity of events based on repeated past experiences of their appearance in sequence. (A general formula for an expectancy might be S-R-S*: the learner expects that, given the presence of a particular sign (S), a particular behaviour (R) will produce a particular consequence (S*). In short, the student learns 'what leads to what'.) As a person becomes aware of novel behaviour and unsuspected relationships, new behaviour will appear – a learning process very similar to the Gestaltist concept of 'insight' (see p. 88), and described by Tolman as 'inventive ideation'. Essentially, said Tolman, learned behaviour comprises *performances* (i.e. acts); these can be understood in terms of end results and are 'patterns of organism-environment rearrangements'.

Reinforcement is *not* necessary for learning to take place, according to Tolman. He suggests that the learner's expectations will not be transformed into behaviour unless he is *motivated*. Motivation (see p. 230) performs two functions: it creates a state of deprivation, that is 'internal tension', which in turn produces a desire for a 'goal object'; it determines those features among the environment to which the learner will attend. Motivation acts as a 'perceptual emphasizer'. According to Tolman, the simultaneous experiencing of events will suffice for the process of learning; reward may affect *performance* where it motivates a learner to show previously learned behaviour, but it will not affect learning.

Tolman distinguished six different kinds of learning, as follows:

1. *Cathexis* (Greek *kathexis*, retention). This is based on a learned tendency to seek one goal rather than another when a certain drive is present. When a goal object satisfies a certain drive a cathexis is formed; the organism has acquired a positive disposition. When the organism has learned to avoid some objects while in a drive state, a negative cathexis is said to have been formed.

2. *Equivalence beliefs*. These are 'cognitions' that, where reward or punishment is found in a certain situation, the situation itself is equivalent to the reward or punishment and is, therefore, in itself rewarding or punishing. It is evident where a student's sub-goals have the same effect as his or her goal.
3. *Field expectancies*. These are built on 'cognitive maps' based on anticipations about the environment in which we function, and resulting from repeated experiences. They make possible short cuts and round-about routes in learning. Tolman spoke of the organization of knowledge into 'field maps' in the following terms:

    > [The learner's brain] is far more like a map control room than it is like an old-fashioned telephone exchange. The stimuli which are allowed in are not connected by just simple one-to-one switches to the outgoing responses. Rather, the incoming impulses are usually worked over and elaborated in the central control room into a tentative, cognitive-like map of the environment. And it is this tentative map, indicating routes and paths and environmental relationships, which finally determines what responses, if any, the animal will finally release.

4. *Field-cognition modes*. These are biases towards learning one thing rather than another, resulting from the discovery of principles and the changing of one's frames of reference. They make possible new strategies of perceiving, inferring and remembering.
5. *Drive discrimination*. This involves a learner's ability to distinguish one kind of internal drive stimulus from another. Where a learner's *needs* are not clear to him, his *goals* are unclear and his behaviour may be inappropriate. An ability to understand one's *drive state* is needed for effective behaviour.
6. *Motor pattern acquisition*. This involves learning by contiguity, which can be viewed in terms of simple conditioning, based on S-R connections.

Research on Tolman's work

Tolman's work has inspired research which is of significance for teachers. Experiments have been carried out, designed to discover the precise nature of Tolman's concept of 'latent learning', that is, hidden learning which proceeds unobserved but which can be revealed in certain circumstances. Work on the 'intervening variables' in his model of the learning process has taken place in Britain and America. In Chaplin's words, referring to Tolman's legacy:[6] 'It may be that once the processes entering into cognitions, capacities, expectancies, and so on, are better known, their manifestations in molar form can be subjected to more precise manipulation'.

In *Social Learning and Clinical Psychology* (1964), the educational research worker, Rotter, building on Tolman's theories but finding an important place for the concept of reinforcement in behaviour, put forward the following points concerning the teaching-learning process.

1. A student's preference for a particular event is determined largely by its reinforcement value.

2. A student will have a subjective expectation concerning the likelihood of obtaining a particular reinforcer.
3. A student's expectation of obtaining reinforcement will be determined largely by the particular situation of which he or she is a part.
4. A student's response to new events will be guided by his or her generalized expectancies based upon past experiences. Rotter defines expectancy as 'the probability held by the individual that a particular reinforcement will occur as a function of a specific behaviour on his part in a specific situation or situations. Expectancy is independent of the value or importance of the reinforcement.' (This is linked to Tolman's idea that the pursuit of unrealistic expectations by students can often cause psychological disturbance.)

Tolman's work and the teacher

Tolman's refinement of early behaviourism has attracted some of the teachers who are repelled by the arid, mechanistic views of Watson and his contemporary advocates. The emphasis on purpose, drive and motivation in Tolman's writings corresponds in many ways to the importance attached by practising teachers to a curriculum and lesson scheme organized around the *needs* of learners. His view of learning as based on 'sign-expectation', that is, as resulting from an individual's expectation that the environment is organized in certain ways and that 'one thing invariably leads to another', has found an echo in the theory and practice of those teachers who place emphasis on the *logical construction* of schemes of classroom work, and who attempt to show students how a topic may be approached by a variety of paths. His insistence on the importance of cathexis – the acquired relationship between an object and a learner's drive – and his belief that cathexes are extremely resistant to forgetting, have been embodied in the views and practice of teachers who construct lessons on the basis of a carefully explored relationship between the perceived needs of students and the objective of those lessons.

Students, says Tolman, must be granted a variety of opportunities in which to test hypotheses. The teacher should assist by formulating hypotheses, arranging conditions for testing, and providing confirming experiences when the hypotheses are accurate. In this way students will compute and develop their own cognitive maps, allowing them to pursue their activities meaningfully. Small tutorial groups may be needed for processes of this nature.

Tolman's view of behaviour in molar terms has drawn the attention of teachers to the need for an overall approach to class behaviour, which is not to be viewed in simple terms. The expectancies of students are to be considered along with their apparent reactions to stimuli. Intervening, interacting variables have an importance which should be reflected in the teacher's overall awareness of the many factors which go to make up learning. Tolman's listing of age, heredity, endocrine conditions and previous training, as influencing learning, reminds the teacher that classroom learning is not the only determinant of overall behaviour and that student reactions have to be understood in wider terms than those constituting the simple S-R schemes of some psychologists.[7]

Gagné: the background

Gagné (b. 1916) is an educational psychologist who has occupied the chairs of psychology at the Universities of Princeton and Florida. His work has been concerned largely with a consideration of the general processes of learning so that the design of instruction might be improved. His most important books are *The Conditions of Learning* (1965), *Essentials of Learning for Instruction* (1974) and *Principles of Instructional Design* (with Briggs, 1988), in which he offers a 'rationally consistent basis' for the design of instruction in the classroom.[8]

'Instruction' is, for Gagné, 'a set of events that affect learners in such a way that learning is facilitated'. Learners may, in fact, be able to initiate and manage some instructional events themselves. The planning of instruction is undertaken so as to support the process of learning.

'Human beings acquire most of their human qualities through learning.' Learning must be linked, according to Gagné, with the design of instruction 'through consideration of the different kinds of capabilities that are being learned'. Those external events we call 'instruction' must have different characteristics 'depending on the particular class of performance change that is the focus of interest'. Instructing means arranging the conditions of learning that are external to the learner. We must not forget that the most important aspects of a learner in relation to his learning tasks are 'his senses, his central nervous system and his muscles'.

Gagné and the learning process

Learning is described by Gagné as '... a change in human disposition or capability, which persists over a period of time, and which is not simply ascribable to the process of growth'. It is a *process* taking place in the learner's brain and is called a 'process' because 'it is formally comparable to other organic processes such as digestion and respiration'. People do not learn in any general sense, but rather in the sense of changed behaviour that can be described 'in terms of an observable type of human performance'. The *change* in a student's performance is what leads to the conclusion that learning has occurred; the 'learning' may be, for example, an increased capability for a given type of performance, or an altered 'attitude' (i.e. a tendency to behave in a certain way).[9]

Gagné enumerates eight *learner characteristics* which will affect instructional design. These characteristics approximate to what he has described as 'internal conditions' which have critical effects on learning; they do not include genetically determined (innate) qualities, such as visual acuity.

1. *Intellectual skills*. These comprise 'learned capabilities which enable the learner to *do* various things by means of symbolic representations of his environment'. Representations include rules, concepts (see p. 295) syntactically organized. New learning will necessitate the retrieval of prerequisite skills, subordinate skills essential for cognitive strategies, and basic skills involved in verbal information.

2. *Cognitive strategies*. These are 'internally organized capabilities which the learner makes use of in guiding his own attention, learning, remembering and thinking'. They comprise procedures that govern the selection and utilization of intellectual skills. New learning requires their retrieval.
3. *Verbal information*. 'Man's primary method of transmitting accumulated knowledge' is composed of 'individual propositions, or networks of propositions, organized around central ideas or generic concepts'. New learning requires the recall of propositions, meaningful contexts and the spread of activation (i.e. recall of key ideas involving related ones also).
4. *Attitudes*. These are 'acquired internal states that influence the choice of personal action'. Gagné supposes that internal states affecting choices of personal action are affected strongly by 'situational factors'; revival of memory of a situation may involve revival of the attitude associated with it. New learning will involve the activation of the learner's motivation.
5. *Motor skills*. These make possible the precise, accurately timed execution of the type of performance involving the use of the learner's muscles. The core memory of such a skill seems, according to Gagné, to consist of a highly organized and centrally located 'motor program'. New learning in this area demands the recall of sub-routines and part-skills (see p. 300).
6. *Schemas*. These are organizations of memory elements (e.g. images) representing a set of information pertaining to some general concept. New learning necessitates the activation of related networks of propositions.
7. *Abilities*. Gagné sees these as fundamental, stable characteristics, persisting over long periods and not easily changed by instruction or practice. New learning involves the adaptation of instruction to levels of abilities.
8. *Traits*. These are tendencies of learners to respond in characteristic ways to a variety of situations. New learning involves the adaptation of instruction to differences in a learner's traits.

Learning is viewed by Gagné as a 'total process', beginning with a phase of *apprehending* the stimulus situation, proceeding to a stage of *acquisition*, then to *storage* and finally to *retrieval*. The teacher must ensure that a student has the prerequisite capabilities for the learning task he or she is to undertake. There is a 'learning hierarchy'[10] which depends on prerequisite intellectual skills. The prior learning, and reinstatement in the memory, of subordinate capabilities is essential for new learning. Gagné enumerates eight *types of learning*, each requiring its own teaching strategy. In each type of learning there is a different state of the learner's knowledge which will produce a new capability for performance.

1. *Signal learning*. Here the learner associates an available response with a new 'signal' (i.e. stimulus). A generalized response to stimuli is made (see Pavlov's work noted on p. 45).
2. *Stimulus-response learning*. Here the learner acquires exact responses to discriminated stimuli.
3. *Chaining*. The learner acquires a number of S-R bonds, such as the sets of motor

responses needed to change a typewriter ribbon, set up a drilling machine, or finger A-flat on the oboe.

4. *Verbal association learning.* Here the learner acquires verbal chains, selecting the links from his previously learned repertoire. 'The chain cannot be learned unless the individual is capable of performing the individual links.'

5. *Multiple discrimination.* The learner acquires the capacity to discriminate between apparently similar stimuli and to make the correct response.

6. *Concept learning.* The learner is able to make common responses to classes of stimuli that appear to differ widely from one another and to recognize relationships, known as 'classes'.

7. *Rule learning.* The learner is able to form 'chains' of two or more concepts. Knowledge of a rule is 'an inferred capability that enables the individual to respond to a class of stimulus situations with a class of performances'. New rules ('the stuff of thinking') are discovered when previously acquired rules are used so as to produce new capabilities. It should be noted that knowledge of a rule involves much more than the ability to state it with accuracy. Effective learning involves the student being able to apply a rule to a variety of circumstances and to retrieve the constituent parts of the rule from memory.

8. *Problem-solving.* This is 'a natural extension of rule learning, in which the most important part of the process takes place within the learner'. It is characterized by discovery of relationships.

Gagné suggests the use of 'instructional sequences' consisting of: informing the learner as to what form of performance is expected after completion of learning; questioning the learner so as to elicit recall of previously learned concepts; using cues eliciting the formation of chains of concepts or 'rules'; questioning the learner so as to obtain a demonstration of rules; requiring the learner to make a verbal statement of the rule.

The phases of learning

The 'information-processing model' is considered by Gagné to represent 'a major advance in the scientific study of human learning'. According to Gagné's interpretation of the model, an act of learning, no matter what its duration in time, comprises several phases. It begins with an intake of stimulation from the learner's receptors and concludes with feedback, following his performance. A number of 'internal processing events' also take place. The teacher's task involves several different types of external stimulation which affect the processes of learning.

The following *phases of learning* are differentiated by Gagné.

1. *The motivation phase.* This involves striving to attain some end. The identification of students' motives and channelling them into 'activities that accomplish educational goals' form a task for the designer of instruction. The generation of student expectancies is essential in this phase; the teacher can assist by informing the learner of the objectives – 'expectancies of the learning outcome'.

2. *The apprehending phase.* Attention and selective perception constitute this phase. The teacher's specific task here is the direction of attention, so that the learner is ready to receive appropriate, prepared stimuli. Selective perception involves the teacher in arranging stimuli which will emphasize those features of his presentation which it is intended shall be stored in the learner's short-term memory (see p. 212). The highlighting of aspects of presentation (by repetition, audio-visual aids, and verbal and pictorial emphasis) is an essential feature of 'foundation learning' in any subject area.

3. *The acquisition phase.* Coding and storage entry characterize this phase of learning. The process of coding involves transforming information into a pattern appropriate for storage in the memory. The provision of learning guidance, the 'stimulation of recall of necessary prerequisites and other supportive material from the learner's long-term memory' comprise the teacher's principal task in this phase. Verbal directions eliciting the utilization of previously learned material are important. Questions and cues have a part to play here.

4. *The retention phase.* Memory storage, following storage entry, is the essence of this phase. Instruction designed to ensure retention – practice, tests, feedback – is necessary here.

5. *The recall phase.* Retrieval is the appropriate internal process for this phase. The provision of a variety of external cues within the learner's frame of knowledge is the teacher's task at this point. Thus, the learner may be required to apply what she has learned to novel types of problem in a variety of circumstances.

6. *The generalization phase.* Transfer of learning (see p. 223) is the objective of this phase; the teacher's task is its promotion. Gagné views transfer of learning as taking the form of lateral and vertical movement. *Lateral transfer* is a process of generalizing that 'spreads over' situations at approximately the same level of complexity, such as where the acquired ability to recognize parts of speech is carried over from English to, say, French. *Vertical transfer* involves the use of learned capabilities at one level of learning at a higher level, as where the knowledge of handling clay is utilized in the design of pots.

7. *The performance phase.* The eliciting of an appropriate performance, reflecting newly acquired capability, is essential if the teacher is to have evidence of the learner having attained his objective.

8. *The feedback phase.* This final phase, in which the learner is made aware of the degree to which his performance approaches required standards, acts as a reinforcement, strengthening newly-learned associations and their recall.

Gagné's essentials of a theory of instruction

Gagné states that a theory of instruction should seek to relate the external events of instruction to the outcomes of learning by demonstrating how these events 'lead to appropriate support or enhancement of internal learning processes'. The theory should set out a 'rationally-based relationship' between the events constituting instruction, how they affect the learning process and how that process results in a learning outcome. The following concepts should underpin the theory.

1. Learning ought to be thought of in terms of sets of processes which are internal to the individual learner and which result in the transformation of stimuli from his or her situation into information which will be lodged in the long-term memory, resulting in qualitative improvements to his or her capacities.
2. A learner's capacities include intellectual skills, cognitive strategies, verbal information, attitudes and motor skills; all are differentiated in ways allowing their differential assessment.
3. 'Different learning outcomes necessitate differential instruction.'
4. The positive features of certain 'time-tested learning principles' would figure large in the theory of instruction. They include: the principle of *contiguity*, so that the stimulus situation should be presented simultaneously with the desired response; the principle of *repetition*, allowing the frequent repetition of the stimulus situation and the desired response; the principle of *reinforcement*, based on the view that the occurrence of a new act (A_2) is learned more readily when followed immediately by an earlier-learned act (A_1) that the learner 'likes to perform,' so that A_2 is made contingent on the learner performing A_1.

Gagné's work and the teacher

The teacher's fundamental task is to assist in making possible the attainment of a set of educational goals; these goals are, according to Gagné, 'those human activities that contribute to the functioning of a society (including the functioning of an individual *in* the society) and that can be acquired through learning'. Deliberately planned instruction by the teacher is essential if the goals are to be attained.

The practical significance of Gagné's work has been recognized by the many teachers who build their lesson schemes and plan their instruction on the basis of the concepts set out in *The Conditions of Learning* (1965). Gagné sees the teacher as a *designer and manager* of the process of instruction and an *evaluator* of learning outcomes. He emphasizes, above all, the importance of the *systematic design of instruction* based on intended outcomes and linked with awareness of the internal conditions of learning. Gagné's view of the 'hierarchical nature' of the learning process serves as a reminder to the teacher that *the learner must be adequately prepared* to enter a particular phase of instruction. The teacher must ensure that 'relevant lower-order skills are mastered before the learning of the related higher-order skill is undertaken ... First, find out what the student already knows; second, begin instruction at that point.'

The *importance of feedback* in the classroom is stressed by Gagné. 'Every act of learning requires feedback if it is to be completed.' This necessitates communication to the student, as swiftly and accurately as possible, of the outcome of his or her performance and calls for careful and regular evaluation in the classroom. The planning of feedback is one example of the design of instruction – with the learner in mind – which characterizes the neo-behaviourism of which Gagné is a powerful and influential advocate.

Gagné's work is of particular importance to teachers because it has, at its centre, the practical problems of class instruction. His theories and the research which underpins them relate to the everyday activities of staff and students. He warns, in the preface to *The Conditions of Learning* (1965), against research into learning which is based on a 'variety of sources, not all of which relate to education'. He also points out that sometimes the source of an original research problem, which may have been educational in nature, 'has, over a period of years, been virtually lost sight of, while the problem itself has become subtly altered in its definition'. Gagné emphasizes that a learning theory which does not take into account the *formal* processes of instruction in school and college may be of restricted value to teaching practitioners. Educational theory must be rooted in educational practice.

Notes and references

1. See generally for this chapter: Hilgard and Bower (*op. cit.*); Hergenhahn (*op.cit.*); 'Behavioural pedagogy' by K. Wheldall in *Introduction to Modern Behaviourism* by H. Rachlin (Freeman, 1980); *The Philosophy of Psychology* ed. W. Donohue (Sage, 1996); *Psychology: The Science of Mind and Behaviour* by R. Gross (Hodder & Stoughton, 1996); *Theories of Learning* by J.C. Malone (Wadsworth, 1991).
2. Behaviourism, said Skinner, is little more than a thoroughgoing 'operational analysis of traditional mentalist concepts': see 'The operational analysis of psychological terms' in *Psychological Review* (1945, *52*). Note the doctrines of the logical positivists who appeared to support Skinnerian operational analysis – see e.g. Carnap, in *Psychology in Physical Language* and *The Logical Syntax of Language* (Harcourt Brace, 1937): 'Every sentence of psychology may be formulated in physical language.'
3. *A History of Psychology* by T.H. Leahey (Prentice-Hall, 1980).
4. 'The current status of behaviourism and learning theory of psychology' in *Behaviourism and Learning Theory in Education* ed. D. Fontana (Scottish Academic Press, 1984); 'Images of man in contemporary behaviourism' by D.E. Blackman in *Models of Man* ed. A.J. Chapman *et al.* (British Psychological Society, 1980).
5. See Hergenhahn (*op.cit.*); 'The organism and the causal texture of the environment' by E. Tolman and E. Brunswick in *Psychological Review* (1935); 'Tolman's cognitive analyses' by D. Olton in *Journal of Experimental Psychology* (1992, *121*).
6. *Systems and Theories of Psychology* (Holt, Rinehart & Winston, 1970).
7. See *Behaviour and Psychological Man* (California UP, 1951).
8. *Principles of Instructional Design* (Holt, Rinehart & Winston, 1988) is an outstanding text which covers in methodical fashion the essence of instructional systems, basic processes in learning and instruction, and delivery systems for instruction.
9. See also 'Contributions of learning to human development' in *Psychological Review* (1968, *75*).
10. See 'Learning hierarchies' by R.M. Gagné in *Contemporary Issues in Educational Psychology* ed. H. Clarizio (Allyn & Bacon, 1974).

Chapter 6

The Neo-behaviourist School (2)

Behaviourism is not the science of human behaviour; it is the philosophy of that science (Skinner, 1974).

This chapter outlines the distinctive contribution to educational psychology made by Skinner (1904–90), one of the most controversial figures in psychology during the twentieth century.[1] In the words of Kovach:[2] '[He] combines psychological creativeness with an inventor's genius for contriving situations in which new principles can suddenly emerge charmingly and cleanly from the underbrush of complications.'

For Skinner, learning was to be studied in scientific terms. Science was 'more than a set of attitudes. It is a search for order, for uniformities, for lawful relations among the events in nature. It begins, as we all begin, by observing single episodes, but it quickly passes on to the general rule, to scientific law.' A science of behaviour is needed to underpin the investigation of learning (and, by extension, teaching). Skinner followed the spirit of Pavlov's dictum: 'Control your conditions and you will see order.' His work was directed to a study of overt behaviour and to the essence of the learning process which became known as *operant conditioning*, whereby responses are rendered more probable or more frequent. An 'operant' is behaviour which operates on the environment and produces consequences: it is considered on pp. 77–8. A coherent theory of operant conditioning could be used so as to allow teachers to mould students' behaviour.

Fundamental to Skinner's concepts of a behaviouristic analysis are the following assumptions which he set out in *About Behaviourism* (1974).

1. A person is, primarily, an organism, a member of a species and a subspecies, possessing a 'genetic endowment of anatomical and physiological characteristics'.
2. These characteristics are the product of 'contingencies of survival to which the species has been exposed in the process of evolution'.
3. The transformation of an organism into a 'person' takes place as it acquires a repertoire of behaviour 'under the contingencies of reinforcement to which it is exposed'.
4. A person's behaviour exhibited at a given time is controlled by 'a current setting'.

5. The ability to acquire a repertoire of behaviour results from the processes of conditioning which are part of the genetic endowment.

Skinner: the background

Skinner, born in 1904, graduated in English and entered Harvard as a graduate student in psychology in 1928. His doctoral thesis investigated the concept of the reflex; his specific interests led to work on operant behaviour, which was carried out in the biological laboratories at Harvard. During the war years he worked on a project involving the training of pigeons to guide missiles; this resulted in his discovery of the techniques of 'shaping' (see p. 79).[3] In 1945 he became chairman of the Department of Psychology at Indiana University, returning permanently to Harvard in 1948 where he held the chair in psychology until his retirement in 1974. The period from 1974 until his death in 1990 was marked by a prodigious output of books and articles, many of which were designed specifically for practising teachers.

The literature

The outlines of Skinner's work may be found in *The Behaviour of Organisms* (1938), *Science and Human Behaviour* (1953), *Verbal Behaviour* (1957), *The Technology of Teaching* (1968) which deals with topics such as the science of learning and the art of teaching, motivation and teaching machines, *Beyond Freedom and Dignity* (1971), and *About Behaviourism* (1974) in which humanity is seen as capable of controlling its destiny 'because it knows what has to be done and how to do it'.

The many texts and articles criticizing Skinner include *The Misbehaviour of Organisms* by Breland (1961), and 'Psychology and ideology' by Chomsky in *The Philosophy of Society* ed. Biehler (1978). *The Selection of Behaviour* ed. Catania (1989) comprises a set of papers by Skinner which are made the basis of commentaries by scholars. (The acrimonious and astringent tone of much of the criticism of Skinner accounts for his final comment in the text: 'Whatever current usefulness this volume may have, it should at least be of interest to the future historian as a sample of the style of discussion among behavioural scientists near the end of the twentieth century'.)

Techniques of investigation

Skinner's techniques of investigation have been applied to a study of the conditions of behaviour of pigeons, dogs, rats, monkeys and children. He claims that, in spite of considerable phylogenic differences, 'all these organisms show amazingly similar properties of the learning process'. The conditioning experiments associated with his name were based upon the use of the 'Skinner box', an apparatus which allowed him to study the responses of a variety of animals. A hungry (but unconditioned) animal, for example, a rat, is allowed to explore the box. When the rat spontaneously presses a small brass lever, the experimenter drops a pellet of food from a magazine into a tray, thus allowing the animal to eat. This is repeated on several occasions until the rat acquires the habit of going to the tray when it hears the sound made by a movement of the food magazine. Later, the lever is connected directly to the magazine so that the rat's pressure results in the presentation of a food pellet. Conditioning then follows rapidly. Accumulated data on the animal's rate of response were used by Skinner in his formulation of the effect of reinforcement in learning. These techniques were later refined and used as the basis of continued experiments in the *modification of behaviour by operant conditioning* (see below) which, for Skinner, is synonymous with the essential characteristic of the learning process.

Catania's comment should be noted carefully: 'Operant behaviourism provides the systematic context for the research in psychology sometimes referred to as the experimental analysis of behaviour. Behaviour itself is a fundamental subject matter; behaviour is not an indirect means of studying something else, such as cognition or mind or brain.'

The basis of behaviour

Much of Skinner's work has involved the functional analysis of behaviour. This type of analysis involves attempting to isolate and identify all the environmental variables of which behaviour is a function.[4] 'Any condition or event which can be shown to have an effect on behaviour must be taken into account. By discovering and analysing these causes we can predict behaviour; to the extent that we can manipulate them, we can control behaviour.' Behaviour is defined by Skinner in highly formal terms, as 'the movement of an organism or of its parts in a frame of reference provided by the organism itself or by various external objects or fields of force'. It is merely part of an organism's biology and 'can be integrated with the rest of that field when described in appropriate physical dimensions'. The fundamental matter for the student of behaviour is solely 'an observed correlation of stimulus and response'.

The behaviour known as 'learning' is manifested in changes in a learner's responses (see below). These changes result in most cases from *operant conditioning*.[5] An 'operant' is a series of acts which constitute a learner's doing something, for example picking up a pen, opening a book; these are voluntary responses emitted by the learner, whose behaviour operates on the environment so as to generate consequences. Operant reinforcement improves the *efficiency* of the learner's behaviour.

Skinner differentiated *operant* and *respondent* behaviour. As noted above, operant behaviour involves voluntary, emitted responses; they are not elicited by any identifiable external stimuli. Respondent behaviour involves responses elicited by known stimuli; an example is the reflex eye blink in the presence of excessive light.

The experimental analysis of behaviour, most of which is a product of operant reinforcement, has led, according to Skinner, to the creation of an effective technology applicable to education. It will be even more effective, he believes, 'when it is not competing with practices that have had the unwarranted support of mentalistic theories'.

Skinner and the learning process

Skinner's analysis of the learning process is based on his view of the importance of conditioning the learner's operant behaviour. *Learning is, in essence, the result of the creation of conditioned connections between the learner's operant behaviour and its reinforcement; it involves a change in the form or probability of the learner's responses.* (The *strength* of a learned response, i.e. the probability of its recurrence, is generally determined by the amount of reinforcement it receives.) Operant conditioning is, therefore, a type of learning that will result in an increase in the probability of a response occurring as a function of reinforcement.

   Reinforcement is 'the process of increasing the frequency of occurrence of a low-frequency behaviour, or maintaining the frequency of occurrence of a high-frequency behaviour'. The terms 'positive' and 'negative' reinforcement are not used by Skinner with connotations of 'good' or 'bad'. Positive reinforcement occurs when a stimulus is presented which, when added to a situation, increases the probability of occurrence of a response. (In simple terms, it may be noted when some expression of approval is made to a person when the desired behaviour occurs.) Negative reinforcement occurs with the termination of some unpleasant (aversive) stimulus, which, when removed from a situation, increases the probability of occurrence of a response (as when something is taken away from a person upon occurrence of the target behaviour). It should be noted that, for Skinner, 'reinforcement' is not to be equated with 'reward'; 'reinforcement' strengthens behaviour, 'reward' implies some kind of compensation. 'The only defining characteristic of reinforcing stimulus is that it reinforces.'

   Positive reinforcement may emerge as the result of the use of primary or secondary reinforcers. Objects or events that satisfy fundamental needs may act as primary (unconditioned) reinforcers. 'Primary' indicates that the relationship between the objects and events and the satisfaction of needs is *unlearned*. (Food is an example.) Objects and events, otherwise neutral, that have acquired desirable, reinforcing qualities, are known as 'secondary (conditioned) reinforcers'; the relationship between the secondary reinforcers and the satisfaction of needs is *learned*. The reinforcing quality of a secondary reinforcer may be the result of its continued pairing with stimuli that satisfy basic needs directly. Approval from one's peers is an example of a secondary reinforcer. (Eventually, says Skinner, generalized reinforcers (i.e. secondary reinforcers that have been paired with more than one primary reinforcer) will become effective, even though the primary reinforcers upon which they are based no longer accompany them. 'Thus, we play games of skill for their own sake.' 'A miser may be so reinforced by money that he will starve rather than give it up.')

   Negative reinforcement, which involves the removal from a situation of an unpleasant stimulus, may have a role in the classroom where it is necessary to induce desired behaviour. The threat to a student of his removal from class is an example of a negative reinforcer; here the threat of an aversive consequence may produce a change in those overt responses which, for Skinner, constitute a pattern of behaviour. One of the problems arising from the use of negative reinforcers is that behaviour other than that desired by the teacher may be discovered by the student as a means of avoiding the aversive consequences. Further, the repeated use of negative reinforcers may create high levels of anxiety which result in unacceptably low levels of student performance. Where 'punishments', e.g. sanctions, result in the temporary suppression of undesirable responses, a *positive reinforcement* may be used so as to elicit new, desirable responses.

Skinner's advice to teachers rests on the necessity to understand the role of reinforcement in the learning process. First, the teacher must define the behaviour he wishes to build; he must remember that operant behaviourism necessitates teacher-centred instruction. Next, he should select as reinforcers those objects and events which, in the context of the class, with its given social and intellectual background, will have reference to the maintenance of desired behaviour. The types of reinforcer should be varied: secondary, or symbolic, reinforcers (a nod of approval, an overt expression of pleasure) might be utilized. When desired consequences fail to emerge, the types of reinforcer should be changed. Reinforcement should be considered as a means to an end; the end is that quality of behaviour from which the acquisition of learning may be inferred.

The shaping of behaviour

Behaviour can be shaped by appropriate reinforcement: this is, perhaps, one of the most striking of Skinner's suggestions. His experiments with animals led to the refinement of a technique known as *differential reinforcement of successive approximations*. Behaviour is shaped through the animal's successive approximations to the desired, target behaviour; each approximation results from the selective reinforcement of some responses, but not others. Verbal behaviour, for example, is seen by Skinner in terms of responses related to reinforcement, so that talking and listening are amenable to the process of shaping. 'Shaping' in the class-room involves reinforcing a student's correct responses to a series of planned stimuli.

When each step in a complex act is reinforced by the reinforcing of the selected responses of which it is composed, chains of reflexes are established. In this process Skinner employs the technique of *reinforcement scheduling*, that is, the systematic application of reinforcement. Types of scheduling include the following.

(a) *Continuous reinforcement*: every correct response during learning is reinforced.
(b) *Fixed interval*: the first correct response made after a fixed interval of time is reinforced.
(c) *Variable interval*: the first correct response made after a variable period of time is reinforced.
(d) *Fixed ratio*: the first correct response made after a fixed number of responses is reinforced.

(e) *Variable ratio*: the first correct response made after a variable number of responses is reinforced.

Schedules (c), (d) and (e) tend to produce high rates of response; schedule (b) is characterized by bursts of response preceding the usual time of reinforcement, with low rates of response following it. It has been suggested that the most effective schedules for the classroom seem to be those initially consisting of continuous reinforcement, followed at a later stage by intermittent reinforcement. A useful rule is as follows: in the first stages of learning, reward *every* correct response; then, in succeeding stages, reward at random or in a fixed manner relative to an interval or ratio basis. In practice, in the early stages of learning this may involve making each successive step as small as possible, so that the frequency of reinforcement can be raised to a maximum, and so that the aversive consequences of errors are reduced to a minimum.[6]

Biehler, following Skinner, states that teachers should be aware of the possibility that the effectiveness of the techniques of shaping can be weakened in three ways.

1. Where too much positive reinforcement is supplied for 'early, crude' responses, the student's willingness to attempt to give more complex and refined responses may be reduced.
2. Where the teacher expects too much progress to be made too soon, so that steps in the sequence of learning become too wide, the likelihood of appropriate responses may be decreased.
3. Where the teacher delays reinforcing the student's terminal behaviour, additional and unrelated behaviours may emerge.

Walker[7] suggests that the modification of behaviour in the learning process should include the following steps (based on Skinner's views) to be taken by the teacher:

● select the target behaviour;
● determine how often the target behaviour occurs in the normal course of events;
● select appropriate reinforcers;
● reinforce successive approximations of the target behaviour each time they occur;
● reinforce the target behaviour on each occasion it occurs, and on a variable reinforcement schedule.

Skinner's direct application of operant conditioning findings to the problems of classroom learning culminated in his advocacy of programmed instruction (see Chapter 29) and the teaching machine. ('We have every reason to expect ... that the most effective control of human learning will require instrumental aid.') The concepts of immediate reinforcement of emitted behaviour and the gradual withdrawal of stimulus support from the learner ('fading' of learning cues), which characterize programmed instruction, were derived directly from his success in the shaping and conditioning of learning through reinforcement.

Skinner's work and the teacher

Skinner's view of the learning process has attracted trenchant and persistent criticism: see, for example, the onslaughts from Chomsky and Koestler. His fundamental belief that psychology must become a precise science has been rejected as a mirage: for example, according to Hearnshaw, 'man's creative potential adds to the uncertainty and unpredictability' which make impossible precise determination of matters which affect the human brain at any given time. He has been accused of 'extrapolating well beyond his data', and his generalizations concerning human behaviour have been attacked as reflecting the study of animals which are totally unlike human beings. The shaped behaviour of a pigeon taught to 'dance' has been held to be irrelevant to an explanation of the complex activities which form human behaviour. Nor, it has been argued, should the conditions of the operant conditioning chamber be used as the basis of suggestions concerning the conditions which ought to exist in the classroom. Additionally, the basic objections to behaviourism's rejection of the mentalistic explanations of human activity have been hurled with special vigour at Skinner and his associates. It is objected, further, that he seems to consider learning to be of two types only, whereas there may be many types.

Some of the assumptions made by Skinner were challenged by Breland and Breland, who had worked in his laboratory and had later become animal trainers specializing in preparing animals for appearances in films by the use of operant conditioning and shaping. In *The Misbehaviour of Organisms* (1961)[8], they gave an account of their failures in applying Skinner's techniques to the control of animal behaviours. Pigs and racoons, for example, had not responded as expected to attempts to chain and shape sequences of complex activities. 'Nothing in our behaviourist background prepared us for such gross inabilities to predict and control the behaviour of animals.' They concluded that they had failed to take into account the natural behaviour of animals in their normal surroundings. Persons who seek to modify behaviour do not, apparently, have the power to do so in any desired direction by the use of reinforcement. Every species has its unique *species-typical responses*, so that problems of training a species are unique. The swift execution of reinforced responses might be delayed or prevented by the 'prepotency of strong instinctive behaviours'. The 'ecological niche' of a species may have been ignored in Skinner's analysis. (For examples of other constraints on response acquisition, see *Constraints on Learning.*[9])

In 'On Responsibility and Punishment',[10] Staddon criticizes the effects on society of some of the principles advocated by Skinner. In particular, he suggests that Skinner's condemnation of punishment as inefficient and ineffective and his promulgation of the doctrine that free will is a delusion have had a deleterious effect on society in that they have contributed substantially to the prevalent decline in social standards.

Skinner has replied to many of these criticisms and has reasserted his views. (A typical reply, in *Beyond Freedom and Dignity*, is: ' "Animal" is a pejorative term, but only because "man" has been spuriously honorific ... Man is much more than a dog, but like a dog he is within range of scientific analysis.') Teaching remains, for him, 'the arrangement of contingencies of reinforcement under which behaviour changes'. This is a view which has important implications for the class teacher. Teaching, he reminds us, should not be a random, hit-or-miss affair, nor is it an unfathomable mystery; it is a process which is amenable to investigation, and which requires the methodological application of techniques based in part on the results of the experimental analysis of behaviour. A student is 'taught' in the sense that '... he is induced to engage in new forms of behaviour and in specific forms on specific occasions'. *The teacher's task is to shape behaviour and this requires an awareness of objectives and the techniques of assisting attainment.* It requires, additionally, a knowledge of the basis of reinforcement, of results of types of reinforcement scheduling, and of the particular importance of a partial reinforcement schedule. Indeed, the infrequency of reinforcement is regarded by Skinner as 'the most serious criticism of the current classroom'. Hence the lecture technique cannot be viewed favourably (see p. 315). In essence, the teacher's role should be that of practitioner of a technology designed 'to maximise the genetic endowment of each student ... [leading him] to make the greatest possible contribution to the survival and development of his culture'.

Skinner has set out interesting views for teachers who are considering the problems involved in teaching students 'how to learn'. 'It is important that the student should learn to solve problems by himself, explore the unknown, make decisions, and behave in original ways and these activities should, if possible, be taught.' But there should be no attempt to teach 'thinking' while subject matter is being taught. If 'thinking' can be analysed and taught separately, that which is known about it already 'can be transmitted with maximal efficiency'. The teacher should define the precise objectives and the required terminal behaviour in teaching 'thinking' as in teaching a more specific subject area. It should be possible to teach the behaviour known as 'thinking' by using material which is already available in areas such as psychology, scientific method and logic.

Dembo[11] derives the following practical advice for teachers from Skinner's work.

(1) In teaching a new task, act so as to reinforce *immediately* rather than allowing a delay between student response and reinforcement.
(2) Reinforce each correct response in the *early stages* of a task. When learning is seen to occur, insist upon more correct responses before reinforcement and move gradually, but methodically, to intermittent reinforcement.
(3) Do not expect a perfect performance of a task by the student on the first occasion; attempt, rather, to reinforce students' steps in the *direction of mastery* (see Chapter 23).
(4) Do not reinforce in any way undesirable behaviour.

(Dembo's comments have particular relevance for the teaching of skills: see Chapter 24.)

In recent years, Skinner has continued to defend his point of view by vigorous condemnation of the 'conspiracy of silence about teaching as a skill ... so that pedagogy is a dirty word'. An article entitled 'The shame of American education' (1984)[12] sets out his responses to a report that, in 1983, the average achievement of American high-school students on standardized tests was lower than it was a quarter of a century earlier. Skinner sees the spread of 'the fallacies of cognitive and humanistic psychology' as an important contributory cause of this state of affairs. His solution is precisely stated: 'Teachers must learn how to teach ... they need only to be taught more effective ways of teaching.' What needs to be done is this: be clear about what is to be taught; teach first things first; allow students to advance at their own rate; program the subject matter. 'Give students and teachers better reasons for learning and teaching.' He concludes his article with these words: 'Young people are by far the most important natural resource of a nation, and the development of that resource is assigned to education ... We would all be better off if education played a far more important part in transmitting our culture.'

In 'What is wrong with daily life in the Western world?',[13] Skinner referred to certain cultural practices which were destroying social life: they included 'alienating workers from the consequences of their work' and 'guiding behaviour with rules rather than supplying reinforcing consequences'. He urged the importance of striving to overcome these practices by a strengthening of desirable behaviour through contingencies of reinforcement.

Skinner continues to emphasize that a really effective educational system cannot be constructed until the processes of learning and teaching are properly understood and accepted. Human behaviour, he insists, is far too complex to be left to casual experience or even to organized experience in a classroom environment which is, by its very nature, restricted, and in which too great an interval exists between student behaviour and its reinforcement. 'Teachers need help. In particular, they need the kind of help offered by a scientific analysis of behaviour.' Skinner's words affirm the importance for the class teacher of practice based firmly on tested theory. Education is, for Skinner, 'the establishing of behaviour which will be of advantage to the individual and to others at some future time'. The role of the teacher is the creating of that advantageous behaviour.[14]

Notes and references

1. See 'Biographical sketch and bibliography of works by B.F. Skinner' in *The Selection of Behaviour (The Operant Behaviourism of B.F.Skinner: Comments and Consequences)* ed. A.C. Catania and S. Harnad (CUP, 1989) and 'Burrhus Frederic Skinner' in *Theories of Learning* by B. Hergenhan (Prentice-Hall, 1997); *About Behaviourism* by B.F. Skinner (Random House, 1974); *B.F. Skinner: A Life* by D.W. Bjork (American Psychological Association, 1997).
2. *Historical Introduction to Modern Psychology* by J. Kovach (Routledge, 1979).
3. 'Pigeons in a pelican' by B.F. Skinner (*American Psychologist*, 1960, *15* (28)).
4. Half a century earlier, Lloyd Morgan had written of 'behaviour' as a term which 'in all cases indicates and draws attention to the reaction of that which we speak of as behaving in response to certain surrounding conditions or circumstances which evoke this behaviour' (*Animal Behaviour*, 1902).

5. 'Operant conditioning shapes behaviour as a sculptor shapes a lump of clay' (*Science and Human Behaviour*).

6. See *Schedules of Reinforcement* by C.B. Ferster and B.F. Skinner (Appleton, 1957); 'Instrumental appetitive conditioning' by S.B. Klein in *Learning* (McGraw-Hill, 1987); *Systems and Theories of Psychology* by J. Chaplin and T. Krawiec (Holt, Rinehart & Winston, 1970); *Learning Theory* by R. Bolles (Holt, Rinehart & Winston, 1979); 'Rational choice theory' by R. Herrnstein in *American Psychologist* (1990, *45*).

7. *Behaviour Management: A Practical Approach for Educators* (Holt, Rinehart & Winston, 1991).

8. *American Psychologist* (1961, *16*: 661).

9. Ed. Hinde (Academic Press, 1973).

10. *Atlantic Monthly* (1995, *2*).

11. *Teaching for Learning* (Goodyear, 1981).

12. *American Psychologist* (1984, *11*)

13. *American Psychologist* (1986, *41*).

14. Skinner's articles, 'Are theories of learning necessary?' (*Psychological Review*, 1950, *57*) and 'The experimental analysis of behaviour' (*American Scientist*, 1957, *45*), were written in response to matters raised by teachers in correspondence with him and will be of particular interest to college staff.

Chapter 7

The Gestalt School

> The harmony that results from the simultaneous sounding of all the strings [of a lyre] is obviously different from the sounds produced by the individual strings ... The totality that emerges from the harmony of all the strings plucked together differs from the totality produced when the strings are plucked individually (Philoponos, c.AD 500).

Gestalt psychology (see p. 37) takes its name from the German word *Gestalt* – a configuration, structure, pattern; it is a 'form' psychology. It stands in total opposition to the principles, methods and conclusions of the structuralist and behaviourist schools of psychology, and states uncompromisingly that the phenomenological experience (i.e. that which is perceptible to the senses) is different from the parts that make it up. Gestaltist theories concerning the nature of thinking, understanding and learning have found their way into classroom procedures, particularly into teachers' concepts of instruction and its component elements.[1]

The Gestaltists built upon the work of von Ehrenfels who, in 1890, had commented on the fact that a melody is recognizable when sung in any one of a variety of keys. He had concluded that over and above the sensory ingredients of a tune (or a painting) there must be a 'form quality' (*Gestaltqualität*) which describes that which is possessed by the tune (or painting) and which is not explicable merely in terms of component tunes (or colours).

The basic theories of the Gestaltists were formulated and elaborated by Koffka, Köhler and Wertheimer. Koffka (1886–1941) graduated from the Universities of Edinburgh and, later, Berlin. He emigrated to America in 1924 and taught at Winsconsin until his death. His *Principles of Gestalt Psychology* (1935) is a compendium of Gestaltist theories and findings. Köhler (1887–1967) received his doctorate from Berlin University in 1909, but left Germany in 1934 and taught in America (at Swarthmore College) for the rest of his life. His most important work is held to be *Gestalt Psychology* (1929). Wertheimer (1880–1943) was a professor at the University of Frankfurt in 1929. He left Germany in 1934 and settled in America, where he taught at Columbia University. His *Productive Thinking* (issued posthumously in 1945) attempted to distinguish the laws of logic (based on imitative behaviour) and the laws of thought (creative acts of thinking).

Gestaltist objections to structuralism and behaviourism

Structuralists, such as Titchener (1867–1927), had attempted to understand mental states and processes by examining and analysing their composition and arrangement. The Gestaltists condemned this 'atomistic' approach, insisting that any analysis of the mind which merely attempted to reduce it to elements was misleading. Mental patterns could not be reduced, they claimed, to combinations of smaller elements, to 'bundles of sensations'. The components of an individual's mental life, such as learning and thinking, could be analysed successfully only when viewed as *organized, complete structures.* Attributes of component parts could be defined only by their relationship to *the system as a whole* in which they are functioning: this is a vital aspect of Gestaltist doctrine.

Behaviourism, as represented by Watson (see Chapter 4), was also rejected by the Gestaltists. The reduction of human behaviour to S-R patterns was criticized as over-simplified. In its place the Gestaltists offered a concept based on a pattern symbolized by S-O-R (stimuli pattern → perceptual organization by the organism → response based on perception). They maintained that 'organisms do not merely respond to their environment, they have *transactions* with the environment'. A person experiences his world by imposing on his perceptions simplicity, regularity, symmetry and stability: this is a key to an understanding of the Gestaltist approach. The behaviourists' denial of the importance of introspection as an analytical tool was also rejected by the Gestaltists.

To cut to pieces living and thinking processes in an attempt to get at the elements of thinking, was to blind oneself to the significance of structure as a whole. It was to the pattern and meaningfulness of the mental process *as a whole* that the Gestaltists turned their attention. Their guiding thesis was formulated by Wertheimer, thus: 'There are contexts in which what is happening in the whole cannot be deduced from the characteristics of the separate pieces, but conversely, what happens to a part of the whole is, in clear-cut cases, determined by the laws of the inner structure of the whole.'

The essence of the Gestaltist approach

'*The whole is greater than the sum of its parts; we are dealing with wholes and whole-processes possessed of inner intrinsic laws*' – this is the essence of the Gestaltist approach to a study of the phenomena with which psychology is concerned. (Some scholars perceive in this approach the influence of the philosopher, Leibnitz (1646–1716), for whom the whole was *prior* to the parts: there is a unity of mind from which constituent parts are differentiated as development takes place.) It is the total structured form of an individual's mental experience with which the psychologist and the teacher ought to be concerned; the attributes of the whole are not entirely deducible from an analysis of constituent elements. The whole itself, as well as its individual components, may be considered as possessing its own properties. The structural form of a Bach fugue is 'greater' than the totality of the notes of which it is made. The structure of a screw-cutting lathe is 'greater' than the mere sum of the carriage, spindle, cutting tool, etc., of which it consists. The complex perceptions which are involved in thinking and learning are much more than mere bundles of sensations of which they are said to be constituted. A learner's experience has a *pattern*, a wholeness, which is more than the sum of its parts; it is a structure of psychological phenomena with properties which cannot be understood by a mere summation of those phenomena.

Wertheimer suggested that a coherent whole possesses properties which are not discoverable in its individual isolated parts. Further, a part possesses properties which it does not possess when in isolation (or when it is a part of some other whole). The character of a whole may determine the properties of an individual part; hence the part has to be understood as a dependent property of its whole. (Köhler stresses that there are cases in physics of functional wholes that cannot be compounded from the notions associated with their separate parts.)

In the process of learning, how do we understand? According to the Gestaltists, understanding necessitates awareness of some required *relations* between facts. The relations will seem to follow on from the facts themselves. But an understandable relation between two terms is not an added third term; given any two terms, a third may be demanded by the situation. Gestaltists have suggested that understandable relations between terms possess a character of 'requiredness'. Thus, when a learner is faced with an incomplete situation, the gap in understanding of that situation has a property of its own that will produce a tendency towards completion.

Productive thinking, said Wertheimer, is the development of new structures, new organizations. The solution to a problem involves a process (not a single act) which begins with a *situation and a goal* that, at a given moment, cannot be reached. The learner's thinking in relation to this incomplete situation leads, it is suggested, to an urge to bridge the gap; this leads to a re-examination of the problem and its component material. The learner reorganizes the material: new relations emerge and lead to a transition to a new, more coherent, point of view. The learner 'centres and recentres' features of that view and builds a structure from which he or she derives detailed steps leading to a solution of the problem. What began with a perception causing disequilibrium in the learner, terminates temporarily in a new balance, based on a new, organized structure of perception.

Past experiences of the learner contribute to the process of understanding and learning but, according to Gestaltists, 'thinking' is much more than mere recall. Selection and reorganization of material retrieved is essential if new structures of perception are to be constructed.

An individual's experiences and his or her behaviour are therefore not explicable, argued the Gestaltists, by 'atomistic' theories. Phenomena such as learning have to be studied as complex, highly organized structures. The aspect of behaviour which we call 'learning' is, in this view, a pattern of activities characterized by *organization*. Fundamental to an understanding of these activities is the Gestaltist concept of *insight*.

Insight

'Insight' is used by Gestalt psychologists in a very specific sense.[2] It is said to emerge when the learner suddenly becomes aware of the relevance of his behaviour to some objective and is the result of an unforeseen *reorganization by the learner of his field of experience*. The learner experiences a 'flash of inspiration', a 'new idea'. Archimedes' legendary cry of 'Eureka!' ('I have found it!') when he unexpectedly discovered the key to the principle of floating bodies – according to the account of Vitruvius – might be taken to symbolize insight in this sense. But insight should not be confused with the random lucky guess. There can be no insight in the absence of appropriate prior knowledge. ('Fortune favours the prepared mind' (Pasteur).)

The sudden 'flash of illumination', the instantaneous perception of how parts are related to a whole, which throws new light on a hitherto intractable problem, is well known in the history of scientific discovery.[3] Poincaré tells of how his discovery of the essence of Fuchsian functions came to him suddenly during a seaside walk. (He noted: 'Most striking at first is the appearance of sudden illumination, a manifest sign of long, unconscious prior work'.) The physicist de Broglie recounts how 'quite suddenly and usually with a jolt there occurs some kind of crystallisation, and the research worker perceives instantly ... the main outlines of the new concepts that had been latent in him'. Nicolle has told of how he solved in a moment of 'creative illumination' the problem of the transmission of typhus by fleas. Kekulé is said to have discovered the concept of benzene rings while 'in reverie' by his fireside. Lombroso,[4] the founder of criminal anthropology records, somewhat dramatically, how the theory that criminals are 'evolutionary throwbacks' came to him in 1870 while he was examining the skull of an Italian brigand, as a flash of inspiration, 'lighting up a vast plain under a flaming sky'. Sir William Hamilton, the Irish mathematician, wrote of how, while walking, he experienced a flash of inspiration involving his 'new algebra' (relating to discarding the communicative postulate for multiplication). Galton records that the solution to the problem of correlation of anthropomorphic data came to him quite suddenly while sheltering from a rainstorm in Naworth Castle.[5] See also Penrose's comments on the birth of the idea of 'trapped surfaces' in relation to black hole theory in *The Emperor's New Mind* (1991). (Note, however, that some scientists are critical of this concept as it applies to a person attempting to construct a new point of view. Gruber,[6] for example, says: 'The sudden insight in which a problem is solved, when it is solved suddenly, may represent only a minor nodal point, like the crest of a wave, in a long and very slow process – the development of a point of view'.)

Insight, according to the Gestaltists, does not result from separate responses to a series of separate stimuli; it is a complex reaction to a situation *in its entirety*, a perception of a *whole group of relationships*, a discovery of 'a previously unrecognized but fundamental unity' in a variety of phenomena, in effect, a suddenly occurring reorganization of the field of experience. Insight and thought are, in this sense, virtually synonymous. (Note the concept of an extension of knowledge, as adumbrated by Confucius, as 'knowing ten after hearing about one'.[7])

Köhler's well-known study of insight learning in chimpanzees[8] involved tests of the animals' abilities in the solution of problems, some necessitating the use of implements. In one of these experiments, the animal under observation appeared, at one stage, to act very suddenly (giving the impression of carrying out some plan of operations) in order to reach bananas suspended out of its reach. It placed boxes on top of one another, climbed them and seized the fruit. In another experiment, it put together, after many attempts, some jointed sticks which it then used to reach fruit placed outside its cage. Köhler interpreted these actions as being discontinuous with the animal's previous trials and errors; he saw them as exhibiting a pattern of learning which he recognized as insight, transferred to conceptually similar situations. The animal had made a 'discovery in thought'.

On a very much higher level the phenomenon is observed in the learner who is struggling to find the correct solution to an algebraic problem. He may seize on an apparently important feature of the problem and reformulate it in terms of that feature. Eventually his perception becomes sufficiently 'structured' to allow him to 'see into' the problem and to solve it. The sudden 'I have it! I need to multiply the square root by 3, and there's the answer ...' is the result of no magic, no fortuitous assembling of the elements of the problem in their correct order; it is, say the Gestaltists, the result of the learner's perceiving *the structural essence of the total situation posed by the problem*. The learner has made an imaginative leap from present facts to future possibilities. ('Making things explicit leads to the construction of a structure which is partially new, even though contained virtually in those structures which preceded it' (Piaget).) The learner 'sees where he saw not before'. The learner's gap in his psychological field has closed at the very moment of the occurrence of insight. It is possible to speak, in terms of an analogy, of insight as a 'closure of the learner's area of perception' (see law 5 below). Gestaltists hold that, in general, learning resulting from insight is characterized by the following features:

(a) the solution to a problem comes suddenly;
(b) the solution can be repeated subsequently and without any error, on the presentation of further problems of the same type;
(c) the solution can be retained for long periods of time and be transposed to problems which possess the same basic features as the original problem, but which are in very different contexts.

The laws of Gestalt psychology

The basic laws of the Gestaltists arise from the belief that the fundamentally biological process of perception is governed by *principles of organization*, so that the human being imposes on his physical environment a certain *Gestalt*. They may be formulated as follows:

1. *Law of figure-ground relationship*. This involves perceiving selected parts of a stimulus so that they stand out from other parts. An individual's perceptions are organized into 'figures' which tend to stand out from their background. Consider, for example, the letters which are printed on this page. They stand out

from the spaces which separate them. Yet, although figures *and* space form the field of perception, the spaces are not 'perceived' by the reader. Similarly, the pattern in which acts take on their meaning from their context in time and place is based on relationships of this nature. (The effect of expectations is also important.) When the learner attends to one aspect of his environment, that becomes the 'figure', and everything else becomes the 'ground'; which aspect of the learner's perceptual field is figure and which is ground is merely a matter of attention.

2. *Law of contiguity*. Things tend to be perceived as a unity according to their proximity in time or space. The closer they are, the more likely are they to be perceived as grouped.

3. *Law of similarity*. Items which are similar to one another in some way, for example form, tend to be perceived in a group or pattern, other things being equal.

4. *Law of Prägnanz* (i.e. *'significance'*). Percepts tend to produce the best patterns possible under the prevailing controlling circumstances, that is, figures will be perceived in their best possible form, in the shapes most characteristic of form or structure. ('Psychological organization will always be as good as the controlling circumstances allow': Koffka.[9]) Wertheimer considered this law as of the greatest importance. He emphasized that grouping will tend to maximal simplicity and balance, that is towards the formation of a 'good form'; the brain tends generally to interpret a form as an integrated whole.

5. *Law of closure*. Figures and actions which are incomplete may be perceived as though symmetrical or complete, for instance, gaps in a learner's visual field tend to close in order that she may recognize complete units. (The behaviour of Köhler's chimpanzee could be interpreted as a 'closing of the gap' in its field of perception.) Tension in the learner impels towards completion of an incomplete task. Additionally, there may be a mental tendency to organize one's perceptions so that they 'make sense'.

6. *Law of transposition*. Patterns may be changed or distorted without their recognizable identity disappearing; for example, the tune of a national anthem will be recognized whether played by a solo piccolo in G-major or a full orchestra in C-major. (Köhler referred to 'perceptual constancies', i.e. when we tend to *see* an object as the same object under a variety of circumstances.)

The laws of perceptual organization have been summarized thus: '... that immediate experiences come organised in wholes; that certain items "belong" to one constellation rather than another; and that experienced features are modified by being together' (Allport).[10] The Gestaltist laws may account for *equilibrium*, enabling percepts to attain a relative stability.

Learning and productive thinking

Learning, in Gestalt psychology, is no mere linking of associations or the workings of formal logic in the mind of the learner; it is a special case of perception, i.e. a cognitive phenomenon. (Indeed, Wertheimer referred to the rules of traditional logic as reminding him of 'an efficient police manual for regulating traffic'; rules of this nature cannot enhance understanding.) It results from the learner's restructuring and reformulating his perceptions of situations involving problems. Emotions, attitudes and intellect will enter into these perceptions, which lead to a sudden solution based on insight and reflect the learner's cognitive understanding of the relevant relationships; this type of learning will persist for a long period and can be applied to other, similar, problems. Learning is a *dynamic process*, not constituted by mere bundles of discrete S-R events which are transformed, somehow, into new concepts acquired by the learner. *The acquisition and retention of insight form, according to the Gestaltists, the core of the learning process.* Persistent changes in knowledge, skills and attitudes constitute learning and this is not always reflected in a learner's overt behaviour. 'Learning by doing' is not recognized by Gestaltists, except where a learner's 'doing' assists in changing his cognitive structures; learning results where the doer is aware of the *consequences* of his or her acts. Koffka defined learning in precise terms which will be of much interest to teachers: '... the modification of an accomplishment in a certain direction ... in creating trace systems of a particular kind, in consolidating them, and in making them more and more available both in repeated and in new situations'. (A 'trace', according to Koffka, is the inferred effect on the memory of some event. Where events are connected in some way they form a unit and a 'unitary trace'; any future excitation of some part of this trace will spread to the whole trace. The stronger the trace, the stronger will be its influence on the memory processes as a whole; hence the improvement of a skill through practice reflects the influence of a trace on the skill pattern.)

An aspect of learning which was of much importance in the theories of the Gestaltists, particularly Wertheimer, was so-called 'productive (or creative) thinking' (in contrast to mere 'reproductive learning', i.e. a replay of the past). Blind attempts to solve a problem, which are typical of a learner's uncritical application of rote-learned formulae, were contrasted with the dynamic creative process in which the learner applies himself with understanding to the discovery of a solution, based on his growing awareness of the structure of the problem. (Bell, describing the process of creating new knowledge, speaks of 'taking fragments of intellectual mosaics whose larger shapes cannot be predicted in advance and fitting them together in different ways or by regarding large conceptual structures from a new angle, which opens up wholly new prisms of selection and focus'.)

Wertheimer's experiments led him to conclude that although a potential capacity for creative thinking may be present in many learners, it is often unrealized and goes to waste because of the blind, drill-like procedures of piecemeal instruction to which they have been subjected. Productive solutions are usually related, said Wertheimer, to the 'whole characteristics', and not the isolated aspects, of problems. Productive thinking, he asserted, necessitated the learner's grasping the essential relationships within a problem, grouping them into 'wholes' and restructuring the problem. (Duncker,[11] (see p. 239), who experimented with university students in problem-solving, concluded that the solving of a problem often demanded its formulation in 'productive terms', i.e. the students had to see the problem afresh in terms of related stages.)

'Productive thinking' was analysed by Wallas,[12] who suggested that thinking of this type usually involves four stages: (1) *preparation*, in which the learner explores the problem and defines it; (2) *incubation*, in which the learner rests and, in effect, dismisses the problem from his conscious thoughts; (3) *illumination*, in which solutions may occur to the learner in an unexpected manner; (4) *verification*, in which the solutions are investigated and checked by the learner.

A summary of the Gestaltists' position in relation to student learning

Chaplin (1978)[13] gives a summary of the Gestaltist position as it relates to the area of *thinking* in the process of student learning. Six (highly simplified) principles are enunciated.

1. Productive thinking may take place when the learner encounters an original problem with which he or she is unable to deal by the application of habitual methods.
2. Thinking, in the face of a new problem with which the learner is confronted, involves a stepwise transformation of the thought processes so that the learner's attempted solutions become more specific.
3. The process of thinking involves the learner in perceptual reorganization based upon concentrating on the gaps in the possible solutions to the problem and filling them.
4. The readiness with which the learner discovers solutions is linked directly to his or her perceptual field, motivation and previous learning attainment.
5. The eventual solution results from sudden 'jumps' from one possible solution to another, reflecting sudden transformations of the learner's field of perception.
6. Where the learner has been able to achieve 'insightful solutions' to problems and has grasped fundamental principles, there is then the possibility of a high degree of transfer of learning to the solution of similar problems.

Gestalt psychology and the teacher

Gestalt doctrine has been criticized by psychologists who insist that its laws were never systematized or explained fully. There may be much agreement with Koffka's comment that measurement is not the sole source of valid evidence; but the general lack of quantification in expositions of the foundations of Gestalt psychology suggests, for some investigators, an absence of hard, empirical fact.

The concept of insight, which is at the heart of Gestalt psychology as it applies to learning, has brought criticism from some psychologists and teachers. It has been suggested that the solutions to some of the Gestaltists' experimental problems arose out of the subjects' transfer of previous learning. Harlow's experiments with monkeys, taught to solve problems based on the presence of an odd object in a group, convinced him that a trained animal might acquire a 'learning set' which allowed it to solve problems without *apparent* trial and error.[14] Yet it may be that what seems to be insight is the result, not of a sudden understanding of the essence of the problem, but of the recall of past learning. Perceptual functioning, in relation to learning, seems to teachers to require an appropriate foundation of prior experience. Teachers have pointed out also that no insight appears necessary for the learning of many things, such as simple facts. (The history student does not learn the names of the wives of Henry VIII by insight.) Psychologists, such as Gagné, have reminded the Gestaltists that insight is not a prototype for a great deal of learning which people generally undertake.

Koestler[15] criticizes Gestalt theory on the basis of a perceived confusion surrounding the use of the term 'insight'. He notes that the German term for 'insight' (*Einsicht*) is rendered in translation as 'insight' *and* 'intelligence' throughout Köhler's text, *The Mentality of Apes* (translated into English in 1957). The term 'insight' has been used, Koestler contends, indiscriminately, so that on some occasions in that text it refers to intelligence, judgment, understanding, and on other occasions it is used in connection with the sudden acquisition of new understanding. On some occasions Köhler writes about 'insight' as characterized by 'the appearance of *a complete solution* with reference to the whole layout of the field'; on others he writes of 'the dawning of a solution' and 'useful errors' made during the process of reaching a solution. Koestler draws attention also to objections raised by Hebb, in his *Textbook of Psychology* (1958), to the concept of 'suddenness' as a criterion of insight': 'All our evidence points to the conclusion that a new insight consists of a recombination of *pre-existent, mediating processes*, not the sudden appearance of a wholly new process'.

In spite of these and other criticisms of the fundamentals of Gestalt psychology, the concept of learning outlined by the Gestaltists has found a sympathetic response in the practice of many class teachers, who are aware that, to understand the responses of students, it is necessary to consider a multiplicity of facts. Learners often mentally organize the components of a task and perceive with 'sudden vision' the solution to a problem (or, as teachers and students might put it, 'the penny suddenly drops'); this is a common experience in classroom teaching. Learners commonly select from new material that which seems important, so that new terms emerge leading to insight. Insight becomes more highly structured until it produces a solution to the problem. To plan a lesson, to arrange a problem situation, to organize the elements of separate exercises into meaningful wholes, so that the learner is able to move to the discovery of patterns, relationships and solutions, is often a difficult, but necessary and worthwhile task. To prepare students for the possible emergence of novel concepts during contemplation of a problem is to assist in the development of insight. 'He who does not expect the unexpected will not detect it: for him it will remain undetectable and unapproachable' (Heraclitus).

The Gestaltists' approach to learning emphasizes for the teacher the importance of so arranging lesson structure that learners find the route to the solution of a problem *and* see their efforts as directed to that end. Considerable progress may be made in lessons in which learners are brought to a particular point and then asked to examine and explain how they have arrived at that point and how they see their work as linked to the next steps in the solution of the problem. In these cases learning will be facilitated where an 'overview' is presented and the interrelationships of course topics have been explained. Conversely, the presentation of disconnected scraps of information in a lesson is to be avoided.

Wertheimer's warnings against mechanical and blind drill based upon rote learning are echoed in those lesson structures based deliberately on comprehension and understanding as opposed to mere memorization. Katona's work,[16] involving experiments inspired by Wertheimer's theories, led him to conclude that the individual who has learned solely by rote memorization has little advantage over an unpractised learner when both are faced with new problems and that, where a skill has been acquired with insight, repeated tests in novel situations often result in a continuously improved standard of performance. (Teachers who have arrived intuitively at similar conclusions or, as the result of careful and direct observations in classroom, laboratory and workshop, will be encouraged to learn that their conclusions are supported by much formal research.)

Retention and transfer of knowledge – important objectives of the teaching process – appear in the light of Gestalt theory not as the product of repetitive drills, but as the result of the learner's discovery of patterns, relationships and principles and their effective transposition to a new, wider range of situations. In short, Gestalt theory suggests that *the teacher should aim to elicit productive thinking based on the perception of phenomena as integrated wholes.* The teacher's task is, in the light of this theory, the arranging of the conditions of learning so that perception of this nature is facilitated. Use of the lecture technique can contribute to this end, provided that it allows student-teacher interaction.

The importance of practice is stressed by the Gestaltists: they suggest that teachers should consider the advisability of providing for students continued opportunities for the observation of novel patterns and relationships. Awareness and understanding of those relationships can be translated by the teacher into a series of planned, systematic exercises, so that problem-solving can be carried out (in Hilgard's words) 'sensibly, structurally, organically, rather than mechanically, stupidly, or by the running-off of prior habits'.[17]

Notes and references

1. See generally for this chapter: *Gestalt Psychology* by W. Köhler (Liveright, 1947); 'Gestalt theory' by J. Hochberg in *OCM*; 'The whole idea: Gestalt psychology' by E. Burton in *Thinking in Perspective* ed. E. Burton (Methuen, 1978); 'Gestalt theory' in *Theories of Learning* by G. Bower and E. Hilgard (Prentice-Hall, 1981); 'The legacy of Gestalt psychology', by H. Helson in *Scientific American* (1990, December); *Productive Thinking* by M. Wertheimer (Harper & Row, 1945; 1959).
2. The term involves the assumption of a learner's conscious capacity to understand. See *The Nature of Insight* ed. R. Sternberg and J. Davidson (MIT Press, 1996).
3. See *Reason and Chance in Scientific Discovery* by R. Taton (Hutchinson, 1957).
4. See *The New Criminology* by I. Taylor (Routledge & Kegan Paul, 1973).
5. See *Life and Labours of Francis Galton* by K. Pearson (CUP, 1926).
6. *Darwin on Man* (Wildwood, 1974).
7. *The Confucian Way* by L. F. Chen (Routledge, 1987).
8. *The Mentality of Apes* (Harcourt Brace, 1925).

9. *Principles of Gestalt Psychology* (Harcourt Brace, 1935; 1963).
10. *Theories of Perception and the Concept of Structure* (Wiley, 1955).
11. 'On problem solving' in *Psychological Monographs* (1945, *58*).
12. *The Art of Thought* (Harcourt, 1926).
13. *Systems and Theories of Psychology* (Holt, Rinehart & Winston, 1978).
14. 'The formation of learning sets' in *Psychological Review* (1949, *56*).
15. 'The pitfalls of Gestalt' in *The Act of Creation* (Hutchinson, 1964).
16. *Organising and Memorising* (Columbia UP, 1940).
17. Hilgard and Bower (*op.cit.*).

Chapter 8

The Cognitive School (1)

Behaviourism ... has found the door, but it still lacks the key to what is beyond. 'We' do not just sit within the skin and observe. 'We' also infer and interpret what 'we' observe. And if 'we' are naught but representational processes, then 'we' know 'we' exist because those processes think (Wyers, 1988).

'Cognitive psychology [see p. 38] is concerned with how organisms *cognize* – gain knowledge about – their world, and how they use that knowledge to guide decisions and perform effective actions' (Bower and Hilgard).[1] The process of cognition is perceived as involving the overall functioning of a complex system of unobservable mental abilities (remembering, reasoning, etc.) which is the key to the manipulation of information. The tenets of the cognitive school are in total opposition to those of the behaviourists; *it is the learner, not the learning task, which is of significance*; the emphasis in any explanation of learning has to be placed on mental structure, strategy and organization, not on the S-R model, and internal processes and innate factors must be emphasized in discussions on learning. (The theory of 'innate categories of thought', suggesting that innate faculties such as causality and necessity give structure and meaning to our experience, was first enunciated by the philosopher, Kant (1724–1804).)

Cognitivism makes wide use of analogies in order to explain the processes of cognition. A popular analogy is that of information processing and the input-output capacity of the computer. The learner is viewed as an information processor who discriminates among the input of stimuli to his or her sensory organs, detects regularities in accordance with his or her patterns of experience, and uses these regularities to solve problems in a manner which renders possible the coding of any further input. The 'cognitive product' is the direct result of 'cognitive processes' transforming, reducing, elaborating and storing cognitive (i.e. sensory) input.[2]

Cognitive processing can be inferred as applying to all types of information. Hence students' learning can be analysed in terms of a single unitary model. Further, in the teaching-learning context, the relation between cognitive processing and environmental events is *reciprocal*. Students are, therefore, not merely passive recipients of information: they 'create' what teaching means to *them*, so that it is incorrect to view their achievements as resulting solely from the teacher's activities. The role of mental structure and its organization should be seen as vital in the learning process. By 'structure', cognitivists mean the properties of intellect that are inferred as governing behaviour. Learning is viewed as the modification of these structures.

Dick[3] emphasizes the significance for cognitive psychology in the area of instruction of '*schemata*', that is the active organization by the learner of his or her past reactions and experiences. Instruction involves the storage of new information in previously created schemata, the recall of previously learned verbal information, the alteration of new information so that it fits in with existing schemata, the enabling of learners to make inferences so as to fill in any gaps in existing schemata, and the general modification of schemata.

The tenets of cognitive psychology have an immediate appeal for many teachers. The teaching environment does appear to convey information which students process. It seems as though students act so as to make sense out of their environment by selecting important stimuli; some aspects of the environment are rejected, some are utilized. Cognitive characteristics, such as prior levels of student attainment, general mental abilities, developed memory functions, do appear to account in large measure for achievement. If teachers wish to understand the processes which are presumed to take place privately within the student, the analogy of information processing does appear to offer some assistance. Dewey, Bruner and Ausubel, whose work is mentioned in this chapter and the next, were involved in an analysis of the purposes of education and the practical problems of the classroom. Vygotsky devoted much of his short career to investigating the relation of thought to language – a fundamental aspect of the process of instruction. For him, and other cognitive psychologists, the task of the teacher is seen as related directly to the development of cognitive strategies within the student, so that he may improve his capabilities in selecting and modulating his internal processes of thinking, perceiving and learning.

Some of the objections to cognitive theory are mentioned below. Skinner, in particular, sought to rebut the arguments of the cognitivists. Thus, in *The Selection of Behaviour* (1989), he makes the following points (see also Skinner's 'Why I am not a cognitive psychologist'[4]):

> I like Marr's statement that 'modern cognitive psychology largely views the behaviour of organs as *symptomatic* of internal information processing – activities comfortably expressed in computer metaphor'. The important word is 'comfortably'. The computer is a model of one kind of human *behaviour*, anticipated thousands of years ago with clay tiles in which information is 'stored and retrieved' for computational purposes. But it is not a useful model of the organism that engages in that behaviour, and the comfort will, I am sure, be short-lived.

> Cognitive psychology has tried to improve both observation and inference concerning the state of the body that is felt as belief, knowledge, intention, or expectation. I think it has faced insuperable difficulties, and in the long run it will have done nothing more than improve a vocabulary useful for non-scientific purposes.

Dewey: the background

Dewey (1859–1952) lived in a period of great change. It has been pointed out that the year of his birth saw the publication of Darwin's *The Origin of Species* and Mill's *On Liberty*; the year of his death witnessed the explosion of the first hydrogen bomb. He became one of America's best-known educationists and made outstanding contributions to several areas of knowledge.[5] His work on education reflects an era of transformation in social, political and technological thought. As a philosopher, he occupied the chairs of philosophy at the Universities of Chicago and Columbia and was one of the founders of *pragmatism* – the philosophy based on the doctrine that the only real test of the truth of philosophical principles or human cognitions is their practical result. As a psychologist, he was a founder of the school of *functionalism*, which viewed mind in terms of its *adaptive significance* for the organism, emphasizing its mediating function between the environment and the organism's needs. As an educationist he helped to mould American thought and practice in the classroom by a prodigious output of articles and books. His systematic philosophy was expounded in *Experience and Nature* (1925). His writings on education include: *Democracy and Education* (1916); *The Way out of Educational Confusion* (1931); *How We Think* (1933); *The Need for a Philosophy of Education* (1934).

Dewey viewed education as 'intelligent action', characterized by the learner's continuous evaluation of his or her experiences, the eventual product of which is a redefinition of purposes. Education proceeds 'by the participation of the individual in the social consciousness of the race', so that a student becomes an inheritor of 'the funded capital of civilisation'. The only true education comes through the stimulation of one's powers by the demands of social situations. 'The subject matter of education consists primarily of the meanings which supply content to existing social life.' An educational process has two sides, one psychological and one sociological; the former is probably the more significant. Indeed, without the educator's insight into the psychological structure and activities of the student, the educative process can be only haphazard and arbitrary.

Education should train one's powers of 'reflective thinking'. Genuine freedom, says Dewey, is intellectual; it rests in the trained power of thought, in the ability to 'turn things over', to examine a problem in depth. Reflective thinking is based on five steps between the recognition of a problem and its solution: *suggestions* for a solution; *clarification* of the essence of the problem; the use of *hypotheses*; *reasoning* about the results of utilizing one of the hypotheses; *testing* the selected hypothesis by imaginative or overt action.

A sound educational theory is essential for sound educational practice, according to Dewey, if one accepts his concept of education as a 'conscious, purposive and informed activity'. There are four central notions involved in education, each requiring deep theoretical analysis. First, *the aim* of the activity – educational ends and immediate aims had to be postulated with care, but the exact aims of instruction could not be 'legislated' because they depended on groups of variables unique to particular times and places. The second notion concerned *the teacher*, whose task was to prompt with enthusiasm ideas of development in the student by providing a setting which would be conducive to learning and to the acquisition of good habits of thinking. (The teacher's enthusiasm 'is an attitude that operates as an intellectual force'.) The third notion concerned *the learner*, whose desires, interests and purposes 'fired and sustained' the educational process. The final notion concerned *the curriculum*, the means by which educational aims were achieved, and this was to be based, not on the dictates of tradition, but on the principle of relevance of live issues which would stimulate orderly thought.[6] (Only upon the live issues of experience could effective teaching be built. But 'mere activity does not constitute experience'; activities constitute experience only where they have become inter-related with awareness of their consequences.)

Dewey and the learning process

In an early seminal article on the reflex arc concept in psychology, Dewey attacked psychological molecular thinking.[7] He argued that the behavioural act in a reflex movement does not remain a 'meaningful' act if reduced merely to its sensorimotor elements. Rigid distinctions between sensations, thoughts and acts were to be avoided; they were no more than artificial abstractions from the 'organic unity' of the arc. Reflexes and all other types of behaviour had to be interpreted in the light of their significance for *adaptation*; isolating single units for study is valueless if the purpose of behaviour is ignored. The study of the human organism *as a whole*, functioning in its environment, was the proper subject matter for psychologists.

According to Dewey, every event, external or internal, calls for some kind of response. All human behaviour is the result of events and is guided by anticipation of consequences and other intervening variables. That behaviour also determines events which follow it. Learning has to be viewed as part of a whole, as part of an interaction of the learner and his environment.

Learning is *'learning to think'*. It arises as the result of the 'formation of wide-awake, careful, thorough habits of thinking'. The process of learning involves the exercise of the intelligence ('every intelligent act involves selection of certain things as means to other things as their consequences') and the comprehending of information so that it can be used in new situations. 'Learning by doing' is impossible, unless the 'doing' effects a change in the learner's cognitive structures; routine fails to develop the ability to understand, 'even though it promotes skill in external doing'.

Dewey warns against the notion that learning suddenly 'blossoms' in adolescence after a period of unreflective thought. 'Adolescence is not a synonym for magic.' The adolescent has to be *guided* towards utilization of his powers of reflective thinking and this is part of the teacher's overall responsibility. Appropriate guidance necessitates viewing the adolescent within the context of his or her environment and developing the cognitive abilities (in particular, inductive and deductive powers of reasoning) so that learning may result from the 'active, persistent and careful consideration of any belief or supposed form of knowledge in the light of the grounds that support it and the further conclusions to which it tends'. Dewey warns also against the tendency of skill studies to become 'purely mechanical'. Mere imitation, dictation of steps to be taken and mechanical drill may give quick results, but they may strengthen 'traits likely to be fatal to reflective power'. True learning of skills necessitates their acquisition as the result of the use of the intelligent powers of the mind.

The concept of *growth as the characteristic of life* is essential to an understanding of Dewey's views on education. Our power to grow depends, he argues, upon a need for others and 'plasticity', and these conditions are at their height in youth. 'Plasticity' is the power to learn from one's experience and this leads to the formation of habits which allow human beings to control their environment for their own purposes. Habits of an active nature (involving thought and invention) form the background of growth; the readjustment of one's activity to meet new situations is, effectively, 'growth'. The true criterion of the value of education is 'the extent to which it creates a desire for continued growth and supplies means for making the desire effective in fact'.

Criticisms of Dewey

During the 1980s and early 1990s, the educational psychology associated with Dewey and the classroom practices which he advocated, came under increasing criticism. He was held partly responsible for the blight which was said to have fallen on those educational practices involving the 'discovery method', the 'democratic classroom' and the 'progressive curriculum'. The philosopher and educationist, Mary Warnock, refers to Dewey's impact on British education as 'on the whole, disastrous'. She writes of 'the considerable degree of obfuscating vagueness ... the sloppiness and ambiguity of most of his writing' and the difficulty of attempting to know precisely what he thought. 'He was what he wrote.' His recipes for educational activity seem, according to Warnock, to be 'linked to a deep philistinism and anti-intellectualism'.[8]

In *Education, Society and Human Nature* (1988),[9] O'Hear seeks to reject Dewey's 'educational populism'. Dewey's concept of the ideal educational institution as a 'micro-democracy', where all students 'make a contribution' and where teachers are viewed merely as leaders of group activities rather than as authorities, involves, he argues, 'a repudiation of the teacher as an authority on what he is teaching', and an assertion of the view that students are in a position to make a contribution to a lesson which is as worthwhile as that of the teacher. This, says O'Hear, is demonstrably untrue; in practice, the concept can be responsible for the growth of cultural mediocrity and 'endless group discussion of all decisions'. Dewey has not shown that all worthwhile knowledge emerges from the problems of 'real life' and he has not proved that the 'democratic classroom' is essential for the effective transmission of society's cultural heritage to its young people.

Dewey's work and the teacher

Dewey places great emphasis on the role of the teacher 'as a stimulus to response to intellectual matters'. Everything a teacher does in the classroom, as well as the manner in which he or she does it, 'incites' the student to respond in some way or other and each response tends to set his or her attitude in some way or other. *The teacher's influence is paramount*, even in those situations which Dewey describes as 'pupil-centred' (i.e. in which the student's personal desires, level of attainment and motivations are taken carefully into account). The teacher's responsibility for the development of 'reflective thinking' in students is also emphasized. If the complete act of thought generally follows the pattern suggested by Dewey and other cognitive theorists (arousal of interest, leading to exploration, selection and verification of hypothetical solution to problems), then teaching must recognize the organizational steps necessary for the training and development of thinking. Instruction should be organized so as to pace development (but not to outstrip it). The motivation of cognitive learning is related directly to the learner's standards of intellectual achievement and to the guidance of his teacher. 'Processes of instruction are unified in the degree in which they centre in the production of good habits of thinking.'

Dewey's stress on the importance of curriculum content – to be related to the student's environment and his or her intellectual needs rather than the demands of tradition – calls for an awareness of the real nature of that environment. This, in turn, demands from the teacher an ability to differentiate the purely ephemeral from the fundamental. Dewey reiterates in his writings his belief that the true centre of correlation of subjects is the student's own social activities.

The classroom cannot be separated from the environment of which it is an important part. Teaching is a process, not simply of the training of students, but of 'the formation of the proper social life'. The real end to be sought by teachers and learners is 'growth' which will emerge from a 'reconstruction of accumulated experience' directed to social efficiency. Classroom activity is not set apart from society's progress; it is a prerequisite of that progress.

The teacher has to keep in mind the purpose of his activities. Dewey sums this up as follows: 'Discipline, culture and social efficiency, personal refinement, improvement of character are but phases of the growth of capacity nobly to share in such a balanced experience. And education is not a mere means to such a life. Education is such a life.' Translated into practical terms, this necessitates a curriculum and modes of instruction designed consciously with the learner's 'purposes' and the aims of society in mind.

In his statement of belief concerning the aims of teaching, *My Pedagogic Creed* (1899), Dewey stressed the nature of education as a social process and spoke of the role of the teacher:

> All education proceeds by the participation of the individual in the social consciousness of the race ... he gradually comes to share in the intellectual and moral resources which humanity has succeeded in getting together. He becomes an inheritor of the funded capital of civilisation ... Every teacher should realise the dignity of his calling, that he is a social servant set apart for the maintenance of proper social order and the securing of the right social growth.

Ausubel: the background

Ausubel (b. 1918) has carried out much of his work in the City University of New York in which he directed the Office of Research and Evaluation. The principles of his thought are set out in *Educational Psychology – A Cognitive View* (1968); his other important writings include *Theory and Problems of Adolescent Development* (1964) and *The Psychology of Meaningful Verbal Learning* (1963).

Educational psychology is, according to Ausubel, concerned primarily with 'the nature, conditions, outcomes, and evaluation of classroom learning'; it should not involve itself with topics such as the nature and development of needs, animal learning and conditioning. Further, it should take into account only those kinds of learning that take place in the classroom – reception and discovery learning (i.e. meaningful 'symbolic' learning). Rote learning and motor learning are considered by Ausubel to be so inconsequential a part of classroom learning as not to warrant consideration in a treatment of educational psychology. Ausubel's condemnation of much rote learning derives from his observation that it is based on isolated units of information that the learner is unable to relate to, or anchor within, his existing cognitive structures. (O'Neil[10] emphasizes this view: 'Rote memorisation usually involves multiple readings of the material with little or no effort devoted to assimilation. Therefore, the material learned through this method usually is not meaningfully related to other stored information, which limits the facility with which such information can be retrieved at a later date'.)

Ausubel and the learning process

Ausubel postulates learners' cognitive structures as 'hierarchically organised in terms of highly inclusive concepts under which are subsumed less inclusive subconcepts and informational data'.

The principal factors influencing meaningful learning and retention are, according to Ausubel, the *substantive content* of a learner's structure of knowledge and the *organization* of that structure at any given time. If cognitive structure is unstable and disorganized it will inhibit meaningful learning; if it is stable and well-organized it will assist in such learning. To have appropriate background knowledge of concepts and principles is essential for problem–solving. Prior experience with related problems is necessary for a learner to deal successfully with novel situations.

Ausubel differentiates carefully 'reception' and 'discovery' learning. In *reception learning* a learner is presented with the *entire content* of what is to be learned in its *final form*; the presentation is meaningful if it allows him to integrate new ideas with existing knowledge schemes and reproduce it, with understanding, at some future date; but it will not be meaningful if it does not assist in the creation of new understanding. The presentation of a geometrical theorem in terms which give the learner an opportunity to comprehend its structure, is an example. *Discovery learning* involves the learner discovering independently the principal content of what has to be learned *before* it can be incorporated meaningfully into already existing cognitive structures. Ausubel suggests that a condition for optimal learning is the placing of newly learned facts within a context for meaning. Following such learning, the student's capacity to transform facts and integrate them into previously acquired experience will be increased.

Discovery learning in Bruner's sense (see p. 118) is criticized by Ausubel. He will not accept that *all* discovery learning is meaningful; indeed, he believes that students who have reached the early stages of cognitive development learn more effectively by reception techniques. Problem-solving ability, he argues, is not necessarily transferred to situations outside the context in which it was acquired. Further, the discovery approach is not always linked to intrinsic motivation. He poses a rhetorical question to those who urge the use of discovery learning in all learning situations: 'Is it intended that a student shall rediscover *every* principle set out in the subject syllabus?'

In rejecting some of Bruner's claims concerning the discovery method, Ausubel emphasizes meaning as involving 'cognitive equivalence'; there can be no meaning for the learner without the existence of a related cognitive structure. In learning, the student 'subsumes' material to his cognitive structure. As a result of methodical expository teaching, students are able to proceed directly to a level of abstract understanding that is 'qualitatively superior to the intuitive level in terms of generality, clarity, precision and explication'. (Ausubel uses 'subsume' in the sense of incorporating material into a structure which has been created by prior learning.) 'In any case, discovery techniques hardly constitute an effective primary means of transmitting the contents of an academic discipline.'

'Meaningful learning' – to which classroom activity should be directed – involves *the acquisition of new meanings*. New meanings allow a learner to relate and anchor new material to the relevant and inclusive concepts in his or her existing cognitive structure, to integrate the essence of new experiences with existing patterns; this is essentially an 'active' process. In contrast, rote learning does not result in the acquisition of new meanings; it involves no logical perception, no comprehension of relationships, but only arbitrary constructs. The basic type of meaningful learning is representational, that is, learning the meaning of symbols. 'Propositional learning' allows the learning of the meaning of verbal propositions expressing ideas other than those of representational equivalence. 'Concept learning' involves the acquisition of generic ideas. Each of these three types is important for true learning.

Ausubel has formulated the prerequisites for meaningful learning under two headings: first, that the learner must be disposed to relate new information to a prior structure in preference to engaging in rote learning (i.e. he must have the correct 'set' to the task); and, second, that the new information presented to the learner must be relatable to his prior knowledge on a non-arbitrary basis, that is the new information and that which is constituted in the learner's prior knowledge must be related conceptually ('the perception of a stimulus will be a function of the learner's background').

Sequential organization of learning (see p. 277) is of considerable importance. The arrangement of topics in a subject matter field should be the result of an understanding by the teacher of the importance of the fundamental 'anchoring concepts'. A learning unit ought to be a link in a chain; its acquisition by the learner should be an achievement in its own right and should provide the appropriate

scaffolding for the next unit in the sequence. Antecedent steps should be consolidated if the learning of subsequent steps is not to be vitiated. Consolidation
requires, according to Ausubel, 'confirmation, correction, clarification, differential
practice and review'.

Ausubel criticizes the Gestaltist concept of insight (see Chapter 7). He stresses
the emergence of insight as dependent on the learner's prior experience. It rarely
appears in the 'Eureka' form; it tends rather to follow 'a period of fumbling and
search, of gradual emergence of a correct hypothesis'. It is important for the teacher
to understand, however, the circumstances in which an apparently unproductive
period of thought is followed by a sudden 'seeing the light'.

Ausubel's 'advance organizers': theory into practice

Ausubel has advocated the utilization of 'advance organizers' in the process of
instruction.[11] Hilgard suggests that the fundamental idea of the organizer rests on
early Gestaltist concepts of a sequence of information as being best learned by
comprehending how it is organized and how its parts fit together. The advance
organizer is a relatively short arrangement of introductory material, presented to the
learner *before* the lesson, designed to cue his relevant prior knowledge, and
presented at *a higher level of abstraction, generality and inclusiveness* than that of the
planned lesson. It may take the form of a short statement in continuous prose, or
prose interlaced with diagrams, or networks indicating relationships.

Ausubel states that the principal function of the organizer is 'to bridge the gap
between what the learner knows and what he needs to know before he can
successfully learn the task at hand'. Davies[12] sees the functions of the organizer as:
the provision of a linking structure; the differentiation of ideas leading to their
acquisition with clarity; and the preservation of the identity of new ideas, ensuring
that they are not absorbed totally into an existing structure with the loss of their
distinctive features. Gagné considers the principal function of the organizer to be the
activation of pre-existing cognitive structures in the learner's memory, involving
recall.

Examples of the use of organizers in courses offered by one college of further
education have included: the issuing of a document on 'The psychological causes of
conflict' prior to a unit of instruction on 'problems of change' (in a course for
supervisory managers); the distribution of an essay on 'Renewal and survival' before
a lesson on 'population density' (in a course planned for A level geography); the
circulation of an article from a trade periodical concerning the long-term future of
computer-generated art, prior to a series of lectures on the topic (as part of a course
leading to the BTEC HNC in Design, Packaging and Display). Ausubel gives an
example of learners' knowledge of the fundamental principles of Christianity
utilized as an organizer in a course leading to an understanding of the principles of
Buddhism.

'Expository organizers' are used whenever the new material is totally unfamiliar; they emphasize *context* and link the essence of the new material with some
relevant previously acquired concepts. They are intended to remind the learner 'of

meaningful context already available in the memory and relevant to the new learning'. 'Comparative organizers' are used when the material to be learned is not entirely novel. They are intended to point out ways in which that material resembles, and differs from, that which is already known.

Mayer[13] has constructed a checklist of questions to be asked and answered by the producer of advance organizers:

1. Does the organizer I have produced allow me to generate all, or some, of the logical relationships in the material to be learned?
2. Does it provide the learner with a method of relating unfamiliar to familiar material?
3. Does it allow the learner to use the content?
4. Is it likely that the student will normally fail to use his organizational capabilities in the case of material to be learned in the forthcoming lesson?

Problems related to the production and use of organizers have been noted by teachers in the further education sector. First, the considerable range of individual differences among learners in a class makes the production of a useful general organizer difficult. Secondly, there are problems in constructing the necessary learning structures in some subject areas: thus the highly structured sciences of physics and biology provide a contrast to the very debatable structures of some of the social sciences. Thirdly, the techniques necessary for designing satisfactory organizers can be time-consuming: Joyce and Weil[14] indicate that teachers intending to produce advance organizers require 'a strong grasp of their subject matter, including an understanding of its propositional structure' – in short, the contriving of an organizer can be a complex, laborious task.

Research into the use of organizers[15] suggests that they might be of considerable value where the learner may not be able to recognize prior knowledge as relevant and where the teacher wishes to focus students' attention on relationships among the linked parts of an idea and on connections between parts and the whole. Ausubel's own research suggests that the use of organizers can enhance the relationship between cognitive structure and new material, thus facilitating teaching and learning.

Ausubel's work and the teacher

Ausubel's emphasis on 'meaningful learning' will remind teachers that learning, designed to ensure mastery of a situation by an extension of the student's powers of reasoning, involves the careful *design of instruction* with that end in mind. His stress on linking units of instruction to form a continuous process necessitates a 'programmed' approach to classwork so that sequential learning might be achieved and the learner assisted in the discrimination of old and new ideas.

The principal function of the teacher is seen by Ausubel as 'the art and science of presenting ideas and information meaningfully and effectively' so that clear, stable and unambiguous meanings emerge in the process of instruction and are retained by the learner over a long period of time as an *organized body of knowledge.*

Ausubel suggests that class learning can be improved through use of the technique of 'progressive differentiation'. The most general, inclusive concepts of a subject discipline should be taught first, followed by the less inclusive concepts, thus setting the stage for the teaching of specific information. Ease of assimilation and retention of information should result, since the learner's cognitive structure will then contain stable 'hooks' on which new material can be placed. The learner must be helped to discriminate between old and new ideas; this may require the paraphrasing of new ideas. Concepts must not be taught in isolation; the teacher must provide a *framework* (related to the learner's existing knowledge) into which new concepts will fit with relative ease. Organizers will assist in relating new concepts to existing pivotal ideas. Ausubel advocates, additionally, the adoption of 'integrative reconciliation' in the classroom. This technique concerns the overall organization of content within a subject area. New ideas must be integrated with those previously learned during a course: it is unhelpful to students to devote one lesson, early in the course, to a discussion of ideas and concepts and to fail to refer to those concepts at later stages of the course. This is to introduce barriers between subject elements and relationships. There should be reference throughout the course to previously learned ideas, definitions and principles, so that they are integrated into course content as a whole.

The provision of information feedback (essentially a task for the teacher) is seen by Ausubel in terms of positive, cognitive effects on learning. Feedback can confirm appropriate meanings, correct mistakes and misconceptions and indicate how well the learning task has been mastered. 'As a result ... the subject's confidence in his learning product is increased, his learning is consolidated, and he is better able to focus his efforts and attention on those aspects of a task requiring further refinement.'[16]

On the matter of teacher responsibility for the content of the curriculum, Ausubel takes an uncompromising stand against the advocates of a system in which student decisions are used to determine that content. 'Teachers cannot in good conscience abdicate this responsibility [of structuring subject matter content] by turning over to students, in the name of democracy and progressivism, the direction of education.' The content of the curriculum takes into account the students' needs; its formulation remains, however, the teacher's, not the students' responsibility.

Vygotsky: the background

Vygotsky (1896–1934) is a remarkable figure in the history of educational psychology. A polymath, who made important contributions to the understanding of drama, the history of art, linguistics, and child development, he spent most of his working life as a teacher and became a professor at Moscow University during the period of consolidation of Soviet power. His most fruitful work, the study of developmental psychology in relation to children and adolescents, occupied ten years of a short, intensely creative, life. Vygotsky's work fell into disfavour in the USSR, following a party decree downgrading pædology (an interdisciplinary approach to child development, with which he was closely associated) to the level of a 'bourgeois deviation'. His work was stigmatized as revisionist and eclectic. In recent years he has emerged, following a revaluation of the roots of Soviet psychology, as one of the honoured founding fathers of Russian educational thought. Editions and translations of his major work, *Thought and Language* (1934),[17] have appeared in western countries and have aroused much interest among teachers.[18]

Three ideas dominate Vygotsky's work; each is of significance for educational psychology. First, psychology needs a new framework and an appropriate methodology; secondly, the study of human development is the key to understanding people; and thirdly, the work carried out on relationships between thought and language demands reappraisal.

Psychology in crisis

Vygotsky found the study of psychology wracked by divisions and argument: behaviourists and Gestaltists, for example, worked on entirely different theoretical grounds, their methods were in conflict, and the views they sought to interpret seemed irreconcilable. Psychology was not seen as a unified study and it lacked a 'world view' necessary for its transformation into a science. If any advances of psychology towards the status of a science were to be made, psychologists would have to consider a new programme: studies would have to be developed; there would have to be a resolution of the problem of interrelation between the higher mental functions and the lower functions; the socially meaningful activity of humans would have to be accepted as a key explanatory principle of thought. Attention had to be given to the fundamental concept of the learner's mind as 'not a complex network of general capabilities but a set of specific capabilities . . . Learning is the acquisition of many specialised abilities for thinking'.

The reconstruction of psychology as a unified social science necessitated an entirely new approach to methodology. Vygotsky called for a new methodology based on the analysis of higher forms of human behaviour. It was essential to observe the process of learning rather than the performance of tasks which had already been learned. *Behaviour required explanation, not merely description*; 'though two types of activity can have the same external manifestation, whether in origin or in essence, their nature may differ most profoundly'. Further, in order to analyse behaviour, it must be 'turned back to its source through experiment'. Only in this way could psychology overcome its threatening divisions; the required programme would need assistance from methods of investigation used in philosophy and the humanities.

In specific references to the problems of educational psychology, Vygotsky insisted on the study of the learner's thinking processes in 'the best cultural laboratories', that is, the schools, colleges and universities. An analysis of the social settings designed to assist in learning is essential if the psychology of education is to be meaningful. For Vygotsky, education is the very essence of the socio-cultural activities which affect cognitive development; its social setting must be understood. Educational psychology is, above all, a practical matter. Leontiev said of Vygotsky: 'He demanded that psychology become more than a scientific study of education and go beyond theoretical knowledge and intervene in human life by actively helping to change it'.[19] It would be best, said Vygotsky, if the psychologist were not only a thinker, but also a practitioner in the educational field.

The study of development

Vygotsky emphasized the complex nature of human development, to which learning makes a vital contribution. It does not follow a smooth, uninterrupted path; on the contrary, it is a 'complex dialectical process, characterised by periodicity, unevenness in the development of different functions, metamorphosis or qualitative transformation of one form into another, intertwining of external and internal factors and adaptive processes'.

Development, said Vygotsky, is 'a key to understanding the mature form'. Because development – historical, social, personal – unfolds in stages, an interpretation of developmental problems at any time necessitates an awareness of earlier developmental stages. It is the task of the psychologist to construct appropriate experiments which will assist in the heightening of this awareness.

The process of human development in general, and of human consciousness in particular, cannot be understood in isolation; it must be seen in a wide, social context. Here Vygotsky is influenced by Marx's celebrated, enigmatic thesis: 'It is not the consciousness of men that determines their existence, but, on the contrary, their social existence that determines their consciousness'.[20] A developmental psychology which fails to recognize the importance of humanity's social existence is, according to Vygotsky, sterile. The psychologist must not ignore the historical and social context of the object of his study.

A complete theory of human development would concern itself, according to Vygotsky and his collaborators, with answers to the following questions: What is there about the special character of human beings which cannot be dealt with fully by the activity known as 'formal education'? What were the historical conditions under which formal education arose? What tasks was formal education intended to perform and what means are employed? What is the impact of formal education on the individual development of students? How does the development of behaviour occur within the settings of formal education?

Thought and language

The key to the nature of human consciousness is, according to Vygotsky, thought and speech. 'The word is a direct expression of the historical nature of human consciousness. Consciousness is reflected in the word as the sun in a drop of water . . . A word is a microcosm of human consciousness.' But thought and speech are not cut from one pattern; they have different genetic roots and their development follows different curves of growth, crossing and recrossing, but always diverging. 'The structure of speech does not simply mirror the structure of thought; that is why words cannot be put on by thought like a ready-made garment. Thought undergoes many changes as it turns into speech. It does not merely find expression in speech; it finds its reality and form.'

A study of the development of verbal thought shows, according to Vygotsky, that it is not an innate, natural form of behaviour, but is determined 'by a historical-cultural process' and has its own specific properties and laws that are not obvious in natural forms of thought and speech. When thought and word interact, the situation can be analysed correctly only when it begins with an investigation of 'the different phases and planes a thought traverses before it is embodied in words'.

The problem of the inadequacy of language as a means of communication is stressed repeatedly by Vygotsky. Thoughts do not have their automatic counterpart in words; 'in our speech there is always the hidden word, the sub-text'. The relation between thought and word is a living process: 'thought is born through words'. Hence – and here is an assertion of profound importance for teachers – 'direct communication between minds is impossible, not only physically but psychologically. Communication can be achieved only in a roundabout way. Thought must first pass through meanings and only then through words.'

How, then, do we understand another's speech? We have to understand his words *and* his thought. But, says Vygotsky, even that is not enough. 'We must also know its motivation. No psychological analysis of an utterance is complete until that plane is reached.'

The most important of Vygotsky's assertions in relation to mental activity were summed up by Blanck, in his article 'Vygotsky, the man and his cause'.[17] Mental activity is to be seen in its context of social learning and social relationships. The learner's mental development is essentially a socio-genetic process, during which he internalizes society's culture (habits, beliefs, behaviours) with a resulting creation of neuropsychic systems which become a part of the brain's activities. The learner's development of a superior type of nervous activity brings the possibility of forming and developing higher mental processes. Social activities in which the learner participates, e.g. in the classroom, facilitate his or her ability to grasp the meaning (and later the significance) of social structures; in this process the role of the teacher is extremely important. The learners' internalization of their higher mental functions will depend very largely on the historical context of the culture in which they participate. It is essential, therefore, that teachers who are guiding their students in the assimilation and utilization of the culture which they have inherited shall understand the nature of the society of which they are a part and, in particular, the basis of its development.

The acceleration of cognitive development: the zone of proximal development (ZPD)

The intriguing possibility of discovering whether it might be possible to hasten a student's cognitive development was explored in some detail by Vygotsky, and the results of his work in this area have been the basis of research in American schools and colleges (see e.g. 'The ZPD as a basis for instruction' by Hedegaard[18]). The essence of ZPD theory is based upon what the student can do on his or her own as compared with what the student is able to accomplish in a social setting in which his or her peers participate. First, the student's *'actual developmental level'* is assessed by means of an individual test. Next, the student's *'immediate level of potential development'* is assessed in the same way. The ZPD is defined by Vygotsky as 'the difference between the actual developmental level as determined by independent problem-solving and the level of potential development as determined through problem-solving under adult guidance or in collaboration with more capable peers'. He thought of ZPD in the following terms:

> The ZPD defines those functions that have not yet matured but are in the process of maturation, functions that will mature tomorrow but are currently in an embryonic state. These functions could be termed the 'buds' or 'flowers' of development rather than the 'fruits' of development.

Vygotsky suggested that students with wider zones of development will probably experience a greater degree of cognitive development when instruction is aimed *just above the lower limit of the ZPD* than will students with narrower zones. A student who is 'on the verge of learning' can be helped to move into 'new learning territory' by being allowed, and encouraged, to work and reason with another student 'who is operating in the other's ZPD', who has mastered the particular concept upon which the first student is working, and who can explain to the first student how to deal with difficulties arising from attempts at mastery. The teacher will guide the process by providing material related to cognitive structuring, in the form of explanations and rules.

Teaching techniques based upon a recognition of the concept of the ZPD would allow, according to Vygotsky, the *possibility* of accelerated learning from which advances in cognitive development might be inferred. The student's intellectual activities can be intensified through use of the techniques associated with the ZPD, and this increase in intellectual ability is a sure sign of learning having taken place. In Vygotsky's words:

> What lies in the ZPD at one stage is realized and moves to the level of actual development at a second. In other words, what the learner is able to do in collaboration today he will be able to do independently tomorrow.

Vygotsky and the teacher

It is probably in the consideration of Vygotsky's attitude to development and the interrelationship of thought and language that the practising teacher will find much to contemplate. Vygotsky's emphasis on the uneven nature of development, on the irregular transitions from one developmental stage to another, may serve to remind the teacher of the difficulties in effecting these transitions smoothly. His stress on the need to understand a person's former stages of development is echoed in the wise practice of seeing instruction as a contribution to a continuing process of change and growth in the student.

The concept of the ZPD has been described as offering to the practising teacher 'a theory of possibilities'. It constitutes a reminder to the teacher that educational settings and practices should not be considered immutable. The settings in which we teach 'are social creations; they are socially constituted, and they can be socially changed'. There is no 'natural law' governing educational practices and there is a continuing need to examine those practices so as to discover how far they assist or hinder students' cognitive development.

Vygotsky's insistence on the inadequacies of speech ('our daily speech constantly fluctuates between the ideals of mathematical harmony and imaginative harmony') has its lessons for the teacher. Utterances have to be considered as processes (and, therefore, defined in terms of what they *do*); the challenge to the teacher as communicator is to understand the cognitive nature of those processes. In the final pages of *Thought and Language*, Vygotsky quotes a short poem by his fellow-countryman, Pushkin (1799–1837). It contains a useful message for the teacher, relating to 'shared apperception by communicating parties as a necessary pre-condition of normal dialogue'.

> Before the judge who's deaf, two deaf men bow.
> One deaf man cries: 'He led away my cow.'
> 'Beg pardon,' says the other in reply,
> 'That meadow was my father's land in days gone by.'
> The judge decides: 'For you to fight each other is a shame.
> Nor one nor t'other, but the girl's to blame.'

Vygotsky's work developed: Galperin

Galperin (1902–88) sought to advance Vygotsky's work by carrying out research in Soviet schools and technical colleges.[21] He formulated a theory of 'learning through the formation of rational concepts'. His colleagues claimed that the application of his theory did result in a raising of students' cognitive abilities. Galperin argued that cognitive development (or 'learning') is impossible without the learners' own participation in activities related to the world of which they are a part. Learning necessitates students conducting 'appropriate operations' in relation to the knowledge which is to be acquired. In practice this necessitates the teacher ensuring that modes of student activity are designed with objectives in mind.

Initially, cognitive development involves *motivation*. Instruction requires *external activities* which must be related carefully to what has to be taught, so that learning may be generalized. The *interiorization of learning* necessitates the rationalization of activities and their eventual 'automation'. Advances in cognitive development involve *rational intellectual activities* which should be the outcome of learning. What the student learns will become embedded in the mind with the heightening of knowledge resulting from practice. Essentially, the intensification of cognitive development demands a continuous period of applying in practice the results of guided learning.

Notes and references

1. See generally for this chapter: 'Recent developments in cognitive theories' by G Bower and E. Hilgard (*op.cit.*), *Cognitive Psychology* by D. Medin and B. Ross (Harcourt Brace, 1996); *Cognitive Psychology* ed. C. French (Longman, 1993); *Cognitive Psychology* by M. Eysenck (Erlbaum, 1996); *Cognitive Psychology and Instruction* by R.

Brunning (Merrill, 1995); *Cognitive Psychology* by J. B. Best (West, 1995); *Dictionary of Cognitive Psychology* by I. Stuart-Hamilton (Kingsley, 1991); *The Science of the Mind* ed. R. L. Solso (OUP, 1995); *How Brains Think* by W. H. Calvin (Weidenfeld & Nicolson, 1997); *Cognition* by D. Reisberg (Norton, 1997).

2. Not all psychologists accept the force of this analogy. Neisser points out that in a computer the hardware and software have no influence on each other, but in the human organism they do. 'The human is a special kind of biological processor and I suspect that surprisingly little of what we know of ... computers applies to the human': D. Norman in 'A psychologist views human processing' in *Proceedings of the International Joint Commission on Artificial Intelligence* (1981).

3. With Gagné, 'Instructional psychology' in *Annual Review of Psychology* (1983, *34*).

4. *Behaviourism* (1977, *5*); see also 'Cognitive science and behaviourism' by B.F. Skinner in *British Journal of Psychology* (1985, *76*).

5. His major writings on education are summarized in *John Dewey on Education* ed. R. Archambault (Chicago UP, 1974).

6. See 'My pedagogic creed' in Archambault (*op. cit.*).

7. 'The reflex arc concept in psychology' (1898), reprinted in *Readings in the History of Psychology* ed. W. Dennis (Appleton, 1948).

8. 'The sage of discovery' (*Times Higher Education Supplement*, 13 December 1996) – a review of *John Dewey and the High Tide of American Liberalism* by A. Ryan (Norton, 1996).

9. Pub. Routledge.

10. *Learning Strategies* (Academic Press, 1978).

11. See 'The use of advance organizers' in *Journal of Educational Psychology* (1960, *51*); 'In defence of advance organizers' in *Review of Educational Research* (1978, *45*); *Psychology Applied To Teaching* by R. Biehler (Houghton Mifflin, 1993).

12. *Objectives in Curriculum Design* (McGraw-Hill, 1976).

13. 'Can advance organizers influence meaningful learning?' in *Review of Educational Research* (1979, *49*).

14. *Models of Teaching* (Prentice-Hall, 1980).

15. See e.g. 'Do advance organizers facilitate learning?' by B. Barnes and E.D. Clawson in *Review of Educational Research* (1978, *45*); 'Advance organizers as a teaching strategy' by J. Lawton and S. Wanska in *Review of Educational Research* (1977, *47*).

16. *School Learning – An Introduction to Educational Psychology* (Holt, Rinehart & Winston, 1969).

17. See *Thought and Language* ed. A. Kozulin (MIT Press, 1987).

18. See *Vygotsky and Education* ed. L.C. Moll (CUP, 1992); *An Introduction to Vygotsky* ed. H. Daniels (Routledge, 1996).

19. *Handbook of Contemporary Soviet Psychology* by M. Cole and I. Maltzman (Basic Books, 1969).

20. *Critique of Political Economy* (pub. 1859).

21. 'Stages in the development of mental acts' in *A Handbook of Contemporary Soviet Psychology* ed. M. Cole (Basic Books, 1969).

Chapter 9

The Cognitive School (2)

> Man is not a naked ape but a culture-clothed human being, hopelessly ineffective without the prosthesis provided by culture. The very nature of his characteristics as a species provides a guide to appropriate pedagogy, and the very nature of his nervous system and its constraints provides a basis for devising reasonable if not inevitable principles for designing a testable pedagogy (Bruner, 1973).

This chapter considers the cognitive educational psychology associated with Bruner (b. 1916),[1] who draws upon a variety of disciplines such as biology, mathematics and social anthropology in order to fashion a doctrine of learning and a theory of instruction intended to assist in the creation of 'a better or happier or more courageous or more sensitive or more honest man'. Bruner speaks of himself as a 'functionalist', that is, one who seeks to investigate the mind by studying the human organism as an entity functioning in its environment. Further, a human being may be thought of as 'an information processor, thinker and creator'. The role of the teacher in Bruner's cognitive theory is seen as vital to the maintenance of our culture which requires the transmission of knowledge to the young. 'Knowledge, we know now as never before, is power ... Let knowledge as it appears in our education be placed within a context of action and commitment.'

Bruner has maintained his opposition to behaviourism and, in particular, to those 'who extrapolate from rabbits and pigeons to the human being'. He rejects the relevance of operant conditioning (see p. 77) for the processes of instruction. Skinner's reply suggests that Bruner has not understood operant conditioning well enough to see its relevance for learning.

Bruner: the background

Bruner was born in America in 1916 and graduated from Duke University and Harvard, where his experimental work in psychology convinced him that the effective instruction of human beings involves leading them through sequences of statements of problems or aspects of knowledge which cumulatively increase the ability 'to group, transform, and transfer what is being learned'. He became professor of psychology at Harvard in 1952 and established and directed the influential Centre for Cognitive Studies. In 1973 he was appointed professor of experimental psychology at Oxford. Bruner's special interest in the craft of teaching led him to a long-term programme of empirical research in schools and colleges and to a lasting interest in the role of the teacher and the relationship between insight, understanding and competence.

The literature

Among Bruner's many writings, the following texts will be of particular interest to college tutors: *A Study of Thinking* (1990), dealing with the formation and use of concepts; *The Process of Education* (1960), reporting a congress on teaching for understanding; *On Knowing* (1962), essays on the phenomenon of human knowledge; *Toward a Theory of Instruction* (1962), perhaps Bruner's most influential text; *Studies in Cognitive Growth* (1966), an examination of development and 'meaningful teaching'; *The Relevance of Education* (1973), learning skills and educational strategies; *Actual Minds, Possible Worlds* (1986), an exploration of the significance of preparing for change.

The essence of learning and development

Learning is viewed by Bruner in terms beyond the mere acquisition of knowledge; he sees its end as the creation of the developed human being. The institutions in which formal learning takes place – the schools and colleges – are responsible for the important task of 'amplification of intellectual skills'. That amplification involves instruction concerning the place of the student in the culture of his society; indeed, intelligence is seen by Bruner as, 'to a great extent, the internalisation of tools' provided by that culture. Cultural variations produce variations in modes of thinking so that a student's cognitive growth will be influenced directly by social patterns.

Students should be trained to develop their capacities to the full. Understanding of principles should be developed if students are to be given confidence in their capabilities. They must be taught *how* to analyse problems. What students should be learning is not 'particular performances', but *competence*, and central to the attainment of that end is the acquisition of *correct modes of thinking*. Bruner's emphasis on understanding of principles mirrors an earlier statement by Whitehead:

> Whatever be the detail with which you cram your students, the chance of their meeting in after-life exactly that detail is almost infinitesimal; and if they do meet it, they will probably have forgotten what you taught them about it. The really useful training yields a comprehension of a few general principles with a thorough grounding in the way they apply to a variety of concrete details. In subsequent practice the student will have forgotten your particular details; but he will remember to apply principles to immediate circumstances.[2]

Bruner's cognitive-development theory is concerned with *how* what one wishes to teach can best be learned; it takes into account both learning and development.

Bruner and the learning process

The cognitive school of psychology is concerned with the 'building of a mental bridge' between the stimulus and response in the S-R process. Bruner emphasizes the role of perception in that process.[3] Perception is the operation by which the learner interprets or gives some meaning to sensory material and that 'meaning' will result from the context of the stimulus (in the learner and his or her environment) and the learner's past experiences with similar types of sensory stimulation. The brain, according to Bruner, selects some stimuli related to the learner's needs, values, attitudes, etc. Stimuli which are of a threatening type are ignored. The process is named 'perceptual defence'. Sensory experience is organized by the learner's brain in relation to past experiences so as to interpret the current situation. As the result of 'fixation' the recurrence of a stimulus is accompanied by the recurrence of the same type of perceptual experience produced on its previous appearances.

Learning is a cognitive process involving the learner *acquiring* new information, *transforming* his state of existing knowledge and *checking* the adequacy of that state of knowledge against the demands of new situations. (In Popper's words:[4] 'Knowledge is always a modification of earlier knowledge ... [it] goes back, ultimately, to inborn knowledge'.) We learn best, not by committing a body of knowledge to mind, but by 'participating in the process that makes possible the establishment of knowledge'. *Knowledge is a process, not a product.* The acquisition of knowledge is an active process and depends for its effectiveness on the learner relating incoming information to previously acquired frames of reference. Learners gradually acquire internal models, giving them a pattern of meaning for their experiences so that they are able to extrapolate on the basis of that pattern. They construct hypotheses to explain incoming information and test them so as to produce meaningful interpretations of reality.

Learners construct models of the external world and those models will be determined largely by *the culture of society*. An adequate model will not only explain objective reality, but will predict 'how the world might be'. The models become expectancies allowing the learner to make short-cuts and leaps from partial evidence, reflecting the human tendency to categorize. The construction of categories involves the learner's ability to create strategies, that is, sequences of mental events related to goals. Inherent in any strategy are three factors. The first is the *informational situation* which will determine whether more information needs to be gathered by the learner before he arrives at a conclusion. The second factor is the *certainty of cognition*, that is, the intensity of the thinking needed to arrive at a conclusion. The third factor is the *general consequence of failure*, that is, the 'risk' involved in the result of cognition. These factors interact to produce a learner's strategy of movement towards a learning goal. (Gagné[5] criticizes this concept of strategies. To know a strategy is not even a substantial part of what is needed. The learner cannot solve problems effectively until he has acquired 'masses of organised intellectual skills'.)

Growth in learning capacity is *not*, according to Bruner, a gradual accretion of associations or S-R connections; it is 'a matter of spurts and rests ... the spurts ahead in growth seem to be touched off when certain capacities begin to develop'. These spurts do not necessarily depend on the learner's age, but rather on his or her ability to organize incoming information within frames of reference and models of reality. *The development of that ability is one of the teacher's principal tasks*. But the difficulties of this task should not be underestimated. Butterfield, the historian of science, reminds us:

> Of all forms of mental activity, the most difficult to induce even in the minds of the young, who may be presumed not to have lost their flexibility, is the art of handling the same bundle of data as before, but placing them in a new system of relations with one another by giving them a different framework.[6]

One of Bruner's most controversial statements is that 'any subject can be taught effectively in some intellectually honest form to any child at any stage of development'. It is merely a matter of 'representing the structure of that subject in terms of the child's way of viewing things', that is, on an intuitive, experiential level; the idea can then be developed and redeveloped as the learner matures intellectually; a 'spiral sequence of learning' is then produced by a periodical recycling of the same ideas at greater levels of complexity. Ausubel has attacked this statement as ignoring the fact that some abstractions are so inherently complex and difficult that they cannot be made understandable to persons below a certain level of cognitive maturity. In a pointed criticism of Bruner's statement, Tyler[7] asks: 'Do common experience and observation not convince us of the impossibility of teaching such a class of responses as "solving linear equations" to a neonate?' (Bruner's response is that he had phrased his statement so as to suggest the possibility of teaching 'meaningful aspects of any subject' at certain age levels.)

The purposes of the educational process

In Bruner's view, education is concerned with the intensification of cognitive skills related to the principles and needs of the community's culture; it should be linked closely to an understanding and development of those 'technologies and their tools' which are a vital part of cultural expression. The purposes of education may be categorized as follows.

1. The development of the student's confidence in his or her innate capacities and their potential for development. This involves a curriculum which will encourage the student to explore strategies of learning through problem-solving.
2. The development of the student's confidence in his or her ability to solve problems of a new type through 'use of the mind'. The development of understanding and a knowledge of transforming one's powers of cognition will be of much importance.
3. The motivation of the student to operate on his or her own with confidence. Location of 'the form of a problem' is important and this requires the study of techniques of interpretation.
4. The development of 'economy in the use of the mind'. This will necessitate

training directed at the skills needed to search for 'relevance and structure', i.e. 'reflective learning'.

5. The development of intellectual honesty in the student. It is the task of the teacher to insist upon rigour and self-discipline in the attainment of goals in the various disciplines of our culture.

A theory of instruction

A theory of instruction appropriate for our day and our type of society must be, according to Bruner, both prescriptive and normative. It must involve the enunciation of rules concerning effectiveness in attaining knowledge and must provide for the evaluation of modes of teaching and learning. Criteria for instruction must be considered. Such a theory can be built around five essential features.

1. It must specify the experiences which will most effectively predispose students to learn. Effective learning will involve a rigorous 'exploration of alternatives', leading to 'learning how to learn'.
2. It must specify ways of structuring knowledge so that optimal comprehension might be attained by students. A general understanding of the fundamental structure of a subject necessitates grasping its inner significance by comprehension of basic, generalized principles, so that knowledge that is of significance can be extracted from information that is less so.
3. It must specify the optimal sequences of presentation of the material to be learned. (For the significance of sequencing, see pp. 277–8.) Subject matters have their own appropriate 'forms of representation', allowing knowledge of their principles to be converted into comprehensible structures.
4. It must specify 'the nature and pacing of reinforcement' in the processes of teaching and learning. This involves examining and correcting the learner during the instructional process in a fashion which will make it possible for him or her to take over the corrective function, thus avoiding the danger of establishing in the learner a permanent dependence 'upon a scaffolding of reward and a rewarder'. (This will necessitate *appropriate feedback of results to the student*. It should come at that point in a problem-solving episode 'when the student is comparing the results of his try-out with some criterion of what he or she seeks to achieve'.)
5. It must seek to take into account the fact that a curriculum ought to reflect the nature of knowledge and 'the nature of the knower and the knowledge-getting process'.

Bruner's work and the teacher

Interpreting the cultural patterns of society for the learner and assisting him or her to achieve mastery of the processes inherent in creative thinking are the tasks of the teacher, according to Bruner. Students must be taught in a manner which allows them to comprehend single instances in terms of broad generalizations and principles. Bruner stresses that the student learning physics 'is a physicist, and it is easier for him to learn physics behaving like a physicist than doing something else'. The class teacher has the responsibility of ensuring that methods of teaching are *realistic* in that they allow *discovery activity*; purely expository teaching on its own is of little value, according to Bruner, in helping a student to acquire the capacity to think creatively and critically.

Bruner's call for 'discovery learning' (or, as he occasionally refers to it, 'inquiry training') reflects his belief that 'the curriculum of a subject should be determined by the most fundamental understanding that can be achieved of the underlying principles that give *structure* to that subject'. Teaching will be most productive where the subject matter is 'gutted' so that its bare bones – its structural elements – are revealed and made a foundation for the acquisition of principles. A student who knows the *principles* of a discipline has the power to investigate and solve problems within its terms; additionally, the student is more likely to remember information associated with these principles.

In discovering the 'meaning' of principles, a student is learning concepts and relationships. Bruner suggests that the activity of discovering has four advantages. (These should be of interest to the further education lecturer involved, in particular, with first-level and foundation courses.) First, there is a growth in 'intellectual potency' – the student acquires the ability to develop strategies in approaching and analysing patterns in his or her environment in an organized manner. Secondly, intrinsic motivation becomes a preferred alternative to extrinsic rewards – the student achieves satisfaction from discovering solutions on his or her own. Thirdly, the student who has mastered the techniques of discovery learning is able to apply them to the solution of real problems outside the classroom. Fourthly, improvements in memory seem to be associated with the organization of one's knowledge – retrieval of information stored in the memory (see p. 212) becomes easier where the student has organized his knowledge in terms of his own system.

Building on Bruner's views, Taba[8] outlines some general steps in discovery learning. First, learners should be confronted with a problem that initiates a 'feeling of bafflement'. No important generalizations should be offered by the teacher at this stage; learners must be encouraged to explore the problem for themselves. Next, they should be prompted to utilize previously acquired knowledge so as to understand new patterns and structures from which will emerge solutions to the problem facing them. They should then be given an opportunity to demonstrate, in relation to other problems, the principles they have now acquired. In this way the teacher has provided the conditions facilitating the learner's discovery of 'organising principles'.

Mastery of specifics is essential if the student is to make progress and it is the teacher's task to ensure such mastery. 'Lower-order regularities' must be mastered if there is to be movement towards higher-order learning. Students must be given an opportunity to master specifics by developing skills related to immediate problems in which their knowledge may be put to use. The 'exploration of alternatives' (i.e. 'diversity of learning') must be part of the instructional process and it should be linked with a 'general understanding of the structure of subject matter'. The acquisition of a generalized set of basic ideas is an important aim of classroom instruction; indeed, according to Bruner, one of the true tests of learning is whether the student has grasped, and can use, 'the generic code' he or she has been taught. Speed of learning, resistance to forgetting, transfer of learning, creation of ability to generalize and to create new hypotheses are some of the criteria of instruction. A curriculum built on rudiments acquired at an early age, moving upwards and circling back to previous understanding is essential for the successful structuring of subject matter. Such a curriculum ought to be built 'around the great issues, principles and values that a society deems worthy of the continual concern of its members'.[9] Development and redevelopment of the learners' capacities, so that they are able to deal with problems at advancing levels of complexity, are the prerequisites of successful learning and this necessitates appropriate planning of instruction in the classroom.

Bruner argues also in favour of students being given training 'in recognising the plausibility of guesses'. Educated guesses, which may possess the elements of an 'intuitive leap' are not to be discouraged. To repress guessing is, in effect, to check some of the cognitive processes inherent in discovery.

From the variety of teaching techniques suggested by Bruner, Dembo[10] selects four which, taken together, could constitute an effective teaching model for many college courses. First, teach the *basic structure* of the subject, emphasizing concepts, fundamental principles and relationships. Next, experiment with discovery learning techniques so that students are motivated and assisted in the acquisition and retention of principles. Thirdly, consider the advisability of commencing instructional periods with a problem that calls for the utilization of previously acquired knowledge in order to assist students in the search for solutions at a new level of knowledge. Finally, pitch the instruction at a level appropriate to a student's overall cognitive functioning so that concept formation is encouraged.

On the teacher's role in reinforcement of learning, Bruner is categorical. He calls for a 'de-emphasis of extrinsic rewards'. Intrinsic rewards should be emphasized: the teacher's task is to arrange instruction so that there is a challenge to their students to exercise their mental powers fully and to heighten their inner sense of accomplishment. The danger of creating dependence upon rewards is to be avoided. In the absence of external rewards, students need continuous knowledge of their progress; this involves effective feedback. 'Knowledge of results should come at that point in a problem-solving episode when the person is comparing the results of his try-out with some criterion of what he seeks to achieve.'

Instruction, Bruner reminds the teacher, 'is, after all, an effort to assist or shape growth'. It is the responsibility of the teacher to seek to understand growth as development, and to link this understanding to an appropriate theory of knowledge and instruction.

Notes and references

1. See generally for this chapter: *Introduction to Cognitive Studies* by A. Asham (Routledge, 1997); *The Conscious Mind* by D. Chalmers (OUP, 1996); *The Idea of*

Consciousness by M. Bennett (Harvard, 1997); *An Introduction to Teaching: Psychological Perspectives* ed. C. Desfarges (Blackwell, 1995); *In the Theatre of Consciousness* by B.J. Baars (OUP, 1997).

2. *The Aims of Education* (Macmillan, 1929).

3. See 'On perceptual readiness' in *Psychological Review* (1957, *64*); 'An approach to social perception' in *Current Trends in Social Psychology* by J. Bruner and L. Postman (Pittsburgh UP, 1948).

4. See *The Self and Its Brain* by K. Popper and J. Eccles (Routledge & Kegan Paul, 1984). See also *Evolution of the Brain: Creation of the Self* by J. Eccles (Routledge, 1989).

5. *The Conditions of Learning* (Holt Saunders, 1885).

6. *The Origins of Modern Science* (Macmillan, 1957).

7. 'Issues related to readiness' in *Theories of Learning and Instruction* (Chicago UP, 1964).

8. 'Learning by discovery' in *School Journal* (1963, *3*).

9. 'Beyond the information given' by Bruner in *Studies in the Psychology of Knowing* (Norton, 1973).

10. *Teaching for Learning* (Goodyear, 1981).

Chapter 10

The Humanistic Psychology School

To be fully human, to trust in persons, to grant freedom with responsibility – these are not easy to achieve. The way we have presented is a challenge. It involves change in our thinking, in our way of being, in our relationship with our students. It involves a difficult commitment to a democratic ideal (Rogers, 1983).

Humanistic psychology emerged in America largely as a deliberate reaction against behaviourism, which was condemned, along with psychoanalysis, as having reduced essentially human qualities to mere physical entities.[1] The leading proponents of the humanistic theory of learning, Maslow and Rogers, advocate principles (a 'third force psychology') based on the 'self' as the essential characteristic of the human being, on the growth, worth and dignity of persons, and on the need for teachers to facilitate the processes which will lead to the 'self-actualization' of students. Education has the task, they say, of 'helping each person to become the best that he is able to become'.

Maslow developed a theory of self-actualization which allows a person to grow to his 'optimal stature'. Rogers fashioned the idea of 'experiential learning', which would give to education a humanistic orientation, leading to true freedom and self-fulfilment. These doctrines are perceived by some teachers as a clear challenge (or threat) to the practice of formal, structured instruction as administered in our schools and colleges.

Maslow: the background

Maslow (1908–70) was professor of psychology at Brandeis University and pursued research which resulted in a distinctive contribution to theories of motivation and to a novel view of psychology which stressed human potential and aspirations. *Motivation and Personality* (1954), *Toward a Psychology of Being* (1968), and *The Farther Reaches of Human Nature* (1971) set out his perception of the tasks of psychology and education as 'the development of the real self'. So-called 'scientific psychology' has given to the subject a narrow, sterile and dehumanized basis; psychoanalysis has shown itself to be grossly inadequate. Maslow demands a psychology based on *the person as a whole*, which recognizes his higher nature and dignity. Human beings have needs, he says, which must be analysed, understood and gratified if full growth is to result. It is the task of the psychologist to uncover the foundations of those needs; it is the task of the teacher to assist in the development of students toward their full worth. The 'need gratification' which Maslow has in mind is perceived by him as 'the most important single principle underlying all development ... The single, holistic principle that binds together the multiplicity of human motives is the tendency for a new and higher need to emerge as the lower need is able to fulfil itself by being sufficiently gratified.'

In his study of motivation, Maslow arrives at a formulation based on a 'hierarchy of needs' (see p. 123). A person's behaviour in the classroom, factory or home is dominated at any given moment by those needs which have the greatest potency. Motivation is to be understood in terms of an individual's striving for growth. In the context of education, motivation for learning may not arise until certain basic needs have been satisfied; that motivation should be recognized as being mainly intrinsic.

Extrinsic and intrinsic learning

Maslow speaks of 'extrinsic learning' as 'learning of the outside, learning of the impersonal, of arbitrary associations, of arbitrary conditioning, that is, of arbitrary (or at best, culturally determined) meanings and responses'. Such learning is extrinsic to the learner and his personality. The learner, conditioned by his teacher, is merely collecting habits and associations, just as he accumulates objects which he puts in his pocket. What he has collected is largely irrelevant to the particular, idiosyncratic human being he is.

'Intrinsic learning' rejects the generality of repetition, of learning by drilling, and involves, primarily, learning to be a human being in general and, secondly, learning to be a particular human being. This necessitates the development of wisdom and life skills. Such learning will not merely reflect the goals of the teacher, but will be based on the values and perceived objectives of the learners themselves.

The teacher who wishes to assist in the process of intrinsic learning must see himself as a helper, counsellor and guide. He must be receptive rather than intrusive; he must accept the student as he is and assist him to learn what kind of person he is. He must acquaint himself with the student's style, aptitudes and potentialities. He will concern himself, above all, with the student's growth and self-actualization.[2]

Optimal persons and peak experiences

Maslow studied the lives of certain historical persons who, he claimed, had fulfilled their basic potentialities and had grown into self-actualized people. They included, not surprisingly, Jefferson, Thoreau, Eleanor Roosevelt and Einstein. These 'optimal persons' had characteristics in common – they had been dedicated fully to causes outside themselves; they had reacted to experiences 'vividly, selflessly, with full concentration and total absorption'; they had been spontaneous, independent, and in tune with their inner beings.

Few persons, said Maslow, experience self-actualization in its full sense; but many have enjoyed occasional moments involving 'peak experiences', such as the vision to be derived from the great classics.[3] The teacher whose advice and guidance can assist in movement toward such experiences is assisting students in their *real growth* and in the realization of their *inner potential*. The emotional reactions which accompany peak experiences have 'a special flavour of wonder, of awe, of reverence, of humility and surrender before the experience as before something great'.

Peak experiences have prologues and consequences of which a teacher must be aware. The experiences may be triggered in a variety of ways. 'Mathematics can be just as beautiful, just as peak-producing, as music', wrote Maslow. Acceptance of this concept will involve the sympathetic teacher in a continuous search for modes of tuition which will lead a student to experience the real pleasure to be derived from discovery. The consequences of peak experiences may involve 'being changed, seeing things differently, having different cognitions'. No teacher, says Maslow, can afford to ignore the significance of changes of this nature.

Motivation and the classroom situation

Maslow's research produced a 'hierarchy of human needs' which affects the pattern of behaviour designed to achieve a goal – we refer to this as 'motivation'. Student X's observable drive to perform well and Y's sporadic work habits may be understood by reference to some kind of internal process which moves X and Y to satisfy perceived needs. Maslow has a pragmatic attitude to human needs; his model may be visualized as a pyramid,[4] see Figure 10.1.

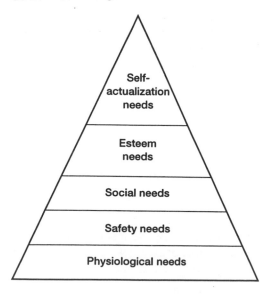

Figure 10.1   Maslow's hierarchy of human needs.

(a) At the base of the pyramid are *fundamental physiological needs*; thus, thirst and hunger lead to the need and desire for water and food. Survival depends on the satisfaction of these needs. Temporary deprivation may override other drives.

(b) The next level is made up of *safety needs*, such as a desire for protection, physical and psychological security, which must be satisfied.

(c) The third level comprises *belonging needs* ('social needs'), e.g. for friendship, affection, affiliation.

(d) The fourth level is of particular significance for adolescents: it is based on the *need for self-esteem* which, in turn, reflects a desire for adequacy and competence, and for attention, recognition and prestige.

(e) At the apex of the pyramid is the *need for self-fulfilment* ('self-actualization').[5] 'What a man *can* be, he *must* be', says Maslow. The need may be met by internal cognitive growth (to which the teacher can contribute much) and by rich and varied experiences.

The first four levels of needs ((a)–(d)) are referred to by Maslow as 'deficiency needs': they motivate the student to engage in activity only when they remain unmet to a significant degree. Self-actualization is seen as a 'growth need': students strive continuously to satisfy it. In his earlier writings, Maslow appeared to suggest that self-actualizing needs would emerge and be activated automatically following the satisfaction of the fourth level of needs (d). He commented later that the move to self-actualization level (e) depends not only on the satisfaction of lower needs, but on an acceptance of certain types of value implicit in 'cognitive needs' (to know and understand) and 'aesthetic needs' (such as the need for order and accord).

Child, in *Psychology and the Teacher* (1985),[6] suggests that 'understanding' and 'knowledge' might be added to the apex of Maslow's hierarchy of needs.)

Maslow's model throws some light on motivation in the classroom. Students' basic needs have to be satisfied before effective learning can take place; the lack of motivation apparent in the physically tired student has to be accepted as a temporary phenomenon only. Students who feel threatened by an environment which they perceive as hostile, or who interpret the demands of instruction as an unacceptable restriction on their 'freedom', may be experiencing a need for security. Class members who esteem acceptance by their peer group as more important than academic achievement may be demonstrating an apparent lack of motivation which reflects no more than the significance they attach to self-esteem and recognition. For the class teacher, Maslow's message is clear: *do not accept the absence of motivation in a student as an unalterable state of affairs*. It can often be analysed adequately in Maslow's terms; it can, therefore, be understood and modified to the advantage of student and teacher.

Deficiency needs and choice

Maslow appears to suggest that, when the need for self-actualization arises, a person will not always choose his or her course of action wisely: a student may, at this stage, make a bad, even seemingly self-destructive choice:

> Every human being has [two] sets of forces within him. One set clings to safety and defensiveness out of fear, tending to regress backward, hanging on to the past, afraid to

grow ... afraid to take chances, afraid to jeopardize what he already has, afraid of independence, freedom and separateness. The second set of forces impels him forward toward wholeness of Self and uniqueness of Self, toward full functioning of all his capacities, toward confidence in the face of the external world at the same time that he can accept his deepest, real, unconscious Self.

The teacher can assist, according to Maslow, in ensuring that the student's choice is at least in the right direction, by ensuring, as far as is possible, that learning situations are not perceived by the student as 'dangerous, valueless or threatening'. The 'growth choice' must be presented so that it is perceived by the student as leading to a desirable outcome. It is for the teacher to help in situations of this nature by urging the student to choose by making the 'growth choice' positively attractive, and less dangerous, and by making the regressive choice less attractive and 'more costly'.

Maslow's work and the teacher

The fundamental tenets of humanistic psychology as expounded by Maslow, his emphasis on realizing human potential, of developing personality and understanding, commend themselves to many teachers. It is, however, the difficulty of interpreting the precise nature and practical applications of the theory which has created scepticism. Much of Maslow's theorizing appears to be based on flimsy speculation: it has been said that it relies for its underpinnings on colourful anecdote, selective case reporting and inconclusive observations. Nietzschean dithyrambs in praise of peak experiences ('... the person at the peak is godlike ...') are no substitute for prosaic facts; the belief that a person's essential nature is 'pressing to emerge' has not been validated; the catalogue of exemplary 'optimal persons' and their characteristics has been interpreted as reflecting little more than American middle-class values and morality of the 1960s.

Yet it is important to take account of the general thrust of Maslow's notions. His motivation model assists in explaining, if only in pragmatic fashion, the nature and quality of some types of student drive in the classroom. His insistence on the value of 'intrinsic learning' should remind teachers responsible for curriculum design and syllabus construction of the significance of insight learning, as opposed to the mechanical acquisition of facts, and of the importance of the enunciation of educational goals that are understood by students, in terms of learning more about themselves and their relationship to others. In sum, those who are assisting the educational growth of students should understand the basis of student motivation if classroom instructional practice is to be successful.

Rogers: the background

Rogers (b. 1902) has occupied chairs in psychology at Ohio State University and the University of Wisconsin. His work in therapy became the foundation of a theory of learning which was outlined in *Freedom to Learn* (1969) and revised in *Freedom to*

Learn for the 1980s (1983). Rogers' thinking on education is similar to that of Maslow: he opposes conventional educational practice and the psychology on which it is based; he calls for student-centred education based on active discovery, in contrast to the essentially passive, conformist, 'accumulation of stored knowledge'.[7]

The humanist approach to education marked out by Rogers places emphasis on feeling and thinking, on the recognition and importance of a student's personal values, on interpersonal communication, and on the development of 'positive self-concepts'. Human beings are innately good[8] and are oriented to growth. Their perceptions of reality determine their patterns of behaviour. Each person has an 'actualizing tendency' which maintains and enhances her experiences and potentialities. As she grows, so she develops self-concepts. The task of the educationist is the construction of situations allowing freedom to learn, and the provision of those conditions in which learning can be generally facilitated. The goal of the educationist should be 'the fully functioning person ... a person who is dependable in being realistic, self-enhancing, socialised and appropriate in his behaviour ... a person who is ever changing, ever developing, always discovering himself and the newness in himself...' The outstanding quality of the successful teacher is empathy – the ability to see someone else's problems through one's own eyes, and to communicate understanding with clarity and care.

The background to Rogers' attitude to the existing, formal education system, which has produced institutions which are 'traditional, rigid, bureaucratic and resistant to change', is to be found in his educational psychology based on the concepts of *organism, self, and congruence*. The 'organism' is the 'total person', with a need for positive regard by others; when its needs are met, it will develop 'a self' which is in congruence with those needs and the environment. Lack of congruence will result in inner conflict, alienation and hostility to the outside world. It is an essential task of education to assist students to deal with manifestations of incongruence. Teachers ought to create, therefore, a climate of trust in the classroom, modes of participating in decision-making, and 'the excitement of intellectual and emotional discovery'.

> If we value independence, if we are disturbed by the growing conformity of knowledge, of values, of attitudes which our present system induces, then we may wish to set up conditions of learning which make for uniqueness, for self-direction, and for self-initiated learning (Rogers, 1963).

Cognitive and experiential learning

Rogers rejects learning which is primarily directed, *cognitive* and basically concerned with 'the fixing of certain associations'. Such learning is often very difficult and is forgotten swiftly. In contrast, 'experiential learning' is meaningful and significant. It arises from the student's appreciation of what he is learning as satisfying his real needs and wants.

Experiential learning has the following important elements: it possesses a quality of personal involvement and stimulates the feelings and cognitive aspects of personality; it is self-initiated, in that the impetus to learn comes from within; it is pervasive and can affect the learner's entire personality; it is evaluated by the learner as satisfying a need; its essence is 'meaning'.

Learning to learn, active involvement in a process of change, should be the primary aims of an education based on experiential learning. But, says Rogers, the assumptions implicit in current educational practice deny the possibilities and value of such learning. It is assumed by those in charge of educational institutions at all levels that: students cannot be trusted to pursue their own learning, so that guidance along approved paths is necessary; learning is little more than presentation; education must be built, brick by brick, on a 'foundation of clearly defined knowledge'; final truth is already known, so that a 'search for knowledge' is seen as unimportant; the constructive citizen will develop from the passive learner; evaluation is education, and education is evaluation.

These assumptions, says Rogers, are faulty and dangerous. When made the basis of practice, they result in a denial of freedom, a stunting of intellectual growth, and the formation of behavioural patterns which are flawed and which prevent the flourishing of students' actualization.

In a paper entitled 'Direct instruction and experiential approaches: are they really exclusive?',[9] Kierstead (1985) attempts to synthesize Rogers' approach and the 'direct instruction' to which he objects. Direct instruction is characterized as including input, modelling, guided practice, checks for understanding, with the teacher controlling the lesson directly. 'Experiential teaching' is characterized by 'flexible use of space, student choice of activity ... the students controlling most of the decisions concerning pace, sequence and control of activities'. Kierstead's conclusion suggests that the *exclusive use* of direct instruction prevents the creation of a 'full range of desired student outcomes'. To share control of a class with students in a 'structured multi-task fashion' gives the students the chance to develop responsibility, independence and higher-level thinking skills.

The humanistic approach

Rogers advocates a humanistic orientation which should characterize an approach to problems of education. The principles of this orientation are set out below. (Rogers' own words appear in quotation marks.)

1. 'Human beings have a natural potentiality for learning.' They are 'ambivalently eager to develop and learn'. This desire to learn and discover can be made the foundation of a new approach to education.
2. 'Significant learning takes place when the subject matter is perceived by the student as having relevance for his own purposes.' Learning takes place more rapidly when a student sees his learning environment as relevant to the achievement of his or her desired objectives.
3. 'Learning which involves a change in self-organisation ... is threatening and tends to be resisted.' Reappraisal of one's values is often painful to the learner.

4. 'Those learnings which are threatening to the self are more easily perceived and assimilated where external threats are at a minimum.' The encouragement of self-evaluation and the freedom to work at one's own pace are relevant here.

5. 'When threat to the self is low, experience can be perceived in differentiated fashion and learning can proceed.' An environment which assures students of personal security will enhance their learning processes.

6. 'Much significant learning is acquired through doing.' The exploration of problems which one is currently experiencing, and their solution as the result of 'experiential confrontation' with practical issues, will enhance learning.

7. 'Learning is facilitated when the student participates responsibly in the learning process.' Participative learning, in which students decide their own course of action, is more effective than passive learning.

8. 'Self-initiated learning which involves the whole person of the learner – feelings as well as intellect – is the most lasting and pervasive.' This kind of learning may occur in the discovery of a new, self-generated idea or in the acquisition of a difficult skill.

9. 'Independence, creativity, and self-reliance are all facilitated when self-criticism and self-evaluation are basic and evaluation by others is of secondary importance.' Creativity involves an atmosphere of freedom and, if creative work is a goal, external evaluation is largely fruitless. The adolescent must come to his or her own conclusions and decide on appropriate personal standards.

10. 'The most socially useful learning in the modern world is the learning of the process of learning, a continuing openness to experience and incorporation into oneself of the process of change.' The survival of our culture depends on our ability to develop persons for whom change is a central fact of life 'and who have been able to live comfortably with this central fact'.

The teacher as facilitator

The translation of Rogers' humanistic approach into a process of teaching involves a total reappraisal of the role and functions of the teacher. Rogers sees the teacher, not as a controller or director, but as a facilitator. He puts forward the following guidelines for the teacher-as-facilitator.

1. The teacher should have much to do with 'setting the initial mood or climate of the group or class experience'.

2. The teacher should help to 'elicit and clarify the purposes of the individuals in the class as well as the more general purposes of the group'.

3. The teacher should rely on 'the desire of each student to implement those purposes which have meaning for him, as the motivational force behind significant learning'.

4. The teacher should look on himself or herself as a 'flexible resource to be utilized by the group'.

5. The teacher should attempt to organize and make available 'the widest possible range of resources for learning'.

6. The teacher should, in responding to expressions from the class group, accept intellectual content *and* emotionalized (i.e. deep and real) personal feelings.
7. The teacher should become a participant learner and a member of the class group.
8. The teacher should share his or her feelings and thoughts with the group.
9. The teacher should remain alert to the expression of deep or strong feelings.
10. The teacher should endeavour to recognize and accept his or her own limitations.

Rogers' work and the teacher

Rogers has thrown down the gauntlet in clear fashion. Current education is hopelessly inadequate, he claims, because it is derived from false premises and a simplistic view of students. In the name of a wider freedom and the continuation of our culture, the education system must be changed and the teacher must rethink his or her role.

The response of teachers to this challenge has been mixed: relatively few have adopted Rogers' tenets in their entirety; some, however, have attempted to organize 'free schools', 'discovery areas' and 'student-centred learning experiences'. The type of criticism levelled against Maslow has been applied to Rogers: there is an absence of compelling scientific evidence in favour of 'experiential learning'; the vagueness of terms such as 'fully functioning person' and 'participative learning' makes interpretation and application of principles difficult, if not impossible. Rogers' view of 'freedom in education' is believed by many teachers to be based upon a misunderstanding of the concept of 'freedom' in relation to the classroom. In *Learning to be Free* (1963),[10] Rogers articulates his beliefs that 'man is essentially unfree in a scientific sense', that 'self-initiated student learning' is critical for freedom, and that it is essential 'to initiate a process in the classroom of learning to be free'.

Skinner has responded repeatedly to Rogers' views. In *The Free and Happy Student* (1973), he argues against the idea of 'the free classroom'. No one learns very much from a 'free world', he suggests. Further, Rogers seems to have forgotten that 'formal education has made a tremendous difference in the extent of the skills and knowledge which can be acquired by a person in a single lifetime'. Rogers' teaching model implies that only what is relevant to the *present* is of significance; it makes no explicit preparation for the *future*. Formal education implies preparation for the student's future. The so-called 'free school' is, says Skinner, no school at all.

> Students are not literally free when they have been freed from their teachers. They then simply come under the control of other conditions, and we must look at those conditions and their effects if we are to improve teaching.

In *The Selection of Behaviour* (1989),[11] Skinner argues that Rogers and Maslow feel threatened by the objectivity of scientific knowledge and its perceived 'impersonal workings'. But, says Skinner, 'personal and social behaviour shaped by social contingencies' has often been 'cold, scheming or brutal'. Social action based upon a scientific analysis of human behaviour is much more likely to be humane.

Criticism of practical experiments in 'free schooling' as carried out in America, on the basis of Rogers' theories, is widespread. Some place responsibility for the perceived decline in American academic standards on confusion over the nature of freedom and misunderstandings fostered by inadequate, albeit attractive, examinations of the 'basic nature' of students. British criticisms of the practical problems arising from attempts to implement facilitative relationships in the classroom often have in mind the history of 'free schools' such as Summerhill and the arguable nature of the results achieved there.[12]

The positive side of Rogers' work is viewed by some practising teachers as being related to his call for the humanization of the classroom. His reminder of the importance of the student in the education process, his opposition to the sterility of dogmatic instruction, and his insistence on questioning what we teach and why we teach it, have acted as an incentive to some teachers engaged in the rethinking of curriculum purpose. The humanist emphasis on a balanced curriculum attuned to the student's social environment and his personal, intellectual and emotional needs, on the integration of studies so that insight might emerge, on activity leading to understanding, and on growth as a desirable educational end, should not be overlooked. Teachers in further education who do not subscribe to Rogers' views of the essential trustworthiness of human nature and the need for self-actualization, may, nevertheless, share his belief in the maximum development of personality as a worthy educational goal.

Notes and references

1. See generally for this chapter: 'Humanistic psychologies' in Murphy and Kovach (*op.cit.*); *Humanistic Education Sourcebook* ed. D.A. Read and S. Simon (Prentice-Hall, 1975); 'Humanistic theories of learning' by W.S. Sahakian in *Learning: Systems, Models and Theories* (Rand McNally, 1976); *Humanistic Psychology* by W.B. Frick (Merrill, 1971); *Psychology Applied to Teaching* by R. Biehler (Houghton Mifflin, 1993); *Humanistic Education* by C. Patterson (Prentice-Hall, 1973).

2. See Maslow's 'Self-actualisation and beyond' in *Challenges of Humanistic Psychology* ed. J. Bugental (McGraw-Hill, 1967); *New Knowledge in Human Values* by Maslow (Harper & Row, 1970).

3. See Maslow's article, 'Music education and peak experiences' in *Music Educators Journal* (1968, *14*).

4. Note 'Two tests of Maslow's theory' by E.I. Betz in *Journal of Vocational Behaviour* (1984, *2*).

5. See Maslow's 'Self-actualising people: a study of psychological health' in *The Self: Explorations in Personal Growth* ed. C. Moustakas (Harper & Row, 1956).

6. Pub. Cassell.

7. See *Carl Rogers: The Man and His Ideas* by R. Evans (Dutton, 1975); *The Carl Rogers Reader* ed. H. Kirschenbaum (Constable, 1990); 'A conversation with Carl Rogers' by M.H. Hall in *Psychology Today* (1967, *12*); 'Carl Rogers and humanistic phenomenology' in *Three Psychologies* by R.D. Nye (Books Cole, 1975). See also Rogers' *A Way of Being* (Houghton Mifflin, 1980).

8. In reading Rogers' arguments for the innate goodness of humanity, and the responses of his critics, one is reminded of the opposing schools of thought in ancient China,

represented by Mencius (c. 370 BC) and Hsun Tsu (c. 300 BC); the former believed that human nature was good, whereas the latter affirmed: 'The nature of man is evil and whatever is good in him is the result of acquired training'. For a brief exposition of the argument, see *Chinese Thought* by H.C. Creel (Chicago UP, 1953).

9. *Educational Leadership* (May, 1985).
10. In *Contemporary Issues in Educational Psychology* ed. H. Clarizio (McGraw-Hill, 1987).
11. Ed. A.C. Catania and S. Harnad (CUP, 1989).
12. Summerhill, in Suffolk, founded in 1921 by A.S. Neill (1883–1973), was a self-styled 'free, progressive school', run on the basis that pupils must never be forced into learning. Neill's philosophy of education has many resemblances to that of Rogers. His views were encapsulated in his credo: 'No one can give another freedom; freedom is a natural state ... the teacher's position in regard to freedom should be a negative one. His motto should be 'Let me keep out''.' For an account of Neill's views, see Bowen and Hobson (*op.cit.*). See also the entry under 'Neill' in *Dictionary of British Educationists* by R. Aldrich and P. Gordon (Woburn Press, 1989). For an updated account of the school's ethos, see 'A different discipline' in *The Times*, 11 April, 1997.
13. See, further, *Carl Rogers, a Critical Biography* by D. Cohen (Constable, 1997).

Part Three

Communication and Control – The Essence of the Teaching-Learning Process

Chapter 11

Fundamentals of Communication in the Teaching-Learning Process

You cannot speak of ocean to a well-frog – the creature of a narrower sphere; you cannot speak of ice to a summer insect (Chuang-Tze, 330 BC).

Consideration of the teaching-learning activities outlined on pp. 7–9 will reveal complex sets of relationships between teachers and learners resulting from *communication*.[1] The process of communication is discussed here; it is explained in terms of 'the exchange of meanings' between teachers and learners, without which effective instruction is impossible.

Much of this chapter is taken up with an outline of models and analogies of the process of communication; these are no more than conjectures based on theoretical and simplified representations of the real world. Deutsch[2] describes a model as 'a structure of symbols and operating rules which is supposed to match a set of relevant points in an existing structure or process'. He outlines four functions of models: *organizing* data so as to show previously unperceived similarities; acting as *heuristic devices* that might lead to previously unknown facts; *predicting* the outcome of specific events; and *measuring* phenomena. Analogies (see p. 24) 'are employed to promote understanding of concepts. They do so by indicating similarities between those concepts and others that may be more familiar or more readily grasped.'[3] Teachers should keep in mind the practical realities of their classrooms, their teaching-learning experiences and their intuitive approaches to problems of communication in considering the abstract models mentioned below. Abstraction can lead to over-simplification, but it may assist in rendering comprehensible a formal analysis of common events in the classroom.

What is communication?

Communicate [L. *communicare* (communis, common)], *v.t.* To impart, to give a share of, to transmit; to reveal; to give Holy Communion to. *v.i.* To share, to hold intercourse, to confer by speech or writing ... communication, *n*. The art of communicating; that which is communicated ... (*Cassell's New English Dictionary*)

The essence of communication is the transmitting and receiving of information through a common system of signals and symbols, whether in the form of writing or other signs, expressive movements, or the spoken word. It takes place when the behaviour of one person acts as a stimulus for the responsive behaviour of another; in the words of Richards, 'Communication takes place when one mind so acts upon its environment that another mind is influenced, and in that other mind an experience occurs which is like the experience in the first mind, and is caused in part by that experience.'[4]

The following definitions of communication are of value in the attempt to understand teaching-learning:

(a) 'the process by which people attempt to share meaning via the transmission of symbolic messages' (Stoner);[5]
(b) 'an interactional process in which meaning is stimulated through the sending and receiving of verbal and non-verbal messages' (Tortoriello);[6]
(c) 'the achievement of meaning and understanding between people through verbal and non-verbal means in order to affect behaviour and achieve desired end results' (Mondy);[7]
(d) 'when two corresponding systems, coupled together through one or more non-corresponding systems, assume identical states as a result of signal transfer along a chain' (Schramm);[8]
(e) 'the transfer of information from the sender to the receiver, with the information being understood by the receiver' (Koontz).[9]

An important characteristic of human beings, which divides them from other creatures, is their capacity for the expressive vocalization which we call *speech*. It may be that the early growth of civilization depended in large part on a person's ability to communicate with his or her neighbour by speaking, and the later stages of civilization have reflected, in some measure, the invention of more complicated media of communication, such as the printing press and the radio. The development of formal teaching, in particular, is linked to the qualitative expansion of communication methods. From the spoken discourse to the printed textbook, the TV lesson and the computer, the teaching process has depended on the ability and technique of the teacher to convey to the learner, in an appropriate form, the fruits of human thought – that is, to communicate.

In the teaching situation, communication by the teacher is generally intended to influence the learner's behaviour. Its mode will be determined, therefore, by that situation which will reflect the lesson's objectives. To that end, communication in the classroom may be verbal or non-verbal, formal or informal, one-way or two-way, designed to elicit a verbal or non-verbal response, intended to state a fact or pose a problem. Its primary function in the teaching process is the creation and maintenance of a *commonality of thought and feeling* which will lead to learning.

The purposive nature of communication

Halliday[10] sets out seven functions of language which indicate the purposive nature of communication. (Teachers should draw on their classroom experience in considering the reliability of this analysis.) First, the *instrumental function* which causes events to happen, e.g. 'Begin writing now'. The *regulatory function* controls events and maintains control, e.g. 'If you score a pass mark you will move to another tuition group'. The *representational function* involves the use of language to convey facts, to explain, to represent reality as one perceives it, e.g. 'You have done well in your test'. The *interactional function* helps to ensure 'social maintenance' by keeping open channels of communication and facilitating social exchange. The *personal function* allows speakers to express emotional, personal feelings which denote individuality, e.g. 'I'm glad to learn of your success'. The *heuristic function* involves the use of language for the acquisition of knowledge, as where questions are asked and answered in class. The *imaginative function* assists in the creation and reception of ideas. (But not always so. Teachers will understand the force of the cynical comment by the statesman, Talleyrand, that the purpose of the spoken word is to conceal one's thoughts from another.)

These functions are not mutually exclusive. The use of language in class by students and teacher may involve a number of linguistic functions simultaneously. In considering linguistic communication in the classroom its *purpose* must be kept in mind. Similarly, in analysing a failure of communication in the classroom it is always useful to consider the purpose of the failed message and to examine the degree of correspondence of function and form of the message used.

Communication in relation to teaching

Class teaching requires the presentation of selected, appropriate stimuli and the eliciting of desired responses from the learner. Effective presentation of stimuli is, in itself, a form of communication. Whether pointing to a chart, tapping on a desk to attract attention or asking a subtle question which demands interpretation and insight for its solution, the teacher is engaged in the process of communicating. Consider, for example, the following situations in typical further education classes:

1. Engineering students are being taught the elements of vehicle maintenance. They and their tutor are examining a mechanism at which he is pointing. He states: 'Our next job is to lubricate the accelerator control linkage and cable and the pedal fulcrum. Here they are.' He then ensures that his statement has been understood by asking a variety of questions.
2. Secretarial students are studying business documents. An overhead projector displays an illustration of a bill of exchange. The teacher says: 'This obviously isn't a cheque, which we looked at a few minutes ago! Why not?' Answers are then elicited and considered by teacher and class.
3. Economics students have been listening to one of their group reading her essay on 'Problems of a single European currency'. She has reached her conclusion: 'I believe that I have shown that this is really a political, and not an economic, question'. The students turn their attention to the tutor, awaiting her reaction. She raises her eyebrows in mock, exaggerated surprise. The students observe,

and interpret, her reaction; some express disagreement with the speaker by shaking their heads; others nod their heads in agreement.

In these examples we can discern a variety of modes and media of communication. They include statements of fact, expressions of opinion, comment on opinion, questions, replies to questions, the posing of problems. The media and channels of communication used here include the voice, gestures (pointing, facial expressions – the so-called proto-linguistic signs, which are of great importance in the classroom), and visual aids. In each of these varied examples of classroom communication the following elements may be discerned:

(a) an *objective* (e.g. to achieve an understanding of the functions of a bill of exchange);
(b) an *awareness* by the class teacher of the path to that objective;
(c) the *creation of a link*, or 'channel', between teacher and class, the effectiveness of which will be determined in large measure by the teacher's skill and the learner's initial motivation and continuing interest;
(d) the adoption by the teacher of *appropriate modes of communicating* his or her 'message', calculated to elicit responses and modify behaviour;
(e) the *reception and comprehension of the message*, of which the teacher becomes aware ('feedback') (see Chapter 12).

Communication in the classroom is, therefore, not merely a matter of an instructor addressing a class; it is the outcome of a number of interrelated activities. Where any one of these activities is omitted, the effectiveness of the communication will be vitiated or destroyed, so that the probability of successful learning is reduced accordingly.

Communication theories

Attempts have been made to analyse the basis of information transmission so as to formulate a general theory of communication. The theories associated with Shannon and Weaver, Osgood, Schramm, Newcomb, Gerbner, Berlo and Barnlund are mentioned below.

The mathematical theory of communication put forward by Shannon and Weaver[11] draws on information theory to present an explanation of communication systems; it has important analogies with the teaching process. (The aim of information theory[12] is the discovery of laws, capable of reduction to mathematical terms, concerning systems designed to communicate or manipulate information. The concept of 'information' is used in a highly technical sense to mean 'that which reduces uncertainty'; it can be measured in terms of changes in probability; it is not to be confused with 'meaning', which refers to 'making sense' of information. In less formal terms, Paisley[13] describes 'information' as denoting 'any stimulus that alters cognitive structure in the receiver ... Something that the receiver already knows, is not information.')

Consider a very simple system of communication, for example that which exists where teacher speaks to student. The system includes the following three elements:

(a) a *source* (or transmitter) – the speaker;
(b) a *channel* – the speaker's voice, travelling through air;
(c) a *receiver* – the listener.

Such a system may be represented by the simple diagram in Figure 11.1.

Figure 11.1 Communication system.

Shannon and Weaver sketched a relatively simple model of the communication process: a message flowed along a selected channel from source ('transmitter') to receiver. Emitted signals were decoded by the receiver. In modelling information flow, the problems to be answered were: 'Who says what, in which channel, to whom, and with what result?' The model was modified later since, in particular, it seemed to ignore the important role of feedback in the process of communication (see p. 151).

Osgood[14] believes that the Shannon and Weaver model has application to engineering problems only; it is not suitable to explain the complexities of human communication in the home or the classroom, for example. Human beings function as sources *and* destinations; each person in a communication event is both transmitter *and* receiver, and each is a 'complete communicating system'. Osgood's model includes total behaviour. Thus, when the teacher (T) talks to the learner (L), T's words, postures, etc., are of relevance as parts of the message sent to L; but there are other parts of T's total behaviour (his reactions to L's posture, for example) that do not derive from his (T's) behaviour. A message is much more complex in structure than it appears to be. Weaver has stressed the *generality* of the theory: '[Our theory] is so general that one does not need to say what kinds of symbols are being considered – whether written letters or words, or musical notes or spoken words, or symphonic music or pictures. The theory is deep enough so that the relationships it reveals indiscriminately apply to these and all other forms of communication.'

Schramm[15] uses the model illustrated in Figure 11.2. This diagram incorporates Schramm's belief that what is communicated is only *what is shared* in the fields of experience of message source and destination (e.g. T and L); it is only that portion of the signal *held in common* by T and L. Schramm noted: '[A communication system] can be no stronger than its weakest link. In engineering terms, there may be filtering or distortion at any stage. In human terms ... if the message is not decoded in a pattern that corresponds to the encoding ... and handled so as to produce the required response, then obviously the system is working at less than top efficiency.'

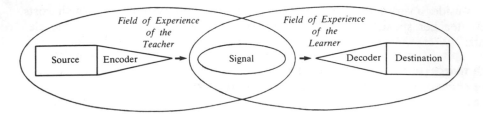

Figure 11.2   Schramm's model of the communication process.

It is for the teacher, in initiating a communication, to be aware of the steps to be taken so as to ensure that the 'communication system' in his or her classroom is working optimally.

Newcomb's 'symmetry' model[16] is illustrated in Figure 11.3. In the act of communication X transmits information to Y about something, Z. That act enables X and Y 'to maintain simultaneous orientations to each other and towards objects (such as Z) in the environment'. Communication between X and Y maintains the symmetry of the relationship between X, Y and Z and allows adjustments to be made in that relationship.

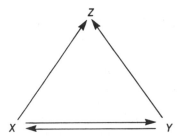

Figure 11.3   Newcomb's 'symmetry' model of the communication process.

Gerbner's model of the communication process[17] has been outlined thus: 'Some person perceives an event and reacts in a situation through some means to make available materials in some form and context conveying content of some consequence.' Gerbner stresses the problems in communication arising from 'variability in the perception of events', and emphasizes the importance of situation and context. Human communication – in street, home, classroom – is of an open nature, in contrast to the closed sequences of a mechanical system; hence it is often unpredictable in its consequences.

Berlo[18] draws attention to the fact that purpose and audience are not separable. 'All communication behaviour has as its purpose the eliciting of a specific response from a specific person (or group of persons).' His model, which is based on the exchange of information between parties, stresses the significance of feedback and the contribution to the process of communication made by cultural influences and communication skills. Concepts such as 'source, encoder, decoder' should not be viewed as entities or people – they are the names of *behaviours* which have to be performed for communication to occur'. The ingredients of communication are not separable.

Barnlund[19] stresses the 'dynamic and transactional nature' of communication, in which perception and attention-giving are vital. Communication is not a reaction to something, nor an interaction with something, 'but a transaction in which man invents and attributes meanings to realise his purposes'. His model shows communication as a *dynamic process* ('continually responsive, continually changing') in which the interaction of all elements within the process must be studied. Each participant shares the processes of coding and decoding; participants 'exchange roles' continually during some types of communication. According to Barnlund, the process of communication should not be viewed as a unidirectional, linear activity, but more in the nature of a mutual, reciprocal, transactional phenomenon.

Certain general features have emerged from the above models. First, communication is viewed best as a process, that is, a series of sequential activities directed to some end. Secondly, communication involves interpersonal relationships. Thirdly, communication involves 'traffic in symbols' which, by their very nature, are mere approximations to the concepts intended to be transmitted. Finally, communication, if it is to be effective, necessitates an accepted commonality of meaning attached to its symbols.

Figure 11.4 is a diagram delineating fundamental features in the communication process based, essentially, on Shannon and Weaver. (Note that 'noise' – see (c) below – occurs throughout the system, and that the dotted line joining sender and receiver should be interpreted as suggesting *an interchange of roles* at many stages in the process.)

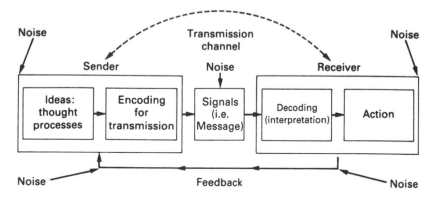

Figure 11.4 Fundamental features of the communication process (based on Shannon and Weaver).

The communication system is made up of the following components:

(a) an *information source* (the 'sender') from which the message material originates;
(b) a *transmitter* which transforms (or 'encodes') the message into a form suitable for the channel;

(c) a '*noise source*' which interferes (not only in the auditory modality) with the flow of information between transmitter and receiver and reduces the probability of the message being received correctly to less than one. (Indeed, as Shannon pointed out, the efficiency of a communication system as a whole is defined in part by the probability that *noise will change the information content of the message.* 'Noise' is used here in its communication engineering sense of unpredictable, random and unwanted signals that mask the information content of a communication channel.) Effectively, it is anything added to the signal that is not intended by the information source.

(d) a *receiver* which decodes the message encoded by the transmitter;

(e) a *destination* for the message;

(f) *feedback* (see p. 151).

The analogy with the classroom situation in which a teacher and learner are engaged in the processes of communication should be apparent. The importance, when designing a lesson, of allowing for the interference of 'noise' is clear. The communication system of a typical lesson may be considered as including the following elements:

(a) an *information source* – the brain of the teacher;

(b) a *transmitter* – the teacher's voice mechanism which produces a signal (words) which will be transmitted through a channel (air);

(c) '*noise*' which distorts the signal and which may result from competing stimuli, e.g. distractions in the classroom environment, or an irrelevant meaning 'read into' the message on the basis of the listener's previous experience;

(d) a *receiver* – the students' sensory organs;

(e) a *destination* – the students' brains;

(f) *feedback* – e.g. by question and answer.

Shannon and Weaver identify three levels of communication problems:

1. With what accuracy can the very symbols of a message be transmitted? – the problem of *technique.*
2. With what precision do the symbols convey the meaning of the message? – the problem of *semantics.*
3. With what effectiveness does the received and perceived meaning affect behaviour? – the problem of *effectiveness.*

These problems may emerge when a teacher analyses the lesson he or she has given and seeks answers to the following questions:

1. 'How accurately have I conveyed the meaning of the lesson, i.e. did I employ the appropriate mode of communication?'
2. 'How precisely, in practice, did the lesson content resemble that which I had in mind?'
3. 'How did perception of the lesson content modify the behaviour of the students as judged by their responses, and, in general, how effective was I?'

The analogies presented by the theoreticians' models emphasize for the teacher the complexities of communication, and draw attention to some of the circumstances which are necessary for the attainment of teaching-learning goals.

Communication theory and the classroom

The elements of the communication process, as they appear in the theoretical models above, are now considered in relation to the classroom.

The information source (the communicator or 'sender')
The communicator in the classroom is a single individual (not a group or collective entity, as in the case of, say, a newspaper or TV programme). The communicator's initial step is *ideation*, that is the formation of an idea, such as a perceived need demanding some activity, e.g. a deficiency in class response, or a recurring error in class written work, both of which require remedial instructional activity. It should be noted that communicators are also receivers (see Figure 11.4) – an effective teacher will be receiving and monitoring 'listener responses' at all times – even though the roles of teacher and student are separately defined.

The message
A message refers to some object in the environment of communicator and receiver; hence it requires *a community of experience* among teacher and students. It may be intended, in the classroom context, to assist e.g. in the reduction or removal of ambiguity. The teacher, as communicator, is conveying *information*, which can be uncertainty reduction, in the signals, i.e. the symbols, which constitute the message. That message need not be verbal; it can be in any form or style than can be experienced and comprehended through any of the receiver's senses.

Encoding
In the classroom, as elsewhere, encoding involves *converting* the communicator's ideas into appropriate message form. The teacher should use a message form based on 'a plurality of signs which have a *common signification* to a number of inter-preters';[20] he or she should consider sign systems other than normal writing or speech. The rules of encoding demand an awareness of classroom conventions and of the necessity of matching the teacher's *intentions* with the students' *abilities* in swift, correct interpretation. A search for 'the right word' may be essential.

Channels of transmission
The effective transmission of communication within the classroom demands not only media of communication (speaking, writing, films, etc.) but *means of transmission*. The selection of *appropriate channels* for the carrying of messages may be determined by institutional rules ('lecturers are expected to distribute printed notes'). Where the teacher is free to select channels, he or she will keep in mind the best possible way, in the circumstances, of gaining and holding the attention of the students for whom the message is intended.

The receiver

In some formal models of communication in the classroom the receiver (the student) may appear to be playing only a passive role – he or she reacts or responds. In practice this is not so: the student is often also the initiator of messages and of processes of selection, interpretation and action. Were this not so, classroom communication would be impossible: the student is expected to discriminate among stimuli (including formal messages), to interpret them and to act. Similarly, the communicator, in interpreting feedback, is acting as receiver.

Decoding

The receiver, that is the teacher or student, must first perceive the message intended for him or her and then act so as to 'interpret' it. The process of decoding is often complex: it is affected directly by the receiver's previous experiences, assessment of the symbols which constitute the message and, above all, the degree of commonality of meaning with the sender. The level of effectiveness of communication will be in direct relationship to the level of 'matching' of sender's intention and 'receiver's' decoding. (Pearce and Figgins note[21] that the 500 most common English words have, on average, over 20 definitions each.)

Feedback

In the classroom, feedback (see p. 151) is a process which begins with a reaction to aspects of the initial message as received by the student. That reaction may be a verbal or non-verbal response (e.g. 'Yes, I understand', or an affirmative head movement) which is transmitted to the teacher. (The student's response is transformed into a stimulus which, when it impinges on the teacher, will produce a response in him or her.) The student's response is interpreted as indicating the level of understanding between parties to the communication. Without responses, the teacher cannot evaluate the effectiveness of his communication; with it, the teacher can *adjust* the content and mode of his or her activities. Feedback is, therefore, essential to good classroom communication; it exerts a *measure of control* over the activities of teachers in their role as communicators.

Noise

The fidelity of the message which is communicated in a classroom is always affected in some measure by a variety of interference known as 'noise'. The causes of this type of interference in the teaching-learning process are varied and are given separate consideration in the next section.

'Noise' as a barrier to effective communication

The best-planned lesson can fall on 'deaf ears' and there must be few tutors in further education who have not suffered the chagrin which arises from the confrontation of a teacher, anxious to present a carefully prepared lesson, and a class, apparently indifferent and unwilling to participate. 'They didn't respond in any way!'; 'I put everything I had into it – diagrams, models, notes – and it fell flat!'; 'As soon as the lesson started, I could tell we weren't on the same wavelength!'

The effectiveness of communication in the classroom may be weakened by the deficiencies of the 'source' and 'transmitter', by 'noise' and competition from a variety of sources, and by inadequacies of the 'receiver'. Often, the very environment in which the class works acts as a 'noise source' which can interfere with and distort reception of the teacher's message. Physical conditions, such as lighting, temperature and seating, may be such as to distract from, and therefore weaken, reception of the message. A badly set-out room in which the teacher can be neither seen nor heard properly is a common source of interference with effective information flow. Where a classroom in a college is set out in formal 'school style', the recall of earlier, unhappy experiences or of failure associated with school may interfere with the effective reception of communication by adult students. Controlling the teaching environment, in the sense of ensuring that it does not function as a 'noise source', is an important task for the class tutor. This is not to be taken as implying that effective communication and teaching cannot take place save in a carefully illuminated, thermostatically controlled room! On the contrary, it is well known that extremely efficient instruction has taken place in ill-ventilated Nissen huts or in badly illuminated laboratories overlooking railway shunting yards. In analysing the reasons for poor communication, however, it is necessary to consider the effect on the class of *all* types of distracting stimuli (i.e. 'noise') including the physical environment. 'The classroom is not neutral!'

The 'source' and 'transmitter' – the teachers themselves – may be responsible for the creation of noise by the conscious or unconscious erection of barriers to effective communication. Their personality and mannerisms will obtrude on the communication process. An aggressive manner, a nervous disposition (which may reflect inadequate knowledge or poor lesson preparation), the proto-linguistic signs which are swiftly interpreted by students as evidence of hostility or lack of interest in the subject matter, may block the pathway to learning. Adolescents are often adept in the swift detection of insincerity, so that there is unlikely to be effective learning where tutors reveal, by an inflexion of voice or a display of indifference in response to a question (so-called 'proto-linguistic symbols') that they are out of sympathy with the class or the purpose of the lesson. (The problems of paralanguage are discussed on p. 146.) An incorrect choice of the medium of communication – a long verbal explanation of the contents of a document, for example, rather than a discussion using its image projected on a screen – may weaken the effectiveness of message transmission. A lesson pitched at too high a level or out of sequence with previous lessons will usually ensure that the class is 'on a different wave-length', so that real communication is impossible. A rate of delivery which is too swift for comprehension and assimilation of the message, or too slow to maintain interest, can prevent effective transmission. A badly structured, disjointed lesson plan may produce signals so erratic that no part of the intended message reaches the class; the signals may also produce 'overtones' resulting in a distortion of meaning. (William James' reminder that 'the mind is, at every stage, a theatre of simultaneous possibilities' is of relevance here.)

The learner – the 'receiver' and 'destination' of the message – may function in a manner which introduces 'noise' and weakens or renders meaningless the communication. He or she may be incapable of receiving or 'decoding' (i.e. comprehending) the content of a lesson because of inadequate preparation. A strong desire to learn how to use a computer to solve network problems will not recompense for a total lack of knowledge of basic computer-handling processes. A well-planned lesson designed to improve speeds of typing, utilizing taped dictation, will have little value for those members of the class whose spelling is poor. Where effective interpretation of messages received by the senses is impossible because of lack of acquaintance with the technical vocabulary employed, 'noise' is intensified and comprehension of the message is impossible. Where there are variations in the learner's level of intensity of interest, the reception of information is influenced directly; there is no real communication where the learner's mind is 'elsewhere'.

Noise may be produced where a teacher is unaware that the language he is using is, by reason of its structure, style, syntax and overtones so far removed from that to which the class is accustomed that the disjunction of transmitter and receiver is almost total. The work of Bernstein[22] in uncovering the different 'class codes' of communication, and their importance in Britain, is of significance for the class teacher. Bernstein draws attention to the existence of two types of language-codes – 'working class language', a highly-predictable, 'public' language in which individual selection and permutation are severely restricted, and 'formal language' in which the speaker is able to make an individual selection and permutation. (For a critique of Bernstein's views see the writings of the American linguistics researcher, Labov.[23])

Parry has enumerated the following factors as barriers to effective communication. (Teachers will recognize swiftly some of the causes of 'noise' and communication breakdown in lessons.) Limitation of the receiver's capacity (e.g. cognitive limitations, preventing recognition of exceptions to generalities – the 'reductive listening' which causes students to think that what is presented as new material is no more than old knowledge 'rehashed'); distractions (often from competing stimuli and environmental stress); the use of unstated assumptions (so that cognitive barriers arise between teacher and students, who are, effectively, at cross-purposes); incompatibility of 'schemes' of understanding (whereby differing reaction patterns and expectancies lead to misinterpretations); intrusion of unconscious or partly conscious mechanisms (such as fear, leading to the rejection of disturbing and unwelcome information); confused presentation of information (which ignores the fact that as information becomes more complex, so, for many learners, comprehension difficulty is intensified). See Pushkin's poem on p. 111 which epitomizes communication breakdown.

Paralanguage

'In every classroom, non-verbal communication is so frequent and important that every teacher needs to understand it and how it works' (Brosin).[24] The totality of a spoken message communicated in the classroom will comprise words, gestures, facial expressions, posture, vocalization, etc. Aphorisms, such as 'actions speak louder than words' and 'it's not what you say, it's the way that you say it' are of relevance to the work of the teacher as communicator. Reference was made above to proto-linguistic signs; these abound in any lesson and form a part of the subject matter of paralanguage. Loveday defines paralanguage as 'the vocal, kinesic (gestural) and proxemic (spatial) channels which accompany, interfuse and partly synchronise the traditionally recognised ones'.[25]

It has been suggested[26] that, for the teacher, communicative competence involves the skilled use of paralanguage, and that the effective direction of classroom instruction necessitates an awareness of one's own and students' non-verbal communication. Three aspects of paralanguage are noted below: kinesics, proxemics and paraverbal features.

Kinesics is the study of 'the communication that takes place through facial expression, gestures and movements' (Birdwhistell).[27] Signals emitted and received during a lesson ('kinesic markers') include, in addition to spoken words, head movements, eye blinks, gaze and gestures which will be interpreted by students. (Indeed, *everything* communicates if one knows how to read the messages.) *Cultural context* is, of course, a vital features of interpretation of a message; thus, direct eye contact is expected in most European classrooms, whereas in some countries in the Far East it is rarely acceptable; bowing before or after a formal conversation is acceptable in Japan, whereas in Europe it is considered as evidence of unacceptable obsequiousness. It is for the teacher to interpret and react to the overt, non-verbal signals from the students, and to be aware that, according to some researchers, we have less control over our non-verbal behaviour than over our verbal behaviour. The teacher as communicator has the special task of ensuring that, as far as possible, his or her gestures, posture and other movements shall be *appropriate to the nature of the communication*. The teacher should remember Freud's dramatic observation: 'He that has eyes to see and ears to hear may convince himself that no mortal can keep a secret. If his lips are silent, he chatters with his finger-tips...!'

Proxemics studies the factor of distances involved in communicative interactions.[28] 'Keep your distance' has a real meaning in classroom communication. The layout of classrooms and the space allocated to the teacher (desk, podium, lectern) will require planning if they are to contribute to teaching effectiveness. The effect of a teacher speaking at a considerable distance from the class, or looming over a 'student's space', may be interpreted by students in ways which vitiate or negate the significance of the message.

Paraverbal features involve the 'non-lexical aspects of speech' – intensity, pitch, intonation, rhythm, speed, pronunciation, vocabulary, for example.[29] They may have a decisive effect on the reception of a message in the classroom. Tape recordings of the teacher's voice made during a lesson can assist in the improvement of vocal delivery. Again, cultural setting is critical: where a message is enunciated in a style or with a vocal pattern which, in the circumstances, enlarges any perceived teacher-student gulf, the partnership necessary for communication disappears, often to be replaced by a growing antagonism.

The fundamental messages from research into paralanguage seem to be: we do not communicate in words alone; our paralinguistic signals confirm, contradict, or are irrelevant to our words; the effective use of paralanguage can be of positive assistance in understanding students; the 'silent yet thunderous impact' of non-verbal language requires study by teachers and those who train them. Abercrombie's words express the essence of paralanguage: 'We speak with our vocal organs, but we converse with our whole body.'[30]

Notes and references

1. See generally for this chapter: *Communication Theories* by W.J. Severin (Longman, 1988); *Communication Theory* by E. Borman (Holt, Rinehart & Winston, 1980); *Understanding Human Communication* by R.B. Adler and G. Rodman (Holt, Rinehart & Winston, 1982); *Communicating* by A. Taylor *et al.* (Prentice-Hall, 1980); *Landmarks in Linguistic Thought* by R. Harris (Routledge, 1989); *Mastering Communication* by N. Stanton (Macmillan, 1996); *Language and Human Behaviour* by D. Bickerton (Washington UP, 1995).
2. 'Communication models in the social sciences' in *Public Opinion Quarterly* (16, *356*).
3. *Models, Analogies and Theories* by Achinstein (Elsevier, 1964).
4. See Severin (*op. cit.*).
5. 'Communication' in *Management* (Prentice-Hall, 1989).
6. *Communication in the Organisation* (McGraw-Hill, 1978).
7. 'Communication' in *Management–Concepts and Practices* (Allyn & Bacon, 1983).
8. 'How communication works' in *The Process and Effects of Mass Communication* (Illinois UP, 1954).
9. *Management* (McGraw-Hill, 1985).
10. *Explanations in the Functions of Language* (Arnold, 1973).
11. *The Mathematical Theory of Communication* (Illinois UP, 1949).
12. See e.g. *Coding and Information Theory* by R.W. Hamming (Prentice-Hall, 1986). For a criticism, see *The Myths of Communication* ed. K. Woodward (Coda Press, 1980).
13. 'Information and work' in *Progress in Communication Sciences* (Ablex, 1980).
14. 'Psycholinguistics' in *Journal of Abnormal and Social Psychology* (1954, *49*).
15. See Severin (*op. cit.*).
16. 'An approach to the study of communicative acts' in *Psychological Review* (1953, *60*).
17. 'Toward a general model of communication' in *AV Communication Review* (1956, *4*).
18. *The Process of Communication* (Holt, Rinehart & Winston, 1960).
19. *Interpersonal Communication* (Houghton Mifflin, 1968).
20. *Communication* by D. McQuail (Longman, 1984).
21. *Principles of Business Communication* (Wiley, 1984).
22. 'Social class and linguistic development in a theory of social learning' in *Class, Codes and Control* (Routledge, 1971).
23. *Language in the Inner City* (Pennsylvania UP, 1976). Labov provides data which he interprets as suggesting that deprived, working class adolescents in the black communities in the USA can handle difficult concepts in their own, restricted linguistic code. For a criticism of Labov, see *The Language Trap* by J. Honey (NCES, 1983). See also 'Language and class' in *The Politics of Discourse* by T. Crowley (Macmillan, 1989).
24. *Lectures in Experimental Psychiatry* (Pittsburgh UP, 1961).
25. *The Sociolinguistics of Learning and Using a Non-native Language* (Pergamon, 1982).
26. See 'Actions speak louder than words: paralanguage, communication and education' by A. Pennycook in *TESOL Quarterly* (1985, *2*).
27. 'Paralanguage' in *Readings in Language and Communication for Teachers* ed. B. Hodge (Longman, 1983). See also *Bodytalk* by D. Morris (Jonathan Cape, 1994).
28. See e.g. *The Hidden Dimension* by E.T. Hall (Doubleday, 1966).

29. See e.g. Loveday (*op. cit.*); 'Non-verbal communication in teaching' by H.A. Smith in *Review of Educational Research* (1979, *49*); *Handbook of Communication Skills* ed. O. Hargie (Routledge, 1997).

30. *The Anatomy of Judgment* (Hutchinson, 1960).

Chapter 12

The Nature of Control in the Teaching-Learning Process

One has control by controlling a few developments which can have significant impact on performance and results. One loses control by trying to control the infinity of events which are marginal to performance and results (Drucker, 1974).

Without communication, teaching is impossible: this was the gist of the previous chapter. But communication will not suffice in itself to create an effective teaching situation. The teaching process, of which communication is a vital part, has to be directed to some desired end, and movement towards the objective necessitates a planned progression. The use of a strategy of instruction designed to attain a learning objective requires *control* – the alternative could be a circuitous meander which may, or may not, bring the learner to that objective. Control, its elements, its application to classroom teaching and, in particular, its relation to the concept of *information feedback* ('knowledge of results') will be examined below.[1]

The argument of this chapter, which seeks to consider control of the specific process of instruction in terms of control of a general system, is based on an extended analogy. The problems inherent in argument by analogy were mentioned in Chapter 2. The use of analogy is not to be rejected outright where its use assists in the assimilation of new ideas to old concepts, or where it allows comprehension of the unfamiliar in terms of the familiar. Where we attempt to correlate a relatively abstract, intangible process with one whose structure is obvious and well known, understanding may be improved. In studying this chapter and its underlying analogy, teachers should keep in mind the classroom as they know it, with its unpredictable nature, its many instabilities and transient features. The validity of the analogy presented here must be judged by the practising teacher. How apt is it? Is it strained? Does it improve one's understanding of the teaching process? Does it hold up under the pressure of any counter-analogy? Above all, does it assist the teacher in understanding his or her everyday tasks of instruction?

Terms such as 'control' and 'manipulation of the environment' are not generally welcomed by teachers, for whom they are associated with undesirable circumstances such as loss of freedom, denial of human rights, etc. At a time in which the very legitimacy of authority as such is being questioned fundamentally, there will be no ready acceptance by teachers of any principles which appear to threaten teacher or student autonomy. But the argument presented below turns on the belief that in *any* system, such as that constituted by a class and tutor, some control is essential, and some manipulation of environmental factors is needed if organizational objectives are to be accomplished efficiently.

> To control does not mean to suppress or impose on the process a course that contradicts its nature. On the contrary, it implies that the nature of the process in question is taken into consideration to the maximum possible extent, and that each influence on the process is applied in accordance with the process's own logic (Talyzina, 1981).[2]

The classroom processes suggested below involve an understanding of, and respect for, the student for whom the provision of effective learning conditions is the essence of teaching activities; they are not based on any desire for suppression of individuality, but are intended to assist in the expression and furtherance of individuality within the context of learning.

The basis of feedback: a control analogy

Information feedback,[3] which is an essential ingredient in any system of control, may be considered as *the return of a signal which indicates the result of an action and which can be used to determine future actions*. Sayre[4] defines feedback in more formal terms as 'a process by which the behaviour of an operating system (e.g. living organism, functioning machine) is influenced in turn by the effects of this behaviour with respect to the system's operating environment'. (For a note on systems, see p. 186.) (In physiological terms, as applied to the learner, feedback is the sensory input resulting from his or her own effector activity.) Consider, for example, seemingly simple feedback actions such as those of a vehicle driver noting a change in the contact between the car tyres and the road surface, thereby sensing the presence of ice and immediately reducing speed, or the automatic excretion of moisture through the pores of the skin in response to signals indicating excessive body heat. Investigation of any system, natural or artificial, the behaviour of which is *purposive* and *adaptive*, reveals some circularity of action between its parts, so that the system's output can be assessed and the input modified. Jacob[5] makes the following observation: 'Feedback operates by introducing into the system the results of its past activity ... Every organization calls on feedback loops that keep each component informed of the results of its own operation and consequently adjusts it in the general interest.'

The basic principles of feedback – which will be considered later in relation to classroom practice – can be illustrated by considering two processes which, outwardly, seem totally different from each other: the steering of a vessel and the lifting of a pencil.

1. Consider, first, a helmsman steering his craft through a turbulent sea, his eyes fixed now on the stars, now on the faint outline of land ahead, sensitive to each movement of his vessel which he is guiding to a selected harbour. Helmsman and craft form a *system* which has a *goal* (reaching the harbour). The process of

control (steering the craft) is determined by the *response* of the helmsman to the information which reaches him (i.e. his *assessment*) concerning his environment (stars, sea, craft, land).

2. Consider, next, a student intending to lift a pencil from his desk. Hand and eye, brain, nerves and muscles which regulate movement form a *system* which at that moment has a specific *goal* (i.e. lifting the pencil). The hand is *controlled* and guided to the pencil by muscles which act on *signals* coming from the body's central nervous system. Signals from nerve endings in the retina of the student's eye result from *responses to information* presented by the position of the pencil (e.g. how far it is from the desired position) and are fed back to the brain, which *assesses* them and *regulates* the action of muscles in the arm and hand. Here is an example of *informational feedback* by which the student learns the effect of his responses on the environment. (The term '*affective feedback*' is used to refer to an organism learning whether a changed situation will be pleasant or unpleasant.)

From these and other similar activities we may generalize concerning feedback, that:

(a) it is a characteristic of a goal-seeking system (e.g. a class and its teacher);
(b) it arises where a system is furnished with continuous signals as to its environment and its functioning within that environment;
(c) it allows the system to respond to information provided by signals;
(d) it enables a response to be made which results from an assessment of signals and an adjustment of activity in relation to the system's goals.

Feedback has been classified as *positive* or *negative*. (It should be noted that these terms do not indicate value judgments regarding their desirability.)

Positive feedback is a process which results in self-administered *positive* reinforcement of an activity. It is a *source of instability* in a system, which, if not checked, may lead in 'runaway fashion' to a breakdown of that system. A simple example is the explosion of gunpowder resulting from heat produced by the chemical combination of its components, leading to an increase in the rate of combination, with more heat, etc. Sayre gives an example of immediate interest to the teacher: an insecure student who incites teasing from his class because of his apparent vulnerability, leading to an increase in his feeling of inadequacy, leading to intensified adverse attention of his class, etc. In cases of positive feedback there is an increase in the rate of some pattern of activity resulting from performance of the activity; in effect, the activity is reinforcing its own performance.

Negative feedback is a process which should lead to *stability and the possibility of control*. It acts so as to prevent (i.e. *negate*) unwanted deviation of a system from some pre-set norm. An example is the effect of light on the retina: when excitation of the retina exceeds a certain level, the eye's pupil contracts so as to decrease the amount of incoming light. A more familiar classroom example may be found in the swift reaction of an experienced teacher to a question and answer session, the results of which indicate a total misunderstanding by the class of a section of the lesson. Content and presentation of the remainder of the lesson would be adjusted immediately. In these examples a part of the output is fed back, making possible the counteracting and controlling of unacceptable deviations.

Feedback in the classroom

The general classroom situation may be considered in terms of *a system*, i.e. a *set of interrelated elements*, characterized by a particular structure and behaviour. In terms of *structure* it consists, basically, of teacher and students each reacting to the other. Its *behaviour* is that of a goal-seeking body, the goal being, at any given moment, predetermined learning objectives. The teacher's activities are directed to the control (i.e. direction) and *transformation* of the system of which he or she is a part, i.e. the changing of the level of class attainment.[6]

Any teaching activity may be viewed usefully in system terms. A lesson designed to increase typing speeds, a class discussion on the problems of town planning – each may be interpreted as a *directed process* intended to alter some element of the system's components, in these cases the speed of response of students, or their understanding of their environment. A directed process, however, demands that the director be continuously *aware of the state of the system*, its approach to and deviation from its goal. Consider the situation of the motorist rendered temporarily blind because of a shattered windscreen, or the army commander who is out of touch with his forward troops. In each of these cases the knowledge which is necessary for the successful control (perhaps survival) of the system is unavailable. Control and, ultimately, viability of the system come to an end. 'When a system's negative feedback discontinues, its steady state vanishes and at the same time its boundary disappears and the system terminates' (Miller).[7] Analogously, *control of the teaching system (i.e. the teacher and class) demands that the teacher shall know its state and its rate of progress towards its goal.*

The nature of the typical lecture or lesson may make a flow of information feedback difficult or impossible. The lecturer engaged in a one-way communication process can have little knowledge of audience reactions save in a superficial way (see Chapter 25). The teacher confronted with twenty students cannot easily monitor twenty different sets of reactions throughout the lecture or lesson. Circumstances such as these, which in theory and practice reduce the general possibility of feedback and control to a very low level, necessitate extraordinary steps by the teacher if some assessment is to be made practicable.

There is the additional problem for the teacher of recognizing the adequacy or representative nature of feedback signals in the classroom. Suppose a departmental head is informed that enrolment for an evening class is below the required numbers and that another six students must be recruited. Here is simple, unambiguous feedback calling for appropriate control by adjustment. Next, suppose a class teacher has completed a section of her lesson plan dealing with, say, positive integral indices. She is anxious to have feedback concerning the level of learning. She puts a general 'overhead' question to the class: 'Assume that m and n are positive integers; then $a^m \times a^n = ?$' She immediately receives the correct response from a student: a^{m+n}. Does this indicate adequate or representative feedback? How many correct answers are required before she can be assured of 'appropriate' feedback? Has the question been phrased so as to test response without the possibility of guessing? Careful questioning and representative samples of answers may provide the sole indicators of the value of responses as feedback in the classroom in a situation of this nature.

But the lesson plan which does *not* allow for the testing of progress, which omits the use of any corrective device allowing the teacher to 'keep on course', has small chance of success – if that success is to be evaluated by attainment of a desired goal. Explanations interspersed with tests, recapitulations followed by question and answer sessions – these are some of the methods of obtaining the signals of progress without which the class teacher's activities may be compared with those of a blind helmsman.

Control defined

'The process through which the teacher ensures that learning performance conforms to the level of desired performance' – this defines what control in the classroom is *intended to achieve*. What is required, however, is an indication of what control *is*. The following, based on Mockler's explanation of management control,[8] is suggested as a working definition.

> Control in the classroom is a systematic effort to set performance standards, to design feedback systems, to compare actual performance with those predetermined standards, to determine whether there are any deviations and to measure and assess their significance and to take any action required to assure the attainment of learning objectives in the most effective and efficient way.

This definition suggests four steps in classroom control: setting standards and deciding on methods of assessing the learners' performance; measuring those standards and assessing the significance of the results by a process of feedback; deciding on the acceptability or non-acceptability of performance; and taking the appropriate adjustive action.

We differentiate carefully 'control' and 'controls'. As Drucker[9] reminds us: synonyms for controls are 'measurement', 'information', etc.; but the synonym for control is 'direction'. *Controls pertain to means; control pertains to an end*. The essence of controls is their *analytical nature* – they are concerned with what was and is; the essence of control is *normative* – its concern is with what ought to be. In sum, the teacher establishes controls in order that he or she might direct the teaching-learning process efficiently and effectively in accordance with the requirements of lesson objectives.

The elements of control

The role of the teacher which is presented in this text is based on a consideration of the tasks of manager, planner, executive and controller. As *controller*, the teacher undertakes the direction of the lesson, with a defined teaching objective as a goal, and a strategy aimed at attainment of that objective. To that end the teacher requires feedback which enables him or her to adjust future conduct by reference to past performance. The control function is not an end in itself, rather it is the general means by which the teacher and students are able to perform a specified function, i.e., achievement of the lesson objective.

The components of a control system may be enumerated in very general terms as:

(a) a *control characteristic*, i.e. an indicator of the performance for which standards need to be set;
(b) a *sensory device* which observes and measures the control characteristic;
(c) a *control unit* (or comparator) which will compare and assess deviations from the desired goal and bring into play a *corrective device*; and
(d) an *activating unit* which will change the basic operating system.

From a consideration of the processes mentioned in this and the previous chapter there emerge the essential constituents of a control activity, whether in the classroom or elsewhere:

(a) *measurement*;
(b) *assessment*;
(c) *adjustment*.

Control (i.e. direction) cannot be effective in the absence of any one of these activities. Thus, the successful driving of a car (an exercise in precise control) involves continuous cycles of measuring distances, assessing speeds, adjusting the position of levers, so that the car's direction and speed are controlled. Effective staff promotion policy in a business organization necessitates a process of measuring staff performance, assessing that performance in relation to potential, adjusting responsibilities, so that total performance is more effectively controlled. Effective teaching demands a process of *measuring* learning performance, *assessing* it in relation to class objectives, *adjusting* teaching plans where necessary.

Control in the teaching situation: an overview

All the activities constituting control ought to be utilized consciously during the teaching process. The 'output of the system', that is its accomplishment in terms of learner achievement, ought to correspond to the teacher's desired objective. Achievement is, therefore, the 'controlled characteristic' which must be assessed. 'Sensory devices' take the form of tests and similar procedures. The 'control and activating units', which respond to an assessment of the learner's deviation from expected performance, are represented by the teacher's application of corrective action.

Where possible the teacher must first *measure* attainment against objectives. This does not necessarily involve absolute precision, although the more precisely he or she is able to measure a learner's level of attainment at any moment, the more effective will be the quality of the teacher's control. The measurement must focus on *critical aspects* of a performance and must be reliable. If the teacher's measurement can be expressed in numbers (e.g. as a percentage, a deviation from an average, a rank order) then the ensuing assessment may be easier. (Lord Kelvin (1824–1907) reminded us: 'When you can measure what you are speaking of and express it in numbers, you know that on which you are discoursing. But if you cannot measure it and express it in numbers, your knowledge is of a very meagre and unsatisfactory kind.' But remember, too, Whitehead's warning against 'false concreteness'.)

The teacher must then *assess* the significance of his measurement – not always an easy task. Consider the case of a student who has scored over 75 per cent in three successive tests and who suddenly plummets to 20 per cent in the fourth test. Consider a situation in which only half of the members of a class respond adequately to a series of 'snap questions' put in mid-lesson. The assessment of the significance of this kind of signal requires a knowledge of one's objectives, of the students' abilities and of those 'boundaries of toleration' which mark out, at their lower level, a 'danger zone'. Upon the teacher's assessment will depend his or her next actions.

The final stage in a cycle of control procedure is reached when the teacher decides to *adjust* the situation and takes steps to do so. This may require remedial work for an individual student or a swift adjustment of the teaching plan as it relates to an entire class. Control demands that the teacher shall act to reinforce success and correct shortcomings. *It is the ability to react swiftly and appropriately to a changing classroom situation which marks out the teacher who has mastered the technique of lesson control.*

The types of controls necessary to give the teacher effective control should be considered in relation to the specifications favoured by Drucker.

1. They should be *economical*. The fewer controls in the teaching-learning situation, the better.
2. They should be *meaningful*. What is to be measured and assessed must have significance. Trivial events can be ignored. Controls should be related only to the major activity within the classroom – learning, its rate and intensity.
3. They should be *appropriate*. Controls in the classroom should indicate 'the real structure of events' therein. Hence the need for carefully constructed tests which can analyse, as far as is possible, the general level of class attainment.
4. They should be *congruent*. A teacher's controls must be congruent with what he or she is attempting to measure. This is an important principle in relation to phenomena such as student interest, motivation and other highly subjective matters.
5. They must be *timely*. Controls which provide information only after a fairly long interval of time may be of little value to the tutor. Information concerning the nature of class responses has to be available swiftly if it is to assist in immediate control.
6. They must be *simple*. Assessment based on a complicated array of gradings, indexes and deviations is rarely appropriate for control in a swiftly changing classroom situation. Complexity and ambiguity must be avoided if learning is to be monitored.

7. They must be *operational*. This involves controls centred on activity, which present results from which necessary changes may be put into operation.

To summarize, the effective direction of a system involves its overall control by means of an appropriately designed group of controls. In terms of classroom activity, control is the *sine qua non* of attainment of learning objectives, and among the necessary controls is the establishing of conditions which will allow swift adjustment of the teaching-learning system, based on feedback.[10] A system of performance appraisal is essential; where information indicates that performance is deviating in unacceptable fashion from the standard, appropriate corrective action must be taken.

In the next chapter we consider the definition of 'learning objectives' – a concept which is linked closely to effective control in the classroom and which seeks to apply to the instructional process the activities of measuring, assessing and adjusting.

Notes and references

1. See generally for this chapter: *Constructive Control* by W. Newman (Prentice-Hall, 1975); *Control in Organisations* by A.S. Tannenbaum (McGraw-Hill, 1968); *Management Control Systems* by R. Anthony and J. Dearden (Irwin, 1980); *Management* by R. Lussier (South Western, 1997); *Introduction to Management* by R. Pettinger (Macmillan, 1997); *Managing in Further Education: Theory and Practice* by H. Harper (Fulton, 1997).
2. *The Psychology of Learning* (Progress Publications, 1981).
3. For an early classic account, see 'Feedback' by A. Tustin in *Scientific American* (1952, *3*).
4. *Cybernetics and the Philosophy of Mind* (Humanities Press, 1976).
5. *The Logic of Living Systems* (Allen Lane, 1974).
6. See, generally, *Cybernetics* by N. Wiener (Wiley, 1948). For a criticism, see 'Cybernetics and all that' by A. Tustin in *Journal of the Institute of Electrical Engineers* (1955).
7. 'Toward a general theory for the behavioural sciences' in *American Psychologist* (1955, *10*).
8. *The Management Control Process* (Prentice-Hall, 1972).
9. *Managing for Results* (Harper & Row, 1964).
10. See, further, 'System and process of controlling' in *Management* by H. Koontz and H. Weihrich (McGraw-Hill, 1988); 'Controlling' in *Management* by J. Stoner and R. Freeman (Prentice-Hall, 1989).

Chapter 13

The Utilization of Learning Objectives – A Behavioural Approach

If you don't know where you are going, it is difficult to select a suitable means for getting there. After all, machinists and surgeons don't select tools until they know what operation they are going to perform ... Instructors simply function in a fog of their own making unless they know what they want their students to accomplish as a result of their instruction (Mager, 1955).

This chapter sets out an important aspect of the process of *control* in the teaching-learning situation, namely, the formulation of *learning objectives*, the attainment of which provides markers along the road to understanding and mastery. Advocates of the utilization of these objectives argue that their nature and composition help the teacher to plan instruction based on logical sequences of thought, to set out patterns of productive class activities and to specify tests so as to determine whether learning has occurred. Opponents of the theory and practice of objective tests claim that the model of learning upon which the tests are based can rarely assist in the actual *processes* of learning. The arguments presented below are not intended to suggest that there can be no successful instruction without the use of objective tests, for that is, demonstrably, not so. What is set out below is the theory and practice associated with one method of seeking to specify with relative precision the outcomes of the teaching-learning situation.[1]

Aims, goals and objectives

A perusal of many of the texts relating to learning objectives (or, as they are alternatively named, behavioural or performance objectives) indicates a move to a standardized nomenclature which differentiates sharply the three concepts of aims, goals and objectives.

(a) *Aims* are general statements representing ideals or aspirations. Thus, the Schools Council defined the aim of humanities teaching as 'to forward under-standing, discrimination and judgement in the human field'. The Business and Technician Education Council (BTEC) described its fundamental aim as ensur-

158

ing 'that students on BTEC courses develop the necessary competence in their careers in their own, employers' and the national interest'. The National Research Council (USA), in its 1989 report[2] on mathematics education, hoped to achieve the aims of 'making mathematics education significant for all Americans' and 'improving significantly students' mathematical achievement'.

(b) *Goals* describe the actual 'destination' of learning, in general terms. Thus the goal of BTEC (in relation to its aim outlined above) is the provision of a series of appropriate courses leading to BTEC awards.

(c) *Objectives* are statements, often of a quantifiable, operational nature, indicating events from which mastery of desired activities may be correctly inferred. An objective is defined by Mager[3] as 'an intent communicated by a statement describing a proposed change in a learner – a statement of what the learner is to be like when he has successfully completed a learning experience. It is a description of a pattern of behaviour we want the learner to be able to demonstrate'.

The essence of learning objectives

How ought a learning objective to be defined?[3] Given the definition of learning which was adopted in Chapter 1, a learning event may be said to culminate in *a change in the learner's behaviour*. The result of that change may be observed (and learning may be inferred) by noting what the learner *can do*, as compared with what he or she was *unable to do* before the learning event. *A statement which describes what a learner will be able to do on the completion of an instructional process is known as a learning or behavioural objective*. In Bloom's words: 'An objective states an attempt by the teacher to clarify within his own mind or communicate to others the sought-for changes in the learner'. Thus we could state that: following an introductory lesson concerning the carburettor, the learner 'will *name* correctly the different components of the carburettor'; or that, following a unit of instruction relating to the industrial trade cycle, the learner 'will *describe* in their correct sequence the events which make up a trade cycle'. The naming and describing refer to types, or to forms, of *behaviour* from which one can observe whether the objectives of the lessons have been attained, or not.

Lesson notes prepared by student teachers may be required to contain statements of the 'object of the lesson'. Often, however, the 'object' is couched in very wide terms ('... to teach the use of the micrometer'), or in a style which makes its attainment incapable of assessment ('... to instil an appreciation of management techniques'), or in a manner so terse as to render impossible any interpretation of the teacher's precise aims ('Ohm's Law'). This latter statement – 'Ohm's Law' – is no more than an indication of lesson *content*. The other examples of statements of 'the object of the lesson' are really means to ends, rather than ends in themselves. The method of defining and stating objectives which is outlined below is rigorous, precise and based on considering those objectives in terms of *student performance* ('the learner will describe ...'), rather than in terms of teacher performance ('... to teach the use of ...') – see further, p. 162.

Two types of learning objectives will be mentioned.

1. The *general* objective: this is usually stated in terms of that section of the general syllabus which forms the unit of instruction.
2. The *specific* objective: this states the observable behaviour of the student which is expected at the end of the period of instruction.

Examples, based on a course in elementary economics, might read as follows:

General objective: At the end of this period of instruction the student shall apply correctly the basic principles of the theory of economic rent to a consideration of a variety of other economic phenomena.

Specific objectives: The student shall:

(a) state the theory of rent in his or her own words;
(b) distinguish correct and incorrect applications of the theory;
(c) outline the concepts of profit and wages in terms of economic rent.

Further examples, based on an elementary science course, might read as follows:

General objective: Following this lesson the student shall demonstrate correctly an understanding of the properties of carbon dioxide and of its production from chalk by the action of an acid.

Specific objectives: The student shall:

(a) recall and make a sketch of the apparatus used;
(b) specify the process of preparation;
(c) identify three properties of carbon dioxide.

The teaching functions of learning objectives

There are *three* principal teaching functions of behavioural objectives, based on their construction and use in the context of classroom teaching. First, they impose on the teacher the discipline of selecting and formulating the steps which he or she considers necessary in the process of instruction. ('I am sure that one secret of a successful teacher is that he has formulated quite clearly in his mind what the pupil has to know in precise fashion': Whitehead, *The Aims of Education* (1929).) Second, they provide him or her with an overall view of the structure of the instructional task. Third, they present him or her with the basis of a suitable assessment and control procedure in relation to standards (i.e. those indices which indicate a desired outcome).

A statement of objectives presupposes *a planned series of precise instructional steps*. Each step has to be seen as a link in a process; each should be considered as starting from an ascertained level of student performance; each should be planned so as to contribute to a movement of that performance to a higher level. This is not an easy task since it involves the teacher posing and answering repeatedly many questions, including: 'What is the student able to *do* before the instruction commences?' 'What do I want him to be able to *do* after the period of instruction?' 'What resources will be available to the class?' and 'What are the constraints (e.g. time available for instruction)?' Without answers to questions of this kind, the defining of learning objectives will be less than precise.

From the pattern of steps formulated in terms of objectives should emerge the *structure of the lesson* designed to achieve the defined instructional ends. The 'total view' of the lesson, or series of lessons, in terms of ends, of the means to achieve those ends and of the modes of recognition of their attainment, is important because it gives the teacher a 'general line of advance' – a prerequisite for the control of instruction.

A further prerequisite for that control is *assessment* of the student's progress. Such an assessment is built into the very process of formulating learning objectives. Attainment of the learning objective can be recognized and, therefore, assessed and evaluated in terms of student behaviour.[4]

The defining and stating of learning objectives in terms of student attainment

Consider a teacher's statement of the lesson objective in the following terms: 'to show students that no loss of matter accompanies chemical change'. Couched in these terms, the objective presents difficulties of interpretation. It views the outcome of the lesson solely in terms of the *teacher's* activities ('to *show* students . . .') as was noted on p. 159. It does not provide a statement of the desirable outcome of those activities in terms of what *the students* will have learned. A teacher could, in fact, 'show students' an experiment designed to illustrate the indestructibility of matter without their learning anything. As a 'declaration of intent' the statement is of some interest; as a formulation of direction and outcome it is of little value.

Consider next a teacher's statement formulated in terms of *lesson outcome* and viewed from the point of *student attainment*. Assume that the section of the general science syllabus on which the lesson or series of lessons will be based reads, simply: 'indestructibility of matter: simple experiments'. The teacher must interpret this phrase and decide on the appropriate teaching method. He should then state the objectives *in terms of the outcome he would wish to see as the result of his teaching*. Next, the teacher should specify how that outcome can be satisfactorily *demonstrated and evaluated*. The teacher's objectives are therefore stated in terms of an *instructional product* which can be assessed, thus:

General objective: Following the series of lessons, the student will:

(a) understand the meaning of the term 'indestructibility of matter';
(b) evaluate correctly the three experiments to be undertaken together with their results.

Specific objectives: The student will, within a period of 90 minutes, and without the use of books or notes:

(a) recall and define the term 'indestructibility of matter';
(b) illustrate in short essay form the concept, 'all chemical changes take place without loss of matter';
(c) analyse in short essay form the results of the experiment involving the burning of phosphorus in a closed flask;
(d) analyse in note form the results of the experiment involving ...

It will be noted that the general objective as stated above involves 'understanding' and 'correct evaluation'. The product of instruction is then stated in the form of a group of specific objectives, that is certain types of behaviour which will demonstrate to the teacher that the students understand and are able to evaluate correctly. That demonstration allows the teacher to assess their progress in relation to the overall objective. In sum, *objectives ought to be defined and stated in terms of learning outcomes, i.e. student attainment.* In that way their use may contribute to the control of the learning event; that is their real significance.[5]

The stating of specific objectives as learning outcomes

Assume that the general instructional objectives have been selected and formulated. The teacher has now defined the general purpose of the lesson, that is the goal to which he or she and the class should move. Specific objectives must be designated next as precisely as possible on the basis of the teacher's personal experience of instructing in the subject area and in relation to the level of attainment of the class.

More precisely, the statement of specific objectives should take into account the *desired terminal behaviour* which will demonstrate the learner's *attainment* of the objective, the *conditions* under which attainment is to be demonstrated and the *criteria of success* upon which evaluation will be based.

1. *Terminal behaviour. This should be couched in terms of the learning* outcomes which the teacher expects; it will *not* refer to the teacher's aims or course content. The terms should be more precise than those used in the general objective – 'lists', 'defines', 'enumerates', as contrasted with 'comprehends', 'evaluates', 'recognizes'. The *action verb* with which the statement of the specific objective begins ought to refer to *observable behaviour*, e.g.:

    (a) '*defines* correctly the terms "profit" and "interest" '
    (b) '*lists* three of the main points of difference between an inland and a foreign bill'
    (c) '*draws* a diagram illustrating the working of a thermostat'.

    The verbs with which these specific objectives begin introduce *behavioural tasks* which can be *observed and assessed* by the teacher. Each refers to a specific learning outcome which will be related to the wider, general objective.

2. *Conditions under which the behaviour is to be demonstrated.* The specific objectives may be formulated so as to include stimulus conditions and desired constraints. The teacher may wish to specify the information, the equipment, the materials which are to be made available to the student, restrictions of time, etc. This is illustrated in the following extracts from specific objectives:

    (a) 'without the use of calculators...'
    (b) 'with the typewriter keys masked...'
    (c) 'within an examination period of thirty minutes...'

3. *Criteria of success.* These will be stated in accordance with the teacher's experience and intentions. Performance will be evaluated in relation to the criteria. An acceptable 'minimal mastery level' should be stated, as in the following examples:
    (a) '...must state correctly at least three of the four principal points...'
    (b) '...must not make more than five errors in the transcription...'
    (c) '...must list correctly all six procedures...'

(See Chapter 23 for a discussion of 'mastery learning'.)

Two views of the statement of objectives: Mager and Gronlund

In *Preparing Instructional Objectives* (1962, 1984), Mager, a pioneer in the field of the construction of objectives, argues that if instruction is to be successful the teacher must decide where he wants to go; then he must 'create and administer the means of getting there and arrange to find out whether he has arrived'. Specific objectives of instruction must then be written on the following basis.

1. Describe what students will be *doing* when demonstrating their achievement and indicate how the instructor will recognise what they are doing.
2. Identify and name the desired behavioural acts of the students, define the conditions under which the behaviour is to occur and state the criteria for acceptable performance.
3. Construct a separate objective for each learning performance.

In *How to Write and Use Instructional Objectives* (1981), Gronlund suggests that Mager's 'specific objectives' are most useful where students are required to demonstrate knowledge of *factual information*. More advanced types of learning seem to require the construction and use of a different type of objective. Gronlund advocates the use of a two-step approach to the writing of more *general* types of objective. After considering what students have to learn e.g. by analysing syllabus requirements, the following steps should be taken.

1. Formulate *general* instructional objectives that describe the types of behaviour students ought to show so as to demonstrate that they have learned successfully.
2. List, under each general objective, up to five *specific learning outcomes*, ensuring that each begins with an action verb and that each indicates specific observable responses.

Gronlund argues that the reasons for beginning with general objectives are: most learning activities are probably much too complicated to be described in terms of a specific objective for each outcome; Mager's specific objectives tend to encourage the memorization of data only; specific objectives involve long lists which result in restricting the flexibility of the teaching process.

Both types of learning objective outlined above are currently in use in the examinations mounted by colleges of further education.

The selection of objectives

Selection will reflect closely the content and requirements of the syllabus to which the class teacher is working. The selection of wide, general objectives becomes relatively easy when the published syllabus elaborates subject headings, rather than when they are stated tersely in a few words. Compare, for example, the following extracts from two syllabuses relating to commercial studies:

Syllabus A 'The modern office'.
Syllabus B 'The modern office: functions; personnel; organization; mechanization'.

Extract A (typical of those syllabus statements which cause some difficulty for teachers seeking to interpret the precise requirements of examination boards) provides little help in the formulation of precise objectives. In such circumstances objectives ought to be selected after an examination of current commercial practice, previous test papers, appropriate chapters in textbooks and manuals, etc. Extract B suggests immediately a number of relevant objectives.

Curriculum guides may provide a further source of general objectives. They may be obtained from teaching institutes, professional and trade educational bodies and, in some cases, examination boards. A fruitful source of examples of objectives and, in particular, their formulation in terms of classroom practice, may be found in the analytical studies of Bloom and Ebel. The taxonomies of teaching objectives which they and others have produced are outlined in the next chapter.

Two matters must be stressed at this point: first, the selection of objectives must be accompanied by the determination of their priorities in a scheme of instruction; second, the determination of priorities must be related closely to the students' needs as perceived by them *and* their teachers. Hence a list of objectives which is, in content or form, unrealistic from the students' point of view will merely reduce the motivation to learn.

Tyler's two-dimensional 'general objectives'

Tyler[6] advocates, in contrast to those who support the writing and use of specific objectives, a concentration on the design and use of *general objectives*. 'More general objectives are desirable rather than less general objectives.' The most useful way of defining an objective is, according to Tyler, to consider two 'dimensions' – *behaviour* and *content*. 'Behaviour' is described by Tyler as 'the kind of behaviour to be developed in the student'. 'Content' means 'the content or area of life in which the behaviour is to operate'. An object requires, additionally, context. What, asks Tyler, is the precise significance of a behavioural objective requiring a student to 'think rationally'? About what ought he or she to be thinking? What is the value of content devoid of context? What is the learner supposed to *do* with the law of diminishing returns or the calculus? Tyler insists on objectives based on behaviour *and* content.

Mere lists of objectives provide, according to Tyler, no real indication of the very structure of knowledge, with which their compiler ought to be concerned. A useful statement of objectives involves the utilization of a graphic two-dimensional chart so as to discover 'concise sets of specifications'.[7] Along one axis is 'behaviour'; along the other is 'content'. Intersections of vertical and horizontal columns are marked where they suggest a direct relationship between content area and behavioural aspect; absence of a mark suggests absence of such a relationship or the presence of a trivial, immaterial relationship. The marked relationships can be used as the basis for a formulation of course objectives. Tyler suggests that, in general, one year's work in a subject area necessitates seven to fifteen behavioural categories and ten to thirty content categories.

Eisner's 'expressive objectives'

In *Curriculum Evaluation* (1970),[8] Eisner criticizes Mager-type objectives, which he defines as 'objectives which specify unambiguously the particular behaviour (skill, item of knowledge, etc.) the student is to acquire after having completed one or more learning activities'. Objectives of this nature appear to have a limited value. Eisner claims that the outcomes of instruction are too complex and numerous to be encompassed by Mager-style objectives. The quality of learning that stems from student-teacher interaction is very difficult to predict, so that the teacher cannot specify, with any accuracy, behavioural goals in advance of instruction. Further, there are subject areas in which the specification of learning objectives is impossible, even if it were desirable. How can one state criteria and objectives in arts subjects? And what of instruction in these areas which yields unpredictable, yet desirable, behaviour which comes as a surprise to teacher and learner? Most of the outcomes of instruction, Eisner argues, need not be specified in advance. The teacher ought not to ask: 'What am I trying to accomplish?' Rather the teacher ought to ask: 'What am I going to *do*?' From the doing will stem the accomplishment. ('We can only know after the fact what we wanted to accomplish.')

Eisner suggests the use of *expressive objectives* in addition to instructional objectives. An expressive objective describes 'an educational encounter': it does not specify the behaviour a student is expected to demonstrate after having participated in learning activities. It is 'evocative rather than prescriptive'; it serves as 'a theme around which a student's earlier-acquired skills can be extended and elaborated'. The reflection made necessary by the expressive objective should result in cognitive development aimed at 'the production of the new' rather than mere 'repetition of the known'. Eisner gives examples of expressive objectives:

- to interpret the meaning of Milton's *Paradise Lost*;
- to develop a three-dimensional form through the use of wire and wood.

The controversy on learning objectives

The principles and use of learning objectives (also known as behavioural objectives) in the classroom have attracted the severe criticism which is levelled against perceived manifestations of behaviourism, such as programmed instruction (see Chapter 29). Education, the anti-behaviourists emphasize, is a process, the outcome of which can be neither defined nor measured in strict behavioural terms. (Objection has been raised, also, to the 'input-output' formulations of some advocates of learning objectives; it has been stated, for example, that 'the terminology of the production line is inappropriate to describe the process of instruction'.) To suggest that overt behaviour is the sole criterion of a learner's cognitive attainment is to miss, it is argued, the 'real point' of education. Further, it is claimed that the learning outcome, by its very nature, defies the precise, quantitative analysis upon which the theory and use of learning objectives rest. To attempt to formulate this outcome in exact terms is, it is claimed, to trivialize the important ends of instruction. How does one 'measure' emotional development or personal enrichment? There is a fear, too, that the minimum requirements of a learning objective may become the maximum level of attainment, so that innovation and exploration could be discouraged.

Hogben[9] has drawn attention to the practical problems of drawing up objectives. He refers to the sheer number of statements and the considerable expenditure of time which would be involved in translating a curriculum into behavioural terms and emphasizes that the type and quality of much classroom learning is largely unpredictable, so that objectives cannot always be stated realistically in advance of the lesson. There is more to education, he urges, than objectives that can be stated unambiguously in terms of student behaviour. In particular, 'responsive diversity' must be encouraged. He makes five suggestions: first, that although some course objectives can be stated, they need not be framed in specific, behavioural terms; second, that long-term objectives (which may not become apparent to students until long after the end of a course) ought to be stated; third, that unexpected and unintended outcomes ought not to be ignored; fourth, that the objectives in their totality ought to mirror the goals which generated them; finally, that objectives which cannot be easily assessed ought not to be ignored in the building of a curriculum.

Popham[10] lists the following arguments against the validity of behavioural objectives. Because trivial learner behaviour is the easiest to cast in the form of objectives, the really important outcomes of education may not receive appropriate emphasis. The stating of explicit goals prevents advantage being taken of those opportunities unexpectedly occurring during a lesson. Behavioural changes are not the only type of important educational outcome. Further, in some subject areas (the fine arts, for example) it is very difficult to identify measurable student behaviour. Finally, measurability generally implies accountability, and teachers might be judged on ability to change behaviour alone.

Macdonald-Ross[11] maintains that most of the claims advanced in favour of the use of instructional objectives are false. If the meaning of the word 'education' is to be taken seriously, then the mere observation of a student's actions cannot be used in order to prescribe objectives of an educational nature. There are no well-defined prescriptions for the derivation of objectives. Defining objectives before the event often conflicts with 'the spirit of exploration' which should characterize the learning process. Unpredicted classroom events cannot be utilized fully in the context of pre-specified goals; indeed, in some disciplines appropriate criteria can be considered only after the instructional event.

Lists of behaviours, argues Macdonald-Ross, do not constitute an adequate reflection of the real structure of knowledge: knowledge (and 'understanding') involve a coherence of ideas, an articulated set of concepts which form a unified whole. Lists of behaviour objectives can make no contribution to understanding structures.[12]

Macdonald-Ross cites with approval the criticisms of Cronbach in 'Test valida-tion' (1971),[13] suggesting that persons who accept the validity of the use of behavioural objectives are denying 'the appropriateness and usefulness of con-structs' (i.e. theoretical terms). Constructs cannot be defined by lists of specific responses to situations because, by their nature, constructs are intended to have application to situations which may arise at some future time and which cannot be specified at the time of the behavioural objective test.

Jarvis[14] states that the usefulness of objectives in cognitive learning courses is questionable and 'contrary to the overall philosophy of adult learning'. Objectives stated in behavioural terms tend to carry the implication that a student is to behave in a manner set out by the teacher, 'like a pigeon or rat'. To designate the manner in which a learner is expected to behave is to undermine his or her dignity.

The case against the use of learning objectives has been summed up in meta-phoric terms thus:

> Education is an exciting journey, the precise destination of which cannot be known in advance. It recognises no bounds, it cannot be constrained by paths and exactly marked roads. It needs no compass, no guide other than the sun, moon and stars. Maps and milestones rob the journey of its real meaning. Those who make the journey must be allowed to wander as they will, to use roads only when they wish, to walk into unknown territory if they so desire. It is better to journey hopefully than to arrive and the exciting prospects of discovery must be allowed to every traveller.

Oakeshott[15] will not accept that the 'goal-directed' model of instruction is valid. He attacks the 'journey analogy' which he perceives as central to the concept of behavioural objectives. Why should we suppose that the analogy of a journey towards a prefigured destination is of any relevance? Such an analogy has no relevance in endeavours such as art, science, poetry and human life in general, but they are not to be considered, therefore, as 'pointless activities'.

In answer, it has been emphasized that the basic rationale of learning objectives takes into account the effective utilization of scarce human and other resources so as to achieve desired ends; this is impossible to attain save by reference to standards and criteria of achievement. It is arguably more interesting to travel hopefully than to arrive, but it is vital to know one's destination and necessary to be able to recognize it. It is also of importance that travellers should not be exposed unnecessarily to the hazards of falling by the wayside and never completing the journey. Nor may we ignore the fact that most educational travellers have a very limited time in which to complete a very arduous journey. The lesson viewed as a planned, exciting journey, with instructional objectives used as milestones along the route, in no way removes the wonder of learning and the satisfaction which comes with achievement. Further, the use of objectives does not necessarily destroy the spontaneity of class response which can enrich a lesson. Nor does it prevent a teacher effectively utilizing the side winds, the unexpected issues, which often arise during a lesson.

In response to the criticism that the principles of behavioural objectives are suspect because they are derived from the principles of behaviourist psychology (see Chapter 4), it has been pointed out that this is based on a confusion, since cognitive psychologists (see Chapter 8) may also infer a student's learning from his or her behaviour. The use of the adjective 'behavioural' in relation to objectives, or other aspects of educational practice, should not be taken as evidence of the user's total adherence to non-cognitive theories of learning.

If a lesson is viewed as an unprepared activity, with no discernible objective, if its content is to be determined by whim and its course by improvization on the spur of the moment, learning goals may be thought irrelevant. If, however, the efficiency of the instructional process is to be tested solely by its success in leading students to desirable goals, then those goals ought to be stated as accurately as possible and the paths of their attainment ought to be charted with precision. The use of learning objectives may contribute to that end.

Learning objectives in the classroom: some practical matters

The following points relating to the use of objectives in the classroom are among those reiterated frequently by teachers in further education who have experimented with the design of curricula.

1. The use of learning objectives in the classroom may involve a complete break with some traditional views of teaching; it necessitates a highly structured and carefully planned instructional activity in which the teacher plays a clearly predominant role.
2. Planning a scheme of objectives is all-important. The objectives, which must never be of a trivial nature or focus narrowly on data or neglect the higher levels of cognitive learning, must be planned and listed in schematic, sequential form on the basis of perhaps two to five per lesson. To have as few objectives as

possible, given the specific demands of the unit of instruction, is a useful practice. (Note the view of Gage[16] that it is not necessary to specify *every* student behaviour that is required, just as roadmaps, to be useful, need not specify every town and stream between points A and B.)

3. The use of time must be planned carefully. Periods of at least 45 minutes seem to be needed where objectives are in use.

4. Gagné emphasizes that the designer of a pattern of objectives must take decisions on whether the *purpose* of the lesson has been kept in mind, whether the planned lesson displays an appropriate *balance* of expected outcomes, and whether the types of objective are *matched* correctly to the selected approach to instruction.

5. Students should be informed carefully of the purpose of this type of instruction, and should be made aware of the relationship of objectives to the subject *as a whole*. Where it is possible to issue lists of learning objectives at the beginning of a session, motivation can be heightened; the objectives can act as a useful reference point, checklist and self-test material for students.

6. Instruction by the use of detailed learning objectives may make unusually heavy demands on a class. Concentrated effort is required from students for extended periods, and control of the class may throw a heavy burden on the teacher. It is advisable that a lesson based on the use of learning objectives be 'broken up' by short 'buzz groups', for example.

7. Failure to attain an objective is not to be viewed by teacher or students as a catastrophe. The aphorism suggesting that 'an unattained objective is an incorrectly drawn objective' is unhelpful: it does not take into account, for example, the phenomenon of unexpected and uncontrollable 'noise' in communication channels (see p. 144).

8. Consideration should be given to the concept of behavioural objectives as providing indicators of progress along roads rather than as terminal points of travel.

9. Complete records of student achievement in relation to tests involving the use of objectives ought to be kept.

Notes and references

1. See generally for this chapter: *Development and Evolution of Behavioural Objectives* by R.J. Armstrong *et al.* (Brown, 1970); 'Formulating and selecting educational objectives' by B.S. Bloom in *Evaluation to Improve Learning* (McGraw-Hill, 1981); *Objectives in Curriculum Design* by I.K. Davies (McGraw-Hill, 1976); 'Preparing instructional objectives' by N. Gronlund in *Measurement and Evaluation in Teaching* (Collier-Macmillan, 1981); *Writing Worthwhile Behavioural Objectives* by J. Vargas (Harper & Row, 1972); 'Curriculum objectives' in *Knowledge and the Curriculum* by P.H. Hirst (Routledge, 1975).

2. *Notices of the American Mathematical Society* (36, 3).

3. See e.g. *Preparing Instructional Objectives* by R.F. Mager (Pitman, 1962, 1984).

4. See *Writing Behavioural Objectives – A New Approach* by H. McAshan (McKay, 1970); 'Which objectives are most worthwhile?' by D. Rowntree in *Aspects of Educational Technology* (Pitman, 1973).

5. See *Mathematics Behavioural Objectives* by J.C. Flanagan *et al.* (Westinghouse, 1971).

6. *Basic Principles of Curriculum and Instruction* (Chicago UP, 1949); 'Some persistent questions on the defining of objectives' in *Defining Educational Objectives* ed. C. Lindvall (Pittsburgh UP, 1964).

7. See Tyler (*op. cit.*, 1964).

8. *American Educational Research Association Monograph Series on Curriculum Evaluation* (McNally Rand, 1970).

9. 'The behavioural objectives approach: some problems and some dangers' in *Journal of Curriculum Studies* (1972, *4*).

10. 'Probing the validity of arguments against behavioural objectives' in *Behavioral Objectives and Instruction* by R. Kibler *et al.* (Allyn & Bacon, 1970).

11. *Instructional Science* (Elsevier, 1973).

12. See also, e.g. 'Some limitations on the use of objectives in curriculum research and planning' by L. Stenhouse in *Paedagogica Europaea* (1970, *6*); 'Behavioural objectives? No!' by G. Keller in *Educational Leadership* (1972).

13. In *Educational Measurement* ed. R.L. Thorndike (American Council on Education, 1971).

14. *Adult and Continuing Education* (Routledge, 1996).

15. *Rationalism in Politics* (Macmillan, 1962).

16. See *Educational Psychology* by N.L. Gage and D.C. Berliner (Rand McNally, 1979).

Chapter 14

Taxonomies of Learning Objectives

It appears that by our very nature we are classifying creatures, that is, we categorise our observations based on patterns of similarities (Langenheim, 1987).

A useful setting in which to consider the problems of definition and statement of learning objectives, which were raised in the previous chapter, is provided by the types of classification known as *taxonomies*.[1] Taxonomy refers to a formal classification (*taxis* = arrangement, *nomia* = distribution) based on perceived relationships. Classifications of this type are used extensively in the biological sciences in which organisms are grouped and classified on the basis of class, order, genus, species, etc. Lower classes are subordinated to higher until, finally, the *summum genus*, or most inclusive category with which the science is concerned, is reached.[2]

The most widely known and influential taxonomy of learning objectives is that associated with the name of the American psychologist, Bloom, of the University of Chicago. It was first set out in 1951 at a symposium of the American Psychological Association at Chicago, entitled 'The Development of a Taxonomy of Educational Objectives'. 'Bloom's taxonomy' (as it has come to be known) continues to be of much importance for the teacher in further education since its influence may be discerned in areas such as syllabus and examination paper construction, objective tests, schemes of marking and evaluation, and the identification of training needs in industry and commerce.

Caution is necessary in interpreting Bloom's use of the term 'taxonomy'; in most areas of science it refers to a strictly ordered classification of objects and phenomena. The categories which Bloom classifies (e.g. 'knowledge', 'synthesis') are neither objects nor phenomena in the usual scientific sense; they cannot be identified, inspected and argued over as can, say, the botanical specimens referred to in a Linnaean classification. It is one thing to classify *Magnolia grandiflora* as a representative of the order *Ranales* (according to Bessey) and give it a precise place in the botanical hierarchy; it is quite another to attempt to place 'analysis' or 'appraisal' at a particular level within an appropriate 'family' or 'category'. Further, it must be remembered that classifications are essentially the result of human processes of thought in defining properties of sets or classes before naming them.[3] The great classifiers, Li Shih-Chen (1518–93)[4] and Linnaeus (1707–78), for example, when engaged in the construction of a taxonomy, were reacting to objects subjectively, albeit in organized fashion. The assumptions of any classification or taxonomy may reflect personal attitudes and values, concepts and perspectives; they are not necessarily aspects of objective reality.

The background to Bloom's taxonomy

'Curriculum theory' in the USA has long been concerned with the search for 'reliable' educational objectives. Thus, Bobbitt, a pioneer in curriculum theory, argued in *The Curriculum* (1918), that the teacher's task is to study life so as to discover the 'abilities, habits, appreciations and forms of knowledge that men need'. These would form the objectives of a curriculum which would be based on the skills needed for their attainment. In *How to Make a Curriculum* (1924) he enumerated 160 educational objectives classified in nine areas. For Bobbitt, an effective curriculum necessitated the clear formulation of specific instructional objectives.

Following a meeting of American college examiners at Boston in 1948, it was decided to mount a series of discussions on the formulation of a theoretical framework to be used to facilitate communication among examiners. Out of these discussions emerged the goal of a systematized classification of educational objectives. The classification was to be derived from three sets of principles, educational, logical and psychological. Value judgments concerning objectives and behaviour were to be avoided. The use of a *taxonomy* might assist teachers in labelling their objectives in terms of 'properties' and in obtaining ideas as to the most appropriate sequences in which objectives should be placed.

Three important questions were raised early in the discussions. First, was it really possible to classify educational objectives? Second, would the availability and use of an educational taxonomy result in stultifying the thinking and planning of class teachers in matters concerning the content of the curriculum? Third, might not the use of a taxonomy lead to an undesirable fragmentation of educational purposes which ought to be considered as integrated wholes?

The first problem was met by the assertion that educational objectives could be expressed adequately in behavioural terms. The second was answered by an expression of hope that the very consideration of a taxonomy would help teachers in their work in the wide field of relating curriculum objectives and teaching procedures. The third question was recognized as embodying a real and very deep fear and was countered by the assertion that, if the taxonomy were to be stated in general terms, educational purpose should not be affected too seriously.

The essence of Bloom's taxonomy

Bloom's taxonomy comprises *general and specific categories* which embrace intended goal behaviours, i.e., the likely outcomes of instruction. What was being classified, Bloom insisted, was the 'intended behaviour' of students – the ways in which they are to act, think or feel 'as the result of participating in some unit of instruction'. The taxonomy would assist in explicit formulations of 'the ways in which students are expected to be changed by the educative process'.[5]

Three major divisions, or *domains*, are delineated:

1. *the cognitive*
2. *the affective*
3. *the psychomotor.*

The cognitive domain is concerned largely with information and knowledge. The affective domain relates to attitudes, emotions and values. The psychomotor domain involves muscular and motor skills.

The cognitive domain

This domain is based on a continuum ranging from mere knowledge of facts to the intellectual process of evaluation. Each category within the domain is assumed to include behaviour at the lower levels. There are six major categories within this domain; they comprise a hierarchy based on a growth in the level of quality, and the higher levels are assumed to be founded on the skills of the lower levels.

1. *Knowledge.* This is based on recall and methods of dealing with recalled information. It comprises:

   (a) knowledge of specifics (terminology and specific facts);
   (b) knowledge of ways and means of dealing with specifics (conventions, trends and sequences, classifications and categories, criteria and methodology);
   (c) knowledge of the universals and abstractions in a field (principles and generalizations, theories and structures).

2. *Comprehension.* This is the ability to grasp and utilize the meaning of material. It embraces 'translation' from one form to another (e.g. words to numbers), interpretation (e.g. explaining, summarizing), and extrapolation (predicting effects, consequences).
3. *Application.* This involves the ability to utilize learned material *in new situations*. It necessitates the application of principles, theories, rules, etc.
4. *Analysis.* This involves the ability to break down learned material into component parts so that organizational structure is made clear. The analysis of relationships and the identification of the parts of a whole are vital.
5. *Synthesis.* This refers to the ability to combine separate elements so as to form 'a new whole'. Deduction and other aspects of logical thought are involved.
6. *Evaluation.* This concerns the ability to judge the value of material, with such judgments to be based on definite criteria or standards.

The affective domain

This domain[6] is 'attitudinal' in concept and ranges very widely, from heeding the simple reception of stimuli to the complex ability to characterize by the use of value concepts. There are five major categories within the domain.

1. *Receiving.* This involves 'attending', that is, heeding messages or other stimuli. Awareness, willingness to attend and controlled attention are subsumed under this heading.
2. *Responding.* This involves the arousal of curiosity and the acceptance of responsibility in relation to response.
3. *Valuing.* This involves recognition of the intrinsic worth of a situation so that motivation is heightened and beliefs emerge.
4. *Organizing and conceptualizing.* This involves the patterning of responses on the basis of investigation of attitudes and values, and the beginning of the building of an internally consistent value system.
5. *Characterizing by value or value concept.* This involves the ability to see as a coherent whole matters involving ideas, attitudes and beliefs.

The psychomotor domain

This domain involves the motor skills. No report has yet appeared from the committee set up to study this field, but some suggestions have been made, based on Bloom's general approach. Harrow's taxonomy[7] based on this domain is as follows.

1. *Reflex movements.* These are the involuntary motor responses to stimuli. They are the basis for all types of behaviour involving bodily movement.
2. *Basic fundamental movements.* These are inherent movement patterns built upon simple reflex movements.
3. *Perceptual abilities.* These assist learners to interpret stimuli so that they can adjust to the environment. Visual and auditory discrimination is an example.
4. *Physical abilities.* These are the essential foundation for skilled movement. Speed, exertion and flexibility are examples.
5. *Skilled movements.* These are the components of any efficiently performed, complex movement. They cannot be acquired without learning, and necessitate practice.
6. *Non-discursive communication.* This comprises the advanced behaviours involved in the type of communication relating to movement, such as ballet. Movement becomes aesthetic and creative at this level of the domain.

Simpson[8] proposes an alternative classification of objectives in the psychomotor domain, based on seven categories.

1. *Perception.* This involves the use of the learner's sense organs in order to obtain

those cues essential for the guidance of motor activity, i.e. sensory stimulation, cue selection, translation (of sensory cases into a motor activity).

2. *Set*. The state of readiness for the performance of a certain action, i.e. mental, physical and emotional sets.
3. *Guided response*. This necessitates performance under the general guidance of an optimal performance model and involves imitation, trial and error.
4. *Mechanism*. The ability to perform a task repeatedly with an acceptable degree of proficiency.
5. *Complex, overt response*. The performance of a task with a high degree of proficiency.
6. *Adaptation*. The use of previously acquired skills so as to perform novel tasks.
7. *Origination*. The creation of a new style performance of a task after the development of skills.

Bloom's taxonomy and instructional objectives: an application

Examples of general and specific instructional objectives (in an economics course) based on the cognitive domain are given below.

1. Category: *knowledge*
(General objective) At the end of the period of instruction the student will know the principal functions of cheques.
(Specific objectives) The student will:

    (a) define a cheque;
    (b) state to which class of document it belongs;
    (c) list the parties to a cheque ...

2. Category: *comprehension*
At the end of the period of instruction the student will understand the principle of diminishing utility. The student will:

    (a) explain the principle in his or her own words;
    (b) illustrate the principle by means of a graph ...

3. Category: *application*
At the end of the period of instruction the student will apply principles so as to predict the effects of some specified changes in the variables constituting the quantity equation of exchange. The student will:

    (a) demonstrate in the form of a graph the result of increased supplies of money on the level of prices;
    (b) relate changes in the volume of trade to changes in the general level of prices ...

4. Category: *analysis*

At the end of the period of instruction the student will analyse the assumptions in an article on the Eurocurrency in *The Financial Times*. The student will:

(a) identify the assumptions of the writer in terms of economic principles;
(b) criticize those assumptions...

5. Category: *synthesis*

At the end of the period of instruction the student will formulate one internally consistent hypothesis relating data on wage rates and unemployment. The student will:

(a) design a simple mathematical model illustrating the relationship;
(b) discuss the relationship using appropriate quantitative terms...

6. Category: *evaluation*

At the end of the period of instruction the student will evaluate the weight of a given argument on population and agricultural development. The student will:

(a) identify the positive and normative statements in the argument;
(b) appraise the basis of the argument in terms of economic principle...

Verbs used in the specification of objectives

Given the behavioural basis of Bloom's taxonomy, the verbs which may be used for the specification of learning objectives are of particular importance. Since the objective states what the student will be *doing* as the result of the learning event, a precise *action verb* must be selected. Commonly used verbs are as follows:

1. *knowledge*: lists, names, describes, states, measures, labels, recalls;
2. *comprehension*: identifies, illustrates, explains, classifies, indicates;
3. *application*: performs, uses, manipulates, assesses, changes, demonstrates;
4. *analysis*: analyses, discriminates, criticizes, infers, concludes;
5. *synthesis*: combines, discusses, argues, derives, reconstructs, designs;
6. *evaluation*: supports, attacks, defends, appraises, judges, justifies, clarifies.[9]

It should be noted that some behavioural-type verbs, such as 'identify' can be used correctly at a variety of levels. Thus, 'to identify' a correct definition, 'to identify' a novel situation and 'to identify' the component parts of a complex sentence, may belong to the categories of knowledge, application and analysis respectively. Hence the use in a statement of objectives of a particular verb will not in itself indicate a particular level in the hierarchy which makes up the taxonomy. Gagné[10] suggests that the verbs used in statements of tasks be utilized 'to imply the capability (learning outcome) that they involve'.

Other taxonomies

Ebel[11] is one of several educationists who have put forward taxonomies which appear to be simpler than Bloom's classification. His taxonomy is based on the following:

1. understanding terms
2. understanding facts, generalisations
3. ability to explain or illustrate
4. ability to calculate
5. ability to predict
6. ability to recommend an appropriate course of action
7. ability to evaluate.

Matten, of the Associated Examining Board, formulated the following taxonomy which, although produced specifically in relation to economics, has a very much wider application:

1. recall of information other than principles or terminology
2. recall of terminology
3. recall of principles
4. comprehension (direct interpretation) of statistics or diagrams
5. comprehension of principles
6. application of a principle (numerical) to a theoretical situation
7. application of a principle (diagrammatic) to a theoretical situation
8. application of a principle (linguistic) to a theoretical situation
9. application of more than one principle to a theoretical situation
10. synthesis of principles and background information to 'real' situations
11. evaluation of theoretical situations
12. evaluation of 'real' situations.

Sullivan,[12] in an argument directed *against* Bloom's taxonomy, presents an alternative system, based on six categories of 'performance terms' which will allow the classification of those behaviours relative to the cognitive tasks involved in learning:

1. identifying
2. naming
3. describing
4. constructing
5. ordering
6. demonstrating.

Gronlund[13] provides a hierarchy comprising nine *learning outcomes*, which he uses to delineate the principal areas in which instructional objectives could be classified:

1. knowledge
2. understanding
3. application
4. thinking skills (critical and scientific)
5. general skills (e.g. communication, social, computational)
6. attitudes (social, scientific)
7. interests (personal, educational, vocational)
8. appreciations (literature, music, etc.)
9. adjustments (social, emotional).

Gagné[14] proposes a five-category taxonomy of learned capabilities from which instructional objectives may be constructed.

1. Intellectual skills (discrimination, identification, classification, demonstration, problem solving).
2. Cognitive strategies (encoding, retrieval of complex material, i.e. 'the internally directed control processes that regulate and moderate other learning processes').
3. Verbal information (i.e. 'knowledge consisting of propositions that are semantically meaningful').
4. Motor skills (i.e. execution of coordinated movements).
5. Attitudes (i.e. choice of personal actions that a learner is expected to exhibit).

The value of Bloom's taxonomy to the teacher

Criticisms of Bloom's taxonomy[15] have tended to be based on three grounds; first, that since it is formulated in behavioural terms, it is derived from the 'fallacious view' of learning inherent in behaviourism; second, that it is derived from a naïve and, therefore, inadequate theory of human knowledge; third, that its cognitive/ affective dichotomy is unreal and, therefore, an unsafe guide to instruction.

The taxonomy clearly accepts learning as a response to stimuli, the desired response being the behavioural outcome, or objective. The armoury of anti-behaviourist arguments has been drawn on heavily for an attack on the implicit assertions of the taxonomy. In general, Bloom has been reminded that educational objectives should not be merely behavioural, and that outcome ought not to be equated necessarily with learning. Conceivably, one may learn without being able to convey to another evidence of having learned. Assessed behaviour, it is argued, ought not to be accepted as the only reliable indicator of the attainment of those goals set by a teacher. The taxonomy is condemned, therefore, as simplistic and inadequate as a guide for the class teacher.

A more fundamental criticism of the taxonomy arises in response to its view of human knowledge. Bloom, it has been argued, has ignored much of the contemporary analysis of the cognitive processes associated with epistemology (that is, the study of the nature, methods and validity of human knowledge, which seeks to answer fundamental questions such as: 'What does it mean to say that "one knows"?' or 'By what means can knowledge be acquired?').[16] Consider the first category in the cognitive domain – knowledge. Has 'knowledge' any real significance in isolation from 'comprehension' and 'application'? Can a student be said to have 'knowledge' of Pythagoras' theorem if he or she is able to recall the precise wording of the theorem, but is unable to use it to solve a simple problem requiring the calculation of the length of the hypotenuse? Does a student 'know' the functions of money if able to recall faultlessly the textbook explanation, but unable to explain whether credit cards are or are not 'money'? 'Knowledge' of the name of the discoverer of 'dephlogisticated air' stands on a different level from that occupied by 'knowledge' of the motives of the Birmingham mob which burned his laboratory and house in 1791. (Consider the precise significance of the word 'know' in the following statements: 'I know his name'; 'I always know when it's time for lunch'; 'I think I know what he means'; 'I know that my Redeemer liveth'. The celebrated translator, Ronald Knox,[17] has written of the difficulty in translating 'know'.)

Bloom's separation of the cognitive and affective domains has been criticized for its reliance on a false dichotomy. Gribble,[18] writing on objectives in literary education, claims that a disjunction between 'cognitive' and 'affective' objectives in education is logically incoherent, and that it is unintelligible to propound 'the education of the emotions' as an aim independent of cognitive development. Bloom fails to see, it is argued, that the cognitive activity of 'judging' is the crucial factor in determining the adequacy of an affective response. Every emotional response involves a judgment, an appraisal of a situation, a perception of some feature of the situation, i.e. some kind of cognition. The attainment of educational objectives in the affective domain 'is necessarily related to the cognitive core of the affective responses, to the appropriateness of the way the object of the affective response is perceived'. More specifically, 'evaluation' (see point 6 of the cognitive domain on p. 173), which comprises cognitive operations, is a logically necessary part of educational objectives in the affective domain of literary studies. Some educationists[19] advocate the doctrine of 'confluence in education' based on the interrelationship and 'flowing together' of the cognitive and affective dimensions of learning; the doctrine stresses the difficulties of isolating intellectual from emotional experiences and calls for recognition of their common factors when lessons are planned.

Advocates of Bloom's taxonomy retort that, in spite of a perceived lack of empirical validation of the hierarchical structure and its domains (which, it is admitted, may mirror the compiler's intuitive, subjective attitudes to matters such as 'sequencing'), it provides, nevertheless, *an organized framework within which objectives can be stated and classified* with some precision. If the defining of goals is accepted as sound educational practice, a taxonomy such as Bloom's is needed to translate those goals into more specific forms. The taxonomy has given, they claim, an intensive stimulus to the search for a means of stating syllabus content in a balanced way and, by grouping together objectives of a similar nature, has made the formulation of instructional strategies easier. Such groupings have assisted in the arranging of sequential units of instruction. The taxonomy obliges examiners to keep in mind that most searching question: *'What are we testing?'* It has acted as a warning against ambiguity in the definition of learning objectives and has assisted in the construction of statements of goals which enable teachers to evaluate attainment by reference to a yardstick – albeit not perfect. Its detailed analysis of the outcomes of instruction provides a new vantage point from which the content of the syllabus and the examiner's scheme might be surveyed and scrutinized in detail.

Bloom's taxonomy may assist the teacher in answering the fundamental questions: *'In what ways should my students have changed as the result of my teaching, and what evidence can I accept as proof of that change?'* The very posing and consideration of these questions may constitute a step towards the provision of some of the essential conditions for effective learning.[20]

Notes and references

1. See generally for this chapter: *Taxonomy of Educational Objectives: Handbook I – the Cognitive Domain* ed. B.S. Bloom (Longman, 1956); *Taxonomy of Educational Objectives: Handbook II – the Affective Domain* ed. N. Krathwohl (Longman, 1964); *Handbook on Formative and Summative Evaluation of Student Learning* by B.S. Bloom et al. (McGraw-Hill, 1971); *Objectives in Curriculum Design* by I. Davies (McGraw-Hill, 1976); *Stating Behavioural Objectives for Classroom Instruction* by N. Gronlund (Collier-Macmillan, 1970); *Educational Psychology* by R. Slavin (Prentice-Hall, 1988); *Psychology Applied to Learning* by R. Biehler (Houghton Mifflin, 1993).
2. See e.g. 'Classificatory procedures' in *The Arch of Knowledge* by D. Oldroyd (Methuen, 1986).
3. See 'Taxonomy as a source of error' by K. Boulding in *Methodus*, June 1990. 'Taxonomy involves the setting up of a series of named "boxes" into which we put our images of the individual objects or realities of the world ... The test of a taxonomy is whether things that are very much alike are put into one box or whether things that are alike are divided among many boxes.'
4. See *Science and Civilisation in China, Vol. VI, No. 1* by J. Needham (CUP, 1986).
5. See 'Testing cognitive ability and achievement' in *Handbook of Research on Teaching* ed. N. Gage (Rand McNally, 1963).
6. See Krathwohl (*op. cit.*); *Behavioural Objectives and Instruction* by R. Kibler (Allyn & Bacon, 1970).
7. *A Taxonomy of the Psychomotor Domain* (McKay, 1972).
8. *Psychomotor Domain: A Tentative Classification* (Illinois UP, 1969).
9. For a detailed list, see Gronlund (*op. cit.*).
10. 'Learning analysis' in *The Conditions of Learning* (Holt-Saunders, 1985).
11. *Essentials of Educational Measurement* (Prentice-Hall, 1979).
12. 'Objectives, evaluation and improved learner achievement' in *American Educational Research Monographs on Curriculum Evaluation* (Rand McNally, 1969).
13. *Measurement and Evaluation in Teaching* (Collier-Macmillan, 1965).
14. *Principles of Instructional Design* (Holt, Rinehart & Winston, 1988).
15. See e.g. 'Bloom's taxonomy: a philosophical critique' by H. Sockett and R. Pring in *Cambridge Journal of Education* (1971, *1*, 2).
16. See e.g. *Knowing and the Known* by A. Bentley (Beacon, 1949); *Conditions of Knowledge – An Introduction to Epistemology and Education* by I. Scheffler (Scott, Foresman, 1961).

17. *Trials of a Translator* (Sheed & Ward, 1949).
18. *Literary Education: A Revaluation (CUP, 1983).*
19. See e.g. *The Live Classroom* by G.I. Brown (Viking Press, 1975).
20. See 'Instructional objectives' in *Teaching for Learning* by M.H. Dembo (Goodyear, 1981); *With Objectives in Mind* by L. Enever and W. Harlen (Macdonald, 1972).

Part Four

Managing the Teaching-Learning Process

Chapter 15

The Teacher as Manager

It is the purpose of organisation and, therefore, the grounds of management authority, to make human strength productive. Organisation is the means through which man, as an individual and as a member of the community, finds both contribution and achievement (Drucker, 1974).

In Part Three, the teacher is considered as 'communicator' and 'controller'. These roles – at the very centre of the teaching process – are but aspects of a wide responsibility which may be described as 'the management of the instructional process'. In the chapters comprising Part Four, the teacher is considered as the *manager* of a situation in which effective teaching is expected to produce a desired standard of learning.[1] This requires from the teacher the exercise of certain functions broadly associated with management, in the formal sense of that term. Provisionally, we define management in Follett's words: 'the art of getting things done through people'.[2]

We are not discussing 'administration', i.e. those aspects of control, associated in a college with the duties of the director, departmental heads and registrar. We are examining *the professional role and responsibilities of the individual tutor in the light of management theory*. Specifically, we investigate later the teacher-manager's tasks in relation to environment, syllabus and course design, the retention, retrieval of knowledge and transfer of learning, the tasks necessary in order to teach students how to study, the maintenance of discipline, counselling, and the teaching of older students. In these complex tasks, the teacher is seen as managing a *system* of which he or she is a part; the teacher is directing an organization, viewed as a unified set of interacting parts.

In essence, this chapter rests on extended metaphor and analogy (see Chapter 2). An attempt is made to understand one phenomenon (the direction of a class of students) in terms of another (general management). The specific experience of teaching is viewed in terms of other experiences with which, superficially, it may share little resemblance; the basis of this analogy is the theory of systems, which considers an organization such as a teacher and a class of students as similar to an organism, i.e. a living, changing system.[3] (It must be emphasized that 'systems are not objective entities – they are only useful conceptualizations of linked segments of our environment'.) The learning situation, of which the teacher and the students are the principal components, is interpreted as amenable to purposeful direction and control.

The organization as machine

Some educationists view the organization (factory, civil service, college) in terms of a 'machine' which will carry out its tasks satisfactorily if all the parts behave exactly according to their design and purpose.[4] This metaphor suggests that, within the college, input is transformed into output, deviations from plans are noted and corrected, patterns of power and control assure a stable environment. The appropriate organizational form is the *bureaucracy*, based on a hierarchy in which everyone knows his place and works for the attainment of organizational goals.[5] In practice, however, this approach to organization invariably creates its own problems: adaptation to changed circumstances often becomes difficult; bureaucracies tend to work in an unquestioning fashion in which predetermined goals rather than innovation dominate; a narrow interpretation of 'efficiency' often becomes more important than flexibility and creative actions. The very term 'bureaucracy' has acquired pejorative overtones, for reasons understood by most college tutors!

An extension to this metaphor is seen in the military organizational model, adapted and popularized by the management theorists, Fayol[6] and Colonel Lydall Urwick,[7] who appear to have absorbed many of the organizational principles advocated by Frederick the Great and Napoleon. The organization is to be based on discipline, authority and responsibility, centralized chains of command, *esprit de corps*, etc. This model is largely irrelevant to the work of the colleges of further education: for example, the motivation of soldiers has nothing in common with that of students; unquestioning obedience to a centralized authority cannot be expected in today's classrooms (or even, for that matter, in some of today's armies).

The organization as an open system

In recent years, under the influence of biological research and advances in cybernetics (that is, the study of organization and communication in human beings and machines), the concept of the *system* has been developed.[8] This concept refers 'both to a complex of interdependencies between parts, components, and processes that involve discernible regularities of relationship, and to a similar type of interdependency of such a complex and its surrounding environment' (Parsons).[9] An organization, such as a group of students and their tutor, may be viewed as a unified, purposeful *system* composed of interrelated parts. *The activity of any part of the organization will affect in some way the activity of every other part.* The conduct of a student in class or, perhaps more obviously, the performance of a tutor, will affect class performance *as a whole*. A system is 'open' if, as in the case of a college, it interacts with its environment; it is 'closed' if there is no such interaction.

The systems model emphasizes, first, the significance of the *environment* in which the organization exists. The college has goals and aims related specifically to community demands; the class within the college operates in the context of those goals and aims. Sensitivity to occurrences in the wider world of which one is a part is necessary for effective management. Secondly, the model stresses *coherence* of the organization; the college is perceived by its staff and students as having purpose, as taking the form of a meaningful entity. Conflict and clash of interests may often be not far from the surface, but systematic, purposeful integration of resources is generally accepted as a goal of the college and its staff. Thirdly, a *structure* (which, in educational institutions, should reflect *strategy*, i.e. purpose and objectives) is significant: the 'structure' of a college, or a single class, is a description of the interrelations among components, the arrangement of its parts, and the potential influence they may have upon one another. (A college organizational chart will usually reveal aspects of the structure of the institution.)

Concepts of systems theory in relation to the classroom

The following key concepts of systems theory[10] should be considered in relation to the classroom and management tasks of the college tutor.

Subsystems

These are the parts making up the whole. Systems, too, will probably be the subsystems of a larger whole. The student is a subsystem of a larger system, i.e. his instructional group, which in turn functions as a subsystem within the college. Subsystems are interrelated, and it is the task of the teacher-manager, in planning and carrying out the processes of instruction, to be aware of the dynamic nature of the relationships. Students are not single, isolated persons: they are parts of a framework within which their personalities, backgrounds, motives and reactions have to be considered.

Synergy

The whole is greater than, and distinct from, the sum of its parts. Students within classes, tutors and departments within a college, can achieve more where they act together than where they operate in isolation. The task of the teacher-manager is to create the links, formal and informal, making this possible.

Feedback

Information concerning the effect of instruction is essential for the functioning of the teaching system. This is discussed on p. 153.

Objectives

A system involves some purpose, such as survival or growth. The objectives of the college will affect the work of subsystems, such as classes or instructional groups.

The essence of management and management skills

We extend the provisional definition of management given above, and now define it as comprising 'those processes by which persons plan, direct and operate organizations so as to meet its objectives and goals'. In general, it involves the planning, direction and coordination of human activities through the medium of organizational structures. Specifically, the manager is concerned with the setting of objectives, the formulation of plans, the organization of activities and the direction and control of operations.[11] In more formal terms, the manager may be considered as engaged in directing the transformation of inputs into outputs.

The essence of management, whether in the context of bank, office or classroom, is to be discovered in its nature, purpose and chosen modes of operation. Its *nature* is that of a 'process' – a continuous and systematic series of activities. Its *purpose* is related, invariably, to the achievement of synergy involving organizational aims and objectives. Its *modes of operation* are based on the techniques of coordination – the assembling of resources and the planning and synchronization of procedures necessary for the attainment of desired ends.

The functions of management have been described as universal, in that they may be discerned, in one form or another, in *any type* of management process. Outwardly, the planning of a production schedule may have little in common with a class tutor's formulation of lesson objectives and appropriate forms of tuition; fundamentally, however, both types of activity may be perceived as reflecting the essence of planning – 'the process of thinking before doing, the devising of a line of action to be followed, the stages to go through and methods to be used'. (Management functions, whether in a classroom or elsewhere, are not always exercised in a fixed sequence; indeed, in some circumstances they will coalesce. Hence a class teacher or personnel director of a commercial enterprise may find it necessary to engage almost simultaneously in direction and control of an activity, for example.)

The teacher's overall function in the classroom, in relation to the process of instruction, may be viewed, in the words of Haimann and Scott (writing of management in general),[12] as 'a facilitating activity that allocates and utilises resources, influences human action and plans change in order to accomplish rationally-conceived goals'.

Three basic skills – technical, human and conceptual – have been identified by researchers as essential for all types of manager. *Technical skill* implies the ability to use specialized techniques: the teacher must be able to utilize appropriate instructional procedures. *Human skill* – of paramount significance in teaching – involves the capacity to understand, motivate and work with other people, individually or in groups, e.g. in instructional classes. *Conceptual skill* is the mental capacity to coordinate the interests and activities of those people (i.e. subsystems) comprising the system, that is, the students for whose instruction the teacher is responsible.

Management style

It will be obvious to experienced teachers that there is no 'one best way' of organizing instruction. The *form* which is considered appropriate (and which will create synergy) will depend on the specific task and the environment with which one is dealing in the classroom; methods which are very effective in one situation may prove unworkable in another.

It is the task of the teacher-manager to identify the particular technique which he or she considers as appropriate to the instructional situation and which will best contribute to the attainment of instructional goals. Thus, for example, where the classroom is seen in terms of subsystems and an open system (see p. 186), management style will be considered as involving a focus on the relationships among the parts of the organization, clarifying those *relationships* and building an appropriate environmental structure. The teacher's work must be concerned with achieving an appropriate fit between the organization of instruction, its environment and goals. He or she may adopt the so-called 'contingency approach' to management tasks in the classroom, based on the principle that no 'universals' will, in reality, fit all situations; the truly appropriate management style will depend on his or her reactions to specific problems at the very time they present themselves.[13]

The teacher as manager must develop a style which reflects an ability to make decisions under *conditions of ambiguity*, i.e. in situations which are novel or are perceived as of a contradictory nature. (For the first time in the teacher's experience, for example, a class may develop a negative or hostile approach to a mode of instruction which has been welcomed in the past.) Lindblom's 'muddling through' model[14] is of interest in this context. He suggests that, all too often, where managers have to deal with problems of this nature, mere theory may be restrictive and inappropriate. The manager should, in these circumstances, cease his search for the 'best solution', and make step-by-step, marginal and incremental comparisons among policies and solutions until the 'better solution' is found and the system returns to equilibrium.

'If the metaphor fits, why not wear it?'

In 1990, an interesting examination of the 'teacher-as-manager' concept appeared in the periodical, *Theory into Practice* (Ohio State University), and the essence is presented here. Practising teachers and educational theoreticians conducted a discussion which began with a caution concerning the use of metaphors in arguments concerning teaching and learning. It was suggested that all language is fundamentally metaphorical and 'words in a language represent ways in which people conceptualize the world'. Terms such as 'teaching', 'learning', 'directing' and 'managing' are associated with specific ways of considering life in colleges and other organizations, so that our acceptance of the validity of a metaphor will reflect our *general attitudes* to the matters under consideration.

In the contribution to the discussion made by Cohen and Lotan ('Teacher as supervisor of complex technology'), organizational theory is deployed in the task of analysing teaching and learning in the classroom setting. The technology of the classroom may be viewed as varying from simple systems (where all the students are carrying out similar routine tasks) to highly differentiated systems (where, e.g. small groups of students are engaged on different tasks). Essentially, the teacher, faced with classroom situations characterized by uncertainty and differentiation (such as where a number of different subsystems are operating simultaneously in the main system), can enhance class effectiveness by adapting some fundamental management techniques, e.g. assessing, organizing and controlling in accordance with pre-set requirements. 'Teachers need to learn how to delegate authority, yet maintain control, and how to avoid "hovering", yet engage students in conceptual tasks ... Students must practise working collaboratively in groups and performing their assigned roles.' Management theory (as it relates to planning and control) can be used, it is argued, to train teachers and students in these tasks.

Berliner suggests, in 'If the metaphor fits, why not wear it?', that the literature of the last few decades, describing the role and functions of management, 'overlaps almost completely with the descriptions of the role of teachers and the functions they must perform'. He notes that one can say of managers *and* teachers that their job is not to tell people what to do, but rather to *enable* them to perform well. Both groups have a 'responsibility for contribution' to the goals of the organization. Further, says Berliner, the classroom can be perceived as a 'workplace' in which the planned output is to be seen in terms of human development, a task which requires the techniques of management.

Six functions of the teacher in his or her role as manager are included in Berliner's analysis.

1. *Planning.* Choosing lesson content, scheduling time, forming groups of learners and choosing appropriate activity structures are analogous to the tasks of a manager. The necessary decision-making which accompanies planning involves complex tasks for both manager and teacher.
2. *Communicating goals.* It is the task of the teacher to communicate expectations of performance, a similar job to that undertaken by the manager who has to convey to subordinates goals and the necessary work arrangements which are involved.
3. *Regulating activities.* The pace of production is analogous to the pace of instruction: both require the exercise of the management function. The sequencing of events and timing require from manager and teacher the abilities to handle information and make decisions swiftly and accurately.
4. *Creating an appropriate work environment.* This is an important task for manager and teacher. In terms of systems analysis, the subsystems which comprise the total system require suitable settings if they are to function in accordance with plans.
5. *Motivating work group members.* Where a workforce or members of an instructional group lack motivation, output is unlikely to be satisfactory. The task of motivation often falls to manager and teacher.
6. *Evaluating performance.* No system will function in accordance with plans in the absence of regular evaluation of performance. Both manager and teacher are

expected to measure and assess the results of those activities for which they have responsibility, as a prelude to corrective action.

In 'Beyond the workplace metaphor', Marshall argues against uncritical acceptance of 'the classroom as workplace'. It is essential, she maintains, to conceptualize the classroom so that 'learning' rather than 'work' is emphasized. The workplace model tends to stress the 'end product' of academic work; this ignores the significance of the cognitive view of learning 'in which the learner is playing an active role in the process of constructing knowledge rather than reacting to external forces'. Given the cognitive model of learning (see pp. 96–112), it is not easy to make a worthwhile comparison of the tasks of the teacher with the 'mechanical, manipulative tasks' of the manager. Learning, Marshall contends, is often an unintended consequence of the teaching process and demands goals which centre on process rather than product. The teacher's tasks are much more complex than those envisaged in the phrase 'enabling students to learn'.

Marshall notes that authority relationships in the classroom are less hierarchical than those which exist in the workplace. The teacher's 'authority relationship' cannot be compared validly to that of the manager. It is necessary, Marshall concludes, to move *beyond* the workplace metaphor so that the unique qualities of the teaching function might be recognized and understood.

Teaching-managing: the relevance of the analogy summarized

It is for the practising college teacher to decide whether or not to accept as valid the analogy which suggests the existence of important similarities between teaching and management, as outlined above. Some teachers will reject systems theory in its entirety as unwarranted 'reductionism' which can never apply to the classroom with its innumerable, rich complexities, its shifting structures, its intensely individual actions and its unpredictable nature (save in some few, trivial matters). Educational activity is unique and its organization cannot be understood by reference to a frame of events from which it is qualitatively dissimilar. It is, say critics of the teacher-as-manager concept, a semantic absurdity to bracket the teacher with the industrial manager; each is engaged in totally different types of activity and each has different ends. Neither would recognize the other as sharing any communality of activity. The teaching-managing analogy is, it is argued, meaningless, save in a very trivial sense.

In favour of the analogy is the perception of the teacher as one who is *objectively* carrying out the functions of a manager when he or she accepts responsibility for the deployment of resources, the planning of instruction and its administration in the interests of efficient learning. Specifically, the teacher has a management responsibility within the college system for each of the following activities:

(a) the creation and maintenance of a classroom environment in which learning can take place effectively;
(b) construction and interpretation of the syllabus;

(c) selection and enunciation of teaching objectives;
(d) selection of appropriate modes of instruction;
(e) class motivation and control;
(f) delivery of instruction;
(g) assessment of student performance;
(h) provision of informative feedback to students;
(i) ensuring retention and transfer of knowledge.

In management terms, these and related activities may be classified under four headings: planning, organization, directing, controlling. As a *planner*, the teacher has to define the necessary instructional objectives (see Chapter 13) based on his or her appreciation of what ought to be achieved, and what can be achieved, given a variety of constraints. As an *organizer*, the teacher has to determine a teaching strategy based on his or her objectives and resources. As *director*, the teacher has to carry out a strategical task which involves the highly important functions of motivating and encouraging students. As *controller* (see Chapter 12), the teacher has to monitor and assess the students' progress and adjust his or her teaching so that objectives can be attained.

In more precise terms, the purpose of management of the teaching-learning situation may be seen as *the modification of the learner's behaviour in accordance with predetermined objectives, the attainment of which should enrich and advance personal growth*. The teacher-manager's functions should have significance only as a contribution to that end.

Notes and references

1. See generally for this chapter: *Images of Organisation* by G. Morgan (Gage, 1986); *Organisational Theory and Design* by E. Gerloff (McGraw-Hill, 1988); *Management* by J. Stoner (Prentice-Hall, 1989); *The Management Task* by R. Dixon (Butterworth, 1994); *Management Concepts and Practices* by T. Hannagan (Pitman, 1995). For the problems arising from the complex interactions of individual members of organizations and the organizations themselves, see e.g. *Organisational Behaviour* by F. Luthans (McGraw-Hill, 1985); *Organizational Behaviour* by J. George (Addison Wesley, 1996); *Organizational Behaviour* by G. Johns (Harper Collins, 1996); *Organization Theory* by M. Hatch (OUP, 1997); *Organizations: Structures and Processes* by R. Hall (Prentice-Hall, 1996); *Introduction to Organisational Behaviour* by R. Pettinger (Macmillan, 1996); *Organisational Psychology* by E.H. Schein (Prentice-Hall, 1980). Schein's often-cited definition of an organization should be of interest to teachers – 'An organization is the planned coordination of the activities of a number of people for the achievement of some common, explicit purpose or goal, through division of labour and function, and through a hierarchy of authority and responsibility'.
2. *The New State* (Smith, 1918).
3. See e.g. 'General systems theory' by F.E. Kast in *Academy of Management Journal* (1972, *12*).
4. See Morgan (*op. cit.*); 'The manager's job – a systems approach' by S. Tilles in *Harvard Business Review* (1963, *41*); *Management Systems* by A.W. Smith (Dryden, 1982).
5. For the topic of bureaucracy, see Morgan (*op. cit.*); 'The concept of bureaucracy' by R.H.

Vallin in *American Journal of Sociology* (1963, *7*); 'Technical characteristics of a bureaucracy' in *Human Relations in Administration* by R. Dubin (Prentice-Hall, 1974).

6. *General and Industrial Management* (Pitman, 1949).
7. *The Elements of Administration*. (Harper & Row, 1944).
8. See 'General systems theory' by K. Boulding in *Management Science* (1956, *4*).
9. *Structure and Process in Modern Societies* (Free Press, 1960).
10. See e.g. 'Definition of a system' by A.D. Hall and R.E. Hagen in *Organisation: Systems, Control and Adaptation* (Wiley, 1969); *Psychology of System Design* by D. Meister (Elsevier, 1991), in which there is an examination of concepts suggesting that: the whole *tends* to determine the nature of the parts; the parts cannot be understood if considered in isolation from the whole; and the parts are dynamically interrelated.
11. For a succinct account of management functions, see 'What is management all about?' in *The Entrepreneurial Manager* by A.L. Minkes (Penguin, 1987).
12. *Managing the Modern Organisation* (Houghton Mifflin, 1978).
13. See e.g. 'A general contingency theory of management' by F. Luthans and T. Stewart in *Academy of Management Review* (1977, *4*); 'The illusion of contingency theory as a general theory' by J.C. Longenecker in *Academy of Management Review* (1978, *7*).
14. 'The science of muddling through' in *Public Administration Review* (1959, *17*).

Chapter 16

The Instructional Setting, Syllabus and Course Design

> Organisation is not mechanical . . . it is organic and unique to each individual business or institution. For we now know that structure, to be effective and sound, must follow strategy. Structure is a means for attaining the objectives and goals of an institution (Drucker, 1974).

In this chapter emphasis is placed on the teacher-manager's functions in relation to *the planning of instructional tasks and the deployment of resources*.[1] The teacher is seen here in the role of controller, as far as circumstances might allow, of the instructional setting (i.e. the classroom) and organizing a teaching strategy appropriate to students' aspirations and needs and the demands of the curriculum. In this role the teacher is viewed within the general pattern of systems analysis (see Chapter 15): he or she is bringing together the components of a learning system – students, teacher, learning environment and instructional materials – in order to achieve a desired objective.

The immediate teaching environment – the physical features of the classroom, shape, size, etc. – ought to be accepted by the teacher-manager as one of the factors constraining the teaching process, which he or she can manipulate only in limited fashion. The classroom as such is a 'given factor'. However, modifications in the use of space may be made, and the teacher may view the instructional setting as an important aspect of a subsystem which can affect the overall instructional process.

Syllabus and course design will be shaped by the teacher-manager's individual interpretation of the wider goals of the curriculum for which the college as a whole is responsible. Eisner defines curriculum as 'a series of planned events that are intended to have educational consequences for students'.[2] In *Curriculum Development: Theory and Practice* (1962), Taba states:[3]

> A curriculum usually contains a statement of aims and of specific objectives; it indicates some selection and organization of content; it either implies or manifests certain patterns of learning and teaching, whether because the objectives demand them or because the content organization requires them. Finally, it includes a programme of evaluation of the outcomes.

The college, through its various committees will have decided on appropriate curriculum goals within the broader setting of community demands; the class tutor will translate these goals into instructional programmes, reflecting availability of resources, chosen modes of instruction and the sequencing of teaching.

The instructional setting: preparing the stage for learning

There can be very few occasions on which the teacher is able to exercise much control over the wider, physical environment in which he or she works. The shape of the classroom, its situation in relation to other rooms, its general facilities, cannot often be altered. But the important details which have a direct effect on the process of instruction – the layout of the room, the relative positions of teacher and students, seating arrangements, the position of teaching aids, temperature, illumination, ventilation – that is, the accommodation arrangements, require organization. Problems of accommodation can often play a disproportionate role in the outcome of the lesson. Classroom temperature, illumination and background noise which are outside the acceptable range may divert students from the immediate learning task. Where such conditions can be controlled, the teacher ought to experiment so as to achieve the most satisfactory environment for the class. In systems terms, the teacher is aware of the fact that *all* the factors which shape activity within the classroom are related to the overall learning process; as far as possible, all should be controlled.

The layout of the classroom is often under the control of the teacher and it is desirable that it be arranged in accordance with the specific requirements of the mode of instruction which is being employed. A discussion group demands a layout of furniture which is quite different from that needed in a formal lecture. The use of an overhead projector or a video recorder necessitates a class arrangement which will differ from that needed in a case study discussion. The teacher in further education ought not to accept as immutable the traditional arrangement whereby a class is seated in neat rows and columns, facing a blackboard which is placed exactly in the centre of the front of the room. Some alternative arrangements have proved successful and experimentation by individual class teachers is essential.

Prints and photographs of late nineteenth and early twentieth century schools reveal an obsession with symmetry, presumably derived from the belief that order and symmetry were equivalent. School buildings laid out with the geometrical regularity of Fourier's phalansteries, or Bentham's Panopticon (the better to observe the prisoners therein), were paralleled by precise rows of fixed desks in each classroom. The teacher's place was usually slightly below the middle of the front row, or on a raised platform in that position. This arrangement, now hallowed by time, is followed slavishly by some teachers, under the impression that 'you can be seen and heard from there by all the class'. This is often not the case; the best position from which to speak, from which to control the class, has to be discovered by individual experiment.

Seating arrangements in class

Seating arrangements in a class should be determined, where possible, by the precise instructional strategy favoured by the tutor. Thus, formal spacing and arrangement of chairs and desks might be considered appropriate for a formal lesson, presentation or lecture. Informal spacing and arrangement might suit a discussion session, with chairs arranged in clusters, with or without tables. The question to be answered by the tutor is: 'In what ways can class seating arrangements facilitate the process of learning, given the particular form of instruction I intend to use?'[4]

Seating patterns in classrooms have been studied repeatedly, and the literature has been reviewed by Weinstein.[5] He concludes that the research is incomplete, inconsistent and often contradictory. But he suggests, nevertheless, that seating position affects student's behaviour and attitudes sufficiently to warrant serious consideration by educators. An observation by Waller[6] that the choice of a classroom seat does *not* appear to be random has been supported by some empirical data. Experienced teachers may recognize Waller's picture of a class seated according to *choice*: in the front row are 'overdependent types', mixed with 'extraordinarily zealous' students; in the back row are 'persons in rebellion'. Walberg[7] concludes that students who prefer to sit in the front of the class generally possess 'very positive attitudes' to learning, while those preferring the back of the class express 'negative attitudes toward their own capacity for success'.

Weinstein suggests that where teachers use a formal seating arrangement (in rows), they should move around the room, directing comments to students seated on the periphery. Where possible, students' seating patterns should be changed periodically so as to prevent the 'permanent relegation' of a section of the class to a zone which may encourage inactivity. The crucial point is, according to Weinstein, that seating must be 'compatible with the nature of the activity and the needs of the persons involved'.

Smith[8] differs from Weinstein: he believes that relatively consistent findings have emerged from research into spatial classroom arrangements. Among these findings, which are of much interest to the practising teacher, are the following.

1. There seems to be a direct increase in student participation in the teaching-learning process with a decrease in distance between teacher and student.
2. Where there is a traditional classroom arrangement, with the teacher standing front-centre, a 'triangle of maximum interaction' may be discerned (see Figure 16.1). Davies suggests that, where the teacher is able to make such arrangements, the 'more introverted, reticent students' should be encouraged to sit within the triangle area, and the 'more extroverted students' should sit outside it. Similar areas may emerge where a teacher moves away from front-centre for a relatively lengthy period of time.
3. A high rate of student participation appears to emerge where the class is based on a U-shaped arrangement and the teacher sits in the centre of the U-gap.
4. Students at college level tend to dislike the formal, standard seating arrangements, i.e. rows of desks faced by the tutor's desk. There appears to be a general preference for less formal arrangements.
5. Students prefer, where places in the classroom have been allocated, to keep their own places: there is a general reluctance to be moved from one part of the classroom to another – 'chairs are territory'.

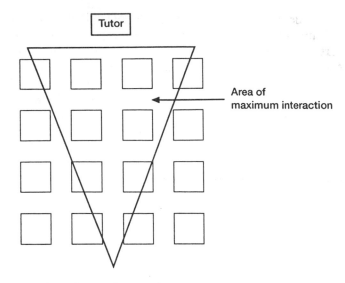

Figure 16.1   Triangle of maximum interaction.

The syllabus: interpretation and compilation

The teacher in further education will usually be involved in the preparation of a class for a public or internal examination and will be expected, therefore, to work to a syllabus. This often determines the general aim and teaching objectives. The teacher's tasks as teacher-manager necessitate interpreting the syllabus so as to plan a programme of work based on objectives and to organize the appropriate resources.[9] (Even where mandatory units are the basis of instruction, as in GNVQ work, the tutor may have to decide upon the sequence in which instruction is to be given.)

A syllabus generally lists a series of topics which should be covered during a course and which may form the basis of examination questions. It may be drawn up in wide terms, which makes the teacher's interpretative task very important; it may, on the other hand, be presented with a wealth of detail which allows for little in the way of individual interpretation. Thus, one syllabus for introductory economics published by an examinations board consisted of sixteen lines. This should be compared with a similar examination syllabus published by another board in the same year which covered several pages. Where there is an absence of detail, the teacher may be at a disadvantage. He or she should then make an appreciation of the situation in the following terms: 'How important is the segment of knowledge, mentioned very generally in the syllabus, in the wider areas of the subject?' 'What details are important to the student at this stage of his development?' 'Will past examination papers and examiners' reports give any indication of the detail required?' The teacher should then 'manage the situation', that is, plan and organize on the basis of the detail he or she considers necessary.

A syllabus will not generally indicate the relative importance of its topics or the order in which they are to be studied. In some cases, those who compile a syllabus tend to follow the traditional textbook 'order of contents', or a pattern prescribed by a logical approach to the subject, or – consciously or unconsciously – the shape of a university or college course in which they may have participated. Often, however, the teacher will feel that the subject demands a different approach. Thus, the fact that many textbooks on economics, and syllabus schemes apparently based on them, begin with a definition of the subject and a discussion on the nature of economic laws, does not invalidate a lesson scheme which begins with that section of the syllabus dealing with a general examination of industry. Where the teaching of the syllabus can be planned so that it coincides with teaching of related areas in other subjects, the probability of 'meaningful learning' occurring is increased. 'Localization of industry', taught as part of an economics syllabus, is enriched when linked with 'the distribution of natural resources', taught as part of the economic geography syllabus.

The *interpretation of the syllabus* presents the teacher with the necessity of making management-type decisions based on answers to the following questions; his or her decisions will result in a plan and an appropriate allocation of resources.

1. 'What ought to be the *content* of my teaching scheme?'
2. 'What ought to be the *shape* of that scheme?'
3. 'What should be my precise *objectives*, the attainment of which will ensure that the syllabus, as I have chosen to interpret it, is largely covered?'
4. 'What *modes of instruction* are necessitated by my choice of objectives?'
5. 'What *modes of assessment* are necessitated by the type of instruction I have selected?'
6. 'What *allocation of course time* is to be made for each part of the syllabus?'

In a few circumstances a teacher may be asked to prepare his or her own course syllabus. A request for a *general syllabus* usually necessitates a comprehensive summary of the course content headings. An *extended syllabus* requires further detail, of the kind usually found in the syllabuses of some major examining bodies, i.e. main headings, sub-headings, specific content. A *working syllabus* generally contains the order of topic development which will be followed by teachers, and which will form the basis of their lesson plans and notes. The compiling of a syllabus by the teacher may draw on standard texts, existing syllabuses and schemes of work, past examination papers and – above all – the teacher's own interpretation of the learner's needs at his or her current stage of development. 'What must the learner know of the subject matter at this stage?' 'What *should* he or she know?' 'What *could* he or she know?' 'What must be known' will form the core of the syllabus. Its outer layers may include 'what should be known' and, where time allows, 'what could be known'. The syllabus content and the suggested allocation of time, as finally decided by the teacher, will reflect clearly his or her personal interpretation and assessment of the needs of the class in relation to their *initial behaviour* (i.e. their level of attainment at the beginning of the course) and their *desirable terminal behaviour* (i.e. their required level at the end of the course).

It is wrong to assume that students attending their first lesson are aware of the published syllabus – many may not know of its existence. The preliminaries of the course ought to include a discussion of the syllabus with the class: its overall purpose, its value, its general contents, its relation to the students' development, order of topics to be followed and allocation of time. Where teachers know that they will be unable to cover all sections of the syllabus, they ought to inform the class of this at the beginning of the course. Plans may then be announced so that the uncovered sections can be learned as part of a private study scheme, which will be organized and directed by the teacher. This may necessitate advice on private study and the teacher must be prepared to suggest schemes of systematic study. The uncovered part of the syllabus must not be forgotten by the teacher, and references to it should be made from time to time. Where the teacher makes a management (planning) decision to omit a section of the syllabus in its entirety – perhaps because he or she considers it irrelevant or out of date – the reasons ought to be made known to the class.

Course design

The task of designing a course in its entirety usually falls to a senior member of staff. It may be delegated, however, on some occasions to other members of staff so that the fundamentals of the task, requiring the exercise of management functions, ought to be known by *all* teachers in further education. Thus, a firm with which the college is associated may ask for a 'six week course for our young supervisory staff, aimed at introducing them to the principles of management' or for 'an intensive week's revision course on motor vehicle maintenance schedule operations'. The course designer must then plan and organize a scheme, taking into account the time available, the number of students and staff, accommodation and other resources.[10] The task of design may be based, initially, on a consideration of the process illustrated by Figure 16.2.

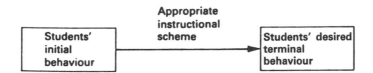

Figure 16.2 The essence of instruction.

What can the students *do* when they enter the course? What must they be able to *do* when they leave the course? The subtraction of one level of behaviour from the other will produce a 'remainder', the content of which should determine the content of the course. Where a course is to be based on the teaching of an industrial or commercial skill a detailed task analysis may be necessary. The Cambridge Industrial Training Research Unit formulated a method of training design based on a classification of the task to be taught according to the specific nature of the learning which is required and the essential nature of the task. Five categories of learning are involved which form the acronym *CRAMP*. The designer of the training course categorizes the objectives of the learning situation by posing five questions:

- is the objective the development of general understanding? (*Comprehension*);
- is it the production of swift and reliable patterns of response? (*Reflex development*);
- is it the development of new attitudes? (*Attitude formation*);
- is it the remembering of specific facts? (*Memorizing*);
- is it to acquaint the trainee with a group of procedures? (*Procedural learning*).

Psychomotor skills – invariably based on organized patterns of muscular activities reflecting responses to signals from the environment – require much practice in coordinated activities (see Chapter 24), and the course design must allow for this.

Whether the course involves skills or wider types of behaviour, its design necessitates that account be taken of the students' levels of attainment *at the point of entry* to the course. What may be expected as a level of attainment, for example, from 'young supervisory staff'? Will they understand the simple organizational techniques upon which general management principles rest? Will the motor vehicle students be acquainted with the general requirements of a maintenance schedule? Discussions with the firm's training officers and, where possible, the administering of pre-course tests, can assist the early planning stages of the course. The desired 'terminal learning behaviour' of the students must be based on a realistic assessment of what is possible, given the limitations of the situation, and this may result in some modification of the original aims of the course.

Course design management is, however, much more complicated than the previous diagram might suggest. The component steps of design and execution should form a coherent sequence which includes those elements of control outlined in Chapter 12. The steps are illustrated in Figure 16.3.

It should be noted, with reference to this chart, that:

(a) the 'suggested course aims' will not often emerge unaltered as the 'agreed course aims';
(b) a terminal test should be constructed as soon as the terminal objectives are drawn up;
(c) the actual programme of work will almost certainly necessitate the agreement of the departmental head;
(d) the results of the terminal test ought to be compared with the terminal objectives and an assessment made;
(e) the feedback loop between 'process of instruction' and 'tests' is a reminder that, without relevant informative feedback, i.e. monitoring and assessment of performance, the level of attainment represented by the terminal objectives is unlikely to be reached.

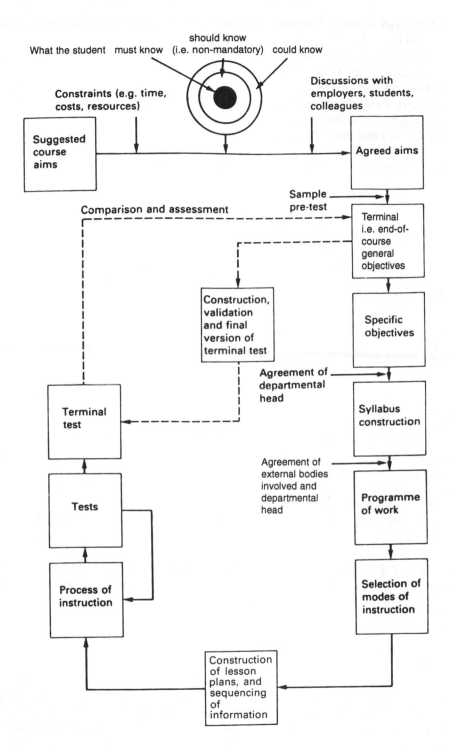

Figure 16.3　Design and execution of courses.

Selecting the mode of instruction: a vital teaching-management task

- 'I understand the content and overall requirements of the syllabus and I am able to identify my appropriate objectives. What must my students do to learn?'
- 'What type of learning do I expect? Surface learning (reflecting extrinsic motivation only) or deep learning (reflecting intrinsic interest in the subject matter), and how do I ensure the one rather than the other?'
- 'How may I best facilitate learning? Ought I to use the lecture form of instruction? Would the formal lesson be more appropriate? Is there a validated programmed lesson which might be useful? Should I use a film which has been produced for this very type of course? Would directed private study on its own achieve the results I desire for my students?'

These and similar questions must be posed and answered by the teacher-manager, who has the responsibility of designing and implementing a strategy of instruction. The most commonly used modes of instruction are considered in Chapters 22–26. A general approach to the selection of these modes is outlined below.

There may, of course, be a very restricted range of choices facing the teacher. He may lack resources in terms of accommodation, audio-visual aids, etc. He may belong to a college in which the form of instruction is decided by a section leader or departmental head. Where the choice is his, however, his first question must be: 'Given my specific teaching objectives, how best do I attain them?' (Gagné suggests two questions: 'What is to be learned?' and 'What kinds of stimulation external to the learner will best support the internal processing necessary for learning?') The subject matter itself may dictate the mode of teaching. Demonstration lessons are likely to be the chosen mode for the instructor working, for example, with engineering students on the techniques of lathe operations. The case study and the discussion group (see Chapter 26) are likely to be selected by the management studies tutor who is instructing an advanced management course in the principles of industrial wage negotiations. A formal lecture might be selected as appropriate by a teacher seeking to outline the structure of the English courts to students who work as legal executives. A brief lesson and test, followed by a short video as recapitulation material, may be selected for the introduction of nursing students to some of the principles of child care.

Lesson objectives interpreted, perhaps, in relation to the structure used by Bloom in his taxonomy (see Chapter 14) could be taken into account when the selection of an instructional mode is under consideration. In very general terms it may be suggested that:

(a) Where the instruction is linked to objectives in the *cognitive domain*, e.g. knowledge, comprehension, analysis, etc., most modes of instruction may be acceptable. In the planning of instruction relating to those parts of the syllabus which involve relatively simple cognitive objectives (such as knowledge of specifics, terminology, conventions or translation from one level of abstraction to another) formally structured lessons and the use of appropriate programmed texts (see Chapter 29) can be considered.

(b) Where the instruction is related to objectives in the *affective domain*, e.g. valuing, organizing, conceptualizing, etc., most modes of instruction may be utilized successfully. Where the objectives are relatively advanced, such as those necessitating the organization of value complexes, the tutor may find that case studies, group discussions, 'low-structure' instruction (see p. 206), directed private study periods and tutorials are most productive. (Kohlberg[11] is one of the few educationists to have published a sample of a prescriptive instructional programme in this domain: he has selected the topic of 'moral education' and begins by eliciting conflicting student issues on a moral question, thus obtaining knowledge of the students' existing level of moral development. The student moves from that 'pre-conventional level' by question and answer to the 'conventional level', when discussions are held on the issue from the perspective of a member of the larger community. Finally, through tutorial groups, the student emerges at the 'principled level', at which point he or she is able to make moral decisions unaided.)

(c) Where the instruction has objectives in the *psychomotor domain*, the 'practical lesson', the demonstration, the employment of visual aids, models, machines and check lists, will be valuable. In particular, verbal instruction based on demonstrations of skills, followed by periods of concentrated practice (i.e. 'high-structure' instruction), is essential if mastery is to be achieved. This applies to diverse and precise objectives such as attaining 40 w.p.m. in typing, decreasing the period of time in which a fractured gas pipe can be repaired, or attaining fluency in the playing of scale passages on the clarinet. (But different types of skills require different treatment in relation to the *pace* of instruction.)

The students' general abilities and attitudes will be an important factor in the selection of the mode of instruction. It has been suggested by Davies that the more able students tend to prefer the so-called 'permissive styles' of tuition (e.g. discussions, directed private study and projects, tutorials), while the less able tend to prefer the so-called 'autocratic styles' (e.g. the formal lesson). In spite of the many exceptions to this generalization – and teachers in further education should refer here to their own experiences with students of varying abilities – it remains a useful rule-of-thumb for the selection of a mode of instruction by the teacher-manager.

A note on objectives

Course design requires that attention be paid to the precise sequencing of objectives, e.g. the acquisition of simple skills must precede the learning of complex skills. The many uses of the term 'objectives' are noted by Gagné,[12] who differentiates their significance carefully. *Lifelong* objectives involve the expectation that acquired skills will continue to be used after the course has ended. *End-of-course* (or 'terminal') objectives set out the performance expected from the student immediately on termination of the course. *Specific performance* objectives (see Chapter 13) state the precise outcomes expected from a student following completion of a unit of instruction. Course designers should state the exact type of 'objective' they have in mind when setting out desired levels of attainment.

Sequencing the content of instruction

'Sequencing' is used here to refer to the process of *arranging the order of events of instruction according to some defined pattern or principle*. The resulting sequences should be those intended to promote effective learning. Essentially this is a management task carried out by the teacher in his or her role as planner. The teacher will have in mind the purpose and content of a particular unit of instruction, the objectives, the existing state of knowledge of the class, the resources and his or her previous experiences in arranging the conditions of learning at this particular level. The importance of sequencing for learning has been emphasized by Ausubel who believes that the learner's 'stability of cognitive structures' and his long-term retention will be influenced directly by the sequences in which learning occurs.

A common-sense approach is the basis of much sequencing in practice. Simple skills have to be taught as prerequisites for the accomplishment of complex skills. Concepts with a relatively low degree of meaning are learned before the student moves to more advanced concepts. Generalities may be taught before specific examples are given: thus an overview will precede a detailed study. Much will depend on the subject matter to be taught: subject areas may have their own distinctive patterns, structures, relationships and inner logic, demanding the learning of one concept prior to the study of another. Thus, the student of law or banking, beginning an examination of the Theft (Amendment) Act 1996, must have prior knowledge of technical terms, such as 'deception', 'money transfer' and 'presentment of a cheque'. The student of operational research, meeting the theory of games, must know something of the elements of probability in order to comprehend 'a game'. The violin student must be proficient in the skills of bowing before he or she can participate effectively in that segment of a sequence of instruction concerning the production of *vibrato*.

Some patterns of sequencing

Herbart (1776–1841), one of the founders of 'scientific pedagogy', advocated a sequencing scheme based on the following structure:[13]

1. *Preparation.* The teacher should arouse the students' interest in a manner which will lead to them being prepared to understand the new material which is to be presented.
2. *Presentation.* The teacher should then present the essential information by means of illustrations, examples, etc.
3. *Association.* The teacher should assist students to assimilate the new ideas through comparison with previously acquired ideas by a consideration of similarities and differences.

4. *Generalization.* The teacher should seek to derive general principles relating to the new material and designed to move comprehension beyond the immediate level of perception.
5. *Application.* The teacher should assign tasks involving the application of general principles so that they are integrated with existing patterns of understanding.

Davies states that, when a teacher has surveyed the material which is to constitute a unit of instruction, a 'general theme' will emerge which will act as a link between sections of the intended lesson. Sequence will be a reflection of the 'general theme and aim' of the lesson and will take into account the *sets of relationships* which constitute the structure of what is to be taught.

Gagné's prescription for the design of instructional sequences is based on decisions which must be taken by the teacher, concerning topics, lessons and lesson components. The general rule is to define aims by constructing a programme based on wide goals down to objectives of an increasingly specific nature. The objectives are then translated into the sequences necessary for their attainment. New skills demand the recall of subordinate skill components; these must be revised initially and extended by the presentation of new topics demanding that type of understanding which can be transformed into 'new skills of learning'

Merrill[14] suggests a path analysis which will allow the teacher to identify the possible paths through a flow chart representing the procedures he or she considers necessary for the attainment of lesson objectives. The material constituting the shortest path is taught first; the remainder of the sequence, involving more complex learning, is taught at a later stage.

Reigeluth's *elaboration approach* is based on the following suggested sequence.

(a) An *epitome* (which is *not* a summary) should present simple and fundamental ideas. Major aspects of the topic to be taught, and major relationships, will be pointed out.
(b) *Elaborations* are then presented. These add detail and complexities to the overview presented in the epitome. Relationships within the topic are considered in more detail. The nature of the teacher's elaborations will be determined by his or her precise objectives. If these objectives are essentially conceptual, he or she will focus on 'what'; if procedural, on 'how'; if based on principle, on 'why'.
(c) *Summaries and a synthesis* are then given. The learner should be able, at this stage, to assimilate the concepts presented, i.e. his or her memory should now contain new clusters of concepts.

Posner[15] has developed a highly systematized scheme for the presentation and sequencing of instructional activities which focuses on instructional content. The following examples illustrate his approach.

(a) Where the principle to be taught is based on 'spatial relations', the sequences of instruction should be ordered in accordance with physical arrangement or position. Example: the parts of a plant should be taught from root to stem, to leaves and flower.

(b) Where 'class relations' dominate the topic, characteristics of the general class must be taught before instruction about the members of the class (or vice versa). Example: sound and light should be taught before proceeding to the concept of wave motion.

(c) Where there are 'logical prerequisites', they must be taught prior to instruction concerning more complex propositions. Example: 'velocity' has to be taught before teaching the concept of acceleration as a change in velocity.

(d) Where 'propositional relations' (i.e. combinations of concepts asserting something) are to be taught, the teaching of a theory might precede the facts which the theory purports to explain. Example: an epitome of the theory of natural selection might precede a lesson on the adaptation of particular species.

In summary, the sequencing of instruction will reflect the long- and short-term objectives of the course, the nature of the subject area, the perceptions of the teacher as to the most appropriate 'learning pathway' for the students, and the teacher's managerial decisions as to the most effective utilization of his or her time and resources. (See p. 277 for a further discussion of sequencing.)

Low and high structure instruction

The instructional approach to be selected by the teacher-manager (in response to the question: 'How do I choose an appropriate scheme of teaching?') is considered by some course planners in terms of the *structure* of teaching. (The exact relation between structure and function remains an unsolved problem in scientific enquiry; what is a structure from one point of view is a function from another.) 'Structure' is used here to indicate a pattern in terms of which action takes place. Teaching can be categorized as 'high structure' or 'low structure'.

High structure teaching involves a precisely stated set of objectives, an ordering of sequences of instruction and a systematic style of presenting information. Where, for example, motor skills are to be taught, an appropriate paradigm might be that of the 'master-apprentice': the instructor selects a task to be taught, discovers what a master (i.e. expert) does when he performs the task, investigates what an apprentice (i.e. novice) does when he performs the task, and finally works out instructional techniques appropriate to teaching the 'difference' to the apprentices. High structure teaching involves moving to one objective, reviewing, assessing the rate of movement and monitoring achievement before moving to the next. Typically, it involves expository teaching in the style of lectures and formal lessons, and tends to be selected where course content is hierarchical, logically structured and amenable to detailed analysis.

Low structure teaching involves a less formal approach. The vital question for the instructor is: 'What is the existing level of my students upon which I can build?' Students are expected to reconstruct their knowledge in terms which indicate a *qualitative growth* in understanding. Mere correction of knowledge frameworks is not enough; fresh insight and rearrangement of cognitive patterns are needed. Alternative modes of perceiving and interpreting data may be presented, so that the student is confronted with a need for alterations to his or her thinking. Low structure teaching involves, typically, an informal style, the presentation of challenges to student thinking, the encouragement of alternative thinking and an extension of students' capacities to explore. Appropriate tasks and activities are presented to students; ends are stated, but means are left (purposely) unclear, in the expectation that discovery based on insight might result.

The systematic design of instruction: the Dick–Carey model

In their manual, *The Systematic Design of Instruction*,[16] Dick and Carey offer a valuable model for the design, development and implementation of instruction based on a systems approach. A series of nine steps is described, all of which receive input from preceding steps and provide output for the next steps. The components of the system are seen as integrated parts of a whole, the purpose of which is to provide effective instruction. The model owes much to the work of Gagné (see Chapter 5), who speaks of instructional systems design as 'the systematic process of planning an instructional system', and instructional development as 'the process of implementing the plans'. These two processes comprise an *instructional technology*.

The choice of systems theory as the basis of the model is justified by the designers on two grounds. First, the instructional system should be thought of in terms of interrelated parts, all working to an end. The focus is on what the student will know or be able to achieve following the instruction. Secondly, each component is linked: each 'participates' in the instructional event; each has its own input and output; the entire system is designed as a whole with the linking of individual components in mind.

The following stages in instructional design are set out by Dick and Carey. First, the identification of an instructional goal. The instructor determines what students should be able to do following the instruction and states this as a goal. The instructor then constructs an instructional analysis, listing the steps and skills within the desired procedures, followed by a task classification and a learning-task analysis, indicating main and subordinate skills to be taught. This information is used for the next step – the identification of entry behaviours and characteristics, which is necessary to identify what the learner must be able to do in order to participate effectively in the instruction.

The next step involves the writing of performance objectives (see Chapter 13) which must be specific and detailed. Skills to be learned, the conditions under which the skills are to be performed, and the criteria for acceptable performance are identified. This is followed by the construction of criterion-referenced test items (see p. 388) which will measure desired achievement.

The development of an instructional strategy is then undertaken so that objectives may be attained. The development and selection of instruction will follow; this may involve the writing of learning material, tests, etc. A formative evaluation is then conducted in order to identify how to improve the draft of instruction. This is used for the revising of instruction. Finally, a summative evaluation is undertaken, perhaps involving some evaluator other than the instructor (see p. 388).

The teacher-manager's role

In carrying out the operations mentioned in this chapter – modifications to the instructional setting, planning, organizing and operating courses, selecting instructional strategies – the teacher is fulfilling a management role. He or she has concentrated on essential tasks, has created structures which reflect teaching strategies, and has taken decisions today that will be the instructional events of tomorrow – the very essence of *managing* the teaching-learning process.

Notes and references

1. See generally for this chapter: *The Management of Learning* by I. Davies (McGraw-Hill, 1971); 'Instructional concerns' by I. Davies in *Instructional Technique* (McGraw-Hill, 1981); *Principles of Instructional Design* by R. Gagné and L. Briggs (Holt, Rinehart & Winston, 1988); *Curriculum Development Theory into Practice* by D. and L. Tanner (Macmillan, 1980); *Foundations of Student Learning* by K. Marjoribanks (Pergamon, 1991); *Curriculum Models in Adult Education* by M. Langenbach (Krieger, 1988).
2. *The Educational Imagination* (Macmillan, 1979). Note also the statement attributed to B. Bernstein: 'Curriculum defines what counts as valid knowledge'.
3. Pub. Harcourt Brace Jovanovich (1962).
4. See e.g. *Adults Learning* by J. Rogers (OUP, 1989); *The Anatomy of Judgment* by M. Abercrombie (Hutchinson, 1960).
5. See 'Seating patterns' in *IETE*.
6. *The Sociology of Teaching* (Wiley, 1965).
7. 'Psychological environment' in *IETE*.
8. 'Non-verbal communication' in *IETE*. See also *Instructional Technique* by I. Davies (McGraw-Hill, 1981).
9. See e.g. Gagné and Briggs (*op. cit.*).
10. See e.g. 'Planning instruction' in *Essentials of Learning for Instruction* by R. Gagné (Dryden, 1974); *Course Design* by G. Posner and A. Rudinsky (Longman, 1978).
11. 'The cognitive-developmental approach to moral education' in *Moral Education* ed. D. Purpel (McCutcham, 1971).
12. *Op. cit.* (1988).
13. *Outlines of Educational Doctrine* (Macmillan, 1904).
14. See 'The structure of subject-matter content and its instructional design implications' by C.M. Reigeluth, M.D. Merrill and C.V. Bunderson in *Instructional Science* (1978, 7); *Instructional Design Readings* ed. M.D. Merrill (Prentice-Hall, 1971).
15. 'Pacing and sequencing' in *IETE*.
16. Pub. Scott, Foresman (1985).

Chapter 17

Facilitating Retention and Retrieval of Knowledge, and Transfer of Learning

> Do not be impressed by all that is presumably known about the psychology of memory. Less is known than you might think ... How do we remember stories, events, experiences? More to the point, how do we retrieve them when least we expect them? (Norman, 1980).

Two further aspects of the teacher-manager's role are discussed in this chapter: first, his or her responsibility for so organizing learning that it is retained by the learner for as long as possible; second, his or her responsibility for the provision of instruction which results in the acquisition by the learner of principles which can be transferred from one type of problem to another, and from the classroom to the world outside. The subject matter of this chapter is the range of processes known as *memory* (remembering and forgetting) and the *transfer of learning*.[1]

The cumulative effects of students' past learning experiences will exert their influence on their present behaviour. The capacity to understand the present so as to plan for the future demands from students some ability to draw on past experiences; they can bridge the present and the future by utilizing their memory of the past. Whether memory exists as an active process or a mere 'storage bin' remains a subject of research from which teachers may learn much. The controversy has stimulated investigation into what is inferred as happening when a student finds one topic 'easy to remember', but has much difficulty in recalling another. It has also provoked discussion and experiment into why retrieval failure is more marked in some circumstances than others. Neisser[2] has suggested that too many laboratory experiments into memory are proving less productive than research based on 'naturalistic study': the place to investigate student learning is, he believes, in the classroom, not the laboratory. Attention has also been drawn to the 'fuzzy' nature of the phenomenon of remembering, often rendering precise investigation difficult. Bartlett states:[3]

> Remembering is not a re-excitation of innumerable fixed, lifeless and fragmentary traces. It is an imaginative reconstruction, or construction, built out of the relation of our attitude towards a whole active mass of organized past reactions or experience, and to a little outstanding detail which commonly appears in image or in language form. It is thus

hardly ever really exact, even in the most rudimentary cases of rote-recapitulation, and it is not at all important that it should be.

Analogies and the use of models (see p. 24) are common in memory research. Memory has been considered in terms of clay tablets on which impressions and traces are made; it has been visualized as a telephone exchange and, more recently, in terms of information processing and the computer. Where analogies illustrate and lead to the construction of hypotheses, they are of value; where they provide the basis for models which rely on some few similarities while ignoring many others, they may have a restricted value. Teachers should keep in mind their own experiences concerning students who seem to remember easily, and those who quickly forget the simplest data. The theories presented below should be considered alongside those experiences.

Retention and recall of knowledge: the problem

'I revised the work with them only last week and today they can't answer a single question about it!' Statements of this nature must have been made in most college staffrooms at one time or another. They express the bewilderment of the teacher confronted by a class unable to recall the content of a recent lesson. For students, too, there is dismay in discovering that, although they can recall effortlessly the words and tune of a song heard (and never consciously 'learned') five years ago, they cannot recall lesson material 'committed to memory' five days ago. It is a responsibility of the teacher-manager to arrange instruction so that knowledge *is* retained by the learner.

Three important questions arise.

1. What is the basis of 'memory'?
2. Why do we forget?
3. How can the process of instruction be structured so as to aid retention and recall?

The memory

Memory, writes Doyle,[4] refers to the ability to bring to mind past events whose characters, locations, happenings, or materials are no longer present to our senses. 'Memory is a bridge over the flow of time ... but many psychologists have concluded that it is both less and more than an inner record of all the events we live through.'

By 'memory' we refer to those processes essential for most intelligent behaviour, including learning, by which a person is able to recall past experiences to his present consciousness. Smith[5] speaks of it as 'an organised and integrative process combining both perceptual and motor activities'. Evans[6] defines it as 'essentially that property, shared by a large number of living organisms, of storing information about past experiences so that these can be acted on later to improve the animal's chances of surviving'. Gerard[7] states: 'Memory involves the making of an impression by an experience, the retention of some record of this impression and the re-entry of this record into consciousness (or behaviour) as recall and recognition'. Adams[8] views memory as 'the habit state of a subject that gives the capacity for correct recurrences of a criterion response'.

There can be no learning without remembering; but learning and remembering are not equivalents, they are different aspects of the same phenomenon. To remember is to retain the effects of experience over a time; to learn is to retain information over a period of time. Hence, memory is implicit in all types of learning. 'There could be no learning if there were no memory, for the effects of experience could not carry over from one time to the next' (Donahoe and Wessells).[9] In order to demonstrate that a student has *learned*, it is necessary to show that he or she has *remembered*, i.e. that, given the passage of time and the effects of interference (see p. 218), the student is able, nevertheless, to retain and retrieve information learned on a previous occasion.

The comments above concerning the phenomenon we speak of as 'remembering' should serve to remind teachers that memory is probably not a 'central storehouse' located at some fixed points in the brain. Rather is it to be thought of as a series of functions of the central nervous system, involving the registration and storing of an individual's experiences and the later recall of what has been stored. The views of early physiologists, such as Gall (1758–1828) and Flourens (1794–1867), suggesting that mental powers, such as memory, were localized in separate, identifiable regions of the brain, seem to have been discredited by the work of Lashley and Penfield. (Lashley has argued that functions are not localized, but that every region of the brain is involved in all functions – the notion of 'equipotentiality'.) Luria, the Russian neuropsychologist, argues that no psychological ability exists in isolation and that human mental processes in general, and conscious activity in particular, require the participation of *all* the appropriate functional units of the brain. A commonly held view of many brain research workers is summarized by Stein and Rosen: 'In contrast to the view of functional localisation, we are proposing that the brain be viewed as a dynamic organisation of differentiated, but highly interrelated, structures ... Input into any one area of the central nervous system can affect activity in all areas of the brain'.[10] Note, however, experiments in electrical stimulation of the brain by Ojemann in 1990 (mentioned by Crick[11]) involving a bilingual person, and suggesting a difference in the location of certain aspects of that person's two languages.

The information-processing model of the memory

In recent years several 'models of memory', i.e. representations of systems believed to account for the phenomena involved in remembering, have been constructed. A number of these models reflect the 'information-processing' approach, which views the memory system as involving three sequential processes – *registration, retention*, and *retrieval of information*. (It will be noted that the language used here is metaphorical, i.e. the processes are explained in terms associated with the storage and retrieval of information in a computer.)

(a) *Registration* comprises the perception, encoding, and neural representation of stimuli at the time of a learning experience. Perception involves the set of events following stimulation that occur in the brain's input part. Encoding involves the selectivity of registration: perceived stimuli are transformed into an organized, conceptual 'meaningful' mode. Encoding processes may emerge as diagrams, images, etc. The teacher should note that a student's motivation, attention, previously acquired knowledge, will affect the selection of stimuli for registration.

(b) *Retention* allows the neurological representation of the student's experiences to be 'stored' over a period of time for later use. (Hence, to 'forget' may be considered as failure to retain that which has been registered.) Tulving[12] has suggested that 'learning' is merely an improvement in the student's power of retention.

(c) *Retrieval* allows the student to have access to information previously registered and retained. It may be that the mechanism of retrieval is distinct from that which places information in the memory. Eccles[13] suggests that 'databank memory' is stored in the brain, especially in the cerebral cortex, and is retrieved by a mental act. 'Recognition memory' then allows critical scrutiny of the retrieval; that scrutiny continues until the retrieval is judged to be correct, or is abandoned. Note Bartlett's suggestion that the act of remembering is more like 'reconstructing' than 'locating or fishing out'.

The Waugh-Norman model[14] suggests that items first enter one's primary memory (PM), which has a very limited capacity. Rehearsal (i.e. 'going over' something in one's memory repeatedly) maintains the items in the PM and assists in transferring them to the more permanent secondary memory (SM). When new material is introduced to the PM, old material is displaced. An item in the PM is in the student's consciousness; an item recalled from the SM has been absent from his or her consciousness.

The Atkinson-Shiffrin model[15] involves three components: a sensory memory, a short-term store (STS), and a long-term store (LTS). The information in one's sensory memory (resulting from simple sensory recognition of stimuli), also known as 'surface memory', lasts only a fraction of a second, depending on the strength of the stimuli (an important point for teachers); such information is made up, according to Houston, of 'very basic, unelaborated impressions of the external environment which decay rapidly unless processed into one of the other stores'. (An example might be a word spoken by the teacher which results in the learner having to integrate his or her changing pattern of auditory stimulation.) Some of the information in the sensory memory is transferred, as the result of maintaining the process of attention, to the STS. (Cognitive psychologists say that the STS defines our immediate consciousness.) Information may be lost from the STS in about 15–20 seconds by a process of displacement or lack of rehearsal; it is transferred to the LTS as the result of processing, i.e. rehearsal. ('Maintenance rehearsal', known also as 'rote rehearsal', or 'repetition' is intended to hold information for immediate use. 'Elaborative rehearsal' attempts to relate newly acquired information to patterns of knowledge stored in LTS.) Information in the LTS may remain there permanently, although it is subject to interference and a process of decay. It is the LTS which is of much interest to the teacher; it represents the permanent part of the learner's memory system reserved for information of high future utility (e.g. one's native language). A much-simplified diagram, illustrating the basic features of this model is given in Figure 17.1.

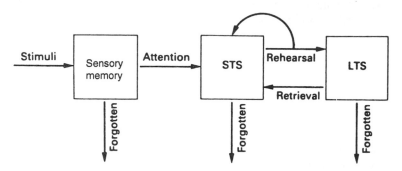

Figure 17.1   The Atkinson-Shiffrin model of memory.

Theoreticians, such as Tulving,[16] have suggested that the long-term memory can be divided into *episodic memory* which stores images of our personal experiences, *semantic memory* which stores facts and general knowledge, and *procedural memory* which stores information about how to perform activities. Johnson[17] states that the long-term memory (LTM) is of particular importance in learning: 'Learning may be said to be *meaningful* to the extent that the new learning task can be related [in the LTM] to the existing cognitive structure of the learner, i.e. the residual of his earlier learnings.' The degree of 'meaningfulness' will depend on the learner's associational background, recorded in his or her LTM. Cognitive psychologists, such as Anderson,[18] have argued that information in the LTM is organised as *schemata*, that is abstract structures of information. The schemata provide expectations about objects and events; when they are properly formed and a particular event is consistent with our expectations, comprehension emerges. Anderson suggests, further, that it is when students do not possess appropriate schemata that problems of memory, comprehension and behaviour may emerge.

Broadbent's model[19] comprises three stores – sensory memory, STS and LTS – and, between STS and LTS, there is an 'address register' which holds information about items that assist in the retrieval of matter from LTS by 'reminding' the individual of what action is to be undertaken in the process of search.

The Craik-Lockhart[20] 'levels of processing' theory states that learners appear to subject stimuli to varying levels of mental processing. Learners retain only that information which has been thoroughly processed so that 'meaning' is given to it. The more attention given to the details of a stimulus, the more likely the student is to remember those details. Bransford[21] has suggested an amendment to this theory by advocating the significance for memory of the *depth of processing* and the *similarities* between the conditions under which the material was learned and those under which its reinstatement is required.

The concept of memory as involving the processing of information in the form of a progression through distinct memory stores has been criticized for failing to stress the *dynamic nature* of memory. It is suggested, as an alternative, that *levels of processing* be emphasized, so that there need be no clear 'terminal points' separating one store from another; memory codes should be characterized according to the degree of processing that created them. Thus, the durability of the memory trace will increase as the depth of processing increases. To retrieve deeply-processed information may require more processing capacity than that needed to retrieve shallow-processed information.

The biological basis of memory

This short sample of some contemporary research is given so that teachers might be aware of the extraordinarily complex nature of memory and so that they might note some of the general trends in current thinking on topics such as 'remembering' – a matter of importance in the management of instruction.

Much research into memory relates to the 'engram' – the inferred physiological change that apparently provides a basis for memory. Researchers seem to accept: that although engrams have not been identified, they must exist; that any change of behaviour reflecting memory must result from some modifications of neural activity; and that these modifications are determined by the organism's experiences and by the physical-chemical properties of the learner's nervous system.

Hebb (1904–85)[22] suggests that an input of information stimulates neural activity in the receptor and effector cells, as a result of which there is 'reverberatory activity' in the brain, thus producing a neural trace (or engram) which lasts for a short time (less than a minute) – the so-called short-term memory. A prolonged or repeated period of reverberation results in the modification of brain structure (perhaps involving protein synthesis) which facilitates the creation and consolidation of connections, perhaps in the form of synaptic growths, between assemblies of cells, known as 'structural traces', forming the long-term memory. (Hebb thought of a trace as a 'construct' inferring a learner's internal representation of specific information about some event stored at the time of its presentation to the learner. Synapses were, according to Hebb, the functional connections between nerve cells, allowing the transmission of nervous impulses from one cell to the next.) The traces can be restimulated, and the experiences which created them can be 'remembered' for as long as the reverberating neural activity continues. The short-term memory is consolidated into long-term memory.[23]

Milner,[24] one of Hebb's students, argues that during the learning process neuronic activity facilitates the release of chemical transmitter substances which make connections between neurons. These connections may become relatively permanent as the result of modifications of the neurons, thus creating 'memory'. (Her views were supported by Kandel,[25] who has referred to the short-term memory as residing in the persistence of a depression in the rate of entry of calcium ions into the cells constituting the presynaptic terminals.)

Developments in cellular neurochemistry, following the discovery of RNA and DNA, have been interpreted as suggesting that RNA may be a 'memory molecule' (i.e. the molecule which acts as some kind of chemical mediator for the memory), the character of which alters with changes in learning.[26] There was some evidence which seemed to point to the conclusion that the concentration of RNA in the neurons tended to increase when they were stimulated during the learning process. Further experiments have suggested, however, that the information-carrying molecule is, perhaps, a soluble protein rather than RNA. Some research workers now hold the view that when learning occurs some chemicals are synthesized and act to direct neural impulses along the brain circuits. (There is evidence to suggest that when a substance inhibiting protein synthesis is administered to a subject soon after a learning event, no long-term memory is established.)

Lashley[27] has suggested, following experiments involving the removal of the cortical area of rats, that the storage of information in the brain seems to be a molar property of the mass of cortical cells. An analogy with the non-localized storage of information on a holograph has been advanced by Lashley's students.

Some types of drug, when administered to learners, appear to enhance short-term memory and to make more efficient, not the recall, but the transfer from short-term to long-term memory. It may be that the effect of these drugs is to modulate the properties of neurones and their synapses.[28]

Perhaps one of the most interesting of recent research programmes into memory is that involving the hippocampus (the region of the brain in the lower part of the cerebrum). It is known that information stored in the brain prior to hippocampal damage seems to be retained, but there is no long-term storage, although short-term memory is, seemingly, unimpaired. There is now evidence that the left hippocampus is involved in the construction and consolidation of verbal memory, while the right is involved with spatial pictorial memory. Injury to the left lobe seems to result in memory loss related to experiences after the injury. Eccles[29] suggests that although the hippocampus itself is not the site of information storage within the brain, the 'self-conscious mind' seems to be dependent on some kind of storage process resulting from hippocampal activity leading to the laying down of an engram.

The complex nature of this research and the relegation of the *tabula rasa* (see below) to the museum of the history of ideas must suggest to the teacher that an explanation of students' failure to recall in terms of 'not trying hard enough' may be simplistic in the extreme.

Reinstatement

William James commented that 'to remember' involves 'the knowledge of an event or fact, of which meantime we have not been thinking, with the additional consciousness that we have thought or experienced it before'. To remember is to recall to one's consciousness. It may involve the *recall of specific information* (in response, for example, to the question: 'Who was the first man to walk on the moon?'). It may be the *recall of contextual experience*, known as 'recognition' ('I know this tune – I can remember it being played at a concert. Of course! It's a nocturne by Chopin!'). It may consist of the process which Gagné names *'the reinstatement of intellectual skills'*, involving those intellectual operations which are necessary in order to operate a typewriter, solve a problem in geometry, or perform on a musical instrument. (Gagné[30] speaks of *schemas*, i.e. networks of memory entities associated with one another; newly learned information 'slots in' to a schema, and information from the entire schema is available for recall.)

Reinstatement may be illustrated thus: a learner faced with a problem necessitating the calculation of the length of a hypotenuse must, first, recall verbal information, such as the meaning of 'triangle' and 'hypotenuse'. Next, he or she must reinstate the appropriate rules of procedure, including Pythagoras' theorem, needed to answer the problem. (The process of remembering has the effect of creating a relationship between past, present and future: we remember how to act so as to set a lathe in motion – knowledge acquired and stored in the *past* is recalled in the *present* so that *future* action is facilitated.) Gagné enumerates three functions of remembering: *temporary holding*, i.e. keeping something in one's mind in order to complete an action; *mediational use*, i.e. facilitating the learning of skills, for example, by the recall of verbal information; *lifetime retention*, i.e. the creation of a store of intellectual skills which can always be reinstated.

How do we store information? What is the precise nature of the neurophysiological changes that occur when information is stored? Early concepts, which appeared long before the investigation of the nervous system, suggested that the human mind was a *tabula rasa* ('scraped tablet') devoid of innate ideas, upon which were imprinted concepts resulting from the senses' reactions to the external world. Aristotle and Thomas Aquinas referred to this theory, which was developed further in the writings of John Locke (1632–1704):

> Let us ... suppose the mind to be, as we say, white paper, void of all characters, without any ideas; how comes it to be furnished? Whence comes it by that vast store, which the busy and boundless fancy of man has painted on it with an almost endless variety? ... To this I answer, in one word, from *experience*. ... The pictures drawn in our minds are laid in fading colours; and if not sometimes refreshed, vanish and disappear. ... Impressions fade and vanish out of the understanding, leaving no more footsteps or remaining characters of themselves than do shadows flying over fields of corn...

This attractive but fanciful view is no longer acceptable but it continues to find an echo in the practice of those teachers who appear to act as though students' minds were 'white paper' merely awaiting the process of imprinting. Complex information is neither received nor retained as the result of a mere statement and its repetition. If that were so, remembering would cease to be a problem in the classroom. It is useful to remember here Trusted's comment that our minds are not like pieces of blank paper, ready to be written on. 'Our minds actively sort and classify sensations, they can be compared to searchlights, directed to and illuminating those parts of the world which they find particularly interesting.'[31] (O' Hear observes that unless the learner is aware of those aspects of his experience to which he should attend, he would probably be unable to note systematically *any* features of his environment; the *tabula rasa* is a flawed concept.[32])

Why we forget

Inability to recall (i.e. the process whereby information in the memory becomes inaccessible) or recognize may range in intensity from the momentary 'slip of memory' (so that one refers to one's friend, George, as John, and quickly corrects the error) to the functional disturbances of the memory such as amnesia, as a result of which the sufferer cannot recall immediate personal history. A variety of reasons for the phenomenon of forgetting can be advanced: repression (i.e. motivated forgetting – a defence mechanism which seems to allow us to set aside and render inaccessible very unpleasant memories); disuse of information (leading, presumably, to the disappearance of the associated memory traces); trace decay; cue-forgetting; and interference.

Trace decay (i.e. gradual decay or loss of clarity in the neural engram) is inferred from the phenomenon which is illustrated in Figure 17.2, i.e. the well-known 'curve of forgetting', representing a decline in the amount remembered over a period of time (if the material learned is not 'practised').

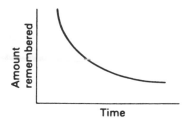

Figure 17.2 Curve of forgetting.

(It should be noted that the amount which the learner tends to forget does *not* vary in direct proportion to the passing of time – there is a gradual levelling out of the curve after an initial steep decline.) It has been suggested that traces in the learner's perceptual system tend to fade rapidly immediately after presentation. Thus, according to Thorndike (see Chapter 4), if actions fall into disuse and are not practised, they weaken and disappear from the memory. (Teachers are often intuitively aware of this.) Guthrie (see Chapter 4) argued that forgetting occurs as the result of competition among responses. Many psychologists now believe that the passing of time does not in itself explain forgetting; the passing of time permits interference from new learning and other memories, which produces forgetting. The nature of the learner's activities between learning and attempted recall is also significant in strengthening or diminishing the capacity to remember. The relevance of this to the place of emphasis, recapitulation and revision in the planning of a lesson should be clear.

Cue-dependent forgetting refers to a failure of retrieval because the cues which were present at the time of learning are not present at the moment of attempted recall. There is a 'trace', but the lack of appropriate cues prevents the learner's access to that trace. Provision by the teacher of contextual cues is useful: 'While you are trying to recall this, think of last week's lesson in which we looked at a video. Can you recall the first event which was shown?'

Interference refers to the inhibition of one 'piece of learning' by another. Where the learner forgets something because of something else he learns *afterwards*, the effect is known as *retroactive inhibition*. Where he forgets something because of something else he has learned before, the effect is known as *proactive inhibition*. Experimental groups have been used to study interference in the following ways:

Experimental group	Learn A	Learn B	Recall A
Control group	Learn A	Rest	Recall A

(Here the measure of *retroactive inhibition* is the difference in recall.)

Experimental group	Learn B	Learn A	Recall A
Control group	Rest	Learn A	Recall A

(Here the measure of *proactive inhibition* is the difference in recall.)

The more similar the subject matter learned (as tasks A and B), the greater is the possibility of interference, resulting in forgetting. The importance of this finding for the management of the teaching process needs to be stressed: time-tables should be arranged so as to separate as widely as is practicable subjects with a similar content, e.g. foreign languages. Further, since interference seems very powerful over short periods of time, the importance in verbal communication of leaving a short gap after a significant statement is based not on any practice of the art of rhetoric but on the need to allow time for some fact to 'sink in' so that its chances of being retained by the learner are increased.[33] (Teachers who are planning lesson content should be aware of the 'primary' and 'recency' effects, which are said to explain the general tendency of students to learn best the first and last things presented in a lesson: the introductory and concluding parts of a unit of instruction are of special significance for the remembering of information. As a consequence, the 'middle of the lesson' should be carefully reinforced. Note also the so-called 'serial position effect' from which is derived the advice: 'Put forward the most important material at the beginning and end of the lesson; do not bury it in the middle'.)

Osgood comments:

> A memory is nothing more than a response produced by a stimulus. It is merely the maintained association of a response with a stimulus over an interval of time. The question of why we forget comes down to this: what are the conditions under which stimuli lose their capacity to evoke previously associated responses? Forgetting is a direct function of the degree to which substitute responses are associated with the original stimuli during the retention interval.[34]

There is also evidence that trying to learn too much may result in forgetting, since the short-term memory may have a capacity of not more than 7 ± 2 separate 'chunks'. (Miller[35] has argued that the short-term memory is limited by its ability to handle only a limited number of chunks of information. In Miller's terminology, a 'chunk' is a unit which integrates a number of smaller elements into a meaningful whole. The size of a chunk can be enlarged by its integration within a hierarchy, allowing the learner's capacity to pay attention to new information to be increased by stages.) This, too, has significance for the planning of instruction, in particular for the timing and spacing of lesson content. Failure of recall may be the result of the teacher's understandable wish to impart as much information as time will allow, without taking into account the possible over-burdening of the students' short-term memory. 'Mental indigestion' may be an imprecise metaphor; it draws attention, however, to the difficulties for the student who is required to assimilate a large mass of material in a short period.

Koestler's 'abstractive' and 'spotlight' memories

In an interesting paper, supported by some experimental detail, Koestler[36] advanced a hypothesis involving two types, or categories, of memory – abstractive and spotlight. Both are different classes of phenomena, based on different neural mechanisms. Abstractive memory generalizes and schematizes; spotlight memory particularizes and concretizes.

Abstractive memory which, in the learner, is related to insightful learning, comprises what we can remember of our life history and the knowledge we have accumulated. A process of filtering 'strips down' input to bare essentials; we condense, remember sequences and reduce experience to a colourless abstract before it moves into the memory store. ('A large proportion of our memories resembles the dregs in a wine glass, the dehydrated sediments of experiences whose flavour has gone.') Learners retain the abstracted meaning of the instruction they have received; particulars may be lost, but they can be trained by appropriate teaching (and by learning from experience) to abstract fine nuances, enabling them to recall detail.

Spotlight memory is derived from our ability to recall episodes from the past with almost hallucinatory vividness. This adds texture and flavour to what is recalled because it is powerfully evocative. Some emotional significance may be involved in retention of this nature; it is as if a significant experience has been imprinted in the memory. The past is continuously recreated in the forms of eidetic imagery (i.e. of a richly pictorial quality). The amalgam of spotlight and abstractive memory affects the content and flavour of our total recall, and the processes involved (which are not yet understood and can only be inferred) are largely of an unconscious nature. 'The canons of perception and memory operate instantaneously and unconsciously; we are always playing games without awareness of the rules.'

The teacher's role in aiding retention and recall

The practical experience of teachers, underpinned by some of the theory discussed earlier in this chapter, may indicate that the learner can be aided in tasks of memorization, consolidation and recall if lesson preparation takes into account certain matters. These are considered under seven headings: timetabling, content, preparedness, presentation, revision, practice and transfer of learning.

Timetabling

The timetabling of a course ought to take into consideration the difficulties which might arise for the learner as the result of proactive and retroactive inhibition. Timetabling should 'space out' similar subjects, should allow for breaks, and should not overload the student with long, unvaried lesson periods so charged with material that acquisition and retention become impossible. (Teachers should note and consider the implications of the discovery by the Gestalt psychologist, Zeigarnik, that interrupting a task in which a learner has become involved, can lead to a higher level of recall of the material being learned. The memory traces which are said to be associated with incomplete actions are thought to remain active until completion of the task.)

Content

The content of the lesson ought to be presented not as an isolated unit but, essentially, as a continuation of that which has been learned previously. It ought to be associated clearly with the learner's existing stock of knowledge. 'The more other facts a fact is associated with in the mind the better possession of it our memory retains. Each of its associates becomes a hook to which it hangs, a means to fish it up by when sunk beneath the surface' (James). (James believed that the secret of a good memory was the forming of 'diverse and multiple associations with every fact we care to retain ... All improvement in memory consists in the improvement of one's habitual methods of recording facts.') As noted above, the provision of cues for the recall of relevant information is also an important contribution the teacher can make to the process of assisting retention and recall. Perhaps above all, the content of the lesson must be *meaningful* to the learner if it is to lead to firm retention and swift recall. Meaningful material is usually remembered more clearly and for longer periods of time than that which has little or no relation to the student's level of learning at the time of the lesson. The statement couched in simple terms, introducing new concepts in terms of those which are already known, has a higher chance of acquisition than that which goes outside the student's conceptual framework, thus making comprehension and retention very difficult. 'If the material is sufficiently meaningful, there may be no forgetting whatever. Content that is not so brilliantly structured, but that still has much meaning, will be remembered in proportion to its meaning. Nonsense material is headed for extinction before the last syllable is uttered' (Stephens and Evans).[37]

Preparedness

Preparedness involves the teacher's explanation, in carefully contrived terms, of the significance and usefulness of the learning in relation to the learner's life style. Seligman has suggested that memory may be related directly to the learner's preparedness. It is for the teacher to motivate the learner in a manner which will arouse and maintain personal involvement with the topic which is to be remembered.

Presentation

Presentation of the lesson, if it is to aid retention, demands a logical, clearly connected and organized sequence. The short-term memory seems to be associated with the organization of information; hence adequate rehearsal is important if information is to be retained more or less permanently. Where the parts of the lesson are organized coherently, comprehension, acquisition and retention of the whole ought to be facilitated since patterns are usually more acceptable to the learner than disjointed fragments. (William James[38] pointed out that, 'of two men with the same outward experiences and the same amount of mere native tenacity, the one who thinks over his experiences most and weaves them into systematic relations with each other will be the one with the best memory'.) A 'warm-up period', particularly before relearning, is usually beneficial to the student's recall processes. Further, the student should be stimulated by the presentation so that his attention (i.e. surface memory) remains focused on the lesson material, thus assisting assimilation and retention. Wherever possible, the presentation ought to avoid an outcome which is no more than rote-learning. (Ausubel describes rote-learned materials as 'discrete and relatively isolated entities that are relatable to cognitive structure only in an arbitrary, verbatim fashion'.) The presenter should aim, rather, at the achievement of insight (see Chapter 7) and the understanding of principles which will facilitate retention. Principles are generally retained much more effectively than a mass of material which has been committed to memory without understanding. Note, also, the *von Restorff effect*, which suggests that the teacher can assist memorization by making ideas stand out, e.g. by verbal exaggeration, underlining, use of bold print and colour in writing.

In *Memory and Program Construction* (1979),[39] Ludwig, who had investigated the problems of retention by students of the content of instruction, argues that where a teacher attempts to make a number of points during a half-hour lesson period, no more than twenty of those points will find a place in a student's short-term memory. Of those twenty points, only six or seven will move into the long-term memory. But the number of points which move into the long-term memory may be doubled where the content of the lesson is repeated some two or three weeks later.

Presentation of the lesson might include training in the use of peg words, key words and mnemonics. Advice from the teacher on the use of a peg words, which, when recalled in the appropriate context, will assist in the recall of associated words, can be valuable. A lecturer dealing with the concept of entropy in a unit of instruction as part of a course in introductory thermodynamics can use as peg words, 'distribution of energy', 'measure of information'. Key words, when supplied by the teacher, can lead to the recall of structures and schemas of thought. An economics teacher conducting a course on 'protection' might use as key words 'dumping', 'diversification', etc. Mnemonics (Greek, *mnasthai* = to remember) can be presented by the teacher as aids to the memorizing of sequences: they are coined words and phrases that use the initials of the words to be remembered in their correct order. Examples: '(Mr.) Roy G.Biv' (red, orange, yellow ... etc. – the order of colours of the spectrum); 'FACE', to indicate the notes in the spaces of the five-line musical stave; the ludicrous, but useful, statement intended to assist students of anatomy in remembering the order of the twelve cranial nerves: 'At an oil factory (*olfactory*), an optician (*optic*) searched for the occupant (*oculomotor*) of a truck (*trochlear*) which...'[40]

Revision and practice

Assimilation, consolidation and retention of lesson content require recapitulation, rehearsal, *periodic revision and review* (i.e. 'practice with an experimental cast'). The teacher's recapitulation at regular intervals of the lesson headings may help in their assimilation. Rehearsal – by which is meant an activity in which the student goes over the lesson material *by himself* after its initial presentation (which may be equivalent to a repetition of the lesson's stimuli) – can take the form of reading a handout which contains a summary of the lesson's main points, or studying and reciting one's own notes. (Such an activity is an example of the 'deep processing' which is said to improve the memory, in that it contributes to the durable encoding of lesson content in the long-term memory.) Revision – which involves re-studying the lesson – should take place as soon as possible after the lesson has ended. (Note the work of Garcia, which throws doubt on the tenet that learning can take place *only* when stimulus and associable events are close in time.) It should be repeated at intervals and, preferably, be linked with tests which examine recall. (There is evidence to suggest that the 'distribution of practice' does affect speed of learning *and* efficiency of recall. The spacing of recall tests is, therefore, of much importance in lesson planning.) The final revision ought to be planned by the class teacher and could be the occasion for a full examination which will test and assess the level of comprehension and recall. Davies suggests that recall tends to rise to its maximum point about ten minutes after the conclusion of a lesson, and that this may be the result of the mind's 'putting material into focus'. A very steep decline in remembering then takes place and, by the next day, approximately 75 per cent of the lesson may have failed to move into the long-term memory. Frequent and spaced reviews of lesson content are essential if learning is to be effective.

The assimilation of material presented in class, the building and maintenance of memory, may be assisted by the process of its being applied in *practice situations*. In particular, where psychomotor skills are being taught (see Chapter 24), practice ought to walk hand in hand with theory rather than follow on its heels. Thus, the theory of the use of the navigational compass is best assimilated by the learner who is able to participate in planned projects involving the practical use of the instrument.

The concept of *circadian rhythms* might be considered by the teacher planning a programme of instruction. It is suggested that there is a daily pattern of physiological change in our bodies which affects our information-processing capacities. Short-term retention, it is argued, is better in the morning; long-term retention seems to be better when the student is learning material in the afternoon. Wingfield argues that biological rhythms have a large effect on performance and memory – up to 10–20 per cent of a total performance score.

Strategies for memorization

In relation to the tasks of verbal learning, Slavin[41] enumerates the following positive methods: use of mental imagery (involving the visualization of 'vivid key words'); use of mnemonics; massed practice (i.e. learning facts by repeating them on many random occasions during a time period); distributed practice (repeating items at fixed intervals during a time period); part learning (learning and seeking to memorize the material, one segment at a time); overlearning (involving practising newly acquired knowledge after the achievement of mastery – see p. 293).

Fontana[42] advises the following routines so as to assist consolidation and improvement of the efficiency of the long-term memory: repeating material and questioning the learner; making instruction relevant, understandable and interesting; introducing practice into the learning process; practising recognition and recall.

Davies recommends employment of the following instructional tactics: concentration on the sequencing of instruction; attempting to stress key points by emphasizing essential facts; organization of teaching material into patterns by the use of diagrams and charts; stressing relationships of newly learned material and that which is already known.

An aspect of behaviour from which effective retention, recall and meaningful application may be inferred is known as 'transfer of learning'. This is considered next in some detail.

Transfer of learning: its essence

In the first chapter of this text education was considered as a *social process* built in large measure on the formal activities of teaching and learning. Learning in the colleges of further education, as in other educational institutions, may be considered to have meaning, significance and value only if it is related to the personal development of the student as a member of society. An important justification of the teacher's role in providing the conditions for effective learning must be, ultimately, the value of that learning to the student in the world outside the classroom. Training in the ability to transfer knowledge, to generalize from learned basic principles, to utilize stored experience in the facilitation of new learning, constitutes therefore, an essential factor in the education of the student.

An important task of the teacher-manager is the planning of instruction so that a high degree of positive transfer shall result wherever appropriate. Transfer of learning has been defined as 'the extent to which the learning of an instructional event contributes to or detracts from the subsequent problem solving or the learning of subsequent instructional events' (Royer). (It has been described also as 'learning to learn'.) The phenomenon of transfer may be described formally, thus:

Where the learning of something (A_1) facilitates the learning or performance of A_2, there is *positive transfer* from A_1 to A_2. Where the learning of A_1 makes the learning or performance of A_2 more difficult, there is negative transfer from A_1 to A_2. Where the learning of A_1 has no apparent effect on the learning or performance of A_2 there is *zero transfer* from A_1 to A_2.

Examples of *positive transfer* are seen in facility in the basic arithmetical processes applied successfully to the use of logarithm tables, ability to ride a bicycle utilized in balancing on a motor cycle in motion, dexterity in the fingering of a tin whistle applied to the playing of scales on the orchestral flute. Subordinate capabilities have been mastered (an essential factor in transfer situations) and applied successfully to more advanced and demanding tasks. An example of *negative transfer* is evident in the confusion of a student trained mechanically in the drills of denary arithmetical processes and confronted, without preparation, by an arithmetic in which $1 + 1 = 10$. A further example is seen in the case of the young mathematician steeped in the tradition of Euclid, which he has acquired in mechanical rote-like fashion, who meets the non-Euclidean geometry of Lobachevsky and Riemann. *Zero transfer* exists where A_1 and A_2 have very little or no relationship as, for example, history and shorthand.

The concept of *proactive interference* has been used to describe a type of negative transfer in which the memory of previous learning experiences slows down, or even inhibits, new learning. *Retroactive interference* occurs when the learning of new information disrupts the retention of previously held information; it is as if the learning of a new response extinguishes the old learned response. Teachers soon become aware, for example, of the phenomenon of failure in one area creating inhibitions preventing future learning in a similar area (unhappy memories of a failure in mathematics creating difficulties in the learning of some aspects of physics) or the learning of idiom in a foreign language driving out acquired formal rules of grammar.

Examples of *lateral transfer* (prior learning affecting new learning at approximately the same level) are seen in the use of mathematics in the solution of problems in physics, the use of principles of geography in the interpretation of problems in military strategy, and the use of scientific method in the solution of a question in applied economics. *Vertical transfer* (prior learning affecting new learning of a 'higher' quality) is exemplified by the progress of the learner from the elements of arithmetic to the use of the calculus, from the knowledge of parsing to the study of semantics, from mastery of the tonic sol-fa to the writing of counterpoint.

Much early speculation on the basis of transfer centred on the 'faculty theory' advanced by those psychologists who held that there existed in the mind separate faculties such as learning, memory, etc. A learner's mind could be trained as a whole, it was suggested, by submitting him or her to a formal discipline which would 'strengthen the faculties', a process akin to the physical training of the athlete. 'Training of the mind' was often the declared objectives of the traditional classical education, consisting largely of mathematics, Greek and Latin grammar and literature. An education of this type was held to accentuate 'mental discipline' to develop the memory and the ability to think clearly – and to prepare the learner for his station in life. ('Bowling is good for the stone ... gentle walking for the stomach, riding for the head and the like; so, if a man's wits be wandering, let him study the mathematics': Francis Bacon in *Essay on Studies* (1597). Sir Leslie Stephen's biography of his brother, Sir James Fitzjames Stephen (1829–94), the legal historian and judge, includes a statement made by their Eton tutor concerning an exercise in 'longs and shorts' (classical versification): ' "Stephen Major", he once said to my brother, "if you do not take more pains, how can you ever expect to write good longs and shorts? If you do not write good longs and shorts, how can you ever be a man of taste? If you are not a man of taste, how can you ever hope to be of use in the world?" ')

The concept of 'transfer of formal discipline' was discredited by the experiments of William James and Thorndike. James undertook to measure the time he spent in learning 158 lines of a poem by Hugo before spending one month memorizing Milton's *Paradise Lost*. He then memorized a further 158 lines of Hugo's poem but found that it took him longer than on the previous occasion. Memory did not seem to be an independent faculty capable of being trained in this way. Thorndike showed by experiment that practice in verbal learning did not by itself improve general learning ability. (For an examination of evidence suggesting the effectiveness of 'formal discipline', see 'Formal discipline' by D. Lehman and R. Lempert.[43])

A later interpretation of transfer of learning was based on the theory of 'identical elements' associated, in particular, with Thorndike and Woodworth.[44] Transfer occurred, they claimed, if tasks A_1 and A_2 had *common elements*. The amount of transfer would be a function of the number of those elements. 'Chief among such identical elements of practical importance in education are associations including ideas about aims and ideas of method and general principles, and associations involving elementary facts of experience such as length, colour and number, which are repeated again and again in differing combinations' (Thorndike). More recent investigation suggests that the amount of transfer might be a function of the level of similarity in the situations leading to the learning events associated with A_1 and A_2; learning for transfer is seen to be largely the result of the teacher's careful organization and reorganization of experience.

Transfer of learning in the classroom

Transfer of learning rarely occurs spontaneously in the classroom; almost always it is the result of a teaching strategy aimed specifically at transfer and emphasizing underlying principles. Such a strategy will generally involve direct methods of teaching and will include the practice of skills and the application of principles in realistic situation. Where the instructional objective is concerned with lateral or vertical transfer, the mastery of subordinate tasks is an essential prerequisite for success. Revision and recapitulation so as to ensure this mastery must have a place, therefore, in a transfer strategy. In particular, the identical elements of the transfer situations must be analysed and presented to students in detail.

In the early 1990s particular attention was given in some British colleges, during a period of research into transfer of training, to the implications for class teaching of *the theory of low-road and high-road transfer* which had been formulated by the American researchers, Salomon and Perkins. *Low-road transfer* applies to an activity in which a previously acquired idea or skill seems to have been retrieved from the memory almost automatically, and is utilized in a similar, current task, such as where a student who has mastered a mechanical task involving one type of motor car is able to carry out the same task swiftly and, apparently, automatically, on a different type of car. This type of transfer (known also as 'near-transfer') involves students being given many opportunities to practise the skill with a variety of materials in different task settings.

High-road transfer involves the formulation of a rule, strategy or schema which facilitates the creation of 'connections' between different high-level tasks, such as where a student of economics was able, without any assistance, to discover for herself the general application of differentiation processes, which she had learned in mathematics classes, to problems involving the calculation of marginal revenue. The 'mindful abstraction' involved in this type of transfer necessitates students being aware of *what* they are doing and *why* they are doing it. High-road transfer appears to be associated with training in the recognition of meaningful cues so as to allow the retrieval of learned information in order to establish appropriate schemas and with the planned development of thinking skills (views which were confirmed by the research in British colleges).

Several key studies in transfer have offered the conclusion that successful retention and transfer may depend on the ability of the learner to *generalize by obtaining insight into the basic principles* underlying his work. (The findings of the Gestalt psychologists (see Chapter 7) are of particular relevance to these studies.) Discovery by the learner of common patterns of content or technique has been said to facilitate the application of principles to novel situations. The necessity for instructional objectives to be concerned with discovery and understanding if transfer is to be achieved, implies the need for careful consideration to be given to those modes of instruction which tend to encourage the comprehension of principles which will be applicable to new learning. Practice in a large and varied number of stimulus situations may be essential if generalization and transfer of knowledge are to result. The classroom teacher should remember two points: that generalization involves an understanding concerning *relationships*; and that training in *when and how to generalize* is of high significance as an aim of instructional activity.

Harlow's work on transfer suggests a further principle of direct importance for the classroom. Whenever the positive transfer of learning takes place, then, according to Harlow,[45] students are 'learning to learn' and acquiring 'learning sets' which facilitate their performance in the situations they encounter. To teach students *how* best to learn is to help in ensuring a fair degree of success in their task of generalization of learned principles.

Notes and references

1. See generally for this chapter: *Human Memory* by A. Baddeley (Erlbaum, 1994); *Theories of Memory* ed. A.F. Collins (Erlbaum, 1996); *Memory in the Real World* by G.

Cohen (Erlbaum, 1996); *Memory* ed. E.L. Bjork (Academic Press, 1996); *The Anatomy of Memory* ed. J. McConkey (OUP, 1996); 'Roads to transfer' by G. Salomon in *Educational Psychologist* (1989, *24*); *Memory* by A. Parkin (Blackwell, 1996).

2. *Memory Observed* (Freeman, 1982).
3. *Remembering* (CUP, 1932).
4. *Explorations in Psychology*, by C.L. Doyle (Brooks, 1987).
5. *Cybernetic Principles of Learning and Educational Design* (Holt, Rinehart & Winston, 1966).
6. *Psychology: A Dictionary of the Mind, Brain and Behaviour* (Arrow Books, 1978).
7. 'The memory' in *Scientific American* (1953, *2*).
8. *Human Memory* (McGraw-Hill, 1969).
9. *Learning, Language and Memory* (Harper & Row, 1980).
10. Note, however, the work of researchers such as Zeki, of London University. He apparently identified the existence and location of a specialized 'colour centre' in the brain: *Nature* (1989, p. 386). See also *A Vision of the Brain* by S. Zeki (Blackwell, 1993); *The Human Brain* by S. Greenfield (Weidenfeld & Nicolson, 1997).
11. *The Astonishing Hypothesis* (Simon & Schuster, 1994).
12. *Elements of Episodic Memory* (OUP, 1983).
13. *The Self and Its Brain* by Sir Karl Popper and Sir John Eccles (Routledge & Kegan Paul, 1984). This notable review of the body-mind relationship contains much information of interest to the teacher who wishes to know 'how we function'. It includes, for example, an explanation of current theories concerning the function of the brain hemispheres. (Note an argument against the 'right brain, left brain' hypothesis in 'Right brain, left brain: fact and fiction' by J. Levy in *Contemporary Issues in Educational Psychology* (McGraw-Hill, 1987).)
14. 'Primary memory' in *Psychological Review* (1965, *72*).
15. 'Human memory' in the *Psychology of Learning and Motivation* (Academic Press, 1968).
16. 'How many memory systems are there?' in *American Psychologist*, (1985, *40*).
17. 'Meaning in complex learning' in *Review of Educational Research* (1995).
18. 'Some reflections on the acquistion of knowledge' in *Educational Research* (1984, *13*).
19. *Perception and Communication* (Pergamon, 1958).
20. 'A framework for memory research' in *Journal of Verbal Thinking* (1972, *11*).
21. *Learning, Understanding and Remembering* (Belmont, 1979).
22. *The Organisation of Behaviour* (Wiley, 1949); 'A neuropsychological theory' in *Psychology* ed. S. Koch (McGraw-Hill, 1959).
23. Popper (*op.cit.*) criticizes this theory – it tends to ignore the role played in learning by interest, or attention, and it does not take into account the tendency of persons to forget unpleasant events. ('The essence of repression lies simply in the functions of rejecting and keeping something out of the consciousness': Freud.)
24. *Cognitive Processes and the Brain* (Van Nostrand, 1965).
25. *Principles of Neural Science* (Elsevier, 1991). See also *Synaptic Plasticity* by M. Boudry and G. Lynch (MIT, 1993).
26. See *Physiological Psychology* by J. Blundell (Methuen, 1975).
27. 'In search of the engram' in *Symposia of the Society for Experimental Biology* (1950, *4*).
28. See *Physiological Psychology* by R.A. Levitt (Holt, Rinehart & Winston, 1981).
29. *Op. cit.*
30. *The Conditions of Learning* (Holt-Saunders, 1985).
31. *The Logic of Scientific Inference* (Macmillan, 1979).
32. *Education, Society and Human Nature* (Routledge, 1981). See also *Human Memory and*

Cognition by M. Ashcroft (HarperCollins, 1994); *Learning and Memory* by J. Anderson (Wiley, 1995).

33. See 'Limits of memory' in *Mind in Science* by R.L. Gregory (Peregrine, 1984).
34. 'Method and theory' in *Experimental Psychology* (OUP, 1953).
35. 'The magical number 7±' in *Psychological Review* (1956, *63*). See also *The Mystery of Number* by A. Schimmell (OUP, 1993).
36. *Bricks to Babel* (Picador, 1980).
37. *Development and Classroom Learning* (Holt, Rinehart & Winston, 1973).
38. *Principles of Psychology* (Holt, 1890).
39. Pub. Buffalo (1979).
40. 'Mnemonic devices: classification, characteristics and criteria' by F.S. Bellezza in *Review of Educational Research* (1981, *51*). See also 'Mnemonic methods to enhance storage and retrieval' in *Memory* ed. E.L. Bjork (Academic Press, 1996).
41. *Education Psychology* (Prentice-Hall, 1988).
42. *Psychology for Teachers* (Macmillan, 1995).
43. *American Psychologist* (1988, *43*).
44. 'The influence of improvement in one mental function upon the efficiency of other functions' in *Psychological Review* (1901, *8*).
45. See 'The formation of learning sets' in *Psychological Review* (1949, *56*).

Chapter 18

Motivation, and Teaching Students How to Study

A motive is simply an impulse viewed as a constituent in a habit, a factor in disposition. In general its meaning is simple. But in fact motives are as numerous as are original impulsive activities multiplied by the diversified consequences they produce as they operate under diversified conditions (Dewey, 1922).

The variability of student behaviour in a classroom is generally taken for granted. Student X works with undiminished vigour in all lessons related to his course; Y shows interest in three out of the six subjects on his timetable, while paying little attention to the remaining three; Z views the course as of no value in his plans for the future and he remains uncommitted to the process of instruction. The attitudes of X, Y and Z may be explained in terms of *motivation* – a psychological construct which infers from a learner's *behaviour* his *perceived need* (i.e. some internal state requiring correction), his *drive* (i.e. the push given to his behaviour as a result of the need) and his *incentive* (i.e. the significance or the importance of his 'goal object', such as achievement of a high standard in his course work).

The psychological basis of motivation will be considered below, together with a short note on its physiological foundation. Suggestions are presented for the maintenance and strengthening of a learner's initial motivation in the classroom. The behaviour of the classroom teacher who is generally an important source of the stimuli which heighten the arousal of students in the learning process is seen in this context as possessing much significance.

The responsibility of the classroom teacher for promoting the conditions for effective learning should be seen not only in relation to the formal presentation of an instructional programme. Efficient *work skills* are needed by students if they are to utilize their time effectively, and this demands from the teacher acceptance of the need to explain to them how to develop productive study habits and maximize learning opportunities. In the second part of this chapter we consider instruction in study techniques.[1]

Motivation: its general nature

Motivation (*motus, movere* = to move) has been defined variously by psychologists as: 'the phenomena involved in a person's drives and goal-seeking behaviour'; 'the tendencies to activity which commence with a persistent stimulus (drive) and end with an appropriate adjustive response'; 'the arousal, direction, regulation and sustaining of a pattern of behaviour'; 'the internal state or condition that results in behaviour directed towards a specific goal'. The term will be used here in a general sense to refer to *a person's aroused desire for participation in a learning process*. ('Intrinsic motivation' comes from the individual; 'extrinsic motivation' is imposed on him by the environment (see p. 233).) Dewey[2] speaks of the teacher in his or her role of guide and director as steering a boat, '. . . but the energy that propels it must come from those who are learning'. The arousal, regulation and sustaining of the student's enthusiasm for learning, that is, the utilization of his or her power of motivation in the service of the learning process, constitute an important task for the teacher. The harnessing of the learner's drive is to be seen as of paramount importance in learning, for drive is the basis of intrinsic motivation in the classroom.

The presence of motivation is considered by most teachers to be essential to effective communication and learning. Davies[3] enumerates specific effects of motivation that are of importance in instruction: motivation arouses, sustains and energizes students; it assists in the direction of tasks; it is selective, in that it helps to determine students' priorities; it assists in organizing students' activities. Tutors in further education are aware of the relative ease of teaching highly and intrinsically motivated students and of the frustrations and difficulties arising from lessons with students who, for example, see no link between their aspirations and the content of a curriculum. The former usually exhibit behaviour which is calculated to assist the process of learning; the latter may display a resistance which makes effective learning difficult or impossible.

Motivation: its psychological basis

Psychologists tend to speak of the concept of 'motive' in terms of that which accounts for a learner's energy, direction and persistence of behaviour; hence it becomes possible to infer a learner's motives from observation of his or her use of learned behaviour, from the direction of that behaviour and from its persistence in pursuing and attaining a goal.[4] A learner's motives include those related to his or her physiological needs (hunger, sleep, etc.) and those related to self-esteem, ability to deal with his or her environment, etc. An individual's 'stored motives' depend on their strength and on the 'cues' in a situation which give him or her information as to the desirability of the goal and probabilities of attainment. Where motives are in conflict, the stronger motive generally prevails; where the motives are of equal strength, compromise, uncertainty and, possibly, inactivity will result.

Some psychologists refer to a 'motivational cycle' which is based on the following components: *need* (which arises when conditions felt to be necessary for optimal chances of survival veer from their optima); *drive* (some purposeful activity initiated by a need state of the organism or, in Woodworth's phrase,[5] 'the force of energy that activates the mechanisms that subserve behaviour'); *goal* (the terminal point of the drive); *satiation* (resulting in the cessation of the drive activity).

It is of interest to contrast the varying attitudes of some of the schools of psychology to the problem of motivation. The *Skinnerian behaviourists* view the concept of intrinsic drive as a useless construct; there is no value in postulating drive intervening in the process leading to operant responses. Purpose as a cause of motivation is seen as a non-scientific intrusion into S-R theory. A learner selects one response rather than another because of his or her genetic inheritance, prior conditioning and present stimuli; so-called 'motivation' is irrelevant. The *Gestaltists* view motivation as part of a total dynamic situation in which the learner seeks to resolve cognitive disequilibrium by overcoming barriers and moving to a goal. The *cognitivists* see external environmental matters as instigating activity which is mediated through the learner's cognitive system, thus providing intrinsic *and* extrinsic motivation. ('The cognition of future outcomes promotes the largest single source of motivation for human action.')

Maslow on motivation

Maslow[6] sees motivation in terms of an individual's striving for growth; he seeks to explain it by reference to a 'hierarchy of human needs' (see p. 123). People are 'wanting animals'. He believes that at any given moment a person's behaviour is dominated by those of his needs which have the greatest potency.[7] As his 'lower', physiological needs are adequately satisfied, motives at a 'higher' level in the hierarchy come into play. The hierarchy is illustrated on p.123.

Alderfer (b. 1926)[8] has reformulated Maslow's hierarchy into three levels:

1. *existence needs*, e.g. physiological and safety needs;
2. *relatedness needs*, i.e. needs involving social and interpersonal relationships;
3. *growth needs*, i.e. all those needs relating to the development of human potential.

In addition to Alderfer's hierarchy being based on a 'need satisfaction process', it incorporates a 'need frustration regression process'. Thus, where students experience repeated frustration in their efforts to satisfy some higher-order needs, they will place greater importance on the preceding lower-level needs.

Herzberg (b. 1923)[9] believes that persons are affected by 'motivators' and 'hygiene factors'. *Motivators* are the factors directly associated with the *content* of an activity. He enumerates, as examples, recognition, responsibility and the feeling of accomplishment. To the degree that they are present in the classroom motivation will occur, having a positive effect on learning. *Hygiene factors* are those primarily associated with the *context* of an activity. As applied to the classroom setting, examples of such factors are the style of instruction adopted by the teacher, security of the learner, interpersonal relationships in the classroom. When met, hygiene factors prevent dissatisfaction, but do not necessarily lead to satisfaction.

Motivation: its physiological basis

The physiological mechanisms behind behaviour directed to fulfilment of goals remain obscure although research continues. Some theories, which have direct implications for teachers, are mentioned here. The concept of *homeostasis* (the tendency for bodily biological processes to neutralize change and maintain a stable equilibrium state) is associated with Cannon.[10] In 1932 he suggested that people sought to maintain themselves 'at an optimum level of functioning'. Any imbalance indicated by internal or external stimuli (i.e. any intimation of the body deviating significantly from that optimum level) resulted in a 'drive' to correct that imbalance. Motivation was the result of drive which arose from disequilibrium in the body's homeostatic process.

Morgan[11] introduced, in 1943, the construct of a *central motive state* (CMS). The CMS is a function of neural activity which is generated by stimuli, internal and external, and the presence of chemical substances in the blood. Stellar,[12] in 1954, suggested the hypothalamus (a group of nuclei in the forebrain) as the brain area which coordinated the stimuli producing the CMS. Motivated behaviour was a direct function of 'the amount of activity in certain excitatory centres of the hypothalamus'. Activity of this nature leads directly to 'drive arousal'.

Hebb[13] put forward, in 1958, a theory of arousal functions. The 'cue' (the message associated with a stimulus) is thought to be transmitted directly to the brain's sensory areas along neural pathways. The resulting stimulation also activates areas of the brain through the reticular activity system (RAS). The RAS stimulates activity and attentiveness throughout the entire cortex. Activation of the RAS defines the arousal function of a stimulus. For any specific activity there is an appropriate level of arousal at which the learner's performance will be optimal. At any given time the learner will behave so as to maintain the level of arousal which is near-optimal for his or her activities. Hebb suggested also that the search for excitement was a significant factor in human motivation: 'It appears that, up to a certain point, threat and puzzle have positive motivating value, beyond that point, negative value'.

Categories of motivation

Psychologists concerned with understanding learning have attempted to formulate 'categories of motivation', i.e. groupings of students' motives for learning. Categories have been presented under four headings: instrumental motivation; social motivation; achievement motivation; and intrinsic motivation. It should be noted that more than one category may dominate learner motivation at a given time. (For details, see e.g. Biggs and Telfer.[14])

Instrumental motivation

This type of motivation, which is purely *extrinsic*, is in evidence where students perform tasks solely because of the *consequences* likely to ensue, for example, the chance of obtaining some tangible reward or avoiding a reprimand. It is in total contrast to intrinsic motivation (see below). In the face of motivation of this nature, the teacher should ensure that the task to be performed is placed in a context perceived as constructive (Biggs and Telfer[15]).

Social motivation

Students influenced by this type of motivation tend to perform tasks so as to please those they respect, admire, or whose opinions are of some importance to them. Rewards are of limited significance even if tangible; the reward here is non-material and is related in direct measure to the perceived relationship between the student and the person whose reinforcement activity (praise or approval, for example) is considered important.

Achievement motivation

This is involved where students learn 'in the hope of success'. Ausubel[16] suggests that there are three elements in motivation of this type:

(a) *cognitive drive* – the learner is attempting to satisfy a perceived 'need to know';
(b) *self enhancement* – the learner is satisfying the 'need for self-esteem';
(c) *affiliation* – the learner is seeking the 'approval of others'.

Intrinsic motivation

In this case there are no external rewards; the task is undertaken for the pleasure and satisfaction it brings to the student. It seems to be central to 'high quality involvement' in a task and to be self-maintaining and self-terminating. Curiosity and a desire to meet challenges may characterize the learning set of students motivated in this style.

Motivation and the problem of perception of irrelevance

Where the content of instruction is regarded by students as irrelevant, that is outside their self-constructed boundaries marking out and separating the useful from the non-useful, there will be little motive to participate in the process of instruction. Consider, for example, the young shorthand-typist attending a part-time skills course, a segment of which involves instruction in some of the finer points of grammar. She views the occupational role of shorthand-typist as that of interpreter, not creator, and may reject involvement in detail which is not perceived at that time as possessing any utility. Consider, next, the law student faced with a short introductory course on jurisprudence. She has a personal schema, based on the utilitarian content of 'black-letter law' – contract, conveyancing, etc.; she sees no point in attempting to digest the brew of philosophy and sociology presented to her. At best, she is convinced that the subject may be treated as a harmless optional extra; at worst it is rejected as an intrusion on the study of 'the real law'. Consider, finally, the teacher in training, who sees as useless and, therefore, irrelevant, the content of a course on the history of English education. The links between his or her perceived immediate need (how to instruct efficiently) and, for example, the minutiae of the 1944 Education Act are viewed as extremely tenuous, so that the subject area arouses no motivation and no drive to study its content.

Situations of this nature will not disappear by being disregarded by tutors. Action by the tutor is required, aimed at the creation or restoration of need, drive and incentive. Analysis of the situation in terms of the theoretical construct of motivation, and an interpretation of the problem from the student's standpoint, are essential.

There must be a full explanation to students of the *significance* of the 'unaccept-able' subject area in terms of content, its links with the subject as a whole, and its contribution to comprehension of that subject. Short-term goals (the passing of examinations, the acquisition of professional skills) must not be deprecated in any way whatsoever; for the student they are, correctly, matters of much consequence. Remonstration based on appeals to 'broaden one's outlook' or 'the importance of extending cultural horizons' is likely to be resented and to go unheeded. A positive approach is needed: links between short-term and long-term goals (professional competence and its requisite, expanding levels of knowledge) should be stressed. The presentation of subject content in an interesting fashion, the utilization of a variety of channels of communication in the search for effective stimuli, must rank high in lesson shape and structure. Instruction related to the students' existing level of knowledge, capable of linking the 'unacceptable area' to the solution of significant problems, is important. Thus, in the case of students who find a discussion of the educational legislation of 1944 of no relevance to today's problems, it might be useful to point out ways in which some of today's debates on education mirror the fashionable educational philosophy of the 1940s. Law students ought to be reminded that current controversial legislation in the areas of welfare, the family, and employ-ment owes much to earlier academic speculation on abstractions such as 'rights' and 'duties'.

Where the teacher is able to implant perception of a need, there exists a probability of its becoming the precursor of a drive which may provide incentive. Lack of motivation is rarely a single problem; it often represents an amalgam of attitudes which require analysis if the attendant difficulties are to be overcome.

Motivation in the classroom

The teacher has the task of creating a learning environment which relates the learner's activity to needs and aspirations, so that competence is developed and strengthened and a sense of self-improvement heightened. In Gagné's words: 'The task of the instructional designer is one of *identifying* the motives of students and of *channelling* them into activities that accomplish educational goals'. This may necessitate a combination of teaching techniques which will deliberately keep alive, utilize and strengthen the learner's initial motivation. These techniques might take into account the following matters.

1. The individual learner's motivations and goals should be understood and the aims of the course should be clearly and repeatedly defined and explained to him or her. 'Establish an expectancy of the performance to be achieved as a result of learning' (Gagné).
2. 'Goals that are too hard or too easy to attain are neither motivating nor reinforcing when attained' (Hilgard and Bower).[17] Performance is probably most efficient when *some* anxiety (but not fear or panic) exists in the situation; some challenge is essential. (Note the research work of Atkinson, suggesting that there are circumstances in the classroom in which 'an overly high probability of success may be detrimental to motivation', and that motivation may be at its highest where the probability of success is neither very low nor very high.)
3. Short-term goals should be explained in relation to long-term achievement.
4. Lessons should be planned by the teacher and seen by the student as part of a sequence eventually leading to the attainment of desirable ends.
5. Tasks set by the teacher should be appropriate to the student's level of abilities. 'Nothing dampens motivation as much as an unrelieved diet of failure and frustration' (Ausubel). Opportunities for success must be provided.
6. Attainment of a required level of competence ought to be explained and accepted, not as an end in itself, but as a key which opens the door to higher levels of understanding and achievement.
7. Lesson material and communication ought to be meaningful and presented with enthusiasm, ought to arouse intellectual curiosity and ought to involve students actively and personally. 'The intensity of our interest in an activity, as well as the amount of effort that we expend on it, depend on our feeling of personal involvement in that activity' (Kolesnik).
8. The level of communication during a lesson ought to be pitched carefully so that there is no 'comprehension gap' between teacher and student.
9. The fatigue which accompanies boredom and which destroys motivation ought to be avoided by a planned variety of teaching and learning activities. Cognitive drive should be maximized by arousing intellectual curiosity.
10. A variety of motivating techniques should be used: vary stimuli; utilize intrinsic motives (curiosity, etc.) as often as possible; employ extrinsic incentives if considered necessary; be aware of differing levels of aspiration among students.
11. Assimilation of lesson material ought to be tested regularly.
12. Evaluation of test results ought to be conveyed to students as swiftly as possible and ought to be interpreted in the context of immediate and long-term aims.
13. Competence and mastery ought to be recognized and reinforced by praise. Satisfaction derived from the learning process is a powerful motivator. 'Learning feeds on success.'
14. Temporary failure ought to be considered by student and teacher as an occasion

for a fresh attempt to overcome difficulties. The teacher should keep in mind, however, that although the concept of 'learning from one's failures' may have positive features, some difficulties, including the disintegration of motivation, may result when a student merely learns from failure that he or she has failed. There is a high probability of a student who has experienced specific failure generalizing to the conclusion that he *himself* is a total failure. Careful handling of the process of assisting a student to learn from failure is essential: positive assistance, intended to demonstrate that the causes of the failure can be discovered and overcome, is vital if motivation is not to crumble.

Does the absence of appropriate motivation invariably preclude the success of a lesson? Ausubel suggests that the teacher should consider ignoring lack of motivation and concentrate on teaching the student as effectively as the situation allows. This, he claims will produce *some* degree of learning, and the motivation for further learning may result. Davies suggests that it is not always necessary to postpone learning until the appropriate motivation exists. The teacher should ignore initial motivational states and rely on a form of lesson presentation which will capture and develop interest.

Teaching how to study: strategies for success

It is taken for granted all too often that college students understand the techniques of effective study, that they understand 'strategies for success'. This is rarely the case: in fact, there are few students in our colleges who would not benefit from methodical instruction in those techniques and strategies. Superstitions highly prevalent among students include the beliefs that repeated readings of a text will, in themselves, ensure learning, that long hours spent in study are not subject to the law of diminishing returns, and that forgetting is almost always the result of an innate, poor memory. Effective teaching involves enlightenment in these matters. O'Neil[18] reminds us: 'By not stressing learning strategies, educators, in essence, discourage students from developing and exploring new strategies, and, in so doing, limit students' awareness of their cognitive capabilities.' The areas outlined below in which instruction in techniques of study might be particularly useful include: the planning of one's time; use of the textbook; making lecture notes; project work; use of the library; retention and retrieval of learned information (remembering); revision; examination technique.

Learning how we learn

Young students embarking on a course of study in a college of further education are generally unaware of the nature and processes of learning. (Elements of psychology rarely figure in pre-college courses.) In some colleges an induction course for students includes lectures and discussions on 'How we learn', 'Study and stress', 'Remembering and forgetting'. Students are introduced to the concept of instruction as an interactive process, are given an outline of elementary theory on the retention and retrieval of information, and are shown the rationale and practical purpose of learning aids such as mnemonics and key words. The theoretical significance of using links with previous experience, of self-testing, of paced learning and of differentiating 'knowing how' from 'knowing why' is explained and translated into practical terms. An explanation of the aphorism, 'Every subject has its own logic', is given. The objective of induction courses of this type is an acceptance by students of the nature of the contribution *they* can make to the process of instruction.

Instruction in study techniques

Included in a college population will be many students whose schooling will have been based solely on the formal class lesson, supplemented by homework. For this group, in particular, the pattern of much college instruction, including private study periods, attendance at lectures and producing one's own notes, may present difficulties. Indeed, inappropriate study skills and undesirable study habits rank high in college tutors' perceptions of the causes of student underachievement and failure. Explanation and demonstration of study skills should be seen in these cases as vital tasks for the teacher.

Demonstrations of appropriate and varied skills – how to take notes at a lecture, for example – ought to be given in the first days of a college course. A lecture on note-taking is rarely effective unless accompanied or followed swiftly by a period of supervised practice in which students test their skills by producing notes (say, of a pre-recorded lecture) which can be analysed by the tutor and compared against a standard set. The 'gutting' of a textbook chapter, so that its overall themes might be discovered, requires several sessions of practice and analysis. In sum, the teaching of study skills must provide opportunities for the practice of those skills. Explanation, demonstration, practice and analysis of results constitute a useful framework for the attainment of study skills mastery.[19]

Planning one's time

Tutors have the task of convincing students that time is very often 'of the essence'. The duration of a course and dates of examinations are fixed, and students should be encouraged to draw up timetables based on a reasonable allocation of available time. Such a plan *must* allow time for revision and consolidation; these phases of study must not be viewed as 'optional extras'. Specimen study plans, illustrating impossible schemes, should be contrasted with schemes within the capabilities of most students.

In the case of part-time students, or those who can attend evening classes only irregularly, the tutor can assist in the learning process by suggesting realistic study plans based on a careful allocation of time. The importance of overall reviews, revision and consolidation must be explained and stressed; assistance may be needed in dealing with the competing claims on the student's time of a full-time job and other responsibilities.

Using one's textbook advantageously

'Some books are to be tasted; others swallowed; and some few to be chewed and digested' (Bacon). Advice to students in selecting and buying texts can be valuable. Students should be made aware of the dangers inherent in purchasing out-of-date editions. Advice to students on the interpretation of reading lists should be offered; important, key texts should be noted; less important, lower priority, items should be differentiated. Where texts are set by an examining body, no advice on choice is needed, save to suggest adjunctive, supplementary or secondary texts. Where choice is a personal matter, the tutor can demonstrate the valuable technique of 'skimming' a text before making a choice. The student should be taught, by example, how to 'taste' a book swiftly – by obtaining an overview from the preface, by selecting a topic from the index and noting the author's method of dealing with it and, finally, by reading one or two sample chapters (always including the first). Demonstrations of 'speed reading' should be arranged for students: its purposes, techniques and advantages will require discussion and illustration.

The detailed methods of 'deep reading' of a textbook should be explained and demonstrated in each case by the use of a class text. The purpose of deep reading – an 'active consideration of the text' so as to absorb its meaning and evaluate its concepts and arguments – has to be presented to students. The '3R' method – read, recite, record – is worthy of consideration, but the tutor has to explain the *precise purpose of each phase*, in particular that devoted to reciting. Robinson's 'SQ3R' method[20] – survey, question, read, recite, review – needs careful demonstration, particularly of the phase demanding readers' ability to 'turn paragraph headings into questions'. (Thus, a paragraph heading, 'Cognitivists' objections to behaviourism', is turned into a question, 'Why do cognitivists object to behaviourism?' and the reader should seek for the answer in the body of the paragraph.) Pauk's well-tried 'OK5R' method[21] – overview, key ideas, read, record, recite, review, reflect – is a valuable method of active reading for students pursuing a full-time course. (Students should be introduced to the 'three readings' method – *first* (swift) reading of a text to obtain an overview, *second* (detailed) reading, *third* (swift) reading for purposes of revision.)

Students can be assisted by directed discussions on the 'writing strategies' adopted by the authors of their texts. Structural patterns of writing soon emerge on examination, and the reader of a text can learn how to follow those patterns to the best advantage. Thus: X's text, *Principles of Economics*, follows a rigid pattern of statement, supporting matter and conclusions; Y's *Elements of Marketing* uses a chapter system in which a thesis is stated, supported and criticized, but no conclusions are reached until the final chapter. Awareness of a book's *structure* can assist in comprehension. Where an author's arguments are presented in hierarchical or branching form, students might be asked to construct a flow chart showing the interconnections of those arguments. This ought to follow from a discussion concerning the purpose and construction of subject trees and flow-charts.

The marking of one's textbook, so as to assist in memorization, should be demonstrated by the tutor. Students should be encouraged to read sections or paragraphs fully before underlining, and should be shown how to use symbols in consistent fashion and in a selective manner and, above all, to mark matter requiring further study or explanation. Making one's notes from a textbook should be demonstrated; this requires from the tutor an explanation of the reasons for using one's own words rather than those used in the textbook.

Helping students to learn how to solve problems

Assisting students to acquire appropriate problem-solving strategies is of much value. Explanation and demonstration are equally important: the teacher should explain, at an early stage of the course, why problem-solving requires a strategy, and should show by a variety of examples how that strategy can be applied. This is a useful contribution to student learning in all subject areas. How do we solve a problem in geometry, in contract law, in mechanical engineering? How ought an argument to be set out and evaluated? Each area of knowledge throws up its own type of problem requiring specific types of solution.[22]

Guided practice is essential, and the teacher who explains strategies of problem-solving is recommended to look at the difficulties in problems *from the point of view of the student*. Practice for students should be related to repeated difficulties experienced by them. Polya[23] suggests that students be helped discreetly and at first unobtrusively. They should be given practice in the type of mental operation useful for the solution of problems of the type with which they are dealing, and they should be trained to think of familiar problems having the same or a similar unknown as that in question. The student must be given the chance of observing some person (e.g. the teacher) engaging in the process of solving problems. 'Trying to solve problems, you have to observe and to imitate what other people do when solving problems and, finally, you learn to do problems by doing them.'

Polya's four-factor scheme for the solution of problems is set out as follows.

1. Understand the problem. What are the unknowns? The data? The conditions?
2. Devise a plan. What are the connections between the data and the unknowns? Will a study of related problems help?
3. Carry out the plan. Check that each step is correct.
4. Look back and examine the solution obtained.

The teacher may be helped by considering the Gestaltists' approach to insight (see Chapter 7). The value to students of working out solutions, first with guidance and then on their own, is high.[24] 'A great discovery solves a great problem, but there is a grain of discovery in the solution of *any* problem ... If you solve [your problem] by your own means, you may experience the tension and enjoy the triumph of discovery' (Polya).

Duncker[25] investigated ways in which students attempted to solve novel types of problem and suggested that they be taught, in formal fashion, the techniques of creating *heuristics*, that is strategies which deal with problems in a manner which, while not guaranteeing exact solutions, may *assist* in moving in their direction. The process begins with a 'means-end analysis', i.e. a general examination of the means by which goal requirements might be confronted and understood, followed by a focus on causes of difficulty and a consideration of ways in which the problem under scrutiny might be dealt with in terms of already acquired strategies. The possibility of novel solutions ought to be welcomed: Duncker wrote of the difficulties in problem-solving which emerge when students are hemmed in by a conscious or unconscious refusal to consider new types of solution. (Koestler has written of 'the stubborn coherence of the perceptual frames and matrices of thought in our minds'. To recognize this and to move beyond the problems it creates, is a valuable learning experience.)

Frederiksen[26] has outlined a teaching programme designed to assist students in learning how to solve 'difficult and unusual' problems, specifically in the sciences. As a first step, the teacher should outline the value of allowing time for the 'incubation' of a solution to a problem and should illustrate the significance of reflecting on a problem and considering alternative approaches to its solution. Next, students should be urged to consider the value of temporarily suspending judgment on those approaches until a forecast of their consequences has been attempted. Only after that should the students move to a considered solution. Frederiksen emphasizes the importance of instructing students in the techniques of analysing the major characteristics of the specific elements of the problem before constructing a final answer.

Developing concentration

Assisting students to develop and maintain powers of concentration is a positive contribution towards ensuring their success in learning. Concentration involves a focus of all one's attention on a task in hand. In essence it is a selective reaction to the numerous stimuli that impinge on the learner's consciousness from many internal and external sources. Students should be helped by discussion and explanation to understand that concentration *can* be improved and that it is the resultant of a variety of factors which are within the learner's control.

Four factors have been put forward as the components of concentration: the development of work study skills; the development of habits of using study time effectively; the creation of positive study conditions; and the presence of an appropriate degree of motivation.

Students should be introduced by explanation and demonstration to the idea of developing work skills appropriate to the task in hand as an aid to concentration. Ends should determine means, so that the study skill to be employed must be selected with the objective of the study task in mind. Revising lists of facts in preparation for a nurses' examination in elementary physiology will demand a different study technique from that required in learning the background to current welfare legislation. Concentration is always improved when the appropriate study skill is selected. The development of efficient utilization of study time involves a planned routine (so that indecision concerning the use of time is avoided) and planned habits of work. Time limits, appropriate pauses in study (between chapters or 'on the hour') should be planned so that concentration during the working period is heightened.

The creation of positive study skills – a vital factor in building powers of concentration – involves a determined attack by the teacher on a most zealously guarded citadel of student superstition. That general noise is a distractor is accepted by students. That concentration might suffer if study takes place to the accompaniment of music is *not* accepted; indeed, a superstition has emerged that concentration is aided positively when there is a background of music. There is no firm evidence to suggest that a musical background aids study, and considerable evidence to the contrary. The 'muzak' background of the supermarket probably does not interfere with the routine business of shopping; but the tasks of studying are not routine and call for as much attention as can be mustered. As Pauk reminds the student: 'Why voluntarily introduce interference when you are studying? It is hard enough to concentrate as it is!'

A linked superstition concerns the advisability of working where possible in crowded, as opposed to silent, conditions – the cafeteria rather than the library, for example. 'Silence is unnatural.' It is for the teacher to point out the falsity of this belief and to explain that concentration is often weakened to the very extent that competing stimuli are introduced into the student's immediate environment. The effects of temperature, ventilation and physical tone (resulting from diet, sleep, exercise, etc.) must not be overlooked in any explanation to students of ways in which they can improve their powers of concentration.

Finally, motivation, as a contributory factor to concentration, has to be explained. An understanding of the *purposes* of one's study is a powerful force in fixing one's attention on the task in hand.

Making lecture notes

Initially, the tutor may have to explain that the lecture provides a means of learning and that it is not merely an exercise in listening. The essence of notes, as opposed to complete transcriptions, should be discussed. ('The student who tries to take literal, detailed notes, can do so only by allocating capacity to this activity ... little capacity remains for the deep processing of the information' (Wingfield).) Students must be shown that the *style* of note-taking should vary according to one's aims and the subject matter. The aim of noting the lecturer's statement of fundamental principles will produce a different kind of note from that intended to record his illustrative material and book recommendations.

The *Cornell system* is worthy of consideration. It is a methodical approach based on three phases. In the first phase, before the lecture, previous lecture notes are reviewed by the students. They then prepare note-taking material, including a margin, to be known as a 'recall column', to be separated from the main column for their notes. In the second phase, which is based on the actual lecture, the students record in the main column the general ideas presented by the lecturer. Abbreviations, sketches and diagrams are used. The third phase, which follows the lecture, involves reading through the notes, underlining important points and using the recall column to note key phrases, definitions, etc., that will bring to mind the material in the main column. Recital of the lecture's main points should follow, to be prompted by reference, first to the recall column and, secondly, to the main column.

Students should be informed of other techniques, such as Buzan's intriguing and helpful method of making 'linking' notes.[27] A tutor's demonstration of Buzan's methods applied to a lecture is likely to be of real assistance to students. The tutor should also warn against making fair copies of notes, transcribing from shorthand notes – activities of this type constitute a waste of valuable time, since none contributes in any way to the retention or recall of information presented at the lecture.[28]

Project work

A large number of college courses demand project work from students, individually or as members of a group. The educational purpose of the project ought to be explained to students. Assistance in choosing, planning, researching and presenting the final material is often needed. Where projects are based on field work or laboratory findings, help may be needed by students anxious to present their material to the best advantage. (Students' work portfolios, required in GNVQ courses, will involve some guidance in presentation techniques.)

Where a project demands the use of a questionnaire, or interviews involving members of the public, tutors can assist by offering advice on the strategy of questioning, with particular reference to formulating and presenting questions and analysing results. The techniques of data analysis, of generalizing and extrapolating should be taught to students.

Assistance in enabling students to recognize and assess what they have learned from the process of producing project material can play an important role in 'rounding off' the activity. It should be emphasized to students that presentation of the project folder is not the end of the process. Tutors should demonstrate how the various activities involved in project work (obtaining, arranging and interpreting data, for example) can provide lessons of long-term significance for students.

Use of the library

The library as a learning centre features all too rarely in students' learning strategies. Concepts of the library as providing services which facilitate study and learning should be developed at an early stage of students' courses. The use of reference books, the study of a variety of texts (and not merely the set book) before embarking upon a written assignment, may have to be demonstrated to students if they are to be accepted as part of learning strategy. Mere abstract statements urging students to 'use the encyclopaedia' may count for little; a demonstration of the utility of this activity will be more to the point. Exercises in the location and use of reference material, preferably in the form of a project, will assist in student comprehension of the purposes of library services. Where the library possesses a computerized information retrieval service or is linked to the Internet, students should engage, initially, in supervised practice designed to help them in some current work schedule.

A talk and demonstration by the college library staff concerning the range of resources should be arranged in the first days of a course. Use of the Dewey system and the catalogue should be demonstrated and the expertise of the library staff in recommending texts and other sources of information should be made known. Where libraries are used as resource centres, offering audio and video cassettes, a demonstration of the range and utility of these aids should be arranged for all students.

Hints concerning remembering

The concept of 'training' one's memory becomes easier for students to accept when the fundamentals of remembering and forgetting have been explained. A short, non-technical introduction to the structure of the memory (see Chapter 17), concentrating on the movement of information to the long-term from the short-term memory should be presented to students in ways which enable them to realize the significance of *activity* in remembering.[29]

The following suggestions might be presented to students as well-tested hints concerning remembering. The 'intent to remember' *can* be developed: full attention to the task in hand and 'active thinking', i.e. working out the implications of what one is reading, and solving related problems, will contribute to the retention of learned material. Recital, review and practice in retrieval contribute to long-term remembering. What has been learned should be used in the unravelling of problems; objective tests are valuable in this process. Seek for associations within the subject area and link the new with the old. Search for pattern and structure and do not learn everything by rote: rote learning has its place in study, but to *understand* what one has learned is a valuable aid in long-term remembering. Finally, be keen to learn; in the jargon of the psychologists, 'create and maintain a positive mental set'.

Some research material suggests that a student's memory in relation to a text he or she has studied may be affected by the *structure* of the text, e.g. by the presence of 'signals', such as summaries and statements of the author's intentions. Asking students to provide their own oral summaries of chapters in a text may intensify the ability to retain and recall.

Frequently, however, students will encounter memorizing difficulties. They should be encouraged to identify the nature of their problems and to experiment with different memorization and learning techniques.

Pre-examination revision

The idea of the pre-examination revision as a 'dress rehearsal' should be explained to students, together with its implications. The revision period should be seen as intensive, wide-ranging and based on the students' own notes. Principles, illustrations and definitions should be checked. Recital of learned material, by writing out selected headings or by working out answers to problems will be a useful component of a revision period. Answering previous examination questions and checking one's answers against text or notes can be recommended. Working in small groups with other students so as to review notes collectively and answer problems is also useful as a revision process.

Advice should be given to students concerning the problems of a 'last-minute cram'. The superstition relating to the advisability of working to the very last minute dies hard among students. Nevertheless, tutors ought to comment on this practice, attempting to explain the dangers of arriving for one's examination in a state of mental indigestion.

Examination technique

There are numerous cases in which the quality of students' examination answers would have been improved significantly by the acceptance of advice on the technique of answering questions. Students must be taught to peruse questions carefully so as to discover their 'essence'. They should be instructed in the significance of the precise wording of the examination question. 'State', 'evaluate', 'justify' and 'compare and contrast' demand particular types of answer. A candidate's answer to a problem such as 'Evaluate Keynes' contribution to our understanding of the significance of the rate of interest', requires a different form and structure from an answer to the question 'In what ways did Keynes alter our understanding of the significance of the rate of interest?' Practice in dealing with the various types of question – factual, discussion, problem – under the supervision of a tutor can be very useful.

The importance of *planning one's answers* cannot be over-emphasized. The techniques of planning answers should be demonstrated by the tutor in relation to the effective utilization of examination time. The significance of allowing adequate time for the revision and amendment of one's answers before handing in the examination script has to be explained. Finally, advice on the writing of answers in essay form is rarely wasted. The purpose and construction of the essay and its underlying structure ought not to be omitted from any discussion of examination technique at further education level.

Notes and references

1. See generally for this chapter: *Introduction to Motivation* by J. Atkinson (Van Nostrand, 1980); *Motivating Students* by R. Beard and J. Senior (Routledge, 1980); *Human Motivation* by B. Weiner (Sage, 1992); *Teaching Students to Learn* by G. Gibbs (OUP, 1981); *A Guidebook for Teaching Study Skills and Motivation* by B.J. Bragstad and S.M. Stumpf (Allyn & Bacon, 1982); *Motivating Students to Learn* by J. Brophy (McGraw-Hill, 1997); *Students: Changing Roles* by H. Silver (OUP, 1997).
2. *Experience and Education* (Macmillan, 1940).
3. *The Management of Learning* (McGraw-Hill, 1971).
4. *Motivation and Teaching – A Practical Guide* (NEA, Washington, 1978).
5. *Experimental Psychology* (Holt, 1938).
6. Maslow's work on motivation is closely linked to his general 'humanistic psychology', which is discussed in Chapter 10.

7. *Motivation and Personality* (Harper & Row, 1970).
8. *Existence, Relatedness and Growth* (Free Press, 1972).
9. *Motivation to Work* (Wiley, 1959).
10. *The Wisdom of the Body* (Kegan Paul, 1932).
11. *Physiological Psychology* (McGraw-Hill, 1943).
12. 'The physiology of maturation' in *Psychological Review* (1954, *61*).
13. 'A neuropsychological theory' in *Psychology* ed. S. Koch (McGraw-Hill, 1959).
14. *The Process of Learning* (Prentice-Hall, 1987).
15. *Op.cit.*
16. *Educational Psychology: A Cognitive View* (Holt, Rinehart & Winston, 1968).
17. *Theories of Learning* (Prentice-Hall, 1981).
18. *Learning Strategies* (Academic Press, 1978).
19. See e.g. *Study and Learn* by S. Ashman and A. George (Heinemann, 1982); *Effective Study Skills* by P.J. Hills and H. Barlow (Pan, 1980); *How to Study: A Practical Guide* by F. Casey (Macmillan, 1985); *Teaching Study Skills* by T. Devine (Allyn & Bacon, 1987).
20. *Effective Study* (Harper & Row, 1970).
21. *How to Study in College* (Houghton Mifflin, 1997).
22. *The Psychology of Study* by C. Mace (Penguin, 1973).
23. *How to Solve It* (Princeton UP, 1945). See also *Human Problem-Solving* by A. Newell and H. Simon (Prentice-Hall, 1972).
24. See 'Helping students to think for themselves' in *Helping Students Think and Value* by J.R. Fraenkel (Prentice-Hall, 1980).
25. *On Problem Solving* (Princeton UP, 1945).
26. 'Implications of cognitive theory for instruction in problem-solving', in *Review of Educational Research* (1984, *54*).
27. *Use Your Head* (BBC, 1989).
28. See 'Note taking in lectures – an information-processing approach' in *Educational Psychologist* (1980, *15*).
29. See *The Psychology of Human Memory* by A. Wingfield and D.L. Byrnes (Academic Press, 1981).

Chapter 19

Class Control and Student Counselling

To understand a phenomenon is to be able to trace its relationship to the conditions and consequences of its occurrence (Sayre, 1976).

The aspect of the teacher-manager's role which is considered in this chapter concerns his responsibility for the formulation, creation and maintenance of the standards of interpersonal behaviour (involving teacher and class) which are appropriate for the reaching of objectives. The subject matter of this chapter is the maintenance of discipline in the teaching situation, and student counselling, that is the process of helping students to learn how to solve some of their interpersonal and other problems.[1]

The appearance in a text dealing with further education of a chapter devoted largely to control and discipline may elicit surprised comment (but not from experienced teachers in the colleges). Discipline is held by some to be a matter for concern only in the school context; a highly motivated student population in the colleges of further education, eager to participate in their lessons, should not create the type of problem associated with a breakdown of discipline. Further, it is suggested, there is little point in discussing the problem of control and discipline with teachers in training: they will quickly learn from experience (and if they do not, they will not survive as teachers); knowledge of how to control a class will emerge quickly enough from contact with reality in the classroom.

The first point suggests an idealized picture of colleges which vanishes in the glare of reality. In fact, a proportion of students in further education experiences behavioural and other problems which can result in difficulties for the teacher attempting to exercise class control; the term 'discipline' is wide enough to cover these problems in the context of further education. The second point is based on the false assumption that one learns a technique best from 'on-the-job' experience. It may be answered that experience is the worst teacher – it gives the test before presenting the lesson.

Theoretical and practical instruction in the understanding and handling of control and disciplinary problems in the college classroom ought to feature in the work of all institutes involved in the training of teachers. Too often, however,

246

requests for practical advice and assistance in comprehending and dealing with problems of class discipline (a matter of concern for many inexperienced teachers) are ignored or turned aside by the use of semantic quibbles seeking to equate 'control' with 'authoritarianism', and by dogmatic pronouncements suggesting, unhelpfully, that misbehavior of students invariably reflects inappropriate instruction. This is on all fours with the inane military aphorism: 'There are no inadequate troops, only inadequate officers'. Many books dealing with class management reveal an ominous gap in the index between the entries on 'direct teaching' and 'discovery learning', preferring, seemingly, to ignore the existence of disciplinary problems.

The view taken in this chapter implies that discipline cannot be considered as a 'thing in itself', that it has to be seen in terms of factors in and outside the classroom, and that its maintenance is essential for overall class control, without which effective learning is impossible. Procedures concerning the maintenance of discipline should be based on an analysis of a variety of problems which *can* be solved. The appropriateness of these solutions ought to be a vital matter for study and discussion in teacher training courses.

The nature of discipline

The word 'discipline' is derived from *discipulus* (pupil) and *discipere* (to comprehend). Dewey[2] warns against its confusion with 'drill'. ' "Drill" is conceived after the mechanical analogy of driving, by unremitting blows, a foreign substance into a resistant material; or imaged after the analogy of the mechanical routine by which raw recruits are trained to a soldierly bearing and habits that are naturally wholly foreign to their possessors.' The term is used in a variety of ways, so that one may refer to the discipline of an army,[3] the discipline of orchestral playing, the discipline of the scholar, and self-discipline (Milton's 'government of the self'). Use of the term generally implies a consciously accepted code of conduct directed to the attainment of some desired objective. In the context of further education, it can be taken to apply to *group conduct held to be essential in the teaching situation and in relation to the personal development of individual students who comprise the learning group.*

Discipline as a universally cultural phenomenon is considered as serving a number of specific functions in the growth process of young people: it assists them in learning those standards of conduct acceptable within society; it helps them to acquire characteristics of a positive nature, such as self-control and persistence; it assists in securing stability of the social order within which the young may achieve security and maturity.

It is important not to confuse 'discipline' with 'order'. Order may indeed be 'heaven's first law'; it is not always a reliable indicator of the presence of discipline. The informality and bustle of students in a motor vehicle workshop, with its apparent lack of order but based nevertheless on a disciplined approach to the task in hand, may be contrasted with the feigned attention of a group of students apparently in a well-ordered class but, in reality, withdrawn from the positive teacher-student relationship which characterizes discipline in its fundamental sense. The shadow must not be confused with the substance. The trappings of a superficial discipline – silent students, instant obedience to a command – have little connection with the core of the controlled and disciplined instructional process based on a voluntary partnership of teacher and class. Order, in the sense of attention – and without attention class teaching cannot begin – is a necessary condition for true discipline seen as a means to an end, but no more than that.

The breakdown of control and discipline

A variety of reasons for the breakdown of class discipline can be enumerated. Their common factor is the provision of explanations of circumstances in which class management proves ineffective, so that learning for the class *as a whole* becomes difficult or impossible. In one way or another, lack of intrinsic and extrinsic motivation (see Chapter 18) may be discerned at the root of the problem. Where a student has no real desire to participate in the process of instruction, he or she will rarely 'enter the class' in the sense of involvement in the lesson; he or she may 'withdraw', which can be expressed by active opposition to the teacher's demands. The student who does not contribute to joint teacher-class effort may provide an example which elicits a like response from other students. It is in a situation of this nature that discipline begins to break down.

We differentiate here those factors in and outside the classroom which can be discerned in an analysis of disciplinary problems. Thus, a student's personal background, home conditions, parental models, perhaps adopted unconsciously, and educational history before entering further education are factors for which the class teacher has no responsibility because they reflect an environment outside the classroom. Membership of a social group with attitudes at variance with the ethos and proclaimed aims of a college may create behaviour problems. McQuail[4] reminds teachers that 'behaviour which seems deviant or disorderly can be reinterpreted ... as reflecting an alternative definition of what is valued or relevant for a given sub-group or sub-culture'.

Some psychologists see behaviour problems in the classroom as resulting from a student's personal environment in which there is generated 'a low tolerance for ambiguous situations'. Such situations are: those that he or she is unable to categorize because of lack of familiarity; those involving complex events that he or she cannot analyse correctly; and contradictory circumstances involving perceptions of different and confusing structures. A student may react to a situation of this type with anxiety, discomfort, avoidance and destructive behaviour. (Experienced class teachers will recognize the aptness of this analysis in relation to some common types of misbehaviour.)

Some of the more important reasons for the breakdown of control and discipline associated more specifically with the situation in the classroom are set out below; they can be considered as the 'triggers' which may set off a pattern of disruption.

1. *Compulsory attendance.* Students may be in attendance at college through no desire of their own. They may work in an industry which insists on attendance at college, or they may be 'sent to college' by an enlightened employer, but against

their will. This can result not only in those passive attitudes indicative of lack of motivation but also in active resentment of, and hostility to, the college, its staff, standards and work. (This is not to suggest that the 'compulsory student' is invariably a source of discontent, for this is, demonstrably, not the case. It is to emphasize, however, the specific disciplinary difficulties which can often stem from compulsory participation in an undesired activity.)

2. *The college seen as an 'extension of employment'.* Young employees may dislike their daily work, so that any activity thought to be associated with it (such as a class held to improve work skills) is also disliked. In such cases participation in college work, with its accompanying demands, may be resented and resisted.

3. *The college seen as a symbol of failure.* Attendance at a college course may reflect, for some students, their inability to obtain full-time employment, which is interpreted as an attack on self-esteem. Resentment directed generally at society's failure to provide work is channelled towards the college and its classes.

4. *Frustration.* The organization, structure, demands and external trappings of the colleges of further education may serve to fan the spark of frustration latent in some students. Frustration may emerge because they see themselves 'back at school' in an atmosphere which may be heavy with unpleasant memories. For some, the course content may be a mere repetition of work attempted unsuccessfully at school, with a consequent blow to pride; for others, the course may necessitate work at an inappropriately high level and may be linked with standards and long-term goals beyond their comprehension and ability. Some may not see the course as having any significance for their personal development; others may see it as forcing them into a pattern which has no relevance to their preferred life style. For some the course will appear unrelated to everyday work; for others the lack of a career structure or general opportunities in their employment can reduce to naught the significance of their efforts in college. Frustration and boredom constitute a fertile breeding ground for uncooperative and aggressive attitudes in the classroom, as elsewhere; the withholding of cooperation from the teacher may be viewed as an escape route from an unacceptable situation.

5. *Distracting personal problems.* A student's anxiety induced by health or financial problems can result in resenting and rejecting the demands of a course of study. (Counselling may help in a case of this nature.) Frequent misbehaviour may, indeed, be a signal to the teacher, indicating the existence of this type of problem. Darkenwald and Knox[5] make the following important observations:

Adults must be sensitive to the fact that late adolescents are going through a period of internal turmoil as they negotiate the difficult passage to full adult status. 'Immature' attitudes and behaviour are symptomatic manifestations of the struggle for identity and independence.

6. *Lack of confidence in the teacher.* Students' confidence has to be earned; it is not there for the asking. It will vanish where, under the critical gaze of a class, a

teacher is revealed as a sham. A teacher's lack of interest in a subject, or poor lesson preparation, or obvious discontinuity and muddle in a programme of instruction, will not remain hidden for long; their emergence often coincides with a decline of confidence in the teacher, which results in a weakening of class discipline.

7. *Resentment of the teacher as catalyst.* Often, but, fortunately, not always, the teacher whose attitudes and probing questions challenge accepted life styles may be viewed by some students as a disturber of their 'mental peace'. Far from the teacher's questions and attitudes arousing an enthusiastic response in the class, they may be resented and may result directly in a withdrawal of coopera-tion. (Some psychologists discern in this situation a reaction to 'cognitive dissonance',[6] i.e. the mental conflict said to arise when ingrained assumptions or beliefs are challenged or contradicted by new information. The resulting ten-sions can be relieved, it is said, by defensive tactics including the deliberate avoidance or rejection of the new information so that inner stability is restored.)

8. *Less tolerance by the young of authority in general.* For better or worse, authority, its representatives, manifestations and symbols no longer automatically com-mand respect. Where a college is viewed as part of an alien power structure linked to 'authority', resentment may build up. Cooperation with a teacher may be interpreted as 'selling out' or 'going over to the establishment'; withdrawal of that cooperation may be equated with the assertion of 'independence'.

9. *Breakdown of communication.* Where communication breaks down, control becomes impossible. An analysis of poor discipline will often reveal a commu-nication channel so affected by 'noise' (see Chapter 11) that teacher and class are rarely in meaningful contact. Badly structured lesson material, inappropri-ate modes of instruction, or failure to monitor the results of class teaching, can destroy communication and, with it, class control.

10. *Immaturity and hostility.* Deliberate attempts to interfere with the conduct of a lesson, often made by an immature 'odd man out', who may be aware of his inadequacies, who is hostile to teacher and class alike, and who is adrift in an environment which he does not understand and, therefore, fears, can result in the breakdown of class control. A firm and controlled response by the teacher aimed initially at effectively isolating the disrupter is necessary.[7]

An approach to the problem

The teacher in further education has almost none of the school-type sanctions with which to challenge an offender. Formal 'punishments' have no place in college life. A partial solution to problems caused by a breach of discipline lies in the processes of *assessment and assertion of control*. Assessment demands a critical appraisal of the situation; control requires action in accordance with that appraisal. It is essential for the teacher to try to see the circumstances surrounding breach of discipline through the eyes of the offender. (Situations in the classroom are, for teacher and students, based on individual perceptions.) Why should a talented student prefer the role of clown to that of scholar? Why should a student of promise suddenly adopt a hostile, uncooperative posture? No answer will easily be found unless an attempt is made to consider the class situation as the *student* might view it. (Personal discussions with the student, or counselling (see below), may assist in discovering the roots of non-cooperation.) It is important, too, that the teacher views, as dispassionately as possible, his or her own contribution (if any) to the breakdown of discipline.

Lack of discipline arising from frustration ought to be dealt with, where possible, at source. The student's suitability for a particular course should be reassessed and a detailed explanation of the objectives of the course and its relation to his or her career development ought to be given. Contact with the student's employer or training officer may be valuable on occasions such as these.

Where college rules designed to help in the maintenance of class control and discipline are published they should be unambiguous, comprehensible and capable of enforcement. An important breach ought to result in prompt action. Rules which cannot always be enforced, so that a blind eye has to be turned to their being broken (e.g. 'unpunctuality can lead to exclusion from classes'), ought to be redrafted in precise terms or withdrawn.

It is extremely important, in relation to the maintenance of class control and discipline, that the teacher should seek to understand the class *as a group with its own internal, informal organization*. A class is more than the mere sum of its individual students; it is a dynamic group, often with its own leaders, its internal tensions, conflicts and crises, which must be acknowledged and understood by the teacher. Mason Haire[8] reminds us of the conflicts between personality and organization: 'Whenever we join a group we give up some individual freedom and therefore the calculus of the balance between the individual and the group is a problem ... As the organisation grows, the force that seems likely to destroy it is the centrifugal force arising from the fact that the members are individuals and tend to fly off on tangents towards their own goals.' The teacher who is able to view the class in these organizational terms and accept the inevitability of tension and occasional conflict (a task which becomes easier as comprehension of class structure becomes deeper) will find that the resolution of class management problems is made easier.

The maintenance of class control and discipline within a college *as a whole* is, of course, the collective responsibility of the entire teaching staff, supported by departmental heads and directors. Lecturers who, in disciplinary matters, find themselves at odds with their seniors, and who are unable to count on their full support, are unlikely to be able to teach effectively. In the college context, discipline is a *social* problem, demanding unity of purpose from all staff.

Hints on the maintenance of class control

There are no golden rules for the maintenance of control and discipline in class (if there were, there would be few unresolved disciplinary problems); each problem requires a separate analysis and set of responses as it occurs. The following hints should be found useful, always provided that they are interpreted, not in a mechanical way, but in accordance with the exigencies of *specific classroom situations*. The strategies involved in class control must always match context.

1. Ensure, as far as possible, that the classroom conditions appropriate to your lesson requirements have been prepared. Seating arrangements are important: thus, to seat students where they are unable to see or hear important parts of the lesson is to create an atmosphere in which order can break down quickly. Set the stage properly before the curtain rises.

2. Prepare your lesson thoroughly. Pitch it at a suitable level so that an appropriate climate of participation is established. Make sure that you do not depress class morale by demanding impossible standards. Ensure, similarly, that students do not feel degraded by being asked to participate in trivial activities which obviously require minimum standards only. Students who believe that their time is being wasted – no matter what the pretext – are unlikely to approach their tasks in disciplined fashion. Provide opportunities for success in class.

3. Where the objective of a task is not immediately obvious, be prepared to explain its significance. Discipline rarely flourishes where students are asked to engage in activities for incomprehensible ends. (Similarly, the objectives of disciplinary policy should be explained to students.)

4. Know your class. The tutor who has taken the trouble to learn the names of the students and to study their occupational backgrounds and academic attainments is demonstrating an interest in those for whose instruction he or she is responsible. Class-tutor cooperation can be intensified in this way, with a corresponding, positive effect on problems of behaviour in class.

5. Adopt an appropriate professional style in the classroom, and keep to it. Students are rarely impressed, and often embarrassed, by tutors who seek to identify with them by affecting an exaggerated bonhomie which, they believe, will bridge the tutor-student gap or eradicate teacher-learner distinctions. Similarly, an austere, autocratic style may have little appeal. The general rule is – as in most matters relating to class control – aim at moderation. To be either too friendly or too remote is, almost always, to forfeit respect, with marked effects on class discipline. To 'be oneself' is probably the best guide.

6. Watch very carefully for early signs of trouble. Try to pre-empt difficulties – prevention is always better than cure. Just as a successful navigator learns to recognize and react to storm signals at an early stage, so the tutor must learn to watch for those events which can presage loss of class control. The conversations which continue after the tutor has complained of their interference with the lesson, the 'clenched silence' which follows a request for cooperation, the continued failure to complete assignments, the record of unexplained absence or unpunctuality – these are signals which tutors ignore at their peril. They demand swift assessment and action.

7. Establish momentum at an early stage: avoid over-long introductions to lessons and focus attention swiftly. Keep up a reasonable pace of class activity and involvement. Periods of inactivity can produce the boredom which spills over easily into indiscipline. Check performance regularly.

8. Do not confuse the trivial and the important. Over-reaction to a minor breach of

a rule can be counter-productive. (Consider carefully the implications of a policy of 'zero tolerance'.) Learn to assess swiftly the real significance of events in class. Studiously ignoring what is, in effect, a challenge to one's authority may be perceived by students as an admission of defeat (see, further, p. 254); reacting intemperately to an unimportant attempt at provocation may be perceived as evidence of unreasonableness. Neither type of response from the tutor is calculated to maintain that respect for him or her which is essential for class discipline.

9. Be seen as fair-minded and impartial. Favouritism of any kind, conscious or unconscious, bias and prejudice, will be interpreted by a class as an indication that fair treatment cannot always be expected. Students have a keen sense of justice which, when outraged, often leads to a withdrawal of cooperation.

10. When you have to issue orders, do so firmly and unambiguously. 'Be sparing of commands. Command only when other means are inexplicable or have failed . . . But whenever you do command, command with decision and consistency' (Spencer).[9]

11. The reprimand is the most common (often the only available) form of primary reaction to misbehaviour in the college classroom. The teacher must know *when* and *how* to reprimand. Reprimands are based on overt responses to unacceptable behaviour; they may be verbal or non-verbal (a gesture or frown), formal or informal. The precise form should be dictated by the situation, the nature of the behaviour, and the effect desired by the teacher. Useful rules are: do not overreact; use the reprimand sparingly; avoid expressions of hostility and idle threats; avoid the 'ratchet effect' statement which can only intensify discord; do not injure a student's self-esteem; consider the effect of the reprimand in the short-term and long-term on the offender and the rest of the class; learn when to ignore a minor, 'one-off', manifestation of misbehaviour, but watch for a build-up of potentially disruptive activities; reprimand firmly any important infraction of previously announced rules, and remember that, through the eyes of students, a teacher's quiescence may be interpreted as acquiescence (see, further, p. 254).

12. If you feel that you have to impose a sanction, ensure that the situation really demands it and that the consequences will be worthwhile. You must decide what constitutes misbehaviour and when it requires a firm response; your judgment as to the necessity for sanctions may vary from group to group, or student to student, but it must be based consistently on principle. The decision to impose a sanction (say, in the form of a severe reprimand, a warning, loss of a privilege) is in no sense a confession of failure. On the contrary, it may be a perfectly appropriate response to behaviour which critically threatens the maintenance of class control. Jones and Page,[10] in a succinct account of the use and abuse of sanctions, stress the importance of disciplinary action being of a consistent nature, and neither random nor haphazard. Let the sanction follow a warning; let it be just and exemplary.

13. Consider without hesitation the sanction (where it is available) of exclusion from class where the continued presence of an offender threatens the main-

tenance of class control. Exclusion can be followed by discussions with the student and, where appropriate, a college counsellor. (Note, however, Dewey's warning on the use of the sanction of exclusion: 'It may strengthen the very causes which have brought about the undesirable anti-social attitude, such as desire for attention or to show off'.[11])

14. Follow up all important disciplinary matters. Analyse what initiated and precipitated the breakdown of discipline. Do not confuse symptom and underlying cause. In the future apply whatever positive lessons you have learned from a successful solution of disciplinary problems.

Reculer pour mieux sauter

There are teachers and writers on classroom management who suggest that, where discipline suddenly disintegrates and a teacher-student confrontation looms, it might be worth considering very swiftly the 'real costs' of a showdown. The tactics of 'positive procrastination', it is argued, might outweigh the possible effects of accepting the 'time-and-place' challenge selected by a student so as to manipulate the situation to his or her advantage. McManus[12] points out that, in classroom confrontations, there are 'three audiences' to be taken into account: students who are present in the room, students who are not present but who will learn swiftly of the incident and its outcome, and the teacher's colleagues who, because they are parts of the college 'system' (see p. 186) will be affected in some way by the event and its results. 'All three audiences contribute to the fear, embarrassment and tension, and accurate perception and balanced judgment are put at risk.' Awareness of the complexities of the situation might provide an occasion, it is argued, for a tactical retreat, where possible, to be followed by a private discussion with the student at some early future date in the hope that the difficulties can be explored and some compromise effected.

Critics of this type of reaction to a confrontation are swift to point out that it may be little more than opportunism (i.e. the sacrifice of a principle so as to gain a temporary, minor advantage), and that it may be perceived by 'the three audiences' as an admission of defeat. Tactical withdrawal is an extremely difficult manoeuvre and is often attended by a high possibility of turning into total defeat. Procrastination carries, and is seen to carry, its own difficulties: to postpone dealing with a problem is not to resolve it – indeed, it may emerge again, but in a much more threatening form. To act with determination, with an awareness of what is at stake but, above all, with a sense of proportion as to the circumstances, is likely to be much more effective in most cases than procrastination.

Assertive discipline: Canter's proposals

The American educationist, Canter,[13] aware of what he referred to as 'the crumbling edifice of discipline in school and college', investigated a large number of educational institutions so as to provide the basis for his model of 'assertive discipline'.

Allowing for differences in social and cultural patterns, the model has aroused interest in some British colleges. Canter's key ideas are formulated as follows.

1. In relation to the role of *teachers* in the maintenance of discipline:

    (a) they must insist on 'decent responsible behaviour' from their students: the community expects it, students need it, and its absence will cripple the process of education;
    (b) they must accept that firm class control, maintained in a balanced form, is 'humane and liberating';
    (c) they must be aware of their basic 'educational rights' within the classrooms for which they are responsible, and these include 'the right to establish optimal learning environments, to determine, request and expect appropriate behaviour from students, to receive help from college administrators when it is needed'.

2. In relation to the role of *students* and the maintenance of discipline, they have basic rights in the classroom, including:

    (a) the right to have teachers 'who will help them to limit their inappropriate behaviour';
    (b) the right to have teachers 'who will provide positive support for their appropriate behaviour';
    (c) the right to choose how to behave 'with full understanding of the consequences that automatically follow their choice'.

3. The rights and needs of teachers and students are best met through 'assertive discipline' in which 'the teacher clearly communicates expectations to students and consistently follows up with appropriate actions, never violating the best interests of the students'.

(It may be that Canter's views are worthy of consideration when colleges draw up 'contracts' which students are required to enter, and which relate to discipline and expected standards of work, before admission to courses.)

Discipline: some concluding remarks

Formal discipline can rarely be imposed on further education classes.[14] Its presence often testifies to class motivation, the tutor's skill in instruction and his or her interest in the progress of the students. Its absence usually reflects a breakdown in the patterns of communication and control, the maintenance of which must be an objective of the teacher-manager. Discipline can and must be *positive and constructive*; it is a worthwhile objective in the classroom. Ausubel[15] sees it in wider terms which are worthy of consideration: '*[Discipline] is necessary for the internalisation of moral standards and obligations – in other words, for the development of conscience*'.

Student counselling in further education: essence and objectives

The refusal by some students to accept the norms of class conduct, the deliberate obstruction of the teaching process and the failure to come to terms with the demands of the further education environment are viewed by some tutors as manifestations of psychological problems which might disappear as the result of active guidance provided by skilled student counsellors. Schertzer and Stone[16] define student counselling as '*an interaction process that facilitates meaningful understanding of self and environment and results in the establishment and/or clarification of goals and values for future behaviour*'. Lewis[17] views it as 'a process by which a troubled person is helped to feel and behave in a more personally satisfying manner through interaction with an uninvolved person'. Rogers (see Chapter 10) writes of effective counselling as 'a definitely structured permissive relationship which allows the client to gain an understanding of himself to a degree which enables him to take new positive steps in the light of his new orientation'. Essentially, effective counselling involves people being taught to help themselves, on the basis of their acceptance of their own potential to change their reactions to a situation and, in doing so, to conquer their attendant problems.

The objectives of counselling include, according to Hamblin,[18] the encouragement of the growth of self-acceptance in the student, the development of internal controls within him, and his acquiring realistic, appropriate strategies of coping with his environment. The goal is the modification of behaviour reflecting insight and changed value patterns; it is achieved when the student understands his emotions and redirects them into new channels of behaviour among which is acceptance of the conditions necessary for effective learning.

Counselling is much more than a mere series of unstructured interviews in which advice is tendered to non-conforming students. The counsellor's overall strategy will determine the structure of the task, which may be considered in the light of various objectives. He or she must attempt, first, to discover, where there is a problem of behaviour in class, the motives of the student's general behaviour and this, in turn, necessitates the establishing of effective communication between counsellor and student, together with the creation of an appropriate level of confidence and trust. Secondly, the counsellor has to understand the student's perception of the college environment. Next, as the result of careful questioning, the reasons for the precise behaviour which has created problems in class need to be uncovered. A diagnosis should then follow, as a result of which the student should be brought to the point of *voluntary acceptance* of all those steps necessary to assist him or her.

Problems in student counselling

The major problems inherent in the counselling process derive from its very nature. It demands certain personal qualities (according to Hamblin, for example, spontaneity, genuineness, 'non-possessive warmth', sensitivity to low-level signals coming from the student); the counsellor must not only possess these qualities, but must convince the student that he or she does possess them. Counselling also requires skills of a high order – an ability to establish a confidential relationship with students of all types, a knowledge of the techniques of eliciting and analysing information, an understanding of the prevalent 'youth culture' and acquaintance with a variety of social environments. Its success involves patience and persistence. In Rogers' words, it requires the creation of *a non-threatening, non-judgmental environment, characterized by an attitude of empathy and respect for the student*. Above all, perhaps, it requires more than a superficial acquaintance with some of the principles of psychotherapy. This formidable list of desirable qualities in the student counsellor is a pointer to, and a warning against, the morass in which well-intentioned, but ill-equipped, amateurs may find themselves.

Further problems may arise from the possible clash of goals and beliefs in the interviewing process, which is inseparable from counselling. How is the strong-minded counsellor, possessed of a morality founded on deeply held ethical principles, to react when faced with the 'values' of an attitude akin to nihilism? How does the professional teacher respond to the expressions of an 'anti-culture' which denies the validity of that in which he or she believes? In short, how does the counsellor achieve the 'understanding neutrality' said to be required in the counselling process?

The complexities of the counselling relationship are outlined by Munro[19] in the enumeration of essential conditions of such a relationship. These conditions are described as 'of an ethical nature' and include: a higher degree of confidentiality than is normally expected from a teacher; an insistence on the essentially voluntary nature of the relationship; insistence on the client's responsibility for his or her own behaviour.

Some further education tutors who have practised as counsellors have reported their feelings of inadequacy when the complex reality of the basic problems of classroom deviance is uncovered. Family backgrounds, financial difficulties, health concerns and emotional entanglements may have woven a web from which the student cannot be extricated, save by a long-term process of adjustment, requiring assistance which is of a type totally beyond the counsellor's power and resources. Frustration on both sides is deepened when the counsellor's diagnosis reveals a situation from which escape seems quite impossible.

The problem of confidentiality often emerges at an early stage in student counselling, sometimes in the first meeting. Where the interviews produce criticism of a counsellor's teaching colleagues, is it to be conveyed to them? Where an interview reveals activities of an illegal nature, are the police to be informed? What is the legal situation of a counsellor who, aware of such activities, fails to inform the authorities? Is it possible to create the conditions necessary for a successful counselling interview if the student is aware that the principle of confidentiality may be breached?

Class teachers as counsellors?

Given the desirability of student counselling, who is to act as counsellor? The student's tutor? An outside expert? The continuing controversy on this question has been reviewed by Ard.[20] On the one side are those who maintain that *all* counsellors must be classroom teachers: they best understand the problems of behaviour in the classroom; they have experience of dealing with aberrant behaviour; they can meet their students as partners in the search for an answer to behavioural problems. On the other side are those such as Ard, who states categorically that 'the nature of the relationship to the student-client must necessarily be different from that of the teacher to the pupil'. Students, it is claimed, feel 'safer' in discussing their problems with someone who does not represent 'authority', and who seems to be neutral in matters concerning the college. Because effective counsellors need to be well-grounded in psychology and its applications, it is not possible for practising teachers to move easily – even should they possess the appropriate expertise – from one role to another. Ard concludes: 'While *some* teachers might become good counsellors, *all* counsellors *need not* be classroom teachers, nor *need not necessarily have ever been* classroom teachers'. A rational division of labour would involve the training of the classroom teacher in the recognition of stress signs (e.g. severe study and learning difficulties, behavioural problems) and knowledge of when to hand over consideration of the problem to a trained counsellor.

The counselling interview

It may be that, in the absence of the division of labour advocated above, the college tutor is asked to undertake the formal functions of a counsellor in a situation resulting from deviant behaviour in the classroom. Some guidelines derived from this type of experience are set out below; as in the case of the discipline hints given earlier in this chapter, much will depend on the nature of the precise state of affairs with which the tutor is faced. The need for some generalization in dealing with deviancy must not result in forgetting the importance of an individual approach to a particular, often unique, situation.

As far as possible, an attempt should be made to set up the physical environment (i.e. the room in which the interview will be held) so as to avoid any suggestion of an authoritative relationship between counsellor and student. One of the objectives of the interview must be to put the student at ease so as to establish a friendly atmosphere in which conversation will flow naturally; this requires an absence of any trappings suggesting an impassable gulf between the parties. Wide tables separating the parties, furniture which stresses hierarchical status, will not be conducive to the creation of a relaxed atmosphere in which confidence is to be established. A couple of easy chairs, not separated by table or desk, is often found to be suitable.

The interview which is designed to build a foundation of trust and confidence requires openness from both parties; this will require patient work on the part of the counsellor. He or she must use a style of language appropriate to the occasion, and must remember the significance of body language (see Chapter 11) and its interpretation by the student. Gestures which might be interpreted as indicating impatience, hostility, incredulity, disapproval, are out of keeping with the nature and purpose of this type of interview, in which existing anxieties may be fed by perceptions of hostility in the counsellor.

Careful questioning, based on the use of open-ended questions (see Chapter 22), and designed to give no suggestion of a forensic cross-examination, is essential. The purposes of questioning in this situation are to elicit information and to present the student with an opportunity of explaining the basis of his or her behaviour and, perhaps, anxieties. Hence, questions must not embarrass; where they do, silence, or obfuscation and evasion will be the response. A teacher placed in the position of counsellor must be prepared to hear unstructured, incomplete, contradictory sets of responses to simple questions; it is for the consellor to *listen*, to ask for elucidation, but not to criticize the form or content of those responses. Probing will be resented and may be perceived as an attack on the student's self-esteem.

Hamblin[21] advocates utilization of the technique of 'funnelling'. This involves the counsellor approaching the particular problem at its 'broad end', with appropriately wide, open questions, and then narrowing the questions until the kernel of the problem is reached. The process requires an atmosphere of confidence and an absence of any mutual suspicions as to integrity. Understanding on the part of the counsellor will emerge, Hamblin suggests, only if he is able to put himself 'in the student's shoes' and is prepared to await results. The diagnosis which may follow the first interview, and the creation of confidence, are to be seen as the most important objectives of that occasion.

A fusion of discipline and counselling

Williamson,[22] in a highly critical study of what he perceives as the dichotomy between discipline ('... repressive, regulatory, imposed ...') and counselling ('... growth-producing, self-regulating, self-initiating ...') suggests that discipline, as such, introduces an unwanted and discordant note into an educational process intended to stimulate the growth of individuality. Discipline on its own, he says, is repressive and growth-arresting; it can be no corrective of misbehaviour in the classroom unless it emerges as the consequence of a counselling relationship. Counselling is 'our present chief prospect for changing discipline from punishment to rehabilitation ... and for aiding the individual to achieve that degree of self-control and restraint so necessary in all members of an interdependent democratic society'.

The most important matter in affairs concerning discipline and student counselling appears to be the need to perceive situations and problems as they are perceived by *the students*. This is not a simple matter, but it has to be attempted. Erich Maria Remarque reminds us of the problem: 'There is a law of the years ... Youth does not want to be understood; it wants to be let alone ... The grown-up who would approach it too importunately is as ridiculous in its eyes as if he had put on children's clothes. We may feel with youth, but youth does not feel with us. That is its salvation.'[23]

Notes and references

1. See generally for this chapter: *Discipline and Morale in School and College* by M. Cleugh (Tavistock, 1971); *Conflict, Decision and Dissonance* ed. L. Festinger (Stanford UP, 1964); *The Teacher and Counselling* by D.H. Hamblin (Blackwell, 1992); *The Psychology of Counselling* by E. Lewis (Holt, Rinehart & Winston, 1976); *The Counselling Process* by L. Patterson (Brooks Cole, 1992); *Counselling* by H. Cowie (Fulton, 1994); *Counselling in Further and Higher Education* by E. Bell (OUP, 1996); *Theory and Practice of Counselling* by R. Nelson-Jones (Cassell, 1995).
2. *How We Think* (Heath, 1910).
3. For an interesting discussion of discipline in relation to the 'military mind', see *The Soldier and the State* by S. Huntington (Harvard UP, 1957).
4. *Communication* (Longman, 1984).
5. *Meeting the Educational Needs of Young Adults* (Harper & Row, 1984).
6. See Festinger (*op. cit.*).
7. See Cleugh (*op. cit.*).
8. *Modern Organisation Theory* (Krieger, 1975).
9. *On Education* (Watts, 1861).
10. 'Punishment – its use and abuse' in *Education and Training* (1983, 2).
11. *Op. cit.*
12. *Troublesome Behaviour in the Classroom* (Routledge, 1989).
13. *A Take-Charge Approach for Education* (Seal Beach, 1985).
14. See 'Good relationships with students' by K. Wadd in *Journal of Further and Higher Education* (1979, 2).
15. *Educational Psychology – A Cognitive View* (Holt, Rinehart & Winston, 1978).
16. *Fundamentals of Counselling* (Houghton Mifflin, 1980).
17. *Op. cit.*
18. *Op. cit.*
19. *Counselling: A Skills Approach* (Methuen, 1983).
20. 'Should all counsellors be classroom teachers?' in *Counselling and Psychotherapy* ed. B.N. Ard (Science and Behaviour Books, 1975).
21. *Op. cit.*
22. 'The fusion of discipline and counselling in the educative process' in Ard (*op. cit.*).
23. *The Road Back* (trans. A. Wheen) (Little, Brown, 1931).

Chapter 20

Teaching the Older Student

The educator of adults must understand the conditions under which adults learn, their motivation for learning, the nature of the community and its structure. Underlying all of these, and essential, is an understanding of oneself, undergirded by a sustaining personal philosophy (Campbell, 1977).

Teaching the older student often presents a variety of unique problems.[1] The 30-year-old engineering supervisor attending a college-based management course requires an instructional environment and programme which will differ from what is considered appropriate for the 17-year-old A level student; the professional workers in the 40–60 age group, who may form the majority of enrolments for an evening course on political affairs, present problems and opportunities for their tutor which differ from those related to the day-class students, whose average age is 18. In this chapter we comment on some important matters concerning the older student – the significance of perceptual theory, instructional strategies and the management of the learning process.

In considering the contribution which can be made by the colleges of further education to the life of adult learners, it is worth keeping in mind Yeaxlee's statement[2] that the *social* reasons for fostering the concept of lifelong education are as powerful as the personal. The work of the colleges in relation to the wider needs of the community now embraces a variety of forms of so-called 'adult education'.

The 'older student'

The age at which a student is classified as belonging to the 'older' age group seems to be purely arbitrary. Terms such as 'young person' and 'adult' have a variety of meanings when used in the literature of educational administration. The phrase 'adult education' has tended to mean education pursued by persons over the age of 18 which is not primarily intended for training or career qualifications; the Russell Committee on Adult Education (1973) seems to have had in mind classes 'for personal and social purposes' rather than 'for work-related purposes'. But the connotations of the term have expanded and now include industrial, commercial and other training.

The average age of students in colleges of further education seems to be under 21, but the number of students aged 21 plus has been increasing steadily, a trend assisted by enrolments of overseas students and the growth in extramural classes, catering largely for older groups. It is no longer possible to speak correctly of further education exclusively in terms of the 16–18 age group. For purposes of this chapter the 'older student' is considered as a person beyond the mid-twenties age bracket; typically, he or she will be, or will have been, in full-time employment.

Perceptual theory and the older student

Perceptual theory, as adumbrated by Coombs and Snygg,[3] for example, seems to have much relevance for the teacher of older students. The theory is built on the concept of our perceptions as the only reality we can know, and the main purpose of our activities as control of the state of our perceived world. Thus, Powers[4] describes human behaviour as 'the control of perception'. Hence, how people view their environment – the people, things and happenings with whom and with which they are involved – will affect their behaviour in large measure.[5] The older person's perception of his or her world must differ, generally, from that of the younger person; in particular, the adult's past experiences which are represented in the totality of his or her past and present perceptions, will be of a different quality from those of the younger person. Lovell[6] reminds us that adults' previous experiences in other groups will influence the way in which they engage in learning and that the most important single factor influencing new adult learning is what has been already learned and organized in conceptual structures.

The determinants of older people's perceptions include their values, beliefs, attitudes, needs and self-experiences. Their feelings concerning their preferred way of life and what they consider to be of lasting value, will affect their perception of their present environment. In the same way, their view of reality will be coloured by their beliefs in the worth of others and of themselves. Kidd[7] suggests that, for the adult, there may be two limits to educational growth – 'the real practical limit of one's maximum ability or potential capacity and the no less real psychological limit which each man places on himself'. Lovell[8] suggests that adult learners tend to underestimate their abilities and often experience difficulties with tasks requiring the interpretation of complex instructions.

Perceptions of 'threat' from the outside world are considered by Verduin[9] as having particular relevance for an understanding of the educational problems of older students. 'Threat is the perception of an imposed force requiring a change in behaviour, values or beliefs. One of the greatest threats to people is the requirement to change behaviour when beliefs, values or needs remain unchanged.' Verduin states that older students may often feel threatened when forced to alter the modes in which they attempt to maintain their self-organization.

In the light of this theory, the teacher of the older student ought to consider, first, removal of any perceptions of threat from the teaching environment. Feelings of safety and security should not be attacked and destroyed; a mere perception of external threat to well-being will put older students on the defensive. The conservatism which often characterizes the 'world-image' of the older person is peculiarly susceptible to perceived dangers stemming from suggestions of the need for fundamental change; hence the somewhat autocratic, highly defensive attitude towards younger students (and teachers) often adopted by the older student. The teacher should attempt where necessary to modify the interpretation of past experiences; those experiences remain the same, but the way in which students interpret them can be changed. Kidd[10] explains: 'All *new* experiences for the learner are symbolised and organised into some relationship with the self, or are ignored because there is no perceived relationship, or are denied relationship, or given distorted meaning because the experience seems inconsistent with the structure of the self'. Clarification of the environment, of needs, attitudes, values and their interrelationships is an important task for the teacher, who has to assist the older students to perceive their goals and their significance, and to perceive their experiences as a *potential asset for learning*. They will learn 'in response to their own needs and perceptions, not those of their teachers'.

Knowles[11] (who popularized the term 'andragogy' as meaning the art and science of assisting adults to learn) sums up by noting that older students are affected by changes in self-concepts, that they have built up valuable stores of mental resources as a result of experience, that they have a high degree of readiness to pursue learning in areas which they perceive as relevant to their lives, that they have developed their own learning styles, and that they are oriented to general learning, resulting in a high degree of intrinsic motivation. Teachers of older students must be prepared to view themselves in 'andragogical' terms, that is, they must be prepared to act as *'facilitators of learning'*.

Problems of learning experienced by the older student

The process of ageing – held by some to commence around the age of 19 to 20 – brings problems and opportunities for the student. In the case of older students, their experiences have multiplied, have been interpreted and reinterpreted and their perceptions of the world may have changed radically. Their rate of learning – but not their efficiency of learning – may have slowed down. Their intensity of motivation – but not necessarily the requisite skills and abilities – may have been heightened. In sum, the older student brings to the process of learning a variety of abilities and previously acquired skills, together with some handicaps, none of which is of an insuperable nature.

The older student will probably have experienced some deterioration in physical agility, in the acuity of his or her senses, in certain intellectual abilities, and in short-term memory. Where learning tasks involve speed, the older student may be at a disadvantage; time may have acquired a particular significance for him or her, so that he or she will be more concerned with accuracy and precision and will tend to work more slowly. Problems in retrieving stored information, arising largely because of lack of rehearsal, may make tasks of memorization increasingly difficult. (It often becomes necessary for the tutor to convince the older student by demonstration that one's long-term memory does not undergo inevitable, swift and irreversible decline as one grows older.) His or her patterns of coordination, rhythm and fluidity, acquired during the process of skills training, may have deteriorated; creativity and flexibility of mind, associated with discovering solutions to problems, may have apparently diminished.

The older student's awareness of a decline in some abilities and associated skills is often mirrored in a lack of confidence and a growth in anxieties; hence the need for a learning environment which will minimize anxieties and improve confidence. As his or her level of achievement moves to a plateau which can presage swift decline, the older learner, conscious of self-image, becomes much more cautious, and can be easily disheartened by temporary failures; hence the need for appropriately designed courses which will help adult learners to compensate for perceived deficiencies. Adult learners tend to resist change, are initially suspicious of novelty and do not always welcome innovation. They may be highly critical of teachers, who are often perceived as lacking the 'practical experience' which the older learner now considers as the root of all worthwhile knowledge.

Specific anxieties related to particular subject areas (e.g. mathematics, languages) and situations (e.g. tests and other activities involving negative comparisons with one's peers) may affect the performance of adult students. One result may be a high degree of 'oral communication apprehension'; another may be continuous distraction from the learning task. (Some psychologists have suggested that this may stem from the 'mobilization of personal defences' and a resulting strain on the learning faculties.) The teacher's reaction should take the form of a methodology of instruction which will ensure that the adult learner is provided with the competence needed for the course of instruction; special introductory classes based on revision of fundamental techniques will be advantageous. Additionally, the adult learner should be made aware of the nature of the learning process; this ought to figure prominently in the early stages of the course. To be aware of one's learning processes is seen by some instructors as a prerequisite for 'learning to learn'.

It has to be remembered that older students are frequently highly – and diversely – motivated learners. Often they will be attending a course of study simply because of a desire to do so, and because of a perception that their own advancement is dependent on the acquisition of further knowledge, or because of a particular interest in the subject matter of that course, with no thought of career advancement, that is, they have developed a 'need to know'. The older student may have long-range goals which have become internalized, allowing him or her to perceive the college course in terms of a direct contribution to the attainment of those goals.

Experience of the outside world may result in the older student having acquired a capacity to make decisions accurately and under conditions of stress. When carried over into classroom conditions, this quality of thought can be advantageous in the processes of learning. A heightened capacity for analytical thought has been noted by tutors of older students, who have been guided through courses involving the exercise of powers of discrimination and investigation. Further, older students who have undergone and assimilated the lessons of events in the wider world outside the classroom, have acquired a 'mental set' of much value in the analysis of apparently complex situations. The contrast between a discussion on, say, trade unionism, involving, on the one hand, young A level students and, on the other, industrial workers, will illustrate well the significance of experience, which comes only with involvement and age, in a deep understanding of social and industrial problems, and their wider implications. Note the significance of Mezirow's words: '[People] move through successive transformations towards analysing things from a perspective increasingly removed from personal or local perspectives'.[12]

Instructional strategies

The essence of a relevant strategy for teaching the older student is the provision of a 'positive supportive-learning' climate in which self-direction will predominate. Verduin's investigation of appropriate strategies culminates in his advocating the techniques of 'explanation' and 'demonstration'. (It should not be assumed, however, that Verduin is advocating these techniques exclusively in relation to the teaching of the older student. Explanation and demonstration are important components of instruction at *all* levels in further education. Verduin draws attention to their peculiar significance for adult learning, particularly where adults experience difficulties of 'unlearning', i.e. of rejecting errors and their consequences after they have once occurred.)

Explanation, as the central component of instruction for the older student, is described by Verduin as 'description, interpretation, analysis, direction giving, and clarification in an informal and conversational manner'.[9] The technique has certain advantages for older students. First, it emphasizes and reinforces what they have been taught previously; additionally, it provides a review of what they have read. Secondly, it summarizes and synthesizes information presented to them; explanation acts, in this sense, to underline the significance of acquired information. Next, it clarifies particular points which might not have been clear to the student initially. It repeats, stresses and reinforces matter presented in outline (generally necessary in a short course). Finally, explanation assists the learner in adapting what he or she has learned to new situations and to other content areas. Problem-based learning situations will assist in developing transfer of knowledge; in particular, synthesis and evaluation, rather than mere conscious memorization, have been found to be useful learning strategies for older students concerned with 'independent learning' leading to transfer.

Demonstration is described by Verduin as 'showing adults how something works and the procedures to be followed in using it'. It assists in supplementing lesson content, translates pure description into actual practice and stimulates a number of senses, with the resulting intensification of learning. The demonstration acts as a focus for attention on correct procedures and applications and assists those older students who may experience problems in reading and comprehending directions. Time, materials and equipment may be utilized economically. Finally, the demonstration constitutes a 'safe approach' to the teaching of hazardous and expensive operations.[13]

Other strategies for teaching the older student may be based on: learning tasks as a whole, rather than by parts, taking particular care to consolidate what has been learned; ensuring 'correct learning' as far as possible in the initial stages of instruction; utilizing self-pacing techniques; and employing practice and review in meaningful situations.

The Keller Plan: a strategy for adult teaching

Tutors of some adult groups have reported success in using Keller's 'personalized system of instruction' (PSI).[14] Keller, an American educational psychologist, devised PSI in the 1960s, believing that individuals, particularly adults, could learn best by using techniques of self-paced instruction. PSI is based on the following approach.

1. *It is 'mastery oriented'.* (See Chapter 23 for a discussion of mastery learning.) Desired outcomes of the adult study course are specified; in particular, the most significant parts of the course are given special attention in the specification. 'Mastery' is defined in terms of an answer to the question: 'What test evidence can I, as course tutor, accept as demonstrating that the desired degree of learning has occurred?' A student will move from one segment (or learning unit) to another only after demonstrating mastery of the first segment.
2. *It is individually paced.* The adult learner moves through the course segments at a speed related to his or her ability (and the general demands on time).
3. *It involves few formal lectures.* Some lectures and demonstrations intended to motivate and stimulate are offered only as options.
4. *It utilizes carefully devised, printed study guides.* Standard textbooks are rarely appropriate for PSI students; special material has to be written and issued in booklet form.
5. *It involves 'proctors'.* When a student has completed an assignment, he or she reports to a 'proctor',[15] who may be a tutor, or even, in some cases, a student working at an advanced course level. The proctor assigns a test, the results of which are discussed with the student, who then moves on to a new segment or is given remedial work.

Reports have indicated that adults do respond positively to the demands of PSI, particularly where skill training is involved. PSI requires careful explanation to staff and students as to its objectives, methods of instruction, evaluation and organization. The part to be played by the college-based instructor has to be explained in detail; the instructor has to respond positively to the organizational tasks, which can be onerous. In his or her role as 'proctor' the instructor may be expected to be available, through the telephone or personal meetings, to organize, explain and encourage.

CPD tutoring

Garry and Cowan[16] developed a scheme for 'continuing professional development' (CPD) based on learner-centred strategies. CPD is taken to mean 'the updating or further educational development required by mid-career adults who wish to maintain or promote their professional standing'. It may be of direct application, therefore, to some types of adult classes mounted by colleges of further education. The strategy advocated seems to owe much to the theories of Rogers (see Chapter 10). The term 'facilitator' is used, implying that the role of staff engaged in CPD tutoring is not to teach, but to 'facilitate' – 'to make learning easier, more efficient, more effective and more comprehensive'.

CPD tutoring is expected to: identify the needs of learners and build on the existing learning level of participants; recognize that the relationships between new and established learning will show marked individual variations within the tutorial group; allow for, and build on, these differences; involve all participants in active learning; and relate the learning process to the professional working lives of members of the group.

Facilitators working in CPD tutoring groups are expected to show a high degree of sensitivity to reactions of students. They are required to listen to participants' views and attempt to understand them, to be ready at all times to respond and adjust to problems posed by students and to relate them to prior experience, and to encourage and reinforce participants' contributions.

The management of instruction for the older learner

The 'supportive-learning' climate needed for the older learner earlier requires careful preparation. Nothing destroys a lesson for adult students more decisively than an inappropriate environment. Wherever possible the tutor should take pains to ensure that the class environment is appropriate. The rearrangement of classroom furniture is, therefore, important. A 'warm-up' learning period before the commencement of the formal part of instruction has been found very useful for older students. During this period the tutor who knows the class (a particularly important aspect of the tutor-class relationship which plays a vital role in effective tuition at this level) can introduce the lesson in personal, informal terms and explain its significance. The objectives of the lesson should always be made clear so that students know their goals, and how to recognize their attainment.

Sensitivity to the problems of the older student should characterize the tutor's approach. Abstraction ought to be minimized, distraction avoided and participation encouraged. Where instructional activities can be task-oriented, individual problem-solving should be encouraged. Group work has been found valuable for the older student: some educational psychologists have suggested that, as a member of the group, the older student is able to retain deeply held beliefs until ready for a change. Direct criticism ought to be avoided, where possible.[17] Achievement should be recognized; indeed, lessons should be so planned that learners are able to see their achievement and evaluate its significance.

For the older student, no less than for all other types of learner, the tutor's style can play a decisive role in the acquisition of knowledge. In the case of the older student, however, reaction to the approach and personality of the tutor is unusually important. Some teachers of adult students emphasize the vital role of the tutor in building up confidence so that the students' self-perception is heightened. A non-authoritarian style, emphasizing self-choice, is likely to win confidence dence. A 'transaction between equals', free from any suggestion of compulsion, has been suggested as an ideal pattern for adult student teaching-learning. The teacher who is able to 'teach without seeming to do so' has a very good chance of winning the confidence of the older student who, in most cases, would prefer to reach his or her destination unaided. Perhaps the words of Lao-Tze (in the 6th century BC), addressed to those rulers who wish to win the hearts of their people and assist them to attain goals, are appropriate:

> A truly great ruler is one who ... when he has accomplished his task ... would hear his people say, 'We've done it ourselves'.[18]

Notes and references

1. See generally for this chapter: *Adult and Continuing Education* by P. Jarvis (Routledge, 1995); *Adult Learning: A Reader* ed. P. Sutherland (Kogan Page, 1997); *Lifelong Learning* by N. Longworth and W. Davies (Kogan Page, 1997); *Key Concepts in Adult Education and Training* by M. Tight (Routledge, 1996); *Teaching Adults* by A. Rogers (OUP, 1996); *Why Adults Learn* by S. Courtney (Routledge, 1992); *Learning in Adulthood* by S. Merriam (Jossey-Bass, 1991); *A History of Modern British Adult Education* by R. Fieldhouse (National Institute of Adult Continuing Education, 1997).

2. *Lifelong Education* (Cassell, 1929).

3. *Individual Behaviour* (Harper & Row, 1959).

4. *Behaviour – The Control of Perception* (Wildwood House, 1974). The author's thesis explains perception as a set of signals inside a system 'that is a continuous analogue of a state of affairs outside the system'. See also 'Perception as hypothesis' in *OCM*. Note also the views of the Gestaltists (see Chapter 7) that humans possess a number of 'inborn organizing tendencies' that make perception possible.

5. See also *The Perception of the Visual World* by J.J. Gibson (Houghton Mifflin, 1950).

6. *Adult Learning* (Croom Helm, 1984).

7. *How Adults Learn* (Association Press, 1975).

8. *Op.cit.*

9. *Adults Teaching Adults* (Learning Concepts, 1978).

10. *Op.cit.*

11. *The Adult Learner: A Neglected Species* (Gulf Publishing Co., 1978).

12. 'Perspective transformation' in *Studies in Adult Education* (1977, *9*, 2).

13. Verduin's advice on this topic applies to the demonstration in lessons in colleges of further education generally.

14. See *PSI: The Keller Plan Handbook* by F.S. Keller and J.G. Sherman (Benjamin, 1974); 'Keller Plan' by J.A. Kulik in *IETE*.

15. The word means, in a strict sense, one who manages another's cause. Keller has in mind a counsellor.

16. See *Learning from Experience* by A. Garry and J. Cowan (FE Unit, 1986).

17. This is a very important matter for the tutor of adults in further education institutions. 'Intimations of incompetence' are not generally welcomed by adults who have chosen to return to education classes. Much tact is needed by the tutor who has to point out errors in these circumstances.

18. See *Tao-te Ching* ed. D.C. Lau (Penguin, 1963).

Part Five

Instructional Techniques

Chapter 21

The Modes of Instruction

> The purpose of designed instruction is to activate and support the learning of the individual student ... The learning it aids should bring all individuals closer to the goals of optimal use of their talents, enjoyment of life, and adjustment to the physical and social environment (Gagné, 1988).

By 'modes of instruction' we refer to the practices, techniques, strategies, rules, routines and procedures employed by teachers involved in aiding learning, often referred to as 'methodology'. This part of the text examines a variety of procedures commonly employed in further education ranging from the formal lesson – the staple fare of English education – to some recent advances in instruction by use of computers.[1]

The importance of discussing modes of instruction methodically in a text of this nature should have emerged clearly from the underlying theme of previous chapters, namely the assumption that instruction, if it is to be effective, needs to be *designed systematically*. The methods of instruction which have grown and which now characterize teaching in further education have their own rationale, techniques and objectives; they will be examined in succeeding chapters as a core of instructional procedures around which may be built *consciously planned instructional systems*.

The significance of instructional methodology[2] has been summarized by Gagné:[3] it is aimed at aiding the learning of individual students; it offers systems of activity which can affect individual human development; it is based on knowledge of how people learn; it takes into account the essential conditions for further learning.

Determinants of an approach to modes of instruction

An 'open system' (see Chapter 15), such as a college of further education, is affected by (and, in turn, affects) the wider social environment of which it is a part. The role of further education is perceived in varied ways by government, college managers, and employers' and employees' associations, for example. Perceptions of the college as basic educator, industrial trainer and social facilitator have figured in the community's expectations concerning the form and content of further education. There have been few college experiments in the Rogers-type 'free-form instruction' (see Chapter 10); in general, formal instruction remains an essential characteristic of further education classes, representing *general community expectations*.

The development of the instruction process in further education has imposed its own logic on many teaching procedures. Colleges grew from, or were grafted on to, secondary schools and 'evening institutes' which had produced their own, somewhat rigid, modes of instruction. Formal lessons and the occasional lecture epitomized the teaching process and passed over into further education as the favoured, primary components of instruction. Small-group tuition and individually tailored courses arrived much later in the colleges.

The *research of educational psychologists* has assisted in the shaping of teaching procedures in further education, but to a relatively limited extent. The obscurity of some research, its concentration on learning in the lower animals, and its apparent irrelevance to classroom practice, may have alienated many teachers. But some research into learning *has* affected current methodology: mastery learning (see p. 293), transfer of learning (see p. 223) and feedback (see p. 151) are examples of commonly accepted aspects of instruction which were developed originally from pure research into problems of psychology.

Another determinant of current thinking concerning modes of instruction is to be found in the *expectations of teachers and students*. These reflect development of the teaching profession, received opinion as to the aims of teaching and the methods of achieving these aims, general career aspirations of students and perceptions of teachers' contributions to the realization of those aspirations. Instructional techniques which seem to reject or downgrade these expectations have little chance of acceptance in our colleges.

The qualitative level of *work in teacher training institutes* has an important effect on professional attitudes to instruction. An institute tied inexorably to the past is unlikely to produce professional teachers who are motivated to experiment with modes of instruction. A training programme which aims at the encouragement of innovation, research into theory and practice, is likely to make a positive and sustained impact on teaching patterns in the schools and colleges.

Types of instruction

In terms of systems analysis (see Chapter 15), instruction may be viewed as the processes whereby classroom input is transformed into output. The learner's capacities, motivation and levels of knowledge are changed during the process of instruction so that standards are improved. In management terms, modes of instruction are made up from *the techniques essential to the learner's directed progress*.

Aspects of instruction techniques presented in the following chapters include the following:

● *the formal lesson*, in which a teacher presents a learning sequence based on the mastery of intellectual skills;

- *the skills lesson*, in which the attainment of a predetermined standard of motor skills emerges from demonstration and practice;
- *the lecture*, in which a speaker engages in a presentation based essentially on one-way communication;
- *the discussion group*, in which a small number of students are encouraged in the collective examination of a problem;
- *the seminar*, in which class members present a thesis or topic for scrutiny by colleagues;
- *the tutorial*, in which tutor and learners discuss in a personal face-to-face setting, problems presented by the tutor;
- *the case-study*, in which a problem, real or simulated, is examined by a group of students;
- *team teaching*, in which numbers of students are taught by teams of teachers working collectively as a unit;
- *audio-visual instruction*, in which auditory and visual aids are utilized as parts of an instructional sequence;
- *programmed instruction*, in which instructional material is self-administered on the basis of the learner's responses to small sequential steps;
- *computer-aided learning*, in which computers are programmed to instruct students.

The acceptance of research into modes of instruction

Difficulties in experimentation and evaluation continue to dog innovations in instructional techniques. Conservatism among educational administrators, planners and examination boards, and caution and wariness among teaching staffs have made the introduction of some new techniques difficult. The almost total rejection of programmed instruction and the unenthusiastic reception accorded initially to computer-assisted instruction exemplify the problems in extending the range of techniques. The dearth of data concerning the general effects of some kinds of instruction (e.g. team teaching) makes their evaluation very difficult.

An uncritical rejection of many of the research findings of educational psychology presents an additional problem to those who seek to extend modes of instruction. It may be that the focusing of attention on the practical outcomes of research into instruction will result in wider examination of those findings. In the meantime, instruction often tends to remain impervious to the implications of much current research (into memory, for example).

The total rejection of *all* methodology of instruction in favour of the practices associated with the 'personality cult' finds favour among some teachers. Briefly, the argument is based on the belief, allegedly evidenced by practice, that if one possesses an 'appropriate personality', successful teaching is assured. 'Personality' is described in terms of a 'magnetism' or 'charisma' which fixes and holds students' attention so that they listen and learn; the precise mode of instruction employed is irrelevant. No proof, save anecdote, is advanced for these beliefs, since none is needed. ('The facts speak for themselves.') This is a powerful superstition, the prevalence of which cannot be ignored. Ultimately, and paradoxically, it is a denial of the worth of teaching itself, since it rejects the necessity and rationality of systematic processes of instruction.

The instructional methods presented in this part of the text are a reflection of current thought among teachers in further education, based on the need to effect successful instruction by means of *techniques underpinned by theory*. In no sense, however, is it suggested that there is any 'finality' regarding the content or appropriateness of teaching techniques. Any suggestion that the final word on modes of tuition has been spoken should not be entertained. Skinner has reminded us that many areas of instruction remain unexplored, 'and the roster of available techniques is certainly incomplete'.[4] Popper's warning remains valid: 'With each step forward, with each problem which we solve, we not only discover new and unsolved problems, but we also discover that where we believed that we were standing on firm and safe ground, all things are, in truth, insecure and in a state of flux'.[5] There remains the need for continuous research into the ways in which teaching is carried out, and it is essential that such research be rooted firmly in what is actually done in the classroom.

Notes and references

1. See generally for this chapter: *Principles of Instructional Design* by R.M. Gagné *et al.* (Holt, Rinehart & Winston, 1988); *Handbook of Research on Teaching* ed. M. Wittrock (Macmillan, 1986); *Research in Classrooms* by L. Anderson and R. Burns (Pergamon, 1989); *Research Methods in Education* by L. Cohen (Routledge, 1987); *Handbook of Educational Ideas and Practices* ed. N. Entwistle (Routledge, 1990); *Research into Teaching Methods in Colleges and Universities* by C. Bennett (Kogan Page, 1996).
2. The term 'methodology' is used here to describe a 'body of methods' used in the practice of teaching. But there is argument as to the validity of the use of the term in this way. See Machlup in 'What is meant by methodology' in *Methodology of Economics and Other Social Sciences* (Academic Press, 1978): 'Although methodology is *about* methods, it is not *a* method, nor a *set* of methods, nor a *description* of methods ... While we use a method, we never "use" methodology; and while we may describe a method, we cannot "describe" methodology.' For an advanced treatment of methodology, which will be of particular interest to science teachers, see *The Arch of Knowledge* by D. Oldroyd (Methuen, 1986).
3. *Op.cit.*
4. *The Technology of Teaching* (Prentice-Hall, 1986).
5. 'The logic of the social sciences' in *The Positivist Dispute* (Heinemann, 1976).

Chapter 22

The Formal Lesson (1)

In his teaching, the wise man guides his students but does not pull them along; he urges them to go forward and does not suppress them; he opens the way but does not take them to the place ... If his students are encouraged to think for themselves, we may call the man a good teacher (Confucius, *c.*500 BC).

Although staff in colleges of further education are known as 'lecturers', they use as modes of instruction the lecture *and* the lesson, which is defined for the purpose of this chapter as *a self-contained instructional session, designed and administered by a teacher, with the intention of attaining a learning objective through guided and flexible class activities involving a variety of teaching techniques.*[1] The preparation of a formal lesson and its structure are considered below, together with associated matters, such as problems of questioning in class.

In systems terminology (see Chapter 15), the lesson involves class and teacher acting as the principal components of a teaching-learning system designed to transform input (teacher's performance, class participation, AVA, etc.) into output (change in class level of knowledge). The lesson will be related to the boundaries of the system (course requirements, departmental policy). Skilful teaching will assure synergy, that is, the attainment of a level of knowledge superior to that likely to be reached if members of the class were to act individually. Linking of all components of the lesson is essential and feedback subsystems (questions, evaluation) must be constructed.

The teacher-manager has the task of planning the lesson on the basis of available resources, and of providing a structure of *direct teaching* which will reflect particular demands of the subject area and patterns of objectives.

Preliminary planning of the lesson

Planning was noted in Chapter 15 as one of the teacher-manager's important tasks, allowing him or her to allocate instructional resources (time, materials, etc.) to the overall demands of the curriculum and syllabus. The planning of a lesson involves similar considerations. Objectives must be established and appropriate instructional activities mapped out before the lesson. Lesson planning should commence with a consideration of ends and means: the topic of the lesson will define its ends; the activities necessary to accomplish the ends will suggest the instructional means. 'Do not take the first step without considering the last.'

Following the selection of his or her objectives, the teacher collects the instructional material related to the students' capabilities and achievements. Sequencing and lesson structure are developed so that a series of instructional events (e.g. oral presentation, tests, reading of notes) emerges, to be modified in accordance with constraints such as the time available.

Time is invariably a constraint on lesson planning.[2] A useful general rule employed in some further education classes is based on the '80–20' principle. Roughly 80 per cent of available time is devoted to the central section of the lesson; the remaining 20 per cent of time is divided between the introduction and the conclusion. (The lesson notes (on p. 277) are based on another widely used pattern in further education: time percentages are, roughly, 15, 75 and 10.)

As with all rules of thumb, time-plans may require modification in the actual lesson: thus, the opening sequence may reveal an unexpectedly high level of class comprehension, allowing immediate movement to the next sequence. But some kind of overall time allocation must be planned if the lesson is to be balanced and if it is to achieve its objective.

Lowman suggests the following routine for consideration at the preliminary planning stage: select the topics to be included in the lesson; formulate the topic objectives; fit goals to realistic constraints (duration of lesson, size of class); arrange to share objectives with students, for instance, by an oral presentation of the objectives.

Lesson preparation

Preparation of a formal lesson demands a consideration of three major factors: the students, the subject matter, and the resources and constraints. Each factor involves a variety of problems which the teacher could examine in the following way.

1. *The students.* 'What is their academic standard?' 'Have they reached the level of attainment required for an understanding of the proposed lesson material?' ('A continuum exists in most content areas, with certain knowledge of skills prerequisite to achievement of more difficult or more complex knowledge and skills' (Hunter)[3]); 'Does my previous experience with them as a class suggest any likely problems?' (The answers to these questions will affect the form of the introduction to the lesson and may necessitate a re-examination of the proposed lesson objective; see Chapter 13.)
2. *The subject matter.* 'How is it related to the syllabus, or scheme of work, as a whole?' 'Does the proposed behavioural objective demand a particular approach?' 'What specific teaching methods might be appropriate?' 'Will audio-visual aids be of assistance?' (See Chapter 28.) 'What ought to be the general headings of the lesson?' 'What type of test should I use to assess and evaluate progress?' 'When ought it to be administered?'

3. *The resources and constraints.* 'How much time will be available?' 'How swiftly should I be able to make progress?' 'At what time of the day will the lesson take place?' (The first hour following the lunch break may demand a very special treatment.) 'Where will I be teaching – classroom, laboratory, workshop?' 'If special apparatus is required, is it available and in good condition?'

The answers to these questions should be reflected in the teacher's lesson notes. The less the teacher's classroom experience, or the more difficult the lesson content, the greater should be the preparation necessary and the more detailed should be the lesson notes. Notes ought to be set out so that they include: the subject heading of the lesson; the learning objective; the subject matter, broken down into approximate periods of time; methods to be used; audio-visual aids; apparatus; tests. An example is given in Figure 22.1. (Lesson notes may be requested occasionally by departmental heads, visiting inspectors, moderators, etc.)

Sequencing lesson content

'Sequencing' refers to the teacher's methodical ordering of *lesson content* in accordance with the pattern of instruction which he or she considers appropriate for the students at their particular stage of development.[4] The process was discussed in

Date: ....Class: ....Title of course: ....
Subject of lesson: ....
Learning objective: ....
Duration of lesson: 1 hour

Time	Lesson content	Method	Aids
10 mins	Test on previous lesson	Q & A	–
5 mins	Statement and explanation of lesson objective	Exposition	o/h projector
15 mins	Concept I	Exposition; Q & A	chalkboard
15 mins	Concept II	Exposition and discussion	chalkboard
5 mins	Recapitulation	Dictation of short note	o/h projector
9 mins	Test and assessment	Q & A	–
1 min	Announcement of title of next lesson	Exposition	chalkboard

Figure 22.1 Outline lesson notes.

relation to course planning in Chapter 16; the general principles outlined there apply also to the sequencing of lesson content. Lesson aims, peculiarities and special qualities of the subject area in relation to students' level of knowledge are factors to be considered when deciding on a pathway to the objective.

There are, however, no immutable rules, no commandments, no prohibitions, in this area. Experience may dictate that the inherent logic of a subject topic is best ignored in the early stages of instruction, or that the time-honoured principle of proceeding from the particular to the general might be reversed ('Here is the general principle ... here are the structural specifics'). Some teachers will prefer sequences which follow the chapter patterns of the class textbooks in use.

A guiding principle (but not a rule) might be derived from the following very general suggestions. Experiment widely, in the early stages of your teaching career, with a variety of sequencing patterns which will reflect *your own view of teaching theory*, and which will answer the question: 'How do students learn?' (By example? By association of ideas? By application of principles to problems?). Try out, initially, the sequences advocated by Reigeluth and Gagné. Evaluate results, modify the sequence where necessary, rejecting any aspects of the sequencing which introduce unnecessary complexity. Aim, eventually, at a simple sequence which carries the learner with relative ease from one part of the lesson to another, which links one segment of knowledge to another, which avoids discontinuities, and which is perceived by students as a progression from one level of understanding to another. Do not hesitate to abandon a sequence where circumstances warrant this. There is no virtue in continuing along a path which leads nowhere.

Lesson structure

Structure reflects and is determined in part by content. The framework of a practical lesson on stock control, designed for part-time management-trainee students, may differ in some ways from that of a formal lesson on the causes of the Second World War, designed for full-time A level students. Structure will also reflect strategy, i.e. the objective of the lesson, the time available, the use to be made of teaching aids and the need for recapitulation and revision. In Davies' words: 'Structure gives form to the learning experience'.[5]

The influence of subject matter on structure must not be overlooked. Thus, lessons on formal grammar may require a structure reflecting the derivation of examples from principles; lessons in geometry will be built around symbolizing and deducing. Lessons in accounting generally rely on a formal structure which emphasizes the significance of rules; lessons in the humanities may adopt a loose structure allowing the opportunity to explore situations. The physical sciences may demand lesson structures based on experiment and induction; where scientific operations are formalized by the employment of quantitative terms, practice in deduction may characterize the form of the lesson.

There are generally four main structural components of a formal lesson: *introduction*, *development*, *consolidation* and *conclusion*. The introduction should state the object of the lesson; the development should present, teach and test the acquisition of the lesson material; the consolidation should strengthen what is being learned; the conclusion should recapitulate and revise. Variations of this basic structure are probably infinite in number. Some familiar examples are illustrated in Figures 22.2 and 24.1. (There is an obvious affinity of the basis of some of these structures with the 'introduction-exposition-development-recapitulation-second theme ... coda' of classical symphonic form in music.)

We now discuss the main components of lesson structure.

The introduction

The arousal of interest, the capturing and maintenance of attention and the 'setting of the scene', are essential in the first minutes of the lesson. A test on previous work should serve to focus class attention and to link the lesson with what has preceded it. (Although the lesson is a self-contained unit of instruction, it must be seen as part of a wider sequence.) Retention, recall and insight may be tested in these first minutes. The lesson objective and its significance should then be stated clearly, so that students are not left without an answer to their unspoken query: 'What are we about to learn?' Long, complicated statements of objective are to be avoided; a short, clear statement is preferable. For example: 'The last time we met we learned that there were three kinds of body surface through which invaders may enter – the skin, the lungs and the alimentary canal. Here they are on the chart. Today we shall learn about the skin and how it guards our body. But, first, a quick test on what we learned last week ...' Another example might be: 'We begin today a new section of our work on the law affecting retailers by examining the Trade Descriptions Act 1968. We shall spend four lessons discussing it and today we shall ask and answer the one question, "Why was legislation of this type necessary?"'

The central section (the development)

The main body of the lesson may consist of the presentation in gradual fashion of a sequence of information linked with previously acquired knowledge. The sequence ought to be logical and (particularly in further education classes) should be designed, whenever possible, to elicit those responses which will develop insight (see Chapter 7). Statements of facts and ideas, illustration by example, demonstrations, discovery by the class of underlying principles, development of facts and ideas and their practical application, may feature prominently in the central section. Full class participation is desirable. Oral questioning and discussion will be useful. Tests and assessments (see Chapter 30) – vital for the process of effective control – should also be included in this part of the lesson structure, not only as a guide for the teacher in assessing and controlling his or her movement to the teaching objective, but in informing students of their progress and maintaining motivation and interest.

The consolidation

The consolidating part of the formal lesson is intended to strengthen what students have learned. It involves review, rehearsal of learning, and a bringing together of the elements of the lesson into an integrated whole. Questioning plays an important part

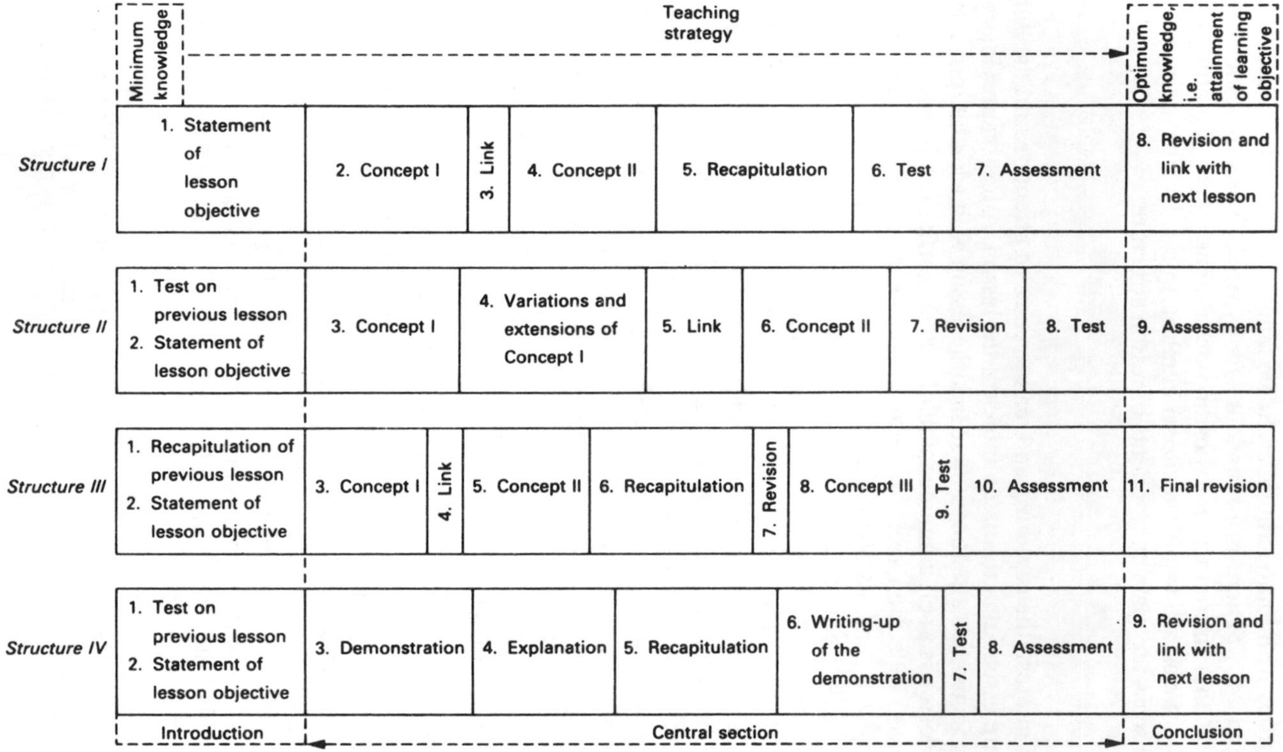

Figure 22.2 Lesson structures. (It should be noted that these diagrams do not specify the instructional media: teaching aids of many kinds (see Chapter 28) can be utilized in most parts of these lesson structures.)

in consolidation. Provision for practising appropriate skills is essential to this phase of the lesson.

The conclusion

The ending of the lesson ought to be planned as carefully as the introductory and central sections. It should not comprise a few hasty words, spoken when it is obvious that time has run out. A conclusion provides a final opportunity of ensuring assimilation and retention and ought to include a revision (perhaps in the form of question and answer), a summary of which can be presented visually. A link with the next lesson in the overall scheme of work can be provided, for example, by the setting of assignments which should be seen as a preparation for that lesson, or by the announcement of the next lesson's title.

Modification of structure

The best-laid plans, however, can go astray and it may be necessary to modify or even scrap the planned structure while the lesson is actually taking place. A failure of demonstration apparatus, an unexpected difficulty in controlling assimilation of a concept, or a class test which reveals a lack of comprehension of important points exemplify some of the circumstances in which a plan may have to be altered or put aside. On occasions such as these, there is no value in 'pressing on regardless' or in going through the mere motions of completing the planned lesson. An alternative structure, based perhaps on revision of a previous lesson or on the relearning of a partially assimilated concept, ought to be readily available; it is not always easy to extemporize in a situation of this nature. (See p. 296).

An example of outline lesson notes (which reveal lesson structure) is given in Figure 22.1.

Lesson structures

Reigeluth[6] proposes the following as a general lesson structure.

1. Stimulate and maintain interest (novel questions, analogies, demonstrations).
2. Create a meaningful context.
3. Present the basic information.
4. Provide enrichment of the presentation (alternative representations, memory devices).
5. Provide practice related to the basic information as soon as possible after it has been presented.
6. Provide enrichment of the practice (repetition at a variety of levels).
7. Provide reinforcement.
8. Obtain feedback.
9. Provide enrichment based on the feedback.

Gagné[7] outlines a sequence of 'events of instruction', formulated as a lesson structure, as follows.

1. *Commence by gaining the attention of students.* There may be circumstances in which attention might be gained by the use of a provocative overhead question (see p. 288) or a short reading related to lesson objectives.
2. *Inform the class of the lesson objectives.* The purpose of this event is to answer the students' question: 'How will I know when I have learned?'
3. *Stimulate the recall of prerequisite knowledge.* This involves the use of teaching techniques aimed at the retrieval of prior learning. Recall questions and short tests are valuable for this event.
4. *Communicate stimulus material to the class.* An appropriate presentation should be aimed at inducing *selective perception*, e.g. instruction in discrimination through the use of a variety of examples, leading to the learning of rules and concepts which can be grasped and used in the solving of problems.
5. *Give learning guidance.* This will involve questioning, hinting, prompting (but not overprompting), priming and cuing retrieval.
6. *Elicit the required performance.* At this stage the teacher should ensure that what has been learned can be applied to a series of examples of different types.
7. *Ensure that feedback is provided.* Knowledge of levels of performance should be conveyed to students so that reinforcement can be established.
8. *Enhance retention and transfer of what has been learned.* (For 'retention', see p. 210; for 'transfer', see p. 223.) The retrieval of concepts and rules will require systematic and spaced reviews. Transfer of learning will necessitate students being provided with varieties of new tasks involving the application of what has been learned.

Ausubel[8] suggests a lesson structure based upon the use of 'advance organizers' (see p. 104) and involving three linked phases.

1. *Utilization of the advance organizer.* Outline lesson aims; present the organizer; provide the context of the new lesson; prompt awareness of the learners' existing knowledge.
2. *Presentation of the teaching material.* Make the logical order and organization of the learning material highly explicit. Arouse and maintain motivation. Present the learning material by use of 'progressive differentiation', i.e. use a stepped progression from general concepts to specific information.
3. *Strengthening of cognitive organization.* Promote active reception learning (see p. 102). Clarify any points arising. Encourage questioning.

Hunter[9] sets out a basic lesson structure built around seven phases.

1. *Create an 'anticipation set'.* Directives and questions are utilized so as to assist in the formation of a mental set appropriate to the nature of the lesson objectives.
2. *State the lesson's objectives and purpose.* Inform the class of *what* is to be learned and *why* it is of importance.

3. *Provide the information input.* The information relating to the lesson objectives should be presented methodically.
4. *Model what is being taught.* Give an indication of the application of the lesson content.
5. *Check for understanding.* Ensure that lesson content has been assimilated.
6. *Give guided practice.* Use the results of practice to provide feedback.
7. *Arrange for independent practice.* This is intended to assist in transfer of learning.

See Figure 22.2 for typical lesson structures.

The lesson in relation to 'information-processing' abilities

Where a teacher decides to use the lesson format for the specific purpose of heightening students' 'information-processing' abilities (see p. 211), the following lesson structure can be considered.

1. Use a variety of techniques which will attract and hold attention. Build on what is known and stress the value of learning new ideas.
2. Allow time for rehearsal of new information and use the technique of distributed practice by organizing short, intensive practice periods at frequent intervals. Utilize the 'serial position effect' by placing the most important items at the beginning and end of the lesson (see p. 218).
3. Stress the meaningfulness of what is being learned and its overall significance. Use analogies where appropriate.
4. Direct the learning experience towards analysis and comprehension of the *essential principles* of what is being taught.

Lesson teaching: some notes on method

The teacher's aim in a lesson must be to motivate, stimulate and communicate, to hold the attention and to achieve a defined objective through class control. The following points are of importance.

1. The lesson must be pitched correctly. The level of the class and its record of attainment must be the starting point for the teacher's preparation. This point cannot be overstressed. Information can only be incorporated in an *existing* scheme of thought. Ausubel is emphatic:

   > If I had to reduce all of educational psychology to just one principle, I would say this – the most important single factor influencing learning is what the learner already knows. Ascertain this and teach him accordingly.

   In the absence of a correct appraisal (which can be made from a swift test), the probability of the lesson's success is low.

2. The lesson objectives must be realistic and clear (see p. 159). This involves careful forecast and design (see Chapter 13). In the absence of objectives, the lesson can become a disjointed, pointless event. The objectives must be explained to the class and their attainment ought to be accepted as a joint teacher-class aim. Lesson objectives must be kept in mind: they represent the *fundamental intention* of the lesson and should be 'balanced' so that expected outcomes are attained. The lesson's teaching plan should be matched as closely as possible to the overall nature of the objectives.

3. Exposition must be ordered, simple and clear. Order and simplicity of presentation are vital if the learner is to achieve mastery of a subject. This must be reflected in the teacher's exposition of the lesson material. New concepts must be linked with previously learned material and must be shown to derive from it. New terms must be explained; it must never be assumed that they are automatically understood by the class ('... there's no need for me to define this, because I'm sure everyone knows what it means'). It follows that the teacher's vocabulary must be intelligible to the class. In the absence of clear exposition effective communication is difficult to achieve.

4. Development must be logical and consequential. Students usually find that continuity in the development of concepts assists in assimilation and retention. Unbridged gaps, unexplained 'jumps' in exposition, make learning difficult.

5. Presentation must be based on the essential 'social character' of the lesson. The essence of a lesson is joint teacher-class activity, so that a 'lesson' made up of a teacher's exposition alone is a contradiction in terms. A lesson is not a solo performance; it will include periods (often alternating) in which either the teacher's stimulus activities predominate or the students' responses are paramount. Discussions and controlled sequences of questions and answers (see p. 286 below) are therefore necessary.

6. Presentation ought to involve a variety of media. The spoken word and the chalkboard are not the sole communication media. The many audio-visual aids (some of which are noted in Chapter 28) can be utilized to constitute an 'assault on the dulled senses' which can bring a lesson to life.

7. Presentation must be related carefully to fluctuations in class attention. Figure 22.3 generalizes the well-known phenomenon of variations in the rate of class attention during a lesson sequence.

    The decline of initial interest, the interference and 'noise'[10] produced by fatigue and diminished motivation, should be recognized by the teacher in the planning and delivery of the lesson. Varied presentation, carefully timed pauses, recapitulation and a variety of class activities may help to offset the tendency to diminishing attention. The use of the teacher's voice, often providing the central communication source in a lesson, is of great importance. Emphasis on key words, variations in pitch and tone so as to prevent monotonous delivery, and clarity at all times, aid the holding of class attention.

8. Presentation should be assisted by appropriate body language. 'Kinesics' (see p. 147) draws attention to the fact that the teacher is 'conversing with his entire body' – his posture, gestures, facial expressions can emphasize, or even contradict, his verbal utterances. Students respond to verbal *and* non-verbal language.

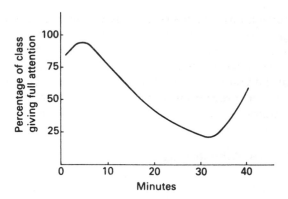

Figure 22.3 Fluctuation in class attention.

Hence the teacher has the responsibility of ensuring that his lesson presentation is assisted, and not hindered, by his non-verbal code.

9. The familiar 'sequence procedures' should be considered.[11] The following procedures are of relevance to lesson presentation.

(a) *Proceed from the known to the unknown.* Students often learn by association, so that the learning of new concepts may be facilitated by their being deliberately linked with what is already known by the class. The student's first-hand knowledge of a motor cycle can be used as the basis of an introduction to theoretical lessons on the internal combustion engine; an awareness of press reports of current economic events, such as levels of inflation, can provide an effective lead-in to a course on the theory of price determination.

(b) *Proceed from the simple to the complex.* A gradual shift in the level of the lesson, so that the class moves from basic principles to more advanced learning, usually necessitates an ordered sequence in the presentation of concepts, e.g. as in a lesson on design, which is based on the preliminary observation of simple, geometric patterns and which moves towards aesthetic considerations and value judgments.

(c) *Proceed from the concrete to the abstract.* Experiments in elementary physics and chemistry are often designed and presented with this procedure in mind.

(d) *Proceed from the particular to the general.* A lesson based on the interpretation of a specific event so that its wider significance shall emerge illustrates this principle, e.g. an examination of a country's decision to devalue its currency, from which some generalizations concerning economic policy may be deduced.

(e) *Proceed from observation to reasoning.* This is a very important principle which draws attention to the development of the powers of reasoning and the gaining of insight as desirable lesson outcomes. To learn to reason from the 'how' to the 'why' ought to be an objective of much of the work in the colleges of further education. ('Men do not think they know a thing until they have grasped the 'why' of it, which is to grasp its primary cause' (Aristotle).)

(f) *Proceed from the whole to the parts, then return to the whole.* This principle is the basis of the lesson sequence which presents its subject matter initially as an entity, then proceeds to an analysis of component parts, finally returning to an overall view.

The techniques of oral questioning

Davies[12] suggests that the planned use of questions is the mark distinguishing a lesson from other modes of instruction. Oral questioning is an integral part of the joint teacher-class two-way activity which characterizes many successful lessons. It has a number of purposes. It may be used to discover the level of class knowledge so that the appropriate starting point for the presentation of new material may be determined. It can provide informative feedback, that is, it can show what progress in teaching/learning has been achieved and what revision is needed. (Indeed, it is by the judicious use of questions that the teacher-manager is able to make the assessment on which his or her control of the lesson may be based.) It can be used also to gain or regain class attention, to fix facts in the memory, to develop a learner's understanding and powers of reasoning and expression, to recapitulate, to produce a dialogue, to prompt students to move to the next mental step, to probe for progressively more precise answers, to challenge beliefs and guide consideration of values, and to develop class participation.[13]

Questions ought not to be selected at random and asked in a perfunctory manner; they require careful preparation, timing and delivery, and should be reasonable (i.e. not impossible to answer) and relevant. Direct, precise and unambiguous phrasing which elicits equally direct and precise answers is advantageous. A long, tortuous question is likely to present the class with the added problem of attempting to understand what the questioner has in mind so that the real problem becomes secondary. The 'closed' question which demands in reply a mere 'yes' or 'no' ought not, in general, to be put, but where such a question has been asked, the reply ought to be followed by a further 'open' question (i.e. non-restrictive, and suggesting a variety of responses), thus:

Q: Now that you have read this newspaper article do you consider the introduction of value added tax to have been based on a wise decision?
A: Yes.
Q: Would you give your reasons?
(A more effective single question would be:
Q: Now that you have read this newspaper article, what do you think of the decision which was taken to introduce value added tax?)

Meaningless, rhetorical questions ('Is that clear?' 'Are you following me?' 'OK?') are of little value in class teaching. (Some communications theoreticians and teachers cite this type of question as an example of the 'blocking' of a communications channel.) Questions which demand obvious answers, and trivial or trick questions, are almost always out of place in a lesson. Where possible, step-by-step questions and answers, each answer giving rise to the next question, should be utilized. (It is worth remembering Steinbeck's comment: 'An answer is invariably the parent of a great family of new questions.')

An entire lesson consisting of questions, answers and occasional recapitulations is possible, but it would seem to require – if it is to be effective – a very efficient teacher, a very small class and subject matter which lends itself well to highly analytical treatment. A prototype is to be found in the teaching methods attributed to Socrates and recorded in Plato's *Republic*. Socrates was famed for his skilled use of the dialectical method in teaching; question and answer dominated his mode of instruction. In his celebrated discussion with Thrasymachus, for example, a vast, complex and renowned exposition of the meaning of 'justice' emerges from the seminal question: 'You say that what is advantageous to the stronger is "just". Now, what do you mean by that, Thrasymachus?' Socrates' 'heuristic method' (in which students are enabled to discover principles for themselves) was based on two phases: in the first (negative) phase, the students' ignorance is exposed by question and answer and their curiosity is aroused; in the second (positive) phase, guidance is given to the students, again through the use of questions and answers, in their search for the correct answer to problems.[14]

Questions should be put one at a time and spread over the whole class, as far as possible, and should not be confined to a small section of 'regulars' who can be relied on to respond. Questions may be put to the class as a whole, or may be addressed to one student by name. A 'wait time' for a response is often advisable. A student's answer ought to be repeated by the teacher if it is almost inaudible. Where no answer is elicited from a named student, or from the class as a whole, the correct answer may be given by the teacher, or instructions given as to how or where it can be discovered. Credit for good answers results in useful reinforcement. Poor answers can be valuable, too, in that they provide the opportunity for further discussion and assimilation; they should not elicit from the teacher an over-critical response. Under no circumstances should a poor answer be mocked; this can destroy motivation and often lead to the student's 'withdrawal' from further participation in the lesson.

Questioning by the class ought to be encouraged as long as it does not degenerate into time-wasting or irrelevance. Where class teachers do not know the answer to a question, they ought to admit this, and promise to seek an answer, which should then be given at the earliest opportunity.

Oral questioning: further problems

Experience in the classroom suggests that the most productive question-and-answer sessions are those placed at 'strategic points' in the lesson process. Dillon[15] recommends the following practice: 'Ask questions during the course of instruction about each point that is important for students to master, rather than depend upon a general, indirect consequence from questioning'. The importance of preplanned questions, inserted in a carefully structured lesson sequence at vital points – where information is to be emphasized, consolidated and organized – must be stressed in answer to the teacher who asks: 'When, in my lesson, ought I to begin questioning the class?'

'*Overhead or directed questions? Relay or reverse questions? Which ought to be favoured?*' An *overhead question* is one asked, initially, of the class as a *whole*. It avoids the problems which may arise from first singling out one student by name; it extends an initial challenge to the class as a whole; it allows the questioner to eventually select the person who is to answer; it may draw from the class a variety of useful responses. A *directed question* is put to an individual, often by name (and often follows an overhead question). It allows the reticent or hesitant student to be drawn into discussion; it enables comment to be distributed; it draws on individual students' capacities. A *relay question* is one put by the student to the teacher, who can respond by putting the question to the group as a whole. Participation is encouraged by use of this technique – and it often allows the teacher time to prepare his or her eventual response. A *reverse question* is one which is thrown back (perhaps in a modified form) to the questioner by the teacher to whom it is addressed. It is said to be a valuable teaching tactic in that it encourages students to think for themselves. But its indiscriminate use can lead to embarrassment for the student and to the drying up of the flow of student-teacher questions.

'*What is the value of the "probing question" in lessons?*' The *probing question* is, in contrast to the superficial query, an attempt to elicit deeper responses which in turn, can be made the basis of further questions (i.e. it acts as a 'springboard'). It may be used to seek further information or clarification of some point made in a previous response, to encourage students to further consideration of the implications of an answer, and to stimulate students to self-criticism in relation to their previous answers. In particular, the probing question may be used for the more difficult questions in a graded series.

> A good questioner proceeds like a man chopping wood – he begins at the easier end, attacking the knots last, and after a time the teacher and student come to understand the point with a sense of pleasure (Confucius).[16]

'*Is it possible to use class questioning to range over the gamut of abilities within the domains of learning?*' It is not only possible, but highly desirable. Research findings suggest that questions requiring higher-level thinking (e.g. in the realms of synthesis and evaluation) produce performance gains much greater than those requiring mere verbatim recall. The following sequence of questions used in the preliminary stages of an early lesson, for non-specialists, on general principles of contract law, illustrates the manner in which the abilities suggested by Bloom as comprising the cognitive domain (see p. 173) might be utilized in question-and-answer sessions.

'Let us begin with the definition of "contract". What would you say in response to a person with no training in law who asked you to explain to him what the term 'contract' means?' (*Taxonomy level: knowledge. Overhead question, involving recall.*)

'One of the phrases used by John in his answer to the previous question was "legal consequences of an agreement". What do we understand by this?' (*Taxonomy level: comprehension. Overhead question, involving understanding.*)

'Let us apply Mary's answer to the last question to the following problem. X, aged 17, after finding his first job, agrees to pay his mother, Y, £25 a week to help towards his food and board. After a month, X refuses to pay Y. Has Y any remedy under the law of contract?' [After a pause] 'Fred, please.' (*Taxonomy level: application. Directed question, involving the use of principles.*)

'Fred's answer and his explanation were correct. Let's go over the points he made ... Now, remember the question I put to Fred. Suppose that X had been aged 19 at the time – would the situation as Fred described it have been any different?' (*Taxonomy level: analysis. Overhead question, involving ability to discriminate.*)

'Now, let's return to John's definition of "contract" – I'll write it on the board. Note the words I'm underlining – "an agreement which the courts will enforce". Can anyone suggest any circumstances in which the courts might insist on an agreement being carried out, even though the parties don't want the courts to interfere?' (*Taxonomy level: synthesis. Overhead question, involving ability to perceive and discuss relationships.*)

'Finally, I would like you to think very carefully about the next question I am going to put to you. Talk it over among yourselves for a few minutes, then I'll call on you for an answer. Here is the question: How *useful* is John's definition – look at it once again – for the "man in the street", who knows no law?' (*Taxonomy level: evaluation. Overhead question, involving ability to formulate a judgment.*)

The growing awareness of the importance of effective questioning technique for the class teacher is evident in the attention being given by some teacher training institutions to the use of 'microteaching' – a process in which teaching techniques are scaled down, allowing a trainee to demonstrate particular skills, such as class questioning, in a short lesson sequence of, say, five to ten minutes. Its objective is to isolate and study a specific teaching skill. Video and audio tapes can be utilized so as to review and analyse the trainee's performance. In this and other ways the vital technique of questioning – 'the core around which most communication during the lesson is built' – can be taught effectively.[17]

Notes and references

1. See generally for this chapter: *IETE*, sections 3, 4, 5; *Essentials of Learning for Instruction* by R.M. Gagné (Dryden, 1974); *The Conditions of Learning* ed. R.M. Gagné (Holt-Saunders, 1985); *The Art of Teaching* by G. Highet (Methuen, 1977); *Instructional Technique* by I. Davies (McGraw-Hill, 1981); *The Craft of Teaching* by K. Eble (Jossey-Bass, 1976); *Mastering the Techniques of Teaching* by J. Lowman (Jossey-Bass, 1984).
2. See 'Time' by W.J. Smyth in *IETE*.
3. 'The teaching process' in *The Teacher's Handbook* (Scott, Foresman, 1971).
4. See 'Pacing and sequencing' by G.J. Posner in *IETE*.
5. *Op. cit.*
6. 'The elaboration theory of instruction' in *NSPI Journal* (19).
7. *Op.cit.*
8. 'Defence of advance organizers' in *Review of Educational Research* (1978, *48*).
9. *Knowing and Teaching* (Alexandria Press, 1984).
10. The term is used here in the context of communication theory (see Chapter 11).

11. The enumeration of these procedures is attributed to Herbart. Continuous citing has given the constituents of the list the quality of clichés; in fact, the procedures continue to influence the basis of many types of lesson in further education.

12. *Op.cit.*

13. See e.g. *Classroom Questions – What Kinds?* by N.M. Sanders (Harper & Row, 1966); *A Guide to Questioning* by C. Kissock and P. Iyortsuun (Macmillan, 1962); *Questioning and Teaching* by J.T. Dillon (Croom Helm, 1988); 'Teaching skill: the question of questioning' by D.R. McNamara in *Educational Research* (1981, *23*).

14. The Socratic principles of education, intended to stimulate careful reasoning and mental self-discipline, are summarized in *Ideas of the Great Educators* by S. Smith (Barnes & Noble, 1979).

15. *Op. cit.*

16. *The Wisdom of Confucius* ed. Lin Yutang (Random House, 1966).

17. Teachers who are interested in the difficult art of forensic questioning (in which the form of the question is almost as significant as its content) should refer to *Questioning Techniques and Tactics* by J. Kestler (McGraw-Hill, 1982); *Interviews and Interrogations* by A. Buckwalter (Butterworth, 1983).

Chapter 23

The Formal Lesson (2)

It is the teaching, not the teacher, that is the key to the learning of students. That is, it is not what teachers are like, but what they *do* in interacting with their students that determines what students learn and how they feel about the learning and about themselves (Bloom, 1972).

This chapter looks at the significance of the assignment and the demonstration as aspects of the formal lesson and discusses so-called 'mastery learning', which is designed so as to ensure that all, or almost all, the students in a class acquire a certain skill at a predetermined level prior to their learning the next skill in a sequence. The significance of teaching concepts (i.e. general categories under which specific elements may be placed in groups) is also noted. Attention is given to procedures for conducting an improvised lesson, and to the teacher's evaluation of the lessons delivered.[1]

Assignments

Assignments may be set because of the rules of a college course or a national examining body, and/or because a tutor considers them as necessary supplements to work done in class. Where set, the assignment should be presented by the tutor as being an *integral* (hence non-optional) part of the course. It is always important to explain to students *why* assignments are set. In the case of classes meeting only once a week and having to attain a high standard of work, assignments may be essential if the syllabus is to be covered.

The aim of assignments may be four-fold: to extend and amplify work covered in class; to revise that work; to provide opportunities for the application of lessons learned in class to the solution of problems arising in novel situations; and to hone students' writing skills. Where assignments are used as an extension of classwork, they should be based on general principles learned during lessons. Where their object is rehearsal and revision, problems may be set which will lead into future lessons. Where practice in new situations is required (a precondition of the transfer of learning) problems demanding recall or reinstatement of skills can be a useful component of assignments.

It is important for the tutor to ensure that assignments are based on tasks which can be carried out within a reasonable time; the expected completion date should be announced with this in mind. Selective, rather than extensive, reading lists ought to be published, together with indications as to where texts and adjunctive material might be found.

The tutor's grading schemes should be made clear: the significance of 'B−', 'C+', and other grades must be explained carefully. How is a pass mark indicated? What weight is given in the final evaluation to content, style, grammatical precision, handwriting? The marking of the assignment should indicate to the student how his or her work might be improved. Where possible, a single-word assessment such as 'good' or 'weak' should be avoided.

Given that the value of feedback and reinforcement tend to diminish with the passing of time, it is essential that assignments be marked and returned to students as soon as possible. Careful timing is essential where an assignment is intended to act as an introduction to the learning of new material on a planned future date.

Demonstrations as part of the lesson

A demonstration is not usually planned as a complete lesson in itself; it should be presented as a part of a lesson sequence, providing a stimulus situation (or 'cue') from which principles may emerge through reasoning. It requires careful planning and presentation if it is to lead clearly to the lesson objective which, in the case of the sciences, may be based on an understanding of principles, causes and effects.

Students must be *prepared* for the demonstration if it is to achieve its optimum effect. Certain preliminary knowledge may be essential and this ought to be tested in the lesson prior to the demonstration. The class ought to be *informed* of what the demonstration is intended to make clear, thus: 'Using this apparatus we shall make chlorine' or 'We shall use this simple apparatus to learn what happens when an electric bell is activated in a vacuum'. The demonstrator ought to give an account of the *pattern of events* as it unfolds ('I'm now pumping the air out of the jar which contains the bell') and, in giving the description, he or she should carefully visualize the apparatus from the students' place in the class ('Look at the bell jar, which is to your left').

Arrangement of the class and the apparatus is important. The students should be seated as near the demonstration as is practicable. Michael Faraday made this point many years ago (with reference to a lecture):

> When an experimental lecture is to be delivered and apparatus is to be exhibited, some kind of order should be preserved in the arrangement of them on the lecture table. Every particular part illustrative of the lecture should be in view; no one thing should hide another from the audience, nor should anything stand in the way of the lecturer.[2]

The demonstration ought not to be too detailed; its main points ought to emerge clearly and be underlined by the demonstrator's emphasis. It should be followed by a recapitulation of the events which the students have seen and by a reasoned statement of the principles involved. The class ought then to write up the demonstration as the prelude to a test which will assess its impact.

Mastery learning and the lesson

The practice of mastery learning which is outlined here places great emphasis on the lesson as a mode of instruction.[3] Mastery learning was developed by Carroll and Bloom in the belief that 80 per cent of students in a class could attain approximately the same high level of attainment that only 20 per cent achieve under traditional instructional methods. Organization and planning are of particular importance in this type of teaching.

Carroll[4] suggested that 'teaching ought to be a simple matter if it is viewed as a process concerned with the management of learning'. 'Mastery' ought to be the goal of all teaching and learning. Essentially, 'mastery learning' is intended to ensure that all, or nearly all, students learn and reach a predetermined level before moving on to the next stage of their learning programmes. The focus of instruction ought to be *the time needed by students to learn the content of a given unit of instruction.* Carroll proposed that:

(a) a student's aptitude should be viewed as an index of learning rate, not learning level;
(b) a student's degree of learning can be considered as a function of the time actually spent in learning.

Bloom, in *Learning for Mastery* (1968), modified Carroll's approach and suggested that:

> Most students (perhaps over 90 per cent) can master what we have to teach them, and it is the task of instruction to find the means which will enable our students to master the subject under consideration. Our basic task is to determine what we mean by 'mastery' of the subject and to search for the methods and materials which will enable the largest proportion of our students to attain such mastery.

He made the following observations:

(a) the student must understand the nature of what is to be learned and the necessary processes for learning it;
(b) specific instructional objectives concerning essential learning tasks must be made clear;
(c) subject matter should be broken down into small units, each unit to be tested;
(d) feedback after each test is essential and must be organized;
(e) the teacher must be able to alter the learning time available for some members of the class;

(f) alternative learning procedures must be available for students.

Bloom's mastery-learning model, as applied to the management of lessons in further education, would involve the following steps.

1. Examine the relevant learning unit which will be the basis of the lesson. Analyse it in terms of items which will be critical to mastery; state them in terms of tasks; set out the appropriate operational instructional objectives.
2. Arrange the resulting lesson objectives into small learning units in a clearly stated, logical sequence.
3. Ensure that the objectives are made known and explained to students, together with the mastery criteria.
4. Develop two similar style tests for the lesson, based upon the mastery criteria, e.g. '95 per cent correct'.
5. Teach the lesson, based upon the learning tasks, using regular class tuition. Each student in the class must be given sufficient time to learn and relearn the instructional material until he or she is able to demonstrate in one of the tests (known as as a 'formative' or 'diagnostic' test) that an appropriate degree of learning has been attained, before being allowed to proceed to the next part of the instructional unit.
6. Failure in a formative test will lead to the student receiving a further, corrective lesson, involving different teaching strategies from those employed in the first lesson.
7. A student who has achieved the mastery criterion in the first test will be given a series of 'enrichment activities' (e.g. a deeper reading schedule) or, in some cases, may be allowed to assist class colleagues who have not achieved the required standard.
8. Students who have received corrective instruction will receive a further test.
9. The final 'summative test' will cover the key aspects of the instruction unit. Where a student fails repeatedly, additional work involving different strategies of instruction ought to be considered, along with the possibility of moving to another, more appropriate, teaching group.

The teaching strategy outlined above differs from conventional lesson instruction: it places emphasis on the mastery of relatively small learning units; it utilizes diagnostic progress tests to inform learners of what has to be done to achieve mastery; it stresses the importance of specific corrective procedures as part of the lesson.

Bloom claims that the model is designed for 'teacher-paced approaches for use in the typical classroom situation where instructional time is relatively fixed and a teacher has charge of 25 or more students'. Lessons designed as part of his mastery learning sequence involve the following management tasks:

(a) careful planning of objectives, and formative and summative tests;

(b) explanation to students of the sequence of activities, together with an explanation of its purpose, with particular reference to tests and gradings;
(c) planning the pace of instruction;
(d) gradually reducing class time spent on corrective activities.

Lessons in concept formation

The teaching of concept formation – the process by which learners recognize how to sort their specific experiences into general classes and rules – presents special problems for the lesson planner.[5] 'Concept learning is probably the most important of all instances of learned behaviour'.[6] Instruction in the categorization of concepts and the acquisition of associated meanings involves careful attention to lesson content and the sequencing of teaching.

A concept is an idea or symbol that brings together a group of ideas or symbols. Hence abstractions or generalizations in the learner's mind which he or she uses to represent some group or class is a 'concept'. We may say that the functions of concepts in learning are: that they are essential to comprehension; that they can act as short cuts to effective communication; that they can assist in the transfer of learning; and that they can promote recall.

Perceptions of concepts tend to change; they develop somewhat slowly and at different rates for different students; their development is fostered where the learner becomes conscious of *similarities* among known concepts. Bruner speaks of concepts as *conjunctive* (where all the values of the attributes of a concept are present simultaneously) or *disjunctive* (where the attributes are not present in all the examples under consideration).

Gagné proposes that in concept teaching the performance criterion should be the identification of a class of things or any member of a class. How do Christianity, Judaism, Islam conform to the concept of 'religion'? Why do we classify the whale as a mammal? How does the use of a jury fit in with the idea of justice? Answers to conceptual questions in this form involve the learned ability to discriminate essential features of things or events and group them systematically into cohesive categories.

Weil[7] advocates the use of lessons based on the presentation of sequences of examples and non-examples, analysing their attributes and building hypotheses concerning the concept in question. Tennyson[8] suggests that concept formation can arise from lessons in which stress is placed on the 'surrounding structure' of a concept; new concepts are taught so as to be seen emerging from those with which the student is familiar. The teacher analyses the 'network location' of the concept he or she intends to teach, and relates it to the student's existing patterns of knowledge. The teacher then defines the concept to be taught and collects examples and non-examples (as contrasts). Matching exercises are used during the lesson to determine 'concept exemplars'. Relationships between larger and smaller entities are emphasized. As a conclusion to the lesson, the teacher suggests new examples based on the structure of the newly learned concept.

A teaching model used successfully in further education for concept formation is based on the following strategy. (It has been used for teaching concepts in economics principles courses, such as 'wealth' and 'utility', and in elementary law courses for teaching concepts such as 'negligence' and 'duty of care'.)

(a) Preliminary definition of the concept is given. (A standard text is used to provide the definition.)
(b) Attributes are identified and 'contraries' are noted.
(c) Examples are elicited from the class and are then discussed.
(d) The concept is redefined.
(e) The structure of the concept (i.e. relationships between its properties) is outlined.
(f) The concept is used in a variety of problem-solving exercises.

In effect, the learner has been taught in this lesson sequence to compare various aspects of an idea and to produce an overview which expresses an important relationship between them.

The improvised lesson

Most college tutors will find that at some stage in their teaching careers they will be asked at very short notice to deputize for an absent colleague. The ability to improvise a lesson with speed and skill emerges after much experience in teaching. For the inexperienced teacher faced with the necessity to plan a lesson with very little time for preparation, and a syllabus scheme which must be followed, the following skeleton plan is suggested.

1.   Examine the *title* of the lesson you have to cover.
2.   What *topics* are suggested by the title? List them.
3.   What *questions* do these topics suggest? List them. (Check that they have not been covered in previous lessons.)
4.   Use the questions as *headings* for sections of your lesson.
5.   The central section of your improvised lesson should comprise a series of *key questions and answers*.
6.   Provide a short *introduction* and *conclusion*.

Personal evaluation of lesson effectiveness

After a lesson the teacher ought to attempt an evaluation of the effectiveness of the learning event for which he or she has been responsible. This requires an assessment of class achievement in relation to the lesson objectives. In particular, the teacher should engage in self-questioning in the following areas.

1.   'Was my introduction effective in arousing interest? Did the class settle down to work swiftly?' Did class motivation appear adequate?

2. 'Was the lesson content adequate, given the amount of time available? Was the time divided adequately among the various parts of the lesson?'
3. 'Was interest maintained? Did I actively promote maintenance of that interest?'
4. 'Was my questioning adequate and how far did the answers elicited help class progress towards the lesson objective?'
5. 'Were my summaries and recapitulations adequate?'
6. 'Were my teaching aids and their use adequate? Did they really assist learning?'
7. 'Were class discipline and control adequate?'
8. 'Does the final test result indicate any specific weakness in my lesson plan or presentation?'

The teacher's answers should seek to be as 'objective' as possible. The result of the final test given to the class will provide an important measure and assessment of effectiveness which ought to assist presentation and control of succeeding lessons.

Notes and references

1. See generally for this chapter: *The Aims of College Teaching* by K. Eble (Jossey-Bass, 1983); *Mastering the Techniques of Teaching* by J. Lowman (Jossey-Bass, 1984); *The College Classroom* ed.R. Mann (Wiley, 1970); *The Skilful Teacher* by S.D. Brookfield (Jossey-Bass, 1990); *Learning for Mastery* by B. Bloom (California UP, 1968).
2. *Advice to Learners* ed.G. Porter (Royal Institution, 1974).
3. See *Implementing Mastery Learning* by T.R. Guskey (Wadsworth, 1985); 'An introduction to mastery learning theory' by B. S. Bloom in *Schools, Society and Mastery Learning* (Holt, Rinehart & Winston, 1974); 'Problems of measurement related to the concept of learning for mastery' by J.B. Carroll in *Mastery Learning* ed. J.H. Block (Holt, Rinehart & Winston, 1971); 'Mastery learning models' by L.W. Anderson and J.H. Block in *IETE*.
4. *Model of School Learning* (Teachers College Record, USA, *64*: 723).
5. See 'The nature of concepts' by V.C. Arnone in *Theory into Practice* (1987, *3*); *Psychology of Education* by E. Stones (Methuen, 1983); *Concept Learning* by E. Hunt (Wiley, 1962).
6. 'A note on two basic forms of concepts and concept learning' by G. Davis in *Journal of Psychology* (1966, *2*).
7. *Information Processing Models of Teaching* (Prentice-Hall, 1978).
8. 'The teaching of concepts: a review of the literature' in *Review of Educational Research* (1980, 50).

Chapter 24

The Psychomotor Skills Lesson

A journey of a thousand miles starts under one's feet (Lao Tze, *c.*480 BC).

Three major categories of skill are generally inferred for purposes of educational psychology and practical class teaching: *mental skills* (e.g. reasoning); *perceptual skills* (derived from the 'mechanisms' underlying perception); *perceptual-motor skills* (based on the coordination of perceptual and motor processes). It is the latter category which is considered in this chapter.[1]

The general principles related to the teaching of a formal lesson, discussed in the previous chapter, apply also to the teaching of 'motor' (or 'psychomotor') skills,[2] that is, *those series of learned acts requiring simultaneous or sequential coordination.* The successful operation of a lathe or word-processor, the correct fingering of a violin or flute, the swift and accurate representation of the spoken word in the form of shorthand symbols involve, essentially, the acquisition of 'a practised ease of execution' in relation to the appropriate sensorimotor activities. ('Habit diminishes the conscious attention with which our acts are performed' (William James).) The principles of instructional technique are basically the same whether the subject matter be welding or economic geography, typewriting or algebra; but 'learning by doing' tends to feature more prominently in lessons aimed at motor skill acquisition. The objective of effective coordination of mind and muscle, resulting in the production of appropriate, swift and meaningful patterns of movement, usually requires a special type of lesson content and an appropriate lesson structure, based on the learning of sequences of unitary motor responses.

The nature of skills

Everyday usage of the word 'skill' implies some expertise in an activity developed as the result of training and/or experience enabling the learner to perform particular tasks; its defining attributes are generally held to be *effectiveness and flexibility.*

The Department of Employment's glossary of terms defined a skill as an '*organised and coordinated pattern of mental and/or physical activity*' in relation to an object or other display of information, usually involving both receptor and effector processes. Mace[3] describes a skill as 'an ability to produce consistently an intended effect with accuracy, speed and economy of action'. Evans[4] describes a skill as 'any ability, generally assumed to have been learned, to perform a complex task involving psychomotor coordination with ease, speed and accuracy'. Welford[5] refers to skill as consisting 'in choosing and carrying out strategies which are efficient'. Howarth[6] regards it, in wider terms, as 'a set of strategic adaptations to the mechanical limitations of the brain and of the body, which enable human purposes to be achieved'. It is built up gradually in the course of repeated training or other experience. It is serial; each part is dependent on the last and influences the next. 'To have a skill,' writes Macdonald–Ross,[7] 'is to have the ability to execute useful tasks to publicly agreed standards of performance'.

Sensorimotor activity, which is at the basis of all skilled performance, is motor activity initiated and controlled by sensory input from the performer's environment and from the performer himself. The systematic motor skills which make up those activities taught in the skills lessons in the colleges of further education are based generally on a series of coordinated movements, the execution of which requires repeated practice and correct timing. ('Certain patterns within the individual are abstracted and carried into new situations.') Performers must learn to be attentive to their environment, to respond to, or ignore, certain types of cue from that environment and to mark their responses by selecting immediately an appropriate and accurately timed movement from the repertoire they have acquired as the result of previous learning. The movement of a needle on a dial, interpreted as the signal for adjustive action, the presence on a sheet of violin music of the symbol *ff*, interpreted as the need for additional pressure of bow on strings, the note in the margin of a manuscript which is being typed, which reads 'CAPS', interpreted as a signal demanding the use of particular keys on the typewriter, exemplify stimuli which ought to result in *swift, precise responses characterized by complete coordination of mind and muscle*. In these examples perception results in linked actions based on manual dexterity and economy of behaviour. The quality of those actions will depend, in particular, on the performer's previous experiences and learning.

The phrase 'coordination of mind and muscle' serves to remind us that skilled performance is an amalgam of motor (MC) and perceptual components (PC). Thus, swimming involves high MC and relatively low PC; playing the piano well involves high MC and PC; reading involves low MC and high PC.

Among the distinguishing features of a skilled activity are dexterity (in which speed and precision are essential), coordination (in which abilities to grasp and manipulate may be vital), the ability to respond quickly, spatial ability (i.e. the capacity to deal with relationships involving more than one dimension), the capacity 'to share attention among a number of more or less simultaneous demands', accuracy in timing, anticipation of movement and perhaps, above all, a smooth flow of movement. These features reflect *the general organization of input data by the performer*. He is able to make sense of what he perceives and to translate his perceptions into organized activity. It is one of the main tasks of the skills teacher to assist in the acquisition of powers of activity organization and learning, and to enable the student 'to obtain the maximum information out of the minimum number of cues'.

The concept of *'flow'* is particularly important in teaching and learning skills. The practical significance of this concept for the teacher who is attempting to inculcate techniques is mirrored in the theoretical view, held, for example, by Smith,[8] in which motor skills are seen as 'multi-dimensional behaviour patterns' rather than as 'temporal sequences of discrete responses'.

The creation and growth of skills

Among the many theories accounting for the creation and growth of skills, the following have been found to be of particular relevance to the work of teachers in the colleges of further education.

Gagné's 'S–R chaining' theory

Gagné[9] considers skills as resulting from the connections of a set of individual associations, that is S–R sequences. Part-skills should be taught, followed by instruction in the 'executive subroutine' which controls their execution in the correct sequence. S–R associations are fixed and reinstated, as the result of guided practice; chains which result are reinforced by further practice. The chains represent mastery of S–R units of activity and result in the appearance of a 'skill'. (Gagné points out that executive subroutines often remain intact for many years even though, as a result of disuse, performance has become uneven. Thus a person who has learned the routine of setting and using a lathe will remember this long after leaving the trade.)

The *conditions for chaining* are described by Gagné in terms which are of particular relevance for instruction in the college classroom and workshop.

1. Previously learned, relevant S–R associations must be thoroughly revised and tested. Reinstatement in correct sequence is essential and this can be assisted by the use of prompting involving external cues.
2. Separate links in the chain should be executed under conditions of contiguity.
3. Repetition of the chained sequence is valuable; this necessitates guided practice. (By 'practice', Gagné has in mind repeated procedure based on the learner's motive to improve performance, and incorporating feedback.)

Crossman's 'selection' theory

Crossman[10] suggests that, in acquiring skills, the learner is refining the process of selecting the most appropriate methods from his or her repertoire. Practice by the learner exerts a 'selective effect' on his or her behaviour, favouring those patterns of selection and action which are quickest, at the expense of others. Hence, according to Crossman, trial and error are not as effective as a process by which the teacher guides the learner through the selection and utilization of the appropriate activity patterns. Speed is acquired as a result of *practice based on an instructor's directions*.

Adams' 'graded-movement' theory

Adams[11] views the learning of graded movements as the essence of skill acquisition. The first stage of such learning involves the establishing of a 'perceptual trace' which the learner uses as the basis of successive movements; this is a verbal-motor phase in which the teacher provides verbal cues concerning the learner's actions. In the second stage (the motor phase), verbal cues are not necessary since the perceptual trace is now firmly established. In practice, therefore, skills acquisition will grow from carefully directed teaching and practice.

Annett and Kay's 'redundancy-appreciation' theory

Annett and Kay[12] have suggested that skills are acquired as the learner is able to understand the redundancy in inputs of sensory information. In the first stages of their learning, learners will observe that signal x is apparently followed invariably by signals y and z. With intensified perceptual understanding they will learn that the probability of signal x being followed immediately by signal y is greater than the probability of its being followed immediately by signal z. They are able to concentrate on useful cues, therefore, by learning to treat certain inputs as redundant. Skill acquisition will be determined by the selection and abstraction from the input of vital relevant information prior to its utilization in the form of an activity.

Fitts' 'three-phase' theory

Fitts[13] believes that the acquisition of a complex skill necessitates the learner passing through three overlapping phases; the transition from phase to phase may take the form of a continuous rather than a sudden change. (Fitts views complex skill learning in terms of the acquisition of a number of semi-independent subroutines which may go on concurrently or successively. Hence, he says, it is essential for success that the teacher shall identify correctly the appropriate 'executive subroutines' concerning sequence rules in a skill.) The phases in Fitts' model are as follows.

(a) *The cognitive, early phase.* The beginner seeks to understand what has to be done and attempts to comprehend the background to the tasks he or she has to master. The teacher guides the learner towards the required sequence of actions and builds on previously acquired part-skills, i.e. the subroutines. Frequently recurring errors are pointed out to the learner. As a result of this phase he or she acquires an 'executive routine', i.e. the required procedure.

(b) *The associative, intermediate phase.* Correct patterns of response are established in the learner's repertoire as the result of demonstrations, imitation and practice. Part-skills are 'smoothed' by the elimination of inadequate movements, and sub-skills are integrated into required total skills.

(c) *The autonomous, final phase.* Skilled acts are now performed automatically, without the learner having to stop to think of 'what comes next'. Errors have been eliminated, speed of performance has been increased, resistance to the effects of stress is built up and improvements in skill continue (although at a decreasing rate).

Miller's 'hierarchical-structure' theory

Miller[14] views the acquisition of skills as the progressive coordination of separate units of activity into a hierarchical structure. He conducted research into 'feedback loops' of activity, using the concept of 'TOTE' units (test, operate, test, exit). The first phase of activity on which skill is based is a 'test', in which the learner assesses whether there is any difference between the actual state of the system and its required state. Any observed difference (of a significant nature) requires an 'operate' phase, followed by a further 'test' phase. The cycle of 'test, operate and test again' will continue until the desired state is achieved, after which activity ends – the 'exit' phase. (Note, for example, how this activity may be observed in the tuning of a violin, the setting of a machine tool, or the seasoning of food.) The use of TOTEs requires a plan, defined by Miller as 'any hierarchical process in the organisation that can control the order in which the sequence of operations is to be performed'. The learning of skill is seen as the integration and ordering of units of sensorimotor activities.

Klausmeier's 'internal program' theory

Klausmeier[15] defines a skill in operational terms as 'the level of proficiency attained in carrying out sequences of action in a consistent way'. He sets out five characteristics of a skilled performance.

1. The learner acquires a 'central motor program' (CMP) by practice as a result of which his or her performance no longer depends on voluntary control or upon continuous attention to feedback; the CMP has attained 'automaticity'.
2. There is increased freedom from reliance on external cues – they have been internalized into the learner's CMP.
3. External 'visual feedback control' becomes internalized in the CMP.
4. Coordinated movement patterns emerge under the control of the CMP.
5. Ability to perform the skill well under different types of changing conditions emerges.

Norman's 'chaos to automaticity' theory

Norman[16] notes the significance of learning and continued practice for any consideration of skilled performance. Five matters are of importance in differentiating the skilled performer from the amateur: skilled performance reveals ease and smoothness in execution of a task; skill brings with it a decrease in mental effort and a lessening of fatigue in performance; stress tends to decrease where the performance is executed with skill; skilled performance involves a wide variety of activities which have coalesced into a unitary skill; skilled execution of a task involves a degree of automaticity.

The importance of 'tuning' one's performance is stressed by Norman. 'Tuning is the fine adjustment of knowledge to a task ... it is, perhaps, the slowest of the modes of learning, but it is what changes mere knowledge of a topic into expert performance.'

Acquisition of a skill generally involves a *sequence of experiences*, necessitating 'moving from whole to part and back to whole again'. Initially, the requisite performance will appear to the learner as chaotic and, therefore, lacking in organization. Systematic analysis, under the supervision of an instructor, will reveal the component parts of the task. It becomes possible to learn the sub-skills separately and then in combination. A synthesis of the sub-skills emerges and 'task structure' appears. Practice and tuning will produce a performance which is 'automatic'.

The psychomotor skills lesson: its essence

The skills lesson is apt to be a relatively slow process; there are very few short cuts to the permanent acquisition of procedural sequences of motor skills. Lesson preparation must take into account the necessity for careful, planned and methodical teaching and learning of the routines of sub-skills out of which mastery emerges.

The skills teacher must cover *all* the tasks which have to be learned. What has to be done? This may involve a detailed *job analysis* (see below). The selection of appropriate audio-visual aids may be determined by a study of the job analysis. How shall competence be recognized and evaluated? The answer may involve a statement of instructional objectives cast in strict behavioural terms (see Chapters 13 and 14).

Job analysis

The *job analysis*, a study of which is essential if the relevant motor skills are to be taught effectively, involves observation (by the instructor, where that is possible) of performance of the job at mastery level. The necessary steps are generally as follows.

1. A description and analysis of the operational system within which the job is carried out should be made so that the job is seen in context. (It is important in teaching a skill that its context be explained.)

2. The relevant job is isolated and analysed in relation to its objectives.
3. Cues and signals involved in the job (e.g. instrument readings, positions of levers) are identified and recorded.
4. Task elements associated with mastery of the job are identified and classified as 'procedural tasks' (such as functional checks) or 'problem-solving tasks' (such as the detection and identification of a malfunction).
5. The analysis is checked in a variety of operational conditions.

A *skills analysis* extends a job analysis through what Davies[17] describes as 'both the overt and the covert manifestations of skill'. Essentially, it is an investigation in depth of skilled performance and is used where tasks involve complex and unusual movements, keen discrimination, and a high degree of information-processing and decision-making. The following questions are generally posed and answered in detail.

1. What are the precise actions performed by an experienced worker during the various stages of the task? How are the actions sequenced and do they involve any inherent difficulties of execution?
2. What information from each of his or her senses is received by the worker during the stages of the task?
3. How does the experienced worker utilize sensory information in deciding how to select and control the physical movements needed for a skilled performance?

Instructors who have examined the job and skills analyses, as they relate to a unit of instruction for which they are responsible (as in some NVQ courses, for example), will find that their work in identifying needs and appropriate instructional strategies will be eased. In particular, instructors will, in Mager's words, 'better avoid the teaching trap of including more theory than is necessary or desirable, and keep the course performance-orientated'.

Lesson planning

Lesson planning in relation to the acquisition of skills can benefit from a study of Miller's identification of the *significant functions* characterizing a process. He notes seven functions which ought to be taken into account when skills techniques are to be taught.

1. The ability to recognize objects and symbols used in the skilled task by name and appearance.
2. The viewing, search and detection of 'task-relevant cues'.
3. The identification and interpretation of 'cue-patterns'.
4. The temporary retention ('short-term recall') of information needed to complete particular sequences.
5. The long-term recall of procedures.
6. Decision-making.
7. Appropriate motor response.

A useful categorization of functions necessary in skill acquisition has been given by Demaree.[18] His scheme of instruction is built on the recognition of four inter-related matters:

1. learning of knowledge related to the task – words, symbols, rules and relationships;
2. learning of skills and task components – perceptual identification, naming, computation, decision-taking (in the face of incomplete information);
3. learning of whole-task performance – procedural patterns, relevant motor skills, complex decision-making;
4. learning of integrated-task performance – coordination and team tasks.

The following principles should be considered in the planning and execution of lessons aimed at the acquisition of skills and based on defined sensorimotor objectives.

1. *The skill ought to be demonstrated initially in its entirely as a fully integrated set and cycle of operations* and it should be stressed from the very beginning that mastery can be acquired by those who are willing to learn; there must be no suggestion that competence can be attained only by a chosen few. The demonstration ought to be accompanied by a clear, non-technical commentary. Above all, it must be a *demonstration of mastery.* The correct movements which go to make up the skill must be in evidence from the outset. The demonstrator must not forget that what is 'second nature' to him or her – posture, the holding of an instrument, the guiding of a tool – must not be taken for granted; it must be seen as part of the skill to be acquired and must be analysed and taught accordingly.

2. *The skill must then be broken down into its component, subordinate activities*; each action should be demonstrated, explained, analysed and demonstrated again so as to emphasize its particular importance and its significance for the skill as a whole. The relation of separate activities one to the other and their integration into a hierarchy of complete routines which make up the skill must be stressed. *Order, sequence, pattern* and *rhythm* must be emphasized.

   (a) Learning of skills should be based initially on units which can be practised with some assurance of success. The reinforcing value of a correctly performed action in the early days of skill acquisition cannot be overstressed. ('Well begun is half-done.') The importance of careful and sympathetic guidance will be obvious. Praise given neither undeservedly nor indiscriminately is a valuable reinforcing agent. The beginner, who has listened with nervous apprehension to the fine musical tone produced by the instrumental teacher, will be assisted by the reassurance that his or her first efforts, when made in accordance with the teacher's directions, are the preliminary steps along the road to competence. The first successful actions of the engineering apprentice working at the bench ought to be acknowledged and praised.

   (b) There are advantages in using 'natural units' rather than unnecessarily small units which have to be combined at a later stage if they are to be meaningful to students. Evidence has been provided to suggest, for example, that the effective learning of typing is hastened by practice based on complete words and sentences rather than individual letters and meaningless syllables.

(c) Sequences of responses must be emphasized. Note Broadbent's comment:[19] 'Continuously the skilled man must select the correct cues from the environment, taking decisions upon them ..., and initiate sequences of responses whose progress is controlled by feedback.'

3. *Skills acquisition lessons require supervised, reinforced, and carefully spaced practice by students.* Technique and understanding must be linked so that the learner attains the objective of an autonomous, overall competence built from those separate activities of which the total skill is composed. Where the skill is linked closely with speed, practice must be arranged so that this feature is stressed. ('Why must the learner practise motor skills? What is the basic significance of practice?' Gagné answers that it is only by repeating the essential movements that the learner can be provided with the exact cues regulating performance. The movements required in the acquisition of motor skills are cued by stimuli that are only partly outside the learner; some are internal and result from feedback to his muscles. Repetition of essential movements in periods of practice allows the learner to discover the 'vital kinesthetic cues which inform him of success'.)

(a) 'Distributed practice' based on activity followed by intervals of rest (in which consolidation can take place) appears to produce better results than those emanating from one long, unbroken period. Two separated 30-minute periods of practice are often more productive than one hour's continuous practice. In this way, 'plateaux', when practice seems to produce no improvement in performance, may be avoided.

(b) Supervision and, where appropriate, physical guidance of all aspects of practice will be vital if errors are to be noted, analysed and eliminated.

(c) The importance of accurate timing must emerge from practice. Timing is not always a matter of the swift response to a stimulus; it must involve an anticipation of 'what is coming next' and a linked ability to select swiftly from one's repertoire of responses. Supervised practice should stress the significance of this concept.

(d) The 'continuous flow' of separate actions combined into a skilled performance has to emerge from practice. This requires that the teacher shall point out the importance of acquiring a 'natural rhythm' in the performance of a task.

(e) There is evidence to suggest the importance of maintaining a minimal rate of information input in practice if the learner is to acquire efficiency in the skill. 'Underloading' may result, for example, from monotonous instruction. 'Overloading' (a more frequent occurrence in skills training) results where the learner's information channel capacity is strained. Miller,[20] in an analysis of much interest to teachers, suggests that skilled operators tend to adopt the following 'strategies of defence' against the stresses of 'overloading':

omission (i.e. not processing information data input); *error* (i.e. processing data input incorrectly and not making adjustments); *queueing* (i.e. delaying appropriate responses); *filtering* (i.e. omitting systematically some categories of information); *approximation* (i.e. making less-than-precise responses to data input); and *escape* (i.e. cutting off the data input). Lessenberry[21] suggests that, in the teaching of typewriting, lessons related to the layout of the keyboard ought to be organized methodically so as to avoid the 'too much, too soon' danger that comes from attempting to cover the keyboard to quickly and the 'too little, too late' boredom that results if the keyboard is introduced too slowly.

(f) The pattern of skill factors making up a task appears to change progressively with practice; hence the content of a practice session must be altered regularly as that pattern is seen to change.

(g) There appears to be evidence that skills are improved by 'immobile practice', in which the learner goes through an activity *mentally* but does not make any of the learned movements; mental rehearsal of this kind assists in the maintenance of a learned skill when full-scale practice is not possible.

4. *Continuous, swift and accurate feedback must be provided for learners* and they must be taught to interpret such information correctly. Learners must be reminded of criterion performance and must be informed of any gap between their achievement and the requisite standard. They must be shown how to close that gap. (Keller[22] has suggested that the perfection of motor skills depends on the increasing refinement of discrimination between the sensory feedback of correct and not-quite-correct muscular performance.) Bartlett[23] points out that the old saying, 'practice makes perfect', is not true. 'But it is true to say that it is practice, the results of which are known, which makes perfect.' Ammons[24] notes that: 'The more specific the knowledge of performance, the more rapid the improvement and the higher the level of performance ... The longer the delay in giving knowledge of performance, the less effect the given information has.'

5. *Tests in realistic conditions ought to be administered regularly.* Insight and retention ought to be evaluated along with the capacity to transfer acquired skills to novel and demanding situations.

6. *Achievement of competence at one level ought to be accepted as a necessary preparation for movement to a higher level of skill.* Relative competence ought not to be an end in itself. The attainment of 140 w.p.m. in shorthand skill practice is one step along the road leading to all-round competence as a secretary.

7. *The development of perceptual skills, i.e. those depending largely on the mechanisms underlying perception, requires discrimination exercises backed up by practice.* The testing of perceptual skills requires a large variety of test settings.

The psychomotor skills lesson: its structure

Some typical psychomotor skills lesson structure are illustrated in Figure 24.1. Experienced skills teachers advocate a structure planned to consist of 25 per cent of available time devoted to demonstration of the skill, or a component part, 15 per cent to verbal explanation and 60 per cent to guided practice. Changes during the lesson, in both activity and pace, are said to assist in reducing student fatigue related to skill acquisition. Lesson structure will reflect the teacher's appreciation of the role of reorganization of sensory input data so that the learner responds swiftly and accurately to appropriate stimulus cues in his or her environment. It will emphasize practice so as to increase precision in the learner's predictive processes, allowing him or her to build up spatio-temporal coordination. Verbal and physical guidance will be given; feedback will be utilized. It will take into account the nature of the ability traits essential in each phase of the skill, and the relative importance of those traits in the overall timing patterns inherent in mastery. It will not overload the learner.

Structure I is derived from a lesson based on an objective concerning the correct use of engineering equipment. It begins with the creation of a link with the previous lesson to create interest and allow the learner to perceive the continuity of instruction. The purpose of the lesson is stated and is followed by an introductory explanation of what will be seen by the students. A complete demonstration is followed by an explanation of the principal features of what has been seen. Students then write up a record of the main features of the demonstration after which they are tested on comprehension of those features. Intensive, supervised practice is followed by a recapitulation of essential matters and further practice.

Structure II is often used in the teaching of shorthand. The aim of the lesson is stated prior to an introduction which will set the scene for what is to follow. The teacher will then demonstrate the shorthand outlines which are inherent in the lesson objectives. Careful explanation is followed by intensive practice after which there is a test. Further, guided practice is the prelude to a final revision.

Structure III is commonly used in the group teaching of musical performance skills. A short performance by the tutor acts as a general introduction to a statement of the lesson objective. A further, intensive demonstration is followed by a technical explanation of what has been seen and heard. Intensive, guided practice is followed by the testing and assessment of individual students' performances.

In a paper presented to the Comparative Education Society meeting in London, the Polish educationist, Okon,[25] outlined an approach to skills lessons in which practical activity played an important role. He spoke of a skill as *the ability to apply appropriate norms (i.e. rules and principles) to the performance of tasks facing an individual*. The following stages in the process of skill formation were delineated.

1. Clarification for the learner of the name, type and significance of a given skill.
2. Formulation of rules to be applied in the activity to be performed, thus providing an appropriate theoretical foundation.
3. Presentation of a model of the activity so that the essence and value of the rules might be recognized.
4. Eliciting from students an attempted performance, under guidance, of the task, and continuous supervision designed to remedy deficiencies in performance.
5. Provision of systematic, independent practice in the use of the skill so that habits are formed that limit the amount of reflection and awareness of procedures needed by the student.

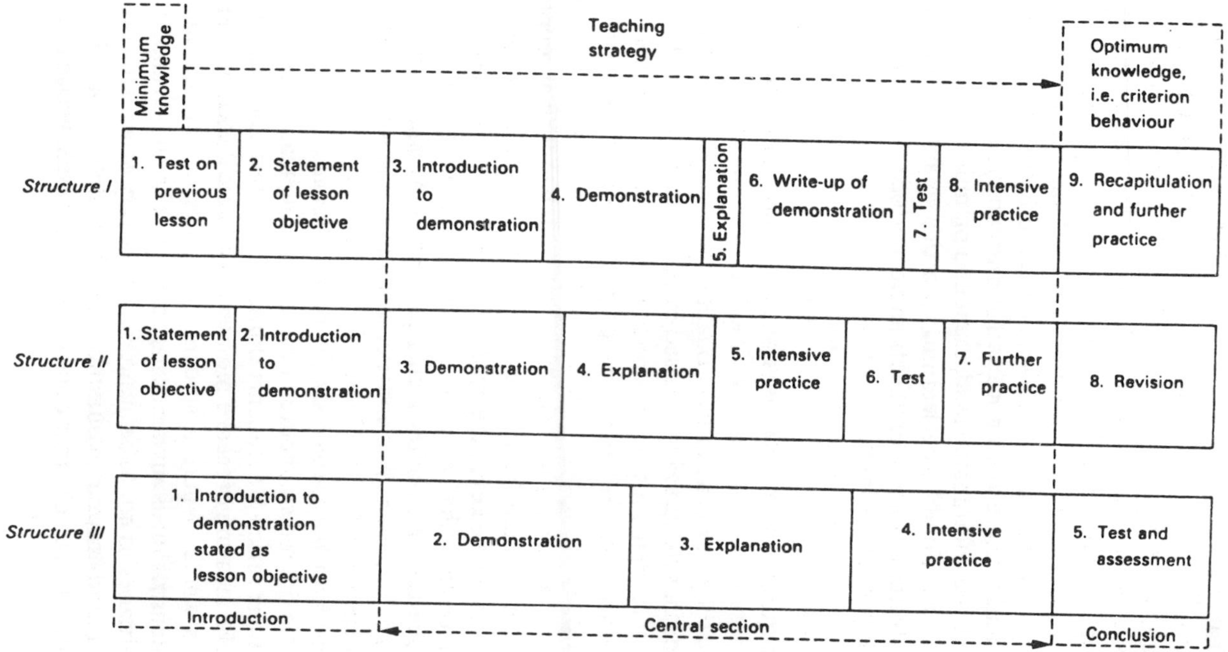

Figure 24.1 Psychomotor skills lesson structures.

Davies' model for the acquisition of complex motor skills

Davies[26] has constructed a teaching strategy model based on three phases (which may overlap).

1. *Introduction*. Tell the learner what to do, how it is to be done and what are the appropriate procedures. Teach the necessary signals and cues. Use short teaching periods based on whole-part-whole learning.
2. *Development*. Gradually remove cognitive and perceptual processes and emphasize physical skills. Allow intensive practice on routines; 'chain' the routines and practise the entire skill. Introduce longer teaching periods and concentrate on coordination, judgment and planning.
3. *Consolidation*. Consolidate learning; practice complete skill until it is over-learned. Increase length of the training period. Wean learners away from reliance on visual feedback.

The use of questions in the psychomotor skills lesson

Questioning as a part of the instructional process was discussed at pp. 286. In the teaching of motor skills, questions raised by instructor *and* learner are of particular consequence.[27] From the instructor's point of view, questions *directed at the learner* encourage participation, initiative, and keep the class 'alive' as to what is going on. Understanding can be checked and learning problems revealed. Specific questions accompanying a demonstration of skills must be pitched at an appropriate level, that is they must take into account the demonstration as a whole and its component steps. 'I kept my thumb on the key at the base of the cylinder while I was removing the cap. Why?' 'In a moment I shall have to remove the disc. What is the safety step I must first take?' Questions may allow a change of roles, as where the learner is asked: 'Here is the welding torch. Will you please tell the class why it is important to hold it in this particular way?'

Questions *from the learner* should be encouraged in a skills lesson. Dillon reminds us: 'No other event better portends learning than a question arising in the mind'. Questions raised by students during a demonstration or explanation may provide a useful measure of feedback and may indicate the level of understanding of the class as a whole. Where a student's question demands from the teacher a practical demonstration as answer or part-answer, it should be undertaken. 'How do we set the carriage?' is not to be answered effectively by a mere verbal reply. Skills concern *doing*, and answers to question relating to skills, should involve an *activity* utilizing the mechanism or other object involved in the exercise of the skill.

A note on skills 'discovery learning'

Student participation and individual problem solving in relation to the acquisition of skills are at the centre of the method of discovery learning developed by E. and M.

Belbin. Some modified techniques of programmed instruction (see Chapter 29) are utilized. Learners who are under instruction in, say, the elementary principles of electrical circuits, are given a simple apparatus consisting of a board on which are mounted batteries, ammeters, switches, bulbs, wire, clips, etc. A written instruction sheet advises on how to carry out simple experiments, on what should be observed and what conclusions ought to be drawn. The learners attain their objective when they construct a circuit without receiving any assistance from the instructor. Questions to the instructor usually result in suggestions only on *how* answers might be obtained by further experiments.

The technique necessitates *careful job analysis*. Its advantages are said to include: total student involvement; step-by-step, intensive learning with students working at their own pace. Its disadvantages include: amount of time needed for effective task analysis and construction of experimental apparatus; possibility of certain important theoretical steps being overlooked by students. There has been criticism, too, of the role of the instructor in merely suggesting modes of discovering answers rather than providing those answers without delay. (Note Thorndike's comment: 'Refusal to supply information on the ground that the learner will be more profited by discovering the facts himself, runs the risk not only of excessive time-cost but also the strengthening of wrong habits'.[28])

Effective skills instruction: a checklist

Fleck and Law[29] put forward the following rules as basic to effective instruction in the skills.

1. Long-term and short-term objectives must be worked out and enunciated clearly at the beginning of instruction.
2. Different types of learning should be encouraged and appropriate instructional methods must be selected carefully.
3. Individual differences among members of the class must be taken into account; hence small groups and alternative instructional strategies are essential if individual learning problems are to be identified and resolved.
4. Demonstrate rather than talk. Avoid verbosity and use speech to reinforce what is being seen by the learner.
5. Invite class participation by specific rather than general questions, and allow time for learners to reflect on what they have observed.
6. Encourage learners to perform tasks unaided and to ask for help only when it is obviously needed.
7. Provide objective appraisals and employ comprehensible strategies for error correction.
8. Check the effectiveness of instruction by methodical questioning and close inspection of learners' work.

Psychomotor skills teaching and the liberalization of education

The work of colleges of further education has assisted in dispelling the myth (largely attributable to the pervasive influence of uncritical acceptance of the doctrines associated with Plato and Aristotle) which suggests that the acquisition of manual skills is incompatible with the aims of a broad, liberal education. It is now realized that a liberal education may depend not on the *subjects* taught but on the *ways* in which they are taught. In Pinsent's words:[30]

> It is possible to teach classics in such a way as to make it a soulless mechanical grind. It is possible to teach handicraft so as to make it a vehicle for a liberal education. The difference lies in *how* the subject is taught.

The challenge to teachers in the colleges in imparting specific skills is to make a deliberate attempt to extend horizons and to develop insight. 'What is taught should be taught in such a way as to promote the general powers of the mind.' This suggestion of the Robbins Committee (1963) requires from the skills teacher provision of schemes of work which will promote the power of judgment, the ability to think swiftly and accurately, and the capacity to discriminate and perceive relationships – all aspects of the 'trained mind' which is associated with the goals of a liberal education.[31]

Notes and references

1. See generally for this chapter: *Fundamentals of Skill* by A. Welford (Methuen, 1968); *The Psychology of Training* by R. Stammers and J. Patrick (Methuen, 1975); *Developing Vocational Instruction* by R. Mager (Palo Alto, 1976); *Selected Readings in Skills* ed. D. Legge (Penguin, 1970); 'Skilled performance' by J. Annett and H. Kay in *Occupational Psychology* (1956, *30*); *Motor Learning and Performance* by R. Schmidt (Human Kinetics Books, 1991); *Learning and Skills* ed. N. Mackintosh and A. Colman (Longman, 1995).
2. See *Learning to Teach Practical Skills* by I. Winfield (Kogan Page, 1979); *Psychology of Motor Learning* by J.B. Oxendine (McGraw-Hill, 1978).
3. *Psychology of Study* (Penguin, 1973).
4. *Psychology: A Dictionary of the Mind, Brain and Behaviour* (Arrow Books, 1978).
5. *Op. cit.*
6. *The Structure of Psychology* (Allen & Unwin, 1981).
7. *Instructional Science* (Elsevier, 1973).
8. *Cybernetic Principles of Learning* (Holt, Rinehart & Winston, 1966).
9. *The Conditions of Learning* (Holt-Saunders, 1985).
10. 'A theory of the acquisition of speed-skill' in *Ergonomics* (1959, 2).
11. 'A closed-loop theory of motor learning' in *Psychological Bulletin* (1968, 70).
12. *Op. cit.*
13. 'Factors in complex skill training' in *Training Research and Education* ed. R. Glaser (Wiley, 1965). See also *Human Performance* by P. Fitts and M. Posner (Brooks Cole, 1967).
14. *Plans and Structure of Behaviour* (Holt, Rinehart & Winston, 1960).
15. *Learning and Human Abilities* (Harper & Row, 1975).

16. *Learning and Memory* (Freeman, 1982).
17. *Instructional Technique* (McGraw-Hill, 1981).
18. *Development of Training Equipment Planning Information* (Smith, 1966).
19. *Perception and Communication* (Pergamon, 1958).
20. 'Input overload and psychopathology' in *American Journal of Psychiatry* (1960, *116*).
21. 'The rationale for a widely used sequence of introducing the letter keyboard' in *Practices and Preferences in Teaching Typewriting* (South-Western Publishing, 1967).
22. *Papers in Psychology* (Doubleday, 1954).
23. 'The measurement of human skill' in *British Medical Journal* (1974, *1*).
24. 'Effects of knowledge on performance' in *Journal of General Psychology* (1956, *64*).
25. 'Formation of the unity of personality' in *Diversity and Unity in Education* ed. L. Holmes (Allen & Unwin, 1980).
26. *Op. cit.* (1981).
27. See *Questioning and Teaching* by J.T. Dillon (Croom Helm, 1988).
28. *The Psychology of Wants, Interests and Attitudes* (Appleton-Century, 1935).
29. *Effective Instruction* (ITRU, 1988). See also *Learning from Experience* by A. Garry and J. Cowan (FE Unit, 1986).
30. *The Principles of Teaching Method* (Harrap, 1962).
31. See *Closing the Gap: Liberal Education and Vocational Training* by R.A. Pring (Hodder & Stoughton, 1996).

Chapter 25

The Lecture

Whatever can be said at all can be said clearly, and whatever cannot be said clearly should not be said at all (Wittgenstein, 1922).

A lecture involves *a continuous oral and formal exposition of, or discourse on, some topic*.[1] Verner and Dickinson define it as an instructional technique through which is presented 'an oral discourse on a particular subject'.[2] The Hale Committee (1964) referred to it as 'a teaching period occupied wholly or mainly with continuous exposition by a lecturer'. It exemplifies the process of 'one-way communication' and, as such, has been criticized severely. And yet the lecture persists as a common mode of instruction in colleges of further education and elsewhere. Typically, it is used to introduce course material, to give groups of students specialized information such as the results of research, or to present a final revision. Its weaknesses and strengths and its peculiar difficulties for the lecturer will emerge in the consideration of lecture structure, planning and delivery which follows.

Lectures can be used in colleges of further education in order to attain objectives of very different types: high-order cognitive objectives, involving the presentation of new, challenging views and attitudes; low-order cognitive objectives, involving explanation and demonstration; affective objectives, involving a deliberate attempt to 'fire the imagination' of the audience. The demands on the lecturer are almost always considerable, particularly in the presentation and transmission of values and attitudes inherent in affective objectives. Effective lecturing has little to do with the ability to write, and read from, one's lecture notes; it calls for a variety of skills, particularly the ability to attract and hold one's audience. Some of the more important skills are considered below.

The management tasks of the lecturer resemble, fundamentally, those of the class teacher involved in a formal lesson: lecture objectives must be planned, resources and constraints must be taken into account, the existing level of knowledge of the audience must be considered, particular attention must be given to the organization of material such as AVA, handouts. The lack of reliable feedback, which can vitiate control to a considerable degree, represents a difficult management problem which may necessitate the creation of alternative control structures.

314

The lecture attacked and defended

Criticisms of the lecture are often uncompromising: lecturing is said to be a negation of teaching; its autocratic form and style necessarily vitiate the partnership considered essential to the facilitation of learning; the 'intellectual passivity and weariness' of the listeners ('the lecturer is a person who talks in someone else's sleep' – an aphorism attributed to W.H. Auden)[3] and the lack of discussion are said to be a contradiction of the process of free flow and exchange of ideas which the learning process demands. The lack of feedback (see Chapter 12) makes real class control impossible, so that the lecture is said to leave much to be desired as a mode of creating the conditions for effective learning.

Over half a century ago, Green,[4] in a series of experiments, demonstrated that students apparently learned as much from reading passages as from hearing the same matter delivered in a lecture. More recently, Bligh,[5] in a detailed examination of lecture techniques, concluded that lectures were not generally effective in teaching students to think. Goolkasian[6] has found that students attending lectures do not always recognize important points better than unimportant details. Kintsch[7] finds that jokes and other types of humorous, extraneous remarks made by lecturers are often remembered by students more clearly than lecturers' major statements.

Critics of the lecture occasionally support their attacks with references to the comments of famous scholars. Thus, Dr Johnson stated, in terms which allowed of little contradiction, 'Lectures were once useful; but now, when all can read, and books are so numerous, lectures are unnecessary'. Charles Darwin refused to attend certain lectures at Cambridge because he was 'so sickened with lectures at Edinburgh'. (His later comment tends to be overlooked: 'I attended, however, Henslow's lectures on botany, and liked them much for their extreme clearness and the admirable illustrations.'[8]) Bertrand Russell is uncompromising: 'I derived no benefit from lectures, and I made a vow to myself that when in due course I became a lecturer I would not suppose that lecturing did any good!'[9]

The argument that 'books are better' is not universally accepted. Saunders,[10] for example, seeks to rebut this view by stating that *the experience of listening* to a lecture differs markedly from reading a printed version. The content may be the same, but the *processes* involved in reading and listening – reception, coding, interpretation and storage of stimuli – are different. Some researchers suggest that acuity of thought is best heightened through the auditory channels. Further, 'a lecturer can be more *flexible* than a written presentation': no author is able to modify presentation, whereas a lecturer who is able to obtain clues from the audience's reception of the material is able to change presentation swiftly. While stressing the 'complementary nature' of book and lecture in the process of instruction, Saunders argues that the lecture surpasses the book in its ability to provide 'a live model of a person thinking'. He writes of an enthusiastic lecturer, posing a problem and moving to its solution step by step, and providing an experience for students which it is 'difficult to duplicate in any other way'.

Saunders speaks for those teachers who reject the view of a lecturer's audience as being invariably 'intellectually passive'. He contends that, while a poor lecturer might induce mind-numbing weariness in the audience, a lecturer who provides a

well-delivered challenge based upon fact and argument can have a positive effect on
the mental activity of listeners. One ought not to draw an inference of mental
passivity from an audience sitting still during a lecture. Saunders cites with approval
Bergman's notion of 'an internal dialogue' taking place within the minds of attentive
listeners:[11] 'Somewhere between the lecture and their notebooks a dialogue had
quietly taken place. This internal dialogue is often as stimulating as, and more open
than, any classroom discussion.' Learning through listening, and reinforcement
provided by the stimulus of internal dialogue, are among the positive advantages of
the lecture.

Underlying this chapter is the belief that a well-constructed lecture which takes
into account the principles of effective instruction can, and often does, succeed in
capturing students' attention and communicating patterns of information.

Types of lecture

The following types of lecture are among those given in our colleges of further
education as components of the instructional process.

1. *The oral essay.* This is a highly structured lecture which presents information
    related to a body of systematized knowledge which is central to a course of
    instruction (see the 'explanation' structure on p. 318 below). Owing to the
    formal nature of this type of 'one-way' presentation, a lecture in this mode may
    lack the dimension of 'interpersonal communication' which is often held neces-
    sary for student motivation. It should be possible, however, where the lecturer is
    aware of this problem, for time to be found for a short question-and-answer
    session after the lecture has ended.
2. *The expository lecture.* Lowman[12] refers to this type of lecture as 'primarily
    defining and setting forth information' (see the 'presenting a thesis' structure on
    p. 317 below). The lecture includes a number of short question-and-answer
    sessions at planned points *within* the structure. Lectures of this nature are
    commonly used in colleges.
3. *The problem-centred lecture.* In this type of lecture students are led through the
    steps necessary to solve a problem which is stated with appropriate emphasis
    during the lecturer's initial statements. A successful lecture presented in this
    style demands a high degree of concentration from the audience and a carefully
    linked presentation if the threads of exposition and comprehension are not to
    snap (see the 'problem' structure on p. 318 below).
4. *The challenge.* The deliberately provocative lecture is intended as a forthright
    challenge to patterns of thought and deeply held values; its objectives are the
    presentation of new perspectives and the questioning of assumptions. Segments
    of lecture time must be given over to questions and answers.
5. *The lecture-discussion.* A very short lecture is followed by a discussion around a
    key point in the lecturer's opening statement. Careful timing is essential.
6. *The lecture-demonstration.* A lecture is used as the prelude to a demonstration,
    the main points of which are summed up in a further, short lecture.

Structure of the lecture

As in the case of the lesson, content will play a large part in the determination of lecture structure. *The purpose of the lecture must be reflected in the way it is constructed.* A lecture on 'the effective utilization of space in warehousing' is likely to demand a structure somewhat different from that used in an exposition of 'recent changes in the law relating to the sale of goods'; the structure of the former lecture is likely to be based on a talk illustrated by much visual display material, while the structure of the latter will probably be based on a verbal exposition only. The major determinant of structure should emerge from the lecturer's instruction strategy, built around answers to the questions: 'What is the purpose of this lecture?' 'Why is it of significance?' 'What are its specific objectives?' 'Does the subject matter demand the use of any visual aids other than a chalkboard?' 'Does the subject matter necessitate a particular approach?'

Four typical lecture strategies are set out below: the first is often used in the presentation of a thesis; the second is designed for the posing and examination of a problem; the third lends itself well to the explanation of an aspect of systematized knowledge; the fourth can be used for the presentation of material in sequential form, leading, by the nature of the logic of the subject matter, to a conclusion.

Presenting a thesis

Examples of this structure might be found in a lecture to business students on an interpretation of some recent research on the location of industry, or to a media studies group on, say, the case against Internet censorship. The structure necessitates a careful presentation of thesis, supporting data and counter-theses. It might take the following form:

A   Statement of purpose and objective of the lecture
B   Statement of the thesis (including stimulating the recall of prior knowledge)
C   Explanation of the thesis:
    1.   Thesis presented as a proposition
    2.   Evidence
    3.   Difficulties in interpretation of the evidence
D   Restatement of thesis and recapitulation of evidence
E   Counter-thesis I:
    1.   Counter-thesis presented as a proposition
    2.   Evidence
    3.   Difficulties in interpretation of evidence
    4.   Thesis in light of counter-thesis
F   Counter-theses II, III ... (presented as in E above)
G   Restatement of thesis and recapitulation of counter-theses
H   Conclusion:
    1.   Statement of conclusion

2. Balance of evidence
3. Restatement of thesis

Examining a problem

Assume that the lecture form has been selected for a presentation to a group of politics students of some of the arguments surrounding proposals for proportional representation, or for the unfolding to management diploma students of the hypotheses underlying the controversial minimum wage. Problem, data, arguments, basic hypotheses and suggested answers can be presented in a logical, patterned structure, of which the following might serve as an example:

A   Statement of purpose and objective of lecture
B   Statement of the problem to be examined (couched in a style which is meaningful to the audience and allowing the recall of prior relevant knowledge)
C   Explanation of the problem:
   1. Its history
   2. Its component features
   3. Its significance
D   Possible solutions:
   1. Solution (a): Statement; argument; reasoning
   2. Solution (b)...
   3. Solution (c)...
E   Restatement of problem and recapitulation of suggested solutions
F   Application of suggested solutions
G   Assessment of validity of solutions
H   Conclusion:
   1. Restatement of problem
   2. Summary of valid solutions

Explanation of an aspect of systematized knowledge

This often provides suitable occasions for the use of the lecture method. Examples might be: an explanation to banking students of the organization and functions of the money market; an analysis for a group of managers of the use of the computer in determining project profitability. The appropriate structure will reflect the hierarchical features of the subject matter, as in the following example:

A   Statement of purpose and objective of lecture
B   Point I...
   1. ...
     (a) ...
     (b) ...

             (i) ...
             (ii) ...
          (c) ...
       2. ...
          (a) ...
          (b) ...
  C Point II ...
       1. ...
          (a) ...
          (b) ...
       2. ...
          (a) ...
             (i) ...
             (ii) ...
          (b) ...
  D Point III ...
  E Recapitulation
  F Conclusion

Presentation of a sequence of information leading to a conclusion

This structure is valuable for an explanation of a series of events or other facts leading to a conclusion. It is useful in mathematics, history and logic – wherever there is a clearly defined hierarchy of facts. Frequent recapitulation and careful definition of terms are necessary to the success of this lecture method. The following form is common in lectures on subjects such as price theory, the use of syllogisms in argument, etc.:

  A Statement of purpose and objective of lecture
  B Short exposition of framework of structure to be presented
  C Point I
  D Links between point I and point II
  E Point II
  F Recapitulation
  G Links between point II and point III
  H Point III
  I   Structure of points and links reviewed
  J Recapitulation
  K Conclusion

Physical environment of the lecture

Where the lecture is to be delivered in a purpose-built lecture theatre, much can usually be done to improve arrangements so that communication is as effective as possible. Audio-visual aids (see Chapter 28) must be set out with care so that their use is not an interruption to the even flow of the lecture. The positioning of screens, blackboards and projectors requires attention prior to the delivery of the lecture.

Where the lecturer is obliged to use a general classroom, seating must be prepared so that notes can be taken without difficulty. The positioning of the lecturer's desk should be determined by experiment; it will not always be at the midpoint of one end of the room. The literature on the subject of spatial arrangements in classrooms repays close study, particularly in relation to the suggestions that the arrangement of a lecture room may have psychological as well as physiological effects on the class as a whole.

Planning the lecture

The lecture plan will be determined most appropriately – as in the case of the lesson plan – by a consideration of three major areas: the students, the subject matter, and the resources and constraints. The problem of pitching the lecture at an appropriate level is often difficult to resolve because the audience is likely to be large in number, so that many different levels of learning are almost certain to be represented. The students' 'learning set' must be kept in mind, and this necessitates making allowance in the lecture plan for time to define terms, to give a number of specific examples, to illustrate and to recapitulate.

The introduction to the lecture, including a clear statement of its significance and objective (reinforced, perhaps, by a visual display), requires careful treatment: it should aim deliberately at stimulating interest and gaining and holding attention, and should attempt to create an appropriate relationship with the audience.

> What you should do in your introduction is to state your subject, in order that the point to be judged may be quite plain ... The introduction is the beginning of a speech, corresponding to the prologue in poetry and the prelude in flute-music; they are all beginnings, paving the way, as it were, for what is to follow (Aristotle, *Rhetoric*).

Constraints include time, the nature of the lecture room and the availability of visual aids. A diagram of the lecture room ought to be studied, so that the precise position of platform, speaker's lectern or desk, chalkboard, projector, screen and other resources can be taken into account when planning the interlocking of speech and visual aids. The conclusion of the lecture requires detailed consideration; its impact is often of much significance.

> In the epilogue you should summarize the arguments by which your case has been proved. The first step in this reviewing process is to observe that you have done what you undertook to do. You must, then, state what you have said and why you have said it (Aristotle, *Rhetoric*).

The amount of material to be presented in the lecture must be planned with care. Lacking the feedback mechanisms available in the normal lesson, the lecturer cannot estimate accurately whether the points he or she seeks to make are being assimilated by the audience. The lecturer should observe the body language of the audience: signs of boredom, obvious lack of rapport, apparent difficulties in comprehension (as where a large proportion of the audience has ceased taking notes), should all be interpreted and acted on swiftly. (Modification of the remainder of the lecture should be considered in these circumstances.) The lecturer cannot take assimilation or comprehension for granted, no matter how carefully he or she plans and delivers the lecture. Lecturers must not fail to take into account the limits of the short-term memory (see Chapter 17). A lecture based on relatively few concepts may have a greater chance of success in attaining its objective, therefore, than one which requires the assimilation of a large volume of information. (Miller's suggestion, noted in Chapter 17, that short-term memory capacity may be limited to approximately seven discrete 'chunks' of information at any time, is of relevance here.)

The lecture plan will reflect the necessity to arouse and keep attention (which may require the carefully planned use of visual material so as to break the monotony of speech), to present appropriate stimuli and to reinforce responses (by correctly timed recapitulation and restatement). The sequence of statement, elaboration, review and recapitulation, based on the sequence procedures outlined in Chapter 22, is worth considering in the planning of a lecture.

Some writers, such as Brown,[13] suggest that a lecture plan can be based on 'keys', that is, key points in the topic which is to form the subject of the lecture. Keys should be expressed as simply as possible should be illustrated by examples, qualified or elaborated and, finally, restated in the form of a conclusion. This is a valuable mode of planning which can be used where there is little time to prepare a lecture fully. The planner begins by noting the subject matter (e.g. inflation) in the form of a question (e.g. 'What are the causes of inflation?'). He or she then uses free association to recall matters linked with the question (e.g. supply of money, pressure of demand), to set out certain keys which are presented in logical form, and adds, finally, an appropriate introduction and conclusion.

The lecturer's own notes, referred to during the course of the lecture, may take the form of a detailed, sentence-by-sentence account (useful for those teachers who have little lecturing experience), or an elaborated plan based on the framework of what is to be said. An example of framework notes is given in Figure 25.1. Note, however, that the fact that detailed lecture notes have been prepared must not result in the lecturer giving the impression of merely reading a prepared statement in mechanical fashion. Some spontaneity of expression and delivery ought to emerge even in the most carefully planned lecture.

How long ought a lecture to last and at what stage does it cease to have any impact? There is no golden rule, because the threshold of assimilation will vary from student to student. One will be unable to concentrate or retain data after ten minutes' unbroken speech, while another will assimilate with ease the contents of a twenty-minute talk. (McKeachie[14] states that studies of student attention during lectures indicate that, in general, 'attention increases from the beginning of the lecture to ten minutes into the lecture and decreases after that point. Evidence of this was that, after the lecture, students recalled 70 per cent of the material covered in the first ten minutes, and only 20 per cent of the material covered in the last ten minutes.') In general, pauses ought to be made in the interests of concentration and assimilation after ten to fifteen minutes of continuous speaking. After that period of time there seems to be a decline in audience attention. The pause may be utilized for

| Date:.....................Group:.........................Subject:........................ |
| Lecture objective(s): .... |
| Time: 50 mins |

Timing	Lecture content	Reference material	Aids
5 mins	Introduction and statement of lecture objectives	–	Chalkboard
15 mins	Key point I: 1. 2. 3.	Textbook, p. 100	–
5 mins	Recapitulation of Key point I	–	Chalkboard
15 mins	Key point II: 1. 2.	Textbook, p. 105 Newspaper cutting	–
5 mins	Recapitulation of Key points I and II; restatement of lecture objective(s)	–	o/h projector
5 mins	Questions. Hand out lecture summary	–	–

Figure 25.1   Lecture framework notes.

the presentation of visual stimuli, such as a chart which illustrates or recapitulates a key point. Many lecturers' experiences suggest that the entire lecture session ought to last not longer than 50 minutes. After that period attention tends to diminish very rapidly and assimilation becomes difficult. Particular use should be made of the short, but marked, peak of audience attention which occurs just before the end of the lecture.

Delivery of the lecture

A teacher's lesson style, mannerisms, speech, gestures, eye-to-eye contact with students, clarity of expression, appearance – so-called 'personality' – can make a considerable impact on the class; positive, where it aids communication, but negative, where it acts as 'noise' which interferes with the transmission and reception of information. Impact of this kind is even more marked in the case of the lecture. It can be said with some truth that, for a lecture audience, 'the medium is the message'. A lecture is dependent for its success – to a marked degree – on the personality and communication skills of the lecturer. That person is the sole focus of attention for most of the lecture period; his or her style of delivery can result in acceptance and assimilation, or rejection, of the lecture content. The lecturer's 'expressiveness', that is, an obvious enthusiasm for the subject, a perceived desire to communicate, and an ability to generate student interest, can 'make or break' the lecture. (Davies cites a study which indicates that only about 7 per cent of a lecturer's message comes from the words; the voice contributes 38 per cent of the message and body language contributes 55 per cent.)

Lecturing technique involves an ability to speak clearly, to modulate voice tone and pitch, to use gestures sparingly, but effectively, and to speak at a pace which does not prevent assimilation and understanding. There is evidence to suggest that 110 w.p.m. may be a 'normal' rate of delivery and that a rate beyond 200 w.p.m. results in a rapid decline in assimilation. The following general points should be considered.

1. The style of delivery ought to be neither casual, nor in the pattern of grand oratory. 'Natural delivery' requires, paradoxically, much practice! It ought to be characterized by clarity, simplicity of expression and planned timing (which may require rehearsal). Michael Faraday comments:

   > In order to gain the attention of an audience (and what can be more disagreeable than the want of it?), it is necessary to pay some attention to the manner of expression. The utterance should not be rapid and hurried and consequently unintelligible, but slow and deliberate, conveying ideas with ease from the lecturer and infusing them with clearness and readiness into the minds of the audience.[15]

2. The emphasis of key points may require variations in the pattern and intensity of speech, a gesture, a pause, a visual illustration. (Actors and musicians, for whom communication and rapport with one's audience are all-important are well aware of the significance and effect of a carefully timed pause. In a lecture it can serve as a 'signal' for a key statement, or as a kind of emphasis.) (Herbart, in *Psychology as Science* (1833) (as translated by James in his *Principles of Psychology* (1890)), notes: 'Empty time is most strongly perceived when it comes as a *pause* in music or in speech. Suppose a preacher in the pulpit, a professor at his desk, to stick still in the midst of his discourse ...; we await every instant the resumption of the performance, and, in this awaiting, perceive more than in any other possible way, the empty time.')[16]

3. Flamboyant, exaggerated gestures rapidly become meaningless, divert attention from the words which they accompany and may snap the thread of communication.

4. Some mannerisms (e.g. of voice, posture) may amuse initially, but in a short time may irritate, even offend and alienate, eventually creating a barrier to effective communication. As soon as lecturers become aware of them they ought to work towards their eradication.

5. It is vital that the lecturer should convey genuine enthusiasm and interest. Non-verbal cues – facial expressions, eye contact (the absence of which is often interpreted by an audience as nervousness, fear or lack of interest), use of the hands – are rapidly communicated to students, who are swift in interpretation (see below). Lecturers would do well to remember the aphorism: 'We speak

with our vocal organs, but we converse with our whole body' (see p. 148). The essential message *content* can be disturbed by non-verbal cues.

6. Where the lecture involves the use of visual aids, they ought to be prepared and ready to hand, so that continuity in presentation is maintained.

7. It is important to keep in mind students' problems in 'receiving a message', in the light of memory theory (see p. 210). A message conveyed by the lectures is stored temporarily in the student's short-term memory for some 30 seconds; it is then forgotten unless it is noted or transferred to the long-term memory. Links between lecture content and existing facts in the student's memory are essential; messages that are incompatible with already acquired knowledge tend to disappear rapidly unless reinforced.

Brown outlines four aids to the achievement of clarity in lecturing. *Signposts* should be used: they give indications as to the structure of a lecture and the path to be taken by the lecturer ('I intend to ask and answer three vital questions concerned with . . .'). *Frames* should be employed to point out the beginning and end of parts of the lecture ('We now move on to our second point . . .'). *Foci* should be utilized to underline and emphasize ('I am repeating the definition so as to stress . . .'). *Links* should be created so as to present the lecture as a cohesive entity ('That, then, is the general rule. But, as always in this area, there are the exceptions, to which I now turn').

In sum, lecturers should remember that, because they are *the focal point of attention*, they are communicating along a variety of channels, some of which are noted by implication in the preceding paragraphs. The *linguistic channel* is, by its very nature, of great importance: choice of words, clarity in syntax, are essential features of an effective lecture. The *paralinguistic channel*, involving the lecturer's vocal tone and quality of expression, provides a vital, individual contribution to overall lecture content and delivery. The *visual channel* involves not only the use of visual aids, but refers to the lecturer's personal appearance, which can introduce unwanted 'noise' into the communication process. The *kinetic channel*, along which the lecturer's body movements are transformed into messages and interpreted by the audience, must not be overlooked; unconscious gestures (e.g. continuous finger-tapping) may convey mixed, often disturbing, messages. (See Chapter 11.)

Michael Faraday summed up the lecturer's task thus:

A lecturer should exert his utmost effort to gain completely the mind and attention of his audience, and irresistibly make them join in his ideas to the end of the subject. He should endeavour to raise their interest at the commencement of the lecture and by a series of imperceptible gradations, unnoticed by the company, keep it alive as long as the subject demands it. . . . A flame should be lighted at the commencement and kept alive with unremitting splendour to the end.[17]

The problem of absence of swift feedback

Where there is no informative feedback there can be no effective control (see Chapter 12). Lecturers suffer from the disadvantage of not knowing the nature of the reactions of the audience, since they cannot generally assess the effectiveness of their efforts to communicate. Lecturers cannot periodically halt the flow of the lecture by a swift examination of the level of assimilation. To rely on the facial expressions of one's audience is of little value ('There's no art to find the mind's construction in the face'). In Gagné's words: '[There is] a *loss of precision* in the employment of instructional events ... The lecturer can only count on the *probable* effects of these events on the many individual students.'[18] A post-lecture discussion or test comes too late to assist assessment and control of the lecture itself. In effect, the lecturer is deprived of the means of measuring *immediate* class reaction and this may account for the learning difficulties of some students whose instruction is based entirely on lectures.

There has been considerable research into aspects of non-verbal communication in relation to lecture-audience feedback. Abercrombie, for example, emphasizes the importance of the lecturer being trained to recognize and interpret the non-verbal elements in language and communication.[19] Argyle and Kendon state: 'Movement may serve to clarify or emphasize aspects of messages transmitted through speech; patterns of looking and movement may serve to regulate the pacing of action in the encounter.'[20] Research of this nature has been interpreted as suggesting that a slight, but useful, element of feedback *is* available to the lecturer who is able to 'read and interpret' the body language of the audience.

Some lecturers have used the 'buzz group' technique to provide feedback and to break up the continuous exposition which characterizes the formal lecture. At carefully selected points in the course of the lecture the audience is asked to *split into prearranged groups* to discuss their responses to a direct question. The groups can be formed by those sitting together in various sections of the room. The lecture is resumed after some of the group comments are reported and, perhaps, discussed.

Lecture notes and handouts

What record of the lecture ought a class to possess? This is a problem which must be faced by every college lecturer. Ought he or she to distribute a printed version of the entire lecture, or rely on students making their own notes during the lecture? Ought he or she to give out notes (to be used as 'organizers' – see p. 104) well in advance of the lecture, or a few minutes before or at the end of the lecture. Ought he or she to dictate a short summary?

The reasons advanced in favour of students making their own notes during a lecture are varied. It is suggested, for example, that the very process of listening and recording by writing forms an important response to the stimuli presented by the lecturer, enabling new impressions to be fixed and assisting assimilation. Note-taking is the student's own work and, it is argued, represents a degree of active participation in an otherwise passive instructional process. (Gagné reminds us that, from the students' point of view, it is they on whom greatest responsibility rests in learning from a lecture.[21]) Further, it helps to overcome the limitations of the short-term memory (see Chapter 17), thereby assisting (so the claim runs) revision, long-term retention and recall. (It is interesting to note that some researchers have found that those note-takers who expressed more ideas in fewer words tended to retain the information better than those who summarized the topics of the lecture in greater detail.)

Difficulties in note-taking, however, abound. Some students are quite unable to write swiftly; others may be unable to discriminate so that they fail to note an important point made by the lecturer; some may have difficulty in concentrating simultaneously on listening and writing. (The many distractions of the lecture room often do not help, and there is a sound case for training students in the skills of listening, concentrating, avoiding distraction, etc.) *The lecturer should not take for granted the ability of the audience to make notes*. For many in the audience it may be a new experience. A few lessons on the technique of note-taking would, therefore, be advantageous for most further education classes. They could include advice and practice relating to the construction and numbering of paragraphs, sections, subsections and cross-headings and to ways of giving emphasis to laws, definitions, formulae, by spacing, underlining, etc. For practice purposes a taped lecture can be played to the class, with prepared transparencies projected on a screen, indicating the points which ought to be noted in writing, and how they ought to be recorded. It assists students to be told by the lecturer of his or her cues which will introduce matter that must be noted, e.g. 'Note carefully . . .'; 'A vital point is . . .' Students must also be shown how to use their notes, i.e. how to expand them (and how to space them for this purpose) and how to use them for pre-examination revision. ('Students must become active learners in their own rights.')

The lecturer should ensure that the environment and the style of delivery allow notes to be taken. The furniture of the lecture room should include some type of notebook rest; illumination which has been dimmed to allow the use of the overhead projector must be increased so that students can see their notes. Short pauses during the lecture (which can be timed so as to coincide with divisions in the subject matter) are of great assistance to the note-writer who is trying to 'catch up'.

The dictation of detailed notes is generally a misuse of lecture time. The practice (fortunately rare) of dictating notes of a lecture in its entirety has been categorized as 'a passage of information from the lecturer's notes to the audience's notebooks without a sojourn in the mind of either'! The writing of the main headings of the lecture on a chalkboard, flipchart or overhead projector transparency may help in the taking of notes and may provide a useful summary of the lecture which can be used for recapitulation and revision.

It is the practice of many lecturers to dictate short statements of principles, theories and definitions. Principles and statements of theories may constitute the essence of lectures and care has to be taken in their communication to an audience. Occasional, *very short dictation* may help to ensure that vital matter is noted correctly. Definitions can be stated in measured tones, allowing students to note them exactly, and can be restated at intervals (perhaps by use of the overhead projector). Koestler's paraphrase of Goethe is relevant: 'When the mind is at sea, a clear definition can provide a raft!'

Some lecturers, recognizing the real difficulties of note-taking, prefer to distribute their own 'handouts', claiming that the advantage of participation by writing is outweighed by the students possessing an authentic record of the lecture content.

Handouts may list lecture objectives, suggest reading, give appropriate references, outline the body of the lecture in précis form and draw attention to difficult points. (Lecturers who prefer not to use prepared handouts claim that their distribution prevents a lecturer changing his or her approach where he or she feels that a point has not been understood – the handout, they argue, fetters the lecturer to a prearranged, unalterable, plan.) The handouts can be distributed well in advance of the lecture, allowing for the checking of references for preliminary reading and the consideration of problems likely to emerge, or they can be given out (as is usually the case) at the point in the lecture when a final recapitulation is about to be made, or when the lecture has ended.[22]

Structured notes which are given to the audience at the beginning of the lecture consist of its main points stated incompletely, so that students must listen very carefully in order to complete them. A completed version may be shown for purposes of checking and recapitulation in the last few minutes of the lecture. An example used in a lecture on the functions of money is given in Figure 25.2.

```
1. Difficulties of barter were:      (a) ......................................
                                     (b) ......................................

2. The use of money overcame
   these difficulties by:            (a) ......................................
                                     (b) ......................................
                                     (c) ......................................

3. Money is, in fact, any
   commodity which acts by
   common consent as:                (a) ......................................
                                     (b) ......................................
                                     (c) ......................................
                                     (d) ......................................
```

Figure 25.2 Structured lecture notes handout.

Short-term evaluation of a lecture

The efficiency of a system demands that the controller of input be aware of its effect upon that system (see p. 154); effective instruction necessitates that the lecturer be aware of the outcome, in learning terms, of the lecture. Although a precise evaluation of a lecture may not be possible in the short run, it is important for the lecturer to have some general indication of the quality of his or her lecture as soon as that can be arranged. The following modes of short-term evaluation can be considered.

1. *Self-evaluation* necessitates the lecturer asking and answering questions such as these: 'Were the key points of my lecture made with clarity? Was there any indication that they were comprehended? Was my timing appropriate and did I

allow sufficient time for questions and answers? Were my visual aids adequate? Was there an indication of effective rapport with the audience?' (It must be stressed that precise answers can be given only after students have been tested methodically on lecture content; the object of a self-evaluation immediately following the lecture is to utilize any feedback which may have resulted from audience reaction.) Some colleges have experimented in the use of video recordings of lectures given by members of staff. The process of self-evaluation can be intensified by a careful analysis of a recorded lecture.

2. *Evaluation by a more experienced colleague* is valuable, either following a lecture or after viewing a recording.
3. *Evaluation by students using a questionnaire* can be instructive. Students can be asked for their reactions to specific aspects of the lecture. 'Was the lecture interesting? Explanatory? Were you given enough time to construct notes? If you were given prepared notes immediately before the lecture, were they of assistance in following the lecture? Did the visual aids assist you in understanding lecture content?'

Evaluation ought not to be considered as a one-off activity to be confined to the initial phase of a lecturer's professional career. It is an essential part of the process of effective lecturing and, as such, ought to be undertaken repeatedly in connection with the feedback which will emerge from formal testing of students.

The lecture in further education

In spite of the weaknesses of the lecture as a mode of instruction and of its general unsuitability for the teaching of skills, it continues to be employed, often with great success, in the colleges of further education. Its advantages ought not to be forgotten; some were enumerated in the *Hale Report on University Training Methods* (1964). They apply, generally, to the further education sector also.

1. Students who are immature learn more readily when they listen than when they read.
2. The lecture is of particular value in introducing a subject.
3. The lecture is valuable where knowledge is advancing rapidly and up-to-date textbooks are not available. (The updating lecture, in which current developments are collated, summarized and explained, is of great assistance to students in areas such as economics, law, commerce and public administration. The lecture has been called 'the newspaper of teaching'; it must be kept up-to-date.)
4. The lecture can awaken critical skills in a student.
5. The lecture can provide aesthetic pleasure.
6. The lecture is economic of staff time, can cover more ground than a tutorial or seminar and can reach large numbers of students.

Course content covered entirely by lectures is rare in the colleges of further education. Courses which include lectures combined with other modes of instruction are common. Thus, lectures may be used to begin a course, to provide a final recapitulation and revision, or in combination with seminars and tutorials. They also figure prominently in some types of team teaching (see Chapter 27).

Carefully prepared, well-timed and skilfully delivered with 'a touch of colour, a hint of wonder', the lecture can be a powerful and stimulating mode of communication and instruction.

Notes and references

1. See generally for this chapter: *What's the Use of Lectures?* by D. Bligh (Penguin, 1972); *The Lecture Method of Instruction* by M. Broadwell (Educational & Technical Publications, 1980); *Lecturing and Explaining* by G.A. Brown (Methuen, 1978); *Instructional Technique* by I. Davies (McGraw-Hill, 1981); *Understanding Academic Lectures* by A. Mason (Prentice-Hall, 1983); 'The lecture-discussion format revisited' by J.S. Bowman in *Improving College Teaching* (1979, *27*); 'Lecturing' by J. Sattersfield in *On College Teaching* ed. O. Milton (Jossey-Bass, 1978); 'Learning From lectures' by V. Hodgson in *The Experience of Learning* ed. F. Martin (Scottish Academic Press, 1984); *Mastering the Techniques of Teaching* by J. Lowman (Jossey-Bass, 1984). For a sceptical comment on Wittgenstein's oracular statement which heads this chapter, see Bertrand Russell's preface to the 1922 edition of Wittgenstein's *Tractatus*.
2. 'The lecture – an analysis and review of research' by A. Verner and T. Dickinson in *Adult Education* (1968, *17*).
3. See *The Life of a Poet – W.H. Auden* by C. Osborne (Metheun, 1979).
4. 'Relative effectiveness of the lecture and individual readings as methods of college teaching' in *Genetic Psychology Monographs* (1928, *4*).
5. *Op. cit.*
6. 'Memory for lectures' in *Journal of Educational Psychology* (1979, *71*).
7. 'Recognition memory' in *Journal of Experimental Psychology* (1977, *3*).
8. *Autobiography of Charles Darwin* ed. F. Darwin (Constable, 1958).
9. *Autobiography* (Allen & Unwin, 1975).
10. 'Lectures as an instructional method' by P. Saunders in *The Principles of Economics Course* ed. P. Saunders and W. Walstad (McGraw-Hill, 1990).
11. 'In defence of lecturing' by D. Bergman in *Bulletin of Association of Departments of English* (1983, *76*).
12. *Op. cit.*
13. *Studies in Higher Education* (Prentice-Hall, 1982).
14. 'Improving instruction' in *British Journal of Educational Psychology* (1980, *50*).
15. See *Advice to Lecturers – An Anthology from the Writings of Faraday and Bragg* ed. G. Porter and J. Friday (The Royal Institution, 1978).
16. A superb example of the pause in music used for dramatic effect occurs in the final nine bars of Sibelius' Fifth Symphony. Those who heard the magnificent reading by Laurence Olivier of the scriptural verse, 'Let there be light, and there was light', will recall the effect of the unexpected, deliberate pause after 'was', followed by an outburst on the final word.
17. *Op. cit.*
18. *The Conditions of Learning* (Holt-Saunders, 1985).
19. *The Anatomy of Judgment* (Hutchinson, 1966).

20. 'The experimental analysis of social performance' in *Communication in Face to Face Interaction* ed. J. Laver (Penguin, 1967).

21. *Op. cit.*

22. See 'On notes and note taking' by J. Hartley and S. Marshall in *University Quarterly* (1974, *28*); 'Using students' notes' by M.J. Howe in *Journal of Educational Research* (1970, *64*); 'Effects of personal lecture notes on recall' by M. Maqsud in *Journal of Educational Psychology* (1980, *50*); 'Note taking – a critical review' by J. Hartley and I. Davies in *Programmed Learning and Educational Technology* (1978, *15*).

Chapter 26

The Discussion Group; the Seminar; the Tutorial; the Case Study Group

> Though all the winds of doctrine were let loose to play upon the earth, so Truth be in the field, we do injuriously by licensing and prohibiting to misdoubt her strength and let her and Falsehood grapple; who ever knew Truth put to the worse, in a free and open encounter (Milton).

The lesson and the lecture, which are discussed in previous chapters, differ radically from the discussion group, the seminar, the tutorial and the case study, which are outlined below.[1] The former are largely *teacher-centred* ('autocratic') modes of instruction; the latter are based on *student-centred* strategies of instruction, directed at facilitating learning within an environment in which *the teacher plays a mediating role and interactive class participation is the norm*. The former generally depend for their success, in large measure, on the teacher's 'solo performance'; the latter achieve success only from the continuing *collective activity* of teacher and class.

Instruction of this nature is not easy to prepare or control. It requires considerable skill to be exercised by the directing tutor who should have some understanding of the rationale of discussion and its techniques, and an appreciation of general group dynamics.[2] The tutor should understand the concept of a 'group' and its nature, the ways in which group members might be expected to interact, the effect of individual differences in status, abilities and expectations on the group as a whole, and the invisible structure of a group (as contrasted with the formal, 'published' structure)[3] from which may emerge the group's real leader and a 'pecking order'. He or she should be trained to understand the use of participation in discussion, the value of reciprocal influence among students in the facilitation of learning, the differences between overseeing, controlling and dominating a discussion, and the types of instructional process which can be served by discussion periods. The decision to enhance learning through supervised discussion will require for its successful implementation, in Lowman's words,[4] 'considerable instructor spontaneity, creativity and tolerance for the unknown'.

It is important to remember that terms such as 'discussion group', 'seminar' and 'tutorial' have not acquired standardized meanings; a tutor who is asked to include 'seminars' in his or her instruction plan should make sure that there is a common understanding of the precise meaning of the word.

The essence and value of the discussion group

A discussion group is constituted by a tutor and class seeking to examine a matter by means of the free flow of argument. Essentially, the members pool knowledge and ideas in the cooperative task of endeavouring to understand a problem by learning from one another. Speaking, listening and observing are essential attributes of the discussion method. The discussion group is free from the relative formality of the seminar and the rigid rules of debate. Its freedom, however, necessitates careful preparation and control by the tutor if the benefits of discussion as a mode of instruction are to be realized in full.

The purpose of a discussion group is usually *the collective exploration and 'public evaluation' of ideas.* ('There must be discussion to show how experience is to be interpreted ... Very few facts are able to tell their own story without comments to bring out the meaning' (J.S. Mill).) Bridges[5] suggests that discussion builds participants' understanding of the topic in question by supplementing each participant's information with information possessed by other members of the group, by stimulating different perspectives on the topic, by allowing conjectures on the subject matter and providing opportunities for criticism and refutation, by encouraging mutual adjustment of opinions. Participants also learn the social and procedural conventions concerning the enunciation and reception of arguments. Two important points should be stressed; first, the discussion must have a clear objective; second, prerequisite knowledge of the elements of the topic to be discussed should be considered in the preparation of the group session.

Necessity for a clear objective

The discussion group ought not to be perceived as a stop-gap in a course. It must be an integral part of the teaching programme, and ought to be accepted by students as such. It may be employed, therefore, when the tutor, in preparing the course work scheme, poses the question: 'Is there a stage in the course when interest and understanding are likely to be stimulated and when the generalization of learned principles is likely to be aided by a collective class exchange of opinions?' and a positive answer emerges. The discussion group might then find a place in the tutor's course scheme with an appropriate, carefully chosen objective. It might serve as a follow-up session to a lecture, as a mid-course examination of ideas or as a recapitulation session.

Prerequisite knowledge

Unless there is in the group prerequisite knowledge of the topic under discussion, there can be no effective participation and the result is likely to be little more than a ritual exchange of loose thinking ('prejudices, platitudes, preconceptions and vague generalities') or of those 'irrationally held truths which may be more harmful than reasoned errors' (Huxley).[6]

Advantages and disadvantages of the discussion group method of instruction

The disadvantages of the discussion group may be summarized briefly. Unless the topic is carefully chosen and the session carefully structured and controlled, there is, it is suggested, a marked tendency for the discussion to degenerate into an informal debate from which a dominant hierarchy of 'star speakers' emerges. A 'pecking order' of participants soon forms, so that the more forceful members hold the floor, while a significant proportion of the group, increasingly hesitant and unwilling to risk public contradiction, become silent observers – a negation of the very purpose of the exercise. Because some groups can be easily dominated, false conclusions, presented in a facile, persuasive manner by a leader on whom the group has become over-dependent, may be accepted all too easily. A tendency for a discussion group to deteriorate into a forum for the exchange of prejudices, so that it resembles 'an athletic contest of closed mind with closed mind', is an ever-present danger. Note also Bridges' comment that, 'since discussion is less structured and certain than lectures, it may provoke anxiety in predisposed students and thereby interfere with their learning'. Finally, the 'real cost' of the small discussion group makes it something of a luxury in the schemes of cost-conscious college administrators.

The advantages of the discussion group are said to emerge, largely, from its 'democratic', permissive, collaborative nature (as contrasted with the 'autocratic' character of the lesson and the lecture). Group experience, it has been suggested, assists 'social facilitation', so that people tend to work more intensely when in a group. Group judgments may sometimes be more accurate than those resulting from an individual examination of problems and membership of a group might benefit those whose thoughts can be clarified by discussion with others. Further, the conflict and disagreement which emerge in any lively discussion group may become the starting point for new exploration, resulting in the group's increased tolerance of varying points of view – and acceptance of Wilde's dictum that 'truth is rarely pure and never simple!' Group discussion also enables a class and teacher to get to know one another's thoughts, opinions and attitudes. It provides for the teacher a useful element of feedback where the discussion has centred on the content of previous lessons and lectures. Bridges mentions research concerning the value of the discussion compared with that of the lecture (at college level) and notes: 'Discussion [has] been found to be more effective for stimulating students to have positive attitudes and motivation.'

Abercrombie[7] reported an interesting experiment in the use of the free discussion method. The experiment grew out of the belief that, in receiving information from a 'stimulus pattern', our selection from that information depends on our making judgments which are *unconsciously influenced* by many factors. The experiment seemed to suggest that more valid judgments might be made if we were conscious of those factors. Our judgment can be improved as the result of a free group discussion in which alternative judgments of the 'stimulus pattern' are explored and evaluated.

Preparing for the discussion

The first stage in considering the mounting of a discussion group session necessitates the tutor being quite sure as to why this mode of instruction has been selected. Has the course reached a stage where collective examination of a problem is essential? Are there sufficient ideas involved to warrant a full discussion? Can the objective which the tutor has in mind be attained by any other form of instruction? To approach the discussion group method merely as a break in the routine of lessons or as a substitute for some other type of instruction is to weaken its chances of success. Next, the aim of the discussion must be clear. This is not to suggest that the discussion must be so planned and manipulated that it will reach a particular, desirable conclusion. 'Aim' implies a discussion having as its objective a reasonable examination of a specific topic.

Preparation demands that the group be active even *before* the discussion session. The group should be told why members will be participating in the discussion, what they are expected to accomplish and what resources will be made available to them. Unity of purpose of the group should be stressed. Group members could be asked to prepare at least one short item to be used as a contribution to the discussion. Reading lists containing suggested approaches to the discussion topic ought to be distributed and announced in advance of the date of discussion. ('When we meet in a week's time we shall discuss the problem of ... Here is a list of topics you might care to consider before that date. The college librarian has prepared a display of recent press cuttings dealing with the problem. At the end of the list you will find some statistics bearing on the matters we shall discuss.')

Boundaries, a general 'line of advance' and the overall pattern which the discussion might be expected to take should be considered by the tutor. Ought the session to begin with a short statement of the problem? By whom? Visual material might be needed so that basic data, maps or statistics can be presented. Is the material available or does it require preparation? Is an explanation of the norms of discussion (and their purpose and enforcement) necessary?

A reporter should be appointed and given the task of noting the gist of contributions to the discussion. Seating arrangements[8] should be made so that the process of 'organized conversation', which typifies the good discussion group, is facilitated. (Small groups allow for more participation from each member.) Face-to-face interaction, enabling all members to communicate, is helpful. A circle of chairs, a U-shaped arrangement of tables and chairs (since communication tends to flow across, rather than around, a group), a chalkboard on which points can be noted and data displayed will require some rearrangement of the conventional classroom. (Abercrombie[9] notes the importance of seating arrangements for a discussion session and comments on the significance of spatial arrangement and group behaviour during discussions.)

Where a class is too large for the type of discussion envisaged here, the 'fish bowl' technique may be used. This allows a small group discussion, with the remainder of the class listening and viewing *beyond* the discussion group; students from the fringe who act as viewers contribute ideas after the formal discussion has ended. The 'jigsaw' discussion method (which presupposes availability of a number of teaching areas, and students who are practised in the use of discussion) allows a topic to be broken down into segments. Different groups meet separately, discuss their segment, and meet later in plenary session to fit together their findings. (In some colleges the general rule is that, when a group is to be broken down into sub-groups, it should be on the basis of the 'square root size', e.g. a group of 16 becomes four sub-groups each of four members.)

Controlling the discussion

The subtle art of discussion control depends largely upon the tutor's awareness of the purpose of the discussion method. He or she must ensure that all members feel free to contribute to the discussion and must be prepared to relinquish some of his or her general, overt authority and control in pursuit of this goal. Members' participation should not be constrained by over-rigid rules, but an accepted framework of conduct is necessary if informality is not to result in mere cross-talk and gossip. (Discussion leaders learn quickly how to anticipate and deal with the side-winds which can blow a discussion totally off course.)[10] Potentially dominant personalities must not be allowed to take over the discussion and the naturally reticent must be encouraged to contribute. Many points of view ought to find expression and the highly unpopular, 'extremist' opinion ought not to be excluded. Three problems of control noted below need to be solved by the teacher as group leader: setting and keeping the discussion in motion; posing appropriate and stimulating questions as a part of the discussion; ending the session. These problems arise from the tutor's need to intervene deliberately in the discussion. Jacques[11] refers to six categories of tutor-intervention: prescribing, informing and confronting (the so-called 'authoritative mode'); releasing tension, eliciting, supporting (the so-called 'facilitative mode'). Deliberate intervention must not become an excuse for the tutor 'taking over' the discussion.[12]

Setting and keeping the discussion in motion

Immediately the opening statement has been made or the first question has been put, it becomes the task of the group leader to initiate and encourage the expression of varying points of view, and to clarify goals. Members ought to be invited to participate at an early stage (since the first few minutes of a discussion period can be the most difficult) with encouragement to the shy, perhaps in the form of a question (based on a common experience) which invites a direct response. The discussion ought to move around the circle of participants, briskly and pointedly. 'Wearing out' a theme or undue concentration on minor matters ought to be politely restrained. Faulty reasoning and circular arguments ought not to remain uncorrected, 'hidden agendas' ought to be exposed, obscure statements ought to bring a request for their clarification and sweeping generalizations ought to be subjected to close examination. Interruptions, irrelevance and invective ought to elicit from the group leader a tactful rejoinder, which does not serve, however, in the manner of a sledgehammer, to terminate the discussion. Occasional summaries of arguments and matters on which there is general agreement should be given and recorded on the chalkboard; differences of opinion should be mediated and clarified. Respect for all group members should be encouraged. The teacher must avoid, however, the type of overall control (or the too-obvious role of 'devil's advocate') which inhibits discussion because it leads the group to feel that it is being 'manipulated' so that a predetermined conclusion will result. Further, the teacher must not interpret a momentary silence as an invariable sign that discussion is flagging; it may indicate a pause for thought and may be a prelude to an improvement in the quality of the discussion. (The use of silence and appropriate, expectant body language by the tutor may indeed stimulate further discussion; a long, contrived pause may create a tension which needs to be broken by contributions from the group.)

Questioning as an aid to discussion

The discussion itself might well result from a single question, but the group leader ought to have available a cluster of prepared questions which can be used to provoke thought and comment, to move the discussion on to a higher level or in a new direction, or to return it to the group's general line of thought. Specific questions to individual members rather than overhead questions to the group in general may serve to bring out the naturally shy and prevent one or two members monopolizing the session, or may be used to draw answers from members who have specialized knowledge. The use of 'probes' to challenge, explore and stimulate is advisable. (The tutor should refrain from answering questions that could, and should, be answered by other members of the group.[13])

Hansen's 'Improving classroom discussion' (1990),[14] enumerates types of question considered appropriate for discussion groups.

(a) *Factual questions*, requiring a specific answer to, e.g. matter arising from pre-discussion reading. Questions of this type are useful in 'bringing out' the more reticent members of a group.
(b) *Interpretive questions*, involving higher-order cognitive skills of comprehension and analysis, e.g. 'What do you think the author of this statement had in mind when he said . . . ?' Questions of this type are valuable for stimulating discussion, since there is no immediately obvious 'correct' answer, and a large area of argument may be revealed.
(c) *Evaluative questions*, inviting the exercise of judgment on a particular point of view, involving the application of personal sets of values, can heighten a discussion.
(d) *Basic questions*, which may relate to the very essence of the matter under discussion, are useful where it is necessary to spark off a full-scale exchange of opinions.
(e) *Supporting questions*, arising from answers to basic questions, assist in moving a discussion forward.
(f) *Probing questions*, used to stimulate discussion in depth, are important in bringing together different points of view.

(g) *Closing questions*, used to bring segments of the discussion or the discussion as a whole to an end, may be employed by the tutor as an invitation to a student to review aspects of a discussion.

Ending the discussion

Intermediate summing-up and recapitulation should occur at several stages of the discussion. A prior indication that the discussion is about to end ought to be given. The final summing-up must not be omitted; it should survey impartially the main points which have been made and should note significant areas of agreement and disagreement. It ought to link the essence of the discussion with previous lessons and should point forward to future classwork in which the discussion will be seen to have played a preparatory role.

Following on the discussion

Monitoring and evaluating the results of the discussion are essential if the tutor is to control the overall instructional process. The tutor should pose and answer the following questions: 'Did the discussion achieve its purpose? Were the prior tasks (e.g. research) carried out by group members? Did members of the group listen to one another, express their ideas clearly, build on one another's contributions? Was everyone, including the quieter members, involved? Did any member dominate? What type of intervention by the tutor was required? Were the norms of discussion accepted and did they help or hinder? Were there any unintended outcomes?'

Answers to questions of this nature will indicate, almost always, that problems are inevitable in mounting and controlling a discussion group. The advantages that can accrue as the result of discussion are considerable, and should be weighed carefully before deciding whether or not to incorporate discussion periods as a part of the instructional programme. Gall,[15] for example, suggests that there is research evidence to indicate that discussion periods do facilitate subject matter mastery and do have a positive effect on communication skills and problem-solving. Additionally, they are said to simulate 'real world' situations in which discussions are often the prelude to decision-making, and tend 'to promote the values and processes of democratic society'.

The seminar: its nature and use

The term 'seminar' is generally used in further education to refer to *a semi-structured group discussion which may precede or follow a formal lecture or a series of lessons and which is introduced by the presentation of a thesis, often in the form of an essay.* Its specialist nature and its more formal setting differentiate it from the discussion group. Thus a course on industrial relations might include a seminar on a topic such as 'Can legislation assist the maintenance of industrial peace?' A seminar on industrial law, for example, might engage in the systematic analysis of an essay presented by a seminar member on 'The history of equal pay legislation'. In general, the seminar appears to be appropriate as a mode of instruction only when the level of attainment of the group is relatively high and the subject matter lends itself to analytical treatment. In the colleges of further education it is often confined to advanced general and professional examination courses.

The main advantage of the seminar as a mode of instruction is its stimulation and testing of students' powers of comprehension and evaluation. The presenter of the thesis from which the seminar stems is tested, in particular, on his or her skill in arranging and formulating a sustained argument. The ability of a student to discover underlying values and assumptions in a presentation, to detect and separate principles from their context, to ponder their application and to question their relevance in certain situations, can be strengthened, it is claimed, by a critical examination of another's thoughts. A principal disadvantage of the seminar lies in the difficulties which can arise where presenter and class are unequally matched so that the group is reduced to the defensive posture of silence and non-participation.

Preparation and presentation of the seminar

The duration of the seminar must be considered by the tutor in his or her preparation. Often the subject matter requires discussion time ranging over several lesson periods. Seminars planned for one hour only may be of little value. Timetable rearrangement may present an initial problem.

Wherever possible, a summary of the paper to be presented ought to be made available to students two or three weeks in advance of the seminar. It should contain information under the following headings:

(a) full title of the paper;
(b) abstract of argument to be presented;
(c) main headings and sub-headings of the argument;
(d) sources, reading list, relevant statistics.

Where members have the opportunity to study a summary of the paper before it is presented, the probability of a total lack of response, which often indicates lack of preparation, is reduced. A feeling of being unequally matched with a specialist may be prevented by prior reading and consideration of the paper to be presented.

Where the presenter is a student for whom the planning and delivery of a paper are novel experiences, it should be the task of the tutor to explain and oversee its preparation and reduction to summary form. Where the presenter is a visitor to the college, the tutor has the responsibility of acquainting him or her with the precise purpose of the seminar and the level of its members. The importance of receiving a summary paper in advance of the seminar must be stressed.

The seminar timetable must be prepared and explained to the presenter. It ought to allow for the following events:

1. introduction;
2. presentation of the paper;
3. discussion – part I;
4. interim review;
5. discussion – part II;
6. summary of discussion (by tutor or member of class);
7. reply to discussion;
8. conclusion.

The preparation of visual aids apparatus for use by the presenter, and planning of seating arrangements so that inter-communication is facilitated, are aspects of seminar organization which should not be overlooked. The lecture environment, where the lecturer stands well apart from his or her audience, is inappropriate for the seminar, which requires an environment in which the presenter's status as a member of the group is recognized.

The general principles of group discussion control (which were outlined on pp. 335–7 above) apply to the seminar also. Where the discussion results in criticism of his or her paper, the presenter may be expected to claim – and ought to be allowed – adequate time for rebuttal, rejoinder and reply. Finally, the concluding section of the seminar should provide a clear link with the next section of the course scheme of work.

The essence of the tutorial

The tutorial is *a meeting between a teacher and a student, or a very small group of students, characterized by discussion and/or personal, face-to-face teaching, generally based on the content of an essay or other material written by the student(s) or on questions raised by the tutor or the student(s)*. It is a mode of tuition associated originally with the older English universities and requires a very generous staff-student ratio. Some colleges of further education have been able to sustain a system of regularly held tutorials for activities such as the following.

1. *Skills teaching groups*. Very small groups meet a tutor for the practice and refinement of psychomotor skills (see p. 298). Individual, face-to-face tuition has been found valuable in gymnastics coaching, the teaching of musical and acting skills, and the practising of some machine production techniques.
2. *Remedial working groups*. In some colleges individual students are encouraged to discuss with a tutor problems arising from difficulties in classwork. Where tutorial periods are used for meetings of this nature, diagnostic and remedial work may be undertaken.
3. *Supervision tutorials*. In this type of tutorial meeting, student and tutor discuss some aspect of the student's work, often in the form of an essay which he or she is required to read and then to support in argument with the tutor. This is the shape of the traditional tutorial and requires very careful preparation by tutor and student alike. Effectively prepared and handled, it can result in a heightening of student cognitive skills, in particular those involving analysis and judgment.

4. *Small-group post-lecture tutorials*. Following a formal lecture or lesson, a very small group of students will meet a tutor with whom they raise individual difficulties, problems of comprehension, etc. The tutor may choose to provide information supplementing or explaining that given in the lesson or lecture. He or she may summarize the main points of the lecture, inviting questions and discussion. The tutor may probe comprehension by discussion of a problem touched upon during the lecture or lesson. The shape of the tutorial will be determined by students' queries; its direction must be in the tutor's hands.

Problems of the tutorial

Group size is all-important; Davies suggests, for a tutorial, 1–3 students.[16] (He cites research pointing to a significant measure of correlation between size of instructional group and achievement.) Because the essential feature of the tutorial is a face-to-face teaching relationship, so-called tutorial groups of, say, 15–20 students are a contradiction in terms. Where a tutorial objective is the improvement of an essential motor technique or the heightening of critical skills, the tutor must insist, so far as is possible, on very small groups.

It is very easy indeed for time to be wasted during a tutorial. Lack of a clear objective, failure by tutor or students to prepare material, failure of a tutor to understand the nature of points raised by students or to comprehend the basis of their difficulties, will lead to little progress. Adequate preparation must be made the rule, so that the tutorial is neither viewed nor used as an opportunity to evade the rigours of the learning process. Where the tutorial involves *a group*, the tutor must ensure the involvement of all members in discussions; the general rules relating to discussions (see pp. 335–7) should be followed.

The posing of questions by the tutor during a formal tutorial session will test to the full his or her competence as 'controller' of instruction. Questions should be designed, fashioned and presented as a contribution to the instructional purpose of the tutorial. They should be adjusted in content, style and presentation according to the quality of the student's responses; hence they should not follow rigidly any scheme designed before the tutorial. Questions should attempt to elicit responses which test capacities to comprehend, analyse and evaluate, rather than the mere capacity to recall. Responses indicating misunderstanding, or based on irrelevancies, should be challenged in a manner which will not destroy the student's confidence. The tutor should not expect answers immediately after questions have been asked; he or she should expect to wait for a considered response. The tutor should remember, too, that his or her gestures and facial expressions may be interpreted by students as a response to their statements.[17]

Tutorials are often criticized as 'too demanding' for students attending further education courses. The criticism misses the essence of the tutorial process. The real value of the tutorial is the intensity of tuition made possible by its very personal form. Its demanding nature is often its essential virtue. Properly planned and staffed, the tutorial should be capable of providing valuable assistance to college students at all levels.

The nature of the case study

The case study mode of instruction is aimed at creative problem-solving and is based upon *a participatory examination, analysis and diagnosis of a real or simulated problem so that general principles might emerge in a realistic fashion.* It is used in colleges of further education to intensify student understanding of the complex, real world relationships embodied in law, economics, business studies, industrial affairs, social work, politics, etc. Designed originally as an aid to the study of decision-making in business, the case study is now utilized in the teaching of many of the disciplines which involve *the identification and selection of a preferred course of action from possible alternatives in conditions of uncertainty.* The aims of the case study may be summarized as: the creation of an active, participatory teaching-learning situation in which the subject matter closely mirrors the outside world; the improvement of the student's ability to identify underlying principles, to think swiftly under pressure and to apply his or her insight and learned principles to the unravelling of a complex knot of relationships and events; the testing of the student's carry-over of class learning to novel situations involving many constraints.

Three examples of the nature of case studies are given below in highly summarized form to illustrate their use in further education courses.

An 'in-tray' exercise

Hospital administrators attending a management development course at a college of further education are presented with the contents of a typical, crowded in-tray. Their tasks are (a) to select, in 30 minutes, the items which they consider most important, to draft appropriate replies and initiate action, and (b) to justify their selection and course of action. The items of correspondence include letters of resignation from senior staff, complaints from union representatives, threats of action by former patients for alleged negligence, etc.

A 'situation' case study

Personnel managers attending a college short course are given a (simulated) letter of complaint from a retail store's graduate manager-trainees, expressing dissatisfaction with their training and career prospects. The group members are allowed a short time in which to analyse and identify the real nature of the complaint, to call for background data and to outline an immediate course of action.

The 'exercise' case study

Financial controllers responsible for very large trading accounts are asked to make a contingency plan involving a 25 per cent reduction in trading revenue. Quantitative analysis is required and a computer terminal link is made available in order to provide a simulation of the effects of decisions taken.

The case study may be used, therefore, to put flesh on the bones of theory and to emphasize to students the real costs (in terms of finance, human relations, goodwill) of decisions taken under stress. It is useful, too, in demonstrating to students, on the basis of an analysis of their errors, the dark areas of real situations which can often be lit only dimly and fitfully by the rays of untested theory. (The words of the editor of the *Harvard Business Review* (July 1981) are of relevance here: 'For the most part, only trivial management problems are neatly structured and quantifiable. All modelling and quantitative analysis directed at a decision are only preludes to subjective judgment. *Vision then must transcend technique.*')

Students using this type of case study should be warned that 'the case study method carries the danger that one "case" may be regarded as typical and generalisations may be drawn, based on a sample that is too small or too unrepresentative to warrant them' (Lee).[18]

Types of case study

Examples of the more widely used types of case study, some of which may be presented by video, are enumerated below.

1. *The 'critical incident' study.* The penultimate event in a chain of incidents leading, say, to an industrial strike, is described. Students must decide on the additional data required in order to obtain a full picture of the circumstances. This can be a useful exercise in analysis and comprehension.
2. *The 'next stage' study.* A case is unfolded, stage by stage. Students must suggest what is 'likely to happen next'. The exercise usually calls for a high order of ability in analysis and synthesis.
3. *The 'live case' study.* The situation presented to students leads to their being asked directly: 'What ought to be done now?' The problem, which may be based on a well-publicized event, such as a breakdown in wage negotiations in the public sector, tests not only knowledge of the factual background of the situation but the ability to think swiftly and to analyse carefully under conditions of stress.
4. *The 'business game' study.* This involves the presentation of a quantitative problem (e.g. pricing, stock control, share price movements). Students compete to arrive at the optimum solution, which may be judged in relation to a computer solution.
5. *The 'major issue' study.* Students are given a mass of data – much of which is deliberately irrelevant to the main issue – and are asked to identify and separate that issue and to suggest remedies for the situation which is revealed.
6. *The 'role-play' case study.* On the basis of an incident (based, perhaps, on a grievance or confrontation) which is reported to them, students are required to act out (in an improvised style) the roles of the central participants, e.g.

industrial relations officer, shop steward, union official, managing director. This technique has been used with success in courses which include training in collective bargaining, arbitrations, etc. (It is important that the roles be allocated with care *and only after explanation*; students may resent what they perceive as mere childish play-acting.)

7. *The 'in-tray' exercise* (see above).
8. *The 'situation' case study* (see above).
9. *The 'exercise' case study* (see above).

Writing and controlling the case study exercise

The writing of case studies is a specialized task which may be carried out best by the course tutor using real-life material (obtained from firms and institutions with their knowledge as to its intended use and suitably disguised by the use of fictitious names and addresses). The case study should be arranged so as to call for the identification of major and minor problems and the preparation of solutions with an awareness of difficulties in their implementation. The content must be appropriate to the students' background, levels of experience and comprehension.

The case study material will include all the important elements of the situation to be analysed. The relevant background must be sketched in, for example, the firm's policies, size of markets, size of labour and entrepreneurial force, etc. Appendices setting out statistical information ought to be supplied. The material ought to be distributed to the group in advance of the study session, together with an explanation of what principle is being investigated and why, the method of investigation which is to be adopted, and the level of analysis required.

The case study session may necessitate the division of the group into syndicates, each with its secretary, chairman and reporter (who will present the syndicate's findings to the groups in the final session). The class tutor moves among the syndicates noting difficulties, providing additional information when it is requested and chairing the final, plenary session. In that session, syndicate solutions must be stated, justified by reference to principle and practice, and criticized. Where the study is based on a real situation which can be discussed without breach of confidence, an explanation and consideration of 'what really happened' can be given during a later lesson; follow-up is vital in these cases.

Yunker[19] recommends the following pattern for the conduct of a case analysis. First, the tutor should study the case carefully, obtain a general feel for the specific problem area, and note the 'pivotal points'. He or she should then decide what concepts emerge and how each ought to be stressed. The following advice should be given to student participants.

1. Take the position of each individual in the case actively and sympathetically, try to establish why they feel or behave as they do. What fears or bias are evident?
2. Isolate the major problems or issues. Examine the case closely for information relevant to those problems or issues.

3. What alternative courses of action are available?
4. Identify the potential risks and benefits attached to each course of action.
5. Select the alternative which, in all the circumstances as you perceive them, is the most satisfactory.
6. Decide how the alternative selected might be implemented successfully.

Eaton[20] outlines a sequential approach to the case study, based on seven steps.

1. Seek to understand and evaluate the information presented. Extrapolate from that information where necessary.
2. Diagnose what appears to be the problem area. Do not mistake symptom for cause.
3. Attempt to generate strategic and tactical alternative solutions to the problem which has been diagnosed.
4. Try to predict possible outcomes of courses of action in terms of risk and uncertainty.
5. Evaluate alternative courses of action and make a considered choice.
6. Consider contingency planning where events might take an unexpected turn.
7. Make a systematic presentation of your analysis and conclusions.

Advantages and disadvantages of the case study method of instruction

The case study as a mode of instruction now has a firm place in the instructional schemes of many colleges where it is often used in the consolidation or revision stage of a course. Its links with reality are welcomed as an aid in removing the artificial barriers of the classroom situation. Its severe demands on a student's powers of analysis, synthesis and general reasoning can be balanced by the high level of interest which is sustained by his or her knowledge of grappling with a 'live' problem, rather than an arid, theoretical situation. Students are 'learning by doing'; moreover, they may become aware of their own prejudices and bias. The sensitive use of case studies is said to improve students' skills in the detection and rejection of irrelevance, in the consideration of the possible results of a decision, in the evaluation of alternative procedures, and, perhaps above all, in the perception of the importance of facts. Case studies also accustom students to working in groups – a useful preparation for the real world of industry and commerce.

Eaton enumerates six skills which can be developed by the case method.

1. *Analytical skills*, involving the classification, organization and evaluation of information.
2. *Application skills*, based upon practice in the use of principles, concepts and techniques.
3. *Creative skills*, which are necessary where alternative solutions to problems must be generated – an essential feature of many case studies.
4. *Communication skills*, arising in the presentation of arguments.

5. *Self-analysis skills*, emerging from an awareness of one's attitudes to the value-judgments which arise in case discussions.
6. *Social skills*, necessary as a member of a group engaged in the social process of collective discussion.

Disadvantages are said to turn on the difficulties attached to the preparation and writing of the studies. The background research, collection and interpretation of data call for much more time than is often available to the college lecturer.

In general, however, the growing bank of outline case studies in textbook form on which hard-pressed lecturers may draw should serve to assist those tutors who feel that direct class participation in the solution of problems drawn from the real world of industry, administration and politics has an educational value in itself.

Tutors involved in case studies presented to students who have experienced only traditional modes of teaching (for instance, lesson and lecture) have found that the initial impact of the case method may produce difficulties in learning. Participants are often unsure as to their precise role in the case study process and are not always sure what 'the problem' is. Student reaction to the tutor's statement, 'there is no unique answer to this problem', is often negative. Further, students may not be immediately aware of what they have learned from a case study; this may be compounded by a lack of precise feedback from the tutor from whom they have been accustomed to expect detailed information.

Effective teaching practice demands an appropriate response to problems of this nature. As a prelude to the case study itself, time must be found for a full explanation of the process. The roles of tutor and student must be made clear; the aims of the study must be set out and some reference should be made, in general terms, to the expected outcome of case analysis.

Small group instruction as an exercise in cooperative learning

The modes of instruction outlined in this chapter are based essentially on cooperative exploration of ideas and group learning. Some teachers in further education feel that this aspect of learning may be of great significance for participants in the long term. Slavin[21] outlines the advantages of cooperative learning: students are aware of their dependency on one another in achieving a common goal; they are motivated to encourage one another to assist in the achievement of group success; their positive contacts with one another in group discussion help to build understanding and tolerance; isolation of students is diminished when all members of the group feel that their contributions are of significance, and self-esteem is increased. A mode of instruction which promises social advantages of this nature certainly has its place in further education.

Notes and references

1. See generally for this chapter: *Instructional Technique* by I. Davies (McGraw-Hill, 1981); *Learning from Others in Groups* by C. Cooper (Associated Business Press, 1979);

'Discussion methods' by M.D. Gall in *IETE*; 'Small group methods' by R.E. Slavin in *IETE*; *Analysis of Groups* ed. G. Gibbard (Jossey-Bass, 1978); *Learning in Groups* by D. Jacques (Kogan Page, 1991); 'Participating in tutorials and seminars' in *A Guide to Learning Independently* by L. Marshall and E. Rowland (Longman, 1989); *Group Communications* by P. Hartley (Routledge, 1997).

2. 'A gathering of people is a "group" when its members are collectively conscious of their existence as a group; when they believe it satisfies their needs; when they share aims, are interdependent, want to join in group activities and to remain with the group': Jacques ('Group teaching' in *IETE*).

3. See e.g. *Group Dynamics* by M.E. Shaw (McGraw-Hill, 1981); 'Two views of discussion groups' by C. Seale in *Journal of Further and Higher Education* (1980, *1*).

4. *Mastering the Techniques of Teaching* (Jossey-Bass, 1984).

5. *Education, Democracy and Discussion* (NFER, 1979).

6. *Collected Essays* (Watts, 1898).

7. *The Anatomy of Judgment* (Hutchinson, 1960).

8. See Davies (*op. cit.*).

9. *Op.cit.*

10. See 'The analysis of a discussion and seminar group' by C. Seale and J. Canning in *Journal of Further and Higher Education* (1978, 2).

11. *Op.cit.*

12. See 'Leading discussions' by P. Barnes-McConnell in *On College Teaching* ed. O. Milton (Jossey-Bass, 1978).

13. See *Questioning and Teaching* by J.T. Dillon (Croom Helm, 1988); 'To question and not to question during discussion' by J.T. Dillon in *Journal of Teacher Education* (1981, *32*).

14. In *Principles of Economics Course* ed. P. Saunders and W. Walstad (McGraw-Hill, 1990).

15. 'The discussion method' by M.D. Gall in *The Psychology of Teaching Methods* ed. N. Gage (Chicago UP, 1976).

16. *Op.cit.*

17. See 'Tutoring' by F.J. Medway in *IETE*.

18. 'Case studies in the teaching of economics' in *Teaching Economics* (Economics Association, 1967).

19. *Instructor's Resource Manual* (Prentice-Hall, 1986).

20. *Learning from Case Studies* (Prentice-Hall, 1982). See also *Teaching and the Case Method* by L. Barnes (Harvard Business Press, 1994).

21. *Co-operative Learning* (Longman, 1983).

Chapter 27

Team Teaching

It is as important to think about the quality of teaching or the quality of the learning situations provided ... as it is about organisation. Many of the benefits of team teaching have been lost at times because of the failure to consider this point. Individual teacher competence is the keystone of team teaching as of any other form of teaching (Lovell, 1967).

The notion of an individual teacher controlling, in its entirety, the progress of a lesson is at the heart of much current teaching practice. The concept of a sole, dominant figure accepting direct responsibility for the planning, execution and assessment of a unit of instruction is questioned, however, by the theory and practice of *team teaching*. The claims made for this practice are wide, ranging from the assertion that it makes teaching more effective, to the highly arguable declaration that the teaching team is the most appropriate instructional organization for the classrooms of a democratic society, in which cooperation at all levels and in many social activities is a worthy aim in itself. An important basic assumption made by some advocates of team teaching is that, where teachers focus their *collective attention* on an instructional problem, the solutions at which they arrive will probably be superior to those presented by each of the same teachers considering the problem in isolation. Put quite simply: two heads are often better than one.

Team teaching in an embryonic sense is evident where, say, two members of staff decide to pool their efforts in pursuit of one specific teaching objective. Thus, where a teacher of design technology, wishing to see an improvement in students' standards of written work, asks an English-teaching colleague to discuss with those students matters such as elements of style, and both undertake to mark the next set of essays jointly (one with content in mind, the other with style), team teaching is being practised. This chapter discusses the more formal aspects of the team, its composition, structure and functions.[1]

The background

The idea of team teaching seems to have originated in the USA, with the publication in 1957 of Trump's *Images of the Future*, written on behalf of the Commission on the Experimental Study of the Utilization of Staff in the Secondary School. One of the conclusions drawn by Trump was that the school of 'the future' would be organized around a range of activities involving large and small groups and individual instruction. Team teaching would be essential for the effective organization of such activities and would necessitate arrangements whereby groups of teachers and their technical assistants would utilize their skills in planning for, and instructing in, a given subject area, involving groups of students equivalent in size to two or more conventional classes. Such teaching would cover groups of students organized in a variety of ways.[2]

The basic reasoning behind Trump's suggestions is not always accepted in this country, and his image of the future of American education and the appropriate institutions may not commend itself to all British (or American) teachers. Nevertheless, some of the potentialities and structures of teaching teams at which he hinted have been explored in this country, so that there now exists considerable experience of the technique in our schools and colleges. In recent years, the introduction of GNVQ courses, involving closely knit course teams and utilizing the procedures of the regular team-organized on-course review process, has led to a valuable re-examination of the rationale of the teaching team.

Essential features of team teaching

Team teaching may be said to operate where *two or more teachers cooperate, deliberately and methodically, in the planning, presentation and evaluation of the teaching process*. In effect, individual teachers sacrifice some of their autonomy, pool their resources and – a vital feature of team teaching – accept *joint responsibility* for the teaching of groups of students.

The practice of team teaching does not necessitate a uniform teaching structure, and in this country a variety of patterns has evolved. Small groups acting under a leader (perhaps a subject specialist or senior departmental member) typify a common form of structure. Large groups – entire departments – coordinated in their activities by a departmental head or senior lecturer exemplify another type. A group might grow spontaneously, with a loosely knit team collaborating to deal with specific, related parts of the curriculum. Another group might be a highly organized, centrally directed unit, working to a planned timetable. In general, the structure of the teaching team will tend to reflect course and departmental objectives, strategies, and the availability of resources. Invariably, it will be based on a *collective approach* to the teaching situation.

A variety of student groupings may be utilized. Lectures to the entire student group, lessons, group discussions involving smaller units, and directed private study will feature in the team's programme. (Joyner suggests that the very success of team teaching reflects directly the team's ability to organize the group activity component of the teaching scheme.[3]) The groupings to be adopted will depend on the team's responses to the questions which are posed later in this chapter under the heading 'The planning and implementation of team teaching'.

Joint responsibility for the teaching of groups, appropriate team structure and student groupings are among the most important features of team teaching, but their presence in a team plan will not necessarily guarantee its success. Of vital importance is the team's conscious unity of purpose. No matter how well-organized the team or how abundant the resources and teaching aids, the chances of the team's success will depend directly on the real cooperation of its members.

Behind the theory of team teaching are the assumptions that teachers working together in a coordinated manner can produce an overall improvement in performance, and that the utilization of experts working in their specialist areas will result in a more effective employment of resources (an important advantage of the division of labour in almost any area of creative activity).

Coordination is much more than the 'working together' which characterizes a college section or department in its daily activities. It involves a set of declared objectives, a common approach resulting from an examination of those objectives, an allocation of teaching tasks based on a team discussion and continuous, collective appraisal of the results of teaching.

The real value of the discussions on team teaching might be found, however, in the challenge it presents to some of the unstated assumptions which often underpin the traditional approach. ('It is one of the canons of national education that a teacher is not only master in his own class but that it is understood that he will perform his function unmonitored, unwitnessed even, by a single other colleague'.[4]) The belief that the size of a learning group ought to remain unchanged no matter what the form of the teaching activity, may stem from exigencies of timetable planning rather than from consideration of the conditions for successful learning. Why should class numbers of twenty be considered effective for, say, science, engineering practice, and geography? Team teaching, with its emphasis on varying sizes of groups depending on the specific educational objectives to be attained, questions this rigid approach.[5] Why is the timetable divided into apparently immutable periods of, say, 50 minutes or one hour? Ought the duration of the instructional period to be the same in *all* cases, no matter what the task? The team teaching concept, with its varying lesson and study periods, calls into question the fixed slots in the timetable. Is the typical classroom layout found in many colleges of further education really appropriate to a discussion session, a large group lecture, individual study and a group project? Team teaching, which makes use of many modes of instructional techniques, draws attention also to the need for experimentation in the design and furnishing of 'learning spaces'.

Structure of a teaching team

A simple team structure may be illustrated by the line chart in Figure 27.1. In this case a small teaching team is administered by a leader who has clerical and technical assistance – vital if the team is to function adequately. A larger operation involving the use of several teams, administered and coordinated by a leader, is illustrated in

Figure 27.2. The first structure (Figure 27.1) is appropriate, say, for a small team within a department; its leader may be a senior lecturer. The second structure (Figure 27.2) might emerge in a department wholly committed to the team teaching principle, with perhaps a section leader acting as coordinator of the three teams.

The team leader (who may also be known as 'the coordinator') has the complex tasks of helping to plan the team's strategy, supervising its operation, controlling clerical and technical assistants, chairing assessment discussions and participating as a teacher in the team's work. Additionally, he or she may have the responsibility of supervising the allocation of teaching space and audio-visual aids and of ensuring that the team's work fits in with the general plans of a wider section or department.

The planning and implementation of team teaching

Team teaching can be introduced into a conventional college environment as the result of a decision 'from the top', such as a resolution of the academic board. Often, however, it appears to have emerged as the result of opinion at staff level that existing teaching patterns required revision. In some colleges the move towards team teaching has begun with the holding of a staff seminar on the topic, or the showing of a video which illustrates a team in action. The preparatory work which then follows may include the study of reports from existing teams and an intensive discussion of the practical problems likely to arise in college. It is at this point that appropriate management techniques should be applied: there must be careful planning, allocation of resources, and the construction of an appropriate teaching framework.

The next stage involves the selection of an appropriate area (according to course, subject and syllabus) for the first trial. A team is then selected, having as its first task a study of the syllabus. A series of weekly meetings is planned, during which the results of the study will be reported and discussed.

Sections of the syllabus are then allocated to and examined by specialist

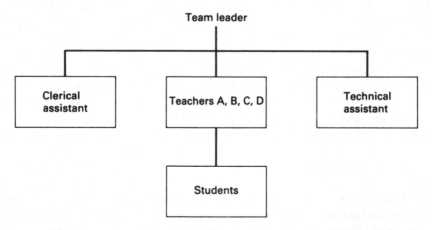

Figure 27.1 Simple team structure.

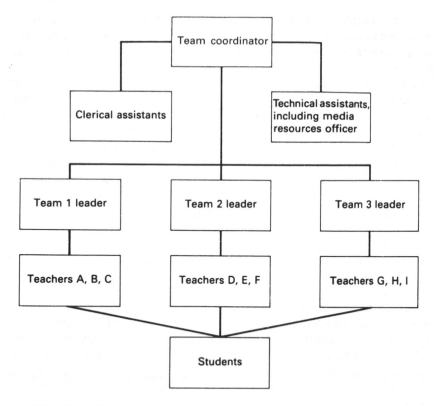

Figure 27.2   Coordinated team structure.

members. Appropriate general and specific objectives couched, perhaps, in behavioural terms (see Chapter 13), are considered. The team then meets under its leader/coordinator to decide on the final version of objectives. (This is essentially a planning matter.)

The stage which follows is of particular importance and is characteristic of team teaching. The team's agreed objectives are used so as to pose a series of questions: 'Which of the objectives can best be attained by a large-group presentation?' 'Which by smaller groups?' 'Which by students working on their own?' The first type of objective may necessitate instruction given to the group as a whole; the second may involve lessons and discussion; the third calls for directed private study. The team then maps out its modes of instruction on the basis of its objectives. (This is an exercise in resource allocation and structure building.)

Large-group instruction, perhaps in the form of a lecture, or a video followed by a lecture, may be used for the 'lead lesson', that is the general introduction to the course of study. It may be used, also, to end the course in the form of a 'coda', in which themes are recapitulated and the threads of discussions and lessons drawn together. Large-group instruction requires the careful preparation which should characterize a lecture (see Chapter 25) and may involve the use of a variety of audio-visual aids. 'Organizers' (see p. 104) are utilized and key-notes or summaries are usually distributed after instruction of this nature.

Small-group discussion and instruction is likely to follow on from the 'lead lesson'. Separate groups may examine the basis of the lesson in detail, work on individual projects and hear and discuss a number of specialist views on the course topic.

Directed private study may be interspersed throughout the course. Students may be advised by team members to read around a topic and to use the resources of the college library. Since the study is directed (and is, therefore, the responsibility of team members) it requires the careful allocation of library space and other facilities. It necessitates, also, assessment by team members of the results of private study. (The importance of furthering students' learning skills (see Chapter 18) often emerges clearly in a team teaching programme.)

Plans for the patterns of team teaching courses are numerous, but several tried and tested structures have emerged, some of which are mentioned below.

The 'thematic' approach

This involves one central theme which runs throughout the course, with relevant, linked topics. Thus, a team teaching project (arranged for an advanced business studies group) on 'the location of industry' has as its central theme the early specialization of production in Yorkshire and Lancashire. The historian deals with the eighteenth and nineteenth century background. The economist/social scientist gives illustrated lectures on the theory of localization and the impact on community life. The geographer (the third member of the team, and its leader) is responsible for directed private study, which involves two essays by each member of the group, selected from a list of geographical topics and related to the two counties.

The 'concentric' approach

The team arranges its syllabus of work so that, from a central thematic point, subjects 'radiate outwards'. Thus, a course on 'the English legal system' (planned by a team for an adult social studies group) takes as its central starting point 'rights and duties' which (presented as the theme of two lectures) leads on to small-group instruction on topics such as rules of law, enforcing the law, making and changing the law, and directed private study on a chosen topic related to a current issue involving legal institutions and the public. Three team members direct the course as specialist tutors in law, social studies and history.

The 'concurrently presented' thematic approach

Two or more linked themes are presented so that each member of the group is studying one of the themes in detail. The group meets as a whole on several occasions so that notes may be compared and links explored. A course on 'the history of scientific thought', for example, is planned by two science specialists and a historian around two central themes (the historian contributing to the study of both themes): 'the birth of modern science' and 'science and the growth of industry'. The students (A level science) produce a group project and individual essays. The team gives a lecture to the full group at the beginning and end of the course.

Team teaching in practice: two examples

The first example reflects the approach of *a small team* within a large department of general studies. The department was not formally committed in any way to team teaching; the impetus was provided by a group of five specialist tutors, three of whom had attended a course at a college of education on the theme of team teaching. With the support of the departmental head, meetings of the five were held for two hours each week over a period of two months and clerical assistance was provided for the tutor elected as team leader. The syllabus in economic history was studied, and a decision was taken that the team would collectively teach that section of the introduction which was stated, baldly, as 'the Industrial Revolution, causes and results'. A list of behavioural objectives was drawn up, modified during three meetings and finally made the basis of a team teaching scheme. (Planning and course structure-building were prominent at this stage.)

The lead lesson, delivered to a class of 40 students, took the form of an introductory talk (30 minutes) given by the team leader (an economist), explaining the nature of the course, the topics to be studied and the methods to be used. A second lecture took as its theme the historical context of the Industrial Revolution, which was illustrated by a video; notes were distributed at the end of the lecture. Members of the three small groups into which the class was divided were later given reading plans and lists of essay projects (to be made the basis of private study). Short reviews of the Industrial Revolution as seen by the economist, historian and geographer of the team were given to each of the groups. The entire group met together on four further occasions to hear a debate between two members of the team, to hear a taped BBC radio talk on the social results of the Industrial Revolution, to question the team members in a question-and-answer session, and to hear the team leader conclude the course with a short lecture on an argument by the historian, Hobsbawm, that the Industrial Revolution 'was not an episode with a beginning and an end ... It is still going on.'

A second example is of team teaching applied to a section of the economics syllabus dealing with problems of population. (This part of the course was also attended by geography students.) Four specialists made up the team. Following agreement on objectives, the lead lesson was given by the team leader in the form of a lecture entitled, dramatically, but pointedly: 'Was Malthus right?' The course was outlined by reference to notes distributed one week before the lecture. References to the doctrines of Malthus (an eighteenth-century demographer) were illustrated by the use of charts.

The second meeting consisted of small group discussions around points raised by the lecturer. The third meeting was used to view a video programme on world population. Directed private study sessions involved work on the calculation of net reproduction rates, population forecasts and guided projects based on this material. Further large-scale instruction consisted of formal lectures by team members on food resources, desert reclamation and the work of the United Nations. The statistician member of the team led discussions and supervised some practical work in each of the small groups on some unexpected problems which arose in the interpretation of statistics. The final session consisted of each member of the team and selected students giving their specific answers to the problem posed at the first meeting. A written examination, set collectively by the team, followed one week later.

Advantages and disadvantages of team teaching

A well-coordinated team will attempt to use the pooled, specialist interests of its members in the best possible way – a considerable advantage of this mode of instruction. The idea of responsibility for an instructional course being shared among a number of specialists may be novel, but ought not to be rejected on that ground alone. There seems to be a distinct possibility, in such a situation, of members of the team learning from one another, of the widening of student horizons and the growth of a collective sense of purpose. Students may benefit from participation in a variety of teaching situations and exposure to several specialist styles of tuition and groupings of resources.

On the other hand, the demands on staff are said to be much heavier than those of the conventional teaching situation. (Apologists for team teaching do not deny this, but point in reply to the *raison d'être* of the technique – a more effective mode of teaching which, they claim, must inevitably involve greater effort.) The large student groups which meet for the lectures in team teaching programmes are said to be difficult to control as units and, in any event, the lecture is often an ineffective mode of instruction. (Apologists will cite, in reply, the positive effects of the carefully prepared and presented lecture.) The special arrangements of teaching space necessitated by the practice of team teaching are said to present many difficulties. (If the principle of the team be accepted, reply its supporters, few of these difficulties will prove insuperable.) The resources necessary for team teaching, it is contended, may be beyond the budgets of many colleges. (This, unhappily, may often be true but it does not weaken the case for the principle of team teaching.) It is claimed that team teaching can function efficiently only by the use of complex administrative techniques, particularly in relation to timetable construction, and this may result in the creation within the department of staffing and structural problems. (That this is an inevitable outcome may be questioned, given the experiences of teams which have functioned successfully without any radical alteration of departmental structure.) Some reports suggest that problems have arisen in teaching teams because of interpersonal strains and general incompatibility of some members of staff. It has been suggested also that there are difficulties in bringing teachers to accept that, as part of teams, they no longer enjoy total autonomy in 'their' classrooms. Further, there is evidence to suggest that team teaching may be unproductive in some subject areas in which large groups generally show many individual differences in ability, for example in mathematics, thus making a common team approach very difficult.

Team teaching is rarely advocated as a cure-all remedy. That there is room for experimentation in the organization and deployment of teaching resources ought not to be denied. What is needed, however, is more information on the level of student attainment in those colleges in this country in which teaching has been carried out by organized teams. Data of this nature would form a useful basis for the continuing discussions on methods of improving the efficiency and effectiveness of staffs in our colleges. What must be remembered, perhaps above all, is that, in Taylor's words, 'the most important resources for team teaching are sustained energy, insight and commitment on the part of the innovators'.[6]

Notes and references

1. See generally for this chapter: *Team Building with Teachers* by J. Chivers (Kogan Page, 1995); *Team Teaching Resources* (MCB, 1985); *Team Teaching in Action* by M. Blair and R. Woodward (Houghton Mifflin, 1970); *Team Teaching* by D. Warwick (ULP, 1971); *Papers on Team Teaching* ed. T. Dudley-Evans (SEAMO Regional Language Centre, Singapore, 1985).
2. See 'Team teaching' by J.L. Trump in *Visual Education* (1966, *11*).
3. 'Team teaching in physics at a college of further education' by T. Joyner in *Vocational Aspects of Education* (1977, *29*).
4. *The Open University Opens* by W.Van der Eyken (Routledge, 1974).
5. On the problem of class size, see *The Management of Learning* by I.Davies (McGraw-Hill, 1971).
6. *Team Teaching Experiments* ed. M. Taylor (NFER, 1974).

Chapter 28

The Selection and Utilization of Audio-Visual Aids

> The selection, orchestration, and delivery of stimulation by means of various sources comprise a large portion of the decisions the teacher must make every day ... The ultimate guide to decisions about the sources of instructional stimulation is the learning objective (Gagné, 1983).

The object of using audio-visual material ('instructional media') in the classroom is the planned communication of information incidental to the total teaching process.[1] Selected and used skilfully – 'the right aid at the right time in the right place in the right manner' – audio-visual aids (AVA) can multiply and widen the channels of communication between teacher and class. Used at random or unskilfully, so that they dominate or distort, rather than assist the instructional process, or without careful consideration of their effect on the attainment of objectives, they can generate sufficient 'noise' (see p. 144) to render communication channels ineffective. The purpose of AVA, the selection of appropriate AVA, the questions which should be asked and answered before they are selected, and some AVA generally available are considered below.

'Media' have been defined by Reiser[2] as 'the physical means by which an instructional message is communicated'. In more formal terms, Gagné uses the following definition of media: 'whatever combination of things or systems of things used to deliver communications or other instructional stimuli to the learner'. Media have been classified broadly[3] as 'criterion' (e.g. maps, pictures), which the learner may have to describe or identify to show that he or she has attained the learning objective, or 'mediating', which have as their function the assisting of the learner by lending insight to an event. The former may require repeated use; the latter may be 'faded' and removed as learning emerges and grows.

Fleming[4] suggests, in relation to the choice of media, that any instructional situation must provide for four learner needs: *stimulation* (selectivity, novelty, etc.), *order* (organization of concepts), *strategy* (mental imagery and elaboration), and *meaning* (meaningfulness and feedback). The utilization of AVA should be related directly to those needs.

The effective use of AVA involves consideration of the purposes of instruction in systems terms (see p. 286). Essentially, AVA function as *input*; their use involves management-type decisions relating to the system as a whole, so that the *purpose and intended outcome* of the AVA require examination. AVA are no more than means to a pre-planned instructional end: the *end* is determined by the instructional objectives; the *means* reflect a considered choice as to the path which will lead to the objectives. AVA ought to be selected and utilized so that the role of the teacher in relation to communication is assisted.

The purpose of AVA

A class acquires knowledge and skills as the result of the assimilation of responses elicited by those stimuli which create sensory impressions. The concept of instruction which is based on the teacher relying solely on his or her voice and personality stems from the belief that communication is best achieved through the medium of sound. The use of AVA in a lesson is based on the consideration of communication as related to *all the senses*; the task of the teacher in providing the appropriate stimuli for desired responses can be *facilitated* by being able to engage the student's senses of hearing, seeing, touching, etc. A verbal description of the River Ganges is strengthened by a short film showing its stretches; a textbook diagram of an economy's income flow takes on added meaning when a class is confronted with a working hydraulic model made from transparent pipes, illustrating by analogy the interconnections and flows of the constituents of the national income.

Because the real thing (an object or process) which is the subject matter of the lesson is unavailable, inaccessible, inconvenient or impossible to handle, or because its essential characteristics can be shown only with difficulty or not at all, AVA may be employed to provide effective substitutes.[5] Films, three-dimensional models, characteristic sounds and enlarged microphotographs, for example, can be integrated into a teaching strategy involving the supplementation of verbal explanation, the focusing of class attention, the stimulation and maintenance of interest, and the promotion of retention of information.

AVA need to be considered neither, on the one hand, as frills ('optional extras') to a lesson nor, on the other hand (and in spite of the claims of their most ardent champions) as the basis of a 'total teaching technology' which may render the class teacher unnecessary. As 'mediating instruments' assisting students to achieve understanding, as components of a teaching situation requiring a combination of instructional techniques, their value is beyond doubt. The use of aids such as the overhead projector or closed circuit television can result in the enrichment and intensification of student learning, improvement in perception, assimilation and retention of learned material, the promotion of transfer of learning and the widening of the boundaries of insight. But a clear analysis is needed of the *total situation* in which they are to be used.

Choice of AVA: some general models

Several models for the selection of AVA have been developed, each suggesting matters which the instructor should consider when presented with a choice of media. We summarize below a group of models based on the fundamental rule of media selection – choice must be made on the basis of potential for implementation of instructional objectives.

Gerlach[6] sets out the criteria to be applied to the process of selection after the teaching objectives are specified and the students' 'entering behaviour' (i.e. prerequisite knowledge) is identified. These criteria are: cognitive appropriateness (can the proposed medium send to the learner the specific stimuli required by the lesson objective?); level of sophistication (will the pattern of communication be understood by the learner to whom the AVA are presented?); cost (will the result justify the real cost?); availability; technical quality.

Knirk[7] calls for the development and specification of instructional objectives, an evaluation of available resources, the matching of objectives, strategies and media characteristics, following which the detailed learning system should be specified. He emphasizes the importance of noting the *domains* of the planned instructional outcomes: cognitive, motor and affective domains require specific types of AVA.

Davies[8] suggests that the instructor take into account the lesson plan he has prepared, the size of the class, the level and background of students. The AVA selected should be simple and relevant (and should be used only where necessary). The nature of what is to be learned and the structural properties of the learning task will also enter into determination of the choice of media.

Gagné[9] notes the significance in selection of AVA of the *characteristics of the learning task* (e.g. motor skills will demand the use of media allowing for the practising of skills and the presentation of immediate, informative feedback). The *physical attributes of the media* (e.g. their capacity to present good visual displays) must be considered. Finally, *learner variables* (environment, preferred learning styles) should be allowed for. 'The primacy of selecting media based on their effectiveness in supporting the learning process is vital for the instructional process *as a whole*.'

Romiszowski suggests that two types of media characteristic be investigated when media are considered for instructional purposes. *Essential media characteristics* are related directly to *clarity* of presentation; thus, the choice of media for instruction in complex manual skills involves a consideration of the visual presentation of the overall skill and its sub-routines. *Optimal media characteristics* are those which concern the *quality* of presentation, e.g. attractiveness to students and links with the instructor's preferred patterns of teaching skills.

Aspects of the use of AVA

The class teacher who is contemplating the use of AVA should have in mind certain questions:

1. 'Does the attainment of my lesson objectives really require the employment of any AVA?'
2. 'What is the precise matter to be learned and how may the probability of learning be heightened by the use of AVA?'
3. 'What are the specific properties of the AVA which will enable me to utilize them so as to attain the required lesson objectives?'
4. 'What particular responses do I require from the use of AVA – e.g. comprehending, consolidating, remembering?'
5. 'What prerequisite knowledge is required from the class if they are to benefit from the AVA?'
6. 'How is the class likely to respond to the AVA?'
7. 'Can the presentation be adapted to student responses?'
8. 'How shall I evaluate the effectiveness of the AVA?'

Unless the behavioural changes which the teacher seeks to bring about are hastened, intensified or consolidated by the use of AVA, he or she may be well advised not to use them. Unless the teaching strategy which is appropriate at a given stage requires the transmission of information in a mode beyond the natural capacities of the teacher, AVA are unlikely to be of value.

The skills instructor, for example, must analyse course content in terms of concepts and tasks, the mastery of which constitutes criterion performance. If an aid is needed to demonstrate and assist the attainment of mastery skills, the various AVA available in the college should be considered, each in turn, in the light of the questions: 'What type of aid is best suited to the purpose of evoking the specific responses necessary at this stage of skills learning?' 'How can this aid be utilized so that the class may benefit from its specific nature?'

Gagné suggests that the use of AVA contributes effectively to the growth of *specific learning capabilities*. Intellectual skills are enhanced by the capacity of visual aids to stimulate the recall of prerequisite skills and to add cues for the retrieval of newly learned skills. Cognitive strategies are assisted in their growth by a variety of visual aids adding cues for the transfer of strategies to novel circumstances. Images used in instruction broaden and add detail to context in which fresh information has been embedded. Motor skills can be improved by the presentation of images encoding 'executive routines and subroutines'. Attitudes are broadened by the skilful use of human models (as represented, for example, in films) and pictorial information in which those attitudes are encoded.

Gagné's analysis[10] leads him to suggest in specific terms that the *exclusion* of some types of media be considered in relation to learning outcome.

1. Where the learning outcome is intended to be the enhancement of intellectual skills or the development of cognitive strategies, media lacking the capacities for affecting learner interaction and *immediate feedback* should be excluded.
2. Where the learning outcome is intended to be a heightening of verbal information, media which cannot present such information and *its elaboration* should be excluded.

3. Where the learning outcome is intended to involve the motor skills, media which do not provide for learner response and *swift feedback* should be excluded.

Types of AVA

Some of the most frequently used aids are discussed briefly below.

The chalkboard

The ubiquitous chalkboard, one of the oldest, cheapest and probably the most used of visual aids, remains the class teacher's stand-by. It is particularly useful for building up maps, graphs and diagrams, for recording the key phrases and important definitions in a lesson or lecture, for building the scheme of a lesson as it unfolds, for recapitulating and summarizing, and for recording impromptu matter. A word or sentence recorded on the board provides an emphasis which may be lacking in the spoken, hopeful, imperative: 'Don't forget this!' or 'Pay special attention to this . . .!' The size of the board is important; it should be large enough to allow the layout of a lesson summary in its entirety.

As the result of experiments in visual perception in the classroom, the erstwhile 'blackboard' now appears in a variety of shades and is imprinted with an even greater variety of coloured chalks. White chalk on a black surface is the most widely used combination, but some teachers prefer yellow chalk on a green surface, which is said to provide an unusually clear effect. Dark blue chalk on primrose yellow is another favoured juxtaposition of colours which is claimed to produce high clarity. Whiteboards and felt-tipped coloured markers are used in some college classrooms, but difficulties of erasure (because of the penetration of coloured inks) make special erasers necessary.

Perhaps because of the very simplicity of the chalkboard, it is often used inadequately. Chalkboard writing, which must be large and legible, and which necessitates careful spacing of words and lines, requires practice. The building up on a chalkboard of notes, or the main topics of a lesson, so that space is uncrowded and important points are emphasized, demands exercise. Cut-outs, templates, the prior preparation of diagram outlines by the use of thinly pencilled lines, can assist the teacher in using the chalkboard to its best advantage.

Charts and models

Charts (i.e. prepared permanent displays) may be used to illustrate, emphasize and supplement verbal comment. They can be designed to clothe an abstraction with greater meaning (e.g. a visual illustration of the components of a free market, or the human family tree), to present factual data or comparative information in the form of graphs, pie-charts and histograms, to focus attention on the characteristics of an object (e.g. the structure of the human skeleton). Used in workshops and laboratories they can act as operational guides, stating factual data and illustrating handling methods and safety rules. Charts clamped together at the top and fixed to a chalkboard can be used in a 'flip sequence' to illustrate the structure of a topic or to summarize in a stage-by-stage fashion.

The most useful charts are often those which are simple and clearly set out and which concentrate on a few points only. Colour contrasts are important and experimental evidence suggests that schemes combining blue, green and red, or blue, orange and red, have high 'attention value' when used in the construction of charts.

Three-dimensional models are valuable where it is inconvenient or impossible to see or use the real thing, or where students might experience difficulty in comprehending a two-dimensional diagram, for example as where interior views are required, or the shape of an object is too complex for adequate illustration on a page or chart, or much detail is needed for the complete communication of a concept, such as the working of a machine. The enlarged working model of a micrometer is often used in the introductory phases of lessons designed to instruct in the functions of its working parts.

Radio

In recent years national broadcasting organizations have transmitted an excellent series of sound programmes intended for students in further education. Produced with skill and with insight into the needs of their target population, the programmes have ranged widely and have been heard regularly by large audiences in many colleges. (There is research which indicates, however, that mere listening to a broadcast does not necessarily lead to learning: few listeners take in more than 30 per cent of the content of a radio talk.) Integration of the programme with departmental timetables and with the course tutor's objectives and teaching strategy is important. The timing of programmes requires careful attention – a problem which can be overcome to a large extent by the recording (with permission) of broadcasts.

The broadcast is best utilized as a teaching aid where it is preceded by an introduction from the teacher which explains its purpose and its place within the instructional scheme and where it is followed by a recapitulation given by the teacher and by use of specially produced subject booklets. Used merely as a 'fill-in', unrelated to previous knowledge and attainment, it can become an irrelevancy. Used in aid of a planned scheme of work, backed by supplementary visual material, it can provide a stimulus for the student's imagination and a widening of his or her horizons.

Tape recordings

The tape recorder, which has revolutionized the techniques and processes of sound recording, works on the principle of imprinting magnetic variations on a tape to produce electric variations which can be amplified and converted into sound relayed through a loudspeaker. The tapes can be erased, thus providing an aid which, like the chalkboard, can be used repeatedly at a low cost.

Tapes can be edited by cutting, erasing and splicing, so that sound stimuli can often be made to approximate very closely to those desired by the teacher. Instant playback and instant erasure provide flexibility of control, while the use of multi-track facilities allows the mixing of sounds. Prepared tapes may allow students to hear the views of authoritative speakers, thus adding the impact of direct sound stimuli to those presented by the printed page.

Tape recordings have been used successfully in the teaching of languages – in particular for the difficult preparatory stages of pronunciation – and in workshops, where recorded instructions on the handling of a lathe, for example, can be programmed so that the learner, to whom the sound is relayed through earphones, can play back parts of the tape and work at his or her own pace. In motor vehicle repair classes the recorder can be used to play back the sound of mechanical faults to students learning diagnostic and remedial techniques. Recordings can be used in conjunction with visual material so that an 'automated' presentation is made possible.

As with all other aids the effective use of the tape recorder demands careful planning. Its real value derives from its ability to augment visual with auditory stimuli. Used in a casual manner its impact declines and diminishing returns set in very quickly. (Tapes used in conjunction with workbooks have been found useful for revision and review.)

The language laboratory

This apparatus allows master tape recordings (usually of language drills and phrase construction) to be used so that a student may imitate what he or she hears, listen to a playback of his or her voice and enter upon a two-way discussion with the tutor. The laboratory attempts to create the conditions under which a language might be learned with speed. The learner is allowed to work continuously, at his or her own pace, on material selected to suit his or her standard of knowledge, and to receive individual attention from the teacher. Practice in listening and pronunciation is emphasized. Comprehension and assimilation of idiom are said to be heightened as a result of language laboratory presentations in which auditory and visual material are linked. But 'leaps' in the pace of acquisition of the structure of a language do not emerge automatically from the use of devices of this nature: aptitude, intelligence and perseverance remain essential qualities in language learning. The language laboratory has provided effective aid in the presentation of linguistic drills; its value in relation to the wider problems of meaning and communication remains, as yet, unclear.[11]

Films and videos

Although the viewing of films and videos as entertainment has now become for many a commonplace event of little or no significance, the film and video properly used in the classroom can be a powerful teaching aid, capable of bringing into the teaching situation a wide range of stimuli (including, in particular, the presentation of current affairs), of assisting in the realization of objectives in the affective domain (see Chapter 14), and of aiding the acquisition of those skills and techniques included in the psychomotor domain (see Chapter 14). In the influencing of attitudes, the intensification of interest and, possibly, the increase in the retention of learned material, the film and video may be highly effective.[12]

Because use of film and video necessitates the teacher handing over his or her active role (since, unlike the situation in which most AVA are employed, the teacher 'disappears from view' and, therefore, must abandon class control during the showing of the film), preplanning is of unusual importance. Choice of appropriate film from among the very large numbers now available is the first planning task. The teacher should answer the following questions in relation to the film or video he or she wishes to select:

1. 'What is its educational purpose?'
2. 'Has it any behavioural objectives and, if so, are they clear?'
3. 'How does it relate to the syllabus and to the objective I wish to achieve?'
4. 'Does it assume, and build on, the previous knowledge of the class?'
5. 'Is its content accurate, up-to-date, well-organized and well-presented?'
6. 'Is the commentary comprehensible and appropriate?'
7. 'Is the sound track clearly recorded?'
8. 'Is its length appropriate?' (30–45 minutes seems to be a maximum time for assimilation.)
9. 'What instructional method (if any) does it employ?'
10. 'Will the class find it interesting?'
11. 'Might it act as a "trigger", generating useful discussion?'

When the film has been selected the teacher may consider that its value as an AVA could be improved if it were to be divided into sequences spaced, perhaps, by recapitulations and tests. In that case careful study of the timing of the film's sequences would be required.

The rearrangement of the classroom (where the college has no separate projection room) is an important part of the planning. Seating and ventilation must be considered, the projector and screen positioned carefully and attention given to the placing of the loudspeaker which should be, preferably, below or behind the screen. Equipment ought to be checked in detail before the showing.

The film and video ought to be introduced and its objectives noted on a flipchart and explained by the teacher. In some cases, where time allows, the film can be shown twice, the second showing following a class discussion of its main points. During the second showing, the sound commentary might be switched off, so that teachers can provide their own, emphasizing the important points of the film or video, restoring their control of the instructional situation and relegating the film or video to its true position as an AVA. (The film or video can – all too easily – become the lesson.) Follow-up study of the film is essential in the form of discussion, recapitulation or test (on prepared questions which can be shown on a flipchart, thus acting as a guide to important points to be noticed).

The advantages of the film and video ought not to be forgotten. They can undoubtedly translate abstract thought into comprehensible, visual terms and, by the use of techniques such as slow motion, close up, and cutting can focus class attention in a unique fashion. Their value as AVA with large groups is considerable. Above all, they bring into the classroom a variety of stimuli presented in an expert and attractive way, thus facilitating the learning process when they are integrated into an overall lesson pattern.

Disadvantages include their association with the relaxed atmosphere which tends to surround the film as a mode of entertainment. The showing of a film or video will not automatically guarantee motivation or attention. Lack of active class participation and the loss of teacher control over the pace of presentation of information can be guarded against, to some extent, by careful planning, the use of attention-directing devices, recapitulation and testing so that the impact of the film or video as an AVA shall be as effective as possible.

Overhead projector

One of the most popular and versatile visual aids is the overhead projector. Little technical attention is required and recent innovations have produced compact, portable machines which project excellent still images free from distortion in rooms requiring no blackout or projection screens (light-coloured walls being quite adequate).

The projector may be used as a 'chalkboard', the teacher writing with a special pen or pencil directly on to an acetate roll, so that the script is projected in magnified form as it is being written. The roll can be cleared and used again. Pre-drawn diagrams can be shown, blank maps can be projected and filled in as the lesson progresses, and recapitulations and prepared summaries, lecture headings (with space for detailed notes), silhouettes and objects such as transparent protractors can be shown with great clarity. In some cases polaroid moving diagrams and 'shapes' of experiments (e.g. on the electrolysis of water) can be projected.

Transparencies in many colours[13] can be borrowed from AVA libraries or can be prepared by the teacher using photographic methods, heat process techniques, dyeline copying or xerography. 'Books' of transparencies can be put together and used on the projector as flip-charts, to illustrate a sequence. (Some microcomputers are able to produce transparencies from designs built up on the video display unit.)

Techniques such as 'overlay' (where additional transparencies are used to superimpose detail on a prepared outline) or 'reveal' (where parts of a diagram are covered by small pieces of paper attached by tape, which are removed to build up detail as required) help in those modes of instruction based on concept analysis in particular. Working models fixed to a perspex plate and constructed from simple metal strips can be projected so that a class may observe elementary mechanical processes.[14]

Transparencies should be simple, their content concise and uncluttered with detail. (In particular, they should *not* consist of printed pages from a textbook: the content of a transparency of this type can rarely be assimilated by a class.) Practising teachers draw attention to some aspects of learner attention which are of immediate relevance to the presentation of visual stimuli, such as overhead projector transparencies: attention is highly selective, so that the impact of the transparency should be powerful; attention is usually drawn to what is novel or different; simple, sparse displays focus attention; realism *per se* seems not necessarily essential for presentations of this type; in relation to the sequencing of transparencies, what occurs in the initial and final units of a display may exercise a disproportionate effect on learning.

Daylight projection and easy control are important advantages of the overhead projector. Even more important is the fact that teacher control of the class is not lost – a fully darkened room is unnecessary and the teacher can face the class while controlling the projector. Thus the apparatus remains an aid and does not at any stage in its use take over the lesson.

The microprojector

This apparatus projects microscope slides and live microscopic material, so that an entire class can view what is usually visible through the eyepiece of a microscope. The need for a large number of costly microscopes is reduced and teacher control, which is not always easy where each member of a group is working with his or her own microscope, remains effective. As a means of providing certain types of visual aids for lessons in hygiene, biology, textile analysis and testing, the microprojector is unequalled.

Television

Uncritical home-viewing habits and the emergence of TV as an entertainment medium may have dulled the educational impact of a wonderful technological achievement. The earlier fears of the replacement of live teachers by a television screen in each classroom have given way to anxieties that the power of TV has not been exploited fully in schools and colleges. All too often the TV programme emerges as a mere intermission or 'audio-visual wallpaper', apparently unrelated to the syllabus or wider educational demands.

Because class teachers are generally unable to preview educational TV programmes, difficulties arise in evaluating their suitability. The guidance notes and leaflets which explain the nature of the programme are often of a high quality but provide no substitute for previewing. Nor are the objectives of the programmes always made clear. Timing of programmes may present a difficulty for timetabling and may necessitate recording.

Many teachers and classes, however, have derived benefit from the wide-ranging and imaginative TV programmes which have been presented in recent years. (At a more advanced level the Open University TV transmissions – often intended as complete lectures – have aroused much enthusiasm.) Where the programme is integrated into a systematic lesson scheme, that is where its presentation is not allowed to dominate an instructional sequence, its impact can be remarkable. The sense of immediacy which is conveyed by television's ability to bring important events into the classroom can be heightened by pre- or post-programme discussions. A scheme of 'introduction by the teacher/TV programme/discussion/lesson based on the programme/test and evaluation', or some similar sequence, can result in a valuable learning pattern in which TV plays a vital role as a learning aid.

Gagné draws attention to the significance of TV by stressing its motivational value and its importance in the 'apprehending phase' of learning (see p. 72) during which it can gain and control the learner's attention. In the 'acquisition phase' (see p. 72) it can provide systems for the coding of concepts and rules and can provide comprehensible contexts for the learning of new information.

As with the use of the film, TV requires a carefully arranged room and timetable. The optimum viewing period for educational programmes seems to be 25–35 minutes so that, where broadcasts can be recorded for later viewing, the breaking of programmes into sequences, divided by discussions or recapitulation periods, is advantageous.

Closed Circuit TV

Closed Circuit TV (CCTV) has become a fast-developing teaching aid. It is essentially no more than a process whereby TV signals are received by private receivers only. It is used, therefore, within colleges to relay, say, a laboratory experiment to groups in a number of classrooms or, within cities, to relay programmes from an education authority's TV studio to its schools and colleges.

The basic equipment of CCTV within the college consists of a TV camera, monitoring and viewing equipment and cable connections. Extra equipment such as zoom lenses and vision mixers allows more imaginative programmes to be designed and produced. Programmes can be recorded and repeated on different days of the week, thus assisting the timetabling of day-release classes in which TV material is used.

One of the dangers of the extended use of CCTV is that it could replace vital practical experience and reduce teacher-student contact. It is indeed valuable for classes scattered throughout a college or city to be able to view on TV an experiment carried out by a team of experts in a central laboratory. It would be a retrograde step, however, if the viewing were to be regarded as a substitute for active class participation in a programme of practical experiments.

Research into AVA

Gagné has noted that the most important function of AVA is 'to make possible *alternate modes of communication in the delivery of instruction*'. Research into the delivery of instruction by means of AVA has been wide but generally inconclusive. Some findings seem to suggest that students can and do learn from the use of AVA, but that the rate and lasting quality of what is learned may be related directly to enhancement by class tutors and to repeated exposure to the media. Research suggests the superiority of visual media over auditory presentations (which, apparently, are not always readily comprehended by some less able students). Clark, in 'Reconsidering research on learning from media' (1983),[15] notes that AVA are no more than channels for instruction, and, *in themselves*, do not have any effect on the level of learning outcome. A further feature which has emerged clearly from research is the relationship between the pictorial representation of information and remembering. Hilgard and Bower[16] cite experiments suggesting that such representation tends to facilitate retention and retrieval of information by factors of 1.5 to 3. Paivio's research findings[17] are based on the so-called 'dual-trace hypothesis', which postulates two different forms of representation, the 'verbal' and the 'imaginal'. If a word is to be remembered, a memory trace enters the student's verbal store; if it is a 'concrete' word (rather than abstract), nodes in his or her imaginal system are activated, so that the student 'sees' a corresponding image, and a memory trace is laid down in the imaginal system. The double traces assist in prolonging memory and – so research appears to imply – the imaginal trace survives after the verbal trace has disappeared. It is reasonable to infer, therefore, that visual aids used in instruction produce traces that might be more resistant to the processes of forgetting.

If the full impact of AVA is to be realized, then, according to researchers, clear introductions to those parts of instruction during which the more advanced types of AVA (such as television and video material) are used, statements of the general purpose and specific objectives of the presentation, summaries and recapitulations of what has been seen and heard appear to be essential. The training of college staff in the principles, preparation, selection and utilization of a wide range of AVA as planned and controlled input to an instructional system should contribute to this end.

Notes and references

1. See generally for this chapter: *Selecting Media for Instruction* by R.A. Reiser and R.M. Gagné (Educational Technology Publications, 1983); *Instructional Technology* by F.G. Knirk (Holt, Rinehart & Winston, 1986); *The Selection and Use of Instructional Media – A Systems Approach* by A. Romiszowski (Wiley, 1988); *Handbook of Educational Technology* by F. Percival and H. Ellington (Kogan Page, 1988).
2. *Op. cit.*
3. See *Management of Learning* by I. Davies (McGraw-Hill, 1971).
4. 'Displays that communicate' in *Industrial Technology: Foundations* ed. R.M. Gagné (Lawrence Earlbaum, 1987).
5. There is no substantial evidence suggesting that 'realistic' materials induce learning, or that 3-D models are particularly advantageous. In many cases, simple line diagrams or drawings will suffice to indicate essentials and relationships. For an example, see the excellent line drawings and diagrams by R. Miller, which illuminate with remarkable clarity some of the complex concepts in the text of Stephen Hawking's *A Brief History of Time* (Bantam Books, 1989).
6. *Teaching and Media* by V.S. Gerlach (Prentice-Hall, 1980).

7. *Instructional Technology* (Holt, Rinehart & Winston, 1986).
8. *Op. cit.* (1971). See also 'Audiovisual aids' in *Instructional Technique* by I. Davies (McGraw-Hill, 1981).
9. *Op. cit.* (1987).
10. 'Selecting and using media' in *Principles of Instructional Design* (Holt, Rinehart & Winston, 1988).
11. Skinner was convinced that 'almost all language laboratories still work in particularly outmoded ways': 'The shame of American education' in *American Psychologist* (1984, 9).
12. Gagné points out that the addition of pictures to verbal instruction enables the learner to 'encode' the events of instruction as 'specific retrievable images'. The learning of motor skills, in particular, is assisted by a pictorial sequence of actions and subroutines: *The Conditions of Learning* (Holt-Saunders, 1985).
13. Schramm noted, in *Big Media, Little Media* (Sage, 1977), that some research indicated that the use of colour does not improve instructional efficiency except where it is a vital factor of what has to be learned.
14. See *Producing Teaching Materials* by H. Ellington (Kogan Page, 1985).
15. *Review of Educational Research* (1983, *53*(4)).
16. *Theories of Learning* (Prentice-Hall, 1981).
17. *Imagery and Verbal Processes* (Holt, Rinehart & Winston, 1971).

Chapter 29

Programmed Instruction and Computer-aided Learning

An educated work force learns how to exploit new technology, an ignorant one becomes its victim (Stonier, 1981).

Programmed instruction (PI) made its appearance in Britain in the 1960s. Drawing on principles based on the work of Skinner (see Chapter 6), advocates of PI claimed that the presentation of highly structured lesson material to an individual student in a carefully prearranged sequence, and at a pace determined by his or her responses, could help in overcoming some of the deficiencies of instruction associated with conventional classroom teaching, the most serious of which was perceived as the lack of swift and continuing feedback (see p. 151). Unfortunately, PI was presented, in its early stages, through the medium of expensive, often unreliable, 'teaching machines'. Additionally, the claims of programmers were often couched in an alien, rebarbative phraseology which antagonized teachers. The PI movement faltered and collapsed under the weight of unsubstantiated claims to have revolutionized instruction. The teaching machine has disappeared from most colleges of further education.

However, the main techniques of PI remain in a variety of forms. They can be very valuable for teachers, since, to construct a program (formerly 'programme') is to see, perhaps as never before, the real foundations upon which one's personal teaching is based. PI techniques continue to be used in a number of college courses. In industrial training PI is used on a wide scale. Some of the world's largest airlines, for example, use PI as a component of skills training for pilots. Two of the most widely used types of PI, linear and branched, are discussed below.

Computer-aided learning (CAL), which burgeoned with the appearance in the 1980s of the relatively cheap and highly versatile microcomputer, is linked to the rapid and extraordinary development of information technology (IT) which, in the words of one commentator, 'has outpaced the ability of teachers to evaluate it properly'. The sustained growth of IT and CAL appears to be limitless, reflecting boundless human ingenuity in the expansion of electronic technology. It would seem to promise well for the enhancement of instructional technology. In Clark's words: 'It seems that each new technological development for storing and delivering information rekindles the hope that we will increase learning outcomes ...'. The general contribution of CAL to the teaching-learning process is considered in the second part of this chapter.[1] (For a discussion of the significance of the variety of acronyms used in this area e.g. CAL, CAI, CAM, CBE (computer-based education), ITS (intelligent tutoring systems), see Levy (1997).)[1] It has been suggested that the acronym CAI (computer-aided instruction) is preferred in the USA, where emphasis is placed on the focus of 'instruction', and that CAL is preferred in Britain, where emphasis is given to the significance of 'learning' in the computer-assisted process.[2])

Skinner's theories and the 'linear' program

In 1954 Skinner published his seminal article, 'The science of learning and the art of teaching'. His earlier book, *Science and Human Behaviour* (1953), and later articles on teaching machines completed the theoretical foundations of programmed instruction. Skinner applied his reinforcement learning theory (see Chapter 6) to the process of self-instruction. A learner's actions which are reinforced are likely to be repeated and learned; actions which are not followed by reinforcement will tend to disappear from the learner's repertoire. *Behavioural learning patterns may, therefore, be shaped at the will of the instructor by use of a series of controlled stimuli.*

Crowder, a psychologist and statistician, writing in the late 1950s and early 1960s, suggested modifications of Skinner's process of self-instruction. He introduced *alternative sequences* into programs which would be related to the student's responses. His types of program (which are outlined on pp. 372–3) are known as 'branching' or 'intrinsic' programs; Skinner's, as 'linear' programs.

The theory of programmed instruction suggests that effective learning can result from the presentation to an individual student of a carefully designed sequence of instructional material, eliciting responses which can be reinforced in the direction of desired behavioural capabilities. A program is, therefore, *an individual lesson, designed and presented as a sequence of relatively small units of information, which lead the student, step by step, to a level of behaviour predetermined by the programmer.*

Features of the linear program are as follows.

(a) Material is arranged in a carefully ordered sequence of very small, cumulative and coherent steps, so that the learner is not aware of any real difficulty in assimilation. ('The whole process of becoming competent in any field must be divided into a very large number of small steps, and reinforcement must be continuous upon the accomplishment of each step ... By making each successive step as small as possible, the frequency of reinforcement can be raised to a maximum, while the possibly aversive consequences of being wrong are reduced to a minimum' (Skinner).[3])

(b) The learner has to make a 'constructed response' in an overt manner (e.g. in writing) to each question arising from the material.

(c) To help the learner in his or her responses, the material includes 'cues and responses' which guide him or her.
(d) Immediately the response is made, the learner is informed whether he or she is right or wrong. The learner acts as his or her own 'response comparator'.
(e) The program (which has been empirically validated) is constructed so that a correct response will be given at least nine times out of ten. This produces satisfaction ('reinforcement') and continuous progress is made more certain.
(f) In the case of an incorrect response, the learner notes the error and moves on to the next unit of information.

A schematic representation of a typical linear program is given in Figure 29.1. The diagram outlines the *strategy* of the lesson, that is the overall steps to be taken so as to achieve the lesson's objective, which is a movement from the learner's state of minimum knowledge (in relation to what is to be learned) to the level of behaviour considered by the teacher/programmer to be desirable at that stage of the learner's development. Small units of information (represented by the numbered squares) are presented to the learner, who constructs his or her responses. The response to unit 1 is assessed and that assessment is presented to the learner before he or she responds to the stimulus of unit 2. A correct response to the nth unit is evidence of having mastered the sequence.

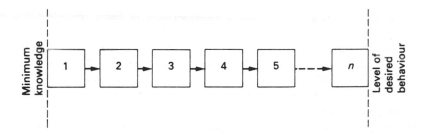

Figure 29.1   Linear instruction program.

Construction of a linear-type program

The programmer must first analyse the area of the subject matter which is to be programmed. What are its boundaries? Its difficulties? Its unusual features? Does its successful teaching necessitate a particular approach? Does it involve an explanation and illustration of technical terms? (These are, of course, among the very questions which must also be posed and answered in the preparation stages of the conventional lesson.) Secondly, the precise nature of the target population, that is the students for whom the program is to be designed, must be delineated. In this context, what relevant behaviour will be available at the start of the program? What relevant behaviour is necessary in order to enter the program? Thirdly, the criterion behaviour which should result at the end of the program should be set out clearly in behavioural terms (see Chapter 13). Fourthly, the sequence of the program and its constituent frames (i.e., separate items of information) must be structured in a coherent manner. Fifthly, the terminal test must be constructed; this ought to elicit from a student who has worked through the program the level of behaviour which the programmer considers as constituting competence in the subject area. Sixthly, the program should be validated by administering it to a representative sample of the target population. Finally, the validation should result in the program being rewritten and restructured, where that is necessary.

For an example of pioneering linear programs (in physics and psychological experimentation) see Skinner[3] and Hergenhahn.[4]

Crowder and the 'branching' program

Crowder's type of program is constructed so as to utilize the learner's responses in the determination of content and actual presentation of the material. In contrast to the linear programmer, he uses *multiple choice questions* (see Chapter 31). Programs built on this basis test the learner's understanding of the materials he or she has studied, and allow the presentation of remedial material where incorrect responses are made.

The branching program begins with a frame which usually contains much more information than that presented in a linear-type step. The information is followed by a multiple choice question. A correct response results in the learner being informed that he or she is correct (and why), and in the presentation of a new unit of information. An incorrect response results in the learner being informed that he or she is wrong (and of the nature of the error). The learner may be instructed to return to the original frame to 'try again', or may be moved on to a 'remedial sub-sequence'. It will be apparent that the amount of material with which the student is presented will be determined by the number of errors made.

A schematic representation of a branching program is given in Figure 29.2. The strategy of the program is to move the student's level of behaviour from that represented by his or her attainment at the beginning of the program, through that represented by frame 4, to the level decided by the teacher as being appropriate in the circumstances. The diagram illustrates the tactical modification of the strategy which may be necessary. A student who is entirely successful moves from frame 1 to frames 2, 3 and 4. Assume that a student makes an error on frame 2. The student will be directed to a remedial frame, 2(i) or 2(ii), depending on the nature of the error, and will be told that he or she is wrong and why. The student is then directed to return to frame 2 to try again. Assume that a mistake is made on frame 3. The remedial sequence 3(i), (ii), (iii) provides further material and allows a move on to frame 4 immediately the error is corrected. The response to the nth unit of information, if correct, indicates mastery of the material in the program.

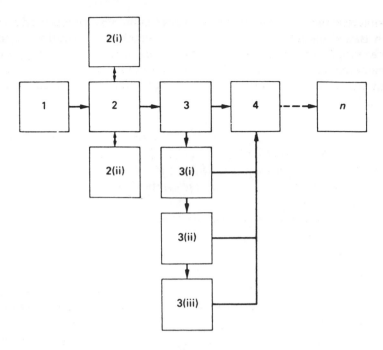

Figure 29.2 Branching instruction program.

Construction of a branching program

The initial stages of preparing a branching program resemble those involved in the linear programme. Subject matter must be analysed, concepts stated and their relationships explored. The presentation technique of the branching program, however, differs radically from that of the linear program in the following ways.

1. A branching frame usually contains more material than that a linear frame. It may consist of one, two or three short paragraphs.
2. The student responds to the material by choosing one of several alternative answers, which appears to him or her to be correct.
3. The frame to which he or she is then directed depends on the answer selected. Consequently, the student does not move straight through the programme, as in a linear sequence.

For examples of early, typical branching programs, see Crowder[5] and Romiszowski.[6]

The use of programmed instruction

The claim of the programmers is that, if a subject can be taught, it can be programmed. There is, therefore, according to this claim, no limit to the areas in which programmed instruction can be effective. It has been applied with some success to subjects as widely separated as statistics (including a widely used program dealing with Bayes' theorem), psychology, logic, economics, operational research and computer programming. Early suspicions that its techniques were appropriate only to primary school subjects have proved groundless.

Programmed instruction seems to have been effective in the following situations.

1.   The learning of a technique which, by its very nature, may be broken down into small steps, e.g. some processes in automobile engineering.
2.   The study of aspects of a subject in which there is a hierarchy of facts, which lends itself to symbolic representation, e.g. symbolic logic, operational research, mathematical economics.
3.   The revision of the outlines of a scheme of work.

In workshop instructional situations a program which is related to psychomotor objectives (e.g. the handling of a tool) can be valuable, particularly because it allows the student to learn at his or her own pace. Similar situations, such as the stripping and reassembling of a machine, have provided useful opportunities for the exercise of the programmer's skill.[7]

Criticisms of programmed instruction

Fundamental criticism continues to be levelled, in particular, at the views of Skinner as they relate to the foundations of programming. Human behaviour is too complex, it is argued, to be described only in terms of his conditioning model. Further, it has been stressed that the model on which the theory of programmed instruction is based does not allow for the high probability of there being different *kinds* of learning which follow different laws. Nor has it been established beyond doubt that confirmation of a learner's correct responses is always a reinforcement, or that learning cannot proceed successfully without swift reinforcement. In McKeachie's 'Decline and fall of the laws of learning',[8] the following comment appears: 'Research evidence on feedback in PI fails to support Skinner's position. The immediate knowledge of results has seemed in several studies to make little difference in learning or even to be detrimental.'

Leontiev[9] stated that PI tended to be concerned with instrumental *output*, while seeming to ignore the student's cognitive processes which produce the output: '[In PI] it is not the student's activity with the material that is corrected or reinforced, but only the result of that activity. Corresponding to this, only a system of influences on the student, a system demanding definite answers, is directly programmed, and not his activity directed towards securing the answers and, even less, the process of mastering this activity.'

The nature and organization of linear programs have also been under sustained attack. They have been held to lead, inevitably, to loss of interest and boredom because of their repetitious, small steps. In particular, their use at the higher levels of learning tends, it has been claimed, to induce a 'pall effect' which rapidly weakens meaningful assimilation. The inflexibility and restricted nature of programs, both linear and branching, fail, it is argued, to make allowances for individual differences in student attitudes and motivation.

The concept of the Socratic dialogue ('one to one') as the prototype of the successful lesson – often suggested as an advantage of programs – is rejected by many teachers who point to the solitary nature of programmed instruction as its major defect. The excitement and stimulation of working in a group, the social importance of assisting, and being assisted by, others, in the common pursuit of knowledge, become unattainable in the programmed lesson.

Bigge[10] has criticized the relationship of programming and 'reflective learning'; the conclusions of a program are decided in advance of the student's learning activities and, therefore, reflective learning cannot be fostered. He criticizes also the concentration on factual learning which seems to him inherent in PI: 'There is little about factual learning as such that contributes to understanding, and little about teaching for understanding in a non-reflective way that contributes to a student's reflective powers and habits'.

In a large-scale survey of experiments in programmed instruction in schools and colleges in the 1980s in the Soviet Union, Talyzina specifically criticizes the influence of Skinner on the principles of programming.[11] His linear program ignores the cognitive activities of the learner so that the probability of acquiring rational forms of 'thinking activity' is low. Nor does the linear program require any application of already developed rational activities. The size of instruction steps seems rarely to correspond to steps in knowledge acquisition; indeed, experiments seem to show that the best results in instruction were obtained where learners were left to regulate the size of their steps. The linear program confuses the reinforcement of responses and their confirmation, and experiments have suggested that substantial delays in reinforcement do not reduce the effectiveness of instruction. Further, the repetition of material (typical of Skinner's programs) does not appear, in Talyzina's survey, to yield any positive effects in instruction.

Leith (1969)[12] argued for a revision of earlier concepts of programming, with particular reference to the problem of negative motivation which appeared to characterize the reported effects of the programmed unit of instruction in some schools and colleges. He made a number of suggestions which pointed the way to a significant modification of PI.

1. The 'small step' which characterized the early Skinnerian approach often induced boredom in users of the linear program. It would be an improvement if students were allowed to take steps of the size with which they are able to cope.
2. It did not seem necessary for the success of the linear program that the student's overt responses had to be in the form of writing: the more mature students do not need to write out all their responses to a frame.
3. Skinner's repeated assertion that, in the case of a linear program, the maximum error rate ought to be no more than five per cent, ought not to determine a learner's progression through a series of frames. Indeed, mistakes may have a

positive instructional value when they lead to correction and eventual reinforcement of instruction.

4. It may be true that, in general terms, self-paced learning is valuable. But all too
    often, the pace selected by learners is much slower than that which they could
    adopt to their advantage. A program which incorporates the techniques of in-
    built pacing, so that learners move at a rate which is expected of them, is likely
    to be useful.

5. Given the rejection of the self-pacing aspect of 'classical PI', group-based PI
    becomes possible, allowing students to work together in pairs or small groups,
    often with advantage.

6. It is not essential to use only one mode of programming in a unit of instruction.
    A combination of linear and branching sequences in a unit is possible, and often
    advantageous to the learner.

(See also Skinner's *Programmed Instruction Revisited* (1986).)

Programmed instruction techniques remain a component feature of some
schemes of work in colleges of further education; its impact on industrial training has
been more pronounced. It continues to provide a useful vantage point for the
observation and analysis of some aspects of instruction. Some of its techniques, in
particular the presentation of information in carefully constructed sequential steps,
were of value in the early development of computer-aided learning, which is
considered below.[13]

Computer-aided learning: a new technology of instruction

Computer-aided learning (CAL) refers to situations in which a computer system is
used in the process of instructing students.[14] It is essentially 'learning *with* (but not
about) computers'. The computer is used in a simulated one-to-one instructional
situation; it presents an analogue of a lesson by providing stimulus information, by
'commenting' and acting on the learner's responses and (in some cases) by dealing
with the learner's additional random queries.

The growth of CAL in colleges of further education is the direct result of three
interrelated factors: the increased use of computers in industry and commerce,
reflected in an extended demand for college-based computer courses; continuing
developments (some of a very sophisticated nature) in computing techniques; and
the vast expansion in microcomputer technology, leading to a steep fall in the price
of components and the availability of cheap computer systems and software.

The range of CAL in relation to courses offered by the colleges of further
education is now very wide indeed: it embraces, for example, computer-aided
language learning, involving interactive, self-paced instruction based on a multi-
media approach; the facilities of the Internet,[15] allowing colleges to exchange
information; personalized learning programs in mathematics and the sciences, and
areas such as geography, utilizing an Ordnance Survey interactive atlas; a CD-ROM,
providing instant access to the half million entries in the twenty volumes of the
standard English dictionary; simulation databases, enabling students to visualize the

effects of their strategic thinking in relation to starting up a new business; voice-recognition software, transforming the spoken word instantaneously into words appearing on the screen; a database of past examination papers and examiners' reports, allowing teachers and students to construct realistic test papers for purposes of revision and assessment practice. IT, in the service of learning, has a versatility which surpasses the predictions made less than a decade ago.

However, problems concerning CAL persist. 'Real costs' remain high: hardware and supporting peripherals require maintenance and replacement, which can drain budgets; built-in obsolescence seems a major feature of some systems, making total replacement almost inevitable when manufacturers announce the appearance of a new 'mark' which promises 'improved capability'. The standard of software (i.e. computer programs) is notoriously variable, often utilizing instructional techniques of dubious style. Nor has CAL won general acceptance from the teaching profession: memories of teaching machine failures die hard, and some staff are unnerved by the repetition of statements such as: 'The central issue in computer ethics during the next two decades will be the replacement of human beings by computers – most probably in tasks that are thought to require judgment and wisdom'. (A recent, highly publicized statement by a leading politician, forecasting the imminent disappearance of the teaching profession which was now 'outdated and increasingly irrelevant to the demands of the new instructional technology', appeared to receive wide support.)[16] Above all, the absence of a *theory* of CAL which will seek to account for the vaunted superiority (in terms of instructional outcome) of the machine over the human instructor, makes the debate on the use of automated teaching procedures difficult to resolve.

Uses of CAL

It is now accepted by college staff that the computer, upon which CAL is based, is neither a mere automated 'textbook page-turner', nor an improved version of the teaching machine of the 1960s. It is a device which is capable of eliciting and assessing student responses to programs of instruction and of evaluating overall learning performance at prodigious speed. In total contrast to the limited, often highly-predictable, range of questions and answers provided by teaching machines, the computer is able to draw on an extensive range of material which can contain elements of randomness.

Reference is made below to some of the principal types of CAL currently in use in the colleges of further education.

Drill and practice sequences

The computer is able to present – tirelessly – long, repetitive sequences of drill questions, suitable for fundamental cognitive skill development. Basic exercises in mathematical calculations, grammar and spelling in foreign languages, equations in chemistry and taxonomic problems in botany, can be generated and presented in non-stop fashion by easily constructed programs. Errors can be checked, error rates measured and assessed, and the attention of the student can be directed by the program to obvious gaps in knowledge. Remedial sequences can be offered.

It is possible, in CAL material of this nature, for students to be allowed a high measure of control over the general processes of instruction: thus, they can select content, choose aspects of presentational form and, to an extent, can modify the learning strategy inherent in aspects of the program.[17] Where a program has been designed on the standard basis of 'present rule, provide examples, give practice', students can be allowed to control the level of presentation, can move away from the program to consult dictionaries, tables and other reference material, and can then retrace their route through the material that has been presented. It has been suggested that there are circumstances in which the learner's control of sequence might be more effective than the program control exercised by the compiler's 'optimum route'.

Problem-solving

Programs consisting of more advanced types of question can be presented, calling for the exercise of the higher skills, such as analysis and synthesis. Student responses can be analysed and patterns of response delineated and 'discussed', with the further presentation of high-order problems.

Information retrieval and browsing

Programs aimed at the higher cognitive skills (e.g. evaluation) can allow the student to 'call up', within a few seconds, outline material which can be skimmed rapidly, prior to the retrieval of more detailed information. There are effective programs of this type in areas such as intermediate economics and trigonometry, in which the student is presented with an on-screen selection of topics, from which he or she selects one or two, prior to examining detailed readings (and graphical material) on the selections.

Tutorials

A typical CAL tutorial sequence may take the following form.

1. The computer presents a unit of information to the student.
2. The computer then presents a test question and waits until the student feeds in a response through the keyboard.
3. The computer scans the student's textual response and categorizes it as correct or incorrect on the basis of predetermined 'key words' identified within it.
4. Where the student's response matches or approximates to anticipated incorrect answers, the computer offers corrective hints; where it does not recognize the

answer, it offers general hints and/or calls for a revised answer, or presents a series of randomly selected problems.

This type of program calls for a highly skilled programmer who understands the general approach of students to problems in the given subject area and is able to anticipate responses, *and the reasoning behind those responses.*

Simulation

It is in this area – based on programmed models of situations or processes reflecting real life – that CAL can excel. The complex, widespread effects of interventions in the operation of a system can be shown instantaneously. Thus, simulation programs are employed in courses dealing with company finance (to trace the knock-on effects of changes in interest rates), biology (to demonstrate the far-ranging results of pollution on ecosystems), and industrial management (to trace the effects on a control system of positive and negative feedback).

The advantages of CAL simulation are considerable. It is able to overcome the prohibitory expense of some types of experiment and field work; dangerous experiments (e.g. dropping caesium into water) can be experienced in safe conditions and impractical experiments can be 'attempted'. The time necessary for some experiments can be compressed into a very short period and levels of complexity can be heightened with relative ease (e.g. the visualization of complex molecular structure). The number of variables can be increased as students learn how to cope with simplified tasks. Disadvantages are said to include the curtailing of real experience in field and laboratory, the over-simplification of reality, and a lack of fundamental understanding if simulation is not followed by a detailed examination of the attendant problems.

Woodhouse[18] suggests that the main advantage of CAL simulation is the possibility it presents of 'enormously extending the student's range of educational experience'. In particular, he believes that it can promote a wide range of educational goals, including motivation for study, discovery learning, skills mastery and concept development.

The integrated 'personalized package'

Given an advanced type of computer installation, CAL can be used to provide an integrated instructional process, *tailored to the student*. It can present tutorial and coaching programmes, can offer '*guided investigation*', enabling the student to work through a programmed sequence, but allowing him or her to explore any side issues raised by the program, or '*free investigation*', giving the student the choice of a variety of alternative paths for the exploration of a topic, and thus allowing a measure of control over the package. Various modes of presentation of information – pictorial, graphical, verbal – can be linked by sound into a full CAL sequence.

Software design and selection

The programming of material for purposes of CAL is a specialist activity, involving a knowledge of programming languages, capabilities of the machines in use, etc. The general criteria of educational program design will be of interest to the teacher who has in mind an objective of transforming an instructional process into a CAL procedure.

General key questions must be asked and answered. What are the precise teaching objectives of the proposed program? What background curriculum material has to be worked through before the program can be utilized properly? How will the program test and evaluate student understanding? Check-lists for CAL construction abound. A typical example suggests the following guides. First, identify subject area and target audience. Next, analyse the task (purpose of program, educational objectives, necessary prerequisite knowledge) and determine the instructional strategy to be employed (drill? deductive, inductive reasoning?). Decide on the mode and style of computer-student interaction, formulate evaluation procedures. Specify the precise requirements of the program, list them in hierarchical order and set out the desired sequence of presentation. (Keith[19] suggests three phases related to the design process of software: *the pre-design phase*, involving a needs assessment and planning for overall content; *the design phase*, comprising the programming of the instruction units; *the post-design phase*, including field-testing, revision and modification of content and sequence.)

The selection of software to be used in CAL should reflect the following requirements: it must meet course objectives and should contribute more to student instruction than a textbook can; it should be constructed on sound educational principles; its instruction should be well-sequenced and capable of providing immediate feedback to users; the system ought to be capable of recording a student's progress in terms of attainment levels.

In general, the questions to be put by a prospective purchaser of CAL software should include the following: What are the precise learning objectives of the program? Where, when and by whom was it compiled? Are there any validated field test results? Is it up-to-date and factually correct? What are its implicit beliefs about student learning? What are the required levels of entry, target population and criterion behaviour at termination? Is its general approach motivating? If it uses graphics and sound, are they useful or merely distracting? Can it be integrated successfully with the overall instructional plan for the class?

Hardware selection

Choice of hardware is now very wide.[20] For those making choices for a system to be used in colleges of further education, a variety of questions needs to be asked.

Is the system of strong construction? (Appearance is relatively unimportant.) Will it withstand 'normal student usage'? What is the cost of peripherals (printers, etc.)? What languages will the machine handle? What are the costs and availability of repair facilities and replacement units? Are the instruction manuals well written and free from error? How many student terminals can be accommodated?

An extensive demonstration of the system's capabilities should be arranged for staff before a purchase is made. On such an occasion, staff should be encouraged to put forward their views on the performance and potential of the system. The views of students should be canvassed wherever this is possible.

Advantages and disadvantages of CAL

The principal advantages claimed for CAL seem to be as follows. The computer-presented program can augment the teacher's capacities and can reduce the time needed for understanding difficult concepts; it can proceed at the precise pace demanded by the student; it can offer swift and accurate feedback. It can offer a very wide range of experiences (e.g. through simulation programs); it can handle very large volumes of data and can be used diagnostically. It may elicit active participation even from the habitually passive, reluctant student. Revision and text enhancement by the use of sound and graphics are areas in which CAL has certainly proved its worth.

Disadvantages seem to emerge from the very design of CAL and the type of software which is in common use. All too often, it is claimed, it is very difficult to provide really individualized tuition: the computer is in control, presenting a fixed sequence of instruction which cannot be varied to suit the infinite capacity of students to respond to material in totally unexpected fashion. Responses by the computer to wrong answers may lack 'comprehension', so that incorrect remedial work is prescribed. (Sleeman and Brown,[21] in an early review of CAL systems, comment that instructional material presented as a response to a student's query or error is 'often at the wrong level of detail – the system assumes too much or too little student knowledge'. Existing systems, they claim, cannot discover, and hence cannot work within, a student's idiosyncratic conceptualization.) Too much drill, too much multi-choice material and a restricted, predetermined range of options in the system's answers, figure large in complaints made by student users of CAL. Boredom caused by lack of human interaction is reported by some learners who have worked through long CAL sequences. Sleeman and Brown comment unfavourably on the tutoring strategies used in many CAL systems, suggesting that they are 'excessively *ad hoc*, reflecting unprincipled intuitions about how to control student behaviour'. Finally, there is the possible emergence of undesirable side effects: a passive learning style 'making learning an instrumental rather than a meaningful activity'; and overdependence on mediated instruction as opposed to enactive learning ('Students are actively involved in the learning process, but their role is that of responder rather than initiator').

Controversy concerning the claimed advantages of CAL has been fuelled by some who fear the erosion of student interest in a 'print culture' dominated by the printed book, as the result of habituation to, and eventual reliance on, screen-presented information. In a highly critical article on the effects of the Internet, the publicist, Simon Jenkins,[22] argues that the book ('a seminal invention of modern civilisation') remains unchallenged by anything electronics has to offer. Books are more convenient than screen-presented information, have a vitality denied to electronically published material, and will certainly outlast the Internet, which will eventually take its place 'in the catalogue of lesser media'.

Views of this nature tend to be dismissed as mere manifestations of Luddite thinking. Others point to the phenomenon of increased book-reading and suggest that there are no signs among the users of the Internet, E-mail or CAL of belief in the irrelevance or obsolescence of books. (A report in *The Times* (27 March 1997) of a survey by the Policy Studies Institute, 'Cultural trends in the 1990s', notes the increased reading of books in Britain in recent years.)

Computer-managed learning

CAL is used to *guide* the learning process: in essence it renders tactical assistance to the student in progress towards a goal of his or her choosing. Computer-managed learning (CML) is different: its use results in decisions of a strategic nature concerning student learning. Typically, the computer suggests, on the basis of an initial interaction with the student, what ought to be an appropriate module of instruction to follow.

First, the learner is tested, through the medium of a computer program, on his or her knowledge of a topic. The results of the test are checked, again by the computer, stored in the learner's individual file and assessed. Deficiencies in attainment are noted, unusual attainment is recorded, and the computer is able to construct a 'student's academic profile'. It is at this stage that the computer is intervening directly in the management function of *control* (see Chapter 12). Student achievement is measured in relation to criterion attainment (based on reference to syllabus demands) and assessed in relation to course requirements as a whole. The computer will then 'suggest' how the student's learning level might be adjusted. Revision of the entire unit? Practice on selected topics? Movement to a new topic, a new module? Remedial module? Enhancement module?

The computer's recommendation, which in some CML schedules is subject to a full tutor-student discussion, constitutes, in effect, the management of the student's conditions of instruction so that efficient personalized learning is made more probable. It should be noted, however, that many CAL packages now in use contain an element of CML procedures in their early stages. Preliminary diagnosis is seen as an essential subsystem in the total system of CAL.

CAL in the future

The growth of IT and its uses in education seem restricted only by the skills of computer designers. The future promises much: distance learning, allowing isolated students instantaneous access to extensive data banks and contact by E-mail with tutors, will be among the most significant advances. Programs will become even more versatile: in the area of algorithms (step-by-step procedures intended to yield optimum solutions to problems) and heuristics (exploratory methods of problem solving), CAL programmers have produced very effective programs pointing the way towards an even higher degree of user interaction in CAL.

CAL has yet to find ready acceptance within the general ranks of a conservative teaching profession. Much more research is needed before teachers become convinced of the veracity of claims concerning the 'infinite uses' in education of computer systems. Such research will concentrate increasingly on the need for a *theory of CAL usage* reflecting, in particular, advances in our understanding of the human cognitive processes, so that 'instead of hardware controlling computer design, the science of cognition will increasingly influence hardware development'. Provision will be made, too, for the involvement of practising teachers in research. Colleges concerned with the training of teachers will include the fundamentals of IT and CAL in their schemes of work at all levels. The teacher will be viewed and acknowledged as a vital factor in the systematic teaching–learning process of which CAL will be a part. In these ways CAL will eventually win acceptance by the profession as a whole.[23]

Notes and references

1. See generally for this chapter: *The Technology of Teaching* by B.F. Skinner (Prentice-Hall, 1968); *Instructional Technology: Foundations* ed. R.M. Gagné (Erlbaum, 1987); *Introducing CAL* by P. Barker and H. Yeates (Prentice-Hall, 1990); *Computers and Learning* ed. O. Boyd-Barrett and E. Scanlon (Addison-Wesley, 1991); 'Learning from computers' by Clark in *Teachers, Computers and the Classroom* ed. I Reid and J. Rushton (Manchester UP, 1985); *Computer-assisted Language Learning* by M. Levy (Clarendon, 1997).
2. *Computers, Language Learning and Language Teaching* by K. Ahmad and G. Corbett (CUP, 1985).
3. *The Technology of Teaching* (Prentice-Hall, 1968).
4. *Introduction to Psychological Experimentation* (Brooks, 1974).
5. *The Arithmetic of Computers* (EUP, 1962).
6. *The Selection and Use of Instructional Media* (Kogan Page, 1988).
7. See *Strategies for Programmed Instruction* ed. J. Hartley (Butterworth, 1972).
8. *Review of Educational Research* (American Educational Research Association, March 1974).
9. 'Learning theory and PI' in *Readings in Educational Psychology* ed. E. Stones (Methuen, 1970).
10. *Learning Theories for Teachers* (Harper & Row, 1976).
11. *The Psychology of Learning* (Progress Publishers, 1981).
12. 'Second thoughts on programmed learning' in *The Selection and Use of Instructional Media* ed. A.J. Romiszowski (Kogan Page, 1988).
13. See discussion in *Computers and Language Learning* by M. & J. Kenning (Horwood, 1990).
14. See *Computing Tips for Teachers and Lecturers* by P. Race and S.M. McDowell (Kogan Page, 1997); *Using IT Effectively in Teaching and Learning* ed. B. Samekh (Routledge, 1997); *Computers: A History of the Information Machine* by M. Campbell-Kelly and W. Aspray (Basic Books, 1997); *Dictionary of Computing* (OUP, 1997); *Designing Interaction* ed. J.M. Carroll (CUP, 1991).
15. See *The Soul of the Internet* by N. Randall (Thomson, 1997); *College Success Using the Internet* by J. Pejsa (Houghton Mifflin, 1997).
16. In the ensuing discussion, much was made of the apocalyptic statement attributed to the

physicist, J.P. Wesley: 'Machines, being a form of life, are in competition with carbon-based life. Machines will make carbon-based life extinct.'

17. See Levy (*op. cit.*).
18. *Computers, Promise and Challenge in Education* by D. Woodhouse and A. McDougall (Blackwell, 1990).
19. 'Designing software for vocational language programs – an overview of the development process' by C.J. Keith and P.A. Lafford in *Teaching Languages with Computers: The State of the Art* ed. M.C. Pennington (Athelstam, 1990).
20. See e.g. *The Principles of Computer Hardware* by A. Clements (OUP, 1994) for an outline of hardware design rules.
21. *Intelligent Tutoring Systems* (Academic Press, 1982).
22. 'No plug, no wires, no rivals', *The Times* (4 January, 1997).
23. See e.g. *March of the Machines* by K. Warwick (Century, 1997); *The Future Does Not Compute* by S.L. Talbott (O'Reilly, 1995).

Part Six

The Assessment and Evaluation of Student Performance

Chapter 30

The Functions and Structures of Examinations

If education is to prosper, teachers and students must learn to welcome regular and systematic testing rather than to regard it as a threat, an intrusion, or a distraction from more important matters (Ausubel, 1978).

Examinations of many types loom large in the working life of the teacher in further education.[1] Most college courses are geared to internal and external examinations so that there will be few members of staff who are not involved in the assessment and evaluation of learning as examiners, assessors, or members of examining panels. Examinations in their various forms are considered in this chapter as an essential component of the system of control which was outlined in Chapter 12.

The essential task of the teacher is to facilitate student learning ... The best way to determine how much learning has occurred is to observe how successfully the student can cope with tasks that require learning; this means testing. It also means grading, for grades can provide concise, meaningful indications of the degree of a student's success in learning (Ebel, 1980).[2]

A note on terminology

The literature on the nature of examinations is not noted for consistency in the use of the specialist vocabulary employed. Terms such as 'assessment' and 'evaluation' are used in a variety of senses, often in contradictory fashion. We set out below some notes on the usage employed in this chapter.

(a) *Examination* (which is derived from *examinare* = to weigh accurately) is viewed here as the methodical testing of attainment, relating to knowledge and capabilities, by reference to agreed standards. *Test* is used as a synonym.

(b) *Assessment* (derived from *asseoir* = to set, settle) involves collecting, measuring and interpreting information relating to students' responses to the process of instruction.

(c) *Evaluation* (derived from *valoir* = to be worth) is based on assessment and appraisal. It is an essentially professional, subjective judgment on the worth or quality of an individual's development at stages in the process of instruction. Unlike assessment, which relies generally on the objective measurement of data, evaluation takes into account congruence between objectives and performance viewed in the light of values. Thus: 'Student X has scored 56 per cent of marks in his examination' (assessment); 'with consistent work, including planned revision, he should achieve credit standard in his final test' (evaluation). (Bloom[3] defines evaluation as 'the making of judgments about the value, for some purpose, of ideas, works, solutions, methods, etc. It involves the use of criteria, as well as standards, for appraising the extent to which particulars are accurate, effective, economical or satisfying'.)

(i) *Formative evaluation* takes place *during* the instructional process; its purpose is to provide feedback to teacher and learner.

(ii) *Summative evaluation* takes place after the instructional process is *almost completed*; its purpose is to show how well the instructional material has been learned.

(d) *Norm-referenced tests* are intended to discover the benefit derived by each student in a class from a unit of instruction. They are usually tests which *compare* an individual student's performance with performance of an entire group of his or her peers. The standard applied to the student's performance has to be interpreted according to the perceived performance of the class considered as a whole. 'Ranking' is typical of this kind of test. Example: 'Student A was top of his class; Student B was in the last place'.

(e) *Criterion-referenced tests* are intended to provide measurements that can be interpreted directly and accurately in terms of predetermined and specified performance standards. Has the learner 'passed' (i.e. scored more than x per cent of the total marks) or 'failed' (i.e. scored below x per cent of the total marks)? Tests of this nature refer to the attainment of requisite levels of achievement and are used frequently in diagnosis of results and guidance of students. Essentially, this type of test compares a student against a standard, rather than against other students. Example: 'Student A is considered to have passed his test' (i.e. A has achieved mastery of the task which was the object of instruction); 'Student B has failed' (i.e. he has not demonstrated the desired mastery of the task).

Examination, assessment and control

Fundamentally, the rationale of formal examinations (i.e. tests administered under controlled conditions in the colleges of further education with which this chapter is concerned) must rest on their importance for the learning process. If that process can be effective without the use of examinations, then they have little obvious value. In Chapter 12 it was suggested, however, that the management of teaching necessarily involves *monitoring and assessment*. Feedback, both to learner and teacher, was noted as being essential for the control of that process. If the teacher's role is accepted as involving the creation of conditions for effective learning, then the

regular assessment and summative evaluation of those conditions and their outcomes would seem to be necessary.

An accurate examination of the learner's *rate of progress* towards the attainment of desired learning objectives serves a number of useful purposes. It provides
the learner with incentive and knowledge of his or her achievement in relation to
those objectives, thus acting as a reinforcer and enabling him or her to take whatever
remedial action may be needed. It provides the teacher with a measurement of the
appropriateness and *effectiveness* of his or her teaching strategy, thus enabling
adjustments to be made where necessary. Therefore, an assessment which results
from the monitoring of a student's achievements during a course of instruction (see,
for example, the technique of continuous assessment) or from the measurement of a
terminal performance (as, for example, the end-of-year examination for a BTEC
National Certificate) forms an essential link in the *chain of control*, enabling the
modification of teaching programmes to attain objectives and to improve curriculum
design and presentation.

The results of formal examinations may have value, therefore, in the assessment
of attainment, the diagnosis of a learner's difficulties and the evaluation and internal
validation of courses and curricula. Another use of examination results which is
growing in importance is concerned with the prediction of a learner's future behaviour. Thus a student's marks in a first-level examination may be used to forecast
performance in an advanced-level course; a student's performance in an advanced-
type test may be accepted by some universities as a prediction of his or her likelihood
of success in a degree course. This function of examinations may help to explain in
part their importance in many colleges of further education.

A case against examinations

The principal arguments presented against examinations[4] are often not so much
attacks on the necessity of assessment (although some will argue against any formal
process of this nature), but rather against their tendency to dominate the curricula in
colleges of further education. Examinations, it is claimed, often become ends in
themselves and exercise repressive and restrictive influences on teachers and students. A syllabus may be determined by an external examining body, after which it
becomes a central task of the teacher to work to its requirements. The teacher's
freedom to decide on the treatment or weight of subject matter is unduly limited and
the learner's liberty of exploring the many side paths in the subject area is curtailed.
Unworthy habits such as question spotting, the learning by rote of model answers,
drill in reproducing the kind of material which examiners are believed to favour are
fostered, while the learner's creative abilities are stultified or denied any outlet.
Learning ceases to be treated as a desirable end in itself and becomes inextricably
interwoven with the competitive demands of the examination system. Further, it is
argued, the course of a person's future may be determined in large measure by a few
anxiety-laden hours in an examination room – a practice which is not easily
reconciled with those theories which draw attention to the uneven rate of development of young persons in their formative years. Attention has also been drawn to the

possible lasting effect on a student's self-esteem of poor performance in examinations designed for candidates with a higher level of abilities.

Examinations as modes of evaluation are, it is contended, demonstrably inadequate. They rarely produce objective assessments and reflect too often the examiner's subjective standards, so that the candidates' true levels of attainment are distorted. They place too much stress on mere memory and, it is argued, favour the uncritical regurgitation of facts (or, as has been claimed, the 'second-hand interpretation' of those facts), rather than the selective application of knowledge. The feedback they provide is all too often judgmental (and, therefore of restricted value), too general (rather than specific),and rarely of a motivating nature. Finally, they place, all too often, an unmerited premium on speed ('answer any six questions in two hours ...') and on those special examination skills which may have little relevance to the world outside the classroom. In effect, it is urged, the examination system is 'an unmitigated blight, and the educational plant, as a result, sickens and droops'.

The value of examinations

For many teachers in further education, the regulative functions of examinations mentioned earlier constitute a conclusive argument for their value. There are, however, other, weightier arguments. If the learner has a right to ask (and few would deny this right): 'How am I progressing in my studies? What, at this moment, is the level of my ability? Am I ready to progress to a further stage of instruction? How do I compare with others in my group?' – then there exists, for the teacher, a related duty to answer the learner on the basis of an objective and valid assessment. If the teacher has a right to ask: 'How effective is my teaching in terms of the attainment of objectives? What, at this moment, are my students' achievements? How well do they carry over their learning into novel situations?' – then there exists a case for the process of evaluation of the kind provided by examinations.[5]

The provision of goals for the learner and objectives for the teacher; the measurement and analysis of progress; the evaluation of merit; the uncovering of weakness and deficiencies in learning and teaching; the motivation and encouragement of students to work steadily and productively over a measured period of time; the inculcation of those communication skills needed to reproduce aspects of one's knowledge in a conventionally acceptable form – these are claimed as among the valuable results of the examination system.

O' Hear[6] sees the value of examinations in the context of their overall significance for students. In the absence of evaluation, there is a risk of education finding itself at odds 'with the needs and achievements of the persons being educated'. Further, tests of students' abilities are valuable in inducing an awareness, of 'the existence and nature of the standards of a discipline'. Objections to the content of some types of examination do not, in themselves, invalidate the value of examinations. It may be that many examination schemes concentrate on the mere recall of too much trivia, that many types of question encourage the unthinking reproduction of unconsidered trifles. This may call for a change in the *structure* of examinations, in the nature of the questions set, in a reconsideration of the fundamentals of mastery learning (see p. 293). It may demand more clarity on the part of examiners as to the very purpose of their papers. It does not, in itself, render nugatory the value of the concept of examining a learner's achievements regularly, methodically and accurately.

The allegedly cramping effects of examinations are not always immediately obvious. The extraordinary range of some A level examination syllabus content in physics, computer studies, or economics, and the scope provided for imaginative teaching permit one to question the validity of the argument based solely on the 'restrictive nature' of examinations of this type.

Examinations can – and often do – test the ability to penetrate to the core of a problem with insight, to marshal one's thoughts with precision and logic, to reduce those thoughts to writing within a given time and to exercise one's powers of recall and discrimination. These are important objectives of the student's personal development, the evaluation of which gives an added dimension to the teacher's record of the learner's progress.

It should be remembered, too, that the very act of answering an examination paper in controlled conditions can be a learning experience of some significance in that the student is obliged to recall, evaluate and integrate subject matter. In answer to the argument which stresses the anxiety caused for many examination candidates it is important to note that the very concept of total freedom from anxiety during a creative achievement may be unrealistic.

> The very act of aspiring to master a body of knowledge or to create something original raises the possibility of failure and depression of self-esteem, and hence is anxiety-producing by definition (Ausubel).[7]

In relation to the argument that failure in an examination has lasting negative effects on students' self-esteem, Ausubel declares that this is exaggerated; further:

> Realistic awareness of our relative intellectual status among our peers is a fact of life to which all of us must eventually adjust and the sooner the better for everyone concerned. There is no profit in sugar-coating the truth or in self-delusion (Ausubel).

Lewin[8] states, in relation to evaluating one's failures: 'This "learning to take it" is certainly one of the most important aspects of learning as a part of the character development of the individual'.

A case for summative evaluation through formal examinations might be stated thus: if the objectives of a learner's course of study are worthwhile, if the syllabus which is to assist his or her attaining those objectives is sound and if the course of study is to result in a systematic movement to increasingly higher levels of attainment, then the repeated measuring and assessing of the learner's skills and the teacher's effectiveness become essential and therefore valuable. Without evaluation, in the form of regularly administered examinations, there is the possibility of goals disappearing from sight all too easily and of inadequate schemes of work and methods of instruction continuing unchallenged. (Additionally, members of the public who finance the work of colleges have the right to receive from time to time indicators of the effectiveness of choices made in the planning of educational activities and programmes, and of the progress of courses and students. Examinations act as one such indicator.) In Bruner's words, examinations 'can be allies in the battle to improve curricula and teaching'.[9] But this is not to forget the importance of a continuous, critical review of their structure and content.

Essentials of assessment

Gronlund[10] suggests that we view assessment as 'a process of obtaining information on which to base educational decisions'. Given the purposes of assessment, certain essential characteristics of a successful process of assessment may be considered. First, the assessment should take place at the appropriate time, which will be determined by the rate of progress of the learner and the duration of the course. Weekly tests and end of term examinations obviously have to be administered at fixed points in the timetable, but should the learner reach the end of a unit of instruction at other times, an evaluation of his or her attainment ought to be made as swiftly as possible if its feedback value is to be realized. Four types of assessment are in common use, the results providing a record of attainment and development over a specified period of time. A *prerequisite test* can be used to determine whether the individual student has reached the level required for entry to the course; if the student has not attained that standard he or she ought not to commence the course without having successfully undertaken appropriate remedial work. A *pre-test* can make apparent to the teacher whether the student has, in fact, attained any of the desired objectives of the course of instruction to be followed; if the student has, then his or her individual objectives should be changed. *Post-tests* (administered weekly or monthly, for example) can be used to measure the learner's standard of attainment following the end of lessons, or groups of lessons making up the course; the results ought to be compared with those of the pre-tests. *Retention tests*, which can include the application of that which has been learned to new situations, can follow at random intervals.

Assessment must be in a suitable form, that is it must be structured correctly in relation to *subject matter and purpose*. A test in typewriting, a practical examination for motor vehicle apprentices on aspects of engine tuning, a post-test on a unit of the business studies syllabus, may call for different structures, dictated largely by what is to be tested, and how. Whether the tests will be wholly practical in nature, or theoretical, or a mixture of both, or take the form of an essay, or objective questions, or both, must depend largely upon the teacher's answers to the following vital questions:

1. 'What am I testing?'
2. 'For what precise purpose?'
3. 'How best can I elicit from the student those responses which will provide an unambiguous indication of what and how well he or she has learned?'

It follows that the test should be at the correct level; mere recall of facts would be quite inappropriate, for example, in the final part of examinations in personnel management.

The assessment must be in a form which is perceived as *valid*. The test should measure as accurately as possible what it purports to measure, that is the outcomes of the learner's study. It should gauge as precisely as possible the gap between actual and expected attainment over a period of time, and should assist in the evaluation of teaching effectiveness. Further, it should range as comprehensively as possible over the content area of the syllabus. Its predictive validity should be high.

The examination ought to be presented to the learner as an integral part of the course, not as an irrelevant imposition. It has to be explained – and accepted – as a necessary step towards the next, higher level of work. The idea of the examination as a 'useful discipline', a desirable end in itself, or as a mere culmination of the learner's activities, has no place, therefore, in this concept of evaluation.

It should be noted that, in NVQ schemes, assessment is viewed as an *integral part of learning*. Favoured types of assessment include: internal continuous assessment; internal testing by designated centres; externally prepared tests; grading, on the basis of highly explicit criteria. Assessment will be worthwhile only if, by identifying strengths and weaknesses, it assists the learner and teacher to move with assurance towards the goal of a desired pattern of learning objectives.

Problems of the essay question

Some of the criticisms levelled against formal tests are based on doubts as to the value of the use of essay-type questions which have tended to dominate the traditional examination.[11] First, it is claimed that there can be no real uniformity (or 'reliability') in marking standards, since strict 'scorer objectivity' is impossible; standards vary, of necessity, from one examiner to another. Given the most detailed marking schemes, the responses of two or more examiners to candidates' answers to open-ended questions, such as, 'Consider the relationship between job satisfaction and productivity', or 'Estimate the effectiveness of the British Government's recent attempts to control inflation', must contain a highly subjective element and may, therefore, differ widely. It could not be otherwise, it is argued; no two examiners have the same background, experience, philosophy, or methods of interpreting and evaluating events. (In addition to variation in the standards of different examiners, it has been reported that in some experimental markings of essays, different marks have been awarded at different times to the same essay by the same examiner.)

Next, it is claimed that, in spite of warnings issued by examining boards, examiners may be swayed unduly, and in different manner, by candidates' actual *presentation* of their answers. The neat, well-turned, correctly paragraphed script may be favoured rather than the script which reaches the same standard in scholarship, but which is difficult to read and presented in crabbed and rebarbative fashion.[12] The value of an assessment and evaluation based on essay-type questions may be vitiated, therefore, by the so-called 'contamination factor' which clouds the real objective of an examination by the testing – often unconsciously on the part of the examiner – of stylistic matters. (Ebel,[13] who opposes the use of the essay test because it does not usually provide valid measures of complex mental processes such as critical thinking, originality, or ability to organize and integrate, states that longer, well-presented essays tend to receive higher ratings.) It is claimed, also, that the presence of a very good, well-presented script in a run of mediocre papers, or of a poor script in a group of otherwise excellent papers, may distort the general pattern of marks which the examiner awards.

Investigations of reliability[14] in essay marking have found that, in typical cases, different examiners tended to vary the emphasis placed on features of the essay, such as skills (punctuation, spelling), ideas (originality, coherence), vocabulary (precision), personal style (individual expression), and organization (structure, general presentation). There seemed little doubt as to the effect of an examiner's personal prejudices on essay marking. Reliability in essay marking can be improved, it was suggested, by the following procedures: 'blind marking' (where the examiner is unaware of the student's identity), 'blind re-checking' (where the original mark is hidden), and 'spot checking' (to be carried out by someone other than the original examiner).

Further, the essay-type questions which make up an examination paper may not be of an equal standard of difficulty, so that they discriminate differently among candidates. Thus, where there is the possibility of choice ('answer any three questions'), and candidate X answers questions 1, 2, 3, while Y answers 2, 4, 6, and Z answers 3, 5, 7, there must be difficulties in evaluating the standard of the paper as a whole, since X, Y and Z have answered, in effect, three different papers. It is objected also that the scope of the typical examination syllabus in further education is now so very wide that it cannot be covered adequately by setting, say, nine questions, from which a candidate may choose 'any five'. In such a case, the student is being tested on a mere portion of the syllabus. A further objection is that the time-consuming process of essay marking and evaluation makes early and effective feedback and reinforcement impossible, so that much of the purpose of the process cannot be realized.

As against these criticisms there are, however, positive features of the essay-type question to be noted. It can test not only the learner's recall and knowledge of the subject matter but also his or her ability to apply that knowledge in the exercise of powers of expression in a creative, cogent and lucid manner. Tests involving the higher-level cognitive processes, such as comprehension, analysis and evaluation often necessitate the learner selecting his or her material and presenting it with care and accuracy. For this, the essay question is often suitable. The ability to select, relate, interpret and extrapolate from facts with imagination and insight ought to be amenable to testing through the writing of an essay. Indeed it has been argued that to exclude the essay question from an examination paper is effectively to deny the student an opportunity of displaying in individualistic fashion that discipline of response and measure of perception which ought to have resulted from the course of study.

Planning and marking the examination

Members of staff of all grades in colleges of further education may be called upon to plan or mark examinations for internal purposes or for external bodies. The following matters need to be considered.

1. The scope of the syllabus must be ascertained precisely and questions must be distributed as evenly as possible over its content. It is unfair for the examiner to assume that any one section of the syllabus is less important than another and, thus, to omit questions based upon it; its publication as part of the syllabus necessitates its being treated by teachers and examiners as material to be taught *and* tested.

2. 'What am I examining?' This question must be kept in mind by the examiner. Essay-type questions, for example, should be related very clearly to the desired outcomes of the appropriate unit of instruction. Given the level of the candidates' attainments, ought the questions to be based on mere recall, or comprehension, or synthesis? Consider, for example, a question set to a first-year business studies class. The syllabus to which they work includes a section which states, briefly: 'Money – elementary treatment of functions and characteristics'. The following questions are among those which have been set from time to time on this unit of instruction.

   Example A: Define money.
   Example B: 'Money is as money does.' Discuss.
   Example C: Which of the following would you consider to be money: (a) cheques, (b) diamonds, (c) credit cards? Give your reasons.
   Example D: In a book recounting his experiences as a prisoner of war, the author states: 'For a time we had no money in the camp, so we used cigarettes'. Define money and use your definition to explain what the author means.

   Example A is a simple recall test, of limited value in an examination at this level; it cannot elicit from the learner any response indicating that the functions of money have been understood. Examples B, C and D demand recall and application of what has been learned and are to be preferred to a mere memory test.

3. 'How can I best test what has been learned?' Essay questions? Objective tests? Data response questions? (These are based on an introductory statement and information, followed by an initial question and sequential sub-questions.) Oral examination? A combination of several types of question? In the case of external examining bodies, the examiner may have no choice as to the *type* of question to be set. For the purpose of college internal examinations, the teacher-examiner ought to experiment widely in the selection and combination of forms of questions.[15]

4. The length of time available for the test will determine the number of questions to be answered. In general, a minimum period of twenty minutes for an essay-type answer is considered desirable.

5. The draft question paper ought to be revised very carefully to avoid possible ambiguities. The examiner's expectations should be stated precisely and in comprehensible fashion. ('State', 'explain', 'outline', 'compare and contrast' have specific meanings and must be used with precision.) Students tend to display a devastating 'logic' in the interpretation of examination questions and ambiguities appear where none was apparent to the examiner. Thus, in a civics

paper set some years ago a question asking for the constitutional significance of 'the Queen's Speech' elicited a large number of answers dealing with the responsibility of the monarch for the setting of standards of propriety in the spoken word!

6. Clear instructions must be given. If there are constraints, e.g. on the use of dictionaries, these must be stated well in advance of the date of examination. (The use of calculators has now to be considered carefully in the design of examinations involving quantitative techniques.)

A marking scheme will reflect decisions as to whether the examination is of a *norm-referenced* or *criterion-referenced nature*, and will take into account the chief examiner's subjective 'weighting' of features of the test. The problem of deduction of marks for incorrect spelling, poor punctuation and grammatical inaccuracy must be studied carefully. Are marks to be deducted for each repetition of an error in spelling, for example? What are the criteria on which pass or fail in an essay answer will be determined? Is the pass mark or grade to be publicized? In the case of internal examinations these matters will call for a full discussion between the teacher-examiner and his or her head of department.

Grading scales and examination records

Student X scores 48 marks out of a possible 100 in an examination. Has he 'passed' or 'failed'? The dividing line between success and failure in an examination must be drawn on the basis of a decision which, inevitably, is somewhat arbitrary in nature. X's mark of 48/100 must be interpreted by the examiner so that it can be evaluated with reference to a variety of criteria. What does this mark tell us of X's level of attainment? How does it compare with the level accepted by the examiner as indicating proficiency or mastery? How does it compare with the level of average attainment? Has it any real predictive value? How does it compare with marks obtained by other candidates in the same group? Does it indicate whether X should move to the next unit of study? In deciding, therefore, whether the pass mark shall be 60, 58, 50, etc., the examiner must consider with care his or her assumptions as to the precise purpose of the test. The basic question, 'What am I examining?', has to be considered afresh on this occasion.

Where members of the class are to be assessed in order of merit, to meet the requirements of a norm-referenced test, an efficient grading procedure is needed. Where the test has been sufficiently 'discriminating', so that it results in a general spread of marks, standards can be graded with relative ease. A simple scale of 'good, average, poor' might suffice. A five-point scale, based on 100 students, might produce a pattern related to the following distribution:

3	very good
22	good
50	average
22	weak
3	poor

A finer, seven-point scale, based on the same number of students, might produce, typically, the following spread:

5	excellent
10	very good
20	good
30	average
20	fair
10	poor
5	very poor

The so-called 'normal distribution curve' (the area under which represents the total number of candidates) tends to resemble Figure 30.1.

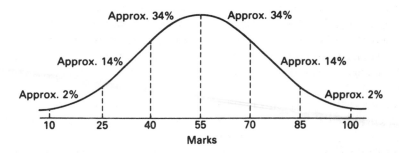

Figure 30.1 Normal distribution curve of students' test results.

The accurate recording of examination results is of great importance in colleges of further education, particularly where the career development prospects of part-time students are linked with the attainment of specified levels in examinations. Ideally, a record ought to contain all the information necessary for accurate extrapolation, thus enabling a pattern of development to be deduced. Such information would include, in addition to personal details relating to the student, statistical data such as:

(a) intelligence quotient (see Chapter 32) where known;
(b) grades in examinations taken before entry to college;
(c) pre-test grades;
(d) post-test grades (which, in the case of continuous assessment, must be kept up-to-date).

The 'practical situation' examination

Where course work involves 'practical objectives', such as operating a power tool, conducting an interview, dealing with a critical event in, say, a laboratory, hospital ward, or workshop, the appropriate examination should place the student, as far as possible, in the relevant practical situation. The evaluation, which ought to be criterion-referenced, should be based upon very precise objectives which will necessitate the student demonstrating his or her ability to perform specified tasks to a previously determined acceptable standard. The nearer the practical examination is to the actual situation it seeks to simulate, the more valuable will be the resulting assessment of the student's performance.

A note on 'open-book' examinations

The open-book examinations allows students to refer to basic material such as atlases, texts of dramas, statutes, etc. (It is necessary to ensure that only standard, unannotated texts are used.) This means, in practice, that the examination does not concentrate on recall of information, but simulates real-life situations which would necessitate a search of reference material. Rather than burdening the law student with the memorization of vast tracts of statute law ('Explain the significance of the Defamation Act 1996, section 1'), the open-book examiner can set questions relating to *the ability to comprehend and synthesize* ('Do you consider that the Defamation Act 1996, section 1, is an adequate revision of the common law defence of innocent dissemination?').

In subjects such as English Literature, the comparison of passages in the texts may be tested with ease, and rote learning and memorization of quotations should be reduced. Geography and physics are examples of other subjects which lend themselves to the testing of the higher abilities where reference to texts is allowed.

It is claimed that the open-book examination reduces nervous strain on candidates, allows them to prepare for examinations free from the burden of recall, and enables them to concentrate on selection of materials and comprehension. It is also suggested, however, that examiners experience difficulty in framing questions which will not result in the mere copying of reference material, and that increased strain on candidates might result from the presence of a plethora of material from which data must be selected with discrimination.

Significantly, the Council for National Academic Awards stated that the best performances in open-book examinations came from those students who chose not to take in texts. Clearly, much research on the efficiency of this type of examination remains to be undertaken and evaluated.[16]

Data response (short essay) questions

An interesting development in examination-question style is the data response item, an example of which is given in Figure 30.2. (This item formed part of an examination at the end of a learning module on 'The historical background of industrial relations'.) 'Stimulus material', which may be hypothetical or drawn from, say, the financial press or government reports, is presented, perhaps in the form of a statistical table or a paragraph of prose, together with a group of questions which are intended to test abilities such as comprehension and analysis. The candidate is invited to respond to the questions by interpreting the data presented, applying

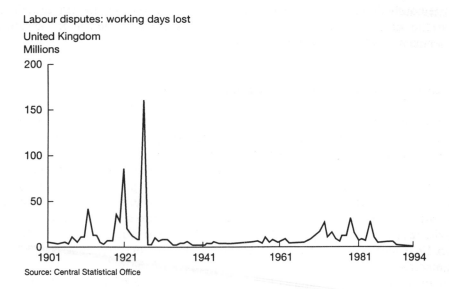

Labour disputes: working days lost
United Kingdom
Millions

Source: Central Statistical Office

(a) Outline the general circumstances surrounding the events which account for the peaks of the 1920s.
(b) Explain the background to the 1984 peak.
(c) Has legislation contributed to the decline in labour disputes shown by the 1994 figures?
(d) Is it possible to extrapolate from this graph a trend concerning the likely incidence of labour disputes in the late 1990s?

Figure 30.2 Data response questions.

principles, analysing the data in the light of principles, and answering the questions, in the form of short essays, by reference to his or her analysis.[17] (It should be noted that questions may be set without specific reference to the data given.)

There is no fixed format for the data response question. Its main advantages are its capability of testing the candidate in the application of theory and principle to the problems of the real world, and its value in testing a variety of abilities.

Continuous assessment

Opposed to the concept of a once-for-all assessment and evaluation in the form of an end-of-course examination, is the principle of continuous assessment. In practice, this substitutes for the single examination *a series of continuously updated measurements and judgments* by the teacher of the learner's attainments. These judgments may be based on, say, weekly tests of the learner's performance in a variety of situations. The learner's written and practical work and his or her contribution to the work of the class as a whole may be taken into account and assessed. (An 'objective-related assessment' is based on a checklist of instructional objectives which the student should have attained by the end of the course.) As a result, a record of changes in the learner's performance is produced. This cumulative judgment, rather than the result of a single examination, forms the basis of the final assessment and evaluation of the student's capabilities.

It has been claimed that an assessment of this nature may provide a much fairer picture of a learner's level of achievement than that given by a traditional formal examination. The strain and anxieties induced by a three-hour test may produce, it is suggested, a distorted reflection of that achievement. The relatively relaxed atmosphere surrounding a test which is administered *as a regular feature* of classroom activity, it is argued, may allow the learner to give a much more reliable account of his or her abilities. The ability to work swiftly in a short period of time and the importance of memory, both of which characterize standard formal examinations, are not unduly emphasized in continuous assessment. Further, the student is supplied with useful feedback relating to his or her achievements and is able to plan immediate remedial action. Finally, and perhaps of the greatest importance, the immediate educational future of the student is not determined by performance in one examination only.

On the other hand, it is contended that for the strain of one examination there is substituted a continuing anxiety spread over an entire term or year. Further, the heavy demands made on teaching staff in relation to the large number of assessments to be made throughout a course may be counter-productive. For some critics the dependence of continuous assessment on the subjective judgment of teachers, and the lack of external moderation of test assessment, are the most cogent arguments against its acceptability. Much research on the effectiveness of continuous assessment as a precise and effective measure of learning remains to be carried out; in particular, investigation is required as to the possibility of compiling an accurate summative evaluation from a series of continuous assessments.

The use of projects in assessment

A project can be made a component of the learning process by students working individually or in groups and generally culminating in the presentation of a report (which may be assessed as part of an overall course evaluation) resulting from personal investigation of a topic, the choice of which has been approved by the course tutor.[18]

Project work is said to motivate students and to raise their general level of interest in the course. It allows for creativity, decision-making and independent work, and may lead to 'the personal development which stems from the acceptance of responsibility'. It is important, however, that the *precise purpose* of the project be explained to students, so that it will be seen as an essential feature of the course, not as an 'optional extra', not merely as a shifting of work from teacher to student, and that it be accorded due recognition in the overall assessment and evaluation of students' course work.

The use of oral examinations

The oral examination, traditionally used in the testing of skills in foreign languages and as a supplementary test in certain types of university course, has been strangely neglected in further education examination schemes, in spite of the fact that oral communication skills are essential in many areas, such as business and management. Its advantages are that verbal fluency and confidence in a stress situation can be assessed; and a student's weaknesses and strengths in expression can be revealed swiftly by detailed probing (so that appropriate diagnosis is made possible). Its disadvantages are said to include difficulties created by reliance on an essentially subjective assessment, high real costs of administering the tests, particularly in terms of time, and restrictions on the amount of learned material that can be examined.

Of crucial importance in oral testing is the role of the examiners, and very careful training for examiners who use this mode of assessment is essential. Oral examiners' subjective judgment is very important, even though the criteria of acceptable student performance are stated clearly and precisely. Examiners must ensure that the testing environment is appropriate (i.e. 'stage-managed'): seating which does not suggest confrontation is essential; eye contact must be possible between candidates and examiners throughout the test. Examiners should be trained so that their questioning is structured and permits free responses from which the candidate's ability to organize and express ideas may be assessed. The examiners' contribution to the test should be reassuring, should not lend itself to being perceived as mere interruption, and should allow the exploration of avenues of discussion opened up by the candidate's responses.

Notes and references

1. See generally for this chapter: *Measurement and Evaluation in Education and Psychology* by W.A. Mehrens and I.J. Lehmann (Holt-Saunders, 1984); *Examinations: A Commentary* by J.C. Matthews (Allen & Unwin, 1985); *Measuring Educational Outcomes* by B.W. Tuckman (Harcourt Brace Jovanovich, 1975); *Evaluation and Assessing for Learning* by D. Harris (Kogan Page, 1996); *Education, Assessment and Society* by P.M. Broadfoot (Open University Press, 1990).
2. 'Evaluation of students' in *New Directions for Testing* ed. W. Schrader (Jossey-Bass, 1980).
3. *Evaluation to Improve Learning* (McGraw-Hill, 1981). See also 'Evaluating instruction' by R.M. Gagné in *Principles of Instructional Design* (Holt, Rinehart & Winston, 1988).
4. See e.g. *School Examinations* by J. Pearce (Collier-Macmillan, 1972). This basic analysis remains of significance today.
5. See *Measurement and Evaluation in Teaching* by N. Gronlund (Collier-Macmillan, 1981).
6. *Education, Society and Human Nature* (Routledge, 1981).

7. *Cognitive Psychology* (Holt, Rinehart & Winston, 1978).
8. *A Dynamic Theory of Personality* (McGraw-Hill, 1945).
9. *The Process of Education* (Harvard UP, 1965).
10. *Op. cit.*
11. See 'Essay questions' by W.E. Coffman in *Educational Measurement* ed. R. Thorndike (American Council on Education, 1971); *Assessment Techniques* ed. B. Hudson (Methuen, 1973); 'Assessment techniques' in *Instructional Technique* by I. Davies (McGraw-Hill, 1981); 'Essay questions and tests' by A. Welsh and P. Saunders in *The Principles of Economics Course* by P. Saunders and W. Walstad (McGraw-Hill, 1990).
12. 'The impact of achievement expectations and handwriting quality on scoring essay tests' by C.I. Chase in *Journal of Educational Measurement* (1979, *16*).
13. 'Essay tests' in *Essentials of Educational Measurement* (Prentice-Hall, 1979).
14. *Measuring Growth in English* by P. Diederich (1974), cited in *The Process of Learning* by J. Biggs and R. Telfer (Prentice-Hall, 1987).
15. See *Designing a Scheme of Assessment* by C. Ward (Thorne, 1980).
16. See e.g. 'An experimental evaluation of the open-book examination' by R. Kalish in *Journal of Educational Psychology* (1958, *49*).
17. See e.g. *Data Response Questions for Economics* by G. Walker (Checkmate Gold Publications, 1988).
18. See e.g. 'Project work' by D.M. Yorke in *Patterns of Teaching* (CET, 1981).

Chapter 31

The Objective Test: Its Rationale and Construction

> If we are really serious about education, we must have precise ways both of measuring learning outcomes in individual students and of ascertaining whether they are consonant with our educational objectives (Ausubel, 1978).

Earlier chapters have drawn attention to the necessity for swift and accurate assessment and feedback of a learner's level of achievement. The previous chapter considered examinations as a mode of assessing attainment and noted some of the criticisms levelled against them, in particular those based on the alleged deficiencies of the essay-type question. Objective tests, which are discussed in this chapter, are presented by some of their advocates as feasible supplements, or even alternatives, to the subjectively assessed essay questions which so often dominate the conventional examination paper.[1] In its multiple choice format, the objective test is now a fully recognized component of the repertoire of assessment methods used throughout the education system. Most students and a large proportion of staff in today's colleges of further education will have been examined at some stage of their educational development through the medium of the objective test, so that its style, structure and purpose are widely known.

Essence of objective tests

An objective test has been defined by the Department of Employment as: 'a test or examination in which every question is set in such a way as to have only one right answer. That is, the opinion of the examiner or marker does not enter in judging whether an answer is good or poor, acceptable or wrong; there is no subjective element involved.' The definition emphasizes the fact that *the term 'objective' relates to the marking of the test*. Whether subjective elements have been eradicated from tests of this type remains arguable. The syllabus content to be covered by the test, the choice of questions, the construction of the alternative answers among which the candidate must discriminate, the abilities to be tested, involve examiners' decisions which must be, to some extent, subjective in their nature.

A test of this type may be made up of 'items' (i.e. discrete questions) which are so constructed and presented that for each item there is one, predetermined, correct answer. Candidates select the one answer which they consider to be correct from a list provided. It is claimed that the objective test, by its nature, design, form and administration, removes from the process of assessment some of the more disadvantageous features of the essay-type examination.

Types of objective test

There are several types of objective test, so that it is not necessary to make up an examination paper from one type only. Indeed, some students who have been tested by objective question papers state a preference for a variety of types of question, rather than a paper made up of only one form of item. Some of the more usual types of objective test are noted below.

The multiple choice (or 'single completion') item

This is made up of a stem and several (usually four or five) choices of answer (often called 'responses' or 'options'). (Note that the number of options is generally a function of the probability of guessing an answer correctly.) One of the options – the key – is correct; the others – the distractors (or 'foils') – are incorrect. The stem of the item may be constructed so as to present an incomplete statement, or so as to pose a question.[2]

Examples of multiple choice items are given in Figures 31.1(a) and (b). This type

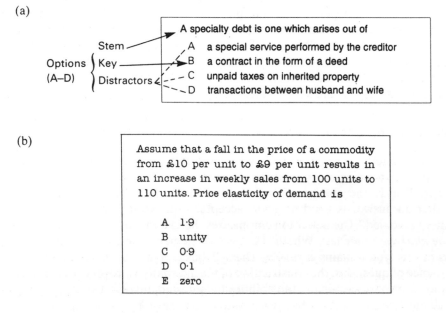

Figure 31.1 Multiple choice items.

of item can be constructed so as to measure a variety of learning outcomes, e.g. simple recall, knowledge of procedure and interpretation of data. The testing of abilities such as synthesis is difficult, however, in this type of objective test.

An interesting variant of the multiple choice format is the 'correct response' item, as in Figure 31.2.

What is meant by the assertion made by some cognitive psychologists that 'our memory structure is analogous to a filing cabinet'?

Indicate your answer by placing a tick on the left hand side of the response below which seems to you to be correct.

When we are given the appropriate clues, we begin a search process in the mind which will lead us to the 'correct drawer and document therein'.

When we recognize general relationships among data, we will move on to a recognition of the appropriate details, and to the activity of remembering.

We can remember only when we are provided with information which allows us to perceive a natural order underlying it.

We must evaluate the quality of the information we are attempting to retrieve before we are able to retrieve it.

Figure 31.2 Multiple choice correct response item.

The multiple response (or 'multiple completion') item

In this type of item more than one of the given possibilities is correct; but there is only one correct answer to the precise question stated in the first sentence of the item. Figure 31.3 is an example. This is a versatile type of objective test, lending itself to the testing of recall, reasoning and the exercise of judgment. Some research has suggested, however, that this test may favour unduly the student who has developed skills in recognizing ambiguity.

The assertion-reason item

This can be a very searching test of analysis and comprehension. A candidate must first decide whether the two given statements are correct or incorrect. If both are correct, he or she must then decide whether the second statement explains the first. It can be used to test some higher cognitive skills. But ability in language comprehension is, inevitably, necessary for success in questions of this nature; hence

---

Which of the following would be included among the functions of a bill of lading?

    I   it is a receipt for goods shipped
    II it is evidence of a contract of carriage
    III it is a document of title to goods
    IV it is evidence of insurance

    A I only
    B II and III
    C III and IV
    D I, II and III
    E I, II, III and IV

Figure 31.3 Multiple response item.

incorrect responses may be elicited from students for reasons which are not relevant to the purposes of the item. Figure 31.4 is an example.

If a firm engages in a wide advertising campaign it must increase the prices of its products.	*Advertising costs enter into total costs of production.*
First statement	Second statement
A Correct	Correct *and* correct explanation of the first
B Correct	Correct but *not* correct explanation of the first
C Correct	Incorrect
D Incorrect	Correct
E Incorrect	Incorrect

Figure 31.4 Assertion-reason item.

The matching list (or 'matching pairs') item

Two lists are presented and candidates are required to match the contents of one list with those of the other. It will be noted that in the example given in Figure 31.5 a candidate cannot use a process of elimination in order to obtain a correct last result, since List II contains more topics than List I. The higher abilities are not easily tested by this kind of item. It has been found useful, however, in testing factual information and allowing a large sampling of learning content area. Both lists must be free of any clues, and the responses in the second list should be short and simple. Marking is generally straightforward.

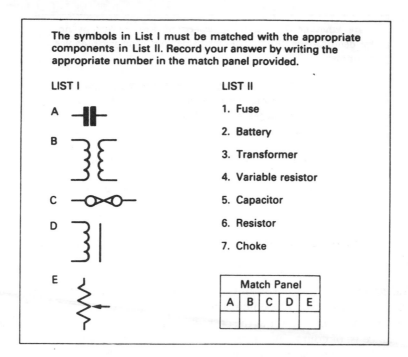

The symbols in List I must be matched with the appropriate components in List II. Record your answer by writing the appropriate number in the match panel provided.

Figure 31.5 Matching list item (from *Objective Testing* (City & Guilds of London Institute)).

True/false item

Statements (usually declarative sentences) forming the item must be evaluated as either true or false,[3] see Figure 31.6. This type of item can be used for examining most concept areas, but there is a danger of it being employed in the testing of trivia. Students are said to feel alienated from a test which is perceived all too easily as downgrading their cognitive abilities. Further, it is not easy to write true/false statements, beyond the elementary, which are unequivocally true or false. A danger of testing 'degrees of correctness' may arise. Words such as 'some', 'often', 'few', 'more' and similar terms, which allow ambiguous interpretation, should be avoided. There is, also, a high probability of students giving correct answers by chance alone.

The problem of guessing

An immediate objection to this kind of test is raised by the possibility of guessing the correct answers.[4] One cannot guess one's way successfully through an essay, it is argued, and wild or unsupported assertions can be spotted easily and penalized accordingly in extended written answers. This does not apply, however, in the case of answers to the questions in objective tests. Guessing – by which is meant making

> State whether the following assertions are correct or not
> by deleting the word 'true' or 'false' (so that your choice
> remains).
>
> (i)   The Queen, advised by the Lord Chancellor, can
>   pardon the commission of a tort.   TRUE/FALSE
> (ii) Puisne judges are entitled to membership of the
>   Judicial Committee of the Privy Council.
>   TRUE/FALSE
> (iii) 'Ownership' and 'possession' are synonymous in
>   English law.   TRUE/FALSE
> (iv) The final court of appeal for civil cases is the High
>   Court.   TRUE/FALSE

Figure 31.6   True/false item (from an introductory module on the English legal system).

'snap' judgments based on uncertainty – is, presumably, not to be encouraged, and the influence of luck should be eliminated.

That a candidate can arrive at the correct answer to a single item by a process of random choice is, of course, possible. That the same process applied to a complete test will result in the award of a pass mark is improbable. In fact, however, a statistical correction for guessing can be made by using the following formula:

$$\text{Candidate's score corrected for guessing} = \text{Total correct answers} - \frac{\text{Total incorrect answers}}{\text{Number of alternatives} - 1}$$

Preparing an objective test

Where possible, the preparation of an objective test ought to be based on *teamwork*, that is the combined operations of a group of teachers acting as item writers, revisers, testers and editors. The steps which these operations involve are outlined below.[5]

1. *A test specification should be constructed.* This necessitates discussion by course tutors and examiners concerning the *syllabus content* which is to be covered by the test, the *purpose* of the test (i.e. whether it is to be criterion-referenced or norm-referenced), the *total number of items to be included* (with reference to the time available) and – of much importance – the *abilities which are to be tested*. A 'grid' can be constructed to weight those abilities in relation to the various sections of the syllabus.
2. *The item must be written.* This involves a consideration of the rules set out in the next section.
3. *The items should then be edited.* The editor should keep in mind two questions: 'Are the items set out correctly?' and 'Are they free from error?' The items ought to be checked so as to ensure that the suggested 'key' is the correct answer

and that none of the 'distractors' provides an alternative which could be correct in circumstances not immediately envisaged by the item writer. Information in the stem ought to be checked for accuracy. The wording of the stem and the options should be free from ambiguity.

4. *The pre-test and analysis of results follow.* The object of the pre-test is the ascertainment of the difficulty of items, of their discriminating power and of the time necessary for completion of the test. As large a group of students as can be made available ought to be used for the pre-test and they should be representative of those for whom the examination is designed. There is little value, therefore, in using a sample of A level students in a pre-test of items designed for a beginners' group.

5. *The results of the pre-test may be analysed* to yield the following statistical measurements: item facility (known also as 'facility value', or FV); item discrimination (known also as 'index of discrimination' or ID); distractor plausibility.

(a) FV is expressed as the percentage of candidates attempting the item who give the correct answer. Thus:

$$FV = \frac{\text{Number giving correct answer}}{\text{Total number of candidates}} \times 100$$

As a general rule, a FV of 90 per cent suggests a very easy item; 70–89, an easy item; 30–69, an item of medium difficulty; and below 30, a difficult item. The average FV of the items to be included in the test should be selected on the basis of an evaluation of the nature of the subject matter, the purpose of the test and the presumed level of attainment of the candidates.

(b) ID will indicate how an item differentiates among candidates who are at different levels of competence in the subject which is being tested. It can be measured, in simple fashion, by the following formula:

$$ID = \frac{\begin{pmatrix}\text{No. in top 27\% of candidates} \\ \text{giving correct answer}\end{pmatrix} - \begin{pmatrix}\text{No. in bottom 27\% of} \\ \text{candidates giving correct answer}\end{pmatrix}}{27\% \text{ of total number of candidates}}$$

The ID will range from −1.0 to +1.0. In general, the higher its value in the case of a particular item, the greater will be the probability that those answering that item correctly will score well on the test as a whole. An ID of 0.4 or above usually suggests that an item discriminates very adequately; below 0.2 suggests weak discrimination (and points to the necessity of rejecting the item).

(c) Distractor plausibility (i.e. the measure of how plausible a distractor was) is the number of candidates who selected it expressed as a percentage of the total number of candidates.

6. Finally, after measurement and assessment of the results of the pre-test, the *structure is adjusted and the test is given its final shape.* Items are selected from

those used in the pre-test, and suitable items which are not included may be assessed, graded and 'banked' for use on other occasions. The final decision on the number of items to be used will reflect the time available for the examination, and its level.[6]

Writing items: some general rules

Gronlund[7] reminds teachers that the construction of good objective test items has become an art, requiring the same skills as those necessary for effective teaching. The test constructor requires a thorough grasp of the subject, clarity in envisaging and defining desired learning outcomes, an understanding of the students to be tested, a 'touch of creativity', and skill in the application of the relevant writing rules. Several of these rules have emerged from the practice of writing and administering objective tests in recent years. The more important are set out below.

(a) The questions must arise from the syllabus of study. Be clear as to what the item is intended to measure.
(b) Questions should be designed to fit the purpose of the test and should take into account candidates' age and educational background.
(c) An appropriate level of language should be used.
(d) Test only relevant abilities.
(e) Ensure that you are not testing English comprehension only.
(f) Items should not be taken verbatim from a set text; in such a case it is probably only memorization that is being tested.
(g) Avoid testing trivia at any level of cognitive outcome. Remember that learning outcomes (which you are seeking to test) are not only *quantitative* i.e. 'horizontal' (relating to the accretion of factual knowledge) but also *qualitative*, i.e. 'vertical' (relating to increases in the level and structure of knowledge so that it becomes 'understanding'). Ensure that your items test horizontal *and* vertical learning outcomes.
(h) The stem and each option should be grammatically correct and as brief as possible.
(i) Stem and options must be linked grammatically.
(j) The stem must be relevant to the options.
(k) Positive rather than negative stems (including, e.g. 'not', 'except') are preferable. A negative stem, if used, should be emphasized by underlining. Double negatives should be avoided.
(l) The question to be answered should, if possible, emerge clearly from the stem on initial inspection. (Some item writers work according to the rule that a good candidate ought to be able to anticipate the correct answer even before looking at the various alternatives presented.)
(m) The correct option (or options, in the case of multiple response items) should be unequivocally correct. None of the distractors should be potentially correct, but they should be plausible (so that if a student lacks information needed to answer the question, any of the choices will seem to be correct).

(n) Avoid options that are synonymous with one another or merely opposite in meaning.
(o) The position of the correct options in a series of items should be based on a random pattern.
(p) There should be no intentional or unintentional clues to the correct answer in the stem or in any of the options, e.g. by the use of 'key words', or by the construction of options which look correct because they are longer than the others. Another kind of unintentional clue, which should be avoided, can be given by the 'self-evident implausibility of the wrong alternatives'. (To give unintended clues is, in effect, to test candidates' ingenuity and their 'test wisdom' rather than their knowledge of the subject matter.)
(q) Try to avoid as a response option 'all (or none) of the above'.

Gronlund's final words of advice should be noted: 'Break any of these rules where you have a good reason for making an exception!'

Reviewing the objective test

Following the administration, checking and marking of an objective test, a general review and evaluation of its utility ought to be undertaken, preferably by a small panel drawn from those who wrote, edited and chose the items. The review should have as its objectives the discovery of information concerning the overall suitability of the test, the exclusion from future tests of unsuitable items, and the banking of suitable questions for use in future tests.

The review should elicit answers to the following questions: Did any administrative problems arise? (For example, was the time allowed adequate? The answer can be discovered by checking the number of those who failed to complete the test.) Were all questions attempted by the majority of candidates? Were some items based on material outside the syllabus? Were any questions too easy? Were any distractors insufficiently misleading? Was average performance satisfactory? What is the relationship between the mean mark in this and previous tests taken by the candidates?

Advantages of objective tests

The advantages claimed for objective tests appear to derive from the nature and form of their design and presentation, for example their comprehensive coverage of the syllabus and its content domain, unambiguous style and ease of assessment. It is argued that the large number of items which can be included in, say, an hour's test, makes it possible to cover very wide areas of the examination syllabus. It has been suggested, too, that, because the candidate has less to write in the answer, he or she will have more time for thinking. Choice of questions is eliminated, so that a candidate's answers are not confined to his or her 'favourite topics' in the syllabus. Question-spotting, too, becomes very difficult. Next, questioning of an exact nature is made possible, so that precision of knowledge can be tested in a way not always possible in the discursive essay paper. Overlap of questions can be avoided completely. Further, the effect of some features of a candidate's work (e.g. 'penmanship' or 'powers of expression') which may not be relevant to the precise ability which is being tested, is reduced. 'Padding' is eliminated.

Walstad[8] argues emphatically that, because there is no bias in scoring the multiple choice test, it offers a much more *objective assessment* of a candidate's *specific achievement* than, say, the essay answer. The very sources of bias (including the mood of the examiner at the time of marking an essay) are absent from the objective test marking process. Further, he suggests that the objective test is a much more *reliable indicator of overall long-term student performance* than the essay question. Precision in marking and consistency in interpretation of student responses make for accuracy in forecasting attainment levels.

The pre-testing of items provides the teacher with a highly selective and diagnostic type of feedback – an added advantage of this mode of assessment. Levels of attainment, gaps in the teaching programme, effectiveness of types of instruction and unforeseen difficulties in comprehension may be discovered by evaluating the results of the pre-test. An important advantage of the test which is eventually administered (after revisions resulting from evaluation of responses to the pre-test) is its capacity to supply candidates with feedback in a relatively short time, as compared with the time required for the assessment and publication of results of an essay question paper.

A further advantage of objective tests is their standardization in relation to preparation, checking and the circumstances of their administration: instructions, time limits, etc., are the same for a large number of examining centres, so that meaningful comparability of scores is ensured. Subjectivity and variability in scoring procedures are eradicated and, finally, there is very high scorer reliability – 100 per cent where the test is marked by a document-reading machine or computer.

Finally, it is claimed that the well-designed objective test can provide useful comparative information about students, that its versatility allows for the testing of a variety of abilities, not merely recall, and that its quality of objectivity is accepted by students as guaranteeing a genuine measure of achievement.

Disadvantages of objective tests

The disadvantages of objective tests also derive, not unexpectedly, from their nature and form. The ability to express oneself coherently and in organized fashion in writing, considered by many teachers to be vital at *any* stage of education other than the most elementary, cannot be tested properly, it is argued, by 'small-answer' objective items. Originality, communication skills, powers of critical analysis and sustained argument, and clarity of expression do not seem capable of appraisal by objective testing. Whether synthesis, comprehension and similar high-order abilities are amenable to assessment in this manner is, it is argued, doubtful. Many teachers remain unconvinced by Ebel's claim that the multiple choice test can be used 'with great skill and effectiveness to measure complex abilities and fundamental understanding'. Teachers' residual suspicions, in spite of assurances to the contrary, that guessing of answers plays too great a role in objective testing, that students may fix in their minds some of their errors of choice in response to distractors, and that the tests make no allowance for the highly intelligent student who sees alternatives which the test writer has not offered, remain unallayed. Teachers have voiced concern, too, at the use of concentrated periods of practice in answering objective tests; it has been said that such practice may be capable of giving increased scores, but with a resulting distortion of the pattern of grades in a norm-referenced objective test.

Ausubel[9] criticizes the undue emphasis placed by objective testing on time pressure.

> It tends to favour the glib, confident, impulsive, and testwise student, and to handicap the student who is inclined to be cautious, thoughtful, and self-critical, or is unsophisticated about testing ... The current emphasis on speed in most standardized tests of achievement detracts from their validity by placing a premium on factors that are intrinsically unrelated to genuine mastery of subject matter.

He emphasizes, additionally, some general limitations of objective testing:

> ... by definition, the tests cannot measure students' ability spontaneously to generate relevant hypotheses ... to marshal evidence in support of a proposition, to design an original experiment, to structure a cogent argument, or to do creative work.

The processes involved – pre-tests, collection and interpretation of results, re-writing and editing – are said to place a disproportionately heavy burden on the teacher who has little time to spare for activities of this nature. The real costs of objective testing in terms of time, intensity of effort and of administration can be very high.

The most serious of the charges brought against objective testing would seem to be that it has a tendency – because of its very nature – to encourage a 'fragmentary' approach to teaching and learning. The whole is greater than its parts, and a test of subject mastery which concentrates on detail while apparently ignoring the *overall significance* of that which has been learned, and which seems to examine the simple components while neglecting the complex totality, may have undesirable effects on the manner in which teacher and students set out to achieve their objectives.

Ausubel's final reminder is of much importance:

> Despite considerable improvement in this respect ... many objective tests still measure rote recognition of relatively trivial and disconnected items of knowledge rather than genuine comprehension of broad concepts, principles and relationships, and ability to interpret facts and apply knowledge.

A general comment

The history of objective testing is brief and research remains too limited to pro-nounce with confidence on its suitability as an accurate mode of assessment. Much more research is needed in order to discover whether objective testing can effec-tively examine more than factual recall and relatively simple application.

As a response to the repeated assertion that the objective test tends to favour those who lack the writing abilities necessary for success in essay-type questions, a large-scale experiment was undertaken in 1989. Economics, English and secretarial studies students completed multiple choice questions in the first half of the examination period, and answered an essay question in the other half of the period. Scores for each half were correlated. It emerged very clearly that students who earned high marks on the essay test achieved a high standard in the multiple choice questions, and vice versa. This result seemed to lend support to the findings of Breland[10] following a similar set of tests in English composition. He concluded that the results of a multiple choice test *did* provide a valid index of students' ability to write an essay.

It would be wrong to assume, however, that the objective test is suitable only for low-level examinations; it is used, for example, in some advanced, post-graduate courses in medical studies. If it can be demonstrated clearly that the higher abilities, such as the perception and analysis of relationships and synthesis, can be tested by objective tests, then much of the opposition to their use should disappear.

There is now an increased willingness by teachers in further education to experiment in the application of a variety of examining techniques. It is possible to foresee, not the total replacement of the narrative-type examination paper by the objective test, but rather an increase in the use of those forms of examination papers consisting of a carefully structured *mixture* of essay-type and objective test questions.

Notes and references

1. See generally for this chapter: *Objective Testing* (City & Guilds, 1984); *Constructing Achievement Tests* by N.E. Gronlund (Prentice-Hall, 1977); *Preparing and Using Objective Questions* by C. Ward (Thornes, 1981).
2. See 'Multiple-choice test items' in *Essentials of Educational Measurement* (Prentice-Hall, 1979); 'Multiple-choice tests' in *Testing and Measurement in the Classroom* by D. Scammell and D. Tracy (Houghton Mifflin, 1980).
3. 'The case for true-false items' by R. Ebel in *The School Review* (1970, 78).
4. See 'Guessing the answer on objective tests' by B. Choppin in *British Journal of Educational Psychology* (1975, 45).
5. See 'Item writing and item selection' by B.S. Bloom *et al.* in *Evaluation to Improve Learning* (McGraw-Hill, 1981); 'Constructing a test' in *Measuring Educational Outcomes* by B.W. Tuckman (Harcourt Brace Jovanovich, 1975); 'Writing the test item' by A. Weisman in *Educational Measurement* ed. R. Thorndike (American Council on Education, 1976).
6. See 'Advances in item analysis' by F.B. Baker in *Review of Educational Research* (1977, 41).
7. *Op. cit.*
8. 'Multiple choice tests for principles of economics courses' in *The Principles of Economics Course* by P. Saunders and W. Walstad (Mc-Graw Hill, 1990).
9. *Educational Psychology – A Cognitive View* (Holt, Rinehart & Winston, 1978).
10. *Assessing Writing Skill* (New York College Entrance Examination Board, 1987).

Chapter 32

The Concept of Intelligence

Intelligence is a disposition or tendency – not a tangible or even intangible possession; but the word provides a convenient *portmanteau* description of the highest level of coordinated thinking by an individual (Butcher, 1974).

The so-called 'intellectual ability' of students is usually assessed by reference to a measurement construct which is said to designate the general level of cognitive functioning known as 'intelligence'.[1] Non-specialist dictionaries define intelligence variously, for instance: 'the ability to use with awareness the mechanism of reasoning'; 'the faculty of understanding'; 'quickness of mental apprehension'; 'the capacity to meet novel situations by novel adaptive responses'; 'intellectual power'. (For Cicero, it was 'the power which enables the mind to grasp reality'.)

Psychologists differ widely in their definitions: the problem of defining intelligence is set out in detail in 'People's conception of intelligence' by Sternberg.[2] Such definitions include, typically: 'the ability to carry on abstract thinking'; 'innate general cognitive ability' (Burt);[3] 'the global capacity of the individual to act purposefully, to think rationally, and to deal effectively with the environment' (Wechsler);[4] 'the ability to respond in present situations on the basis of cogent anticipation of possible consequences and with a view to controlling the consequences that ensue' (Bigge),[5] 'the capacity to apprehend facts and propositions and their relationships and to reason about them' (Ebel);[6] 'a hypothetical factor of wide generality that is presumed to underlie an individual's conpetence in performing cognitive tasks' (Biggs);[7] 'the ability to face problems in an unprogrammed (or, as we often say, creative) manner' (Gould);[8] 'the general ability common to all problem-solving abilities' (Kline).[9]

Neisser,[10] however, warns that 'there are no definitive criteria of intelligence, just as there are none for chairness; it is a fuzzy-edged concept to which many features are relevant'. Nevertheless, there seems to be an element of general agreement among many psychologists on the nature of intelligence as displaying some type of *capacity for rational responses to the stimulus of the environment*.

Doubts continue to be cast, however, on the very existence of the phenomenon of intelligence. In a celebrated aphorism, Boring, of Harvard University,[11] stated:

'Intelligence as a measurable capacity must at the start be defined as the capacity to do well in an intelligence test. Intelligence is what the tests test.' Others reject the possibility of the existence of a single generalized capacity responsible for a person's abilities, related to use of language, comprehension of symbols, perception of complex relationships and the solving of problems.

Latterly, concern with the implications of some aspects of intelligence theory and the procedures of intelligence testing has spilled over from the teaching profession to the social and political arenas, producing much controversy. Many teachers have questioned the very basis of intelligence theory which, they claimed, ignored the phenomenon of pupils of high ability earning relatively low test marks, which often seemed to reflect disadvantaged backgrounds and restricted horizons, levels of expectation and achievement. Public anxieties have mounted: the 11+ selection examination procedures are widely perceived as being based on a dogmatic attachment to belief in an innate, fixed quantum of intelligence, allowing children to be classified according to their test scores. This is viewed as incompatible with egalitarian doctrines and aspirations and is held by some as providing a theoretical underpinning of a social hierarchy which mirrors divisions resting on 'superior' and 'inferior' intelligence. Further, some interpretations of intelligence theory (associated with the American psychologist, Jensen) are held to have given aid and comfort to the proponents of racialist doctrines. Finally, to add to the discomfiture of the psychometricians (who seek to measure intelligence), evidence has been adduced which appears to point to the fraudulent manufacturing of data by one of the founding fathers of intelligence testing.

Nevertheless, the acceptance of intelligence testing remains widespread in colleges of further education and elsewhere. The tests are considered to provide a useful indicator of existing and potential levels of students' abilities. Kline argues that intelligence tests do correlate significantly with educational achievement and occupational success and are useful, therefore, for purposes of educational and vocational guidance.

Concepts of intelligence

The following theories should be of particular interest to teachers.

Spearman (1863–1945)

Spearman[12] propounded a *two-factor theory of intelligence* which became highly influential in the practice of intelligence testing. Data collected from the many psychological tests he administered were interpreted as showing the existence of a *g* factor – meaning general intelligence – *a fundamental, quantifiable factor which entered into all cognitive processes*, which was inherited, or at least inborn, and which could not be affected by training. It consisted of 'something of the nature of an "energy" which served in common the whole cortex'. The *s* factor, which recorded the effect of training ('certain neurons become habituated to particular types of action'), indicated the 'specific, unique information' peculiar to the results of a given test and not related to any other test; it could be considered as the ability to grasp and use relationships swiftly and effectively.

Spearman's analysis of intelligence was held to be of momentous importance. Here was a justification of intelligence testing, of educational theory and practice based on the concept of a 'fundamental, unchangeable, scalable reality' to be found in the very structure of the human brain. (In his later work, Spearman suggested the existence of three additional general factors (*p, o* and *w*): *perseveration* (the inertia of a person's mental energy), *oscillation* (the extent to which mental energy fluctuates), *will* (a motivational-personality factor which can be inferred from intelligence test achievement).)

Gould[13] has attacked Spearman for his determinism (see below) and its effect on political programmes concerned with education, and for his adoption of the fallacy of reification, that is the tendency to convert an abstract concept, such as intelligence, into an entity. Gould sees intelligence as a wonderful, 'multifaceted set of human capabilities', not as a unitary quality which can be expressed as a single number valuation.

Burt (1883–1971)

Burt[14] was for many years the official psychologist of the London County Council. His interpretation of data derived from tests of school pupils resulted in a *four-factor theory* which was based on, and extended, Spearman's concept of intelligence. (The theory provided an underpinning for the ideology from which the '11+' examinations later emerged.) Burt's four factors were: a *g* factor and an *s* factor (both according to Spearman), 'group' factors (relating to abilities classified according to their form or content), and 'accidental' factors (attributes of single traits measured on a single occasion). These factors were, however, not lodged in separate organs of the brain; they were merely 'convenient mathematical abstractions'.

Education, said Burt, could affect the quality of *s* and 'group' factors; it could *not* affect the *g* factor. (The *g* factor 'appears to be inherited, or at least inborn. Neither knowledge nor practice, neither interest nor industry, will avail to increase it.') A person's innate, all-round intellectual ability (the *g* factor) was amenable to unilinear ranking. Burt regarded intelligence, fundamentally, as specifying 'certain individual differences in the structure of the central nervous system'; these differences could be described in terms of histology (i.e. the study of tissues).

Criticism of Burt has tended to stem from his fundamental hereditarianism. In recent years, however, it has been suggested that he falsified some of his data.[15] As a result, considerable portions of his published findings are now viewed with some suspicion.

Thurstone (1887–1955)

Thurstone[16], a pioneer in psychometrics (mental measurement), postulated 'vectors' representing independent, primary mental abilities (PMAs). They included verbal comprehension, word fluency, computational skill, spatial visualization, associative memory, perceptual speed, and reasoning. The PMAs were *irreducible mental entities*; the *g* factor was a delusion. Thurstone wrote of the *g* factor in the following terms:[17]

> So far in our work we have not found the general factor of Spearman ... As far as we can determine at present, the tests that have been supposed to be saturated with the general common factor divide their variance among primary factors that are not present in all the tests. We cannot report any general common factor in the battery of tests that have been analysed in the present study.

Unilinear ranking had no place in Thurstone's system: each person should be described 'in terms of a profile of all the PMAs which are known to be significant', and which make the person unique. (In practice, a student's test score in relation to each PMA is expressed in terms of percentiles, and a 'psychogram' of his or her pattern of abilities is compiled. For the use of 'psychometric profiles' in relation to apprentice training, see *The Times Educational Supplement*, 21 March 1997.) Mental abilities *can* be trained, but will merely enhance innate differences: 'arguments of the environmentalists are too much based on sentimentalism'.

Hebb (1904–85)

Hebb[18] distinguished two concepts applicable to the term 'intelligence': 'intelligence A' is a person's *innate potential* derived from 'the possession of a good brain and a good neural metabolism'; 'intelligence B' is no more than *the brain's actual functioning at any given time*. 'Intelligence B' is the resultant of 'intelligence A' *and* the learner's strategies and concepts emerging from his or her responses and reactions to the environment. Intelligence tests, according to Hebb, seem to measure 'intelligence B'; 'intelligence A' can never be measured directly. (In line with this general concept, Ausubel[19] states that the weight of evidence indicates that intelligence consists of a general unitary ability *plus* a 'constellation of separately measurable abilities or aptitudes'. Bigge,[20] for whom learning is, essentially, the enhancement of intelligence, views intelligence as the number and quality of one's insights. Successful behaviour can be called 'intelligent' only when a person 'might have done otherwise and his actions were premised upon envisaging what he was doing and why'.)

Guilford (b. 1897)

Guilford[21] advanced a theory in 1967 which sought to explain the structure of the human intellect in terms suggesting that intelligence is *multidimensional*. He argued that an 'intelligent act' comprises three elements: the *contents* of a problem are considered first and are then subjected to *mental operations*, as a result of which *products* emerge. Sub-categories of these elements are hypothesized thus:

- *contents*: figural, symbolic, semantic, behavioural;

- *operations*: cognitions, memory, divergent thinking, convergent thinking, evaluation;
- *products*: units, classes, relations, systems, transformations, implications.

In general, Guilford contended, the content of a problem with which a student is faced may be of a symbolic nature, which requires operations, involving cognition and evaluation, which may produce a solution. Guilford suggested the existence of 120 possible separate mental factors (i.e. $4 \times 5 \times 6$), each of which could be tested. In the event, Guilford's colleagues claim to have discovered evidence for the existence of 75 factors.

Kline[22] notes that Guilford's model has been criticized on several counts: the 'operations' category appears to reflect neither theory nor empirical study, and seems to be an intuitive classification; the 'products' category is incomplete; there is little recognition of what is known about cognitive processing; most of Guilford's observations from which the model is constructed involve a group which was of above-average intelligence.

Cattell (1866–1944)

Cattell[23] employed the techniques of factorial analysis in order to distinguish a group of 'primary factors' which should be taken into account in studies of human ability: they included verbal ability, word fluency, meaningful memory, spatial and numerical abilities, perceptual speed, general motor coordination, judgment. Five fundamental capacities essential to human ability appear to emerge from Cattell's analysis: visualization, fluency, cognitive speed, fluid and crystallized intelligence.

Fluid intelligence, which can be measured, indicates the influence of genetic, heritable factors on intellectual development. It involves reasoning and insight, tends to deteriorate after the age of 15, and may be viewed in terms of 'pure ability'. Cronbach[24] sees it as a Spearman-type *g* factor. *Crystallized intelligence*, which can also be measured, indicates the general effect of environmental experience on intellectual development. It involves knowledge and learned skills acquired through experience over time and can continue to develop throughout life. Tests of crystallized intelligence are generally based upon culturally significant skills: hence, measures of this type of intelligence may differ according to time, place and cultural patterns.

Cattell emphasizes that both types of intelligence are involved in tests and other tasks. Measurements of fluid and crystallized intelligence can be of value, it is claimed, in assessing academic and occupational achievement.

Vernon (1905–87)

Vernon[25] describes intelligence in terms of a hierarchical structure which comprises several abilities. At the top of the hierarchy is a *general ability factor* (resembling Spearman's *g* factor). At the next level are *major group factors*: they are verbal-educational (i.e. involving the type of ability essential for successful learning in, say, English and history) and spatial-practical (needed for successful performance in, say, draughtsmanship). The next level comprises the *minor group factors*: these are subdivisions of the major group factors, and include verbal understanding, musical ability and manual ability. At the lowest level are *highly specific factors*. A student who is to achieve success in, say, a verbal test, requires a combination of the general ability factor, a less general verbal factor, appropriate kinds of verbal ability, and other abilities highly specific to the tasks involved in the test.

Vernon noted many cases of significant differences in intelligence among children in the same family who had grown up in similar environments. He argued for a recognition of the significance of genetic endowment in any analysis and evaluation of intelligence, but stressed the importance for teachers and others of neglecting 'neither nature nor nurture' in the furtherance of human development.

Gardner (b. 1921)

Gardner's structural theory of intelligence[26] rejects the significance attached to the *g* factor in most factorial studies. He proposes the concept of 'multiple intelligences', which include, for example, linguistic and musical intelligence, logical-mathematical and spatial intelligence, bodily-kinesthetic intelligence, and interpersonal and intra-personal intelligence. In general, multiple intelligences involve a competence which enables individuals to resolve problems and to acquire new knowledge.

Sternberg

Sternberg[27] interprets the concept of intelligence in terms associated with the contemporary analysis of information-processing. In general, information-processing involves five components:

1. *Metacomponents* are the higher-level processes that plan and 'take decisions' in situations involving problem-solving.
2. *Performance components* are those processes used in the execution of a strategy of problem-solving.
3. *Acquisition components* are used in the acquisition of knowledge through learning.
4. *Retention components* account for the retrieval of previously acquired information.
5. *Transfer components* allow the generalization which results from transfer of learning (see p. 223).

Sternberg views the metacomponents (organizing, planning, decision-making, mental activities) as the all-important, overriding factors which determine the extent and quality of a person's ability to acquire, interpret and utilize information presented by the environment. This inferred ability is to be regarded as 'intelligence'.

Nature and nurture: the biological-determinist controversy

The 'nature and nurture' controversy, generated by some psychologists' perceptions of the basis and structure of intelligence, is of great significance, not only for the teaching profession, but for students, educational policy makers and all those responsible for the quality of education as a social process.[28] Tutors in further education are aware of the phenomenon which can be interpreted as 'an improvement in a student's performance'. A variety of factors may be responsible, but, according to the biological determinists, there has been no improvement in the student's level of intelligence, for that is inherited, innate, fixed and, therefore, unalterable. Teaching may improve some aspects of a student's capacities associated with learning, but it cannot affect intelligence, any more than, by 'taking thought', one can add a cubit to one's stature. This is the determinist position: *as we are born, so we shall develop*. To state otherwise is to practise a cruel deception. The non-determinists – known also as 'environmentalists' – seek to reject these views, emphasizing empirical studies which appear to prove convincingly that environmental factors *can* affect scores on intelligence tests to a significant degree.

The core of the determinist position

Writing in 1920, Goddard[29] (an American educationist) stated his thesis as follows:

> The chief determiner of human conduct is a unitary mental process which we call intelligence ... this process is conditioned by a nervous mechanism which is inborn: the degree of efficiency to be attained by that nervous mechanism and the consequent grade of intellectual or mental level for each individual is determined by the chromosomes that come together with the union of the germ cells ... it is but little affected by any later influences except such serious accidents as may destroy part of the mechanism.

Six years earlier, Spearman[30] had written:

> The effect of training is confined to the specific factor and does not touch the general one ... Though unquestionably the development of specific abilities is in large measure dependent upon environmental influences, that of general ability is almost wholly governed by heredity.

In 1959, Burt[31] wrote:

> A definite limit to what children can achieve is inexorably set by the limitations of their innate capacity.

The essence of the environmentalist (non-determinist) position

The environmentalists are prepared to accept, in general, the heritability of characteristics and abilities which are held to constitute 'intelligence'. But they will *not* accept the idea of an immutable genetic inheritance in relation to intellectual abilities.[32] The very rationale of teaching rests in the presumption of the possibility of improving the quality of some inherited traits. There is considerable anecdotal evidence, too extensive to be rejected out of hand, suggesting that individual IQ test scores *can* be improved as the direct result of training (for 'IQ' see p. 424). Environmental changes, it is argued, can and do affect those fundamental abilities which are said to determine the evaluation of intelligence. Thus, research reported in *Nature* (1989, August) suggests that children adopted at birth by 'educated, prosperous foster-parents' grow up to be 'much brighter than the average child'.

The literature is replete with examples and research findings emphasizing the significance of 'nurture' for intelligence.[33]

A continuing controversy

The discussion as to the links between heredity and environment is set to continue in relation to our understanding of the concept of intelligence. Thus, in '*Familial studies of intelligence: a review*' (1981),[34] Bouchard and McGue state: 'After reviewing 111 separate studies giving 526 IQ correlations drawn from some 55,000 pairings of relatives, we conclude that IQ has both a genetic and an environmental component in proportions unknown.' Kline[35] states that it is possible to demonstrate that environmental factors can create differences 'as large as 38 IQ points'.

In 1994, Herrnstein and Murray[36] provoked further debate concerning intelligence and biological determinism. They made the following wide claims.

1. Differences in basic intellectual capacities reflect 'a general factor of cognitive ability' which 'is measured reasonably well by a variety of standardized tests, best of all by *IQ* tests designed for that purpose'.
2. Social status is ruled by biological factors. The lower classes comprise, in general, those who lack intellectual competence; the upper classes include those whose intellectual merit has enabled them to rise in the social hierarchy. IQ tests would reveal these fundamental differences.
3. Innate, inherited *racial* differences are a fact and cannot be altered by any compensatory social and educational programmes. Inborn cognitive limits of this type, which are manifested in relative IQ scores, cannot be transcended by any amount of socially administered teaching programmes.
4. There is a danger of a growing 'underclass', unable to rise beyond the low levels of achievement fixed by innate intelligence (as amenable to measurement by standardized IQ tests), presenting, in increasing fashion, a threat to the very stability of our society. This situation must be recognized and transformed.

Gould[37] rejects completely the arguments of Herrnstein and Murray. Intelligence, he contends, cannot be depicted accurately in single-number format; it is not genetically based; its levels are not immutable, and Herrnstein and Murray have fallen into the semantic confusion of seeing 'heritable' and 'immutable' as synonyms. Essentially, the thesis of Herrnstein and Murray is based upon the well-known arguments of biological determinism which are fallacious because the features invoked to make distinctions among persons and groups are usually the products of cultural evolution. Herrnstein and Murray are merely repeating, with elaborations, a 'hard line version' of Spearman's *g* factor explanation of intelligence in terms of 'a unitary, rankable, genetically based, and minimally alterable thing in the head'. According to Gould, the concept of intelligence advocated by Spearman, and adopted by Herrnstein and Murray, is false, being based on the fallacy of 'conversion of an abstract into a putative real entity'.

The racial implications of the Herrnstein and Murray thesis are viewed by Gould and other critics as a dangerous repetition of the fundamental theses attributable to Jensen (see below). Critics argue that Jensen's work is discredited and any thesis built around it has no credibility.

The 'race and intelligence' controversy

In 1969, the American psychologist, Jensen, published an article entitled 'How much can we boost IQ and scholastic achievement?'[38] It purported to reveal the existence of a significant 'genetic difference' in intelligence between American racial groups (classified on the basis of colour) and was based upon Jensen's interpretation of IQ test data which appeared to show overall and significant differences in the scores awarded to children in those groups. Jensen rejected the view that the differences which he claimed to perceive among racial group scores could probably be explained solely as the result of environment.

Jensen's views caused an eruption of disquiet and received little support from other psychologists.[39] Critics, such as Gould, attacked the very basis of Jensen's work, which seemed to rest in part on the '*g* factor' presumption. Gould commented: 'The chimerical nature of the *g* factor is the rotten core of Jensen's work and of the entire hereditarian school'. The fraudulent nature of some of Burt's published data, which were linked closely to arguments in favour of the *g* factor explanation of intelligence, assisted Jensen's critics in their attempted demolition of his theoretical edifice. Thus, Kamin and others pointed to the many empirical studies which appeared to contradict the fundamentals of Jensen's thinking.[40] It was argued, additionally, that the tests he had used were not culture-free and could be interpreted as showing a bias in favour of the highly verbal aspects of American, white culture.

More disturbing reactions came from some psychologists and teachers who claimed to hear in Jensen's defence of his findings, overtones of the discredited pseudo-scientific doctrines of Gobineau (1816–82),[41] whose racist theories were taken over by the ideologists of German National Socialism. There followed widespread condemnation of Jensen by many who perceived his views on intelligence as constituting an academic justification of some aspects of racial discrimination.[42]

A detailed account of the principal arguments involving Jensen is given in *The IQ Controversy*.[43] Among the contents is Bereiter's important 'Genetics and educability'.

Piaget and the development of intelligence: a note

Piaget (1896–1980) stresses the biological significance of intelligence, which he views as a quality of the learner's adaptation to his or her environment enabling a state of equilibrium to be achieved between his or her actions and those of the environment.[44] Birth to maturity involves a process of development which can be considered in stages.

1. *The sensorimotor stage.* In this stage, which involves an infant's first activities, actions begin to be coordinated and there is evidence of intention; elementary differentiation of ends and means intensifies.
2. *The pre-conceptual thought stage.* This period continues until the child is aged about 4 years and is characterized by the intensification of symbolic functions in play and a general integration of activities with the acquisition of language. Intuitive and operational thought begin to develop.
3. *The concrete operations stage.* When the child becomes capable of varying a number of relationships simultaneously he or she reaches the stage of operational thinking, but only in relation to that part of his or her environment which is familiar.
4. *The formal operations stage.* Following the onset of puberty a person is able to detach operational thinking from the familiar experiences which make up his or her environment. There is a qualitative improvement in his or her thinking so that the person is able to generalize and to solve problems by the construction of hypotheses and the deduction of consequences.

The measurement of intelligence

Terman (1877–1956), drawing on the work of the German psychologist, Stern (1871–1938), constructed the index which is known as the intelligence quotient (IQ).[45] It is usually calculated as follows:

$$IQ = 100 \times \frac{\text{Mental age}}{\text{Chronological age}}$$

(The multiplication by 100 avoids the use of decimals.) Mental age is determined by the individual's score in a standardized intelligence test.

An often-used interpretation of the range of intelligence quotients was given in 1938 by Merrill,[46] thus:

IQ	*appropriate description*
140+	very superior
120–139	superior
110–119	high average
90–109	average
80–89	low average
70–79	borderline
below 70	retarded

A revised version of this interpretation, published in 1960, makes possible the computation of an individual's IQ from tables. IQ is calculated on the basis of the index, but the tables are used to interpret the quotient for the individual's age.[47] For an explanation of the use of the standard deviation in the interpretation of degrees of dispersion in distributions of IQ scores, see Slavin.[48]

Intelligence tests, their basic concepts, administration and interpretation continue to be criticized sharply.[49] It is contended that they measure naught save some specialized skills (which can be taught and exercised for purposes of the tests), that they over-emphasize verbal ability, that there is a socio-cultural bias in their construction and interpretation, and that their importance is over-stressed. There is important evidence to suggest that the IQ may not be constant throughout a student's period of development. Further, some investigators believe that the development of some aspects of intelligence may cease on the attaining of adulthood, so that there is little value in the measuring of an IQ after development has ceased.[50]

There are teachers in further education who have rejected the intelligence test as worthless. Intuitively – and understandably – they suspect the validity of a test which seems to separate 'tested intelligence' and 'everyday intelligence'. Staff room anecdote has provided many examples of people with high IQs who were notoriously 'lacking in common sense'. Moreover, the single-valued IQ is not always perceived as meaningful. 'It seems likely that there are innate differences in intelligence. But it seems almost impossible that a matter so many-sided and complex as human inborn knowledge and intelligence (quickness of grasp, depth of understanding, creativity, clarity of exposition, etc.) can be measured by a one-dimensional function like the IQ' (Popper and Eccles).[51]

Among teachers in further education who accept IQ testing because of its predictive value, for example, are many who are aware of the difficulties inherent in the attempt to understand the essence of the human characteristic which is being evaluated. Most will keep in mind the importance of a comprehensive assessment based on standardized tests *and* informal evaluation. Non-discriminatory testing requires not only the assessment of ability to learn, but also an indication of other general capacities. The significance of the environment in the task of improving human abilities will not be overlooked.[52]

Envoi

Throughout this text we have sought to stress the positive role of the teacher in the development of human capacities. We give the final word in this chapter – and in the text as a whole – to Bloom (in his 'Reply to Dr. Jensen', 1969):[53]

> The psychologist and the geneticist may wish to speculate about how to improve the genetic pool – the educator cannot and should not. The educator must be an environmentalist, bridled or unbridled. It is through the environment that he must fashion the educational process. Learning goes on by providing the appropriate environment. If heredity imposes limits – so be it. The educator must work with what is left, whether it be 20 per cent or 50 per cent of the variance.

Notes and references

1. See generally for this chapter: *What is Intelligence?* ed. J. Khalfa (CUP, 1994); *Intelligence and Development: A Cognitive Theory* by M. Anderson (Blackwell, 1992); *Intelligence, Heredity and Environment* ed. R. Sternberg and E. Grigorenko (CUP, 1997); *A Model for Intelligence* ed. H.J. Eysenck (Springer, 1982).
2. *Journal of Social Psychology* (1981, *41*). This is a fundamental analysis of considerable significance.
3. 'The evidence for the concept of intelligence' in *British Journal of Educational Psychology* (1955, *25*).
4. *The Range of Human Capacities* (Baillière, 1952).
5. *Learning Theories for Teachers* (Harper & Row, 1976).
6. 'Abilities and the measure of achievement' in *New Directions of Testing and Measuring Achievement* (Jossey-Bass, 1980).
7. *The Process of Learning* (Prentice-Hall, 1987).
8. *The Mismeasure of Man* (Penguin, 1981, 1997). This is a detailed examination of attempts to measure human intelligence. The writer, a geologist and zoologist from Harvard University, rejects the concept of IQ testing as essentially 'reductive', with clear overtones of 'biology as destiny'.
9. *Intelligence: The Psychometric View* (Routledge, 1991, 1996). This is an outstanding exposition of the essential features of intelligence measurement and related topics.
10. 'The concept of intelligence' in *Human Intelligence: Perspectives on Theory and Measurement* ed. R.J. Sternberg (Norwood, 1979). See also 'Definition of intelligence' by H.B. Barlow in *Nature* (1970, *228*).
11. 'Intelligence as the tests test it' in *New Republic* (1923, *35*). Kline observes that Boring's statement is not as circular as it seems: psychometricians claim to be able to specify empirically that which is measured by the tests.
12. See e.g. *The Nature of Intelligence and the Principle of Cognition* (Macmillan, 1923); 'Determination of factors' in *British Journal of Psychology* (1939, *30*).
13. *Op. cit.*
14. *The Factors of Mind* (London UP, 1940); 'Factor analysis and its neurological basis' in *British Journal of Statistical Psychology* (1961, *14*); 'The inheritance of general intelligence' in *American Psychology* (1972, *27*). See also *The Essentials of Factor Analysis* by D. Child (Cassell, 1990).
15. See *Cyril Burt, Psychologist* by L.S. Hearnshaw (Hodder & Stoughton, 1979). For a rejoinder to the charge of falsification of data, see *The Burt Affair* by R.B. Joynson (Routledge, 1989). See also 'The nine lives of discredited data' by D.P. Paul in *The Sciences* (1987, May); *Cyril Burt: Fraud or Framed?* ed. N. Mackintosh (OUP, 1995).
16. *The Nature of Intelligence* (Kegan Paul, 1924); *The Vectors of Mind* (Chicago UP, 1935).
17. *Primary Mental Abilities* (Chicago UP, 1938).
18. *The Organisation of Behaviour* (Wiley, 1949).
19. *Educational Psychology – A Cognitive View* (Holt, Rinehart & Winston, 1978).
20. *Learning Theories for Teachers* by M. Bigge (Harper & Row, 1976).
21. 'The structure of intellect' in *Psychological Bulletin* (1956, *23*); *The Nature of Human Intelligence* (McGraw-Hill, 1967).
22. *Op. cit.*
23. 'Theory of fluid and crystallised intelligence: a critical experiment' in *Journal of Educational Psychology* (1963, *54*).
24. *Essentials of Psychological Testing* (Harper & Row, 1984).

25. *Intelligence and Cultural Environment* (Methuen, 1976); *Intelligence, Heredity and Environment* (Freeman, 1979).
26. 'Theory of multiple intelligences' in *Handbook of Educational Ideas and Practices* ed. N. Entwistle (Routledge, 1990); *Frames of Intelligence* (Basic Books, 1983).
27. For a summary, see 'Intelligence' by R.J. Sternberg in *OCM*.
28. See e.g. Gould (*op. cit.*); Klein (*op. cit.*); Sternberg and Grigorenko (*op. cit.*); *Intelligence: The Battle for the Mind* by H.J. Eysenck and L. Kamin (Penguin, 1981).
29. See Gould (*op. cit.*).
30. 'The heredity of abilities' in *Eugenics Review* (1914, *6*).
31. 'Class differences in general intelligence' in *British Journal of Statistical Psychology* (1959, *12*).
32. 'I have long felt that the prevailing tendency to regard all the marked distinctions of human character as innate, and in the main indelible ... is one of the chief hindrances to the rational treatment of great social questions, and one of the chief stumbling blocks to human improvement': John Stuart Mill in *Autobiography (1873)* (OUP, 1969).
33. See, for example: *The Science and Politics of IQ* by Kamin (Penguin, 1974), in which the significance of genetic factors in the determination of intelligence is contested; *The Milwaukee Project* by Garber (AAMR, 1988); 'The nature and nurture of cognitive abilities' by Plomin in *Advances in the Psychology of Human Intelligence* ed. R. Sternberg (Erlbaum, 1988).
34. *Science* (1981, *212*: 1055–9).
35. *Op. cit.*
36. *The Bell Curve: The Reshaping of American Life* (Free Press, 1994). (The term 'bell curve' refers to the assumption that intelligence is 'normally distributed' within the general population, so that this distribution when plotted as a graph produces a symmetrical, bell-shaped curve.)
37. See 'A critique of the bell curve' in *The Mismeasure of Man* by S. Gould (Penguin, 1981, 1997). See also *In the Blood* by S. Jones (Flamingo, 1997).
38. See also Jensen's *Bias in Mental Testing* (Free Press, 1980) and 'The nature of the black-white differences in various psychometric tests' in *Behavioural and Brain Sciences* (1985, *8*); *Harvard Educational Review* (1969, *33*: 1–123).
39. Support came from H.J. Eysenck in *Race, Intelligence and Education* (Library Press, 1971).
40. See references in Kamin (*op. cit.*), Kline (*op. cit.*); *Psychology for Teachers* by D. Fontana (Macmillan, 1997).
41. See e.g. *Essay on the Inequality of Human Races* (1855, English translation pub. Constable, 1967).
42. It is of much interest to note that Kline (*op. cit.*) refuses to report the detail of Jensen's 1980 and 1985 publications (see note 38 above). He refers to 'a moral dilemma' in such reporting, notes that studies inferring the inferiority of racial groups provide grist for the mills of reaction, and insists that setting out scores on IQ tests of various racial groups adds nothing to our theoretical understanding or to social and educational practice.
43. Ed. Block and Dworkin (Quartet Books, 1977).
44. See *The Psychology of Intelligence* (Routledge, 1950) and *The Essential Piaget* ed. H. Gruber and J. Vaneche (Routledge, 1978).
45. This was based on a test drawn up by Binet and Simon in 1908.
46. See 'The significance of IQs on the revised Stanford-Binet scales' in *Journal of Educational Psychology* (1938, *26*).
47. See 'Intelligence: its assessment' by A.W. Heim in *OCM; Mental Testing: Its History, Principles and Applications* by F.L. Goodenough (Staples, 1949).

48. *Educational Psychology* (Prentice-Hall, 1988).

49. See *IQ and Mental Testing: An Unnatural Science and Its Social History* by B. Evans and B. Waites (Macmillan, 1981) in which the authors emphasize the origins of IQ testing in psychometrics which, they claim, was preoccupied with the spectre of 'racial degeneration'; 'Five myths about your IQ' by M. Bane and C.Jenks in Block and Dworkin (*op. cit.*); *Race and IQ* ed. A. Montagu (OUP, 1996).

50. Ausubel has estimated that academic achievement generally correlates about 0.5 with intelligence test scores.

51. *The Self and Its Brain* (Routledge, 1984).

52. Jones (*In the Blood* (Flamingo, 1997)) notes that in Japan, some 50 years ago, the mean IQ was estimated at about 100. In the late 1990s it stands at around 112. Jones suggests that this must be the result of improvements to the environment since there has been insufficient time for the occurrence of any genetic change in the population of Japan. He draws attention to the significance of parental demands and students' hard work, both of which are important aspects of the prevalent socio-cultural environment in Japan.

53. See *Teaching for Learning* by M. Dembo (Goodyear, 1981).

Appendix

Topics for Discussion

Set out below is a selection of epigrams, aphorisms and judgments from the published writings of educational psychologists, philosophers and practising teachers. The statements are presented for use as the basis of discussion. Consideration might be given to their relevance for further education in particular, in the light of theory and practice.

The selection is presented in random manner with no indication of authorship or date of publication. This is deliberate. The object is to avoid producing a 'halo effect' ('If X says this, it must be a valid argument because he is a highly respected educational philosopher') or a demonic, 'horns and tail effect' ('If Y says this, it cannot be correct because he is a dyed-in-the-wool behaviourist/cognitivist/ Gestaltist'). Each statement should be evaluated solely on its apparent merits.

1. Education is not merely preparation for life but an experience in present living that unites thought with action.
2. Teaching may be said to be a two-fold activity of communicating information and communicating judgment, and learning may be said to be a two-fold activity of acquiring information and coming to possess judgment.
3. A master teaches essence. When the essence is perceived he teaches what is necessary to expand the perception.
4. A human being may become 'free' in many different respects ... becoming educated is itself an emancipation.
5. A science of behaviour cannot limit itself to a discussion of observable responses, for responses take place within the organism that cannot be readily observed. A science that limits itself to a discussion of only the observable would contain a very naïve body of knowledge.
6. Be suspicious of the objectivity and accuracy of all measures of student ability and conscious that human judgment is the most important element in every indicator of achievement.
7. Language most showeth a man. Speak that I may see thee.
8. The authority of those who teach is often a hindrance to those who wish to learn.

9. All pedagogic action is, objectively, symbolic violence in so far as it is the imposition of a culture by an arbitrary power.

10. Of all the baleful dichotomies that stymie our understanding of the world's complexity, nature versus nurture must rank among the top two or three (a phoney division only enhanced by the euphony of these names).

11. Education is the fundamental method of social progress and reform.

12. The process and the goal of education are one and the same thing. The goal of education is disciplined understanding: that is the process as well.

13. A curriculum should be prepared jointly by the subject matter expert, the teacher and the psychologist.

14. So long as a subject seems dull, you can be sure that you are approaching it from the wrong angle.

15. No one starts out teaching well.

16. What we have to learn to do, we learn by doing.

17. Any of the objections given by teachers to instructional objectives seem to be predicated upon inadequate conceptions of education, curriculum or instruction.

18. The business of the teacher is to release his pupils from servitude to the current dominant feelings, emotions, images, ideas, beliefs and even skills, not by inventing alternatives to them which seem to him more desirable, but by making available to them something which approximates more closely to the whole of their inheritance.

19. Take something like 'the ability to solve problems'. What is meant by this phrase? Can we assume that the ability to solve mathematical problems is the same as the ability to solve problems in morals?

20. All learning is 'discovered'. Even when we tell students something, they must perform mental operations with the information to make it their own.

21. That is what learning is. You suddenly understand something you've understood all your life, but in a new way.

22. All problem-solving is creative. The very essence of problem-solving is that the solver *invents* a solution.

23. One of the ironies of classroom research is the great difficulty we have as researchers attempting to describe and understand a phenomenon that appears to us so complex, but to the participants so mundane.

24. Men must be taught as if you taught them not.

25. Educate, not with reference to the present condition of things, but rather with regard to a possibly improved state of the human race – that is, according to the ideal of humanity and its entire destiny.

26. No one will doubt that the legislator should direct his attention above all to the education of youth ... The citizen should be moulded to suit the form of government under which he lives.

27. Once the basic techniques of instruction have been acquired, it is important to begin looking at the craft from the viewpoint of the artist ... At times, as in any art, it is necessary to throw some of the basic techniques out of the window.

28. Learning has to confer an advantage to learners. Otherwise, why should they bother? Sometimes the advantage is self-evident. More usually, teachers have to point it out.

29. The learning process is, somewhat paradoxically, easiest to visualize as a reversal of the hierarchic sequence of operations which will characterize performance when learning is completed.
30. Style and tone have always been ignored in pedagogical theory, but they are of the greatest importance.
31. The decrying of the wholesale use of lectures is probably justified. The wholesale decrying of the use of lecturing is just as certainly not justified.
32. What is all education except a strenuous and systematic effort to give the whole character a certain turn and bias which appears on the whole desirable to the person who gives it?
33. Assessment procedures provide crucial messages to students about the kinds of learning they are expected to carry out.
34. Teachers must recite less facts, ask more questions, give fewer answers ... The intellectual process must be stirred. A feeling for knowledge for its own sake must be engendered.
35. Teachers must be prepared to meet the challenge of the new technology if they are not to be partly superseded by it.
36. The objective of education is the acquisition of a pre-programmed system of external responses, i.e. a behaviour set.
37. The principal task of instruction is the development of reasoned approaches to cognitive activities.
38. The theory of learning must be directed at studies of the principles bearing on the transformation of phenomena of social awareness into phenomena of individual awareness.
39. Few pedagogic devices in our time have been repudiated more unequivocally by educational theorists than the method of expository verbal instruction.
40. Instead of speaking *at* or even *to* students, the teacher should strive to speak *for* them.
41. Methods of teaching should be designed to stimulate students actively to construct meaning from their own experience rather than stimulating them to reproduce the knowledge of others.
42. Significant learning rests not upon the teacher's lectures and presentations but upon certain attitudinal qualities which exist in the personal relationship between the facilitator and the learner.
43. Evaluation is a two-edged sword which can enhance student learning and personality development or be destructive of student learning and personality development.
44. Intelligence is quickness to apprehend as distinct from ability, which is the capacity to act wisely on the thing apprehended.
45. Helping students to learn more about themselves, helping them to relate to others, preparing them for future society, encouraging them to think for themselves and to make their own decisions – these are the goals of education.
46. The first essential of good teaching is that the teacher must know the subject. That really means that he must continue to learn it. The second essential is that he must like it ... The teacher who dislikes his subject or is indifferent to it always runs the risk of becoming a hypocrite.

47. What education can do is to affect a man's desires and his concept of what counts as a good or happy life, and bring about the reality-desire match by working on his desires rather than by helping him to produce appropriate changes in reality.

48. Intelligence is to a great extent the internalization of 'tools' provided by a given culture. Thus, 'culture-free' means 'intelligence-free'.

49. A truly skilled teacher will see to it that each day students, to a safe degree, will leave the class with unanswered questions.

50. Understanding occurs in its best form when students come to see how to use productively, in ways they care about, a pattern of verified general ideas and the facts that support them.

Name Index

Subject Index